BRAZIL
1994

Other Fielding Titles

Fielding's Australia 1994

Fielding's Belgium 1994

Fielding's Bermuda/Bahamas 1994

Fielding's Britain 1994

Fielding's Budget Europe 1994

Fielding's Caribbean 1994

Fielding's Europe 1994

Fielding's Far East 1994

Fielding's France 1994

Fielding's The Great Sights of Europe 1994

Fielding's Hawaii 1994

Fielding's Holland 1994

Fielding's Italy 1994

Fielding's Mexico 1994

Fielding's New Zealand 1994

Fielding's Scandinavia 1994

Fielding's Spain & Portugal 1994

Fielding's Switzerland & the Alpine Region 1994

Fielding's Worldwide Cruises 1994

Fielding's Shopping Guide to Europe 1994

BRAZIL 1994

The Sensual And Entertaining Guide To Adventure In Brazil

Pamela Bloom

Fielding Worldwide, Inc.
308 South Catalina Avenue
Redondo Beach, California 90277 U.S.A.

Fielding's Brazil 1994
Published by Fielding Worldwide, Inc.
Text Copyright ©1993 Pamela Bloom

All rights reserved. No part of this book may be reproduced, transmitted or utilized in any form or by any means, electronic or mechanical, including photocopying, recording, or by any information storage and retrieval system, without permission in writing from the publisher. Brief extracts for review purposes for inclusion in critical reviews or articles are permitted.

FIELDING WORLDWIDE INC.

PUBLISHER AND CEO **Robert Young Pelton**

PRODUCTION SUPERVISOR **Michael Rowley**
PRODUCTION MANAGEMENT **Beverly Riess**
ELECTRONIC FORMATTING MANAGER **Tony E. Hulette**
ELECTRONIC PUBLISHING MANAGER **Larry E. Hart**
EDITORIAL MANAGER **Wink Dulles**
OFFICE MANAGER **Christy Donaldson**
CUSTOMER SERVICE MANAGER **Theresa Martin**

EDITORS

Linda Charlton	Kathy Knoles
Tina Gentile	Evelyn Lager
Loretta Rooney Hess	Jane M. Martin
Dixie Hulette	Reed Parsell
Ann Imberman	Paul Snapp
Norm Imberman	Jean-Marie Swann
Forrest Kerr	Gladis R. Zaimah

PRODUCTION

Jon Davis	Lyne Lawrence
Kenneth Garges	Chris Mederios
Norm Imberman	Kip Riggins
Kang Hyang Kil	Patrick Roebuck
Ely Kreisel	Denise Saunders
Bryan Kring	Munir Shaikh
Ken Kuniyuki	Chris Snyder
Sutter Kunkel, Jr.	Lillian Tse

COVER DESIGNED BY **Pelton & Associates, Inc.**
COVER PHOTOGRAPHERS — Front Cover **Jim Zuckerman/Westlight**
Background Photo, Front Cover **Jim Zuckerman/Westlight**
Back Cover **Nachtlokal Leben Tanzerin/Westlight**
INSIDE PHOTOS **Pamela Bloom, Don Klein, and Claudio Heckmann**
MAPS **Geosystems**

Although every effort has been made to ensure the correctness of the information in this book, the publisher and authors do not assume, and hereby disclaim, any liability to any party for any loss or damage caused by errors, omissions, misleading information or any potential travel problem caused by information in this guide, even if such errors or omission are a result of negligence, accident or any other cause.

Inquiries should be addressed to: Fielding Worldwide, Inc., 308 South Catalina Ave., Redondo Beach, California 90277 U.S.A., Telephone (310) 372-4474, Facsimile (310) 376-8064, 8:30 a.m. - 5:30 p.m. Pacific Standard Time.

ISBN 1-56952-005-4

Printed in the United States of America

Dedication

To Maneco Bueno, whose record collection recharted the course of my life

And to mother, who continues to survive beautifully *my* trips to Brazil

Letter from the Publisher

In 1946, Temple Fielding began a remarkable series of well-written, highly-personalized guide books for independent travelers. Temple's opinionated, witty, and oft-imitated books have now guided travelers for almost a half-century. More important to some was Fielding's humorous and direct method of steering travelers away from the dull and the insipid. Today, Fielding Travel Guides are still written by experienced travelers for experienced travelers. Our authors carry on Fielding's reputation for creating travel experiences that deliver insight with a sense of discovery and style.

Pam Bloom has created a unique travel guide to one of the world's most mysterious and unexplored regions. Fielding's *Brazil* is a thoroughly intriguing book that conveys the real Brazil through an injection of sensitivity, excitement, and adventure. Pam's intimate knowledge of Brazil's people–from their music, arts, and language, to their world-renowned passion for fun–elevate this book above any other guide to Brazil.

In 1994, the concept of independent travel has never been bigger. Our policy of *brutal honesty* and a highly personal point of view has never changed; it just seems the travel world has caught up with us.

Enjoy your Brazilian adventure with Pam Bloom and Fielding.

Robert Young Pelton
Publisher and CEO
Fielding Worldwide, Inc.

Fielding Rating Icons

The Fielding Rating Icons are highly personal and awarded to help the besieged traveler choose from among the dizzying array of activities, attractions, hotels, restaurants and sights. The awarding of an icon denotes unusual or exceptional qualities in the relevant category. We encourage you to create your own icons in the margin to help you find those special places that make each trip unforgettable.

TABLE OF CONTENTS

IMPORTANT! xxi
ABOUT THE AUTHOR xxiii
TO MY READERS xxv
ACKNOWLEDGMENTS xxix
INTRODUCTION 1
DIRECTORY 7
    BEFORE YOU GO 7
    WHILE YOU'RE THERE 19
FIELDING'S BEST OF BRAZIL 33
HISTORICAL ROOTS 35
INSIDE BRAZILIANS 49
CUISINE 55
TRAVELER'S GUIDE
   TO BRAZILIAN SPIRITS 59
CARNAVAL 67
    BEGINNINGS 68
    THE PARADE 71
    BAHIA 74
    PERNAMBUCO 74
    THE ESSENTIAL CARNAVAL 75
        RESERVATIONS 75
        CARNAVAL BALLS 75
        CARNAVAL REHEARSALS 76
        STREET CARNAVAL 76
THE SOUNDS OF BRAZIL 77
RIO DE JANEIRO 87
    RIO'S PAST GLORIES 91
        RIO: A BIRD'S EYE VIEW 94
        RIO'S SCENERY 95
            CORCOVADO 95
            PÃO DE AÇÚCAR 97
    RIO BY FOOT 101
        SANTA TERESA 110
        GREEN RIO 111
        FAVELA TOURS—NOT FOR THE FAINT OF HEART 115

RIO—ESPECIALLY FOR CHILDREN	118
RAINY DAYS IN RIO	119
USER'S GUIDE TO THE BEST BEACHES IN RIO	120
BEACH BLANKET SURVIVAL GUIDE	122
COPACABANA	123
LEME BEACH	125
IPANEMA	126
ARPOADOR	128
LEBLON	128
FLAMENGO	129
BOTAFOGO	129
PRAIA VERMELHA	130
VIDIGAL	130
SÃO CONRADO	131
BARRA DA TIJUCA	132
FARTHER WEST	133
MUSEUMS IN RIO	133
SPORTS IN RIO	137
ART AND RELIGION IN RIO	141
SHOPPING	142
HOTELS	150
IN RIO	152
BARRA DA TIJUCA	163
CULINARY RIO	164
RIO BY NIGHT	180
WHERE TO FIND NIGHTLIFE IN RIO	182
THE MOST ROMANTIC THINGS TO DO IN RIO	187
EROTIC RIO	188
HANDS-ON RIO	191
AN A-B-C GUIDE	191
GREENER RIO	201
NORTH OF RIO	203
PETRÓPOLIS	203
TERESÓPOLIS	206
THE ESSENTIAL NORTH OF RIO	207
WHERE TO STAY	207
WHERE TO EAT	207
COSTA DO SOL	209
BÚZIOS	209
THE ESSENTIAL BÚZIOS	210
GETTING THERE	210
GETTING AROUND	210
THE BÚZIOS SCENE	210
BEACHES	210
SPORTS	211
SHOPPING	211
WHERE TO STAY	211
WHERE TO EAT	212

COSTA VERDE 215
ALONG THE WAY 215
CRUISES 216
ILHA GRANDE 219
THE ESSENTIAL ILHA GRANDE 221
WHERE TO STAY 221
WHERE TO EAT 221
PARATI 223
SIGHTS 224
EXCURSIONS 225
THE ESSENTIAL PARATI 226
WHERE TO STAY 226
WHERE TO EAT 226
NIGHTLIFE 226
SERRA DA BOCAINA 227
THE ESSENTIAL SERRA DA BOCAINA 228
WHERE TO STAY 228
GETTING THERE 228
GETTING OUT 229
HOT FLASH FOR 1994 229
GETTING THERE: 229

MINAS GERAIS 231
BELO HORIZONTE 235
PAST GLORIES 235
MUSEUMS 238
THE HISTORICAL CITIES 238
EXCURSION 240
THE ESSENTIAL MINAS GERAIS 242
WHERE TO STAY 242
WHERE TO EAT 243
NIGHTLIFE 246
SHOPPING 247
HANDS-ON BELO HORIZONTE 248
OURO PRETO 249
WHEN TO GO: 250
PAST GLORIES 250
A BIRD'S EYE VIEW 252
SIGHTS 252
THE ESSENTIAL OURO PRETO 258
WHERE TO STAY 258
WHERE TO EAT 260
NIGHTLIFE 261
SHOPPING 261
HANDS-ON OURO PRETO 262
MARIANA 263
SIGHTS 264
EXCURSIONS 266
THE ESSENTIAL MARIANA 268
WHERE TO STAY 268

WHERE TO EAT	268
NIGHTLIFE	268
SHOPPING	268
CRAFTS	269
HANDS-ON MARIANA	269
SÃO JOÃO DEL REI	**271**
PAST GLORIES	272
A BIRD'S EYE VIEW	272
SIGHTS	273
EXCURSIONS	275
THE ESSENTIAL SÃO JOÃO DEL REI	277
WHERE TO STAY	277
WHERE TO EAT	277
HANDS-ON SÃO JOÃO DEL REI	277
TIRADENTES	**279**
THE ESSENTIAL TIRADENTES	281
WHERE TO STAY	281
WHERE TO EAT	281
SHOPPING	281
HANDS-ON TIRADENTES	281
CONGONHAS	**283**
PAST GLORIES	283
A BIRD'S EYE VIEW	284
ALEIJADINHO:	284
SIGHTS	285
THE ESSENTIAL CONGONHAS	288
WHERE TO STAY	288
WHERE TO EAT	288
SHOPPING	288
HANDS-ON CONGONHAS	288

THE SPA TOWNS

SÃO LOURENÇO	**291**
SIGHTS	291
THE ESSENTIAL SÃO LOURENÇO	293
WHERE TO STAY	293
WHERE TO EAT	293
SHOPPING	293
HANDS-ON SÃO LOURENÇO	293
CAXAMBÚ	**295**
SIGHTS	296
EXCURSIONS	298
THE ESSENTIAL CAXAMBÚ	298
WHERE TO STAY	298
WHERE TO EAT	298
NIGHTLIFE	299
SHOPPING	299
HANDS-ON CAXAMBÚ	299
SÃO TOMÉ DAS LETRAS	**301**

SÃO PAULO ... 303
SÃO PAULO (CITY) ... 307
PAST GLORIES ... 307
A BIRD'S EYE VIEW ... 308
SIGHTS ... 309
OTHER OUTINGS ... 309
MUSEUMS ... 311
THE ESSENTIAL SÃO PAULO ... 312
WHERE TO STAY ... 312
WHERE TO EAT ... 315
NIGHTLIFE ... 319
SHOPPING ... 321
HANDS-ON SÃO PAULO ... 322
GUARUJÁ ... 325
THE ESSENTIAL GUARUJÁ ... 326
WHERE TO STAY ... 326
WHERE TO EAT ... 326
NIGHTLIFE ... 327
SHOPPING ... 327

FOZ DO IGUAÇU ... 329
THE FALLS:
THE BRAZILIAN SIDE ... 330
THE ARGENTINE SIDE ... 333
OTHER SIGHTS ... 333
THE ESSENTIAL FOZ DO IGUAÇU ... 335
WHERE TO STAY ... 335
WHERE TO EAT ... 336
NIGHTLIFE ... 337
SHOPPING ... 337
HANDS-ON FOZ DO IGUAÇU ... 337

SANTA CATARINA ... 339
FLORIANÓPOLIS ... 343
BEACHES ... 343
THE ESSENTIAL FLORIANÓPOLIS ... 344
WHERE TO STAY ... 344
WHERE TO EAT ... 345
NIGHTLIFE ... 345
HANDS-ON FLORIANÓPOLIS ... 345
JOINVILLE ... 347
SIGHTS ... 347
THE ESSENTIAL JOINVILLE ... 349
WHERE TO STAY ... 349
WHERE TO EAT ... 349
NIGHTLIFE ... 350
SHOPPING ... 350
HANDS-ON JOINVILLE ... 350
BLUMENAU ... 351
SIGHTS ... 352

THE ESSENTIAL BLUMENAU 352
  WHERE TO STAY 352
  WHERE TO EAT 352
  NIGHTLIFE 353
  SHOPPING 353
  HANDS-ON BLUMENAU 354
CAMBORIÚ 355
  SIGHTS 355
  THE ESSENTIAL CAMBORIÚ 355
    WHERE TO STAY 355
    WHERE TO EAT 356
    NIGHTLIFE 356
    HANDS-ON CAMBORIÚ 356

RIO GRANDE DO SUL 357
PORTO ALEGRE 361
  THE ESSENTIAL PORTO ALEGRE 361
    WHERE TO STAY 361
    WHERE TO EAT 362
    NIGHTLIFE 362
    HANDS-ON PORTO ALEGRE 362
    SHOPPING 363
GRAMADO AND CANELA 365
  SIGHTS 365
  THE ESSENTIAL GRAMADO AND CANELA 367
    SPAS 367
    WHERE TO STAY 367
    WHERE TO EAT 368
    SHOPPING 368
NOVA PETRÓPOLIS 371
  SIGHTS 371
  THE ESSENTIAL NOVA PETRÓPOLIS 372
    WHERE TO STAY 372
    WHERE TO EAT 372
    SHOPPING 372
    HANDS-ON NOVA PETRÓPOLIS 372
TORRES 375
  BEACHES 376
  EXCURSIONS 376
  THE ESSENTIAL TORRES 376
    WHERE TO STAY 376
    WHERE TO EAT 377
    SHOPPING 377
    HANDS-ON TORRES 377

WINE COUNTRY
CAXIAS DO SUL 379
  THE ESSENTIAL CAXIAS DO SUL 380
    WHERE TO STAY 380
    WHERE TO EAT 380

CONTENTS

SHOPPING	380
HANDS-ON CAXIAS DO SUL	380
FARROUPILHA	**381**
GARIBALDI	**383**
THE ESSENTIAL GARIBALDI	383
WINE-TASTING	383
WHERE TO STAY	383
BENTO GONÇALVES	**385**
THE ESSENTIAL BENTO GONÇALVES	385
WINE-TASTING	385
WHERE TO STAY	385
WHERE TO EAT	385
CARLOS BARBOSA	**387**
BRASÍLIA	**389**
PAST GLORIES	390
A BIRD'S EYE VIEW	393
DAILY LIFE	395
SIGHTS	396
SPIRITUAL BRASÍLIA	399
NIGHTLIFE	402
THE ESSENTIAL BRASÍLIA	403
SHOPPING	403
HEALERS	403
WHERE TO STAY	404
WHERE TO EAT	406
HANDS ON BRAZÍLIA	407
POINTS BEYOND	408
BAHIA	**409**
SALVADOR	**411**
PAST GLORIES	413
CULTURE	414
A BIRD'S EYE VIEW	417
SAFETY IN SALVADOR	418
BEACHES	418
SIGHTS	420
MUSEUMS	428
BOAT EXCURSIONS	430
RAINY DAYS	431
THE ESSENTIAL BAHIA	432
WHERE TO STAY	432
RESORTS IN BAHIA	435
WHERE TO EAT	436
WHAT TO DO AT NIGHT	440
GAY SALVADOR	441
SHOPPING	441
SPORTS	443
HANDS-ON SALVADOR	443
WHEN TO GO	445

CACHOEIRA 447
   SIGHTS 448
   CANDOMBLÉ 450
   THE ESSENTIAL CACHOEIRA................................... 451
      WHERE TO STAY 451
      WHERE TO EAT 451
      NIGHTLIFE 451
      HANDS-ON CACHOEIRA 451
PRAIA DO FORTE 453
   SIGHTS 454
   EXCURSIONS 455
   THE ESSENTIAL PRAIA DO FORTE 456
      WHERE TO STAY 456
      WHERE TO EAT 456
      HANDS-ON PRAIA DO FORTE 457

PARTY BAHIA
PORTO SEGURO 459
   SIGHTS 460
   THE ESSENTIAL PORTO SEGURO 460
      BEACH EATERIES 460
      PARTY SCENE 461
      WHERE TO STAY 461
      WHERE TO EAT 462
      NIGHTLIFE 462
      SHOPPING 462
      HANDS-ON PORTO SEGURO 462
ARRAIAL D'AJUDA 465
   BEACHES 465
   THE ESSENTIAL ARRAIAL D'AJUDA 466
      WHERE TO STAY 466
      WHERE TO EAT 467
      NIGHTLIFE 467
      HANDS-ON ARRAIAL D'AJUDA 467
TRANCOSO 469
   THE ESSENTIAL TRANCOSO................................... 469
      WHERE TO STAY 469
      WHERE TO EAT 470
      HANDS-ON TRANCOSO 470

THE NORTHEAST 471
   MACEIÓ 475
      A BIRD'S EYE VIEW 476
      BEACH SCENE 476
      EXCURSIONS 477
      THE ESSENTIAL MACEIÓ.................................... 479
         WHERE TO STAY 479
         WHERE TO EAT 481
         NIGHTLIFE 482
         SHOPPING 482

CONTENTS

HANDS-ON MACEIÓ 483
RECIFE AND OLINDA 485
   HISTORY 485
   A BIRD'S EYE VIEW 486
   SIGHTS 487
   BEACHES IN RECIFE 492
   BEACHES NEAR RECIFE 492
   THE ESSENTIAL RECIFE AND OLINDA 494
      WHERE TO STAY 494
      WHERE TO EAT 496
      NIGHTLIFE 497
      SHOPPING 497
      HANDS-ON RECIFE 498
NATAL 501
   A BIRD'S EYE VIEW 502
   BEACHES IN NATAL 502
   BEACHES NEAR NATAL 503
   EXCURSION 504
   THE ESSENTIAL NATAL 506
      WHERE TO STAY 506
      WHERE TO EAT 508
      NIGHTLIFE 510
      SPIRITUALISM 510
      SHOPPING 510
      HANDS-ON NATAL 510
FORTALEZA 513
   HISTORY 513
   SIGHTS 514
   BEACHES IN FORTALEZA 515
   BEACHES BEYOND FORTALEZA 516
   EXCURSION 517
   THE ESSENTIAL FORTALEZA 519
      WHERE TO STAY 519
      WHERE TO EAT 520
      NIGHTLIFE 522
      SHOPPING 523
      HANDS–ON FORTALEZA 523
FERNANDO DE NORONHA 525
   PAST GLORIES 526
   SIGHTS 527
   THE ESSENTIAL FERNANDO DE NORONHA 528
      WHERE TO STAY 528
      HANDS–ON FERNANDO DE NORONHA 528
SÃO LUIS 531
   PAST GLORIES 532
   SIGHTS 532
   BEACHES 535
   EXCURSIONS 536

THE ESSENTIAL ALCÂNTARA	538
GETTING THERE	538
PARQUE NACIONAL DOS LENÇOIS	538
THE ESSENTIAL SÃO LUIS	541
MUSEUMS	541
WHERE TO STAY	541
WHERE TO EAT	543
SHOPPING	543
HANDS–ON SÃO LUIS	544
AMAZÔNIA	545
A BIRD'S EYE VIEW	546
PAST GLORIES	548
A QUICK RAINFOREST TOUR	554
OPTIONS FOR TRAVEL	557
THE AMAZON SURVIVAL KIT	559
SANTARÉM	563
PAST GLORIES	564
A BIRD'S EYE VIEW	565
SIGHTS	566
EXCURSION	568
EXCURSION PACKAGES	570
THE ESSENTIAL SANTARÉM	571
WHERE TO STAY	571
WHERE TO EAT	572
NIGHTLIFE	572
SHOPPING	573
HANDS-ON SANTARÉM	573
BELÉM	577
SIGHTS	578
MORE SIGHTS	582
EXCURSIONS	584
THE ESSENTIAL BELÉM	589
WHERE TO STAY	589
WHERE TO EAT	590
NIGHTLIFE	591
SHOPPING	591
HANDS-ON BÉLEM	592
MANAUS	595
SIGHTS	596
MUSEUMS	598
JUNGLE EXCURSIONS	601
THE ESSENTIAL MANAUS	602
JUNGLE LODGES	602
WHERE TO STAY	603
WHERE TO EAT	605
NIGHTLIFE	606
SHOPPING	607
HANDS-ON MANAUS	608

ALTA FLORESTA ... 611
CULTURE ... 612
THE ESSENTIAL ALTA FLORESTA ... 614
WHERE TO STAY ... 614

THE PANTANAL ... 615
HOW TO VISIT ... 617
PANTANAL SURVIVAL KIT ... 619
CUIABÁ ... 621
A BIRD'S EYE VIEW ... 622
SIGHTS ... 622
MUSEUMS AND ZOO ... 623
THE ESSENTIAL CUIABÁ ... 624
WHERE TO STAY ... 624
WHERE TO EAT ... 624
NIGHTLIFE ... 625
SHOPPING ... 625
HEALERS ... 625
HANDS-ON CUIABÁ ... 625
CHAPADA DOS GUIMARÃES ... 629
ON THE WAY TO CHAPADA ... 629
A BIRD'S EYE VIEW ... 631
MYSTICAL THEORIES OF CHAPADA ... 632
SIGHTS ... 632
EXCURSIONS ... 633
OTHER FAZENDAS ... 635
BOTELS AND BOAT CRUISES ... 637
THE ESSENTIAL CHAPADA DOS GUIMARÃES ... 639
WHERE TO STAY ... 639
WHERE TO EAT ... 639
SHOPPING ... 640
HEALERS ... 640
HANDS-ON CHAPADA DOS GUIMARÃES ... 640

SPECIALTY TOURS ... 643

LANGUAGE ... 647

HEALTH KIT FOR THE TROPICS ... 659

BOOKS AND FILMS ... 667
BOOKS ... 667
FILMS ... 670
RAINFOREST INFORMATION ... 671

SELECTED DISCOGRAPHY ... 673

INDEX ... 679

IMPORTANT!

INSIDER TIP:
One of the most unique features of this guide are the discounts on hotel accommodations awarded readers of The Fielding Guide to Brazil. Here's how it works: To receive the stated discount (anywhere from 10 percent-50 percent), you must present the book in hand to the manager of the hotel. This will prove you are a Fielding's reader. (Sorry, but that means you will have to travel "with" the book!) While all these offers were confirmed to me in person and in good faith, I cannot be responsible for any last-minute changes of policy. Given the variable economic situation, anything can happen in Brazil, but do notify me immediately if you encounter trouble. (The service was instigated only as a courtesy to my readers, and I receive absolutely no kickback on the transaction.)

INFLATION WARNING

Inflation in Brazil transcends the unbelievable. In 1993, prices in *cruzeiros* were rising 30 percent per month, without any relief in sight. The value of the dollar is therefore extremely volatile, but because prices in *cruzeiros* are always being revised, prices in U.S. dollars tend to rise only about $10-$15 each year (following the general international trend). However, *nothing* is predictable in Brazil; as such, prices quoted in this book (always in dollars) can only be considered a good estimate.

DISCLAIMER

While every effort has been made to assure the accuracy of facts mentioned in this guide, human mistakes are inevitable, not to mention the ever-changing landscape of the Brazilian tourist industry. All opinions expressed in this book stem from the author's personal experience only; consequently, neither she nor the publisher can be held accountable for a reader's personal experience while traveling. Any comments, suggestions, and ideas for future editions may be addressed to the author, Pamela Bloom, c/o Fielding Worldwide.

LATE-BREAKING FLASH FOR 1994

In the summer of 1993, the Brazilian government changed the currency to the cruzeiro real by knocking off three zeroes from the cruzeiro. By itself, this maneuver (which was designed simply to make calculations easier) does not affect prices in dollars, nor even "real prices" in Brazilian currency, beyond the ever-present, ever-rising inflationary affects. As of September 1993, the government has begun to issue new paper and coin money, but the change will take some time to become fully integrated. As such, you may be presented with "old money" whose value, as printed on the money itself, should not be allowed to confuse you. Do keep an eye out for mistakes.

Pam Bloom, Author

ABOUT THE AUTHOR

Pamela Bloom is a music and arts critic, travel writer, and fiction writer whose work has appeared in such publications as the *New York Times, Chicago Tribune,* and *Los Angeles Times,* as well as *High Fidelity, Musician, Downbeat, Seven Days, Connoisseur,* and *Elle* magazines, among others. She received a B.A. in comparative literature from Trinity College (Hartford, CT), attended Dartmouth College, and also studied opera at Indiana University and the Juilliard School of Music. She teaches the history of Brazilian jazz at the New School for Social Research in New York and also presents a multimedia lecture series on Brazilian music and culture at the Ballroom Club in Manhattan, in conjunction with their annual Brazilian jazz series. A world traveler, Pamela Bloom has pursued writing assignments in China, Spain, Greece, and the Caribbean, as well as throughout the U.S.A. As a dedicated Brazilophile, she has danced in Rio's Carnaval with the Portela Samba School, interviewed many of the country's top musicians, and traveled extensively throughout the country. A native of Houston, TX, she presently resides in Brooklyn, NY.

TO MY READERS

One day late in the summer of 1985, I was walking down West 65th Street in Manhattan, wondering why the Brazilian at my side was not as madly in love with me as I was with him, when suddenly he handed me his headphones and purred, "Pamela, you must *leesen* to *deese.*" From that moment on, when I first heard the voice of the great Elis Regina singing the songs of Milton Nascimento, my life irrevocably changed. Like many before and after me, it was the wings of song that carried me into the heart and soul of Brazilian culture, one that at first seemed so exotic but has since come to feel like second skin. As a music critic, I have had the rare opportunity of sitting down to talk with the country's greatest musicians, visiting their homes in Brazil, watching them record, and listening like a child at their feet as they discussed their dreams and visions and the ineffable power of their music. In 1986, I even had the wondrous joy of dancing with the Portela Samba School in Rio's Carnaval. But nothing can match the privilege of writing this book, of being able to travel to over 55 cities and villages—meeting the locals, tasting their food, surfing their waves, tramping their forests, and yes, even getting bitten by their bugs, to begin to understand what makes up Brazil, and, more importantly, what makes a Brazilian. The very size and diversity of this tropical country defies simple stereotype, but there is one thing that is certain: anyone who travels to Brazil with an open heart is sure to return home with an incurable case of *saudade* —an indefinable Portuguese word that is translated most often as unrequited longing. Composer Tom Jobim immortalized that feeling in *bossa nova*, but for travelers it can mean only one thing: book a return passage as fast as you can.

Frankly, I wrote this guide book for the kind of tourist who wants to engage himself body and soul in Brazil and Brazilian culture. In fact, I have written the guide book *I* wanted to read—hopefully, one that not only inspires adventure but also demystifies any obstacles to travel. As such, you'll find not only straight–from–the hip tips about hotels, restaurants, and tours, but also first–person narratives and interviews that bring the color of Brazil to life. In fact, there's enough information and background here that non–Portuguese speaking tourists may never have to hire a private guide to explain what they're looking at. In this first edition, I have tried to include all the major tourist destinations, though a few may seem "off the beaten track" for the more Western–oriented traveler. And incredible as it may seem, I personally inspected 99 percent of the hotels included in this book. Like anywhere else in the world, in Brazil you get the room you pay for, but no travel writer can foresee quirks in personal service, change of administration, and just the plain bad luck of getting that one room where the air–conditioning is busted and the sewage has backed up. Brazil is a country of continuous movement and unpredictability, and a guide book at its best can only point to the way, not carve it in stone.

A most important section of this book is dedicated to Eco–Brazil. In an era when clean air, pure water, and rich soil is at a premium, Brazil remains one of the leading destinations in the world for those who want to scale mountains, traverse rainforests, veg out on beaches, or trek through the backcountry on horseback. As you'll be able to tell from my first–person accounts, I managed to happily survive all these adventures, proving you don't have to be in Olympic-quality shape to enjoy yourself in Brazil. But even before you turn a page, make a promise to me that you will become the most eco–conscious traveler ever. This means traveling light, disposing of garbage properly, not throwing cigarette butts on the forest or beach, and not unduly disturbing fauna or flora above or under the sea. In other words, as they say in Brazil, *"Preserve a Natureza"* and by doing so we'll preserve the planet.

Most importantly, I have taken the issue of my readers' personal safety deeply to heart. More than anything, I want to see you return

TO MY READERS

home from Brazil happy, healthy, and with your valuables intact. As with all large cities throughout the world, the major cities of Brazil do have their share of crime, but there is absolutely no reason why anyone should be deterred from visiting Brazil. Mostly, safety is a matter of common sense and caution, and throughout this book I have given numerous safety tips which, if followed *precisely,* can go a long way to ensuring your well-being. While incidents do occur, not one threatening situation happened to me during twelve months of travel, though I did return from the Amazon with a few nasty tics. For eco-travelers, included in the back of the book is an extensive health kit, one which you should study *months* prior to a trip to the backlands.

With apologies to any real mothers out there, being the sole author of a guide book to a country bigger than the continental United States can only be compared to giving birth to triplets and then adopting four other children all at the same time. As such, I ask your indulgence for any mistakes that may have incurred between hastily taking notes in a canoe in 100° heat all the way to deciphering my Porto-English scrawl back home in Brooklyn—not to mention, that kind of Jekyll/Hyde personality some computers adopt right in the middle of life-and-death projects. In any case, I would love to hear from you about *your* trip, your likes and your dislikes, and any suggestions or tips you would like to contribute to the subsequent editions of this guide. After all, it was thousands of 18th-century *bandeirantes,* not just one, that opened up the interior of Brazil to the rest of the world. If only we in the 20th century could be half as adventurous.

So get out the suntan lotion, pack your sexiest swimsuit, and head out with me to one of the most glorious spots on this Earth. As they say in Brazil, *Vai com Deus* (Go with God), and, as I like to add, *May you return with a song in your heart.*

PAMELA BLOOM

ACKNOWLEDGMENTS

A book of this magnitude could never have been written without the support of literally hundreds of people, both in Brazil and back home. My deepest thanks goes to the offices of the Brazilian Tourist Office in New York and Fundação Turismo (Fun Tur) in Rio, especially Gloria Britto Pereira, Priscilla Monerrat and Eliane Freitas, for their active support throughout my entire Brazilian sojourn. Also instrumental was Ana Maria Almeida and her staff at Embratur. Special thanks go to Trajano Ribeiro, President of Rio Tur, his colleague Aniko Santos, and her staff, who helped to make my hard work in Rio more like fun.

My wonderful moments in São Paulo were all due to the lively, super-efficient staff of the São Paulo Convention Bureau headed by Sylvia Mangabeira. A kiss and hug to Christine Baanwaart, Gabriella Esgaib and Cecília de Oliveiro Barbosa.

The deepest thanks are extended to the tourist boards of each state and city I visited, with special mention for outstanding assistance by the staffs of Santa Catarina, Paraná, Pará, Amazonas, and Rio Grande do Sul. Many thanks goes to the staff of Bahiatursa, who helped me realize a demanding schedule. Special gratitude must be accorded the staff of Belotursa, spearheaded by Neiva Duarte, and the state tourist board of Minas Gerais for giving me so much superb assistance.

A special *beijo* goes to three Secretaries of Tourism who kept me awake and entertained beyond the call of duty: José Luiz Nogueira of Caxambú, Ivan Canzioni of Farroupilha, and especially, Fernando

César Mesquita of the state of Maranhão, who introduced me to the unforgettable dunes of Parque dos Lençois.

Deep gratitude is extended to Maureen Callanan and Andrea Leal of Varig, and their ever-supportive staff throughout my entire project.

Special mention of gratitude must be made to Claudio Heckmann and Robert Falkenburg of F&H Consulting and André von Thuranyi of Expeditours, who never let me down when I most needed them. Thanks also to Vania Leite of the Luxor Hotels, Paulo Gustavo Reis do Vale of the Horsa chain, and Fabiana Espanhol of the Hotel Glória in Rio. Many thanks go to Beatrice Imbiriba of Lago Verde Turismo in Santarém.

Among the many guides who gave of their time and knowledge, many thanks go to the following: Kim Kamel and Paulo César in Rio; Silvia Vannuci Chiappori in Salvador; Rosane Freitas, Secretary of Tourism in Torres; Antônio Augusto in Belo Horizonte, Beto Westphal in Florianópolis, Berenice Pereira in Porto Alegre; Denise Gonçalves Borges de Medeiros in São João del Rei; Silvio Benedito Pereira da Silva in Alta Floresta; Chris Moraes in Blumenau, Gia Nilce and Teodoro Gruber in Rio Branco; and Tony Rocha and Miraya Lima in Belém.

Special credit is extended to Vera Lucia Régis for her research assistance in Rio.

Mystical thanks goes to Fernando do Oxalá, *pai de santo* in Belo Horizonte, for his words of wisdom and encouragement, União Vegetal's Mestre Felipe Belmonte in Brasília and Mestre Alberto in Salvador for several nights of illumination; Marilena Simões in Belo Horizonte for her accurate psychic readings, and Vida Vidmar at Transamérica Hotel for her enlightening lunch.

For saving me on a crazy day in Salvador, thanks go to Sérgio Pessoa for the use of his car and driver. A special kiss to Graça in Brasília for making my stay in her city such a joy.

Special holistic thanks to Dr. Andrea Brito in Rio, shiatzu practitioner Patrick Sasso in Rio, acupuncturist Homero Bernardo in Brasília, and the community of Vale do Amanhecer for saving my life.

For memories that will last a lifetime, a large *abraço* goes to: Mássimo Ferrari of São Paulo for a night of unsurpassable dining; Túlio Marques Lopes Filho of Belo Horizonte for a superlative

ACKNOWLEDGMENTS

weekend on horseback; Humberto Morim of TV Amazonas in Manaus for making me feel like a star, and Luis Claudio Ferreira and Celso Losado of Arraial d'Ajuda for being themselves.

Traveling through Brazil would mean nothing without making friends. The deepest love goes to Diana Figueroa and Jorge Magdalena of Buenos Aires for two perfect days in Angra; Sonia Gomes in Salvador for her hospitality and kindness; Ma Prem Dwari in Cuiabá for her Bach Remedies dispensed at the end of the world; Vera Régis in Rio for her hospitality; a special double kiss to Neiva Duarte in Belo Horizonte for her laughter, constant support, and true beauty; to Itamar and Mirta in Rio for their friendship; and most of all, to Carlos Alberto Saldanha Leite in Rio, without whose love, support, *jeitinhos,* and packing genius I would never have been able to return home.

In New York, many thanks to Dr. Marsha Woolf for tips on how to stay holistic and healthy abroad; Master Alan Lee for care and support during the second revision; Deborah Wolf, for spiritual assistance; Tobias Nascimento for his Portuguese lessons and unbounded enthusiasm for Brazilian culture; Faye Hammel, travel writer extraordinaire, for her commiseration; Carol, Gary, Rachel, and Andrew Shaffer for culinary support; Eva Franklin for her weekly support calls and uncanny ability to find articles on Brazil in the strangest of places; and especially to "Shtevie" Katz for a few lifetimes of friendship.

A nod of deep gratitude to Georgia Christgau of *High Fidelity* magazine, Don Shewey of *Seven Days,* Jon Pareles of the *New York Times,* and Cathy Cook of *Taxi* magazine, who welcomed my articles on Brazilian music, and especially to Mark Rowland of *Musician* magazine, who sent me off on a wild, unforgettable roadtrip with Milton Nascimento.

A big *beijo* to Altamira Leite for his indefatigable linguistic support. Eternal gratitude and a pocketful of miracles to Steve Perine for his emergency editorial assistance.

Special thanks to Robert Pelton of Pelton & Associates for having a vision and the energy to implement it. Extra special thanks is extended to the Toshiba Corporation for the loan of a wonderful laptop computer. May I not send it through an airport x-ray machine the next time.

And finally in Houston, to Dr. Kim Bloom and family for the generous gift of a hard drive and modem; to Dr. Kerry Bloom and family for finding me in the jungle and getting me home for my mother's surprise birthday party; and most of all to my parents, Mitzie Muntz Bloom and the late Dr. Manuel G. Bloom, for their love, support and patience beyond all common cents.

INTRODUCTION

Brazil is a land of exotic collision. Cows lumber across multilaned highways, battery-powered TVs blare away in the jungle, and some of the world's most sophisticated music wafts from its sorriest ghettoes. In Brazil's modern metropolises, skyscrapers surge like icons toward heaven, while only blocks away languish beaches of such incredible beauty they can only be called paradise. Hot spices, hot rhythms, hot climes all jangle together to produce a multicultural mélange that favors mystics and marketplaces and marginal societies. And yet, just kilometers away, are cold winters, sauerkraut, and European-style beer fests. Simply, Brazil is a third-world country with a sometime first-world face, a persona that often tricks not only its own people but even the savviest travelers who venture to its shores.

Long called the sleeping giant, Brazil is just now wiggling its gargantuan toes and waking from a hibernation that has, with a few notable exceptions, kept it politically and economically dazed for most of the 20th century. To some keen observers, Brazil has been likened to an adolescent struggling to find itself in the face of an enormous but chaotic inheritance. From its birth as a Portuguese colony with unlimited promise, it has steadily passed from being an unwieldy empire, an ambitious republic, and a repressive dictatorship into the still-struggling democracy it is today, supported firmly, if cautiously, by the world's major powers. As the biggest country in South America, Brazil boasts both some of the greatest wealth and the greatest inequality in the world—at times, even the sunshine seems unfairly distributed. Yet what makes Brazil so attractive as a travel destination is its diversity. Just as there is no one topography that represents the richness of the nation's resources, there is no one color of Brazilian, though the stunning coffee-colored *mulata* has come to represent, for better or worse, a definite standard of national beauty. But to the surprise of most tourists, there are also German blue-eyed blondes in the South, Indian-angled cheekbones in the Northeast, Japanese almond eyes in São Paulo, and dark Italian features in the extreme south, not to mention the black-faced descendants of African tribes, whose religious beliefs, music, dance, and cuisine support the very core of Brazilian culture itself.

Travelwise, Brazil has lain buried under a burden of misconceptions. Ask the average American to name the first thing that comes to mind at the thought of Brazil, and the answer will probably be: monkeys, Spanish, elephants, naked pretty girls, and Carnaval—though not necessarily in that order. In truth, there are monkeys in Brazil—in the rain forest, not roaming the streets; Spanish is spoken by a few, but it's Portuguese that is the national language; elephants, to my knowledge, have never, *ever* been sighted in the jungle, but there *are* definitely lots of pretty girls, though not necessarily naked, except during Carnaval, when flinging off one's brassiere becomes nearly an act of national pride. As for other easily puncturable myths, the Brazilian bombshell Carmen Miranda probably did more than any other "goodwill ambassador" to perpetuate the idea that all Brazilians walk around with fruit on their heads. Sure, in the interior, particularly in Bahia, women gracefully carry piles of laundry, luggage, yes, even crates of fruit on their head without missing a beat, but visit a disco in a big city like Rio or São Paulo and you'll find Brazilians more stylishly dressed than most North Americans.

What Brazil is today is a country where you can travel between centuries in a matter of hours. There's the Amazon jungle where Indians live in the Stone Age; 18th century historical villages where you'll find horses hitched to posts; 19th century *fazendas,* or ranches, where cowboys still ride the range; fashionable 20th century cities like Rio and São Paulo, where international trends set the style, and even one arresting city called Brasília, whose avant-garde sculptured buildings proudly face toward the 21st century. There are even tiny villages, like São Tomé das Letras in Minas Gerais, that seem totally out of synch with time—dare I say *otherworldly.* It's not for nothing that Brazil has gained the reputation for hosting some of the most famous UFO sightings in the world.

The continuous clash between first-world and third-world values is something that no tourist can escape when he visits Brazil. Even within the same city, such as Rio, upper-class grande dames take afternoon tea in plush beachside hotels while only blocks away, high up on the hillside, families of ten crowd into huts that disappear regularly under mudslides and rainstorms. It's impossible to travel through the country without taking both realities into account, and yet most tourists, unless they travel far into the backlands, will not be assaulted with a continual display of wretched poverty. Somehow the tropical beauty, especially along the seashore, seems to soothe some of the harsher social realities—even for Brazilians, who appear able to delight in the simple pleasures of sun, surf, and sand, even when there are no other amenities in sight. This is not to discount the very real problems faced by a majority of the population, particularly in the Northeast: high infant mortality rate, drought, homelessness, malnutrition, and disease. But even in the worst possible circumstances, there seems to be an indefinable Brazilian spirit that manages to transcend human misery and extreme hardship, or at least absorb and transmute it into song, dance, and religious fervor. Frankly, I have never seen such shining, luminescent eyes than in the faces of some hearty souls who struggle to survive everyday life in the Amazon jungle.

THE ESSENTIAL BRAZIL

WHERE TO GO

Most travelers light down in **Rio de Janeiro** as their first Brazilian destination. Next to Paris, London, Tokyo, and New York, Rio is one of the great cities of the world—a treasure that proved its worth when it was successfully invaded by hundreds of thousands of foreigners for the Rio '92 ecological conferences. **São Paulo,** the Brazilian Big Apple, is also easily accessible from New York City, but with direct flights also now available to **Recife** and **Salvador** from the States, the Northeast of Brazil has opened up as a tourist destination in its own right. It's perfectly possible to spend your entire trip journeying from Salvador north, first enjoying the center of Afro-Brazilian culture, then venturing northward along the coast to savor the beaches of **Recife, Maceió, Natal,** and **Fortaleza**. From **São Luis,** a revived colonial capital right on the beach, you can easily enter the Amazon region, landing either in **Belém, Santarém,** or **Manaus,** from which you can actually enter the jungle. And once you're settled in Manaus, a flight to **Cuiabá** in the Pantanal is as easy as making a reservation. Planes do get smaller as you plow further into the interior, but I never felt unsafe, and no professional airline I rode ever approached the kind of rickety bumper planes you see in Hollywood-made movies.

Today, perhaps Brazil's biggest draw, and least publicized asset, is its amazing array of ecologically oriented vacation adventures, many of which are included in this book. If the **Amazon** rain forest is your thing, you can stay overnight in a treehouse lodge in the jungle, float down one of the Amazon's many tributaries in a canoe, fish for man-eating piranha during the day, or hunt for alligators at night. To relive the 18th-century wanderings of Brazilian explorers, you can make an overnight horseback trek through the mountains of **Minas Gerais** (the eco-trip I consider the best in Brazil). If exotic birds and animals are your fancy, you can traipse through the **Pantanal** on horseback, in canoe, and by jeep, depending on the time of the year. There are mineral water spa towns for health-oriented fanatics and there are national parks where you can camp next to waterfalls or sling a hammock under natural stone houses.

For history and architecture buffs, the historical villages of **Minas Gerais** offer a plethora of artistic treasures.

HOW TO GO

The most important thing to decide before you go to Brazil is what kind of traveler you are. Do you want adventure, and how much? How self-reliant are you, or do you prefer to be coddled? Would you rather have an agency make all your reservations, or do you want to wing it alone? Is your idea of a vacation a deserted beach where you can snooze all afternoon, or do you prefer to be revved up by physical challenges? Are you traveling with children or with valuable equipment that can't be replaced? Do you like to mingle with the upper crust, or would you rather meet locals who live a simpler life? Every single possibility can be found in Brazil, and you must gauge your accommodations and activities accordingly. If you communicate clearly to your travel agent or tour operator, even trips through the Amazon jungle can be arranged to suit your particular state of fitness, age, and ecological desire. Believe it or not—even senior citizens over seventy have been glimpsed hooting up a storm in the rain forest.

IS BRAZIL EXPENSIVE?

Can I afford Brazil? is the question most asked by tourists, and while the answer depends on your personal tastes and available purse, the answer in general is a resounding yes. The airfare from the States will be one of your biggest financial setbacks, but there are ways to scope out reduced fares through package deals, air passes, advance purchases, and courier services. Once in Brazil, you can go the luxury route and relax at fabulous beachside resorts or stay in relatively low-priced *pousadas* or inns, even bargaining for a hammock on the porch of a local. As of 1993, a good meal practically anywhere in the country could be had for under $5, an excellent one for about $10, and world-class *haute cuisine* for no more than $25 per person. If you start off the day with a big breakfast (a substantial buffet is included in the rate of most hotels) you could probably get by on just one more meal a day (fueled, perhaps, by a few inexpensive snacks). Depending on the exchange rate (which is as variable as a bad love affair), you may often discover that your dollar is worth much more by the time you leave Brazil than when you arrived—a quirk of international travel that inspires in most tourists a strange mixture of glee and regret.

WHY GO?

If you're still looking for one overriding reason to go to Brazil, here it is: Brazil is just plain fun—as are Brazilians, who are among the warmest and most hospitable people in the world. It's been said that you could put any Brazilian on a stage anywhere in the world and he or she would instantly become a star. Simply, in Brazil emotionality is an art form, the ability to dance second nature, and even young boys from *favelas* can beat out complicated sambas on the side of a beer can. All that pent-up passion to sing and dance explodes come Carnaval every February when Brazilians in every part of the country take to the streets to celebrate the coming of *Quaresma* (Lent) with parades, masquerades, and an explosive effusion of rhythms. Known worldwide is the gargantuan parade in Rio's Sambódromo—a highly organized yet exuberant parade involving over 70,000 dancers, singers, and models. The party, countrywide, is open to tourists, who need do nothing but hang loose in a flow of merrymaking that ranges anywhere from the merely joyous to the outrageously sexy. (For more on Carnaval, see the chapter titled *Carnaval*.)

BIRD'S EYE VIEW

Brazilian explorer José de Paula Machado wrote that "Brazil is a country in which space is its most important heritage, the ecosystem its language, and the natural resources still its greatest secret." Space, indeed, is Brazil's middle name. The fifth largest land-rich country in the world, Brazil is also the most populous country in Latin America with over 150 million people. With the exception of Chile and Ecuador, Brazil's borders touch every country in South America—a fact that requires continual diplomacy. Although the country boasts a landmass larger than the continental United States, its people are crammed into a very small area. Forty-five percent of the total population crowd the southern region, which represents only 14 percent of the total territory. The Amazon rainforest occupies 42 percent of the total mass, although it is home to fewer people than live in New York City. Despite the construction of the ultramodern capital, Brasília, the Central Plateau remains relatively uninhabited.

Brazil thrives on its **colorful regionalism**. There are six distinct regions, each with its own geography, climate, racial makeup, and cultural traditions. To meet the political and social needs of each, however, is an ongoing challenge for the federal government.

The area most known to tourists is the **Southeast**, dominated by the beachside city of **Rio de Janeiro** and the industrial capital of **São Paulo**. Also here is the mining state of **Minas Gerais**, its fashionable capital **Belo Horizonte**, and the small legion of historical towns that continue to preserve the flavor of 18th century Brazil. Geographically, the region is divided between a slender coastal zone and an elevated plateau banked by a narrow mountainous range. With the exception of the ports of Rio and Santos, most of the region, sculpted by rolling hills, enjoys a temperate climate with a clear winter and summer.

The smallest of Brazil's regions, the **South**, makes up 7 percent of the national territory and has experienced a boom since the 1950s. Located below the Tropic of Cancer, it boasts a subtropical climate with all four seasons, including frosts and occasional snowfall during winter. In the states of **Paraná**, **Santa**

Catarina, and **Rio Grande do Sul**, there is a distinctive mix of Italian, German, Polish, and Russian immigrants, many of whom continue to speak their native languages and perpetuate their homelands' cuisine. Home to the Brazilian cowboy, called the *gaúcho*, the extreme south is blessed with magnificent rolling hills, picturesque valleys, and a fertile wine country; but the region's greatest natural wonder is the **Iguaçu Falls**, which plunge through a gorge of the Iguaçu River along the Argentina-Paraguay border.

The **Central West** is an elevated plateau that reaches 3,300 feet above sea level and is called the **Planalto Central**. It is divided into areas of forest (mostly in the north) and woodland savannas known as *cerrado*. This scrubland, when cleared, has actually proven quite fertile, inspiring southern farmers to develop large soybean and cattle-grazing plantations. In the middle of this plateau stands the nation's futuristic capital, **Brasília**, a mirage of modernism in an otherwise sparse region.

The **Northeast** is the third largest region, covering 18 percent of the country. Once the center of the sugar industry during colonial times, it has remained underdeveloped due to life-threatening droughts, but it is not underpopulated. Some of the best beaches in Brazil are located here, its coastline rewarded with sunshine year-round. Among the best coastal resort cities are **Aracajú** in the state of Sergipe, **Maceió** in Alagoas, **Recife** in Pernambuco, **João Pessoa** in Paraíba, **Natal** in Rio Grande do Norte, **Fortaleza** in Ceará, and **São Luis** in Maranhão (all capitals of their respective states). Located here is also the state of **Bahia**, and its capital, **Salvador**, the center of Brazilian black culture and one of the most colorful and folkloric parts of Brazil.

Legend and harsh reality come together in the region known as **Amazônia**, home to the vast, mysterious Amazon jungle and the enormous river of the same name. Modern cities, quaint port villages, and isolated jungle huts all await the intrepid tourist who may indulge in a variety of adventures over land, swamp, and river. Just south of Amazônia is the magnificent swampland known as the **Pantanal**, a veritable paradise of exotic animals and birds whose migrations depend on biannual flood tides.

BEACHES

Brazil is best known for its fabulous beaches—over 4,600 miles of Atlantic coastline. The sophisticated beach scene in Rio de Janeiro stands in a class by itself, but each Brazilian city with a beach boasts its own personality. After Rio de Janeiro, Salvador is the second most frequented coastal destination in Brazil, enjoying a massive bay and numerous primitive beaches in its outlying districts. One of the most memorable beach diversions in all Brazil is the *jangada* boat ride in Maceió, matched only by dunesurfing in Natal. Beaches outside the city of Recife are known for their wild, unspoiled locales, while some of the most exotic beaches (colored sand, wind-swept dunes, moonscape rocks) are situated outside Fortaleza. Some of the best scuba diving in the world can be found off the northeastern coast, on the island of Fernando de Noronha. Encroaching upon the edge of the Amazon, the city of São Luis combines picturesque beaches with a rich folklore and a beautifully restored colonial center. In the extreme southern state of Rio Grande do Sul, the beaches of Torres boast craggy grottoes and wooded cliffs that often seem reminiscent of Druid country.

HOW TO USE THIS GUIDE

The best way to get acquainted with Brazil through this book is to read the first chapters up to Rio, followed by the introduction to each region. Then, according to your interest, move on to the introduction to each city, also perusing the descriptions of the beaches, as well as the boxed "Excursions." Hotels and restaurants have been listed in such a way as to facilitate clarity and to give you a quick idea of what's available in all price ranges. Because the "culture" of Brazil differs drastically from region to region, I have included this kind of information within each particular area to preserve their distinctive flavors.

DIRECTORY

Rio's Copacabana

BEFORE YOU GO

ACCOMMODATIONS

Accommodations in Brazil run from the fantasy resort hotel to the jungle lodge adorned with mosquito nets. In between are reasonable, air-conditioned hotels, as well as simple pensions with ceiling fan. Most hotels are rated by EMBRATUR, the official tourist board, according to a 5-star scale whose values are not always equivalent in different regions of the country. The quality of 5-star properties in Rio and São Paulo, however, are nearly competitive with top-class hotels around the world and offer an array of facilities, including excellent pools, gourmet restaurants, fashionable decor, exercise equipment and/or sauna, boutiques, and fine service. As you move up the northeast coast and into the Amazon region, 3-star hotels will sometimes challenge American standards of cleanliness, and 2-star hotels, unless otherwise stated, can only be recommended for backpackers. (Do note that the "stars" next to hotels, restaurants, sights, etc. are my own personal rating system.)

A recent tourist trend, particularly in Rio, São Paulo, and Belo Horizonte, are apart-hotels, which are often exquisitely decorated apartments that cost much less than 5- and sometimes 4-star hotels. They are excellent choices for families, large groups, or anyone wishing to escape the tourist hubbub of larger hotels. Youth hostels are generally upbeat and clean, do not discriminate by age, and provide a social network that often proves extremely valuable.

The prices of hotel rooms fluctuate greatly throughout the year, not only because of inflation, but in response to the various seasons. During low season (March–June and August–November), you can often receive up to a 20 percent discount, but you or your travel agent must ask for it directly. Accommodations December–February, the month of July, and especially the weeks around Carnaval are at peak rates. A major perk for *Fielding* readers is that they may receive special discounts on specific hotels (as designated) if they show the book to the receptionist. (This means you must travel *with Fielding's Brazil*—as you should!)

Reservations for all accommodations should be made in advance; during Carnaval and other regional folkloric events, such as Oktoberfest in Blumenau, they should be made 6 months in advance.

Excellent package deals can be obtained through various private tour companies that you will find listed under "Package Deals" below and *Specialty Tours* in the back of the book. If you fly on Varig Airlines, you can receive up to a 10 percent discount on Varig hotels, which often includes a transfer from the airport. (Varig properties include the Tropical Hotels in Santarém, Manaus, and Iguaçu Falls.)

AIR TRAVEL TO BRAZIL

International flights from the United States to Brazil run between 5 and 12 hours, depending on where you leave from and where you arrive.

Flying **Varig** airlines (☎ 800-468-2744), Brazil's national carrier, is one of the best ways to start off your Brazilian vacation. While other airlines may be cheaper, Varig is known throughout the travel industry as one of the best carriers in the world—consistently providing punctual arrivals, excellent food, and cheerful, efficient service. Executive class seats are considerably more comfortable than tourist class, and their meals (along with those of first class) include extensive hors d'oeuvres and desserts; one might even complain that there is too much food! Films (generally two) shown throughout the long flights are usually the latest releases. Best of all, the Brazilian stewards and stewardesses give you the opportunity to try out your Portuguese and will answer any questions you may have about traveling.

From North America, Varig offers wide-body services to Brazil through 5 gateways: New York, Chicago, Miami, Los Angeles, and Toronto. From Miami, there are 17 weekly flights, including daily nonstops to both Rio and São Paulo, plus one flight each to Manaus, Belém (continuing on to Fortaleza), and one to Recife and Salvador. From New York, there are 8 weekly nonstop flights to Rio and/or São Paulo. Chicago offers 3 flights weekly to Rio, with continuing service to São Paulo. Los Angeles operates 6 weekly flights to Rio and São Paulo, 3 via Lima, 1 via Manaus. In addition, Varig flies 3 times weekly from Los Angeles to Tokyo. For Canadian travelers, there are 6 weekly flights from Toronto.

The cheapest fare Varig offers is an excursion package, with a minimum stay of 21 days (maximum 3 months), with the ticket purchased 14 days in advance (about $1,362, tax not included). Another excursion package (minimum 7 days, maximum 21 days, 14-day advance purchase), must be combined with a land tour, hotel, or package booked through Varig. About $100 can be saved during low season, which runs August 8–December 9, and January 11–June 20. First-class tickets in any season run about $4,960; executive class about $3,230.

NEW IN 1994

Varig passengers traveling to Rio de Janeiro, Brasília, Porto Alegre and Curitiba may now reserve a cellular phone to use during their stay, with more cities being added. Daily rental fees, minimum usage fees, and security fees are all waived; renters receive a 10 percent discount on all calls. Reservations for the service must be made 72 hours in advance through a travel agent or Varig.

United Airlines (☎ *800-241-6522*) offers nonstop flights from New York and Miami to Rio. Although rates fluctuate depending on season, the lowest ones are awarded for 14-day advance purchase and a minimum stay of 21 days (maximum 90 days). Highest rates are generally between December and January. A New York-Rio roundtrip runs about $1,210 in low season (with advance purchase).

American Airlines (☎ *800-433-7300*) flies Miami-Rio nonstop (for about $1,102 coach low season) and New York-São Paulo nonstop. For information about packaged vacations and discount flights, see "Package Deals" below.

Aerolinas Argentinas (☎ *800-333-0276*) flies New York –Rio nonstop for $1,180 coach low season), New York–São Paolo nonstop, and Miami–São Paolo and Miami–Rio.

For information regarding cruises to Brazil, see under *Specialty Tours*.

AIR TRAVEL WITHIN BRAZIL

Brazil is a *big* country (as the musician Caetano Veloso once said, "kinda *too* big"), and the distances between major cities are enormous. If you are planning to visit more than one city in Brazil, do seriously consider buying **Varig's Brazil Airpass**. For a basic cost of $440, you receive 1–5 flight coupons (6 if Santarém is included), which allows you to make that many flights within a 21-day period. (You are also allowed to make 2 connections via any of the following cities: Brasília, Fortaleza, Manaus, Recife, Rio, Salvador, and São Paulo.) Additional coupons can be purchased for $100 each. Do note that you must plan your itinerary carefully, as some cities, especially in the Northeast, will require several connections. Also, the Airpass must be purchased outside Brazil (though you need not be flying internationally on Varig), and it may be used only on domestic Varig flights. It is not valid on the Rio/São Paulo shuttle between Congonhas and Santos Dumont airports. Nevertheless, this Airpass, depending on your itinerary, can save you hundreds of dollars, since domestic travel within Brazil is extremely expensive.

Other airlines within Brazil are **Transbrasil** and **VASP,** but airfare bought within Brazil can run into hundreds of dollars. Transbrasil flights are usually at night and connections aren't always convenient.

For travel by bus, car, and train within Brazil, see "Travel Within Brazil" below.

BEST TIME TO VISIT

Anyone interested in Brazil must experience Carnaval *ao vivo* at least once in his life—whether it's in Rio, Salvador, Recife, or a folkloric city like São Luis (for dates, see *Carnaval*). Do avoid July, a school vacation month, when hotels are packed and rates excessive. Regional folkloric festivals are great fun, such as the beer-swilling Oktoberfest in Blumenau (October), Círio de Nazaré in Belém (second Sunday of October), and Bumba-meu-boi in São Luis (June). New Year's Eve in Rio and Salvador offers huge processions of white-clad celebrants who perform ceremonies on the beach. Wine-tasting in the state of Rio Grande do Sul is best done January–March while the grapes are still on the vine. The best time to visit the Amazon and Pantanal is in August. (For more information on climatic conditions and when to visit, see the "Hands-On" section of each city.)

CHOLERA

Cholera was declared epidemic in Brazil in 1992, but it need not scare away informed tourists. Long called the poor people's disease, it largely attacks populations with untreated sewage and no access to clean drinking water. Unless you are traveling in rural areas and/or drinking tap or river water, you stand almost no risk of getting sick. The U.S. Centers for Disease Control also recommend that all visitors to Latin America avoid consuming ice, salads, tap water, foods sold by street vendors, raw fish, and cooked food served cold. For more information, see the chapter *Health Kit for the Tropics*.

CONSULATES

The **Brazilian Consulate General** in the U.S. is located at *630 Fifth Avenue, New York, NY 10020; (☎ 212-757-3080)*. Brazilian consulates are also located in Chicago, Houston, Los Angeles, Miami, San Francisco, Washington D.C., and Puerto Rico. Visas may be obtained from these offices, as well as general information.

In England, the embassy is located at: **Embassy of Brazil** *(32 Green St., London WTY 4AT England)*.

For American consulates in Brazil, see "Hands-on" in each city.

CUSTOMS

Upon arrival from any international flights, all foreign visitors pass through customs—usually a quick and painless process. Follow the crowd to the inspection site and have your passport, visa, and card of embarkation ready for viewing by the passport inspector. (On the flight over, the flight attendant will have handed you the card of embarkation—a declaration card—to fill it out. Guard this card with your life and do not lose it, because you *must* show it on departure. Best bet is to attach it securely to your passport as soon as possible.)

Besides clothing and personal belongings, travelers to Brazil may carry a radio, a tapedeck, a computer, a typewriter, and cameras for their personal use only. Though luggage is usually not inspected, it will be difficult, for example, to explain why you personally need ten radios, if discovered. Also permitted is $500 in gifts (an additional $1,000 in taxable gifts), and $300 of duty-free goods (liquor, cigarettes, etc.) bought at the airport.

DOCUMENTS

A valid passport is required for entering into Brazil, and you must also obtain a visa prior to arrival. Visas may be obtained in person at the Brazilian Consulate (for addresses in the U.S., see below under "Consulates," or you may write the head consulate in New York). You'll need one 2" x 2" photo (black-and-white or color), your passport, and your airline ticket (or itinerary confirmed by your travel agent), as well as a completed and signed application. Tourist visas obtained in person are free; those transacted by a messenger cost $10; you may also use local visa service agencies.

Tourist visas last 90 days, renewable for a second 90 days. If you plan to stay longer, do not, under any circumstances, forget to renew your visa at the nearest Federal Police office or immigration office in Brazil. If you are late, you will be fined and given 8 days to leave the country, unless you are a fast talker with a keen sense of theatrics. It's rumored that offenders are placed on a computerized list that makes returning to the country difficult.

Business visas may be obtained by showing a passport (valid for at least six months), photo, completed application, and a letter from your company detailing the purpose of your trip. Business visas are processed in 24 hours and cost $30 ($40 by messenger).

If you need to stay longer than 6 months (3-month visas are only renewed once, for a 6-month limit), you must prove you are financially able to remain in the country without working. Check with the Federal Police or immigration office to determine your applicability.

You should also carry with your passport the official record of your vaccinations, particularly if you are planning to go into the jungle. If you become sick or if an epidemic breaks out, a physician can determine your susceptibility. If you pass into bordering countries, you may be required to show it.

Brazilians love letters of introduction, so if you are doing special research, collect as many signed references as you can. Business cards are also impressive and prove you are a serious professional.

JET LAG

International flights from New York and Miami usually leave at night and arrive in Rio between 7:00 a.m. and 9:00 a.m. Although there are no remarkable differences in time zones from most U.S. destinations (see "Time Zone"), you may be exhausted from fidgeting in your seat all night long. For tips to combat travel stress, see *Health Kit for the Tropics.*

LANGUAGE

Brazilians are not at all like the French when it comes to foreigners speaking their native tongue. In fact, Brazilians will deeply appreciate the slightest effort you make to speak in Portuguese, even if it's a garbled mess. In general, Spanish is a help, but it will only get you so far. Brazilians have the uncanny ability to *understand* Spanish, although if you speak only Spanish, you will be floored when you first *hear* Portuguese—the rhythm, accent, and sensibility are totally different, although more than a few words may be similar. (Written Portuguese, on the other hand, is much easier for Spanish-speaking travelers to decipher.)

Even if you speak Portuguese, you will find that regional accents vary profoundly. Southerners actually speak with a kind of cowboy twang, and Northeasters speak extremely fast and clipped. Sometimes even Brazilians don't understand each other, and actors from the interior have been known to undergo diction classes before they're allowed on stage or screen.

Still, it's very possible to travel throughout Brazil without any facility in Portuguese or Spanish. Just make sure all your travel arrangements are made in advance, and join group tours rather than wander around alone in the backcountry. In fact, Brazil without Portuguese (or even *"Portu-Spanglish"*), can be a great international adventure. In southern cities like Blumenau, Nova Petrópolis, and Gramado/Canela, German is spoken as a second language, and throughout the southern wine country in Rio Grande do Sul, many of the Italian-born families are well versed in their mother tongue. There is also a large Japanese-speaking community in São Paulo.

As for finding English-speakers in Brazil, if you stay at 5-star and 4-star hotels, you are sure to discover receptionists who do, as well as at some travel agencies in Rio, Salvador, São Paulo, and Manaus. Usually, at least one person at a city or state tourist information center speaks English. *Fluent* English, however, is another matter. Although many can understand English because of the huge influx of foreign music and film, Brazilians have little opportunity to practice speaking and, hence, are extremely shy. If you are speaking English to anybody in Brazil (no matter how fluent they may *seem*), speak slowly (but do not shout!), use simple words and grammar, and be on the lookout for misunderstandings. Brazilians tend to mix up *he* and *she,* and often confuse negative constructions. They also speak more through body language than through words.

MONEY

Traveling to Brazil with a large amount of cash is risky (because once it's stolen, it's gone). However, in a wildly fluctuating economy like Brazil's, with the value of the dollar rising daily, it's your best bet for value, particularly if you exchange only small amounts at a time. Your second-best option is to carry a mixture of cash, credit cards, and traveler's checks. Credit cards (the most widely accepted are MasterCard and Diner's Club, followed by American Express) can be used at most 5- and 4-star hotels, but not all restaurants accept cards (particularly American Express) because the delay in payment causes them to lose money. Clothing stores and boutiques often give discounts if you pay in Brazilian currency or dollars, and/or charge 20 percent extra if you pay by card.

If you are traveling into the interior (away from large cities), make sure you have exchanged enough money to pay for everything in Brazilian currency because you will be hard pressed to find anyone who will accept traveler's checks or dollars.

If you run out of money while traveling, the easiest way to receive extra funds is through cash advances on your credit card, but note that you can only receive the money in Brazilian currency. Remember to bring personal checks with you to facilitate this negotiation.

American Express will cash up to US $1,000 on green cards and $5,000 on gold once a week, exchanged at the official tourist rate (offices can be found in Rio, São Paulo, Manaus, and Salvador). Banco do Brasil also handles money forwarded on Visa. In New York the **Brazilian American Cultural Center** (☎ 212-730-1010) does make transfers in dollars to Brazil.

It's best to have already exchanged some Brazilian currency (small bills) before you arrive to pay for airport tips and taxis. There is usually an exchange house or bank in the airports of major cities.

PACKAGE DEALS

The cheapest way to get to Brazil is to buy your transcontinental ticket through a wholesaler. These independent operators and travel agents buy tickets in bulk and sell them at discounted rates and/or arrange package tours that include ground transportation, hotels, transfers from airports, and stops in several cities. Many agencies work on an FIT system, which allows them to contour a package vacation according to your specific needs. Carnaval packages often include tickets to the Sambódromo parade. Do note that prices from year to year can change drastically, depending on inflation in Brazil (and in the U.S.!), as well as the agency's ability to obtain discounts. Your best bet is to call around to many operators and find the lowest price for your particular itinerary. Three reliable wholesalers are:

The Brazilian American Cultural Center *20 West 46th Street, New York, NY 10036;* (☎ *212-730-1010) or toll free 800-222-2746* is not only a wholesaler but a membership club that requires a $20 fee. The BACC membership allows you to take advantage of round-trip fares that are sometimes $400 below fares listed by the airlines. Included in the membership fee is also a subscription to *The Brasilians*, the organization's newspaper, which gives up-to-date news from Brazil. For a $15 fee, BACC will also secure a visa for you. You must first request an application, then mail them the completed form with one 2" x 2" photo and a check or money order payable to BACC. The company will then process your papers through the Brazilian Consulate. This service is especially good for travelers who don't live near a consulate.

Ladatco *2220 Coral Way, Miami, FL 33145;* (☎ *800-327-6162)* A specialist in Latin American travel, Ladatco has been in business for 26 years. President Michelle Shelburne offers numerous packages (one 14-day itinerary includes Salvador, Rio, Brasília, Manaus, and a stay in the jungle). She can also arrange discounts on air travel and tailor-make any agenda.

Ipanema Tours *8844 West Olympic Blvd., Suite C, Beverly Hills, CA 90211 (☎ 800–421–4200)* offers a 5 percent discount to clients, 10 percent to travel agents on all international flights. The agency handles all of South America and can custom-tailor itineraries. Carnaval packages are also available.

For more package tours, charters, and cruises, see *Specialty Tours* in the back of the book.

PHOTOGRAPHY

Film and developing often costs twice as much in Brazil as it does in the States, so stock up before you come. Carry all film in a protective lead-lined bag to protect it from damaging x-rays at airport security stations and take it out of your hand luggage before you pass through any metal detectors in airports. Do not pack expensive equipment in checked baggage; it could get damaged or stolen. In the rain forest, keep film well protected from moisture and humidity.

SAFETY

Brazil has received an undeserved reputation for being dangerous. True, in the big cities such as Rio, São Paulo, Salvador, and Recife, you must exercise extreme caution and not walk around like a neon sign for robbers. In general, this means carrying as little money on your person as possible, not wearing jewelry (leave gold watches at home), and not brandishing expensive-looking cameras. Don't leave valuables strewn about your hotel room; do use the safe inside your apartment or at the receptionist's desk. Take taxis, especially at night, and don't exchange money with people you meet on the street. Use your common sense.

As you move into the interior, away from the big cities, you'll happily discover laid-back, crime-free areas. In some cities, like Nova Petrópolis in Rio Grande do Sul, the residents don't even bother to lock their car doors. The trick is to look like you have nothing to steal.

You can do a lot for your own safety by becoming an expert traveler. This means double-checking your airline schedules, keeping a consistent check on your passport and travel documents, and carrying your cash, credit cards, traveler's checks, and ID in separate places. Never carry your wallet in a back pocket. Carry backpacks in front of you. Invest in a money bag that straps inside your clothes around your stomach, chest, or ankle.

DIRECTORY

And don't think crime only happens in Brazil. There's been a rash of airport thefts reported in the U.S.; the most targeted ones are Kennedy, LaGuardia, Newark, Boston, Miami, and Los Angeles. Entire bags have been stolen, or relieved of packed cameras, laptops, credit cards, portable phones, jewelry, scuba equipment, and even golf clubs. For protection, don't carry expensive-looking luggage or attach American Express platinum card tags. Buy adequate locks and use them. Pack only clothes and carry anything that is valuable with you on board. The motto is: If you don't want to lose it, don't check it.

VACCINATIONS

Yellow fever vaccination is highly recommended if you are visiting rural areas or the Amazon jungle. Immunizations for hepatitis and typhoid are suggested for rural and jungle travel. It's always a good idea to update tetanus vaccinations. For in-depth information, see *Health Kit for the Tropics* in the back of the book.

WHAT TO PACK

Before going to Brazil, it's important to check the climate of the areas you will visit (see each region) and also consider whether you will be spending most of your time in metropolises, small back-road towns, or the jungle. In very hot weather, tropical clothing (light cottons or silks) are *de rigueur*. Businesspersons in Brasília and São Paulo wear suits and dresses, but in general, jeans and T-shirts are the fashion, all worn with a sexy, stylish flair. In fact, most Brazilian fashion feeds on extreme seduction—skirts are very short, pants are tight (or very baggy), and tops for women are skimpy. Think anti-dowdy. Although you may not want to do as Brazilians do, it is a good idea for safety's sake not to look like a tourist. This means don't even think about wearing a loud, garish tropical shirt, any T-shirt with BRAZIL or I LOVE RIO blazoned across it, or any large handbag that looks like you're carrying a microwave oven. Instead, invest in a waist-pouch to carry your small necessities (cheap ones can be bought from street vendors in Ipanema and Copacabana in Rio) and/or consider carrying your money in a body pouch underneath your clothing.

For most Americans, what to wear on a Brazilian beach is a dilemma. If you want to look like a Brazilian, probably no bathing suit you can buy in the States will be small enough. Simply, most

Americans on the beach look like they are either dressed for winter or wearing a diaper. On the other hand, if you are anything but petite, most Brazilian bathing suits will not fit you, or at least certainly not cover what you are used to covering. One option for women is to buy a large scarf and tie it native-style around your waist; you can also buy adjustable bathing suit tops that can regulate the amount of flesh you expose. Fair-skinned travelers, however, should give real consideration to coverups for skin protection; the tropical sun is much more intense than it seems.

What you wear on your feet is a prime factor in determining your trip's pleasure quotient. Most of Rio's streets are cobblestone or uneven pavement, and you won't be happy in anything that has a high heel. Flat, lightweight tennies or well-grounded walking shoes are best, though Brazilian women do wear high heels at night (okay if you take cabs). A pair of sturdy sandals is also important, as well as a cheap pair of beach sling-ons. Cowboy boots tend to be too hot (not to mention bulky to pack), but fashionable Brazilians have taken to the miniboot, the kind that just grazes the top of your jeans. If you run, you'll want to throw in your jogging shoes to join the throngs that turn out dusk and dawn in nearly every seaside city.

Brazilians live to dress up at night. They take hours after work getting ready to go out for dinner, even though they may end up looking nonchalantly casual in an open shirt and nice slacks, or a short sexy dress. Only in the very elite restaurants are men required to wear ties; a jacket is sufficient in most cases. If you are going out with Brazilian friends, they will, upon meeting you, check out just how fashionable and coordinated you look, even in the smallest city. If you're going high society, matching shoes and bag is expected, and fashionable (if fake) jewelry is a must. No matter what one's social class, in Brazil taking care for one's physical appearance is a sign of self-respect.

I'll discuss jungle attire at more length in the chapters on the Amazon regions, but do note that at some point you will have to come out of the jungle, and Brazilians don't take kindly to muddy, smelly, wild-looking barbarians, no matter how great their jungle stories are. Make sure you bring an extra pair of pants or a skirt, a clean pair of shoes, and a nice shirt, if you want to partake of anything in the city that's civilized.

WHILE YOU'RE THERE

AIRPORT TAX

You will be charged US $18 for international flights (if you stay in Brazil over 24 hours) and US $1–$3 on local flights, payable when you check in. To facilitate matters within Brazil, have small change in Brazilian currency ready.

AIRPORT TRANSFER

Taxis are always available at airports. Buses into the city are much cheaper, but are awkward if you're juggling lots of luggage, and they may not drop you at your hotel's front door. Special taxis can often be obtained at a central post near the exit of the airport, where you pay in advance, then give your receipt to the driver. These special taxis generally cost about 10 percent more than the regular fare but are considered safer and are guaranteed to get you to your destination. Have the name and address of your hotel readily available. Some hotels, especially those booked through package deals, will provide transfers to and from the airport, so check in advance.

BRINGING HOME BRAZIL

Varig Airlines is entirely accommodating when it comes to traveling home with a *berimbau*—a large, one-stringed instrument attached to a round gourd. Wrap the bow separately in heavy packing paper and send it through with your luggage. Carry the gourd with you as hand luggage.

U.S. Customs allows returning residents of the United States to bring home duty-free articles totaling up to $400. This includes up to 100 cigars, 200 cigarettes (from one carton), and one liter (33.8 fluid ounces) of alcoholic beverages. When shipped, gifts up to $50 in fair retail value may be received by friends and relations in the U.S. free of duty and tax.

Among prohibited articles considered injurious to the public welfare are: absinthe, liquor-filled candies (where prohibited by law), narcotics, obscene articles and publications, and switchblades (unless you are a one-armed person who uses a switchblade knife for personal use). Most fruits and vegetables are either prohibited from entering the country or require an import permit. Meat, livestock, poultry, and their byproducts (sausage, paté) are either prohibited or restricted from entry, depending on the animal disease condition in Brazil.

If you are traveling with medicines containing habit-forming drugs or narcotics (i.e., cough medicine, diuretics, heart drugs, tranquilizers, sleeping pills, depressants, stimulants, etc.), you must properly identify all drugs, carry only the quantity you will normally need, and have ready a prescription or written statement from your personal physician confirming you are under a doctor's care and in need of these drugs for your personal health while traveling.

Plants, cuttings, seeds, and certain endangered species either require an import permit or are prohibited from entering the U.S. Wildlife and fish are subject to certain import and export restrictions, prohibitions, and quarantine requirements. All ivory and ivory products—except antiques—made from elephant ivory are prohibited. If you are contemplating purchasing articles made from wildlife, such as tortoise shell jewelry, leather goods, or other articles from whalebone, ivory, skins, or fur, contact—before you go—the U.S. Fish and Wildlife Service, Department of the Interior, Washington, DC 20240.

BUSINESS HOURS AND HOLIDAYS

Most businesses and stores open at 9:00 a.m., break for lunch between noon and 2:00 p.m., and reopen from 2:00 p.m. to 5:00 p.m. Monday–Friday. Shops in Ipanema and Copacabana in Rio tend to open 9:00 a.m.–1:00 p.m. on Saturday. Banks are open 10:00 a.m.–4:30 p.m. Monday–Friday. Many businesses close up shop for the five days of Carnaval leading up to Ash Wednesday. Museums throughout the country are generally closed on Monday.

Businesses, but not restaurants, shut down completely for the following Brazilian holidays. (As in the States, some offices may shut down not on the official date, but on the Monday closest to it, for a long weekend.)

January 1 ---------------- New Year's

Carnaval ---------------- 5 days leading to Ash Wednesday

March/April ------------ Good Friday and Easter Sunday

April 21 ----------------- Tiradentes' Day

May 1 -------------------- Dia do Trabalho

June 10 ----------------- Corpus Christi

September 7 ----------- Independence Day

October 12	------------	Nossa Senhora da Aparecida (Our Lady of the Apparition)
November 2	-----------	Dia dos Finados (All Soul's Days)
November 15	----------	Proclamation of the Republic
December 25	----------	Christmas (most restaurants closed)

CLIMATE

If you're coming from the Northern Hemisphere, remember that the seasons are inverted. For more information, see under individual regions.

COMPUTERS

Laptop computers should be carried on board airplanes with you in your hand luggage, but *don't ever* send them through a Brazilian x-ray machine. Otherwise, you may find your entire program and files wiped out, as I did. Travelers headed for the rain forest should protect the computer and diskettes from humidity and moisture by wrapping the case in an extra plastic bag.

CONSULATES

In the case of *any* emergency (health, safety), immediately contact your own consulate in the nearest city.

CURRENCY EXCHANGE

One of Brazil's ways to handle inflation is to knock off zeroes from its present currency and change its name. At press time, the currency is the *cruzeiro real*, though it may have changed by the time you read this. Contrary to popular belief, there is really no longer a black market for exchanging currency in Brazil. There are, however, three levels of exchange: the *oficial*, or official rate, which Brazilians pay to buy air tickets and foreign currency; the slightly higher tourist rate called *dólar turismo*, generally offered to tourists at official exchange offices called *câmbios*, and the even higher parallel rate, called *dólar paralelo*, which is so rarely made available to tourists that it's not worth thinking about. Rates vary daily, and you should check the newspaper before exchanging money.

With the *cruzeiro* wildly out of control, everybody in Brazil will want to exchange your dollars, from the man on the street to your hotel's porter. The safest places to exchange money is at banks or at officially recognized *câmbios*, where you may be taken to a back room to make the transaction in private. Exchanging money on the street with people you don't know is asking for trouble; you might as well just give your wallet away. Hotel employees, especially in 5-star properties, are generally honest, but check the newspaper first for the official tourist rate. Hotel exchange houses usually give the lowest rate around, so try to avoid them, though they are often more convenient. Do note that traveler's checks often receive a slightly lower rate than the tourist dollar because of the paperwork involved.

One word of advice:

Travelers have been known to ruin their trips obsessing over the exchange rate and how to get the best deal. Frankly, it's not worth it, but there are some guidelines to keep you sane: exchange only small amounts at a time (for 2 or 3 days' expenses); exchange in reputable places and keep the receipts; use a pocket calculator and be clear how many dollars you are spending on a purchase; exchange money in big cities, where you will get better rates. At some point you will have to give up and realize it's a gambler's game, and often the amount you would be saving adds up only to a few dollars. At last call, remember you are in Brazil for a good time.

CUTTING COSTS

Because severe inflation and the fluctuating fees of air travel make determining costs difficult, prices quoted by travel agents may change weekly. On the bright side, if you spend substantial time in Brazil, you will usually discover that over time your American dollar is worth much more than when you arrived. Traveling at off season is the best way to save money since most hotels offer discounts if you ask. Other tips include: join a pre-packaged tour; take full advantage of your hotel's large "American" breakfast and skip lunch; forego a hotel with a pool in a seaside city; rent a room without a view; buy an air-pass for travel within Brazil; and carry a map so you won't get cheated by taxi drivers. Soda, bottled water, and candy bars in your minibar can run up to $2 each; make a stop at a neighborhood store or bar and stock up. If you need to travel with your own bottle of scotch or whiskey, buy some at the duty-free shop before you leave the States. Don't use credit cards, to avoid the surcharge. Make overseas telephone calls direct or at the public phone company. Lunching at a *rodízio* (an all-you-can-eat steak house) could last you all day. Regularly verify all meal checks and hotel bills for accuracy;

"mistakes" are often made. Become well acquainted with the currency before using it so you won't confuse the bills.

DISEASES

Brazil now has the third largest number of recorded HIV infections in the world (about 1 million people infected, twenty percent of them women). Among the factors contributing to its proliferation are a large amount of bisexual activity, heterosexual anal sex, an active gay population, a lack of efficient blood testing practices, and the sharing of needles, particularly in the upper class, where drugs were deemed fashionable in the late 1970s and 1980s. Young prostitutes who come down from the *favelas* often believe in magical potions made by the Indians or think using a bidet is sufficient for cleansing germs. Despite a television blitz campaign warning about the danger of unsafe sex, and the omnipresence of Benetton billboards featuring enormous multicolored condoms, few couples take preventive measures. Brazilian men often refuse to use condoms out of ignorance or inconvenience, and women are loath to press the issue. Furthermore, the quality of Brazilian condoms is vastly inferior to the ones you may be familiar with, and prone to breakage.

A foreign traveler's best bet is to pack a sufficient supply of American condoms, use them unstintingly, and give the leftovers to Brazilian friends, who will be delighted to receive them. If you must buy condoms in Brazil, they can be found in most pharmacies, under the name *camisinha* or *camiseta de Vênus* (note the word *camiseta* alone means T-shirt).

For information regarding jungle diseases, see the *Health Kit* in the back of the book.

DOCTORS AND PHARMACIES

If you have a medical emergency, ask your concierge to recommend a doctor (some 5-star hotels have doctors and nurses on call). If the problem is extremely serious, contact your consulate and ask for help in returning home as quickly as possible. Simply, Brazilian hospitals tend to be overcrowded and not up to American standards.

The good news: if you find a competent doctor (usually referred by a friend or your concierge, and they do exist!), he/she will probably give you more time than their American counterparts, exhibit more gracious behavior, and even call you at home to follow up on your condition. Frankly, all private health care I received in Brazil, from traditional western medicine to more oriental practices, turned out to be excellent.

If you travel with prescription drugs, carry a copy of the prescription with you (for customs and emergency refills), but be sure to pack more than enough of your own supplies. Do note, however, that many drugs that are available only through prescription in the States are purchasable over the counter in Brazil, though their quality can't be vouched for. Other products, such as homeopathic remedies (Bach Flower Remedies, in particular) require a prescription from a certified practitioner.

Receiving prescription drugs (or even vitamins) from home while in Brazil is often tricky. All overseas packages are opened, and you will be required to pick up the box at a government agency, as well as show three copies of the prescription and a letter from the doctor stating why these products cannot be bought in Brazil. (To the country's credit, a care–package of vitamins I never picked up in Rio was actually returned to my mother, the sender—totally intact!—a mere 12 months later.)

Shiatzu and acupressure practitioners are well trained in Brazil and provide excellent service. Make sure, however, that any needles have been disinfected before they are used on your body, or carry your own.

DRIVING

No room for contest—Brazilian drivers are maniacs. (Is there a better reason why the Formula One races are held in Rio?) They ride on each other's bumpers, turn left from left-hand lanes, run stop signs and red lights, and most of all, love to swoop down and park on the sidewalk next to your foot. Unless you have the mind of a madman, I wouldn't suggest driving a great deal in Brazil unless you are settling down there and have no choice. Outside the large cities, which usually have paved and/or cobblestone streets, roads run from passable in the South to awesomely hazardous in the Pantanal, where four-wheel drive is an absolute necessity.

If you insist on renting a car, you will find car-rental agencies in most airports and in all major cities. Officially, you are required to have an international driver's license, but a few extra bucks might curtail that requirement. Gas in Brazil is more than twice the cost in the U.S., while the state-subsidized alcohol is slightly less.

Pedestrians should note that the police in Rio advise drivers not to stop at red lights at night to avoid being held up. So whenever you're crossing the street, look both ways several times and keep an eye out for speeding cars. Pedestrians in Brazil do not have the right of way.

ELECTRICITY

Electric voltage is not standardized in Brazil. What we consider "house current" in the States can generally be found only in Manaus and some 5-star hotels. The general current is 127 volts, while the city of Brasília uses 220 volts. Plugs have two round holes, so if you want to use hairdryers, shavers, or other appliances from home, you will need a converter kit that has an adapter. Check your appliances before you leave: some have a switch that can be turned to 110- or 220-volt current (110-volt appliances work normally on 127-volt current.) Computers should always be used with a surge protector because they draw more power.

Most 5- and 4-star hotels supply hairdryers in the bathroom, or you can ask for one. Just check the voltage before plugging anything in. One warning: even with a converter, my electric steamer pooped out after only a few weeks.

FLIGHTS

You must confirm all flights at least 24 hours in advance, and international flights, 48 hours; otherwise you will risk losing your reservation. And keep a check on the weather at your destination. Some of the planes flying between Northeastern destinations and in the Pantanal are small.

HAIR SALONS

Excellent hair salons and barbershops can be found in most 5-star hotels. The best private salons in Rio and São Paulo are listed in their respective chapters. I would suggest not getting your hair colored or permed anywhere in Brazil. Products tend to be harsher than their American counterparts, and my own hair actually started to fall out from a combination of bad products and overbleaching from the tropical sun. Manicures are cheap (about $2–$5), but bring your own utensils; I never saw any disinfecting equipment that satisfied me. And don't be startled—Brazilian manicurists have a way of globbing polish all over your fingers, then cleaning up the residue later, but the final result is usually excellent.

LUGGAGE DAMAGE

Luggage has been known to get damaged on the finest airline carriers. Reports may be made to an airline official at the airport, but unless the bag is totally dysfunctional, you are better off biting the bullet, especially if you are not staying long in that city. In general, suitcases are taken to be repaired, not exchanged, a delay that could cause you even greater grief.

Do make sure that all luggage (hand and checked) is well identified with your name and home address.

MAIL

On a good day, it takes about 5 days to a week for a letter from Rio to reach New York. On a bad day, it might take a few years. Anyone sending packages to Brazil should note that all packages are opened by post office officials and that strict restrictions apply.

The easiest way to mail an envelope is to hand it to your concierge, who will mail it for you or sell you stamps at a small markup. There are usually post offices in major airports. Postcards from Brazil to the States cost about $1 to mail, as do letters up to 20 grams. Express post, registered mail, and parcel service operate both domestically and internationally.

NEWSPAPERS

Most major cities have at least one newspaper, if not two, which will offer listings of local events in music, theater, film, and dance. *O Jornal do Brasil* is Rio's version of the *New York Times,* as is *A Folha de São Paulo* in São Paulo. In Rio, São Paulo, and Brasília, it is relatively easy to locate the *International Herald Tribune,* the *Miami Herald,* and the *Wall Street Journal,* as well as international versions of *Newsweek* and *Time* magazines. A daily English-language newspaper, the *Latin America Daily Post,* circulates in Rio and São Paulo. I've even glimpsed copies of *Musician* and *Downbeat* magazines in Rio—for more than twice the price. At larger newsstands and airport bookshops you can find other foreign newspapers and magazines, and possibly some paperback novels in English.

POLICE

Contrary to popular belief, the police in Brazil can often be helpful, especially in Rio, where special forces maintain watch over the beaches. If you are in trouble, don't hesitate to approach one even if he doesn't speak English; he will find someone who does. (I was saved during Carnaval by one charming officer who made sure I got to my proper samba school.) If you are the victim of petty theft (camera, wallet, etc.), the best thing to do is notify the concierge and manager of your hotel. Filing a complaint with the Federal Police may be a waste of time unless you want to file an insurance claim.

Don't get nervous if you see armed policemen stopping cars on the street or highways near *favelas* (slums). They are most probably making routine searches for drugs.

RESTROOMS

Memorize this phrase: *"Onde fica o toalete?"* ("On-gee fee-cah oh twah-letch-ee?") That will get you a finger pointed to the nearest restroom. Women's restrooms (also called *banheiros*) are usually marked *M* for *mulher*, and, for men, *S* for *senhor*. Adequate facilities can be found at most restaurants, and if you are not trailing sand, the more casual ones will probably let you use them without dining. Toilet paper is not uniformly present in public restrooms, so I'd suggest carrying your own supplies (like Handiwipes) or snitching a few sheets of tissue from your hotel room. Bus stations usually have clean facilities, with an elderly woman handing out a stiff, torturous paper for a few cents. Most hotel rooms come with regular toilets, as well as European-style bidets. If you're camping out, you'd better go prepared with something other than leaves.

SHOPPING

Fine clothes, though stylish, have become extremely expensive in Brazil, often costing more than comparable items in the States. Centers of fashion are Rio and São Paulo, which boast extremely modern shopping malls, as well as chic neighborhood boutiques. Best buys are leather shoes and bags, particularly if you take advantage of end-of-season sales (look for the words *promoção* or *liquidação*).

Most native crafts can be bought in Rio, but they will usually cost twice as much as they do in their states of origin. Unabashed bargaining is expected at open-air markets and bazaars, but use discretion in finer stores and boutiques, although you might be able to wrangle discounts on large purchases, such as jewelry, if you speak to the owner or manager.

TAXIS

Taxi drivers, particularly in Rio and Salvador, have long been notorious, but are slowly being educated that their honest service deeply affects tourism, and thus the country's economy. Here are some tips for avoiding being carried miles out of your way and stiffed for an outrageous fee.

- Know where you're going and have your destination written in Portuguese on a piece of paper, as well as the best route there, recommended by your concierge.

- Because of inflation, rates are constantly changing, but up-to-date prices must be displayed on a chart pasted on the back window. See that the taxi meter, located in the front seat next to the wheel, starts when you do, and check the chart yourself at the end of the ride. A surcharge is collected on Sunday and after 10:00 p.m., so check the second table of prices.

- If you are returning to your hotel, call out to the porter to verify the charge, or hail a policeman if you see one.

- Special air-conditioned taxis, which are safer, are usually found lined up in front of fine hotels, but they invariably run almost twice as much as the normal fee. Rates are determined in advance, so ask.

- Hire a car and guide for the day or by the hour.

- Attend nighttime shows with tour groups, which provide transfers by private coach.

- If you're hailing your own cab, stand on the curb and point your index finger down to the ground, not up!

- Always carry the name, address, and telephone number of your hotel tucked inside your shoe in case your wallet or purse gets stolen.

TELEPHONES

The phone line in Brazil has a mind of its own. Many numbers seem perpetually busy, and you can be suddenly disconnected for no apparent reason. Be patient. Local calls can be made from your hotel usually free of charge (though do check ahead of time), but you can also make them from city streets at phone booths that require tokens. You can obtain these tokens, called *fichas*, quite cheaply at any newsstand; buy at least two packs of five at one time, since each *ficha* lasts only for about three minutes. When you first pick up to dial, put 2 or 3 in at once, since disconnections come fast and without warning.

☎ Calling Brazil/Calling Home

It's cheaper to call Rio from the States than vice versa. Since AT&T offers no weekend rates, the best time to make a call to Brazil from the States is between midnight and 8:00 a.m.: a 10-minute, call from New York to Rio costs about $7.59; between 6:00 a.m. and midnight about $9; and between 8:00 a.m.–6:00 p.m., about $11.86. In Brazil, the same Rio-New York call runs about $26 during the week (all hours), with a 20 percent discount on Sunday. Some 5-star and 4-star hotels offer direct dialing; when the hotel operator becomes involved, calls can often take up to a half hour or more to place. Hotels often charge up to 25 percent service fee or more for international calls; to save money, patronize the city phone company called EMBRATEL, where you will be directed to a private booth and given a key that opens the phone. You pay the receptionist after you make the call. Phone companies operate at most airports as well.

☎ To Brazil

From the States, dial 011–55, followed by the area code and number.

☎ Within Brazil

For direct-dial: 0 plus the area code plus the number. For collect calls (not in a hotel): dial 107.

☎ From Brazil

For direct international calls to: **U.S.** 00–1–area code-number; **Great Britain** 00–44–area code-number; **Ireland** 00–353–area code-number; **Australia** 00–61–area code-number. For collect calls: dial the International Operator, 000111.

Direct calls from Brazil to the U.S. and Canada run about $4 per minute before 8:00 p.m., about $3 after 8:00 p.m., and Sunday until 8:00 p.m.

TIME ZONE

Brazil has three time zones, though most of the country is located 3 hours behind Greenwich Mean Time. This region occupies eastern Brazil and parts of central (including Rio de Janeiro, Salvador, São Paulo, Brasília, Recife, and Belém.) That means when it's noon in New York, it's 2:00 p.m. in Rio de Janeiro. The second zone, which is 4 hours behind GMT, encompasses the states of Mato Grosso and Mato Grosso do Sul and most of Brazil's north (such as Manaus, Corumbá, Rio Branco, Porto Velho, Cuiabá, and Campo Grande).

Far-western Brazil (Acre and the western edge of Amazonas) are 5 hours behind GMT. For Daylight Savings Time, clocks go forward an hour on the second Sunday in November and are set back on the second Sunday in March. The city of Belém is not in the habit of following this schedule, so double check your flight schedules.

TIPPING

There are no service taxes charged in Brazil, but most hotels and restaurants add a 10 percent service charge unless otherwise specified (look for the sign *não taxa de serviço* or *serviço não incluso*). If none is added, or if you want to leave more, feel free—remember, you're in a third-world country where maids, waiters, manicurists, porters, and other service people barely subsist on minimum wages. In Rio and Salvador (and most anywhere, actually), especially if you are sitting at a sidewalk café, street children or beggars may ask you for money or food. Follow your conscience, but be aware that the request is sometimes a ploy to divert your attention while a third party lifts your belongings.

On a good tour, tip a guide between $1 and $5 (half-day tours). They usually make very low wages, despite being multilingual and well educated. Do note that they probably receive commissions from any stores they steer you to.

TRAVEL WITHIN BRAZIL

Bus

Bus travel through the country can be an invigorating way to see the countryside, if a little demanding. Most buses are not air-conditioned, but the breeze is refreshing, and the tickets are cheap. Sharing the bus with you may be chickens and other small animals that are riding with their owners (I have yet to see a pig). In most cases, seats are reserved by numbers, which are taken seriously. Ask for a seat next to the window *(janela)*, which is generally cooler. Buses stop frequently, about every 3 or 4 hours, and bus terminals, with snack bars, casual restaurants, newsstands, and bathrooms, can provide colorful glimpses of native life. A viable trip by bus is down the southern coast from Rio to the seaside cities of Ubatuba and Guarujá. Another well trod bus trip is the Rio-São Paulo route, which is about 6 hours, for $25. Reservations for buses should be made as far as possible in advance, especially on weekends and during high season.

DIRECTORY

Custom-designed, air-conditioned buses called *leitos* are more expensive but luxurious, sporting reclining chairs for overnighters and sandwiches and cookies in cardboard boxes. The Salvador-Ilhéus route in the state of Bahia is an excellent overnight trip.

In seaside cities, such as Salvador, Maceió, Natal, and Recife in the Northeast, **special tourist buses** take bathers down the main beach drag to the various beaches.

City buses are boarded from the back and payment in exact change is given to the cashier, who sits in the rear. You exit from the front. City buses, however, are usually not the best form of transportation for a first-time tourist. They are almost always packed, and crime is prevalent.

Train

There are few trains in Brazil, and you are generally better off taking the bus. A few daily trains run between Rio and São Paulo, and 2 trains weekly between Rio and Belo Horizonte.

TRAVELING WITH KIDS

Brazil is an extremely family-oriented country. High chairs are available in numerous restaurants, and many hotels do not charge for children under 5. Baby-sitters are often available at resort-style hotels, whose private grounds and excellent security make them ideal for families. Best examples of this kind of resort-hotel are the Rio Sheraton in Rio de Janeiro, Nas Rocas Resort in Búzios (near Rio), the Transamérica Hotel and Praia do Forte in Bahia, and the Pratagy Eco-Hotel in Maceió. Kids love the jungle lodges in the Amazon and would do well taking a lazy boat trek through the Pantanal. However, a child who goes on an adventure tour must be accompanied by an adult, and should be old enough to take directions without misinterpreting or balking.

Throughout the book, suggested activities geared especially for children are highlighted.

WATER

For health reasons, you must drink *only* bottled water wherever you go in Brazil. Even in small towns, you will be able to order it at bars or in restaurants; even Amazon jungle lodges serve bottled water. If you are camping, you must carry your own; you're asking for cholera and any other number of diseases if you drink river water, or in some cases tap water, purified or not. Most hotel rooms are supplied with bottled water in the minibar. Avoid brushing your teeth with tap water. For more tips, see *Health Kit* in the back of the book.

WOMEN ONLY

I have yet to accurately nail the quality of machismo in Brazil. It is more charming, more subtle, yet at times more brutal than in other Latin American countries. More and more women are working outside the home, but a woman's first responsibility is still to her family, and she is rarely allowed the freedom to come and go as freely as a man. Consequently, a foreign woman traveling alone in Brazil is still a point of enormous intrigue. Blondes, in particular, seem to evoke the same kind of fantasies that darker-hued women inspire in Northerners, but pinching is rare (more common are intense stares and lighthearted flirtation). How you dress and carry yourself will determine how you are received. If you don't want undue attention, you might consider wearing a fake wedding ring, although this will only slow down action, not stop it. In no circumstances, should you go off into dark places with a man you do not know, or traipse off alone into the jungle with only a male guide. On the plus side, women traveling alone are often treated with great deference; old ladies will be glad to watch your luggage at bus stations while you use the bathroom. Just use your head about whom to trust. If you are traveling to São Paulo or Rio, the Caesar Park Hotel is especially attentive to single women, and the southern states of Brazil are particularly hospitable, in the European fashion.

YOUTH HOSTELS

For a list of youth hostels and addresses throughout Brazil, write: **Youth Hostels Contej** *(Estácio de Sá/ Rua Vinícius de Moraes 120/Rio de Janeiro, Brasil).*

FIELDING'S BEST OF BRAZIL

Best Hotels: Sheraton Rio (Rio), Caesar Park (Rio and São Paulo), Maksoud Plaza (São Paulo), Hotel Tropical (Manaus), Sofitel Quatro Rodas (Salvador), Laje de Pedra (Canela).

Best Restaurants: Satyricon (Rio), Mássimo (São Paulo), Claude Troisgros (Rio), Mariu's (Rio), The Place (São Paulo), Saint Honoré (Rio), Café Colonial Bela Vista (Gramado), Raízes (Recife), Lá Em Casa (Belém), Tia Lucinha (Belo Horizonte), Recanto do Tio Flor (Porto Alegre).

Best Eco Trips: Horseback riding outside Belo Horizonte, *jangada* rides in Maceió, dune surfing in Natal, dawn cruise to Parrot Island near Belém, Expeditour's Pantanal Triangle Cruise, camping and trekking in Chapada dos Guimarães, hiking through Serra da Bocaina, scaling the mountains of Petrópolis, traversing the Pantanal's Transpantaneira Highway.

Best Resorts: Transamérica Hotel (Comondatuba Island), Praia do Forte (Bahia), Pratagy Eco Hotel (Maceió), Floresta Amazônica Hotel (Alta Floresta, MG), Genipabú (Natal), Hotel Casa Grande & Senzala (Recife).

Best Beaches: Grumari Beach (Rio), Piatã (Salvador), Praia do Forte (Bahia), Praia de Ponta Negra (Natal), Praia de Francês (Maceió), Jericoacoara and Taíba (Fortaleza), Caeheta and Porto de Galinhas (Recife).

Best Ranches and Jungle Lodges: Ariaú Jungle Tower (Manaus), Fazenda Xaraes and Pousada Caiman (Pantanal).

Best Pousada: Pousada do Vale dos Veados (Bocaina National Park).

Best Historical Sites: Parati (Rio de Janeiro), Ouro Preto and Mariana (Minas Gerais), São Luis and Alcântara (Maranhão), Olinda (Pernambuco).

Most Spiritual Sites: Rio and Salvador on New Year's, Ouro Preto, São Lourenço and Caxambú (Minas Gerais), Iguaçu Falls, Chapada dos Guimarães.

Most Artistic City: Congonhas (Minas Gerais).

Best Scuba: Island of Fernando de Noronha.

Best Outdoor Market: Belém (Pará).

Best Party Towns: Porto Seguro and Arraial d'Ajuda (Bahia).

Safest Locations: Transamérica Hotel (Bahia), Fernando de Noronha (island), Praia do Forte (Bahia), Chapada dos Guimarães (Mato Grosso), historical towns and spa towns of Minas Gerais, Santarém (Pará), Blumenau and Joinville (Santa Catarina), Nova Petrópolis and Torres (Rio Grande do Sul).

Best Sites for UFOs: Sugarloaf (Rio), São Tomé das Letras and São Lourenço (Minas Gerais), Chapada dos Guimāraes (Mato Grosso), Alta Floresta (Mato Grosso), Amazon jungle.

HISTORICAL ROOTS

16th Century Depiction of Amazon Indians

Pristine beaches, crystalline waters, luxurious vegetation—the Brazil the first European explorers saw was nothing less than a terrestrial paradise: *"one so well favored that if it were rightly cultivated it would yield everything,"* said one enthusiastic chronicler. Today, after 500 years, that sentiment of perpetual promise is still being bantered about by supporters and critics alike, and exactly how to cultivate that wealth has remained a continuous challenge. If Brazil has had one major obstacle through its tumultuous history, it has been its gargantuan size—a girth so preposterous as to make near impossible any attempt to maneuver a reasonable distribution of wealth. Ever since the first explorers ventured onto Brazilian shores in 1500, their primary approach has been the Manifest Destiny creed of "explore and conquer"; today, that philosophy cuts at the heart of the world's ecological debates regarding the importance of Brazilian rain forests to the planet's survival.

The First Europeans

The Portuguese were the first Europeans to set foot in Brazil, and in the late 15 and 16th centuries, they were already a mingling of many cultures—Iberians, Celts, Phoenicians, Greeks, Carthaginians, Romans, Visigoths, and Muslims. In a society dominated by the Church, religious motives for expansion played at least a superficial role—the hope was to defeat the enemies of the Christian faith in Africa and carry the word of God to the continent. The Crown's more pressing goal, however, was to create a direct all-water trade route with the Orient that would break Italian domination and bring a cascade of riches to Portugal. Not surprising, then, that crass materialism and the most sublime spiritual intent mingled in the Portuguese seaman with almost fanatical fatalism. Those who sailed across the vast sea to the New World had to be not only adventuresome and fearless, but also unquestionably loyal to the Crown.

Under the appointment of Manuel I, the explorer **Pedro Alvares Cabral** set forth with 13 ships and 1,200 men to follow up Vasco da Gama's claims, departing from Lisbon on March 8, 1500. The voyage to India began routinely enough, but on April 20, after a whirlwind storm, the fleet unexpectedly sighted weeds and reeds in the ocean. Two days later, at approximately 17 degrees south latitude, land appeared, which Cabral christened **Ilha da Cruz** (Island of the Cross). Some say his fortuitous discovery was a nautical mistake; others believe he intentionally veered off course, either on a hunch or on instructions from the throne. In any case, the Court paid little attention until French and British pirateers began to raid the spice ships. Later merchants, attracted to the plentiful stands of brazilwood, a source of excellent red dye, would rename the new territory *Terra do Brasil* (Land of Brazil).

The native people who shyly met those first expeditioners at what is now **Porto Seguro** in Bahia were friendly, even generous in their innocence. According to conservative historians, there were around 2-1/2 million native Indians living in Brazil at the start of the 16th century, the population having lived there undisturbed for hundreds of thousands of years (possibly having migrated from Asia over 430,000 years before). Fragmented into small tribes, the majority were **Tupí-Guaraní**, who tended to be short and bronze-colored, with long straight black hair. Though the Tupis tended toward cannibalism when provoked (they ate the first bishop to arrive in Bahia), they had become masters of tropical survival, cleaning and pruning just enough land for their own crops, wearing no clothes, and indulging in intricate body designs. Although they were not equal in culture to the sophisticated Aztecs of Central Mexico, the Mayas of Yucatan and Guatemala, and the Incas of Peru, they had developed a strong tradition of spirituality, in which the *pajé,* or shaman, communed with nature spirits and prescribed herbal medicines culled from the forest. What their visionaries did not manage to foresee was their disastrous future.

A New Race

To be fair, the first white men the Indians encountered were not exactly the cream of humanity, but they had their strong points. As was the case with most New World colonies, among the first to inhabit Brazil—its first progenitors, actually—were *degredados,* exiled criminals ordered to live among the Indians and learn their language. While they may have been rough and uncouth, these *degredados* were at least equipped with the one thing upon which the future of the Portuguese colony depended. According to Brazilian sociologist Gilberto Freyre, the blending of the Lusitanian and Amerindian cultures was facilitated primarily by one major factor: a favorable attitude toward miscegenation—in other words, lust. Since Portuguese women were excluded from the first colonies, the conquerors, who were already accustomed to the dark-skinned beauty of the Moorish, African, and Asian females, soon discovered a veritable paradise. Some men, like **Diogo Alvares** (renamed **Caramuru**) in Bahia, actually sired an entire village of miscegenated offspring. As a result, a new race quickly appeared—the *mameluco* or *caboclo*—a blend of European and Indian blood well adapted to the physical demands of the land. In return, the Indian taught the white man the best methods for farming and hunting, introduced him to new crops like manioc, and showed him the best way to pass the night in the tropics—in a hammock.

Missionaries

As ship captains bartered with the Indians, exchanging trinkets for brazilwood, a temporary truce was enjoyed. But soon enough, **Jesuit missionaries** set out to convert "the heathens," supervising their education and encouraging them to dress like Europeans. At the same time, the arriving colonists, supported by daring explorers, were rounding up conquered Indians as candidates for enforced labor. In time, the Jesuits would severely antagonize the Court with their viewpoint that the enslavement of Indians was contrary to Christian intent, but the fathers themselves managed to violate their subjects' basic human dignity by systematically stripping them of their animistic beliefs and instinctual lifestyle. Though some Indians became acculturized, most either rebelled or ran away or, more frequently, succumbed to death when their immune systems proved too weak to fight even the slightest Western cold germ.

By the end of the 16th century, about 100 ships were sailing annually from Lisbon to Brazil. To discourage the French privateers scoping the coast, **King João III** in 1532 sent **Martim Afonso de Sousa**, plied with colonists, plants, seeds, and animals, to found the first settlement at **São Vicente** (somewhere near Santos). Established at this time was the pattern of land distribution that would influence Brazilian history for centuries—15 captaincies of about 60 leagues in length, divided among 12 donnees and extending all the way to the Tordesillias Line. The owners could tax, impose justice, divide the land into *sesmarias,* and be expected to rent their land in the name of the king. The majority of captaincies failed but two survived—Pernambuco, where sugar plantations flourished, and São Vicente.

Disappointed by the lack of progress, João III appointed **Tomé de Sousa**, a loyal soldier who had served in Africa and India, as the first governor in charge of all military and civil administration. Beyond the French, Portugal's biggest headache was the Dutch. (Owing to a legitimate right of succession, the Portuguese Crown in 1580 had passed to the heir of the Spanish throne—making both Portugal and Brazil dominions of Spain for 60 years.) Although the Dutch, in the guise of the Dutch West Indies Company, occupied the Northeast for 30 years, they were eventually defeated in a near-massacre campaign that pitted Catholics against Protestants. In 1555, the French occupied what is now the city of Rio de Janeiro, but few colonists were seduced away from Europe, and they were finally driven out by the Portuguese in 1565. In 1624, a Dutch fleet off the coast of Salvador took the governor by surprise, burned the Jesuit College, and massacred priests until they were expelled nine months later by a hastily assembled Spanish and Portuguese fleet. The occupation of

Recife by the Dutch lasted a brutal 24 years, replete with ambushes, outrageous taxes, and mounting hostilities, until the colonists themselves sent them packing.

Motley Crews

The conquest of the vast, mysterious Brazilian interior was due mostly to the *bandeirantes,* a rugged breed of men, propelled as much by their own personal dreams of glory as by loyalty to the throne. Ever in search of gold, diamonds, and Indians, these Brazilian explorers set out mostly from São Paulo, on mules, on foot, and in canoes, forging waterways and paths that would eventually appear on the maps of the coming empire. The motley crews that banded together under their own flag almost always included a priest (sometimes craftier than his colleagues), a few fierce Indian fighters, and, later, botanists, who dared to explore the Amazon, Uruguay, and Paraguay rivers. It was the *bandeirantes* who led the first expeditions to Minas Gerais, when gold was discovered in Sabará in 1695 and then later in Ouro Preto, Mariana, and elsewhere. In 1719, the gold rush opened the path to Cuiabá in Mato Grosso—a 3,500-kilometer obstacle course from São Paulo that led through hostile tribes, voracious mosquitoes, sweltering heat, and dangerously flooded rivers. The herculean efforts of the *bandeirantes* finally paid off: By the middle of the 18th century, it was Brazilian gold that was keeping the Portuguese throne afloat.

Brazilians are fond of saying that they have never had a bloody revolution. In truth, Brazil does enjoy the reputation of being the only South American colony to have achieved independence through peaceful means, but that doesn't include the many who died trying to amass power before and after. The most famous of the aborted rebellions was the **Inconfidência Mineira**, hatched by 12 prominent citizens in Ouro Preto, who were inspired by the success of the 13 former British colonies up north. The conspirators betrayed each other before they even began, except for the self-avowed leader, **Tiradentes**, whose gruesome execution would make him a national hero after Brazil gained its independence. In 1807, Napoleon's invasion of Portugal forced the royal family to take refuge in Rio, declaring it the temporary capital of the Portuguese Empire. On the suggestion of French minister Talleyrand, the portly, good-natured prince named João III made his tropical home into an official kingdom and actually grew genuinely fond of it, despite the constant complaining of his wife, the Spanish princess **Carlota Joaquina**. In 1816, following the death of his demented mother, Maria I, he ascended to the Portuguese throne in his own right as King João VI and did not return to Lisbon until liberal revolts demanded his presence back home five years later. When he finally bid farewell to Brazil, he felt quite nostalgic about leaving the cosmopolitan city he had transformed from a small, unimposing village.

Constitutional Emperor and Perpetual Defender of Brazil

As João VI sailed home, he left behind as regent his 23-year-old son **Pedro**, with the advice that he should take up the crown of Brazil if it should part from Portugal, lest it fall into the "hands of an adventurer." Although Pedro was a talented and complex young man, his education had been sorely neglected and his undisciplined childhood eventually gave way to a lusty adulthood. A dashing horseman, composer, and friend to the Italian composer Rossini, he lived openly with his mistress, the beautiful **Domitila de Castro**, in a relationship considered one of the great love stories of the Americas. (She bore him five children.) Unfortunately, as a ruler, Pedro alternated between autocratic and democratic behavior, eventually battling the Côrtes, the parliamentary body, which demanded his return to Portugal. On September 7, 1822, the short step to independence was taken on a dusty road between Santos and São Paulo when Pedro received a slew of messages: one from the Côrtes reducing his power, others from friends pushing for independence, and the most powerful one from his wife, who urged him to fight with the words: "Pedro, this is the most important moment of your life." With the fire of a *bandeirante,* Pedro unsheathed his sword right on the banks of the Ipiranga River and gave the infamous cry "Independence or Death." On December 1, 1822, in typical royal splendor, he was crowned "Constitutional Emperor and Perpetual Defender of Brazil."

The United States became the first country to recognize the newly independent empire on May of 1824, when President James Monroe officially received José Silvestre Rebelo as chargé d'affaires. By the end of 1825, Portugal acknowledged the independence of its former colony in return for 2 million pounds sterling, though the "bill" and Pedro's allowance to use the honorary title of Emperor of Brazil infuriated Brazilians, further enflaming anti-Lusitanian sentiment. A disastrous war with Argentina, domestic disorganization, and a rampant money crisis, aggravated by promises to free the slaves, eventually forced Pedro to abdicate with the following announcement: "I prefer to descend from the throne with honor rather than to go on reigning as a sovereign who has been dishonored and degraded. Those born in Brazil no longer want me for the reason that I am Portuguese. My son has the advantage over me that he is Brazilian in birth. He will have no difficulty in governing." The son he was talking about—the one he would leave behind as he sailed for Lisbon—was a five-year-old child.

Although **Pedro II** was a mere pawn of his courtiers when he mounted the throne at the age of 14, he achieved full maturity in only a few years. By 1847, he was ruling firmly, free of all political influences, emerging as a symbol of order and prosperity for various regional groups. At the time Brazil was overwhelmingly rural, and Pedro II reasoned that he needed the support of those who dominated the fields—namely the plantation owners (sugar, coffee, and cacão). In retrospect, most historians praise Pedro for his honesty, integrity, and moderation, though a few have complained that his tolerance dampened any progressive vision.

National Unity

The presence of the royal **Braganças** in Rio for 30 years forged a most needed sense of unity in the new empire. In fact, they became the only European monarchs to ever set foot on their American domains. During their reign, Brazilians acquired the habit of looking to Rio as the center of power, and they saw in the monarchy a guarantee of national unity and security. At the urging of the emperor himself, a constitution was written advocating some of the major tenets of early 19th-century liberalism—free trade, sanctity of private property, and capitalistic incentives. Unfortunately, these directives proved disastrous and had the effect of further subordinating the Brazilian economy to the needs of the capitalistic markets of the North Atlantic.

The relative sense of national unity, however, gave emotional space for long-repressed tensions in the interior to arise. Black slaves rebelled against masters; Indians rose up against whites; old scores with Portuguese noblemen were settl/oed. The **Cabanagem Rebellion**, a bloody ten-year uprising of the dispossessed, exploded in the Amazon, when mixed-breed rebels invaded Belém and killed the governor of Pará. Uprisings in Maranhão, Pernambuco, Bahia, and Rio

Grande do Sul further threatened the stability of Pedro's administrative powers. Although he was ostensibly an intelligent ruler, Pedro's foreign policy led Brazil directly into the bloodiest war in South American history—the **War of Triple Alliance**, from 1864 to 1870. Although Paraguay initially started the hostilities by invading Uruguay and parts of Mato Grosso, Brazil had antagonized its neighbor by blocking access to the sea. Though Paraguay was deeply humiliated, losing over 75 percent of its male population, it did fight gallantly and caused great damage to Brazil.

Slavery

Due to the rise of the plantation culture in the interior, the color of the average Brazilian began to change drastically. As sugar and tobacco industries dominated the economy, the need for extensive labor ballooned, and when Indians proved unsuitable, millions of Africans were stripped from their tribal communities and shipped to Brazilian ports beginning in the 17th century. For 300 years, the ignominious **slave trade** continued, and some historians claim that Brazil imported a half million *more* slaves than did all of Spanish America. Most labored under hot suns on the sugar plantations of Bahia and Pernambuco; in Minas Gerais, slaves toiled under even more inhumane conditions in the underground gold mines. While many tried to preserve their African culture through food, dance, religion, and music, others fled to refugee enclaves called *quilombos*. As the winds of abolition wafted through Brazil on a British current, the backlash to preserve slavery incited even more racism and bloodshed. Although the slave trade was finally abolished in 1854, slavery itself remained legal, requiring the impassioned oratory of lawyer **Joaquim Nabuco** to turn the final tides of sentiment. On May 13, 1888, Brazil achieved the notorious distinction of being the last country in the Americas to abolish slavery.

The End Of The Monarchy

The political fallout from such a humanitarian gesture did not ultimately serve Pedro's administrative position. Threatened by the loss of labor, enraged landowners turned on him, as did the liberal intellectuals clamoring for a republic; even the military had not forgiven the debacle of the Paraguayan War. Without a shred of resistance, military forces led by **Marechal Deodoro da Fonseca** marched into Rio on November 15, 1869, effectively announcing the end of the monarchy. Though invited to remain, Pedro II insisted on exile, dying impoverished in a humble Parisian hotel.

The end of the monarchy ushered in an era of military involvement that would color Brazilian politics up to the present day. Twenty years after marching into Rio, Fonseca declared himself a dictator, but unsupported by his own troops, he was forced to resign two weeks later. His successor, **Marechal Floriano Peixoto**, took command, proving himself even more incompetent, until finally stepping down in favor of the first elected civilian president, **Prudente de Morais**.

The Good, The Bad, And The Ugly

For the first 30 years of the 20th century, Brazilian leaders oscillated between the good, the bad, and the ugly. The surge of the coffee industry shifted the base of power away from the sugar fields of Bahia to the coffee fields of São Paulo and the dairy farms of Minas—a political trend that came to be known as *café com leite* (coffee with milk). Between 1890 and 1930, large-scale immigration further spiked the ethnic mix, as the Japanese headed to São Paulo, Italians to the wine-conducive lands of the extreme south, and Germans to the cool, fresh climes of Santa Catarina. Rubber joined the boom-bust economy as millions of *nordestinos* (northeasterners) moved into the Amazon to tap rubber—that is, until a sly British conspiracy to smuggle seedlings out of the jungle eventually exploded Brazil's world monopoly.

World War II

As regional interests began to dominate the federal scene, political graft slowly set in. During World War II, Brazil passively sided against Germany; on the homefront, the economy was weakened by the disastrous collapse of the coffee market as 2 million sacks of beans lingered unwanted in storage—a million more than the world consumed in one year. The year 1929 marked the beginning of an 18-year domination of government by one single man—**Getúlio Vargas**. Though he lost the 1929 presidency in a legitimate election, a military junta immediately seized power from the elected opposition and eventually passed Vargas the sash of office four days later. In one dramatic act, the old republic ended just as it had begun—with military intervention.

For nearly a generation, Vargas managed to rule the country from every possible political position: as chief of a provisional government

(1930–1934), as constitutional president elected by the Congress (1934–1937), as dictator (1937–1945), and finally as constitutional president elected by the people (1951–1954). Born to a rich ranching family in Rio Grande do Sul, Vargas proved to be gifted with unusual political acumen, though he never quite demonstrated the megalomaniacal tendencies of Latin dictators like Juan Perón of Argentina (to whom he was often compared). Urged on by a group of young, idealistic supporters, he managed to nationalize the oil, steel, and electricity industries and standardized a health and social welfare program that brought him working-class kudos long after his death. But to effect such drastic changes, Vargas had to create his own power, which he did by declaring himself dictator and renaming his regime *O Estado Novo* (The New State). World War II found Vargas siding with the Allies, only after the U.S. offered massive aid in return for naval bases, but it was his own army that forced him to resign upon their return from fighting troops in Italy. From 1945 to 1950, **Marechal Eurico Gaspar Dutra** ran an insipid regime, opening the door to Vargas' defiantly triumphant return in 1950. This time, however, military enemies and crushing inflation undermined his popularity, particularly when he raised middle-class taxes. Events turned tragic when Carlos Lacerda, a famous journalist who had publicly called Vargas a communist, was nearly murdered when a shot meant for him killed one of his bodyguards instead. Evidence pointed to one of Vargas's own bodyguards, though the president was never directly implicated. Nevertheless, when the High Command eventually demanded Vargas's resignation, the politician countered with a swift response that left behind a country in shock. After writing a dramatic farewell note, he retired to his bedroom in the Palácio do Catete in Rio and shot himself through the heart.

Brasília

An interim government ruled until a most industrious, truly visionary physician from Minas Gerais turned the country on its head. **Juscelino Kubitschek** (known to his supporters as **JK**), marched into Brazilian politics with faith in the interior and a commitment to modernism, all symbolized in the construction of a new, decidedly futuristic capital called Brasília. Suddenly, with new highways, avant-garde architecture, and a thriving automotive industry, Brazil shot into international prominence as a modern country to contend with. Although JK can be credited with bringing Brazil out of the horse-and-cart era, the administration his successor, **Jânio Quadros**, inherited was a financial nightmare, riveted by debts incurred in the construction of Brasília, and worsened by Quadros's own autocratic temper and his friendliness to Cuba (the latter shocking the military). When Quadros suddenly resigned seven months after taking office (citing "terrible forces" against him), the military stepped in, severely reducing the power of his succeeding vice president, **João Goulart**, and instituting a parliamentary system. A plebescite in 1963 returned the full power of the presidency to Goulart, whose land reforms and social programs veered him dangerously to the left. As the cost of living soared and middle-class opposition swelled, the military accused Goulart and his government of being communists and again usurped power in a bloodless coup on March 31, 1964. Within four hours of taking power, before Goulart had even fled to Uruguay, the leaders of the coup received a telegram from President Lyndon B. Johnson congratulating them on their maneuver. Generous American aid and loans would soon follow.

Trials and Tribulations

For the next two decades, Brazil was at the mercy of a military dictatorship, where presidents were chosen in secret by the army and where individual human rights were severely abused. The regime never hesitated to resort to violence to achieve its agenda. The most repressive era was the **Médici** years, between 1969 and 1974, when "subversives" were tortured and killed and even the lyrics of popular songs were censored. Nevertheless, aided by harsh measures, the economy surged between 1974 and 1979, giving rise to the "**Brazilian Miracle**," as it was called—boom years of unprecedented prosperity, though its riches barely touched the legions of the impoverished majority. The 1980s reverted to hard times as the Latin American debt crisis exploded and foreign loans dried up; just the interest alone on Brazil's foreign debt outstripped the nation's ability to pay. The last military president, **João Baptista Figueiredo** intentionally paved the way for the end of the regime—rescinding press censorship, calling for an amnesty for political prisoners, and even allowing Congressional elections—but he could not surmount growing public hostility over the failing economy.

Democratic Elections

It seemed as if the sun would finally rise in Brazil in 1985 when 75-year-old elder statesman **Tancredo Neves** was elected by an electoral college comprised of Congressional and state delegates to be Brazil's first civilian president in 21 years. Aided by humanitarian insight, Neves, considered the most competent moderate to oppose the military, was able to unite rival factions—until he was rushed to the hospital with a bleeding tumor the night before he was to take office. Thirty-eight days and seven operations later, he died of septicemia, though a few suspected foul play. (In 1991 his surgeons were still on trial for incompetency.) His vice-president, **José Sarney,** a staunch conservative from the northeast state of Maranhão, attempted to gain the support of liberals through populist land reforms, but his indecisive nature, not to mention institutionalized government corruption, helped to fuel the foreign debt that reached a devastating $120 billion by the end of his term.

By the time he left office, Sarney was so out of favor that crowds regularly greeted him with showers of bricks. Still, nationalistic fever had gained prominence, leading the government to declare a moratorium on the foreign debt and instigate strict measures against foreign investment. By 1988, inflation, up to 700 per cent, had become so outrageous that a new, powerful president was needed to avoid another military takeover. In 1989, **Fernando Collor de Mello** became the first president elected by popular vote in 30 years—the scion of a wealthy Alagoas family, who as governor of his home state had become famous for hunting down *marajás*—retired generals and former public servants who were living illegally on multiple pensions. Beating out the Worker's Party, Collor brought a new sophistication to Brazil's international image with his movie-star good looks, beautiful wife, and personal derring-do. (He once took over the controls of a 727 jet on his way to the White House to meet President Bush.) Only hours after taking office, however, he totally shook up the country when he froze the banks—an anti-inflationary plan that pleased those without money (their buying power remained stable), but infuriated those who had any assets. (No one could withdraw from their accounts for at least a period of six months.) Eventually, most of the money was returned—with interest—but not before many in the middle class had to drastically change their lifestyles.

Scandal

The **Collor Plan**, a complicated financial agenda geared toward salvaging the failing economy (including the privatization of government-owned industry) has generally been hailed as a positive step, but its workability has been obscured by scandal after scandal that has erupted throughout Collor's administration. To the zeal of the press, the first brouhaha began with his minister of economy, **Zélia Cardoso de Mello** (no relation to Collor), an extremely intelligent but somewhat graceless woman who eventually resigned under political pressure, but not before her illicit affair with a married Cabinet member was uncovered. Collor's own wife, Rosane, in a series of scenes straight out of a Brazilian soap opera, was accused of illicit spending and deposed from an honorary position (her public tears upstaged only by her husband's dramatic disposal of his wedding ring into a lake before they were subsequently reconciled). Finally, on the eve of Rio '92, the finance manager of Collor's election campaign was accused of embezzlement by the president's own brother, who also publicly accused the president of using cocaine. (Complicating the scenario was the fact that the finance manager was trying to compete with the Collor family's newspaper and radio conglomerate in Alagoas, "coincidentally" run by the brother.) In June 1992, Collor addressed the public in an impassioned six-and-a-half-minute speech denouncing the scandal, effectively clearing the way a few days later for a monumental repackaging of the foreign debt with the International Monetary Fund. Yet, as Congressional investigations provided more evidence of fund-milking by Collor, his wife, and key administrators, public and legislative pressure swelled, demanding the president's swift resignation.

Itamar Franco, Collor's low-profile vice president, succeeded to the presidency in the fall of 1992, quickly losing popularity through indecisiveness, lack of humor, and a penchant for changing his cabinet ministers on a moment's whim. (In the meantime, Collor, along with his wife, prepared to face criminal charges.) In spring 1993, a bid for the return to a monarchy was overruled by popular vote, though many supported it not as a joke but as a desperate attempt to change the dire economic crisis. By the summer of 1993, the political situation in Brazil seemed to be enduring a standstill as the public, fed up with a 30 percent rise in inflation per month, looked hopefully toward the next presidential elections set for 1994.

INSIDE BRAZILIANS

Anything is possible in Brazil. That's the attitude to adapt if you're planning to do any traveling or business. Given the Brazilian temperament, however, nothing is ever accomplished by a push and a shove. The currency in this country is not so much money but charm (though a few discreetly placed bucks never hurt anyone). Even though most of Brazil remains a third-world country, the sophistication of the upper-class has filtered into every level of society, mostly through the extravagant soap operas that dominate the air waves. Simply, Brazilians are worldly and should be treated as such—some remote farmers I met in the Amazon jungle had just watched the entire coverage of the Gulf War on their battery-powered TVs.

There's no question that Brazil labors under a seemingly perpetual economic crisis, and anyone in possession of the more stable U.S. dollar holds the power. Most prices can be bargained down, but it depends on your attitude and technique; even with a street vendor, you should negotiate with grace, humor, and dignity. *It is totally tasteless to bargain in restaurants or commercial stores, though if you are Brazilian, it's perfectly fine (nearly expected) to complain about the high prices.* Hotels in low season tend to respond favorably to the word *desconto*, or discount (see *Accommodations* in *Directory*). The same holds true for a fashionable boutique or jewelry store, particularly if you are buying a substantial amount of goods. The thing to do is smile, look beseeching, then offer to pay in cash (especially dollars).

A Difference of Culture

Brazilians often experience American straightforwardness as brusqueness, and if you learn to soothe your western impatience, you will find many more social doors opening. Unfortunately, numerous Brazilian women have complained to me that American men tend to treat them all as (pardon the language) whores. To be politic, I think the misunderstanding mostly has to do with **sexy standards of tropical dress**, which must be reinterpreted by us northerners as merely national style. True, in the big cities, around touristic hotels, there are lots of prostitutes, but you will rarely find them among the legion of professional guides and shopgirls, many of whom are quite conservative, no matter how short their skirts are. If you want to date a Brazilian, ask with the same grace you accord women at home.

Social kissing is one national habit that causes undue consternation among North Americans. Even when meeting professionally, most women kiss each other hello and good-bye on both cheeks (really, two pecks in the air), though two men (or a man and woman) in a corporate situation usually just shake hands. Industries like tourism and arts and entertainment usually find everybody kissing everybody, no matter how well they know each other. If a Brazilian acquaintance introduces you to his or her mother, especially if you've been invited to dinner, get ready to kiss. When in doubt, you can always shake hands; the thing to remember is that this kind of double-cheek kissing has really nothing to do with deep-seated affection, though it is a sign of how important even superficial displays of warmth are to Brazilians. If you feel awkward or mess up, those acquainted with American mores will probably forgive you.

In terms of **personal address**, Brazilians can be both respectfully formal and charmingly casual. When introduced socially, a Brazilian might give only his or her first name (indeed, at times in Brazil it seems that nobody has a last name). The truth is, most people have four or five names, the combination of which—if you were told—you would probably promptly forget. While first names are commonly used, titles of respect—*senhor* for men and *dona* for women—are also used as a sign of politeness with strangers and also to show respect to an elder or someone from a different social class. As such, guides or hoteliers often addressed me as Miss Pamela, and I always addressed my elderly landlady in Rio as Dona Vitória. Children always address their parents as *o senhor* or *a senhora* in place of the equivalent "you," a form also expected in matters of business. A pleasant way to address a government official or older colleague is to call him *Doutor*, followed by his or her first name (i.e., Doutor Fernando, or Doctor Fernando.) The trick is to keep the sarcasm out of your voice.

Family life is important to most Brazilians. Due to the financial crisis, adult children often live at home long after their American counterparts would, a condition now identified by Brazilian psychologists as severely extended adolescence. Until 1985, divorce was illegal in this Catholic country, giving rise to a subculture of adultery (the poet and lyricist Vinícius de Moraes was famous for his numerous wives/lovers/companions). Today, you will find many men over 40 already on their second wife—usually young, pretty women in their 20s—while the legion of divorced upper- and middle-class women continues to swell. Both married men and women tend to take lovers, but given the machismo still rampant, women must remain more discreet. In fact, men accused of murdering their wives for adultery often go unconvicted, as do rapists in general. A feminist movement is only now beginning to have a voice in Brazilian politics, but most women will admit that they are still judged on the basis of their looks, not their capabilities.

What truly separates Americans from Brazilians is **punctuality**. Basically, *never* expect a Brazilian to be on time or to apologize for being late (yes, even up to one or two hours). Tardiness is simply not considered a problem in Brazil, and if you ever comment on it adversely, you will only be met with a quizzical look. On the other hand, every time *I* was late for a business meeting, it always seemed to matter to somebody. The rule in Brazil, I guess, is expect to wait, but never keep anyone else waiting.

Smoking seems to be a universal activity among Brazilians, even including those who live in the Amazon jungle. While respect for nonsmokers is not yet officially entrenched in the culture, I was surprised at how many times I was politely asked if smoking would bother me. Nevertheless, I had the distinct impression I was expected to say no, and, in fact, most Brazilians are too socially accommodating to ever admit to offense. If you really can't stand the smoke, the best way to curtail it is to plead severe allergies.

Brazilians, in general, have impeccable **table manners**, and are often shocked by more casual American mores. They eat nearly everything (including pizza) with knife and fork (held in the right and left hand respectively, European-style, without changing), and the habit runs deep. It was not until I brought a Brazilian friend to New York that he saw for the first time "sophisticated" people eating barbecue ribs with their fingers.

Among habits that will shock you is the Brazilian manner of getting a person's attention, particularly in stores or restaurants. It's common to snap one's fingers, hiss, and make a sound like *sssh* (as if telling one to be quiet). Waiters are accustomed to these signals, though you may feel a bit uncomfortable using them. Also, Brazilians (more men than women, but not exclusively) use toothpicks found on the dining table to clean their teeth after meals, though they always shield their mouth with one hand. Like Italians, Brazilians love to color their conversations with dramatic **hand gestures**. The first time I saw a native frantically shaking his hand from his wrist and snapping his finger I thought he was having an epileptic fit. (The gesture, common among all classes, actually means "a long time ago.") "Thumbs up" (a raised thumb rising out of a fist) is a commonly used gesture by all sexes to mean "great." One gesture you should totally avoid is the common American gesture for *okay* (thumb and forefinger touching with the last three fingers raised). In Brazil, it's equivalent to a four-letter word.

Most **business** in Brazil is done in social situations: over drinks, during two- to three-hour lunches, and at evening receptions and cocktail parties. While laws exist to be broken in Brazil (a favorite national saying), bureaucratic **red tape** has felled many a foreigner, particularly those trying to acquire permission from federal agencies in Brasília. What you need most are personal contacts: that is, friends (or at least friends of friends) in high places. Most important, however, is your own behavior, especially if you can acquire the reputation of being *simpático*. The word variously means you are a joy to be with, you are not an American boor, you can be trusted in delicate situations, and, just possibly, you might make a good lover. The next best thing to be called is *esperto*, or clever. Maybe it's a sign of the financial times, but these days *esperto* is most often applied to somebody smart enough to have made a million dollars, no matter how.

The Amazon jungle is at the heart of heated political controversy these days, so for those heading to the wilds, here's a word of advice: *Don't go with the self-righteous attitude that Brazil is destroying the rain forest and the rest of the world is innocently suffering from it.* Keep your mind open, talk to as many people as possible, and don't come to hasty conclusions. Brazilians complain that tourists blame *every* Brazilian they meet for the ecological destruction of the planet. It's not a fair assumption, and worse, you will lose out on developing a lot of great friendships.

As for **romance**, Brazilians are just plain sexy, and there's no getting around it. Even those lacking in traditional physical charms have a certain *je ne sais quois,* a way of expressing their life force that can have devastating effect. Even in normal conversation, Brazilians like to look their partner straight in the eye, and in true Latin fashion they love to touch (though a light finger on your arm doesn't necessarily signal sexual interest). On the other hand, many Brazilians might say, "*What doesn't signal sexual interest?*" Simply, Brazilians are big flirts, big heartbreakers, and totally irresistible.

CUISINE

A Waiter Delivers a Plate of Grilled Lobster at a Jangada Party

Brazilian food is hearty, colorful, and delicious.

Brazilians are big meat eaters—and for good reason: southern beef from Rio Grande do Sul and cuts imported from Argentina are among the tastiest in the world. If a small town has only two restaurants, at least one of them is sure to be a **steak house**: a *churrascaria*, where you can order grilled beef à la carte, or a *rodízio*, an all-you-can-eat buffet—where formally dressed waiters rotate, serving you up to 18 cuts of meat until you yell quits. For a single moderate price, you start off with chicken hearts, ham, sausage, and gizzards, then work up to chicken, filet mignon, and prime rib. Most often included in the price are dozens of side dishes or an extensive salad bar. If you pace yourself properly, one meal at a *rodízio* could hold you for days.

The **national dish** in Brazil is *feijoada*. Throughout the country most restaurants serve it on Saturday, though it can often be found on Wednesday (especially in the finer hotels of Rio). The original version was invented by black slaves during the colonial period, who creatively employed the leftovers from their master's table. Today, making a good *feijoada* is a fine art (it takes all day to prepare), and you're expected to eat it at a leisurely pace, among good friends or family. The basic element is a black bean stew, to which is added an intriguing lineup of dried, salted, and smoked meats, including pork, tongue, pork loin, ribs, sausage, and bacon. (Chefs at more sophisticated restaurants tend to leave out some of the more traditional ingredients like pig's ears, tail, feet, and snout.) Uninitiated foreigners are sometimes put off by the dark, "witchy" look of the simmering pots, but steel yourself and dig in: the dish is truly delicious, if a bit heavy.

Nearly every region, however, boasts its own delicacies. **Rio's cuisine** is as international as they come, but local specialties focus on excellent grilled fish, lobster, fine **fish stews** called *caldeiradas,* and some of the best **pizza** in Brazil. Cuisine in Minas Gerais tends toward short ribs, heavy bean dishes, and to-die-for *torresmos*— **fried pork rinds**. Bahian cuisine is spicy, most often orange in color (from the *dendê* palm oil), and based around seafood. The most exotic **fish** dishes can be found in the Amazon, where anything from *piranha* to *pirarucu* is fried, stewed, broiled, and poached. In the more German-inspired cities like Blumenau and Joinville in the state of Santa Catarina, superb wienerschnitzel, spätzle, and sauerkraut are washed down with dark, frothy beer. Some of the best **pastas** can be found in the Italian wine country of the extreme south.

Vegetarians need not worry in Brazil. While you should avoid eating raw vegetables or unpeeled fruits, rice and beans are unilaterally served in every restaurant, omelettes are easy to find, and *legumes cozidos* (cooked vegetables) can be prepared by any chef if you ask. In some of the larger cities, like Rio, São Paulo, and Brasília, there are good macrobiotic restaurants, as well as a variety of health-conscious vegetarian counters. Delicious **tropical fruits** are among Brazil's natural wonders, replete with shapes, sizes, and colors you have probably never seen before, among the best of which are made into ice creams, smoothies, and compotes. Among the more familiar are apples, melons, strawberries, and bananas—as well as mangoes, pineapples, guavas, passion fruits, persimmons, and tamarinds, not to mention the more exotic specimens like *bacuri* and *cupuaçu.*

A committed café culture has developed numerous ways to pass leisure time through noshing and drinking. *Cerveja* or **beer** seems to be a national battle cry, and Brazilian natives seem to have an uncanny ability to drink all night and not get unduly drunk. Even children sip *cerveja.* (Best names are Brahma and Antarctica). *Chopp* is draft beer, which usually runs under a dollar and goes best with tiny hors d'oeuvres. *Caipirinha,* a lethal concoction, is made with lime slices crushed inside a glass full of sugar, ice, and *cachaça,* or sugarcane liquor. Competing with the ubiquitous Coke is the native-made *guaraná,* a tangy carbonated soft drink distilled from the berry of the same name. (Diet Coke is usually available only in figure-conscious cities like Rio.) Good before or after meals, *batidas* are rum-based liqueurs made with various flavors like coconut or chocolate.

Wines produced in the south of Brazil are quite fine. Among the best names are **Casa Valduga** (available in 5-star hotels and restaurants), **Maison Forestier,** and **Peterlongo** (champagne). When in doubt, ask the maitre d' for suggestions. *Tinto* is red, *branco* is white, and *rosé* is rosé; dry wines are referred to as *seco,* sweet wines as *suave.* As for spirits, there are few good Brazilian whiskeys, and imports are usually expensive.

Brazil takes great pride in one of its most important exports—**coffee**. Nearly a ritual, *cafezinho* (sugar-laced coffee served in tiny cups) is taken frequently throughout the day and you are sure to be offered one at a business meeting (it's a little impolite to refuse). Most Americans find Brazilian coffee too strong, but *café com leite* (coffee with hot milk), served at breakfast, helps to cut some of the tang. *Finding fresh milk for coffee at any time other than breakfast, however, will prove a challenge,* though fine restaurants may have delicious whipped cream called *chantilly.* (Ask for it—it's great in *cafezinho.*) The best place to buy packaged Brazilian coffee is at the airport's duty-free shop on your way back home.

Bottled **mineral water,** *água mineral* (a must for all travelers; see *Health Kit*) can be found in nearly all restaurants and counters and is happily delicious. You can order it carbonated *(com gás)* or not *(sem gás)*. The best name is Caxambú.

(For more information regarding cuisine, see under the individual regions.)

Insider Tip:

Food in Brazil comes heavily salted, and if you are used to cutting back, you will find your first bite a veritable shock. Don't be shy when ordering to ask for "sem sal" (without salt). You can always add more yourself.

TRAVELER'S GUIDE TO BRAZILIAN SPIRITS

Church in Olinda

It's common knowledge that although 98 percent of Brazilians are Catholic, 100 percent believe in something else. That "something" ranges from African spirits, Indian fetishes, and gypsy love potions to trance channelers, psychic healers, and extraterrestrials. No matter where you go in Brazil, you are sure to run into something or somebody that smells otherworldly. Most commonly heard is the phrase: *"I'm not a real believer, but you can never tell..."* In my own travels, I've met government officials who are self-proclaimed *bruxos* (witches), and even respected businessmen who regularly consult psychics. Prior to her son's election in 1989, the mother of President

Fernando Collor secretly met with an American trance medium to scope out her son's political chances. It's public knowledge that the federal government annually consults the *Umbanda* roll, which predicts events for the coming year. These practices so exasperate the Pope that rumors of excommunicating the entire country regularly abound.

Catholic worship itself at times reaches fanatic proportions in Brazil. On October 12 of each year, hundreds of thousands flock to the Basílica of Aparecida on the highway between Rio and São Paulo to celebrate the founding patron saint of Brazil, Our Lady of Conception. The city of **Congonhas,** which displays the sculpted prophets of the artist Aleijadinho, has long been the site of spontaneous healings. In Belém, religious tensions reach such a fervor during the Círio de Nazaré parade that fights break out among penitents pushing each other to catch hold of the rope shielding the sacred Madonna. In cathedrals throughout the country, there are special rooms full of letters, photographs, and plastic heads and body parts symbolizing prayers that have been answered. At a famous grotto outside **Torres** in Rio Grande do Sul, you'll find staunch believers climbing up the torturous stone staircase on their knees. In small villages, devotees elect to carry immensely heavy crosses for hundreds of miles in payment for healings.

The syncretism of Catholicism and the African Yoruban religion finds expression in the Afro-Brazilian cult worship called *candomblé*. During colonial times, slaves were not allowed to practice their native trance religions, so they clothed the African divinities in the guise of Catholic saints—a double-faced identity that's been preserved to this day. *Candomblé*'s basic principle is that the body of the believer through possession becomes the instrument of communication between divine forces and mortals. Worshippers who receive signs by the spirits of their potential mediumship undergo extensive training, including months of seclusion, ritual baths, and initiations that involve smearing animal blood and chicken feathers on their foreheads. The religious ceremonies themselves are great shows of African drumming and frenetic dancing, all designed to provoke the initiate to fall into a trance. Although white upper-class devotees are rare in *candomblé*, the maternal heads of these *terreiros*, or churches, are often powerful spiritual figures in the community; among the most famous was **Mãe Menininha,** the supreme priestess of Gantois (one of the oldest *terreiros* in Brazil) and a favorite amo҆ such as novelist Jorge Amado and composer Dorival (Although Mãe Menininha was a staunch traditionalist, she wa true daughter of syncretism; her office, where she received v҆ was decorated with pictures of Jesus, Omulu (an African divi and John F. Kennedy.

An underlying theme of Brazilian spirituality is the cult of the feminine. It's no wonder that in this beachfront country the Goddess of the Ocean would arise as a major power symbol. Considered the syncretistic equivalent of the Virgin Mary, the Afro-Brazilian goddess **Iemanjá** inspires reverence on a national scale: witness the celebrations held on New Year's throughout the country. On December 13 in Praia Grande near São Paulo, December 31 in Rio, and February 2 in Salvador, her worshippers offer flowers, perfume, and lipstick at the edge of the sea. In the south of Brazil along the seashore of Torres, the mesmeritic power of Iemanjá has been transformed into legends of mermaids who seduce unsuspecting sailors with their siren-like beauty and song.

Among the most democratic of the visionary cults is **Umbanda**, which arose in 1908 when a 17-year-old boy questioned during a spiritualist session why the spirits of *caboclos* (mixed breeds), blacks, and Indians were never channeled. Subsequently, he began to channel the spirit of an enlightened Indian named Seven Crossroads, as well as a Preto Velho (old black man), who cured sick people. Today, *Umbanda* sessions, which are free of charge, are performed only for the sake of healing, and, in contrast to *candomblé*, use no drums or chanting. Many of Brazil's artists and musicians participate in *Umbanda*, however fleetingly; during the 1980s, Gilberto Gil entitled one of his records *Um Banda Um,* a play on words between the name of the cult and the phrase "One (Music) Band."

Along the beach of Copacabana, as well as in forest grottoes and near waterfalls, you'll no doubt stumble upon the remains of a Macumba ritual. Erroneously equated with *Umbanda*, **Macumba** is actually a form of black magic that arose out of Quimbanda Bantu fetishes and witch doctor rituals. Public sessions are held after midnight in dark forests; the spirits are supposedly of the lowest level, and *trabalhos,* or work, is performed ostensibly to undo evil. Dishes of food and candy are often left out as appeasement to the gods, and under no circumstances should the offerings ever be disturbed; even dogs have the good sense to sniff and walk away. Cigars, popcorn, bowls of manioc flour, and black candles and ribbons are sure signs of Macumba.

Although the Portuguese colonialists were raised on the mystical stories of their black nurses, the enlightened whites of Rio longed to find a seemingly more "civilized" way of believing in spirits. The court of the Emperor Dom Pedro II was well peopled with shamans, including a doctor who did laying on of hands and another who communicated with spirits. In 1858, the work of French spiritualist **Allan Kardec** was brought back from Europe by a nobleman who had it translated into Portuguese, which immediately inspired a subculture of white spiritualists who began experimenting with automatic writing, table rapping, and healing. Today, numerous adherents of Kardec-inspired philosophies practice healing, laying on of hands, and exorcisms without the benefit of drumming, drugs, or the incentive of money.

Today, *candomblé* and spiritualistic practices in Brazil have reached far beyond their own membership. Upper-class Brazilian families sometimes sneak patients out of mental hospitals to be healed by a *mãe de santo* with spirit medicine. Anyone visiting the dressing room of singer **Maria Bethânia** after a show will be greeted in a darkened room thick with incense and cluttered with dripping candles, with pictures of her favorite spirit guides placed before her mirror. In the darker cults, however, spirit possession is used to manipulate clients and to provoke fear, and, even in *candomblé*, one *mãe de santo* has publicly admitted that not all examples of trance possession are real. Fights have been known to break out in *terreiros* when two members claim to be receiving the same spirit simultaneously—a sticky situation that must be resolved by the *mãe* or *pai de santo* with Solomon-like diplomacy.

Long before black slaves arrived in Brazil, however, native **Indians** were practicing **shamanistic rituals** that required the services of a *pajé*, or medicine man, who understood the therapeutic power of plants and allowed himself to be possessed by nature spirits in order to cure disease. Throughout the Amazon, legends arose that are still believed today, mostly regarding the *matita pereira* and the *pai do mato*, sylvanlike spirits who love to befuddle humans. Today, *candomblé do caboclo* and a cult called *batuque* call upon such legendary Indian spirits as Iracema and Peri during ritual trance work. Travelers to the Amazon may actually inquire about meeting a *pajé*—a request still so rare that you are bound to meet the real thing.

The native use of **hallucinogenic jungle plants** has given rise in this century to two popular cults that use an organic mixture known in the States as *ayahuasca* to invoke spiritual visions. Branches of the independent organizations **Santo Daime** and **União Vegetal** can be found throughout the country (though mostly in Rio, Salvador, and the Amazon), having attracted adherents from all walks of life, including celebrities and artists who gleefully retell their psychedelic experiences on talk shows. Although the drug (actually, a ritually prepared concoction of two Amazonian plants) was illegal for many years, recent government research has proved the thick, bitter liquid (poetically called *chá,* or tea) to be neither addictive nor harmful, despite its side effects of extreme gastrointestinal distress (most first-timers succumb to intense vomiting or diarrhea). Men, women (sometimes during childbirth), and children are known to partake of this drug, though advisories are given to forgo meat, alcohol, and, in some cases, sex prior to the ritual. The more orthodox of the two cults, **Santo Daime** often makes participants stand or dance in one place for hours, while the more liberal **União Vegetal** plays classical and Brazilian music to accompany the seated group ritual. American travelers should note that it is illegal to transport *ayahuasca* back to the States, and that there have been numerous cases of confiscation at customs. If you are interested in participating in any of these groups, it is best to do so through personal contacts.

Psychics and psychic healers have many adherents in Brazil. One of the most famous and respected is **Francisco Cândido Xavier** (nicknamed Chico). Born in 1910 of humble origin, this craggy-faced mulato barely managed to finish primary school, but one day, while working as a day laborer, he began channeling poetry from 56 dead writers. The poems were so good that Brazil's finest literary critics were unable to dispute their authenticity. The book, published under the title *Parnassus Beyond the Grave,* became the first of hundreds Xavier would write regarding spirituality and health. For years, Xavier has given psychic medical consultations to thousands who stream to his home in Uberaba, Minas Gerais, though last reports have found him extremely ill.

Another famous psychic was **José Arigó,** who, with the supposed help of the spirit of a dead German physician known as Dr. Fritz, was seemingly able to perform psychic surgery using only a rusty paring knife. Despite persecution by the government, Arigó was, over a number of years, apparently able to heal thousands of people; it was rumored he even received a silver box inscribed with thanks from Pope Pius XII. Following Arigó's death, at least 13 other Brazilian psychics have surfaced, claiming to channel the same Dr. Fritz and performing operations (though, apparently, none have yet gotten Dr. Fritz's German accent quite right). That the establishment now accepts such activities as more or less believable was made apparent in a recent report by *Veja* magazine (the *Newsweek* of Brazil), which only half-jokingly asked, "Would the real Dr. Fritz please stand up?"

Given the above interest, it's not surprising that one of the most popular American writers in Brazil is Shirley MacLaine, whose latest esoteric-oriented book *Dancing in the Light* describes two other astounding Brazilian psychics. Among the middle-class, New Age interest is intense, and yearly conventions featuring crystals, psychics, and astrologers are often held at 5-star hotels like the Bahia Othon in Salvador. Although Brazil is home to enormous pockets of natural **crystals,** they were not considered much more than pretty rocks until about five years ago, when the demand from the States made Brazilians reconsider their esoteric (and, hence, commercial) value. Now you can find traditional jewelers setting stones for "healing purposes," and you can also purchase excellent raw crystals and rocks. The best place to buy them is in the state of Minas Gerais.

There is also a thriving **holistic health** community found not only in the big cities, but in such remote areas as Cuiabá in Mato Grosso. There you'll be able to find shiatzu practitioners, acupuncturists, masseurs, and homeopaths. The city of Brasília, in particular, is populated with numerous healers who use extraordinary means, such as color, sound, and aroma. Brazilians adore natural health cures; spa towns featuring mineral waters and baths attract millions of health seekers in the south of Minas. And ever since the singing superstar Xuxa began taking dips in waterfalls on the advice of her personal psychic, Marilena Simões of Belo Horizonte, thousands have been flocking to *cachoeiras* around the country. Herbs of all kinds, cultivated throughout the Amazon, are generally accepted as medicine; available at homeopathic stores and herb markets, they are said to cure anything from impotence to heart, lung, and blood disease.

As for extraterrestrials, it is difficult to travel through Brazil without meeting numerous people who have sighted **UFOs.** Among the most famous locations are the Amazon jungle, Brasília, Rio de Janeiro, Chapada dos Guimarães, and São Tomé das Letras in Minas Gerais—the latter an entirely eccentric village made of stone where some residents claim to have conversed with extraterrestrials for the last 30 years. A half-hour from São Tomé is a highly respected community of contemplatives founded by **Trigueirinho,** a former film director turned guru and author who claims to have continuing contact with beings from outer space.

A deep strain of **millennarianism** has run for centuries throughout Brazilian history; today, religious groups like the **Euboise Temple** in São Lourenço, Minas Gerais, fervently hold to the conviction that the birthplace of the Third Millennium will take place in that area. Groups in Brasília feel the same way about their own city, as do individuals in the town of **Chapada dos Guimarães** in Mato Grosso, the geocentric point of South America. A community already gearing for the end of the world is **Abra di Garça,** an alternative village in the interior of Mato Grosso where only the international language Esperanto is spoken.

One of the most unusual communities, which incorporates spirits from all races and planetary systems, is **Vale do Amanhecer,** or Valley of the Dawn, a dusty, nearly handmade village outside Brasília. Founded by a feisty ex-trucker known as Tia Neiva (Aunt Neiva), the community is based on her channeled visions and has trained over 3,000 mediums. Brazilians from all over the country descend on the village to be healed inside a brashly colored temple full of icons of Indian, black, and extraterrestrial spirits. As per the group's philosophy, no money is charged and no religious dogma other than a form of open-ended spiritualism is promoted. According to local police, the village is a model of harmony. While the outer visuals of the community look silly—residents dress in tacky Renaissance outfits (according to channeled injunctions from Tia Neiva)—its inhabitants all seem to be "normal" people and are particularly gracious to visitors. One young psychotherapist I met there was developing her psychic skills to deal more skillfully with her patients. Despite the community's eccentricities, the national press is always petitioning it for spiritual advice during such phenomenon as eclipses, harmonic convergences, and general disasters.

CARNAVAL

Dancers at Carnaval
Samba: "*the capacity for sustained episodes of intense unambivalent joy.*"

From ***Samba*** by Alma Guillermoprieto

Brazilians didn't invent Carnaval, but probably more than any other country in the world, they *sustain* it. A festival of unbridled emotion, Carnaval in Brazil has many faces—from the televised grand parade in the Sambódromo and the fashionable upper-crust balls in private clubs to the streetside frenzies that anyone can join. For four days businesses close, drinks flow freely, inhibitions of body and mind are shed without caution. To an outsider, it looks like so much indulgence, but for those who live in the *favelas*, where the so-called samba schools were first born, Carnaval invokes a fierce sense of tradition, a unifying force that gives political, emotional, and even spiritual nourishment to those who feel deeply disenfranchised from the (mostly white) center of power.

But Carnaval is hardly about race. No matter what one's social status, sexual preference, or style, it's a time to be whatever one *isn't* during the rest of the year—to inhabit for a brief moment the cloak of a prince, the skirt of a vamp—to have a stage big enough and brash enough to express one's deepest desires and not be condemned. Yet Carnaval is also about music—the color, rhythm, and soul of samba. If you've never had the urge to sing and dance in the greatest Broadway musical in history, you cannot begin to understand the joy Carnaval enflames in its most willing victims.

Beginnings

The Bacchanalian urge dates back to Greco-Roman times, when during late fall, hierarchy was happily dissembled and princes, politicians, philosophers, and paupers all mingled with lower-class ladies in orgiastic assembly. As the Catholic Church slowly usurped control, the festivities were severely condemned, but nevertheless allowed to flourish in a tamer version restricted to the days preceding Ash Wednesday. With a nod to their own appetites, food-loving Italians adopted the phrase *Carne Vale*—farewell to meat—a salute that soon included all kinds of flesh.

In Brazil, the origins of Carnaval were more impish than erotic. The festival entered the country on the wings of the Portuguese *entrudo*—a term used to describe the naughty if somewhat childish acts of mischief performed by the Portuguese in the name of religiously sanctioned fun. In the middle of the 19th century, *cariocas* took to the streets on the Sunday before Ash Wednesday to lance water bombs and rotten lemons; a painting by the French artist Debret shows a young Rio man giddily dousing the face of a black slave girl with flour. After a parade of upper-class young men managed to secure a proper brass band, a Portuguese shoemaker, considered "an athlete at beating soles," invented a unique bass drum beat that immediately took root—later becoming the *Zé-Pereira,* or percussive fanfare that begins every Carnaval samba. While waltzes and polkas were played at the Parisian-inspired masquerades, a class war was being waged on the street, with police trying to quell the raucous African *candomblé* drums and ordering drunken revelers back home. But the upper classes could not control themselves either; at one memorable São Cristavão ball, even the Emperor Dom Pedro II, a self-avowed party boy, got himself pushed into a fountain.

The First Samba

It was not until samba was born as a musical form that Brazilian Carnaval found its true dancing legs. Historians claim the infectious rhythm slipped into Rio from Bahia around the turn of the century, conceived in the backyard of Tia Ciata, a well-to-do black woman who opened her home to the aspiring musicians of the neighboring hills. Out of those fiery jam sessions in 1916 sprang the first samba, "*Pelo Telefone*" (On the Telephone)—a jovial if saucy tune, with insinuating comments about the chief of police. Inspired by their own creativity, the *favelados* didn't take long to complain that only middle-class whites and blacks had the privilege of parading down the main avenues of Rio. Since they used to rehearse near an old teacher's college, they called their makeshift organization an *escola de samba* (samba school) and dubbed themselves "*Deixa Falar*"— Let Them Talk, a definite uppercrust snub. Their debut was dazzling, and by the next year, five more black communities were following in their footsteps.

Out of this early creative explosion was forged the irrepressible personality of the *sambista*—one who not only plays samba, but eats it, loves it, and dreams it morning to night. As one observer wrote, "A sambista happens to be a human being in whom the soul is more apparent than the flesh, his spirit more recognizable than substance." Uninhibited but generous, and bohemian to the core, the sambista can invent great poetry despite being illiterate and compose great tunes with no knowledge of music. Invariably, even the greatest sambistas never make money, but their friendships and contacts cross cultural bounds. At the funeral of Sinhô, one of Rio's most famous sambistas, hundreds of prostitutes, *malandros,* and underworld characters crowded in next to intellectuals, then headed out to grieve at a neighborhood bar.

The building boom in Rio after World War II profoundly affected Carnaval. As numerous dwellings were razed in Botafogo and Copacabana to make way for middle-class housing, thousands fled to the squalid shantytowns, taking with them their passion for music, dance, and most of all, *desfile* (the parade). By 1935, rules fixed by the city carnaval commission banned any other musical instruments except percussion and the omnipresent mandolin to accompany the parade singer. During the early 1960s, before the coup that would submerge Brazil into its 21-year-long dictatorship, white journalists, artists, and musicians slipped into the blackest *favelas* to soak up "root"—a collaboration that would soon birth samba's cooler child—sweet bossa nova. Though middle-class whites were still a rarity in the late 1960s, by the 1970s they were a welcome minority, and by the late 1980s some schools, like Mangueira, were not only boasting white *alas* (wings), but black chiefs in charge of the most expensive white wings.

Sambódromo's Parade

In 1983, architect Oscar Niemeyer changed the face of Carnaval when he built its new home, called the **Sambódromo** (or Sambadrome)—actually, nothing more than a wide cement pavement hugged on both sides by bleachers and boxes. The overwhelmingly bland features of the structure shocked many a devotee, but as soon as the extravagant color and panache of the parade filled its empty spaces, the stadium's very insipidity showed itself as a virtue. Today, tickets for the Sambódromo's parade (which lasts for two consecutive weekends) are outrageously expensive, and although you can fully watch the festivities on TV, there is nothing like being so close to the dancers that you can swim in their passion and get wet from their sweat.

Better than watching the Sambódromo parade, however, is to dance in it. Tourists are welcome in a variety of possibilities (see p. 75), but if you don't have the time (or courage), do read *Samba*, Alma Guillermoprieto's stunning account of what it takes to pull off a parade—from the inside of the *favela*. Amid drug trafficking, murders, poverty, and despair, Verdi-sized productions are designed, carpentered, sewed, sequined, and rehearsed to reasonable perfection, and most often at the price of great personal sacrifice. Individual costumes have become so pricey lately (sometimes two or three times the monthly minimum wage), that sambistas sometimes go for days without eating just to save up. To *sair* (go out) at Carnaval is not only a matter of pride; for many it's a condition of soul. For those fanatics who can afford it, parading with two or three schools per Carnaval is not uncommon; a friend of mine in New York with unearthly endurance manages five!

Is the real spirit of Carnaval dying? The death knell has been rung ever since the 1800s, when it first began to lose its folkloric elements. What has transformed Carnaval over the years, however, has been the natural creative fervor of the people themselves, who seem to perpetually rise each year to the awesome occasion. Today, the real thief of Carnaval is the economic crisis and its uncontrollable inflation, which has given rise to the desperate need to attract international tourists. Although exhibitionism is at the heart of the Brazilian personality, even hard-core sambistas today complain that the blatant nudity and lascivious role-playing is eating away at the true spirit of Rio's Carnaval—all done, they say, for the sake of the camera. In actuality, the truly "uncivilized" behavior takes place these days in the upper-class balls, where outlandish sexual displays are photographed in every detail for late-night TV. It's no exaggeration to say that the sex channels on American cable have nothing over these televised Roman orgies, among whose guests are numbered famous politicians, celebrities, and girls from "good families." Tourists who venture forth to such parties should at least be forewarned; though some, like the Gay Balls, are outrageously funny, anyone burdened with an extreme sense of prudishness will be happier staying home and watching the events tubeside.

The Parade

At first glance, the Sambódromo's parade can seem as mystifying and chaotic as the trees of the rain forest, but once you know what to look for, you'll become as discerning as the panel of judges. Since the parade is actually a fierce competition between 14 schools, a certain regulated structure is adhered to, around which the creativity of each school is allowed to flourish. Annually required of each school is an overriding theme, which unveils itself like an operatic plot through costume, decor, song, and dance. Since sambistas have a great passion for "roots," historical themes are often favored; the best are those that tap the dreams of the masses, like "The Brazilian Utopia," which Portela boasted in 1985 when I danced with them. Political barbs in Carnaval can get sticky, however. In 1960, Império Serrano was actually petitioned by the Paraguayan embassy to change its theme ("The Paraguayan War") to avoid re-humiliating Brazil's now friendly neighbor. Designing the productions for each school is the *carnavalesco,* most often a white stage designer (and, more recently, art school graduates), who must invent original designs at the same time remaining true to each school's personality.

Portela, for example, is known for its muscular verve, Beija-Flor for its extravagant lushness, and Mangueira for its populace appeal.

School Parades

Each school's parade usually opens with the *abre-alas*, which may consist of a very simple painted sign or an elaborate float recounting the major theme. Directly afterwards is the *Comissão de Frente*—consisting of the directorate of the school usually attired in silk hats, gloves, and spats. After pausing before the judge's box for a quick inspection, they execute a well-drilled maneuver and step aside as the school passes in front of them. Behind them are the children's wings, followed by the Bahianas—usually older woman of enormous girth, or at least of enough personal stature to carry off wearing the traditional hoop skirts that are so heavy they must be suspended from the shoulders by straps. (In olden days, men used to dress as Bahianas, because the costume's skirts provided an ideal hiding place for knives and other weapons.) Today, the heart-felt spirit of the Bahiana wing carries the soul of the school; Mangueira's is the most famous and most traditional. Other schools have taken to dressing their "mothers" in newspaper clippings or, as in one year, Statues of Liberty—an artistic license that caused wild controversy.

In between elaborate floats full of half-naked women dances the most important member of the school—the *mestre-sala*. The majordomo of the parade, the **mestre-sala** is the pivot around which all the choreography revolves, best performed by a tall, slim fellow who is both graceful and agile. Usually dressed like a Dumas musketeer or a Louis XV courtier, he accompanies the *porta-bandeira*, or flag-bearer, often the prettiest girl in the school. As he pirouettes around her, she gracefully twirls about holding the school's flag—not such an easy task since many a girl has gotten tangled up in the folds. Appearing singly or in pairs among the many *alas* are the *destaques*, fabulously dressed women and men of great beauty whose sequined and pearled costumes are usually heavier than they are.

Native Instruments

The guts of the parade, however, is the *bateria*, a percussion ensemble of 300 men (and women of late!) who march forward looking as though they're on their way to slay Goliath. Although the uninitiated observer may hear only a Mack truck wall of sound, the beauty of the percussion section is its intricate interplay of rhythm and color, created by a wily assortment of native instruments that are played with so much force that blood often runs. The *surdo,* or bass drum, sets the two-four beat of the samba, a dull thud achieved by dampening the skin of the drum with one's hand. The gypsy-style *pandeiro* is beat like a tambourine, its metal disks jingling as the performer, usually a great ham, twirls it up over his head, between his legs, and around pretty women. The *tamborim,* a small round shallow drum, is played with two long thin sticks, effecting a velvety rat-ta-ta-tat. In contrast, the *agogô,* a short iron bar with two or three hollow cups, adds a shrill piercing tang, like the beating of an anvil. *Chit*-chit *chit*-chit *chit*-chit is provided by the *chocalho* (or *ganza*), a rattle from the Northeast made of sheet metal and filled with pebbles. Add to the mélange a couple of frying pans, and last, but not least, the *cuíca,* the Carnaval clown—a small steel barrel open at one end and skinned on the other, into which a stick is attached to the center of the membrane. Great *cuíca* players can cajole sighs, screams, laughs, smirks, and sneers from their instrument, and even seem to engage in prolonged conversations. To coordinate all these intricately timed instruments is a steely-eyed conductor of enormous discipline, whose stop-and-start whistles must be considered God's law by his troopers.

Holding this opera together is the school's song, written anew for each year's Carnaval and sung by dancers and audience alike. Usually, the songs have been played on the radio for weeks, but lyrics can be found in the program. Even if you don't speak a word of Portuguese, or don't understand anything about the schools' themes, you will instantly recognize a good samba. The best ones are the infectious, irresistible ones that don't dissolve into monotony during the 80-minute parade of each school, the ones that grab your heart, pull you to your feet, and, along with the screaming crowd, carry you off into ecstasy. Believe me, it won't pass you by.

For those who don't make it to the Sambódromo or the balls, there's always Street Carnaval—in Rio, led by neighborhood *blocos,* an old tradition, who carry out their parades all throughout Ipanema and Copacabana, as well as the colonial sections downtown.

Museu do Carnaval *Avenida dos Desfiles (Praça da Apoteose, entering from Rua Frei Caneca. Tuesday–Sunday 11:00 a.m.–5:00 p.m.) Planned by world-class architect Oscar Niemeyer, who also designed the Sambódromo, this museum was inaugurated in 1984 to display the cultural, historical, and folkloric aspects of Carnaval. Posters, pho-*

tos, costumes, instruments, videos, and written literature tell the story from 1840 to the present. There is also a video room, an exhibition hall, and a consultant room.

Bahia

Salvador's Carnaval couldn't be more different than Rio's—some connoisseurs claim that it's better. In Salvador, the entire festival is a street affair, the linchpin of which is the *trio elétrico,* a blaring flatbed truck that harks back to a hillbilly duo in the 1950s who toured the city during Carnaval in a beat-up Chevy playing pop and folk tunes. Today, the *trio elétricos* feature three musicians, flashing lights, and thousands of people trailing them through the city streets. At some point during Carnaval, the various bands meet in Praça Castro Alves, playing anything from samba to *frevo* to a new rock-influenced samba called *deboche.* During the 1980s, even reggae infiltrated the menu, creating a new hybrid by the 1990s and new superstars like the dynamite performer Daniela Mercury. Some of the best music comes from organized cultural groups like the Grupo Cultural Olodum, on the Pelourinho, and the Ata Ketu, at the Praca da Sé. In the weeks preceding Carnaval, their *blocos* hold fabulous rehearsals near the clubhouse that are as exciting as the real thing.

Also, don't miss the *afoxés,* or spiritual processions of the Filhos de Ghandi, located on Rua Grégorio de Matos, near the Pelourinho. You'll locate them by their white papiêr-maché elephants or by their mascot, who looks uncannily like the original Gandhi. For other outdoor parties, check the northern beaches near the Hotel Rio Vermelho and Ondina. The Bahiatursa office can provide you with schedules, parade routes, and tickets where necessary. Also check the special supplements in the newspapers on Thursday and Saturday.

Pernambuco

The stars of the Northeastern Carnaval, Recife, and its colonial sidekick, Olinda, explode with *frevo*—a feverish, fast-stepping rhythm that sounds like it's stuck on a perpetual upper. Instead of the hip-swinging samba, *frevo*-ites seem to spend most of their time jumping up and down in a vertical fashion, twirling huge parasols that seem to hark back to the ones carried by slaves to shade their masters. The costumes of the *frevo* dancers tend toward knee-britch stockings and floppy shirts, but anything is allowed. Some even indulge in Indian headdresses and lots of body paints.

Although Recife does have street celebrations, you'd be a fool to be so close to Olinda and not drop by its city-wide party, filling the historical cobblestone streets with a panache all its own. Strewn with streamers and gas lanterns, the colonial city takes on the look of a Christmas tree, the sidewalks becoming cement beds for the thousands of drunken revelers who can't make it home. (Many local residents escape to the nearby Jesuit seminary for four days of peace and quiet.) The festivities start the Sunday before the official opening of Carnaval, when the Virgem do Bairro Novo, a traditional *bloco*, parades down the seafront road followed by huge crowds. On Friday night and during the day, huge *bonecos*—papier-maché stuffed puppets representing folk heroes or savage caricatures of local personalities—are also paraded over the cobblestones. *Pinga* flows like water, revelers take baths in the public fountains, and at some point the major *blocos* all meet at the junction of four corners with a rousing hurrah. Accommodations must be made months in advance: all or part of a house may be rented out for the four days ($150–$800), or you can knock on doors and bargain.

THE ESSENTIAL CARNAVAL

Reservations

Hotel reservations in Rio (and in Salvador and Recife/Olinda) should be made as far in advance as possible; for the best rooms, call at least six months prior.

You can buy tickets for the Carnaval parade at the Sambódromo starting in December at the Meridional Bank, or call Alô Riotur; ☎ *242-8000*. After January 16, Rio Tur will sell tickets for tourists in Setor (sector) 9; ☎ *297-7117*. The concierge of your hotel may be able to obtain tickets for you at the last minute, but rest assured he will charge a hefty commission. Better bet is to ask at travel agencies—they receive a 10-percent commission. In 1993, the price for a numbered chair was about $450, grandstands about $145 (one person, one night).

For tickets to the Carnaval balls, inquire directly at the clubs in advance. (See addresses below.)

Carnaval Balls

Roda Viva
Avenida Pasteur, 520; ☎ *295-4045* Mostly attended by tourists.

Yacht Club
Avenida Pasteur, 333; ☎ *295-4482* Mostly high society.

Clube Sirio Libanês
Rua Marquês de Olinda, 38 (Botafogo); ☎ *551-9942* Mostly artists and tourists attend this ball, which goes under various names: Atlantic Ball, Tourists' Ball or Artists' Ball.

Scala
Avenida Afrânio de Melo Franco, 296 (Leblon); ☎ *239-4448* is famous for its flamboyantly outrageous "Gala Gay" ball, which is attended by all sexual persuasions, including tourists.

Hippopotamus Prive Discotheque
Rua Barão da Torre, 354; ☎ *247-0351* High society with *feijoada* on the Saturday of

Carnaval week starting at 8:00 p.m. You must buy a T-shirt in advance to wear on the date.

Clube Monte Líbano
Avenida Borges de Medeiors, 701; ☎ 239–0032 Artists and high-class prostitutes usually frequent the "Night in Bagdad" ball on the Tuesday of Carnaval week.

Help Discotheque
Avenida Atlântica, 3432; ☎ 521–1296 A popular ball on the touristic side, but a good price.

Carnaval Rehearsals

Even though you might not be in Rio during the actual Carnaval events, you can still visit the samba schools during their practice sessions to watch them rehearse. All rehearsals start at 10:00 p.m. on Saturday night unless otherwise indicated. Call first to verify the day. The most popular performance is the Beija Flor samba school on Morro da Urca, every Monday night at 10:30 p.m., where you can see snippets of one of Rio's best *escolas* against a beautiful natural backdrop. For reservations, ☎ 541–3737. In high season, they also perform Thursday and Saturday nights at other locations in the South Zone. Check the newspaper. Also entertaining, if touristy, is the floor show at Sugar Loaf, where you can take good photos. Other school locations are:

Portela *Rua Clara Nunes, 81 (Madureira);* ☎ 390–0471.

Beija-Flor *Rua Pracinha Wallace, Paes Leme, 1562 (Nilópolis);* ☎ 791–2866.

Acadêmicos do Salgueiro *Rua Silves Teles, 104 (Vila Isabel);* ☎ 238–5564 Saturday at 11:00 p.m.

Estação Primeira de Mangueira *Rua Visconde de Niterói 1072 (Mangueira);* ☎ 234–4192.

Street Carnaval

If you'd rather go the street route, you won't have to look far in Copacabana or Ipanema to find *blocos* parading the street and partying on the beach. Day and night, the area around the Garota de Ipanema Bar is crammed with the most colorful transvestites in Rio.

CARNAVAL DATES FOR THE 1990S

February 12, 1994
February 25, 1995
February 17, 1996
February 8, 1997
February 21, 1998
February 13, 1999

THE SOUNDS OF BRAZIL

In Tutola, Authentic Folk Song and Dance is Performed from the Heart

The majority of Brazilians may be poor, but they boast one of the richest musical cultures in the world—a sensuous mélange of African, Indian, and European influences. Nightly in any major city, you'll find jazz artists of international renown, regional musicians specializing in native rhythms, and even world–class dancers executing the sexy moves of *samba* and *lambada*. Some of the best music can be found at impromptu jam sessions on the beach or in tiny bohemian bars where guitar–strumming singers croon out cool *bossa nova*. And no world–music fan should ever miss the big arena concerts given by riveting performers like Milton Nascimento, Gilberto Gil, and Caetano Veloso—proponents of a highly sophisticated strain of pop music called **MPB**, or *música popular brasileira*.

Roots

The rhythmic vitality of Brazilian music harks back to the native Indians, who accompanied their pantheistic rituals with an exotic blend of rattlers, shakers, and panpipes. Starting in the 17th century, black slaves imported from Africa brought along the hot, impassioned drumming of their *candomblé* rituals. Slow, heartbreaking ballads were added by the first Portuguese colonists, who accompanied themselves with *cavaquinhos* (similar to the ukulele), the *bandolim* (mandolin), bagpipes, and the Portuguese guitar.

Sensual body movement has always been second nature in Brazil. From the *lundu* of the Portuguese court to the hip-grinding *lambada* of the last decade, Brazilians have consistently demonstrated their knack for inventing undulating dances. Many were inspired by the erotic dances of African slaves, traveling with only a little refinement to the salons of the ruling class. *Samba* itself is said to have been derived from the slave dance called *umbigada*, where each successive soloist is signaled by a sharp pelvic thrust. Even European-imported dance rhythms like the polka and the mazurka were soon tropicalized into the *maxixe*, a flamboyant tango that became the rage during the 1920s.

Slowly, a passion for gorgeous melody began to surface in Brazil. During the 1930s and 1940s, the songs of **Dorival Caymmi**, one of the country's classic songwriters, romantically evoked the seaside sensuality of Bahia. **Ary Barroso's** "Aquarela do Brasil" (known to most of the world as "Brazil") signaled to North America that something languid and subtle was happening down south. In 1958, however, a brand-new sound called *bossa nova* rocked the Brazilian music scene and eventually the world's.

Bossa Nova

Musically, the times were ripe for revolution. Optimism was high; JK was pushing Brasília; film, theater, and painting were thriving. Bohemian musicians gathered in the cafés of Ipanema and Copacabana to jam and write songs. The singer Johnny Alf and the composer Luis Bonfá were already shaping the loud, brassy strains of *samba* with a soft jazziness, but it was the strange harmonies and cooled-down beat of the song "Chega de Saudade" that truly shocked the public and marked the beginning of MPB. The composer was the yet–unknown **Antônio Carlos Jobim** and the performer was **João Gilberto,** an eccentric musician who managed to simultaneously recreate all the rhythms of a samba band on his solo guitar. His awesome technique would influence generations of musicians to come, but it was Gilberto's voice—a feather–light timbre suggesting a sad teddy bear—that perfectly embodied the tender wistfulness of *bossa nova*. Even today, Gilberto still plays so softly that audiences must sit on the edge of their seats to hear him.

Jobim (who is often called Tom) remains the undisputed master of *bossa nova*—a classically trained musician who infuses his songs with Ravel–inspired harmonies and unexpected blues notes. Over the next 35 years, Jobim's songs, often written with Vinícius de Moraes, one of Brazil's greatest poets, would be recorded by literally thousands of musicians worldwide—the most prominent among them being Frank Sinatra and the American saxophonist Stan Getz. The peak of *bossa nova* expression was the 1960 movie version of *Orfeo Negro*— Jobim and Moraes' musical play that retold the Orpheus myth through the eyes of two poor lovers during Carnaval. (Fans should *run* to rent the Academy Award–winning movie, now available on video.)

Though many singers, including Astrud Gilberto, Flora Purim, and Gal Costa, became famous for singing *bossa nova*, there was one voice that gave it its soul. Born in Porto Alegre, **Elis Regina** was called *furacão*, or hurricane, by her public. Not particularly pretty or glamorous, she was enfused with a naturalness of voice and spirit that seemed to render anything she sang a hit. Those who loved her singing style were swept away by her prodigious emotionality that could swing from intense joy to profound sorrow in seconds. A favored muse of Jobim's, she also recorded renditions of Milton Nascimento's greatest hits that nearly eclipsed his own. In 1982, Elis died from an accidental overdose at the peak of her career—a tragedy deeply felt by the entire country.

Tropicália

By the late '60s, *bossa nova's* sweet strains weren't sufficient to quell the public's growing despair over the military regime. A cult of the absurd emerged from the state of Bahia, calculated to shock the middle class from their complacency. Spearheaded by singer/songwriter **Gilberto Gil** and his best friend, **Caetano Veloso**, the movement called

Tropicália pitted electric guitars against *berimbaus* (a native one–stringed instrument), freely borrowing from international influences in what was dubbed "neo–cultural cannibalism." At a time when all Brazilian singers wore dark suits and ties, Gil and Veloso bounded on stage with long hair and bellbottoms, spouting Dada–esque lyrics that few understood. Their eccentricity got them arrested and eventually exiled from Brazil, but when they returned two years later they reactivated careers that have since become the most enduring in the country.

If any one Brazilian musician represents the successful synthesis of disparate parts, it is Gilberto Gil. Raised the son of a doctor in a country village near Salvador, Gil absorbed a musical environ that included not only the nasal cries of street singers, *trios elétricos*, and the folk accordion of Luiz Gonzaga, but also the Beatles, the Rolling Stones, and Bob Dylan. The passion to make sense of this international collusion has underscored Gil's entire career and ever since his return to Brazil in 1972, his albums have shown an ever–increasing knack for being primal, contemporary, and futuristic all at the same time. A consummate lyricist, Gil writes about a wide range of concerns, from the profoundly spiritual to the hotly political. A song lambasting the Pope was banned from Brazilian TV in 1985, but it didn't diminish Gil's popularity; in the early '90s he was elected to the city council in Salvador and remains a leading force in the Green movement.

Born in Santo Amaro, a small coastal town near Cachoeira in Bahia, **Caetano Veloso** is considered one of Brazil's greatest poet–composers. Although few of his 20–odd albums have gone gold, he has emerged at the age of 52 as a world–class performer, still mesmerizing audiences with his doelike good looks, sweetly-seductive presence, and a searing intelligence partial to irony. Caetano's styles run the gamut from *bossa nova* and rock to avant–garde, but his lyrics are the true standouts: full of Joycean–invented words, internal rhymes, and cryptic allusions. In 1986, his American debut on Elektra/Nonesuch was heralded by many American critics as one of the top ten albums of the year.

The ultimate muse of the Tropicália movement, and Brazil's biggest singing star today, is **Gal Costa**. A fellow Bahian, she met Caetano as a young girl and recorded her first song (his "Domingo") in 1967. While Gil and Veloso were living in exile in London she interpreted their songs with a raw, earthy voice that has since grown into a reedlike instrument of astonishing flexibility. Part hippie, part torcher, part elegant lady, she is painfully shy in person, but her self-consciousness becomes transformed on stage into shining vulnerability. Her repertoire ranges from *samba* and rock to folkloric rhythms like *frevo* and *baião*, but she truly excels in *bossa nova*.

The sister of Caetano Veloso, singer/songwriter **Maria Bethânia**, has carved her own niche in MPB, despite her brother's fame and her own anti–diva personality. In 1978, she became an overnight sensation when she replaced the ailing singer Nara Leão in a highly controversial stage show, but it was her 1979 album *Álibi* that shot her to national prominence—a lush collection of ballads sung in her inimitable husky croon. In recent years, Bethânia (as she is called) has added socially conscious songs to her repertoire, a gesture that has lent her the persona of a mystical Joan Baez.

Minas and Milton

Arguably, the most important Brazilian songwriter in terms of international influence is **Milton Nascimento**, who hails from a constellation of musicians from Minas Gerais, a state known for its introspective people and deep religiosity. Blessed with one of the greatest voices in jazz history, Milton can soar effortlessly from a heartfelt baritone to an angelic falsetto, but he is also equally revered for his profound melodies and rhythmic ingenuity that derives from an exotic cache of influences, including the Portuguese *fado*, the Mineiro folk ballad called *toada*, the Beatles, Gregorian chants, and *nueva canción*. Among Milton's best early albums, the 1971 *Clube da Esquina* featured such other local artists as Lô and Marcio Borges, Beto Guedes, Ronaldo Bastos, Fernando Brant, and Toninho Horta, all of whom would later establish their own impressive careers. Although Milton ascribes to no one religion in particular, his albums are infused with a profound spirituality and almost prophet-like affinity with the human condition. In 1973, when the military dictatorship censored his lyrics, the wordless cry of his falsetto on the album *Milagre dos Peixes* expressed more political protest than words ever could. In his latest album *Txai*, he incorporates chants and percussion from Amazonian tribes to riveting effect.

The most ingenious ensemble from Minas is **Uakti,** a quartet of classically trained musicians who make their own instruments. Other notable Mineiros, whose records you might find only in Minas, is the singer/songwriter **Flávio Venturini**, keyboardist **Túlio Mourão**, and singer **Tadeu Franco**, a heartthrob who often performs in local clubs.

More MPB

MPB has been pushed forward by the creative musicianship of many who continue to transcend genres while carving out their own unique identities. **Chico Buarque,** the son of one of Brazil's greatest intellectuals, has written not only an impressive array of songs but novels, plays, and literary analyses. Another songwriter with an instantaneously recognizable sound is **Ivan Lins**. A former chemical engineer, Lins was brought to the public eye by Elis Regina, who propelled his song "Madalena" into posterity. Although many of Lins' songs have been recorded by such American artists as Patti Austin, Ella Fitzgerald, and Dave Grusin, Lins is often his own best interpreter. His concerts are always joyous explosions of romantic sentiment.

A born rhythmist, **Jorge Ben** developed his own unique guitar style because he couldn't imitate João Gilberto's. "Mas Que Nada," his biggest hit, shot to international fame in 1966 in the hands of Brazilian bandleader Sergio Mendes. Still thriving 25 years later, Ben is known for shows that turn into tribal parties pumped by a transcontinental black groove.

João Bosco is one of Brazil's most daring songwriters, a post–modern troubadour who wildly flips between boleros, flamenco, jazz, and classical styles. With his lyricist, the ex–psychiatrist **Aldir Blanco**, he has written songs that range from the surreal to the socially conscious, in languages as diverse as Tupi, French, Yoruban, and his own invented phonemes.

Though born in the northeastern state of Alagoas, singer/songwriter **Djavan** has long transcended his folkloric roots to create a pan–American sound hailed internationally for its radiant melodies and jazzy, undulating rhythms. Steering clear of political controversy, Djavan focuses more on love songs and highly danceable tunes; one of his best albums, *Luz*, features Stevie Wonder.

Northeast

During the late '70s and '80s, singers and songwriters from the Northeast and Amazônia have catapulted to national attention as regional beats like *forró* and *maracatú* proved themselves disco-friendly. Part court jester, part serious balladeer, **Alceu Valença** is a perennial presence in Olinda's Carnaval and the king of *forrock*—an explosive mix of *forró* amplified by electric guitars and rock drums. His songs, written with partner **Geraldo Azevedo,** are much like *cordels* —the pulp–story narratives that document the misery and miracles of northeastern existence.

Entering her fourth decade as sexy as ever, singing sensation **Elba Ramalhho** continues to magnetize fans worldwide with her irrepressible energy and infectious repertoire that marries northeastern rhythms with Caribbean dance mixes. Other prominent names in the Northeast are **Dominguinhos**, one of Brazil's greatest accordionists, **Zé Ramalho,** a *sertanejo*–styled guitarist, and **Fagner,** a romantic pop balladeer. From Amazônia has sprung the popular singer **Fafá de Belém,** and *lambada* singer, **Beto Barbosa.**

The South

The musical traditions in the south are just now enjoying a surge of popularity, especially among youths looking to revitalize their *gaúcho* roots. Among their role models is the hippie–looking **Renato Borghetti,** a young accordionist who plays folkloric tunes with a modernistic flair. More mainstream, **Kleiton and Kledir,** two brothers from Rio Grande do Sul, achieved national fame with their "country rock" sound during the late '70s and '80s; more recently, Kledir has been pursuing a fine solo career.

Tropical Rock

For the last three decades, Brazilian rock has been brewing underground, slowly working its way up in the '80s to guitar–slashing anger. The father of the movement was singer **Roberto Carlos,** who, with his partner, **Erasmo Carlos,** promoted a good–time rock that counterbalanced the social concerns infiltrating *bossa nova*. Today, Roberto remains Brazil's best–selling artist, having savvily maneuvered his Lothariolike image into that of a slick, middle–aged balladeer. Also an early proponent of Brazilian rock, **Rita Lee** began her career with the Dali–influenced **Os Mutantes** (The Mutants), but later evolved into a light, sassy pop singer trading on native rhythms and sly humor.

Irreverence reaches state–of–the–art with rocker **Ney Matogrosso,** whose outlandish stage attire situates him somewhere between Elton John and Carmen Miranda. Despite his feminine voice (higher than most females) and his flagrant strutting, Matogrosso continues to draw crowds that defy sexual definitions or age categories. His contributions to the rock genre have included a spirited fusion with *virá*, a syncopated Portuguese folk style played with great verve on the accordion.

As the democracy of the '80s took hold, a new generation of rockers, freed from censorship, conquered the air waves. The wildly theatrical **Blitz** opened the door for other hard rockers like **Barão Vermelho** and **Kid Abelha,** who took the 1985 Rock in Rio concert by storm. The most ingenious rock group of the '80s and '90s is **Os Paralamos do Successo,** a bass, drum, and guitar trio (filled out with brass) who have incorporated *lambada, afoxé,* and *coco* in a wild Caribbean party mix. Nearly as ebullient is the work of **Lulu Santos,** who describes his own style as "Brazilianized, tropicalized, Latinized rock."

It's not surprising that Brazilian punk emerged from the sons of the military in Brasília, a city where the monotony of the architecture alone is enough to make a kid crazy. One of the most popular has been **Legião Urbana,** who in 1983 stumbled onstage in disheveled jeans and torn T-shirts (unheard of in Brazil) and reveled in a frenetic, *Cure*-influenced protest rock. The city of São Paulo has also spawned hundreds of rock groups; among the biggest sellers has been **RPM** and **Titãs,** the latter a group of young men who sing everything from *brega* (old-fashioned) ballads to two-chord punk, reggae, and funk.

The rock star who most deeply affected Brazilian society in the last two decades was **Cazuza,** an electrifying performer whose venom-filled lyrics attacked social hypocrisy and political deception. An open bisexual, Cazuza discovered he had AIDS in 1987 but courageously continued to perform in public, sharing the reality of the epidemic with his fans. By the time he died in 1990, his last two albums had reached multiplatinum success.

Avant-garde

Full-dimensional musicianship reaches its pinnacle in two Brazilian composers revered worldwide by jazz fans for their inventiveness, prodigious output, and sheer genius.

An albino who looks uncannily like Santa Claus, **Hermeto Pascoal** can coax a musical sound out of any object that dares cross his path—from a blade of grass to teapots, sewing machines, kitchen utensils, and even bleating piglets. Despite his stubby fingers, Hermeto is a piano virtuoso, master accordionist, percussionist, and wind player, capable of improvising profoundly-moving melodies, as well as the most intricate of rhythms. Accompanied by his tightly rehearsed band, his shows are always exhilarating and full of invention. Many musicians (foreign and Brazilian) make pilgrimages to his commune outside Rio just to audit his all–day rehearsals. As iconoclastic as Hermeto is the composer **Egberto Gismonti,** a conservatory–trained guitarist and pianist whose works are fascinating abstractions of Brazilian folklore, world–beat music, and free–form jazz. Ever since 1978, he has been influenced by an ongoing relationship with Amazonian Indians, whose percussion sounds are often heard in his work.

Percussionists

It's not surprising that some of the best percussionists in the world have sprung from Brazil. Among them is **Airto Moreira,** who along with his Brazilian–born wife, singer **Flora Purim,** has profoundly influenced American jazz, bebop, funk, and pop. Approaching genius is the work of **Naná Vasconcelos,** a virtuoso on the *cuíca* and *berimbau,* whose provocative stage presence often resembles that of a jungle shaman. The most famous of *samba* percussionists is **Marçal**, the former director of the Portela Samba School. **Olodum** is the Bahia–based pop group, propelled by *afoxé* percussion and vocals, that was heard on Paul Simon's *Rhythm of the Saints* album.

Other Instrumentalists

The list of Brazilian jazz artists who thrill fans around the world is seemingly endless.

Among guitar masters is **Baden Powell,** an early *bossa nova* advocate who has made extensive research into Afro-Brazilian traditions. An early colleague of Jobim's but now based in the States, **Oscar Castro–Neves** is one of the most enduring *bossa nova* composers continuing to spin out beautifully evocative albums. **Ricardo Silveira,** a former lead guitarist for Milton Nascimento, has tackled the international jazz scene with his fusion–driven albums. In a more classical vein is the **Duo Assad**, two guitar–playing brothers whose superb repertoire ranges from baroque airs to free–form jazz. On the horizon is the brilliant guitarist **André Geriassati**, whose superlative technique and profound lyricism pushes the edges of jazz, fusion, and the avant–garde.

The most talented jazz pianist to come out of Brazil today is **Eliane Elias** (now based in New York), acclaimed for her impressive piano technique, deep lyrical affinity, and rhythmic inventiveness. Running in close competition is the effervescent **Tânia Maria**, who has maintained a successful transcontinental career as a jazz singer, pianist, and composer for several decades. Young keyboardist **Rique Pantoja** also has recorded several fusion albums in the States, the latest with trumpeter Chet Baker.

Other fine instrumentalists include: trumpeters **Claudio Roditi** and **Márcio Montarroyos**, both of whom have carved solid reputations in the jazz field; fusion sax player **Leo Gandelman** and the avant–garde saxophonist **Ivo Perelman**. Among the best ensembles is the long–running trio **Azymuth**, whose numerous albums have been well received in the States. Formed in 1988, **Banda Savana** is a 19-piece jazz band whose lush, sophisticated arrangements of Jobim and others are dedicated to preserving the roots of Brazilian music.

Among singers not already mentioned, the best are **Simone**, an ex–basketball player known worldwide for her husky near–baritone voice; **Marisa Monte**, an instant success in her twenties and the most likely heir apparent to Gal Costa; **Zizi Possi**, an impeccable stylist whose voice approaches Barbra Streisand's in terms of purity and control; and newcomer **Adriana Calcanhoto**, whose punklike irreverence is matched only by her masterful jazz chops and superb writing skills. Among popular *samba* singers, the best are **Beth Carvalho**, **Alcione**, **Martinho da Vila, and Paulinho da Viola**. *For a selected discography, see the back of the book.*

Insider Tip:

*The newest flash of light on the Brazilian scene is **Daniela Mercury**, a samba-reggae singer/dancer who began by attracting thousands in her home state of Bahia and is now conquering fans worldwide. A forceful voice, admirable looks, and a magnetic presence inspired a New York Times critic in 1993 to aptly describe her as "sex on two feet." Don't ever miss her shows!*

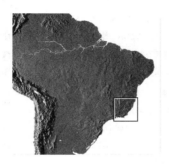

RIO DE JANEIRO

Sugar Loaf Mountain

Few people escape that catch in the breath when they first glimpse Rio from the window of a plane. That fabulous white shoreline curving crescentlike around the azure-blue ocean, the mysterious jungle-like mountains towering above the city's sinuous streets, the hundreds of tiny tropical islands that dot the natural southern bay—all combine to make Rio a city of startling beauty, if not perpetual promise. For the 10 million strong who live here, Rio is like a tempestuous lover one can never imagine leaving. Other cities may have more money, others more culture, but none have the beach, the sun, and the *joie de vivre* of Rio de Janeiro.

An intricate weaving of man and nature, Rio is unique among the cities of the world in that most of its important landmarks are natural rather than man–made: Corcovado Mountain, with its imposing **statue of Christ the Redeemer**; **Sugar Loaf Mountain**, standing guard at **Guanabara Bay**, and **Copacabana Beach**, that irrepressible stretch of sand as alive in legend as it is in fact. Against this sensual backdrop, and behind the facade of first–world glamour, however, lies a more bitter reality that engulfs at least 40 percent of the city's population—pit-level poverty. Crowding into slum dwellings, called *favelas,* that hang precariously from the mountainsides, these rural poor, many who fled to Rio from the droughts in the Northeast, only now have begun to receive a voice in a culture that has traditionally separated them from the upper-class neighborhoods lining the shore. Rio may have fine restaurants, ultra-chic shopping, and exotic nightlife, but for many, the very heart of the city lies in these more downtrodden neighborhoods, for it's from here that **Carnaval**, *Rio's greatest theatrical production, is constantly being reborn and reinvented—a free-for-all celebration fueled as much by creative passion as it is by living life on the edge.*

But pleasure in Rio doesn't end with Carnaval—in fact, the city's sensuous delights last year-round. And they can be exceedingly simple: an early-morning jog down a fabulous beach, an afternoon hike through a tropical rain forest, an exquisite sunset-splashed vista overlooking the city, or just the cool taste of a delicious *água de coco,* coconut water, straight from the shell. For the shopper, there are bustling open-air markets, boutiques with tight sexy clothes, and some of the best jewelry stores in the world. For the gourmet, there are some of the finest chefs in South America. For the adventuresome, there's scuba and skydiving and treks up the mountains. And for the soulful, there is music and art, dance and magic, and black voodoo cults. To be in Rio is to be in tune with the ever-changing play of the sunlight, with the eternal movement of the rushing waves, with the incessant beating of *candomblé* drums, and with the ubiquitous rhythm of samba tapped out on the side of a matchbox.

Carioca is the Indian word given to the first settlements of Rio, but the word has also come to refer to the stereotypical personality of Rio's inhabitants—sensual, indolent, uninhibited, and irrepressibly hedonistic. A *carioca* is an improviser, a jester, a creature whom somehow the sea has made asystematic. For a *carioca,* nothing is certain and anything is possible—especially if one has mastered the art of *jeitinhos,* clever little maneuvers that are always helped by a handful of cruzeiros. In contrast to the hardworking *Paulistanos* (from the city of São Paulo), *cariocas* know how to party and they have, it's been claimed repeatedly, no inhibitions. But there's a sadness that underlies their esprit. "The same satirist [who can joke about Rio] can sit down and cry in the street," says the writer José Augusto Ribeiro, who's talking not only about the nature of the carioca's personality but about carioca street life itself. Day and night Rio's sidewalks and plazas are crowded with shoppers and vendors, lovers and loners, a cacophony of bargaining and negotiating and flirting filling the air. On a perfect Friday afternoon, with a hot sun and a clear sky, you won't find many people left in the office.

Dream Assignment

I'll never forget the first time I met the *carioca* spirit face to face. Several years ago, I was sent by a magazine on a dream assignment—to join a samba school in Rio and dance in Carnaval. Since I would be staying on for several months, I rented a small room in Copacabana from Dona Vitória, an elderly widow who rose at dawn every day to bake cookies for high-society parties. One night, when we were discussing whether she should leave the door unlocked for me, I muttered something about having found a new boyfriend, and was perhaps—well—not coming home. For a moment she looked confused, then suddenly she threw out her arms and hugged me. "Ah, *querida*, go! Have fun, eat, dance, laugh, make love! Life is so short!" In that brief moment, the joy of her *carioca* spirit blazed through me, and as I shut the door behind me, I felt somehow I'd been blessed.

These days there is still great joy in Rio, but there's also much that reminds me of the Wild West—hot, gritty, chaotic, not a little dangerous, yet always exciting—a fount of nonstop stimulation. Indeed, after a visit to Rio in 1993, it seemed to me that New York City was moving in slow motion. Of course, there's no denying it—against the great inequality of wealth, tourists in Rio can become a magnet for petty crime, but you don't have to slink around being paranoid. (The saddest stories I've heard are from tourists who didn't dare leave the vicinity of their hotel from fear of being mugged—this is ridiculous.) While you don't have to pack a shotgun, you do have to arm yourself with a '90s attitude toward health and safety. The kind of New York street savvy I've developed over 15 years of living in Brooklyn is exactly the kind of awareness you need to brave Rio—no more and no less. Through this chapter you'll find insider tips and safety guidelines that you should follow without thinking twice — they will save your life, your wallet, and your good memories of Rio. Most important is your attitude. Remember that no matter what your standard of living is, it will be considered princely by most citizens of Rio.

Exotic Adventures

Yet no tourist should think of Rio as merely one city. These days, the trend among travelers is to think of Rio as the center of a larger environ that holds a myriad of eco-travel possibilities. Simply, you should never get stuck for your whole trip in Copacabana, no matter how much you may love it. Within hours of Rio proper there are so many fascinating day trips and overnight excursions that you can have the most exotic adventures without ever flying to another city. Years ago, travelers would spend a week or 10 days in Rio glued to one beach; today, using the information in *Greener Rio*, you can use the same time exploring the beach resorts of the Costa do Sol, the deserted islands of Angra dos Reis, the historical city of Parati, or the magnificent forests of Serra de Bocaina with a minimum of effort and a maximum of pleasure. The new Rio is simply a multifaceted treasure that's still being developed and awaiting explorers. For anyone looking for the ultimate in fantasy as well as adventure, Rio remains, as it has for centuries, the superlative paradise.

RIO'S PAST GLORIES

As with the discovery of Brazil just two years earlier, the Portuguese stumbled on the future city of Rio de Janeiro by nautical mistake. On the first of January, 1502, a fleet sent by the King of Portugal to survey the newly found territories sailed merrily into Guanabara Bay, thinking it was a river. Even after the confusion was cleared up, the name stuck—hence, Rio de Janeiro, or River of Janeiro. In 1555, desperate for their own stake in the New World, the French, under the command of the Vice-Admiral Durand de Villegaignon, reconnoitered an area around the bay and dubbed it France Antartique. The Portuguese governor Mem de Sá, valiantly attacking the invaders on several occasions, even established a fort on the Morro do Castelo (where the Santos Dumont Airport stands today), but it was not until after a prolonged siege in 1567 that he was able to expel them. Once relieved from French hands, the city grew rapidly, supported by the excellent harbor and the fertile soil, which proved perfect for sugarcane.

In the 15th and 16th centuries, to be Portuguese was to be Roman Catholic, and one of the earliest records of Rio contains an account of a Portuguese bishop who warded off shipwreck in 1647 by praying to Our Lady of Copacabana and, in gratitude, rebuilt the chapel. The bishopric of Rio was established in 1676, but it wasn't until 1763 that Rio was made the capital of the colony, not only because it was closer to the military threat but also because it could serve as a lookout for the flow of wealth from the mines of Minas Gerais. As gold was discovered in the hinterlands, Rio quickly became home to a small affluent class. Despite the filth, the stench, and the overwhelming heat, a mid-18th-century visitor could still describe a certain elegance prevailing in the streets—ladies appeared impeccably arrayed in public wearing black veils over one eye and men were carried about in chairs or hammocks, trailed by at least one or two barefoot servants dressed up in finery. Meanwhile the port, an important leg in the South American-European-African trade and a magnet for contraband, throbbed with activity. Most of what remains from that time can be found close to the harbor, notably the beautiful São Bento Monastery, the Convento de Santo Antônio, and the Praça XV, full of colonial administrative palaces.

Dom João's Reign

With the arrival in Rio of the Portuguese court of Dom João VI, the city suddenly gained a caché of glamour. The city Dom João and his 1,500 nobles discovered on arrival was a sleeping beauty; of its 60,000 inhabitants, 24,000 were Portuguese, 12,000 were slaves, and the rest a contingent of English and French looking for something to do. Immediately the ruler threw open the port to free trade, but by 1808 the harbor was so full of foreign ships that nary a Portuguese one could be seen. Still, the presence of the royal family helped focus Rio as the center of power. In the first decades of Dom João's reign, universities, medical schools, and naval academies were established, while the newly made printing press churned out the first issues of *Gazeta do Rio de Janeiro*. Curious visitors from the remote provinces even made the long trek to the tropical city, invariably surprised to find such a European mode of life.

Rapid urbanization began to alter Rio. By the end of the 1850s, Rio had become the largest city in South America, with a population exceeding a quarter of a million. Large numbers of aristocratic planters were now indulging in the pleasures of the city, dividing their time between the noisy, friendly streets and the more sedate salons. Women went mad over French fashions, an obsession that has remained to this day. The crown even honored that obsession by inviting a French cultural mission to Rio and years later founding the French-staffed Academy of Fine Arts. Most notable in this group of talented French instructors was the artist Jean Baptiste Debret, whose brush depicted memorable scenes of that epoch.

By the last half of the 19th century, Rio had become a bustling metropolis. The English traveler William Hadfield, returning after a 16-year absence, marveled at how the population had burgeoned to 600,000. All the principal streets had been paved and an efficient drainage system installed. The new streets were wide and lined with buildings whose beautiful architectural style Hadfield commended. New public markets and shops provided a variety of wares, and coaches, carriages, and omnibuses pulled by mule teams crowded the main streets illuminated by gaslight. Even then, the infamous *carioca* personality was already beginning to form. In a French memoir of the 19th century, the author observed that young ladies from the best families of Rio were flirting outrageously with lads right inside the Imperial Chapel—exactly as they would 100 years later in the cafés along the city's most beautiful beaches.

Throughout the last half of the 19th century, hundreds of mule trains headed for Rio, discarding their cargo of precious coffee at the train station to await shipment to foreign ports. By 1890, the capital had more than a million inhabitants and boasted many characteristics of a first-class American city, with one exception—no good hotel. Students and other visitors were forced to find lodging in monasteries that were no longer functioning. Still, the American traveler Maturin M. Ballou reveled in the hospitality of the city, with its beautiful fruit trees and gardens enlivened by monkeys and caged parrots, as well as its wonderful French meals. Ice-cream, a miracle food in a tropical country, was first spotted at the Hotel do Norte during the early days of Pedro II, and the novelty spread throughout the century. Francioni's, the first ice cream parlor to boast tropical flavors, became a popular meeting place, with its enormous shade trees and exotic fruit drinks.

Of course, not a few travelers complained about the heat and the beginning of the slums that would later climb up the mountainsides as eternal proof of the inequality of wealth. But by the end of the century, colonial mercantilism had given way to the modern pulse. Trams and trains were installed, and the first tunnel through the mountains of Alaôr Prata was built in 1892. Additional access was provided with the Leme Tunnel in 1904, all providing impetus for the transformation of Copacabana into single family houses.

In the early 20th century, Copacabana and Ipanema were nothing more than sleepy fishing villages. But accelerated growth during World War II began to see the first high-rises dot the strand. During the '30s, the international jet set swarmed down on Rio, stimulated by a handful of Hollywood movies, like Fred Astaire's *Flying Down to Rio,* with its chorus line of beautiful girls doing the samba on the wings of a jet. Composer Antônio Carlos Jobim still harbors nostalgia for that Ipanema of the pre-bossa nova wave, "when the streets were empty and the fish were so big we were afraid to go in the water!" Yet it was Jobim himself, with poet Vinícius de Moraes, who put Rio on the map during the '60s with "The Girl from Ipanema" and other beautiful songs like "Corcovado" that later became international jazz standards.

Even as Rio surrendered its status as the country's capital to Brasília in 1960, a new building boom began to transform the shoreline. Luxury hotels like the Caesar Park, the Rio Palace, the Meridien, and the Sheraton Rio were added to a lineup that had traditionally centered around the elite Copacabana Palace Hotel. At the same time, the *favelas,* or slums, were burgeoning with the influx of immigrants from the arid Northeast, forging a subculture of despair and poverty beneath the glamorous sheen of *carioca* life. With the commercialization of Carnaval in the late '60s and the building of the Sambódromo in 1975, what had once been a folkloric festival of the masses was now being transmitted worldwide through satellite TV, popularizing the culture and drawing new fans from the States, Europe, and even Japan.

In the '90s, the advent of AIDS, as well as the severe economic crisis, somewhat dampened the sense of outrageous licentiousness that had characterized the Carnavals of years past, but what has started growing in its place has been a new sense of responsibility, foresightedness, and cooperation, particularly in light of the United Nations Conference on the Environment that was held in Rio in 1992. For the first time in years, roads have been improved, taxi drivers reeducated, and the general public enlisted to renew the sense of hospitality that has made Rio such a *cidade maravilhosa* for hundreds of years.

RIO: A BIRD'S EYE VIEW

The city of Rio de Janeiro is two longitude lines east of New York City, putting it two hours later on the Greenwich Mean Time scale. Smack on the Tropic of Capricorn, it shares the same longitude (and the same hot, humid climate) as much of the Kalahari Desert in Botswana, Africa. Rio is the capital of the state of Rio de Janeiro (one of the smallest states in Brazil), which is flanked to the south by the state of São Paulo, in the west by Minas Gerais, and in the north by Espirito Santo. With an area of 728 square miles, the city of Rio is only second in size to São Paulo, and is the third largest port in the country.

The modern city of Rio is divided into two separate zones: **Zona Sul** (south) and **Zona Norte** (north). Downtown, the commercial center of the city, lies in between and is the site of a number of historical blocks (see "*Rio by Foot*"). In general, most tourists avoid the more industrial North Zone and spend their time on the beaches, all of which are located in the south. But you will certainly make a pilgrimage to the North Zone if you visit Rio's great temple to soccer, the world-class Maracanã Stadium.

Neighborhoods in Rio are called *bairros*. In the South Zone, the name of the bairro is synonymous with the name of its beach. The most famous, of course, are **Copacabana** (with its extension called Leme) and **Ipanema** (with its extension called **Leblon**). A few miles west along the southern shore lie **São Conrado** and **Vidigal**, the home of Rio's most luxurious resort hotels. Even farther to the west is **Barra da Tijuca**, a 9-mile beach that's considered to be the Mercedes Benz of beaches and the most promising development area in the city. Following the southern shoreline of the Atlantic Ocean, you will eventually reach the most remote beaches of **Recreio dos Bandeirantes**, **Grumari**, and **Guaratiba**. In 10 years' time, these outlying primitive beaches will probably be as developed as Ipanema—so go now.

Less touristic neighborhoods with their own beaches also include **Botafogo** and **Flamengo**, situated to the northeast of Copacabana. Both are fashionable middle-class neighborhoods that enjoyed their heyday a few decades ago, although Botafogo still boasts some of the best restaurants in the city. **Urca**, situated at the base of Sugar Loaf Mountain, is a quiet, elite neighborhood that offers a spectacular view of the city from its unassuming shoreline.

RIO'S SCENERY

CORCOVADO

Perhaps the greatest symbol of the soul of Rio de Janeiro is the enormous **statue of Christ the Redeemer** that towers over the city on the 2,400–foot–high mountain called **Corcovado**. Clearly seen from numerous points throughout the city, the 120-foot-high figure of Christ, with his arms outstretched to an expanse of 75 feet, seems to be welcoming, if not embracing the multitudes that throng to the city seeking work, pleasure, and a pocketful of dreams. At night, illuminated in lush, golden light, the statue takes on a preternatural glow, appearing almost to rise mystically from the dark sky. No matter what your religion, it takes only a few days in Rio to orient yourself to the statue's omnipotent presence as you travel throughout the city.

The massive mountain of Corcovado was a focal point for *cariocas* long before the soapstone-and-concrete statue was completed in 1931 to commemorate (albeit 10 years late) the centennial of Brazilian independence. Dom Pedro I, in particular, loved to trek up and down the trail to escape his more princely duties—but no doubt he was also greatly influenced by the stunning panoramic view of his kingdom. In 1885, in an effort to entice less athletic visitors, Dom Pedro's son (later Pedro II), commanded the construction of a passenger train that would rise to the peak through lushly forested landscapes. Thankfully, that forest is still intact, and today one of the best ways to reach the monument is to follow this same path on a much modernized tram.

Visit Corcovado early in your stay; the view will convince you that Rio is still one of the most beautiful cities in the world. Locating your hotel may be difficult from the south side of the platform, but you can follow the voluptuous curves of Copacabana and Ipanema Beach all the way to Leblon, as well as to the crystal blue waters of the Lagoa Rodrigo de Freitas. Closer in, you'll be able to glimpse the leafy backstreets of residential neighborhoods like Botafogo, Cosme Velho, and Laranjeiras, and there are excellent views of Sugar Loaf, Guanabara Bay, and Flamengo Park. From the northern platform, you can locate the most industrial parts of the North Zone, but don't miss the glimpses of the encroaching vegetation that represents some of the last untouched Atlantic rain forest on the east coast (and the home of some very poor *cariocas*). Don't forget to look up into the eyes of the Christ—to catch the entire figure on film, you'll have to somehow find a way to lie down and shoot upwards.

The best time to visit Corcovado is on a clear day around three or four in the afternoon to catch the drama of dusk as it sets over the city. However, don't ignore cloudy days—one of the most exciting moments is when the sun finally breaks behind the statue, magically illuminating it. The tram ride lasts about 20 minutes, after which you must climb about 220 semichallenging steps to the base of the statue. (Although there are various levels for rest, refreshment, and observation, anyone with a heart condition should think twice about this climb.) The wind is strong as well, and on overcast days, in particular, hats and sunglasses may take flight. Unfortunately, during high season, the numerous crowds can turn your visit into a push-and-shove affair, particularly at peak hours. And don't be surprised if you're accosted on the way down by a salesman with a ceramic plate embossed with your face—your photo was secretly snapped on your way up—but don't feel obligated to buy. Postcards, film, and souvenirs are often much more expensive here than down below in the city.

VITAL STATS
- The Christ weighs over 1,000 tons.
- Its hands and face were sculpted by French artist Paul Landowski, with the help of Brazilian engineers.
- The lighting was designed by Marconi.

Getting There

The easiest way is to sign up for an organized tour (see the list of travel agencies in *"Hands-on Rio"*) that either takes you to the Cosme Velho train station or to the base of the statue. You can also take city bus #583, which leaves from Copacabana and goes to the train station. Private car or cab can also take you to the base of the statue (or train) and wait for you while you tour the site. The train, winding around a tropical paradise, leaves every 20-30 minutes from 8:30 a.m.-6:30 p.m. and costs about $2.50 round trip. Agency tours usually cost $20-25 and include both Corcovado and Sugar Loaf in a half–day itinerary.

PÃO DE AÇÚCAR

If Corcovado is the soul, Pão de Açúcar must be the rock-solid heart of Rio. This huge granite and quartz mountain sits on the edge of the shoreline of the Urca peninsula, staunch and immovable, like a sentinel protecting its charges from a threatening ocean. Thousands of years ago, the 1,500-ft.-high mountain must have made an excellent lookout for the Tupi Indians who populated the area and were rumored to have cannibalized not a few colonists. Though no one really knows the origin of the mountain's name, it does sound remarkably like the Indian phrase *pau-hn-açugua,* meaning a high and pointy hill. Others scholars believe the name originated from the Portuguese, who thought the shape of the hill resembled a loaf of sugar cane, or *pão de açúcar.*

That Pão de Açúcar is a classic tourist attraction should not daunt the more esoteric traveler. From its peak of 1300 feet can be seen a view as stunning as Corcovado's—and in fact includes the best view of Corcovado itself. To the west can be seen the entire scope of Copacabana and Ipanema beaches, to the north the district of Botafogo with the Corcovado behind, to the east the neighborhoods of Laranjeiras, Flamengo, Santa Teresa, and Guanabara Bay, and to the south the Atlantic Ocean. In 1912, a rickety cable of wooden carriages probably frightened more visitors than it thrilled as it rumbled up the mountainside, but today you can ride to the top in a modernized cable car that holds up to 75 passengers.

The most romantic time to visit Sugar Loaf is at sunset, when the mountain is bathed in ever-deepening hues of pink. Even the twinkling lights of the slums fiercely clinging to the hillsides seem picturesque in the glow of twilight. The cable-car trip, in two stages, first stops at the Morro da Urca, where there is a large restaurant and entertainment complex. The second stop takes you to the peak, which can become quite windy on overcast days. At night the temperature turns decidedly nippy, so take a sweater and take care that your sunglasses don't go sailing off toward Copacabana.

With some inventiveness, you could actually spend the entire day here. There is a great tropical bird collection with screaming toucans and macaws, as well as a small playground (but, seriously, was that an alligator I saw slithering about, or just a big lizard?). Every Monday evening at 10 p.m., the Beija–Flor Samba School presents a well-received show featuring authentic Carnaval costumes and near-naked sambistas. Rock concerts are often held in the amphitheater, and during the afternoon you may overhear some young bloods or even famous artists practicing for their shows.

The latest eco-trend at Sugar Loaf is to forego the sissy cable car and actually climb the damn thing. (The first recorded scaling was made by an Englishwoman in 1817.) Though I personally cannot attest to the glories of this trek, it's rumored to take about two days and you don't need a special permit. You do, however, need a special guide, which you can obtain by calling Rio Tur (☎ 242-8000).

Getting There

Many travel agencies offer half-day and full-day tours that include Sugar Loaf. It's very easy to go by yourself, however. Every taxi driver knows where it's located (just make sure he/she takes the direct route). From Copacabana you can take the #511 bus. The entrance fee is about $3. Cars run from 8 a.m.-10 p.m. at 30-minute intervals, or continuously if the demand is heavy. A tourist information booth manned by Rio Tur can answer any questions you may have about Rio in general. For more information call ☎ *541-3737*.

Insider Tip:

Film, batteries, and souvenirs bought at Sugar Loaf will usually cost about two to three times the normal rate, so stock up before you go.

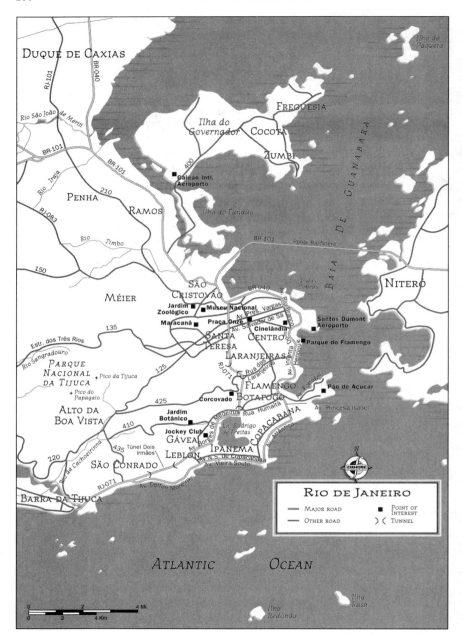

RIO BY FOOT

This is an energetic walking tour of town, which focuses on what's left of historical Rio. On this route, however, are also shopping diversions and enjoyable pit stops, so you can make the excursion a full-day outing. Of course, many travelers will not want to give up their day at the beach to see churches and old palaces, but for architecture buffs and art connoisseurs, this walk through downtown can give an exciting glimpse of what it was like to live in Rio from the 17th century on.

Insider Tip:

Best time to take this historical walking tour is on Thursdays and Fridays to catch the outdoor markets. Weekends will give you more breathing space, but stay alert for anyone eyeing your handbag or backpack.

The best place to enter into the heart of historical Rio is where Dom João VI did—at

Praça XV. It was here at the waterfront in 1808 that the King of Portugal, fleeing Napoleon's conquering armies, first arrived in Southern Brazil, and where 81 years later, his grandson, Pedro II, would be forced by the newly declared republic to return to Portugal in exile. A few steps from the docks, on the square originally known as **Largo do Paço** looms the

Palácio Imperial, a formidable white palace with green shutters and grilled balconies that was originally built in 1743 to house the local governor of what are now the states of Rio de Janeiro and Minas Gerais. Later, it was where Dom João and his family both lived and worked. It was also here, on the palace steps, in 1888, that Princesa Isabel proclaimed all of Brazil's slaves free—an act that was accompanied, at least for the moment, by cheering crowds and dazzling fireworks. In recent years, the magnificent architecture of the palace has been restored to reflect its former glory in the 1850s and is primarily used for concerts and exhibitions.

Walking down Rua Premiero de Março, you'll come to the

Cândido Mendes Escola Técnica de Comércio, now a law school but formerly a monastery where the colorful Queen Maria I of Portugal (the mother of João VI) often resided while in Brazil. Known as Dona Maria, she was officially declared a madwoman by the powers that be (epilepsy—the true cause of her raving fits—was not medically recognized until 200 years later), and she spent the rest of her years here, until her death in 1816, under house arrest.

Walking towards the overpass, turn left at the sign

"Antigo Cais do Periodo Canal." Soon you'll come upon an 18th-century fountain, where servants had to arrive by canoe to fill their jugs with water (the ocean at that time flowed up this far!); notice that the stonemaker showed himself to be a nationalist by incorporating gray Brazilian granite with Portuguese white marble. Walking along the side of the imperial palace you'll meet the statue of General Osário—hero of the Paraguayan War in 1894; his mummified body is actually buried underneath.

On the northern side of the square is the

Arco de Telles, a colonial arch dating back to the 18th century built by a rich traditional family named Telles and the same architect who built the imperial palace. Behind the arch runs one of the most charming streets in Rio—

Travessa do Comércio, a narrow cobblestone alleyway with authentic, centuries-old architecture. In the 18th century, this street, definitely the boulevard of power, linked the Palace to Rua Ouvidor, where the common folk lived. The first building to the right of the arch is the

Bolsa de Valores, home of Rio's stock exchange. During the 19th century, the grilled verandas, tall roofs, and neo-classic columns of the upper-class homes above street level contrasted starkly with the Mack-the-Knife set of beggars, prostitutes, and thieves who populated the seedy taverns below. Dom Pedro I, a libidinous fellow, loved to frequent the *travessa's* bars in disguise, and the stories are numerous; it's been said that one night, as a group of hooligans unwittingly harassed him, a young man who suddenly recognized the ruler jumped up and yelled, "At your service, Your Majesty!" and at that the drunken Pedro dubbed him his personal secretary on the spot.

On Thursdays and Fridays, the square bursts with old–world energy as vendors cram into the cobblestone plaza hawking every item imaginable—from clothes to handicrafts to typical foods and antique coins.

If you choose to walk down

Travessa do Comércio, you find the house where Carmen Miranda, the Brazilian bombshell, lived with her family during the '20s and '30s (#13, second floor). Her mother owned a cheap restaurant down below on street level. As you follow the street, note that it becomes so narrow that an antique lamp connects to both sides of the street.

Turning right on

Rua do Ouvidor, you'll eventually come across some good restaurants (lunchtime only) on the cross street Rua Mercado (one of the most noted, Cabeça Grande, is over 70 years old). Turning left on Rua Rosário to Rua dos Mercadores (a street so narrow it makes a pretty frame for the church at its end), you'll discover the brand-new art gallery

Galeria Paulo Fernandes *Rua do Rosário, 38, 2nd floor (corner at Rua dos Mercadores);* ☎ *253-8582. Tues.-Fri. 10 a.m.-8 p.m., weekends 2 p.m.-6 p.m.* The exhibition is sure to be among the most avant-garde in Brazil; even the skylight is impressive, left-over from colonial times, and the balcony gives a connoisseur's view of the street below. Beside the building housing the gallery, you may find a superb outdoor brass sculpture by artist Nelson Felix, nicknamed "La Donna é Mobile," because of its identifiably female shape which blows in the wind.

At this point you may return the way you came, back to the Imperial Palace, and cross Av. Primeiro de Março to the Nossa Senhora do Carmo da Antiga Sé (see below), or you may continue to walk down the street beside the gallery to Rua Visconde Itaboraí to what was formerly Banco do Brasil, and which is now an impressive cultural center called

Espaço Cultural dos Correios (Cultural Corridor). One hundred and ten years old, the bank was founded by a Portuguese family in 1808 and now houses the pride of Rio—an impressive array of cultural events throughout its 6 floors, including art exhibits, videos, historical archives, and free musical performances. Do go up the stylish green Greek Revivalist elevator to the charming teahouse on the second floor, where you may take lunches and afternoon tea. At several locations throughout the center, there is also a computerized information center with what-to-do-listings in the city in English. (The center is opened *10 a.m.-10 p.m. Tues.-Sun.*)

On the right of the bank is the white-and-orange Customs House called

Casa Franca–Brasil, the most important Classic Revival building in Brazil. Do walk into the interior, an enormous hall that suggests the facade of a Greek temple (though the columns are wood); interesting temporary exhibitions are often held here. Do go outside to look at the *palmito decorativo*, a most unusual tree whose branches seem to stream down like a cascade of dreadlocks.

If you have returned to the Imperial Palace and Praça XV, cross Av. Primeiro de Março to the

Nossa Senhora do Carmo da Antiga Sé (1750s), where Dom Pedro I was crowned as the first "Constitutional Emperor and Perpetual Defender of Brazil" in 1822. Since 1808 it had been used permanently as the city's cathedral until the 1970s, when the New Cathedral was built. It's a fine example of Portuguese rococo in Rio, with its pure-gold adornments and original Portuguese blue tiles still intact. Visit the cathedral store and check out the eerie plastic heads bought by parishioners who have prayed for their loved one's healing and received success. The heads are then placed on one of the

side altars in the cathedral as tokens of gratitude. Mass is held on Wed. at 9 a.m. and Fri. at 12:20 p.m.
Next door is an even more beautiful church,
Igreja da Ordem Terceiro de Nossa Senhora do Monte do Carmo, founded in 1761. The magnificent rococo facade is matched only by the chapel's stunning silver altar, decked with arabesque flowers, candelabras, and a multitiered throne featuring statues of the Divine Mother and Jesus. The stalls housed the rich families, who most often came to church not to pray, but to be seen. The seven altars along the wall represent images of Christ in his various worshipped forms. Today it's considered very fashionable to be married here. Mass is held daily on the hour from 8 a.m. to 1 p.m.
At the end of Rua Primeiro de Março you'll emerge onto Praça Pio X, where stands the 18th-century

Igreja de Nossa Senhora da Candelária Constructed between 1775-1898, this neoclassical structure, with a stunning painted cupola, ranks as the largest and richest church of Imperial Brazil. Its origin harks back to the 17th century, when a Portuguese couple, about to be shipwrecked, prayed to Saint Candelária and promised to build a chapel in her name if their boat did not sink. Miraculously, they were saved and, in gratitude, they built a small chapel at the first harbor they met. The present structure, a marvelous marriage of baroque and renaissance revival styles, took over a century to complete and was fashioned after the Basilica of Estrela in Lisbon.
Walk back toward Nossa Senhora do Carmo and turn left at Beco dos Barbeiros to watch the vendors in the streets sell tickets for the lottery called
Jogo do Bicho (The Animals' Game). The illegal (but usually tolerated) game, which run daily at 2 p.m., with results by 3 p.m., was invented by the baron who owned the old zoo to advertise its treasures to the public. Today, I'm told, the game is so honest that nobody would dare not pay you, although the bankers of the game, who are shunned by high society, are forced to find their social status as presidents of samba schools. (In 1993, a scandal ensued when I was in Brazil when a group of so-called "bankers" were arrested for gambling, an event which threw the samba schools into disarray.) Usually, however, the areas where the tickets are sold are among the safest in the city, since hidden security is always on patrol. While you're deciding whether to play, stop on the corner for a *cafezinho*, or maybe a fresh *suco de maracajú* (fresh juice) at
Café Sublime. This kind of juice bar, called a *botequim*, is where *cariocas* come after work to relax, schmooze, and show off their new girlfriends.
Turn down the cobblestoned Rua do Carmo to the

Livraria São José, a fascinating antique bookstore where you may find old maps of Rio, as well as used books on anything from music and poetry to physics. Walk to

Rua do Ouvidor, which during the 19th century was the street of fashion, filled with French corsets and gowns, as well as fashionable cafés and restaurants. Walking toward Av. Rio Branco down the cobblestone street, look right and left down the pedestrian streets that cross Rua do Ouvidor, full of *camêlos*, street vendors who peddle everything from cheap cosmetics to dubious cassette tapes and batteries. Take the time to browse and use your best bargaining tricks; if you look hard, you may find some extra locks for your luggage. Lining Rua do Ouvidor are several banks where you may exchange money and traveler's checks.

Eventually you will arrive at

Avenida Rio Branco, the city's center of commercial power ever since it was inaugurated on Nov. 15, 1905, under the name Avenida Central. In 1912, it was renamed Rio Branco to commemorate the Baron of Rio Branco, José Maria da Silva Paranhos Júnior, whose brilliant legal defenses of Brazil's borders added over 342,000 square miles of land (approximately the size of France) to its territory. Conceived originally as the Champs Elysées of Rio, the avenue during the early 1900s was dotted on both sides by fashionable cafés and boutiques and frequented by upper-class ladies who leisurely strolled down it, followed by their colorful retinues of well-dressed, but barefoot servants.

Crossing Av. Rio Branco, walk toward Rua Gonçalves Dias, where you will see the remains of a group of old Rio buildings. Once fashionable homes, these three-story buildings, with their pink, white, orange, and light-blue facades, are now restaurants and shops. From Av. Rio Branco, turn left on Rua Gonçalves Dias, heading for the

Confeitaria Colombo *Rua Gonçalves Dias 32/36;* ☎ *232-2300; open 8:30 a.m.-6:30 p.m.* a traditional *fin-de-siècle* teahouse that is a masterpiece of art nouveau. Originally a meeting place for the intellectuals and artists of Rio, it has retained its magnificent tile floors, stained glass ceiling, and humongous Belgian mirrors framed in jacaranda wood. Order a complete tea (*chá completo*) to feast on a parade of dishes that include sweets, breads, and salty hors d'oeuvres, or indulge in some luscious Viennese-style pastries while the piano player bangs out old-fashioned waltzes.

If you're interested in more involved dining, head back toward Av. Rio Branco to

Praça Floriano, an area of Rio that looks like Paris revisited. Since the elite *cariocas* of the late 19th century aped everything Gallic (French was their second language), it was only natural that the city's finest buildings should also emulate Louis XVI style.

The Teatro Municipal is a small-scale replica of the Paris Opera, which has hosted international artists of ballet, opera, and theater ever since its opening in 1909. (To make a tour of the theater, you must make an appointment in advance; English-speaking guides will probably be available.) If you didn't fill up at Confeitaria Colombo, do stop for lunch at the theater's adjacent restaurant, known as

Café do Teatro, considered one of the best in Rio, as well as being one of the most flamboyantly appointed. Affecting the atmosphere of a chic underground cave, the restaurant boasts huge ceramic tableaus of Assyrian-influenced Persian themes, marked by marble columns and elegant piano music. Even the outside foyer is magnificently arrayed with a tiled tableau of Moliere's *Le Bourgeois Gentilhomme,* among others.

Across the street stands the

Museum of Fine Arts (Museu Nacional de Belas Artes) *Av. Rio Branco, 1991;* ☎ *240-0068. Tues.-Fri. noon-4:30 p.m., Sat., Sun., and holidays 3-6 p.m. Free.* In 1816, the French Artistic Mission arrived in Brazil to arrange the official teaching of art, ten years later founding the Imperial Academy of Fine Arts, which exhibited works of both students and teachers as well as those donated by the Imperial family. When the school went public, its name was changed to the National Fine Arts School, which was housed in this building beginning in 1908. In 1937, the museum was officially installed to house the school's collection, which now numbers over 20,000 pieces. As such, it is the best place to view 19th-century academic Brazilian painting. (One sidelight: when the holes for construction were made at the turn of the century, builders found the remains of boats, suggesting the waters of the bay had once flowed this far north.)

Next door is the

National Library *Av. Rio Branco, 2191;* ☎ *240-9229. Mon.-Fri. 9 a.m.-8 p.m., Sat. 9 a.m.-3 p.m.* This is one of the most important libraries in South America and the sixth largest in the world, with over 4 million books, including documents brought by the royal, family as well as important treaties. If it looks like the Military Academy of Paris, it's because it was patterned after it, evoking Louis XVI style. Situated on the steps around the buildings are numerous vendors selling used records and books, where you might try your luck picking up some old bossa nova classics. All these buildings are part of the district called Cinelândia, so named for the many old-fashioned cinemas that dot the area. These days the neighborhood has been all but usurped by the gay community, which uses the area as a hangout,

RIO DE JANEIRO   107

although singles of all sexes tend to congregate during the day at the numerous cafés and bars.

> **Insider Tip:**
> Rua Quintanda at Rua 7 de Setembro, in the nervous heart of downtown, is a magical crossroads. Crowds form at the slightest influence; once at noontime I witnessed a hawker of Amazonian aphrodisiacs vie for attention next to a tender-faced young man playing great classical guitar. Up and down the closed-off avenue are shops, restaurants, and places to perch for people-watching during the week. Near Avenida Rio Branco, at the corner of Rua 7 de Setembro and Rua Rodrigo Silva, try a hot pão de queijo (cheese roll) and a delicious espresso.

From the Museum of Fine Arts, find the street on the right of the Opera House—Março de 13—and walk direct to

Largo da Carioca, a colorful public square where street vendors hawk their goods, and where artists and like-minded bohemians traditionally congregate.

Church and Convent of Santo Antônio, built between 1608 and 1620, is situated on a low hill overlooking the square. Also, the exquisitely adorned Church of Saint Francis dates from the 18th century. The hill on which the two churches stand are the final remains of the landfill that was excavated to become Flamengo Park. Santo Antônio (Saint Anthony) is the patron saint of marriages, and young carioca girls still come here to light candles in the eternal hope of landing a mate (a perpetual ritual for some, since eligible men in Rio are scarce, so I'm told). June 13 gets practically every single girl and her mother out of hiding when a huge celebration for the saint's birthday is held. If you're in a marrying mood, here's how to make a *pedido*. At the vendor stalls in the church's courtyard, buy a little silver-colored statue of Saint Anthony holding the baby Jesus (called *Santo Antônio com o menino Jesus solto para arranjar um namorado*), then remove the baby Jesus and tell Saint Anthony you will only return the infant when your lover appears. (For the sake of my readers, I actually tried this ploy, but eventually gave up in frustration and returned the baby to Santo Antônio out of pity.) If this strikes you as too religious, another fine remembrance is the key chain made in the shape of a tiny *cachaça* bottle with the image of Saint Anthony inside! As you wander through the church, note the turquoise cherubs sitting on the organ pipes, the Portuguese-crafted image of Christ adorned with a crown of thorns, and the authentic yellow and blue-and-white Portuguese tiles. Before leaving, you can even place a written wish in the crack of the picture frame of Saint Anthony with the Madonna and Child.

Next door is the

Igreja da Ordem Terceira da São Francisco da Penitência *Largo da Carioca, 5 (Centro);* ☎ *262-0197. Mon.-Fri. 1 p.m.-5 p.m.* initiated in the mid-18th century (although the order was constituted as early as 1610). This is the second richest church in Rio, a true example of baroque style (remember that the baroque era arrived late in Brazil, dependent on the discovery of gold in Minas Gerais). The church will probably be closed for repair, but you may call ahead and request special permission to enter. The visit will be worth it, as the images inside are of great beauty and artistic value, in particular the tableau of Saint Francis and the Crucified Jesus at the altar.

To reach the

Metropolitan Cathedral (Catedral Metropolitana) *Rua dos Arcos, 54 (Lapa);* ☎ *240-2669. Mon.-Sat. 7 a.m.-6 p.m., Sun. 9 a.m.-6 p.m. Note: bathing suits and shorts are not permitted, but culottes are acceptable.* Take the underpass walkway (more or less safe) in front of the convent. You'll be passing under the 36 arches of the **Aqueduct da Carioca,** one of Rio's best landmarks, designed to carry fresh water from the Santa Teresa neighborhood to the public fountain in the **Largo da Carioca**. Inaugurated in 1976 after 12 years of work and still unfinished today, the cathedral's stark modernistic construction has been the center of controversy among cariocas—one that seems to be falling on the side of those who can't stand it. Actually, the huge cone-shaped construction (83 meters high) resembles one of the great Mayan pyramids, and I personally find its airy, New Age spaciousness appealing, though perhaps not exactly appropriate for a baroque Catholic mass. The main door itself, sculptured with 48 bronze reliefs, is considered the Portal of Faith, and each of the colors used in the imposing stained-glass windows variously symbolize the doctrine of faith (blue), the one gospel for all races (red), and the victory of the Crucifixion (yellow). Beside the main altar stands the protector saints Sebastian and Anna. In the basement is the

Capela das Almas, where a 17th-century book recording the baptism of slaves can be seen. Walk through the parking lot to visit the Ossário, a bathhouse-type crypt where the bones of former parishioners are kept, but don't get nervous: the sign reading "Don't leave your ashes on the floor" refers to cigarette smokers!

If you're aching by this time to **return to your hotel** (probably in Zona Sul), walk up Av. Rio Branco to the bus terminal on Rua São José, where you can take an air-conditioned bus. Best bet, however, especially if it's hot, is to grab a taxi.

For Relaxation au Natural

Walk back under the aqueduct to Largo da Carioca, then left along Rua Carioca, arriving soon at **Praça Tiradentes,** named after the leader of the so-called Minas Conspiracy of 1789, a complicated political plot that attempted to overthrow the Portuguese rule. (For more information, see the chapter on Minas Gerais.) Three blocks west, along Rua Visconde do Rio Branco, is the

Praça da República in the Campo Santana. Spurred on by the arrival of the Portuguese royal family to Rio, the Count of Rezende started to urbanize this area in 1808, and the park was inaugurated in 1880, becoming the site of the court's most popular parties. In 1889 the square was the site for the proclamation of the republic by the Marechal de Deodoro da Fonseca, at which point it got its official name. Today the beautiful green landscaped park, suggesting an English style, is an oasis from the agitation of downtown. Unfortunately, it's not considered a safe place to kick back.

A Must on Sundays

São Bento Church *Rua Dom Gerardo, 68 (downtown);* ☎ *291-7122. 8 a.m.-5:30 p.m. Sun. mass at 10 a.m.* Built in the neighborhood of Saúde on one of the original four hills that once marked colonial Rio, São Bento ranks as one of the most beautiful and richly adorned churches in the country. Construction was begun in 1617, on land bequeathed to Benedictine monks who had sailed from Portugal via Bahia; the architect, sculptor, and painter were all priests who lived on the site as it was being constructed. The entire facade remained simple in contrast to the deeply baroque interior—an intentional device to create a sensation of shock among the parishioners as they entered through the portals. When the French invaded Rio in the 18th century, a cannon was placed in the temple to protect it against incipient bombing. In 1938, the church, monastery, and hill became a national patrimony.

The dark and humid atmosphere inside the church is steeped in mysticism. Large silver censors handmade in the 18th century hang from the ceiling, and the seven-tiered, gold-inlaid altar is strewn with gold-leafed curlicues, saints, and candelabras in every possible nook. Particularly exquisite is the rendering of the Madonna breast-feeding the baby Jesus surrounded by cherubs. On Sunday, a marvelous choir of monks singing Gregorian chants accompanies the high Benedictine mass replete with incense and carillons, making it one of the most transcendent musical experiences in Rio. The officiating priest may go on interminably about such favorite Latin topics as infidelity, but feel free to leave early or take photos, as long as you don't disturb the other worshippers. Also, leave time to stroll around the lovely landscaped gardens that look down on Guanabara Bay and Praca Mauá, once a seedy port that's now being renovated.

GETTING THERE:

The church is located on a slight incline that can be reached by an elevator at Rua Dom Gerardo, 40, or you may walk or drive up the hill. After services, walk to Av. Rio Branco and catch a taxi.

Insider Tip:

The church fills up fast on Sundays, so get there early. Shorts worn by either sex are not allowed, and one of my companions was even prohibited from entering for wearing stylish culottes.

SANTA TERESA

If old Rio exists anywhere, it is in the winding cobblestone streets and Victorian mansions perched precariously on the hillside in the district of Santa Teresa. During the 19th century, prosperous landowners and businessmen constructed high-walled gardens and fabulous homes here to take advantage of the cooling winds and remote privacy, and even today the isolated neighborhood retains much of its distinctive, if slightly bohemian charm. For years the most colorful way to appreciate the neighborhood was to take the *bonde*, an open-air streetcar that moseys over an antiquated track from a station near the New Cathedral in Largo da Carioca. Unfortunately, in recent years the trolley has been a major target of lightning-fast assailants who jump on and off the usually jam-packed trains while they're in motion. These days, policemen ride shotgun on most trams, but they can't guarantee you safety. If you do decide to brave the trolley, leave all valuables at home and sit near the security guard. The better way to see the neighborhood is to hire a private car (see "Private Cars" under *Hands-On Rio*.)

One of the major stops in Santa Teresa is the **Chácara do Céu Museum** *Rua Almirante Alexandrino, 316, store B;* ☎ *232-6570. Tues.-Sun. noon-10:00 p.m.* This modernist mansion was formerly the home of Raymundo de Castro Maia, one of Rio's leading industrialists, whose dabblings in the art world managed to amass one of the greatest private collections in Brazil. Adorning the walls are works by Brazil's finest modernists, such as Portinari, Di Cavalcanti, and Volpi, as well as impressive originals by Picasso, Matisse, Dali, Modigliani, and Monet. Outside, the landscaped gardens invite contemplative walks, as well as offering awesome views of the bay and downtown Rio. Afterwards, gear up for a slightly uphill traverse to the district's most bohemian hangout—**Bar do Arnaudo**—where you're sure to find some of the city's best artists and intellectuals passionately discussing the day's latest political mess.

> **Insider Tip:**
>
> *If you do take the tram, don't take your camera, and carry only the money you need for the day, preferably inside your clothes.*

GREEN RIO

Outdoor Rio isn't just a bunch of fabulous beaches. The city has more than its share of forests, parks, and mountains, and a committed outdoorist can hike through a jungle, paddle a canoe, and take a dip in a waterfall without ever leaving the city. Only in Rio!

TIJUCA FOREST

Long before the first colonists arrived, 95 percent of Rio and much of southern Brazil was blanketed with dense tropical rainforests that cooled the heated air and provided a magnificent self-sufficient ecosystem for literally thousands of life-forms, both flora and fauna. Sadly, only 9 percent of that chain, known as the Atlantic forest, remains in any visible form (having endured a rate of destruction decidedly more devastating than that of the Amazon forest). The good news, however, is that a sizable portion of this forest can be found right in the middle of Rio—in the **Tijuca National Park**. By some estimates the largest city forest in the world (about 175 square km), the area of the park was once the property of a wealthy nobleman who slashed and burned the forest to make way for coffee plantations. By the 1850s, however, the city managed to replant 100,000 trees and a second growth flourished. Today the park is an *eco–paradise of stunning waterfalls, exotic jungle trails, tropical flowers, and even Tarzan-like swinging vines*—a must for anyone with a green itch. Tour buses usually stop at the best views: the **Vista Chinesa**, 38 meters high, with a homage to the Chinese immigrants who came to work on tea plantations; the **Mesa do Imperador**, where the Dom Pedro I and his family loved to romp, and the **Dona Marta Mirante**, with a riveting view of Botafogo, Sugar Loaf, and Guanabara Bay. The **Mesa do Imperador** is the best place to picnic, and if you follow the map, you can hike the trails alone. However, if you want to do the kind of eco-trekking you will remember for a long time, hire a private guide, such as those from **Expeditours** (☎ 287-9697), who can provide expert leadership, security, and even specialized training in birdwatching and botany. And whatever you do, don't forget to wear your swimsuit under your hiking shorts: taking a dip in one of the many exotic waterfalls is a sensuous experience you will never forget. Near the **Cascatinha de Taunay**, one of the most delightful waterfalls, is the rustic **Mayrink Chapel**, most notable for the altar painting by the great Brazilian 20th-century master, Cândido Portinari. Two restaurants within the park offer dining options from rustic to more-than-rustic. The better one, called **Os Esquilos** (The Squirrels), serves merely adequate international cuisine, but the environs, surrounded by enormous trees and the chirping of birds, is of God's making. ☎ 224-3242. *Hours: 8 a.m.-5 p.m. daily. Free entrance.*

Getting There

Many travel agencies offer bus tours through Tijuca Forest, but in most cases you'll just see the trees from the window and miss the forest. A great guided trek through the forest (a superb way to experience the wet, moist, and cool crunchiness of the Atlantic chain) is supplied by **Rubéms Topelem** ☎ *256-8297, 236-6400* the owner of **Bicho Solto**, a two-person eco-agency, and a former physicist with poetry still in his veins—he knows enough about tropical botany to make tangled roots and slimy fungus a joy. Tours last about 2-1/2 hours (about $35) and you can extend it by visiting a **favela** (see p. 115). During winter, the forest can get cool, so take a jacket; it's a great option for a gray Rio day since sun rarely penetrates the forest anyway.

If you want to take **public transportation** (*not recommended*), catch bus 221 from Praça XV de Novembro, or #223 or 234 from the main bus terminal.

> **Insider Tip:**
> For an extra special experience of the Atlantic rainforest, consider a 2 day/1 night excursion to the city of Arcadia (about a 90-minute drive from Rio). Jeeps will transfer you to the small village of Lagoa das Lontras, where you commence a 3-1/2 hour trek through the rainforest (classified as "easy"). After a refreshing swim in the São Pedro River, another trek ("medium-hard") lasts about 1-1/2 hour. A campsite is made in a natural granite cave that accommodates up to 12. The following day a visit to the ruins of a church is followed by a feijoada lunch and eventual return to Rio. A biologist guide accompanies the tour, and rucksack, mattress, raincoat and sleeping bag are all provided. For more information, contact: Diana Turismo Av. N.S. de Copacabana, 330/Co. 01; ☎ 255-2296. Access to the park is from Praça Afonso Vizéu (Alto da Boa Vista). Take bus 221 from Paça XV de Novembro #233 or 234 from the main bus terminal.

JARDIM BOTÂNICO

This luxurious ecological paradise was the creation of Dom Jōao VI, who designed a living laboratory to test the many exotic spices and plants his farmers imported from the East Indies. The 34-acre Botanical Garden boasts over 8000 different kinds of trees and plants, as well as 268 enormous royal palms majestically lining the main promenade like courtiers posed at attention. The grounds, part cultivated, part jungle, is a relaxing place to stroll, picnic, and birdwatch among its many ponds, shady leafed clearings, and stunning 18th-century bronze fountains. There is also a museum, a botanic library, and an exotic plants collection, including the famous Victoria Régis water lilies from the Amazon that look like Mad Hatter saucers. *Rua Jardim Botânico, 10008;* ☎ *274-4897. 8:30 a.m.-6 p.m. Mon.-Fri. Fee is about $2.*

QUINTA DA BOA VISTA

Formerly owned by the Jesuits, the sprawling grounds of this natural park were later appropriated by Dom João VI for the private use of his family. Today, the city-owned complex, which can be enjoyed in a full day, includes the **Jardim Zoológico** (the zoo) and the **Nacional Museu** (National Museum), as well as hundreds of acres of fine shaded park.

A wonderful place to watch Brazilian families in action, the Zoo also offers an exciting closeup of Brazil's finest jungle creatures, even if the caged animals do seem to be a little depressed. Alligators, monkeys, snakes, and big cats abound, as do some impressive elephants from Africa. And the tropical bird collection is out of this world. The star of the zoo, however, is Tião, a big black ape who became famous for throwing water on the mayor and still seems to be in a perpetual funk. With a bit of teasing, you, too, can get him to roar.

Children will adore taking the little train through the park, which ends at the National Museum, a palatial estate displaying prehistoric fish skeletons, artifacts from Pompeii, crafts by American and Amazonian Indians, macumba statues, and folkloric crafts. Within the park itself, canoes can be rented for paddling around the ponds, and shows are often performed on a Grecian-columned stage in the middle of a lake. The sprawling park is a perfect place for picnics and long strolls, but note that the weekends are often crowded.

Getting There

Take the metro to the Estação Cristóvão stop, or bus #472 or #474 from Copacabana.

Insider Tip:

The unshaded sidewalks of the zoo can get extremely hot, so don't forget to take a sun hat, shades, and lots of suntan lotion. Most important, keep track of young boys who may be enviously eyeing your camera equipment.

PARQUE DO FLAMENGO

Mostly frequented by residents of the neighboring bairro of the same name, Flamengo Park is the biggest city park in the world. Stretching from Botafogo Beach to the Santos Dumont airport, it runs alongside the Marina da Gloria, as well as Flamengo Beach, and was the vision of the famous botanical professional Paisagista, who utilized to majestic effect the landscaping artistry of Roberto Burle Marx (the latter managing somehow to situate over 13,000 trees representing nearly every Brazilian species). Completed in 1960, the complex boasts two restaurants, excellent jogging and biking trails, basketball, soccer and tennis courts, playgrounds, and a sports arena. On Sundays, northbound traffic is closed so that visitors can stroll, play, and flirt in the street. The park also houses the Museum of Modern Art and the Carmen Miranda Museum, as well as the World War II Soldier's Memorial. Wonderful for children, the park is best visited in the accompaniment of a private guide. *Av. Infante Dom Henrique, 85.*

EXCURSION: PAQUETTÁ ISLAND

A half hour away from Rio across the Guanabara Bay lies **Paquetá Island**, once the summer nesting roost of Rio's upper class. These days, the island is packed on the weekends with the populace of Rio, especially families who spend the day on the island's various beaches. It's best for foreign tourists to come during the week, when there is less people-traffic. Cars are banned on the island, but you can rent bicycles and rowboats, and a real treat is the 40-minute, horse-drawn carriage that will carry you around the perimeter of the island. Tiny beaches are good for families with children. The best beach is José Bonifácio.

Paquetá is also called Lover's Island because of a romantic legend involving a young *morena* (girl with brown hair) who was waiting patiently for her lover beside a large rock. Couples write their names on the boulder, and you can even climb to the top.

There are no vendors or snack bars on the beaches, but a good restaurant is the Praia da Moreninha on Moreninha Beach (about $12). The **Lido** also has good fish. Hotels (more like *pousadas*) are few on the island, but a moderately priced one is **Flamboyant** *Praia Grossa, 58;* ☎ *397-0087.* Doubles with air conditioning and minibar run about $40.

FAVELA TOURS—NOT FOR THE FAINT OF HEART

They sit on the sides of the mountains in Rio, their golden lights twinkling under the cover of dark like a storybook picture. During the day, the tumbledown, pastel-colored shacks of Rio's *favelas,* or slums (nearly 534 in Rio, 7 on the mountainsides) still look picturesque from a distance; it is only up close that the harsh daily reality of almost 40 percent of Rio's population becomes painfully apparent. Although *favela* tours have never been on the typical tourist agenda, a new breed of travel guides are now offering intimate supervised jeep tours of these neighborhoods. The word *favela* itself means a yellow flower that proliferates fast—an apt description for Rocinha, the largest slum in South America, which over the last 40 years has burgeoned from a miserable dump to a population of 350,000 with a political voice. Today Rocinha actually functions as a viable city, with restaurants, businesses, neighborhood associations, day-care center, and its own samba school in the secondary division.

In truth, one of the "best" things I ever did in Rio was to visit Rocinha, accompanied by travel guide Rubéms Topelem, owner and chief guide of Bicho Solto, his alternative travel agency. Secure in Rubéms' jeep, we roared off from my hotel in Copacabana to the treacherous mountainside roads of Rocinha 15 minutes away. (Rocinha is where many of the taxi drivers, hotel clerks, and maids of the South Zone live). On our way up the mountain, we stopped at some of the most magnificent vistas of Rio while Rubéms offers an explanation of "*favela* law": since 600 kilos of cocaine pass through Rocinha every month, the drug dealers of the *favela* rule something like Robin Hoods, maintaining the welfare of the community in return for nepotism. It's said that little violence takes place among the *favela's* residents, though drug busts occur all the time, and I even witnessed a troop of police entering one house with their guns drawn. (The arrival of the police is always heralded by firecrackers set off by the residents on the lower levels, so keep an ear out.)

The tour of the *favela* proper bashed all my preconceptions. Accompanied by Rubéms, who seems to know everybody (don't ask how), we traipsed through narrow alleyways and stony staircases, strolled past busy barbershops and noisy chicken coops, and browsed through the bustling market square. To my eyes, Rocinha looks very much like the rustic country villages of the interior, except that everything is pushed and jumbled into a very small space. Most importantly, far from being a show of miserable poverty, the ambiance is extremely lively; children can be seen traipsing home from school with their backpacks, and the tour the day before mine actually stumbled upon a samba/pagode jam at lunchtime and got out and danced. Rubéms also makes a stop where the Carnaval costumes are made, and I even visited a private apartment picked at random (inside the tiny, clean, three-room dwelling at the end of an alleyway was a CD player, a color TV, and a cassette player!) A stop for a *caipirinha* at an open-air bar gave us time to peruse the exotic fruits and vegetables in the market square and eavesdrop on the card games going full blast in the street. Surprisingly, as a tourist, there was nothing embarrassing about this tour—since you go as a "friend of Rubéms'," everyone is friendly and you don't feel as if you're gawking at the less privileged. In truth, nothing will give you a clearer picture of the underside of Rio's glamour than this kind of tour—a necessary view, in fact, if you want to truly grasp Brazilian life in all its extremes.

While I highly suggest this 2-1/2 hour tour (about $25), I must add a few warnings.

- Although Rubéms has taken groups of 30 (all in jeeps) to Rocinha, I would suggest it's best to go in small groups.
- Because some of the climbs are steep, you should be in good shape.
- Wear tennis shoes and dress low-key; that means absolutely no jewelry, extra money, or important documents.
- Always ask permission before you take a photo, and don't take any photographs if you see something strange happening.
- Don't give money to beggars (though you may tip people who help you).
- Don't accept any drugs whatsoever (or you might get busted on the way down).
- Drink bottled water and eat nothing that has not been well cooked.
- Don't go during or after a heavy rain because mudslides are common and in recent years have killed numerous people and destroyed housing.
- Most of all, go to a favela only with an experienced guide who knows the people well. For more information, contact **Rubéms Topelem c/o Bicho Solto** ☎ *(21) 256-8297, 236-6400.*

Insider Tip:

Besides Samba *by Alma Guillermoprieto (a look at Carnaval from inside the favela), another excellent book to read in preparation for this tour is* Child of the Dark, The Diary of Carolina Maria de Jesus, *translated into English by Penguin Books, 1963. Written on scraps of paper picked from the gutter, it's the raw, primitive journal of a favela survivor who fought daily to feed herself and her three illegitimate children in a São Paulo slum. At times horrifying, at other times inspirational, the book instantly became a best-seller in Brazil during the '60s and today remains a minor classic.*

RIO—ESPECIALLY FOR CHILDREN

You may find it a horrifying thought, but children will love Rio. And there are plenty of things to do that will keep them entertained, happy, and safe. Rio-friendly children should either be so young they won't remember the trip or old enough to follow directions immediately. Hotels like the Inter-Continental and Rio Sheraton, which are more isolated from the hubbub of the city, should prove safer for small children. The following are some suggested activities for kids of all ages, even the ones over 40.

Fazenda Alegria ("Happy Farm") *Estrada da Boca do Mato, (Vargem Pequena);* ☎ *342-9066. Sat., Sun. and holidays 10 a.m.-5 p.m.* A popular ecology farm for kids with waterfalls and animals (including lambs and miniponies) that are pettable. Lunch available.

Jardim Zoológico (Zoo) *Quinta da Boa Vista;* ☎ *254-2024. Daily 9 a.m.-4:30 p.m.* Besides 2,500 animals, there are snack bars, clean toilets, and acres of adjoining grounds for picnics. About $2. (See *Green Rio.*)

Mini–Rio Barra Shopping *Av. das Américas, 4666;* ☎ *325-5611. Daily from 10 a.m.-10 p.m. About $6.* While the adults shop, kids will enjoy the playground on the first level, which almost rates as a small circus. Bumper cars, airplane rides, and boat rides for the wee-sized.

Tivoli Parque *Av. Borges de Medeiros (Lagoa);* ☎ *274-1846. Thurs. and Fri. 2-8 p.m., Sat. 2-10 p.m., and Sun. 10 a.m.-10 p.m. About $6.* An amusement park open every day during the afternoons in Lagoa, with a special Mini-Tivoli for children 2 to 10. *Cariocas* usually spend 2–3 hours there; you can go anytime and find it full.

Flamengo Park The largest landscape project in Rio, with jogging and bicycle tracks, tennis courts, places for picnics, museums, and restaurants. (See *Green Rio.*)

Planetário (Planetarium) *Rua Padre Leonel Franca, 240 (Gávea);* ☎ *274-0096.* See *Green Rio.* Special shows for adults and kids.

Barra da Tijuca

If you're bathing at the beaches in Barra with children, don't miss a trek to **Lokau** (The Spot). Built on a small estate, it hosts a menagerie of animals, including ducks, toucans, monkeys, and peacocks, as well as an expensive open-air restaurant. Children can be let loose to roam around on their own. Eat on the outdoor deck facing the Lagoa of Marapindi, full of tiny alligators that are being preserved. (See *Culinary Rio.*)

Baby—sitters

The concierge of your hotel will most likely be able to find you a reliable baby-sitter. One whom I personally recommend is **Patricia Régis** (☎ 541-6701), a young woman who speaks excellent English.

RAINY DAYS IN RIO

There may come a day in your stay in Rio when you've either overstayed your time in the sun (and you're so red you can't sit down) or, God forbid, it's raining. Rio is a sad city on a rainy day; the sea turns mopey gray, the sky hangs ominously over the mountaintops, and even Corcovado disappears in the fog. To keep you from moping in your hotel room and complaining about how much money you're wasting, here are some suggestions to take up the slack.

- Visit the **Museum of Fine Arts** and take a long lunch next door at the elegant **Café do Teatro**.

- Browse through the chic stores at **Barra Shopping Center**, followed by lunch at **Guimas**, a movie, then a few rides at the amusement park.

- Visit a great health club like **AKXE**, where there's a fantastic Olympic-size pool, great-looking members, and up-to-the-minute equipment.

- **Souvenir shop** for the perfect crystal-carved bird or chess set down Rua N.S. de Copacabana.

- Visit the **Carmen Miranda Museum** and learn to sing "Down South American Way" with the right accent.

- Visit the **H. Stern Museum** and workshop (they'll pick you up), design your own jewelry, then pay for it with your credit card.

- Visit the **studios of up-and-coming artists**, followed by **afternoon tea** at the Caesar Park Hotel or the Meridien Hotel.

- Check what's playing at the **neighborhood cinemas** in Copacabana and Ipanema—usually new American films with Portuguese subtitles (an interesting way to learn bad words in Portuguese).

- Sleep in, take brunch or afternoon tea at the **Confeitaria Colombo**, take another nap, then indulge in an all-night-long orgy of Rio by dark.

- Get drunk at the **Garota de Ipanema Bar** and try to whistle all the bossa nova classics you know.

- Check out the **record stores** and listen to the latest releases.

USER'S GUIDE TO THE BEST BEACHES IN RIO

My first experience of Copacabana was on a hot weekday in December. I had plunked down my towel on a clean strip of beach, but not far from me was a tanned, muscular young man with two beautiful girls in bikinis. When the redhead jumped up to take a dip in the water, the young man and the brunette started making out like crazy, and I said to myself, "Ah, so this one is his girlfriend." But then the brunette went swimming, and the redhead returned, whereupon she and the young man immediately fell into a mad clutch. I had started to worry what would happen when one girl found out about the other when suddenly the brunette came back and everybody laughed and the scene started over. All I could do was shake my head and say, "So, this is Brazil."

"An artist in Brazil must suffer deeply," Tom Jobim, the great bossa nova composer, once told me, "otherwise he'd never have reason to leave the beach." And though he was laughing, he was also dead-serious. Unless you're afflicted with some tragic skin disease, there's no escaping the beach in Rio. Behind every business deal, behind every high-powered lunch or political negotiation is someone thinking about how to get to the beach, what to wear, whom to meet, and where to eat. It's a mentality that quickly envelops any tourist who comes here, and makes the more serious-minded workaholics from São Paulo shake their heads in disgust. But to the *carioca*, the beach is more than a pastime; it's where life itself is played out. For some, the 90 kilometers of beach that run from Guanabara to Sepetiba bays is a vast natural playground, a kind of personal backyard; for others, it's a muse, a bedroom, a runway, a place to make love, fake love, even stake out love. For those Brazilians with voodoo in their veins, the long stretches of Copacabana and Ipanema beach are sacred altars ruled by the dazzling but dangerous Iemenjá, goddess of the sea. Cross her, so the saying goes, and you better get your butt off the shore.

There are no bad beaches in Rio. There are beaches for swimming, for surfing, for mere strolling; even the polluted ones along the bays are excellent for tanning. And none of them are dirty: an urban cleaning company, supported by the city, cleans the beaches daily with imported equipment from Italy and France. Where the beaches differ is in personality. Exactly with whom you want to hobnob may color which hotel you choose, where you eat, and where you want to party. But remember: nobody owns any stretch of beach in Rio, and everyone, from rich to poor, native or foreign, male, female, and "ambisextrous," can wriggle toes in sand anywhere he or she want to. In a city full of inequalities, the beach at least is the one great equalizer.

There is, however, one great "disequalizer" that has tourists quaking in their sandals: there is absolutely no cellulite on Rio's beaches, except for that brought in by the foreign trade. Although this is perhaps a slight exaggeration, do be fully prepared for the most glorious figures—male and female—that God has ever wrought. Considering the Brazilian diet of red meat and heavy sweets, there is no accounting for this phenomenon of nature, except that *cariocas,* when they're not on the beach, are usually dieting fanatically or killing themselves in a gym. For those who can't afford the luxuries of a health club, it's been said that walking up and down the mountains of the *favelas,* not to mention years of hip-pounding samba, has produced some of the best thigh muscles in the world. And, of course, it's Brazil which gave birth to one of the world's most famous plastic surgeons, Ivo Pitanguy, whose services are utilized as much by Brazilian grand dames as by international jet-setters.

However begotten, the *carioca* body remains a noble work of art, one that is continually inspiring a multitude of variations on the near-nonexistent mini-bikini. For years the prevailing rage has been the *fio dental* (or dental floss)—so named for the tiny string that serves to cover (or uncover) the derriere. More recently, the larger triangular style of the *asa delta* has dominated the scene—its shape (and name) reminiscent of the outspread wings of the hang–gliders who soar over São Conrado beach. The latest fashions can always be found in boutiques along Ipanema's Rua Visconde de Pirajá.

Perfect Tans And Tight Muscles

But whatever they're wearing, *cariocas* seem to excel in the art of beach-bathing. Perfect tans and tight muscles are surely the prime obsession of most of Rio's beachgoers, but they pursue it with such grace: it will astound you the first time you see a beautiful, nubile 16-year-old gently lower herself to a towel without getting one drop of sand on her body. But no one on the beach stays immobile for long. Most likely you'll find a volleyball game nearby; there's always the mandatory dip in the sea; there are fruits, chips, and drinks to buy from picaresque vendors. And then there's strolling—the sensuous art of display made famous by the original girl from Ipanema. Brazilian women seem to have learned in the crib how to show off their bodies with maximum pride and an admirable lack of shame. And as liberating as that can be, the effect, for some less tropical tourists, should come with a warning. I knew one poor American fellow who had to sit out his first few days in Copacabana with a towel on his lap.

The following User's Guide will help you decide where to spend your beachtime in Rio. Following the descriptions of each beach is a list of the best hotels and restaurants in the area. For more information, check the Hotels and Restaurants sections.

BEACH BLANKET SURVIVAL GUIDE

SAND Think light when you go to the beach. Most *cariocas* get through a beach day with nothing more than their towel, suntan lotion, and a few bills stuffed into a plastic neck purse. Whatever you do, follow their form. Tourists who have gotten ripped off at the beach insisted on walking up and down the strand with a handbag of valuables, something you should never do, particularly at night. If you insist on taking your camera to the beach, go only for a photo shoot, then return it to your hotel before taking a dip in the water. Of course, there are plenty of nice people on the beach who will watch your belongings when you go for a swim, but entrusting anything more than a towel to a perfect stranger is asking for trouble. (On the other hand, once when I forgot where I left my things, a wonderful little girl came running over to point out my towel!)

SUN Don't forget you're in a tropical country. The sun is hotter and the UV rays more deadly. Time your first few days in the sun carefully, using lotion with a high-protection factor, or you will get so red you will become a social embarrassment. (*Cariocas* in general have darker skin that absorbs the rays more easily.) Anyone with color-processed or permed hair should also use a protective gel. (My own highlighted hair turned white–blond and broke off after repeated harsh exposures.)

SEA The undertow in most beaches is fierce. The seabed drops off sharply and currents can either pull you under or far away from where you left your towel. Copacabana, in particular, boasts strong waves. As such, don't swim far out, keep track of the height of the waves, and mark the place where you left your towel. (A friend of mine, a travel writer no less, failed to heed these warnings and had to be saved from the undertow by a gracious but fortunately strong stranger.)

SNACKS Most of the food sold on the beach, whether by vendors or makeshift bars, is safe—*mais ou menos*. Personally, I'd avoid anything with mayonnaise (like tuna sandwiches) that may have been left out too long in the sun. Soda pop bottles should always be returned to the vendor who sold them. Once you get accustomed to the terrain, you might want to pick up some drinks or a box of cookies or chips at a neighborhood deli. Coconut milk, only available seaside, is a fabulous sunstroke reliever.

SECURITY Recently Rio has beefed up its beach security, with a 600–man police force that patrols the strand. The number of plainclothes policemen has also been increased, as well as the telephone-equipped police posts. In addition, the Meridien and Caesar Park conduct constant surveillance of the beach in front of their hotels. Lifeguard posts are marked by white flags; those with a red cross indicate that swimming is prohibited. If anything happens to you, however, try shouting "*Polícia*" (poh–lee–sée–ah) or "*Socorro!*" (soo–cor–roo).

COPACABANA

VITAL STATS

- A half–moon curve of beach 2 miles long, from Av. Princesa Isabel to the military-owned Copacabana Fort.
- Mass-market appeal, with lifeguard, toilets, and security posts stationed at intervals.
- Rough for swimming, good for people-watching.
- Half a million visitors during summer weekends.

Copacabana—the very name itself still shivers with the excitement it first inspired during the 1920s, when gambling was king and the Copacabana Palace Hotel first opened its luxurious doors to international jet-setters. Since the 1960s, when the hotel boom began to define the high-rise skyline that now characterizes the 4-km strip, the population of Copacabana has steadily expanded to become the most populous neighborhood in Rio, and one of the most densely populated areas in the world. Apartments lining the beach drag called Avenida Atlântica are still expensive, but behind it, in the 109 narrow streets and alleyways that mark the neighborhood, more than 10 people are often crammed into 2-bedroom apartments. Nevertheless, many of the best hotels are still located here, and the area is packed with fine restaurants, souvenir shops, and moderate-priced shopping along Av. N.S. de Copacabana, parallel to the beach drag.

The downside is that Copacabana Beach, today more populous than elite, is one of the most vulnerable neighborhoods in terms of petty thievery and assault. During Rock in Rio, the international rock festival, it was rumored that even George Michael, the rock star, was robbed walking out the front door of his hotel. And a few years back, marauding bands of teens from the favelas one day attacked bathers, right under the eyes of the helpless police. Although nobody should be scared away from Copacabana, even the natives who live there take special precautions for their personal safety. And although I've been told it's okay to walk on the beach until 11 p.m., I wouldn't step on the sand anytime after dark, and I *certainly* wouldn't do so carrying anything valuable.

Personally, though, I love Copacabana exactly for its raucous, boisterous joy. During high season (Dec.–Mar.), the strand is nearly an invisible blur of towels and umbrellas, as well as a musical cacophony of radios vying with the nasal-hard yells of vendors selling everything from beer to natural sandwiches. It's a great place to see Brazilian families in vacation mode, and between 5 and 6 p.m., a microcosm of Rio—rich, poor, old, young, loners and lovers—strolls up and down Av. Atlântica in various stages of beachwear and jogging attire. A perfect way to cool down after a hard day of tanning is to browse through the crafts stands on Av. Atlântica, where everything from Brazilian maps and bikinis to crystal-carved birds and leather bags are sold. After dark, it's the only beach where the floodlights are turned on so that volleyball can be played.

Feast Of Iemenjá

One of Copacabana's greatest events, which shouldn't be missed, is the **Feast of Iemenjá,** held yearly on New Year's Eve. Starting at 7 p.m., thousands of white-clad adherents of Afro-Brazilian cults of *candomblé, macumba,* and *umbanda* congregate on the beaches of Copacabana and Leme and set up sand altars. Initiates are baptized, and at midnight they launch scores of handmade wooden boats out to sea laden with gifts for Iemenjá. Meanwhile, the cults' spiritual leaders, smoking huge cigars to maintain their trance states, receive petitioners on the beach, giving blessings and conducting healing "passes" over their bodies. At the stroke of midnight, dazzling fireworks explode from nine different positions along the strand. The crowds and the seeming chaos may look forbidding, but don't be afraid to approach and participate, as long as you've left your valuables at home. All night long, the air will be thick with ritual, incense, and passionate drums, and even at dawn you're sure to see some lone celebrants making their private offerings with coins or flowers. The best view for the rituals is from above the beach, and if you're lucky enough to have a friend who lives on Av. Atlântica facing the strand, wangle an invitation for the evening. Or reserve a prime hotel room with a balcony or bay window at least six months in advance.

Best Hotels:
Rio Palace (expensive), **Copacabana Palace** (expensive), **Rio Atlântica Suite** (expensive), **Ouro Verde** (moderate), **Toledo** (inexpensive).

Best Restaurants:
Le Bec Fin (French, expensive), **Copacabana Churrascaria** (steak, moderate), **Ouro Verde** (French and Swiss, expensive), **Da Brambini** (Italian, moderate), **O Crack dos Galetos** (grilled chicken, cheap).

LEME BEACH

VITAL STATS
- About 3000 feet long, just to the southeast of Copacabana Beach, where it connects without interruption at Av. Princesa Isabel, and extends to the Morro de Leme.
- Family-style beach a tad less rambunctious than Copacabana, but still full of local color.
- Rough for swimming, good for surfing.

Since there are no signs, Leme Beach to the uninitiated looks like the same stretch as Copacabana, but officially it begins where the Meridien Hotel reigns on Av. Princesa Isabel. A relatively calm, middle–class residential district, Leme is a wonderful neighborhood to browse through, with its winding leafy streets and small but excellent restaurants like Shirley's and Crepe D'Or. **Caminho dos Pescado-**

res (or Fishermen's Walk), located at the very end of Leme Beach, offers a fantastic view of Copacabana that shouldn't be missed. From this privileged site you'll see the entire expanse of Copacabana, including Sugar Loaf and Gávea Stone. Crabs can be seen crawling over the rocky sand, while *cariocas* meditate or relax after a jog. Courageous surfers battling the crashing waves add to the drama, but note that the area is not safe to visit at night—not only because of thieves, but because people have been swept off into the ocean by high winds in inclement weather. From the outcropping of rock called **Pedra do Leme**, you can stroll around the cement walkway at the base of the cliff and join the amateur fishermen with their poles hanging over the side. (These crusty, colorful fellows start to congregate around 5 a.m.). You may also see, tucked into craggy coves, remnants of recent *macumba* rituals, an African-derived spiritual practice that uses candles and food as offerings to the gods, but under no circumstances should you disturb them. Guaraná (a soda pop) and candies are signs that a special rite for the spirits' children have been held, but tradition says that only dogs are allowed to walk away with the treats.

Insider Tip:

Since the Meridien Hotel maintains a tight security watch on the beach near the hotel, it's not a bad idea to locate your towel near their official cabana, even if you aren't a guest.

Best Hotels:

Meridien (expensive), **Rio Copa** (moderate), **Predia Leme** (inexpensive).

Best Restaurants:

Mariu's (steaks, moderate), **Le Saint Honoré** (French, expensive), **Príncipe das Peixadas** (fish, inexpensive), **Yes Salads** (crepes, cheap).

IPANEMA

VITAL STATS

- Stretching due north from Copacabana for about 1.5 miles, from the far side of Copacabana Fort to the canal that flows off from the Lagoa Rodrigo de Freitas, a large inland lake.

- A step up in "cool" from Copacabana—it's been said the best bodies, male and female, can be spotted here. More a lover's beach, where attitude is everything. No unfashionable swimsuits allowed.

Ipanema Beach burst into international prominence one day in 1960 when two starving artists decided to immortalize the gorgeous *garota* (chick) who daily strolled past their bar stools with an insinuating walk. Three decades later, the bar is still there, the composer, Tom Jobim, is known worldwide for his cool bossa nova, and the original *garota* is now a mother of four grown children and reportedly still beautiful. (Lyricist Vinícius de Moraes went on to become one of Brazil's best-loved poets.) These days, nostalgia buffs should head for a drink at the bar now christened (of course!) **Garota de Ipanema**, where you can sit outside and watch the '90s version of beauty stroll back from the beach. During Carnaval, however, this corner of Ipanema is infamous for attracting the most flamboyant personalities, including transvestites who sometimes look better than the real girls.

Chic and upper-class, Ipanema attracts bathers similar to its own fashion-conscious residents who shop on **Rua Visconde de Pirajá**, two streets in from the beach drag, where some of Rio's best fashions can be found. (See Shopping). The safest areas of the beach may be near the Caesar Park, which conducts secret surveillance of the strand for its own clients. On Sundays the main beach drags—Av. Vieira Souto and Av. Delfim Moreira—are closed to traffic as roller skaters, skateboarders, and joggers take to the pavement. A stroll through the large **food and flower market** on Praça da Paz on Fri. will give you a chance to see *cariocas* do their weekly shopping. A beautiful sight at dusk and dawn are the free group classes of **Tai Chi Chuan** held in the Praça da Paz—feel free to join in. And obligatory is at least one trip to the **hippie fair** at Praça General Osório held on Sundays, although be forewarned that crowds may be dense during high season and the crafts are sometimes less than inspiring.

Best Hotels:

Caesar Park (expensive), **Mar Ipanema** (moderate), **Ipanema Inn** (inexpensive).

Best Restaurants:
Porcão (steak, moderate), **Torre de Bebel** (funky, cheap), **Grottammare** (fish, expensive), **Satíricon** (Italian, expensive), **Alberico's** (grazing, inexpensive), **Pax** (continental, moderate), **Garota de Ipanema** (nostalgia, inexpensive), **Caravella** (pizza, moderate), **Chaika's** (ice cream, pizzas, and hearty, fast meals, inexpensive).

ARPOADOR

VITAL STATS

- Slice of beach 400 yards long on the eastern tip of Ipanema.

- Rough sea excellent for surfing. Surfers congregate on this tiny stretch of beach for some of the best waves in Rio.

LEBLON

VITAL STATS

- Beach runs almost a mile along Av. Delfim Moreira until it turns into Vidigal Beach at Av. Niemeyer.

- Separated from Ipanema by a small canal that connects the ocean to the Lagoa Rodrigo de Freitas.

- Upper-class neighborhood that abhors rowdiness.

As Leme is to Copacabana, Leblon is the sister beach to Ipanema, separated only by a small canal that runs from the *lagoa* (lake) to the ocean. With few exceptions, buildings along the beach drag tend to be only 5 stories high in accordance with zoning regulations; hence the visual effect is definitely less high-tech and much homier. Dotted with leafy, shady streets, Leblon exudes an atmosphere of cool sophistication that is felt even surfside. Hotels tend to be quieter, the nightlife less dramatic, and even the crime rate lower. Of all the beaches in the Zona Sul (South Zone), Leblon is probably the safest.

Best Hotels:
Marina Palace (expensive), **Marina Rio Hotel** (moderate), **Hotel Carlton** (inexpensive).

Best Restaurants:
Antiquarius (very expensive).

FLAMENGO

VITAL STATS

- Over half a square mile of prime oceanfront from Enseada da Glória to the Bay of Botafogo.
- Beach nearest downtown.
- Restaurants are cheap.
- Calm sea that facilitates sports (except swimming).
- Lots of tennis courts and soccer fields.

Flamengo is the only beach in Rio adjacent to a park—in this case, a luscious forest of vast green lawns and tall palm trees designed by the Brazilian landscape architect Roberto Burle-Marx. One of the largest land reclamation projects in Brazil, the Parque do Flamengo sweeps from the Enseada da Gloria to the Bay of Botafogo on about 1.2 square km of prime beachfront. Although the beach, which runs alongside the park, is pristine for tanning, the polluted waters should deter anyone interested in bathing—*cariocas* don't even think about swimming here. On the plus side are the attractive foresty environs of the park, which include a tractor train for children, a large playground, and sports facilities. An excellent view of Nitéroi, across the bay, can be seen. Also located at the park is the **Modern Museum of Art,** as well as the **National War Memorial for the Dead of the Second World War**—a powerful sculpture of two large pillars upholding a curved slab. Many of the remains of Brazilians who fought for the Allies in Italy are buried near the Tomb of the Unknown Soldier.

Best Hotel:
Hotel Glória (expensive-moderate).

Best Restaurants:
Rio's (romance with a view, expensive), **Kioto** (Japanese, expensive).

BOTAFOGO

VITAL STATS

- 600 yards of beachfront.
- Good for sunbathing, poor for swimming.

Botafogo's curving beachfront is much more popular with its middle-class residents than with outsiders, but the charming neighborhood boasts some of the best restaurants in Rio.

Best Restaurants:

Sol e Mar (Spanish-style fish with a view, expensive), **Clube Gourmet** (French peasant-style, expensive), **Adega do Valentim** (Portuguese, expensive).

PRAIA VERMELHA

VITAL STATS

- 100 yards long, located below Sugar Loaf.
- Sheltered environs makes it perfect for swimming.

Praia Vermelha (or Red Beach) is the only strand in Rio with thick golden sand. Sunsets are spectacular, as is the swimming, which takes advantage of the sheltering rock.

VIDIGAL

VITAL STATS

- 656 yards long.
- About 1/2 hour from the South Zone of Rio by car.
- Access on weekdays from the Tunel Dois Irmãos, weekends from Av. Niemeyer.

Although all beaches are city property, Vidigal Beach has, for all intents and purposes, been appropriated by the Rio Sheraton Hotel, whose sole staircase to the beach is constantly being surveilled by hotel security. For guests, the limited access makes Vidigal one of the safest beaches in the city, as well as one of the loveliest—boasting a magnificent craggy coastline and tumultuous waves. Nearby, unfortunately, is the Vidigal favela, one of the largest slums in Rio, which is why you may see cars on the highway being stopped and searched by police. (The machine guns look daunting, but tell yourself it's for your own good.) As for activity on the beach, you'll be hard pressed to find a wandering vendor, but the Sheraton offers a full array of excellent, if pricey, restaurants and snack bars.

Best Hotel:

Sheraton Rio (expensive).

Best Restaurant:

Valentino's (Italian, moderate-expensive).

RIO DE JANEIRO 131

SÃO CONRADO

VITAL STATS

- 1.6 miles long.
- 1/2 hour from Copacabana by car.
- Official landing strip for hang gliders.
- Chic, exquisite, and deserted during the week, packed in high season.
- Excellent for surfing.

Embraced on three sides by densely forested mountains, São Conrado Beach offers the best combination of surf and turf. Thirty years ago the strand was practically virgin; in the last ten years musicians, artists, and high-class rollers have moved into the pricey condos that precariously hug the mountainous cliffs just below Rocinha, one of Brazil's largest *favelas*. (It's said that in Rio only the very rich and the very poor are crazy enough to live on the sides of the mountain.) São Conrado Beach, however, is thrilling even before you arrive. The roller coaster ride from the South Zone on Av. Niemeyer curves dramatically around the edge of the cliff and sometimes looks straight down to the sea. The trip's climax, however, is in the last few kilometers, when the avenue descends dramatically for a breathtaking view of the massive Gávea Mountain. Bathers enjoy watching daredevil hang gliders perform the 1,680-ft. jump from atop Gávea and land on the beachfront—right next to their towels. Clients of 5-star hotels are invited to make use of the 18-hole Gávea Golf Course, which cuts through the middle of the beach, but arrangements must be made in advance. To get here by bus, take #500, which originates in Urca and passes through Copacabana on Av. Atlântica, Av. Vieira Souto in Ipanema, and Av. Delfim Moreira in Leblon.

Best Hotel:

Inter–Continental (expensive).

Best Restaurants:

All located in São Conrado Shopping Mall: **Guimas** (chic lunch, moderate), **Lagostão** (lobsters, expensive), **Alvaro's** (fish and beer, moderate).

BARRA DA TIJUCA

VITAL STATS

- Immense sand reef 12–1/2 miles long.
- Deserted during the week, full of chic *cariocas* during the weekends.
- Good swimming, perfect for families with a car.

What's become most chic in Rio is anything that's hard to reach. The beach of Barra da Tijuca is about 45 minutes from the South Zone, and though you can take bus #553 from Copacabana (it's going to be a very long ride), you will probably need a car once you get there. Still, Barra is beautiful, the future of Rio, and the weekend escape for industry execs and their families, who dote on the small intimate strands, the quaint fishing villages, and the casual seaside eateries. For years the last undeveloped stretch of sea front in the city, Barra was built up during the late '70s: now apart-hotels and condo complexes dot the beach drag along Av. Sernambetiba, which, during the weekends, is packed bumper to bumper. Paes Mendonça, one of the largest supermarkets in South America, is located here, as well as hundreds of love motels frequented by Brazilian couples (legal and illicit) who need a change of romantic environ for all different reasons. Swimming is excellent, and bird-sighting of tropical species is common since the surrounding marshes serve as a natural habitat for wildlife.

Restaurants in the neighborhood of Barra lean toward the rustic and romantic; also lining the strand are dozens of trailer cars that hawk drinks and sandwiches during the day and turn into beachside discos at night. One of the most well-known vending stands is Pepê's, which sells great natural sandwiches on the northernmost part of the beach in front of Barão, a windsurf rental shop. If you can't find Pepê's green and white hut, look for the bevy of beautiful bikinis that always surrounds it.

Best Hotel:

Barrabela Hotel (apart-hotel, moderate).

Best Restaurants:

Ettore (Italian, inexpensive), **Baby Beef** (steak, moderate), **Nau Catarineta** (rustic pizza, inexpensive).

FARTHER WEST

Recreio dos Bandeirantes, surrounded by fields of wildflowers and tall grasses, is located at the southern tip of Barra—a small community of chic summer weekend homes and simpler but colorful shanties. If the crowds at Barra become intolerable, follow the sharply rising road past the rock formations at the end of Recreio to the more deserted stretch of **Prainha**, or Little Beach, one of the best places for surfing in Rio, along with **Macumba Beach**, right next door. Prainha is small but enticing. (Surfers should bring their own boards, as there are no rental shops around, but Brazilians are so friendly that you could just ask to borrow one.) Ten minutes up the road you'll reach an even more primitive beach called **Grumari Beach** (where the movie *Blame It on Rio* was filmed), perhaps the very image of tropical splendor and untouched beauty that foreigners still harbor about Brazil. Tall slender palms and Brazilian cactus coupled with crystal-blue seas will make you feel as if you've stumbled into paradise. Another 15 or so minutes to the west lies **Pedra da Guaratiba**, where the beach is dirty but is considered medicinal, so the villagers say. (People with skin problems flock to the beach just to smear their bodies with the muddy-colored sand.) There's no swimming here, however, and the narrow roads are often not big enough for two cars. Full of quaint seamen's houses as well as luxurious summer homes, the area is reminiscent of the Greek islands, with lots of simple restaurants that offer a hearty plate of fried fish for about $5. Lately, *cariocas* have been traveling the one-hour-plus ride from the South Zone to Guaratiba just to patronize Cândido's, a near-shack of a restaurant that serves superlative seafood dishes.

Best Restaurants:
Cândido's (fish, expensive), **Tia Palmira** (fish, moderate).

MUSEUMS IN RIO

Fine Arts

Museu de Arte Moderna (Museum of Modern Art) *Av. Infante D. Henrique, 85 (Parque Brigadeiro Eduardo Gomes, Flamengo);*
☎ *210-2188. Tues.-Sun. noon-6 p.m.* In 1952, the architect and urbanist Afonso Eduardo Reidy received an area of 40,000 square meters on the landfill of Flamengo to construct Rio's Museum of Modern Art; inaugurated in 1958, the hangar-type construction is considered to be the acme of modernist style (others think it looks

merely like an airport hangar). More than a museum, MAM (as it is affectionately called) has become a space for innovation and the ever-changing showcase of local culture, hosting the main artistic movements of Rio, such as the "Neoconcretism" of the '50s and the "Nova Figuração" (New Design) of the '60s, among others. A fire in 1978 destroyed 90 percent of its collection, but in recent years, about 4,000 important works have been donated by Gilberto Chateaubriand, one of Brazil's most renowned collectors, including works by Anita Malfatti, Do Cavalcanti, Portinari, Panceti, and Djanira. Besides a library that specializes in the arts, you'll also find a fine movie collection, a research center, art workshop, and arena for fairs. A restaurant makes the museum a nice stop for lunch, particularly if you are visiting Flamengo Park and beach.

Museu Nacional de Belas Artes (National Fine Arts Museum) *Av. Rio Branco, 199 (downtown);* ☎ *240-0068. Tues.-Thurs. noon-4:30 p.m., Sat. and Sun. 3-6 p.m.; free.* One of the most beautiful buildings in downtown Rio, the National Museum of Fine Arts was constructed in 1908 in French renascent style to imitate the Louvre, but was first used to house the National Academy of Fine Arts. Since 1937, when the museum was installed, the collection has grown to over 20,000 pieces, including paintings and sculptures of both native and international artists. The layout of the permanent exhibition offers an interesting overview of Brazilian culture as it developed over the centuries. Photography is prohibited. If you'd like a specialized guide who speaks fluent English, call for an appointment To get there, take the metro to *Carioca* station or a city–bound bus to Av. Rio Branco.

Historical

Museu Histórico Nacional *Praça Marechal Ancora;* ☎ *220-5829 and 240-2092. Tues.-Fri. 10 a.m.-5:30 p.m., weekends and holidays 2:30-5:30 p.m.* An architectonic treasure, the building that houses Rio's National Historical Museum boasts its own colorful history. Once the site of the 17th-century Santiago fortress which was constructed at the base of Castelo Hill to defend Guanabara Bay, it later became a military prison where slaves were detained and tortured. Since 1922, after the building was utilized for exhibitions during the Centennial celebrating Brazil's independence, the museum has remained in effect. The collection of over 130,000 objects from furniture and weapons to painting and sculpture tells the story of Brazilian history from the moment Cabral discovered its shores up to the time of the Republic in 1889. There is also a research library and an archive of manuscripts.

Museu da República *Rua do Catete, 153;* ☎ *225-4873 and 225-4875. Tues.-Sun. from noon-5 p.m. Free.* From 1887-1960, when the capital of Brazil was transferred to Brasília, the Catete Palace was the private residence and headquarters of the country's presidents. Today it's a historical museum starting where the national historical museum leaves off—at the beginning of the republic—featuring presidential memorabilia, including the bedroom where President Getúlio Vargas committed suicide. In 1985 the museum was restored; in evidence still are exquisite stained–glass windows and an impressive skylight. The Folklore Museum (see below) is located nearby. To get there, take the subway to the Catete stop.

Museu da Imagem e do Som *Praça Rui Barbosa, 1, Praça XV (downtown);* ☎ *262-0309. Mon.-Fri. 1-6 p.m.* The development of Brazil's social history as told through the media of books, film, photos, records, and tapes. Fascinating photos of Rio from the first 40 years of this century. Call to verify that it's open.

Music and Theater Museums

Museu Villa–Lobos *Rua Sorocaba, 200 (Botafogo);* ☎ *266-3845.* Established in 1960, in honor of Brazil's most famous classical composer—Heitor Villa-Lobos. If you don't know his works already, look up his *Bacchianas Brasileiras No. 5* for high soprano. There's also a display of personal possessions and original scores. Tapes and records are on sale.

Museu Carmen Miranda *Parque Brigadeiro Eduardo Gomes, in front of #560 of Av. Rui Barbosa (Flamengo);* ☎ *551-2597. Tues.-Fri. 11 a.m.-5 p.m., weekends and holidays 1-5 p.m.* Revel in the fruit-basket headdresses and tight ruffled dresses of the Brazilian songbird whose memory still lingers on in the drag queens of Miami. Stock up on T-shirts, postcards, and records. Located in Flamengo Park, near the Hotel Glória.

Native Culture

Museu do Indio (Indian Museum) *Rua das Palmeiras, 56 (Botafogo);* ☎ *286-8899. Mon.-Fri. 10 a.m.-5 p.m., closed weekends.* A must if you're headed for the Amazon, this small but discriminating collection of Indian artifacts tells the story of native life in Brazil. Exhibitions range from dress, jewelry, weapons, and daily utensils to a fascinating selection of native music and language. Researchers will also find the stock of documentary films on contemporary aboriginal issues provocative.

Museu do Folclore *Rua do Catete, 179;* ☎ *285-0441. Fri. 11 a.m.-6 p.m., weekends and holidays 3-6 p.m.* A wealth of art, artisanry, costumes, and utensils by popular Brazilian artists working within the various folk traditions of the country. A good introduction if you're headed to the Northeast.

Rocks, Gems, and Jewelry

Museu Amsterdam Sauer *Rua Garcia D'Avila, 105 (Ipanema);* ☎ *512-4746.*

Museu H. Stern *Rua Visconde de Pirajá, 490.* One of Brazil's greatest natural resources are the scores of semiprecious crystals and gemstones discovered mostly in the state of Minas Gerais since the 18th century. The art of creating fine jewelry from these semiprecious gemstones is also a well-developed Brazilian craft—a process that can be seen in the lapidary workshops of one of the country's leading jewelers, H. Stern. A free 15–minute tour conducted in a multitude of languages (through earphones) will guide you through the making of jewelry from the cutting and polishing of the stone to the design and construction of the finished piece. In the small museum on the same site you'll be able to view some of the world's largest uncut gemstones, both polished and raw. For big purchases, helpful salesmen who speak excellent English will assist you in private. Most clients at 4-star and 5-star hotels receive invitations that include free transportation, but you can also call one of the company's many outlets and arrange an appointment.

Astronomy

Planetário da Cidade do Rio de Janeiro *Praça Padre Leonel França;* ☎ *274-0096.* A bit disappointing if you've visited Epcot Center, but Rio's only planetarium should attract anyone interested in the constellations of the southern hemisphere. Forty-minute shows are held on Sun.: 4:30 p.m. for children, 6 p.m. for teenagers, and 7:30 p.m. for adults, with all explanations in Portuguese. The classical music soundtrack is both relaxing and inspiring. On Wed. when the sky is clear, an astronomist allows visitors to peruse the night skies through a telescope around 6:30 p.m.

Museu de Imagens do Inconsciente (Museum of Images of the Unconscious) *Rua Ramiro Magalhães, 521 (Engenho de Dentro);* ☎ *592-3242.*

SPORTS IN RIO

With its brilliant sunshine and magnificent shoreline, Rio is made for the outdoor life. Fueled by their passion for perfecting the body beautiful, *cariocas* can be seen jogging up and down the beaches from morning till night, riding bikes along the newly paved track beside the shoreline, and even chinning themselves on bars along the beach. Serious pumping and aerobics, however, take place inside the 3000 gyms in the city—many open to tourists on a special pass. Perhaps because of the heat, tennis is not a popular sport, nor is golf. However, for the eco-tourist, there are dozens of options for hiking, scuba, and boating in Rio, as well as in its surrounding environs. (See also *Green Rio* and *Greener Rio*.)

Equipment
Mako Sub
Av. Ataúlfo de Paiva, 1321-D (Leblon); ☎ 239-0899.
One of the most complete lines for sportswear and equipment for skiing, tennis, surfing, and scuba.
Escola de Vela
Marina da Glória; ☎ 285-3097.
Windsurfers and sailboats for hire.
Centro de Atividades Subaquáticas
Marina da Glória; ☎ 265-0797. and
Subshop
Rua Barata Ribeiro, 774; ☎ 235-5446.
These firms rent scuba-diving equipment and boats.

Hang Gliding, Paraflying, and Ultra-Leve
For thrills, sail off the 510-meter-high Pedra Bonita rock at São Conrado. This hang gliding flight, which costs about $75 and includes transportation from your hotel, lasts between 7 and 45 minutes, depending on the air currents. Landings arrive (hopefully) at Pepino Beach, also in São Conrado, with an ice-cold *água de coco* awaiting your pleasure. For more information, contact:
Super Fly Agency
Av. Epitácio Pessoa, 3624, room 201 (Lagoa); ☎ 322-2286 or 226-5207.

Owner Rui Marra, a super-champion among South American hang gliders, is considered a great pilot—and very handsome to boot! To share a flight on the same wings with an experienced pro (the first-timer's best bet), also contact
ABVL
Associação Brasileira de Vôo Livre
☎ 322-0266.
The public is free to watch the takeoffs at Sitio das Três Pedras, in the district of Pedra Bonita in São Conrado.
Participation in **ultra-leve (ultralight)** flights happens every third Sun. of the month, 8 a.m.-6 p.m. at the
Clube Esportivo de Ultra-Leve
Av. Embaixador Eduardo Bueno (next to the race track), gate 7, door 7 (Jacarepaguá); ☎ 342-8025.
This sport can be practiced in three types of ULM: amphibian, hydroplane, and land. With the ultra-leve sports club equipment, longer flights above the city up to 2-1/2 hours are possible. The land "ultralight" will carry two people and is available Tues.-Sun. 8 a.m.-6 p.m. for about $12.

Golf
Gávea Golf Club
Estrada da Gávea, 800; ☎ 322-4141.
Only accepts tourists staying at the Intercontinental and Rio Sheraton hotels. Available hours are Mon., Wed., and Fri. from 9 a.m.-7 p.m., and Tues. and Thurs. from noon on. Court rents for $40 per hour, plus equipment. On Sat. and Sun. you must be in the company of club members.
Itanhangá Golf Club
Estrada da Barra da Tijuca, 2005; ☎ 399-0507.
Tourists can play on weekdays. Weekends you must be accompanied by a member, when you may play free. If you play alone, the rent of the court is $100 and the equipment (clubs are called *tacos*) is $15. All nationalities converge here.

Health Clubs

Branches of the **Corpore Health Clubs** are some of the best places for like-minded, health-oriented singles to meet. Branches are located in Copacabana, Leme, Leblon, Ipanema, Barra, and São Conrado. Nautilus machines are available, as well as aerobic classes and juice bars. Tourists can pay for one session (about $6), or buy a special tourist 2-week pass. Locations include: *Rua Visconde de Pirajá 365;* ☎ *247-4049. Mon.-Fri. 6:00 a.m.-9:00 p.m., Sat. from 8:00 a.m.-11:00 a.m., 3:30-7:00 p.m. and São Conrado Estrada da Gávea, 468. Mon.-Fri. 6:30 a.m.-11:30 a.m. and 4:00-9:00 p.m.*

Heavy Duty Gym
Rua Barata Ribeiro, 181, loja I (Copacabana); ☎ *542-3045.*
800 meters of an excellently equipped gym, unabashedly based on "modelo Americano." Also classes in aerobics, ballet, stretch (*alongamento*), and children's judo.

AKXE Club
Av. Canal de Marapendi, 2900 (Barra da Tijuca); ☎ *325-3232. 7 a.m.-11 p.m.*
Here's a superlative club with a racing-size pool, tennis courts, volleyball and soccer fields, aerobic classes, and the most advanced weight equipment in the city. Price is about $12 per day including the sauna and pool. The **Top Bell Club**, at the Sheraton Rio and the Inter-Continental, accepts guests from other hotels for classes and weight lifting for about $11 an hour. Also, the best hotel pools can be found at the Rio Sheraton, the Inter-Continental, the Othon Palace, and the Rio Palace.

Helicopter Flight

Super Fly Agency
Av. Epitácio Pessoa, 3624, room 201; ☎ *322-2286.*
Flights for 10-15 minutes start at Jacarepaguá Airport for $75.

Hiking

Expeditours
Rua Visconde de Pirajá, 414/room 1010; ☎ *287-9697.*
The premier travel agency for outdoor hiking, Expeditours can arrange a myriad of options: treks through Tijuca Forest, treks up Alto Mourão Peak near Itacoatiara Beach, hikes through the Serra dos Orgãos National Park, and others. For more information, see *Greener Rio.* Several camping clubs in Rio offer group treks for minimal fees and provide a meeting place for like-minded enthusiasts:

Camping Club Turismo
☎ *240-5390 or 210-3171.*
A camping club favored by *cariocas*. The price depends on the trek.

Clube Excursionista Carioca
Rua Hilario de Gouveia, 71, room 206 (Copacabana)
The group meets *Wed. and Fri. at 9:00 p.m.*

Horse Racing

Jockey Club
Praça Santos Dumont (Gávea); ☎ *274-0055*
Night races are held Mon. and Thurs. with post time at 7:30 p.m. The last race finishes at 11:45 p.m. (Note that it is dangerous to leave very late at night. Security remains only inside the club.) Races on the weekend start at 2:30 p.m. The Brazilian Derby, the event of the year, is held the first Sun. of Aug. Tourists only pay $1 and are allowed to enter by the members' entrance; dining is available in the air-conditioned restaurant. Bets are made starting from a half hour to five minutes before each race, and can range from less than a dollar to $16. An official program lists the schedule and the favorite horses, and races run every half hour.

Jet Ski

At the **Lagoa Rodrigo de Freitas,** in front of the Corte do Cantagalo, is the principal point where jetski enthusiasts congregate for action. Also constantly utilized is the **Lagoa de Marapendi** in Barra. Demonstrations to the public are made Sat. and Sun. from 11 a.m.-5 p.m., weather permitting.

Jogging

Jog or bike in Tivoli Park around the lagoon or along the strand in Copacabana, Leme, Ipanema, and Leblon. The latter is packed in the early morning and evening.

Sailing

Foreign boats can dock at the Marina da Glória for up to six months. For more information on sailing equipment, contact:
Captain's Yacht Charters
☎ 252-4715/252-2227.

Scuba Diving

Hundreds of deserted islands, caves, and shipwrecks in Angra dos Reis (south of Rio) present the ideal conditions for scuba diving for both beginners and more experienced divers. Aquamaster in Rio has more than 25 years of experience in providing training and trips (including accommodations, food, transfer, and equipment). Complete instruction by accredited guides is offered, as well as housing, meals, equipment for rent, tanks, refills, and boats. In Rio, contact:
Aquamaster
Marina da Glória, counter 7;
☎ 205-7070/287-8015.
In Angra, contact
Aquamaster
Praia da Enseada, Estrada do Contorno, 100; ☎ *(243) 65-2416.*

Soccer

Cariocas, like all Brazilians, are mad about soccer, which they call futebol (footch–baw). Loyalties for home teams are nearly thicker than blood, and games held in **Maracanã** ☎ *(264-9962)* the world's largest stadium, are spectacles of passion—and I'm talking about the crowd. With firecrackers marking the goals and fierce drumbeats throughout the game, the sport played by fiercely competitive athletes is often more exciting than Carnaval. (The former soccer star Pelé is still considered one of the most beloved celebrities in the country.) The home teams of Rio are Botafogo, Flamengo, Fluminesne, and Vasco, and you might as well buy a team flag and wave it around like everyone else. Official schedules don't exist, but the season for city and state championships usually runs between March and Sept. National championships begin in Oct., with the finals held in Dec. or Jan. The cheapest way to see a game is to take a cab or bus to the stadium, located north of downtown, and buy a $2 ticket. That will get you a hard seat on the bleachers, but for $10 you can occupy a cushier reserved seat. Tour operators often sponsor group excursions that can minimize the chaos. If you go alone, check with your concierge first about the schedule and the availability of tickets.

The public may visit Maracanã Stadium Mon.-Fri. from 9 a.m.-4:30 p.m., and Sat. from 9 a.m.-1 p.m. There are no visits on Sun. except at games, which usually start at 5 p.m. The stadium holds 180,000 seats, with 480 special seats for journalists, and it takes its name from the river that flows through the area. (As well, the Indians used to call the birds who sat alongside the river *maracanã*.) Right beside the stadium is **Maracanazinho** (or small *maracanã*), which has been the stage for many important shows and sports competitions.

Tai Chi Chuan

In the **Praça Nossa Senhora da Paz** in Ipanema, free group classes of tai chi are held daily at sunrise and at five in the afternoon.

Tennis

The few public tennis courts available in Rio are generally not available to tourists because of long waiting lists. Foreign visitors, however, may book courts at the Rio Sheraton, the Inter-Continental, and the Nacional Hotels, even if they are not guests. The following private clubs accept bookings by tourists, but do call in advance:

Lob Tênis
Rua Stefan Zweig, 290 (Laranjeiras); ☎ *205-9997*

$20 for 1 hour to rent the court. Daily classes from 6 a.m.-10 p.m. Games played until midnight. Courtesy games are held on Sun.

Canaveral Club
Av. das Américas, 487 (Barra da Tijuca);
☎ *399-2192. 7 a.m.-6 p.m.*

Synthetic and sandy courts available. Sat. and Sun. are best in the afternoon.

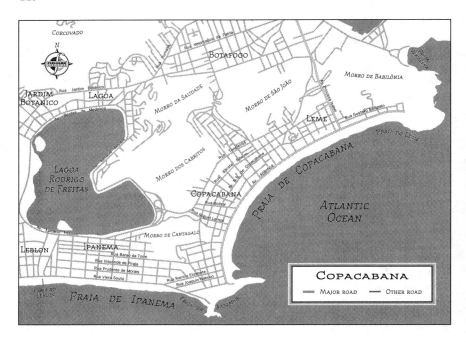

ART AND RELIGION IN RIO

RIO'S ART SCENE

There is a thriving art community in Rio, with numerous galleries. Some of the finest are listed below. Check the newspapers for announcements of openings, or ask the concierge if you're staying in a 5-star or 4-star hotel. Personal tours of galleries and museums may be guided by **Paulo César** ☎ *(21) 208-8369*, who himself is an up-and-coming abstract and naif artist.

Naif Art
(African and folkloric tendencies):
Galeria de Arte Jean Jacques *Rua Ramon Franco, 49 (Urca);* ☎ *542-1443.*

Contemporary Art
Galeria Saramenha *Shopping da Gávea, Rua Marques de São Vicente, 52, loja 165;* ☎ *274-9445.*
Galeria Bonino *Rua Barata Ribeiro, 578 (Copacabana);* ☎ *235-7831.*

Traditional Art
(Brazilian artists in European styles):
Galeria Europa *Av. Atlântica, 3056 B;* ☎ *256-4574.*
Galeria de Arte Borghese *Shopping da Gávea, Rua Marquês de São Vicente, 52;* ☎ *259-6793.*

Artist Studios

Buying work at the artist's studio is usually about 50 percent cheaper than buying from a gallery. You also get the opportunity to meet the artist in person and discuss his work (not to mention, snoop around his studio). The following artists open their studios to interested clients. Call to make appointments in advance.

Contemporary Abstract and Naif:
Barão de Morallis *Rua Torres Homem 440, casa 14 (101), Vila Isabel;* ☎ *208-8369.*

Conceptual Colorist:
Anisio Carvão *Rua Souza Lima, 138, apt. 1301;* ☎ *287-6800.*

Academic and Abstract Painting:
Rubens Monteiro *Rua Evaristo da Veiga, 35, apt. 1513;* ☎ *240-2751.*

Northeast Regionalist and Abstract:
Wanderley Santana *Rua Mem de Sá, 72, apt. 502;* ☎ *222-4772.*

RELIGIOUS SERVICES IN RIO

When you're far away from home, you may want to attend church services of your own denomination, or even visit others out of curiosity. One Sunday mass not to be missed is at the São Bento Church, where a group of monks chant Gregorian tunes.

Catholic masses performed in English:
Capela de N.S. das Mercês *Rua Visconde de Caravelas, 48 (Botafogo);* ☎ *246-5664 Sat. 6 p.m., Sun. 9:30 a.m.*

Jewish:
Sinagoga Beit Aron *Rua das Laranjeiras, 346;* ☎ *245-8044 Fri. 7:30 p.m., Sat. 9:15 a.m.*
Associação Religiosa Israelita *Rua General Severiano, 170 (Botafogo);* ☎ *295-6444. Fri. 6:30 p.m., Sat. at 8:30 a.m.*

Presbyterian:
Catedral Presbiteriana do Rio de Janeiro *Rua Silva Jardim, 23;* ☎ *262-2330. Sun. 10 a.m. and 7 p.m.*

Umbandista:
Tenda Espírita Mirim *Av. Marechal Rondon, 595 (São Francisco Xavier);* ☎ *261-3160.*

Candomblé:
Palácio de Iansã *Estrada Santa Efigênia, 152 (Taquara);* ☎ *342-2176. Sat. 10 p.m.*

Spiritualism:
Centro Espírita João Evangelista *Rua Mena Barreto, after Rua Conde de Irajá. Fri.–night sessions are open to the public.*

Yoga and Meditation:
Academia Brasileira de Yoga *Rua Visconde de Pirajá, 318, sobreloja 204;* ☎ *287-7048.*
Centro do Tibet *Rua Ribeiro de Almeida, 50 (Laranjeiras);* ☎ *205-0583.*
Lotus Center for Yoga *Rua Voluntários da Patria, 375, casa 2;* ☎ *246-2573.*

SHOPPING

As the largest shopping center in South America, Rio is an exotic blend of first-world and third-world goods. You can browse for designer labels in the most modern of shopping malls, bargain wildly for native crafts at street fairs, or negotiate wholesale prices in some of the finest jewelry stores in the world. Whether you're looking for a last-minute costume for Carnaval or the latest mini-bikini, you'll be able to find it in Rio.

The two main shopping drags in Rio are **Rua Visconde de Pirajá** in Ipanema and **Avenida Nossa Senhora de Copacabana** in Copacabana, both only a few blocks from the beach. They are, however, as different as day and night. Ipanema, of course, is the much more chic place to shop; the main drag is full of tiny, expensive boutiques with merchandise of international quality, including exquisite luggage, gorgeous evening dresses, fine leather jackets, and elegant men's wear. Some of the snappiest stores, however, are tucked into the many sidestreets that cross Rua Visconde de Pirajá both perpendicularly and at an angle. Days could be spent just wandering up and down, perusing the small but highly selective stocks.

Heart Of Rio

Experiencing the vibrancy of Copacabana's main shopping drag, however, is a must for those who want to throw themselves into the heart of Rio. Avenida Nossa Senhora de Copacabana stretches for about 2 miles, from Avenida Princesa Isabel (where the Meridien is located) to Rua Francisco Otaviano, but most businesses and vendors are concentrated between Rua Sá Ferreira and Avenida Princesa Isabel, with the busiest blocks directly behind the Copacabana Palace Hotel. The name of the street means Our Lady of Mercy and it dates back to the 18th century, when some Peruvian Quechua Indians gave a statue of the saint to the city. The avenue is so popular that sometimes you have to squeeze your way through crowds, but you will no doubt also pass homeless families of young women and children camped out on the sidewalk—if you feel like giving money, follow your conscience. From the boutiques to the streetside vendors, shoppers will discover everything they need (and don't need)—from fresh fruits, shoes, and lingerie to batteries, cheap watches, and even those complimentary airline slippers resold for a buck. (In 1994, the massive proliferation of these sidewalk vendors can only be attributed to the economic crisis.) There are also cinemas and record stores and tiny malls with restful benches and even waterfalls. And there are dozens of luncheonettes, juice bars, and casual restaurants where you can fill up on salads, rice, and meat for under $4.

Along the sidewalk on **Avenida Atlântica** in Copacabana, especially on weekends, street vendors set up stands of bikinis, towels, leather bags, maps, and various sculptured art made out of semiprecious rocks. (Other crafts fairs are listed below.) Stone-carved birds precariously perched on chunks of crystal are great buys and are usually half the price of those found in stores. If you become obsessed with these birds (as I did), you will find that the better ones evoke unique personalities. They make excellent gifts (even the tiny ones that go for around $3-5). Just make sure you repack them exceedingly well in newspaper—don't depend on store-wrapped techniques to be sufficient. Sadly, many birds in my crystal menagerie arrived home with their heads snapped. Soapstone sculptures don't travel well either.

Fairs are a good place to pick up souvenirs and less expensive craftwork, and a number of them, like those in Copacabana and Ipanema, are directly geared toward the tourist. Here, you should bargain like crazy, but watch your purse at all times, particularly when you take your money out to pay. Wandering through the vegetable and flower markets held weekly in the South Zone is also fun, and pretty girls are usually offered free samples.

Other fine souvenirs include the *figa* (a charm or statue made in the shape of a clutched fist, a sign of good luck in Brazil, though tradition says you can't buy one for yourself); folkloric-dressed dolls, Indian artifacts, *berimbaus* (stringed instruments made out of a gourd), clocks, coasters, letter openers, and chess sets made out of semiprecious stones, rose-quartz crystal balls, lace handiwork from the Northeast, hammocks (though they're much cheaper in Amazônia), music tapes, and tropical bird calendars.

Insider Tip:

Any boutique at a 5-star or 4-star hotel, while it may be convenient, is most likely to be outrageously overpriced. But only bargain on the street or at a fair. If you want a lower price in a fine store, discreetly ask if there is a promoção (sale) or if you could get a good rate for the dollar. Most often, if you pay in cash (as opposed to credit cards), you'll receive up to a 20 percent discount.

Choice stops for shopping are listed below. General business hours are from 9 a.m.-6 p.m. Mon.-Fri. and 9 a.m.-noon on Sat. Shopping centers are generally open Mon-Fri. 10 a.m.-p.m. and Sat. 10 a.m.-8 p.m. Stores usually don't close for lunchtime siestas.

WHERE TO SHOP IN RIO

Clothes: For Women Only

Insider Tip:
Unless you are petite, Brazilian clothes, which are already cut tight to hug the body, may not fit you. Best buys are leather jackets and leather shoes, but, in general, fine clothes and classic sportswear are more expensive in Rio (and Brazil) than in the States.

Blu 4
Rua Visconde de Pirajá, 444, # 126/129 (Ipanema). Mon.-Fri. 9 a.m.-7 p.m., Sat. 9 a.m.-2 p.m.
Brightly colored T-shirts and jersey dresses.

Daboukir
Rua Visconde de Pirajá, 225 E (Ipanema). Mon.-Fri. 9 a.m.-7 p.m., Sat. 9 a.m.-1:30 p.m.
Classy short and long beaded and chiffon gowns for last-minute affairs.

Elle et Lui
Rua Visconde de Pirajá, 393A (Ipanema). Mon.-Fri. 9 a.m.-7 p.m., Sat. 9 a.m.-12:30 p.m.
As boring as sophistication comes in Brazil—seriously yuppie fabrics and cuts at very high prices. If you wear clothes like this, why not just buy them in the States?

Folic
Rua Visconde de Pirajá, 540, loja B (Ipanema); ☎ 239-8997
Exquisite women's clothing with high-class sexy touches. A branch in Rio Sul Mall and Barra Shopping and downtown at Rua Gonçalves Dias, 49.

Heckel Verk
Rua Visconde de Pirajá, 547, loja E (Ipanema); ☎ 239-8891
Fine Brazilian designer with one-of-a-kind outfits. Just don't run into the glass door (everybody does).

Krishna
Rua Garcia D'Avila, 101 (Ipanema). Mon.-Fri. 9 a.m.-7 p.m., Sat. 9 a.m.-1 p.m.
Exquisitely stylish silk and linen separates. Stores in Leblon and Barra Shopping, with a special children's section in São Conrado Fashion Mall.

Optimo's by Leilah
Rua Visconde de Pirajá, 351/loja 109 (Ipanema)
Exquisite handmade leather and suede dresses. It's just a hunch, but if you really want something, bargaining with sophistication might bring down the high prices.

Piccola Gente
Rua Visconde de Pirajá, 371 (Ipanema). Mon.-Fri. 9 a.m.-7 p.m.
Stylish baby clothes.

Sagaró
Rua Visconde de Pirajá, 295 (Ipanema)
Good-quality, stylish women's shoes.

Comercial SA
Rua Visconde de Pirajá, 592, loja B (Ipanema).
The shop that entranced me—where upper-class madames buy their maids, valets, and chauffeurs their near-colonial-style uniforms.

Mariazinha
Rua Visconde de Pirajá, 365-B (Galeria Fiamma/Ipanema).
Chic women's shoes and handbags.

Pucci
Rua Visconde de Pirajá, 371 (Galeria Paranhos/Ipanema).
Excellent-quality women's shoes.

Bikinis

Miss Bikini
Rua Visconde de Pirajá, 177 (Ipanema); ☎ 521-1574.
Full line of one-and two-piece suits. All cards.

Bum Bum
Rua Visconde de Pirajá, 187, loja C (Ipanema); ☎ 287-4493.
"Bum Bum" in any language probably means the same thing. No cards.

Sunkini
Rua Visconde de Pirajá, 602, loja B. (Ipanema). Mon.–Fri. 9 a.m.–7 p.m., Sat. 9 a.m.–2 p.m.
Snappy collection of bikinis and one–piece suits—both the kind you could wear back in the States and the kind you can't.

Clothes: For Men Only

Eduardo Guinle
Rua Visconde de Pirajá, 514-A (Ipanema).
Elegant men's sports clothes, including oversized tropical shirts that won't embarrass you when you wear them in Boise.

Giorgio Armani
Rua Visconde de Pirajá, 559-A (Ipanema).
The name speaks for itself.

Pullman
Av. N.S. de Copacabana, 897 (Copacabana).
Fine men's wear.

Saint Gall
Av. N.S. de Copacabana, 420-C (Copacabana)
Chic, understated men's wear.

Dijon
Rua Garcia D'Avila, 110 (Ipanema)
Stylish men's wear.

Costume Jewelry, Etc.

Alana Bijoux
Rua Visconde de Pirajá, 580/103 (Ipanema); ☎ 259-7794. Mon.–Fri. 9 a.m.–7 p.m., Sat. 9 a.m.–4 p.m.
Small but excellent selection of knockoff watches, earrings, hair pieces, and whatnots for startling prices. All cards (but 15 percent added).

Shok Presentes
Rua Visconde de Pirajá, 580-A (Copacabana).
Perfumes, cosmetics, and costume jewelry.

Cosmetics

Boticário
Rua Visconde de Pirajá, 540 (Ipanema).
One of Brazil's great success stories, Boticário has its own factories that make all-natural perfumes, anti-allergic cosmetics, shampoos, and soaps. The masculine line is also very popular. You can find these stores throughout Brazil. All cards.

Fine Jewelry

Fine jewelry stores seem to be situated everywhere you look in Rio—from the lobby of your hotel to the airport and in every main shopping street and mall. As one of the world's largest suppliers of gold and semi-precious stones, Rio can offer anything from diamonds and emeralds to aquamarines, blue and gold topaz, tourmalines, and rubellites. Unless you're a pro, stick to the top stores, which can guarantee the quality of your purchase and will treat you with deference. **H. Stern**, perhaps the biggest name in Brazil, makes it easy for tourists at 5-star and 4-star hotels by inviting them to a free tour of their workshop and main headquarters, located at Rua Visconde de Pirajá, 490; transportation is included. The other big names in Brazil are **Amsterdam Saeur**, as well as **Moreno**, **Natan**, **Masson**, and **M. Rosenmann**.

> **Insider Tip:**
>
> If you do buy jewelry, you'll be better off paying in cash (or dollars), as you will not receive a good exchange on your credit card. Also, take your purchase immediately back to your hotel and secure it in the hotel safe until you are ready to leave for home. Whatever you do, avoid the impulse to wear it in Rio.

Records

One of the best ways to remember Brazil is to go home with its music. In Rio, you can find not only the best albums of Brazilian popular music, but also a smattering of various regional artists as well. And don't forget the great masters of Brazilian classical music, like Heitor Villa-Lobos. What's terrific is that you can usually listen to recordings on the store's equipment before you buy them (this habit began a few years back when customers kept bringing back records they didn't like and demanding refunds). Salespersons will usually be helpful, and in fact, checking out the newest recordings is a great way to while away a rainy day in Rio. It's also not a bad idea to check whatever you do buy before you leave the store; the sealed cassette I bought of sexy Bahiana Daniela Mercury turned out to be Roberto Carlos singing out-of-date love songs.

Sad to say, recorded music is much more expensive here than in the States; as of 1993, the latest cassettes (*fitas*) run about $10, while CDs run about $20. You can usually receive a 20 percent discount if you pay in cash. Some of the best buys are videos—of carnaval, bossa nova, and even erotica. If you're a fan of Caetano Veloso, look for his newly released concert performance entitled *Circuladô*.

Gabriela Discos
Av. N.S. de Copacabana, 683 (Copacabana); Rua Visconde de Pirajá, 422 (Ipanema) and Rio Sul Shopping Center
One of the best record stores for new releases.

Cocoon
Av. N.S. de Copacabana, 98–A (Copacabana); ☎ *295-2596 and Rua Gustavo Sampaio, 676 (Leme);* ☎ *541-2596*
A full line of jazz, pop, and videos. The store in Leme is the best.

Copadisco
Av. N.S. de Copacabana, 340 (Copacabana); ☎ *235-2977.*
A full line of MPB, rock, jazz, lambada, and video tapes of Carnaval and erotica. *Cards: V, DC.*

Souvenir Shops/ Crystals/Semiprecious Gems

Ely's Gem, Jewelry & Souvenirs
Av. N.S. de Copacabana, 249, loja D–E (Copacabana). Mon.–Fri. 9 a.m.–7:30
p.m., Sat. 9 a.m.–6 p.m.
Some of the best selections of crystal-carved birds, as well as jewelry, coasters, clocks, and chess boards made out of semiprecious stones. The huge raw amethysts are gorgeous. To ship large rocks (25 kilos) to the States will run about $150. *All cards (dollars and traveler's checks).* Fielding's readers who show the book receive a 20 percent discount.

Rio Souvenirs Ltd.
Rua Fernando Mendes, 28-D, at the corner of Av. N.S. de Copacabana (Copacabana). Mon.–Fri. 9 a.m.–7 p.m., Sat. 9 a.m.–3 p.m.
Largest collection of *mulata* samba dolls dressed à la Carmen Miranda and in a variety of Carnaval costumes—excellent for little girls. *No cards.*

Rising
Rua Santa Clara, 50, room 301-302 (Copacabana); ☎ *256-3287. Mon.–Fri. 9 a.m.–10 p.m., Sat. 9 a.m.–4 p.m.*
A small, soothing gem-and-crystal store most conducive to clients who are seriously into healing. Owner Miumar Mothé, who comes from a traditional family rooted in the mining business, can speak only a little English, but she is one of the foremost esoteric experts on crystals in Brazil. There's a good selection of raw crystals and semiprecious stones, but most charming are the amazingly lifelike wood carvings of gnomes. Courses (in Portuguese) are also given on UFO-ology, tarot, runes, Bach Flowers, and numerology. Open house is held on Fri. night at 8 p.m. for those who want to meet like-minded souls.

Pharmacies
Pharmacists give shots and also dispense advice freely. You can also buy some toiletries, and there's usually a big scale in kilos. The following pharmacies are open 24 hours and some English is spoken:

Farmácia Piauí
Av. Ataúlfo de Paiva, 1283A (Leblon); ☎ *274-8448.*

Farmácia Piauí
Rua Barata Ribeiro, 646 B (Copaca-

bana); ☎ 255-7445.
Farmácia do Leme
Av. Prado Júnior, 237 (Copacabana); ☎ 275-3847.

Books/Magazines

Alpharrabio
Rua Visconde de Pirajá, 365-B/loja B (Ipanema).
Duck around the bend in this shopping center to find a funky antique bookstore full of 30-year-old Brazilian magazines and even older books. Sifting through dust piles, I even found a pre-*Manchete* magazine with pictures of the 1956 Carnaval for only $6.

Astral e Magicos
Rua Visconde de Pirajá, 595, loja 108 (Ipanema); ☎ 512-3365. Mon.–Sat. 9:30 a.m.-7 p.m.
A small book and crystal store with New Age paraphernalia, including tarot cards, runes, incense, and trance music.

Casa Piano
Rua Visconde de Pirajá, 365 (Ipanema). Mon.–Fri. 9 a.m.–6 p.m.
Best newsstand in Rio, where you're likely to see Tom Jobim sniffing through the French and English newspapers and magazines. Good American paperbacks for a hefty price. Located across the sidewalk from Casa Piano is a travel agency with a reputable *câmbio* (money exchange).

Kosmos
Rua do Rosário, 155 and in front of the Copacabana Hotel, Av. Atlântica, 1702 (Copacabana).
Excellent coffee-table books on Brazilian subjects, prints of old Rio perfect for gifts, and calendars with photos of the exotic birds of Brazil. However, everything here will be extremely expensive.

Nova Galeria de Arte
Av. N.S. de Copacabana, 241, loja D. (Copacabana); ☎ 255-4055. Mon.–Fri. 9 a.m.-7 p.m., Sat. 9 a.m.-5 p.m.
A fine bookstore in Copacabana where you can buy such classics as *Brazilian Cookery, Traditional and Modern* by Margarette de Andrade, and the beautiful picture book *Botanical Gardens of Rio de Janeiro* by Tom Jobim (the composer) and Zeka Araújo. *All cards.*

Livrarias Sicilianas
Av. N.S. de Copacabana, 591 (Copacabana).
One of the biggest and best chains in Brazil, with an impressive selection of American and foreign magazines, including the *Harvard Business Review* and lots of rock magazines. Also, a lot of esoterica, including the works of French psychic Alan Kardec, who profoundly influenced the spiritualist movement in Brazil.

Unilivros
Av. N.S. de Copacabana, 445/A (Copacabana); ☎ 235-1594.
Full of interesting books on esoterica and spirituality in Portuguese. Also unearthed were several copies of *Birds of Brazil* in English and Jacques Cousteau's *Amazônia*, a classic adventure-photo album.

Luggage/Handbags

Victor Hugo
Rua Visconde de Pirajá, 507 (Ipanema). Mon.–Fri. 9 a.m.-7 p.m., Sat. 9 a.m.-4 p.m.
Best name for leather in Brazil, with finely crafted women's purses, wallets, and exquisite luggage. Luscious leather backpacks run about $125. A branch can also be found in Rio Sul Shopping Center.

A Mala do Rio
Rua Dias da Rocha, 9-A (Copacabana); ☎ 237-7021.
Good luggage for last-minute overweights. Just one note: if you buy luggage in Brazil, be careful when picking it up at the airport in the States; there'll be many Brazilians with similar luggage on your flight.

Foods

Kopenhagen Chocolates
Av. N.S. de Copacabana, 583A (Copacabana). Mon.–Sat. 9 a.m.–9 p.m., Sun. 10 a.m.–6 p.m.
Simply, the best chocolates in Brazil. A gift from here would be most appreciated by any Brazilian. Get some for yourself. *All cards.*

Paes Mendonça Hipermercado
Av. das Américas (Barra da Tijuca). Mon.

2 p.m.–10 p.m., Tues.–Sat. 8:30 a.m.–10 p.m.

"Hiper" is even bigger than super in Portuguese—here is the country's most famous oversized supermarket, and probably the only one in the world that doesn't allow you to take photos. Which is unfortunate, because pretty young clerks zoom through the aisles on roller skates wearing very short skirts. Anything that's available in Brazil is here at good prices, including gourmet cheeses, Argentine butter, and all sorts of dietetic products. More important, this is the place to see Brazilian culture in action, but notice that you will rarely see a single woman shopping alone. Expect crowds, watch your wallet, and whatever you do, don't stand on the orange lines in front of the checkouts, or the roller skaters will zoom you down.

Natural Food Stores

Amigos do Trigo
Rua das Laranjeiras, 462, loja 7;
☎ 255-5590. Mon.–Sat. 7 a.m.–5 p.m.
A bakery and natural foods stand since 1984, Amigos offers freshly baked, 100 percent whole-wheat loaves of bread, cookies, cakes, oatmeal, and other products. Another larger health food store is right around the corner in the same shopping center.

Cereal Panificação Integral
Rua Siqueira Campos, 143, loja 87;
☎ 237-2999.

Vida Integral Produtos Naturais
Rua Figueira Magalhães, 741, loja H;
☎ 237-0748.

Macro Nature Produtos Macrobióticas e Naturais
Rua Miguel Lemos, 51. loja F;
☎ 247-3941.

Photo Development

Klub Foto
Rua Visconde de Pirajá, 318 (Ipanema)
Two nice Jewish brothers who do excellent development, fast.

Kronokoma Foto
Rua do Russel, 344–loja E (Glória);
☎ 285-1993.
The most professional photo lab in Rio. Slides developed in 2 hours, contact sheets in

6. Prints take a week. Near the Hotel Glória.

Revelação
Rua Visconde de Pirajá, 511 (Ipanema).
Mon.–Sat. 8 a.m.–7 p.m.
One–hour express development. One-hour development stands can also be found at Rio Sul and Barra shopping centers.

Shopping Centers

I have a deep passion for the shopping malls of Rio. The top three, Rio Sul, São Conrado Fashion Mall, and Barra Shopping Center, are all modern, with-it malls where you can pick up anything from toothpaste and fine shoes to evening clothes and sexy beachclothes. Not to mention jeans, jeans, jeans—a Brazilian obsession. If you get overwhelmed by the third-world buzz, these air-conditioned oases make for a few cool hours of diversion or even a full day's distraction, such as at Barra, with its myriad forms of entertainment.

Rio Sul
Rua Lauro Muller, 16 (Botafogo). Mon.–Sat. 10 a.m.–10 p.m.
Closest shopping center to Copacabana, Rio Sul is a modern multilevel mall of 400 shops with a great ice cream and yogurt stand on the first floor and a culinary floor of intriguing fast foods on the top. The shopping center is about a $2 ride from the Meridien Hotel, but don't walk as you have to go through a tunnel. Many hotels have complimentary bus service. Best bets include Bee Infantil for children's wear, Sapasso for shoes, Canteen for women's wear, Ocean Pacific for surfwear, Bijoux Access for costume jewelry and accessories, and 1 Hora Revelações for photo development.

São Conrado Fashion Mall
Estrada da Gávea, 899 (São Conrado).
Mon.–Sat. 10 a.m.–10 p.m.
About a $5 cab ride from Ipanema, this sophisticated 2-level mall near the InterContinental Hotel has the classiest stores in Rio. Best bets are highly fashionable children's clothes at Joanna João, knitwear at Asparagus, Carmen Miranda T-shirts at Boy's House, leather bags, shoes, and belts at Carmen, teen sportswear at Philippe Martin and

Company, traditional Northeastern lace at Borogodó, fine linen dresses at Chocolate, expensive Brazilian shoes at Mezzo Punto (they give a tiny gold shoe as a present that allows discounts on future purchases), women's clothes at Champagne, Banana Republic styles at Bill Bros., and Livrarias Sicilianas for books. Hair stylist Alan Duran at Parruchiere is one of the best in Rio.

Barra Shopping
Av. das Américas, 4666 (Barra da Tijuca). Mon.–Sat. 10 a.m.–10 p.m.

Some consider Barra to be the best mall in Rio. Located in Barra da Tijuca, it boasts 3 cinemas, an amusement park for children, an ice-skating rink, Rio's only bowling alley, video games, and restaurants from fine foods to McDonald's. Air-conditioned buses run from most hotels to the mall. Best bets include Bee for unisex wear, Gabriela Discos for records, Temper Roupas for men's wear, Formosinho for sportswear, Love Rio for souvenirs, and Le Postiche for leather goods and accessories.

Rio Design Center
Av. Ataúlfo de Paiva, 270 (Leblon)

is a mecca for interior designers, with numerous showrooms featuring the finest in home furnishings. There are also several art galleries, as well as antiques stores.

Shopping Center Casino Atlântico
Av. Atlântica, 4240 (Copacabana).

Attached to the Rio Palace Hotel, this small mall features souvenir shops, jewelry stores, and antiques shops with inflated prices. There's also a tea room and a dark, relaxing atrium.

Fairs

Hippie Fair (Copacabana)
Praça do Lido. Sat. and Sun. 8 a.m.-10 p.m.

About 300 artisans exhibit and sell paintings, sculptures, ceramics, leather goods, jewelry, clothing, and dolls. A fine place to bargain for the perfect gift. Remember, the knickknacks that look like nothing always seem to look ten times better when you get them home.

Hippie Fair (Ipanema)
Praça General Osório between Ruas Jangadeiros and Teixeira de Mello Sun. 9 a.m.–6 p.m.

A large, crowded open–air market that has rarely lived up to its reputation. The stop is obligatory, though, for first-time tourists, who may find the leather bags, lace embroidery, and hippie-style jewelry enticing. Don't carry snatchable bags and keep your wits about you. Bargain like crazy.

Daily Fair (Copacabana)
In front of Rio Othon Hotel, Av. Atlântica, 3264

Various handicrafts, paintings, and sculptures can be purchased daily 6 p.m.-midnight.

Northeast Fair
Sun. from 6 a.m.–1 p.m. in the Campo de São Cristavão, close to the Quinta da Boa Vista Vendors in traditional Northeast clothes sell a variety of crafts, typical foods, and clothing accompanied by the strains of the *zabumba* (bass drums) and *sanfonas* (accordions). Good buys are colorful hammocks, leather sandals, and straw items. Take the bus marked São Cristavão 461 from Ipanema or #463 from Copacabana.

Praca XV Square
near the Arco dos Telles. Thurs. and Fri.
One of Rio's oldest fairs peddles everything from typical foods to handicrafts and coins.

Antiques Fair
Praça Antero de Quental (Leblon)
Held by the Rio de Janeiro Antique Dealers Association on *Sun. from 10 a.m.–6 p.m.*

Antiques Fair
Praça Marechal Ancora (downtown). Sat. from 8 a.m.–5 p.m.

You can bargain for pricey European antiques from the 18th century.

HOTELS

Whether you stay three days or three weeks in Rio, choosing the accommodation appropriate to your needs can go a long way toward assuring a happy, even safe vacation. As a city geared for pleasure, Rio offers hotel rooms for every sized wallet—from the most princely suites with wraparound verandas to more modest digs for under $20 a night. If you've come to Rio to tan, you'll be glad to know that most of the best hotels are located right in the Zona Sul (or South Zone), along the beaches of Copacabana, Ipanema, and Leblon. In fact, if your hotel boasts an address on Avenida Atlântica or Avenida Delfim Moreira, all you'll have to do is cross the street and throw yourself into the waves.

Although EMBRATUR, the official tourist board of Brazil, rates hotels according to stars, the results are not really comparable to North American standards, though they do suggest the availability of certain facilities, as well as prices. In general, all 5-star hotels have a pool, nightclub, at least two excellent restaurants, a bar, gym, sauna, and hair salon. Four-stars generally boast a good restaurant, bar, and sauna. Three-stars usually differ from 4 only in a slight downgrading of decor, while 2-stars, with no extra amenities, offer only breakfast. Every hotel room has air-conditioning. Where you'll really feel the crunch is in the quality of the "American" breakfast included free of charge in all rates. Five-star hotels outdo each other with fabulous spreads of breads, cheeses, deli meats, fruits, and often freshly made omelets, while a 2-star hotel won't serve much more than a roll and coffee.

Location is important. A quick perusal of the section on beaches will give you an idea of the neighborhood behind each strand. In general: Copacabana, while one of my favorite places, is not the safest or quietest place to stay these days; however, it is at the heart of the city's pulse, and many of the best restaurants, as well as nightly hangouts, are within walking distance. The beaches of Ipanema and Leblon attract more "beautiful people," while Barra these days is considered the hippest beach, with the most preserved shoreline and the highest quotient of celebrity sightings.

If you're concerned about **safety**, the Caesar Park and the Meridien Hotel both provide excellent beach security, with hidden patrols surveilling the strand in front of the hotels at all times. The safest beachside hotel is probably the Sheraton Rio, on an isolated strip of sand that is closely patrolled by its staff. Unfortunately, it's located about 30 minutes from the South Zone. As for valuables, the best hotels have safes in the rooms, as well as professionally secured drawers behind the reception desk. If you stay at a 3-star or 2-star without safes in the rooms, don't bring any valuables, and think twice before you rent a security box at reception.

No question about it—staying in a luxurious hotel like the Caesar Park or Rio Palace can be a memorable experience, but if you can't swing it, here's how to **save substantial bucks** without feeling the pinch. Hotels located a few blocks from the main beach drags are generally cheaper, and the walk isn't bad—*cariocas* are used to seeing bathers stroll through the streets wearing only a coverup. And who needs a pool in Rio, anyhow? Restaurants, hair salons, bars, and nightclubs at fine hotels are always open to the public. And as for exercise equipment, you might have more fun buying a tourist pass at a neighborhood gym, where you're bound to meet more natives.

For some, a good option is one of the newly trendy **apart-hotels**—residences that are run like hotels but are actually private, completely stocked apartments that may be rented daily. They usually run half the price of hotels and often are better decorated. Those in Barra have all been built in the last five to seven years. Breakfast and maid service is usually included, although the kitchen is fully equipped for cooking. These accommodations are especially good for families or large groups of singles wanting to budget, although the quality of some apart-hotels is so superb you often can't believe the price. A medium-priced two-bedroom apartment runs about $50 a day.

As for **reservations**, anyone arriving in Rio without one is living life on the edge. During high season (Dec.–Feb.), the best rooms are sure to be taken, and you will be lucky to even find a suitable option. Reservations for Carnaval and during New Year's must be made six months in advance.

If you want to stay at a 5–star hotel anywhere in Brazil and don't want to take the trouble to research them, the American-based, Brazilian-owned **F & H Travel Consulting** can steer you to excellent accommodations and make all arrangements. *Contact in California: 2441*

Janin Way, Solvang, CA 93463; ☎ (1-800-544-5503); FAX (805) 688-1021.

WHERE TO STAY

IN RIO

Rates:
Room rates given in this guide usually refer to high season, but note that rates around Carnaval and other prime holidays may be doubled. Discounts during low-season sometimes run as high as 20 percent; Fielding's readers (with book in hand!) can receive an extra 10 to 15 percent on choice hotels, as noted by this icon:

Very expensive -------- **Over $140**

Expensive -------------- **$80–$140**

Moderate --------------- **$40–$80**

Inexpensive ------------ **Under $40**

Insider Tip:

Do "use" your concierge for everything; that's his job. He can make and confirm reservations at restaurants, tell you what musical performances are happening; arrange excursions, etc. It's also best to have him check whether restaurants and clubs you are headed for are still open; things change very fast all over Brazil.

5–star Hotels

★ **Caesar Park**
Av. Vieira Souto, 460 (Ipanema);
☎ (21) 287-3122; FAX 247-7975.
Perhaps the most elegant hotel in Brazil, the Caesar Park in chic Ipanema winningly combines first-class professional service with the kind of luxuries international tourists demand. And for good reason—the Japanese management is part of the Leading Hotels of the World. Which is not to say that Brazilian charm does not abide everywhere; from the mints on your pillow at night to the excellent *feijoada* buffet on Sat., the hotel does everything to make its guests feel the high rates are worth it. The lobby, with its oriental rugs, tropical flowers, and huge grand piano, is immediately inviting, though not exactly the place for screaming kids. The private rooms are just as lavish. The standard, superior, and deluxe suites differ primarily in the view and floor level. Becoming a preferred choice for singles is the *solteiro*, a nook of a studio with single bed, special furnishings, and a magnificent mahogany desk. The white-and-wicker breakfast room resembles a charming teahouse; breakfast is an impeccably arrayed buffet with a chef who prepares fresh omelettes. The Petronius, long considered one of the finest restaurants in Rio, is now undergoing a change to classical European cuisine; there's also an outrageously expensive Japanese sushi bar. An English-style pub, the prettiest around, nightly offers the kind of soft bossa nova you rarely hear on the radio. A small pool is easily usurped by the beach across the street, but it does offer private tanning space. The hotel's special security force takes the sting out of beachcombing: two lifeguards (one stationed rooftop) constantly keep sight of clients, who may be identified by the yellow beach tag supplied to each room. A special Carnaval kit includes a ball for guests and visitors, as well as samba shows during meals. In 1993, the hotel began sponsoring music and arts programs throughout the city; if you attend these performances, you can receive a 20 percent discount at their most prestigious restaurant, Petronius, overlooking the shoreline of Ipanema. 221 apts. *Very expensive.* All cards.

Copacabana Palace
Av. Atlântica, 1702 (Copacabana);
☎ (21) 255-7070; FAX 235-7330.
Certainly one of the oldest landmarks along the southern beach drag, the Copacabana

Palace has never lost its reputation as the most elegant address in Copacabana; in fact, its palatial facade always reminds me of a great white wedding cake. Inside, old money talks loud; unfortunately so does old furniture. Thankfully, the English group Orient Express has recently purchased the hotel and is making extensive renovations. Photos from 1923 show the newly built hotel surrounded by untamed space; now it's wedged in by high-rises, elegant jewelry stores, an exotic flower shop, and dozens of apartment buildings. The Palace's enormous pool has been compared to that of the Beverly Hills Hilton, not only for its size but for its social-climbing activity. Guests might be lucky enough to stumble over a society wedding, held in the chandelier-filled Salão Nobre, with its massive wraparound veranda. The main building has 10 floors, the annex has 6, filled with 75 suites. Deluxe rooms hold double beds, a desk, and art deco lamps; standards are somewhat smaller. Any room with a veranda overlooking the beach is the place to be on New Year's Eve. Newly decorated rooms, seen in 1993, are cheerful and light; rooms have also been soundproofed. The breakfast room is one of the most pleasant in Rio, with freshly made pancakes and omelettes, and the highly formal Bife de Ouro restaurant serves international cuisine with an Italian buffet every Thurs. Teatime, a tradition among Brazilian women with stiffly teased hair, is a cultural event not to be missed; make reservations a week in advance. For high-season, rooms must be booked 6 months in advance. 223 apts. *Expensive*. All cards.

Everest Rio Hotel
Rua Prudente de Moraes, 1117 (Ipanema); ☎ *(21) 287-8282; FAX 521-3198.*
Tucked into a side street of Ipanema a few easy blocks to the beach, the 17-year-old Everest Rio is a 5-minute walk from Chaika's, one of my favorite stops for pizza and ice cream sundaes. The lobby makes an elegant statement without overwhelming, the burnt–orange leather couches warm the speckled marbled floors. Mon. through Fri. the hotel is filled with executives; weekends

attract pleasure-seeking tourists. Promotions are available year-round. Standards have only a slice of ocean view squeezed between high-rises; deluxe rooms look out to the Lagoa and Corcovado. Families will particularly appreciate the suites, which easily sleep four: the bedroom is twice the size of most rooms and the living room comes with a couch bed. The pool on the top floor lies under an open sky, and a separate playground will keep children occupied. Sauna is available for men only. An elegant restaurant with live music is open to the public, and the coffee shop off the lobby is especially attractive, with flowered banquettes and a fast-food counter. Three convention salons cater to large groups. A hair salon and small boutique are also on premises. 166 apts. *Expensive*. All cards.

★ **Glória**
Rua do Russel, 632 (Glória); ☎ *(21) 205-7272; FAX 245-1660.*
One of the most beautiful white facades in the city, the recently refurbished Glória is actually two hotels in one—the first, a 5-star page out of *Art and Antiques* magazine, and the second, a budget alternative for large and small groups. The owners, who live on the 10th floor, are antiques fiends who shop the world to furnish the Glória's rooms with an individuality unsurpassed in Brazil. The classical lobby brings back memories of *Dangerous Liaisons*, with sculptured ceilings, love seats, crystal chandeliers, and antique phones that really work. The suites are just as lavish; incredibly enough, there's never been one theft. Suites with two rooms are individually designed and boast some kind of objet d'art in every corner. The best buy is the Imperial Suite, for about $110/night: draped in satin and brocade, with Oriental carpets, an antique French receptionist desk, and sculptured arches over the bed. Only the standard rooms remain nearly featureless, though they are large enough to fit three single beds with room to spare. Do ask for a reformed standard, which usually includes Oriental rugs and antique sofas. Singles may love Room 802, which, despite a strangely skinny bed, boasts an exquisite mahogany desk and col-

ored chandelier. A few suites and superiors on the 4th floor have sit-on verandas. With its full view of downtown and the Marina da Glória, the panoramic pool is a lovely place to relax as the sun goes down on the city. The gourmet restaurant La Grita offers a different cuisine daily; there is also an indoor pool restaurant where Cokes run about $2. The dark, sexy, cavernlike bar is open till 1 a.m. During Carnaval, the Glória hosts the Concurso de Desfile—a costume competition famous in the city. Security is tight because the vice-governor lives here. 700 rooms. *Moderate-expensive. All cards.*

Inter–Continental Rio
Av. Pref. Mendes de Moraes, 222 (São Conrado); ☎ *(21) 322-2200; FAX 322-5500.*

The Inter-Continental is a large, sprawling hotel situated in one of the recently developed condo areas outside Rio proper. Despite its size, however, the hotel is so intelligently designed that it is virtually impossible to get lost. More dated than the Sheraton, the hotel is set to be refurbished; presently it's reminiscent of a Club Med. An elegant arcade of shops and restaurants winds around to a sensuous pool complex, which includes a children's pool and several waterfalls. Breakfast is served poolside in an open–air restaurant, which doubles as a breezy lunch buffet. Perfect for families are the 20 cabanas that face the pool. Appointed in lime green, beige, and mauve, the spacious standards differ only from the deluxes in view; in fact, many prefer the standards for their eclectic vistas of ocean, mountain, and Corcovado. All rooms have direct–dial telephones and safes; most bathrooms have tubs and hairdryers. A business center includes a stunning meeting room with free drinks and canapés, international access TV, video and journals, and a multilingual secretary. Tennis courts are not gratis. Guests may use the *Gávea Golf Club* (for about $100). Dining options are richly varied: French candlelight dinner at Monseigneur, pasta at Alfredo (from the man who invented Fettucine Alfredo), and "the best hamburgers south of Miami" at a '50s-style luncheonette. Im-

probably hungry guests can also walk a block to São Conrado Fashion Mall, the chic-est in Rio, which is packed with other eateries. Special activities in July will keep children out of the hair of their parents, who can spend their day drinking *cachaça* at the bar inside the pool, or sunbathing at the beautiful beach across the street. The hotel is also a perfect spot for viewing the hang gliders diving off Lookout Rock. 463 apts. *Expensive. All cards.*

Internacional
Rio Av. Atlântica, 1500 (Copacabana); ☎ *(21) 295-2323; FAX 542-5443.*

Two years old, the Internacional Rio is a well–coordinated, well-organized hotel that serves executives, as well as international tourists. A sleek modern sheen characterizes the decor of both the corridors and the apartments. Deluxe rooms are extremely spacious, in black, white, and gray decor, with muted lighting and verandas that make them an excellent choice for New Year's, especially if you're looking to party. The marble bathrooms are particularly attractive and come with tub/showers. In the suites, a Japanese sliding door separates the bedroom from the sitting room. All apartments have safes and a telephone in the bathroom. A gastronomic festival featuring the cuisine and music of different cultures is held every two months. Breakfast is taken in a sleek and modern wraparound restaurant with a fabulous view of the beach. The 6th–floor business center is stocked with computers, telex, Fax, typewriters, and multilingual secretaries. Compact and sleek, the lobby bar is known for its special *caipirinhas*—honey, *cachaça*, and a few drops of Cointreau. The designer of the building, João Fortes Co., is now invading Barra, with a resort opening soon. Fielding readers receive a special discount. 117 apts. *Expensive. All cards.*

Marina Palace
Rua Delfim Moreira, 630 (Leblon); ☎ *(21) 259-5212, FAX 259-0941.*

Located along the beach drag in the high-class neighborhood of Leblon, so expect only similarly rich people to sun on the sand dunes beside you. An elegant hush seems to pervade this hotel; corridors are wood-paneled and illuminated with muted light. Bedrooms, individually decorated, all have brightly colored spreads with enamel and wood headboards; wicker chairs and glass-topped tables make a stylishly upbeat effect. Safes can be found in the closets. Standard rooms offer a lateral view of the beach, but also a peek at the rooftops of the neighboring apartment building—terrific, considering all the nude suntanning. Suites face the ocean. Clients include lots of Americans, Japanese, French, and Germans, who appreciate the fine service. The pool on the open rooftop is minuscule, but it does offer a wraparound view of the city. There are two restaurants and a hair salon. Fielding readers receive a 20 percent discount. 160 apts. *Expensive. All cards.*

Le Meridien
Av. Atlântica, 1020 (Leme);
☎ *(21) 275-9922; FAX 541-6447.*
One of Rio's most lavish hotels, the French owned Meridien knocks itself out to provide the best possible service for its international clientele. One of the Meridien's best advantages is its location in the family–filled neighborhood of Leme—5 minutes from Rio Sul shopping center, around the block from excellent restaurants and fast-food joints, and across the street from some of the most exotic shows in Rio. Entrance into the hotel is dramatic: escalators quickly skirt you up to the 2nd–floor reception, where elegant red-suited clerks greet you in a lobby lush with huge crystals and overstuffed banquettes. Even the young elevator boys, their chinstrap caps perched jauntily on their heads, look like they just stepped out of an MGM movie. Standards—spacious, with an added entrance hall—are done in shades of blue, with plush carpets and a lateral view of the sea. Superior rooms boast a full view of the sea, though windows are not uniformly clean. Most impressive are the enormous luxe suites, with raised living area, pillow couches, queen-size bed, two bathrooms, and trellised shutters opening onto the sea. All bathrooms have tubs, make-up mirrors, and Hermès toiletries; all rooms have safes

and 110 volts. The hotel's special festivities are legendary: the New Year's Eve Ball, the Carnaval Costume Parade and Competition, and Oct. international backgammon tournaments. A strong conciergerie takes care of all tickets for excursions and entertainment. The troop restaurants are all first-class. Café de la Paix is a Toulouse-Lautrec-style salon where society ladies gather each afternoon for extravagant teas; Le St. Trop Café, overlooking the beach, is *the* place to sample French pastries and Brazilian delicacies. Around the pool, a daily barbecue buffet serves four kinds of meat and numerous salads; and Le Saint Honoré, on the top floor, not only won best restaurant in 1991 but also offers the best nighttime view of the beach. For late–night music, Le Rond Point Bar, on the first floor, is a chrome-and-glass wonder, with real Magrittes, a stunning wraparound bar, backgammon tables, and sexy maroon couches. 496 apts. *Expensive. All cards.*

Nacional Rio
Av. Niemeyer, 769 (São Conrado);
☎ *(21) 322-1000; FAX 322-0058.*
The best thing about the Nacional Rio is the Free Jazz Concerts held annually in its massive convention center. In fact, everything about the Nacional is massive; unfortunately, it lacks the warmth necessary for a top-class resort. Built in 1972, it is located on an isolated though pristine beach in the poshly developed area of São Conrado; however, the beach can only be reached by crossing a major highway. The hotel is primarily frequented by large groups—the kind that enjoy loud samba bands during lunch. Perhaps the most intriguing feature is the aesthetic beauty clinic, which includes a gym, treatments for body and hair, weight and cellulite reduction programs, makeovers, and massage. Vaguely stylish standards offer either a large lateral view of the beach or a mountain vista; superiors are oceanfront. Only a few rooms have tubs; all have safes and walk-in closets. Tennis courts are available, as well as 24-hour room service. Guests must take either taxi or bus to Rio proper. 510 apts. *Expensive. All cards.*

★ Rio Atlântica Suite Hotel
Av. Atlântica, 2964 (Copacabana);
☎ *(21) 255-6332; FAX 255-6410.*

Just built in the last couple of years, the Rio Atlântica Suite Hotel has been carefully designed to remain beautiful for years to come. Despite its slick, modern facade, many have observed that the hotel's interior "looks just like Rio," perhaps because of its natural lighting, raw brick walls, and sand–colored decor that recalls rolling waves. The marble lobby comes complete with waterfall, and you must pass an irresistible deli counter before you even reach the reception. Half–Swiss, half–Brazilian owned (50 percent belongs to TV Globo), the hotel brings a Swiss sense of organization to its 228 rooms (120 of which may be booked as two-room suites). Children up to 12 stay free; all suites hold two adults and two children, or three adults and one child. The bedrooms, a delightful mix of mauves and gray-greens, are filled with fine furniture; showers hanging from the ceiling are perfect for tall people. Contrary to other 5-star hotels, here all apartment floors are tiled, not carpeted, in order to avoid the mustiness that pervades many seaside accommodations. There are also three handicapped suites, as well as some nonsmoking rooms. The outdoor pool has been so designed as to make swimmers feel they are on a boat in the middle of the ocean. Health-minded guests will adore the gorgeous weight room stocked with Nautilus: imagine pedaling away on a bike in full view of the sea. Dry and wet saunas are also available for a fee, as is massage. A real plus is the 70-seat mini-theater, which hosts premieres in simultaneous translations. A 24-hour takeout service offers some of the best Swiss pastries and pastrami in Rio; even if you're not a guest, stop by for some beach snacks. The Café ao Ponto coffee shop, with its pink luminescent lighting and art nouveau ceiling, looks transplanted from New York. A more formal Swiss-style restaurant serves top-class cuisine. A drugstore, Timberland shoe shop, and H. Stern jewelry store completes the picture. 228 rooms. *Expensive. All cards.*

Rio Othon Palace
Av. Atlântica, 3264 (Copacabana);
☎ *(21) 521-5522.*

The flagship property of the Othon chain, which has 9 hotels in Rio alone, the Rio Othon is much more family style than the Meridien or Copacabana Palace. The lobby is dark, cool, and intimate, with numerous couches; the only blemishes are the H. Stern and Amsterdam Sauer employees, ready to pounce on you as you walk by. Standard rooms with lateral ocean views offer adequate space, attractive quilted spreads and plush carpets. The bathrooms in marble and tile are smallish, though each contains a scale, hair dryer, and makeup mirror. Executive suites with two bathrooms are bright and sunny, with terrific views that nearly extend out over the beach; the master bedroom is separated from a sitting room by sliding doors. Deluxe rooms can hold an extra bed and sport tiny verandas. The pool is located on the top floor, and the skylight bar gives a wraparound view of the Forte de Copacabana and the west end of the beach, including the Vidigal favela. The VIP floor has a 24-hour butler, an executive breakfast room with open bar at night, and a small living room with international newspapers. The coffee shop is a tropical wonder, with waterfalls gracing the back walls. A fancier restaurant, Estância, overlooks the ocean. The gym, with weight machines and sauna, alternates days between the sexes, and the house masseur will even come to your room. Hair styling for women is also available. The lobby bar, a nice place to crash, features a Brazilian singer nightly. 581 apts. *Expensive. All cards.*

★ Rio Palace
Av. Atlântica, 4240 (Copacabana);
☎ *(21) 521-3232; FAX 227-1454.*

Enough said that Frank Sinatra and Paul McCartney stay here. Big, posh, and splashy, the Rio Palace fulfills a tropical dream some tourists still pine for—like having brunch on your balcony overlooking the beach. That's why the twin–tower hotel is usually sold out for New Year's Eve—its verandas offer a perfect view of the *macumba* rituals down below. Moreover, the hotel is extremely user-friendly; clerks are fluent in English, and a special guest-relations director will even do your personal shopping. The pool complex can only be called gloriously self-indulgent; two large pools front and back are so situated as to catch the rays of the sun all day long. Medium-sized rooms are brightly decorated with brocade spreads and dark maroon rugs; all bathrooms come with hairdryers, toiletries, and phone, as well as tub/showers. A glass-enclosed restaurant serves one of the largest breakfasts in the city, with health-food options and a dazzling array of breads, croissants, and tropical fruit juices; you can also eat outside on a terrace overlooking the beach. The 8th-floor Imperial Club, for executives, offers a butler, open bar, and full secretarial services, as well as exceedingly elegant meeting rooms. A wraparound salon with wicker chairs and a great view of the beach makes afternoon tea a special event. A panoramic elevator takes you to a 5-star French restaurant, Le Pré Catalan, and to the Horse's Neck Bar, a dark English pub with live jazz nightly. Replete with antiques from the era of Dom Pedro II, the lobby itself makes an elegant statement, even if the adjacent bar seems to attract certain high-class "ladies" looking for business. The hotel is also connected to the Casino Atlântico, a shopping mall open from 10 a.m.-8 p.m. One warning: Guests must take caution entering and leaving the hotel as it's a prime target for thieves. Security, however, is always on hand. 415 apts. *Expensive. All cards.*

★ **Sheraton Rio Hotel & Towers**
Av. Niemeyer, 121 (Vidigal);
☎ *(21) 274-1122; FAX 239-5643*
A 40-minute drive out from Copacabana lies one of the most complete beach resorts in Brazil. With a circular driveway opening onto its Hollywood-style lobby, the Sheraton offers a 5-star ambience compatible with any top-class hotel in the world. In fact, guests may completely miss the sense of being in chaotic Rio. With the hotel situated on a lone cliff overlooking an isolated beach, security is excellent; access can only be made by a lone staircase constantly patrolled by the staff. The 45 special suites, nearly apartment-like, are the stuff honeymoon dreams are made of: gauze-canopied beds, bamboo and brocaded walls, thick shag rugs, potted plants, and white-shuttered windows opening onto dramatic crashing waves. Even the pastel-colored standards are highly stylish, with verandas, carpeted floors, and sliding glass doors. All rooms have safes and bathtubs; most have hairdryers—the only difference in rooms is the amount of ocean view. VIP services are available for the first 4 floors, known as the Towers, including a business center, private breakfast room, and courtesy tea and bar. A nonsmoking floor is also available. The Sheraton has the best gym in Rio—with a full line of exercise equipment, all-day classes, massage, and sauna. Five restaurants include a top-class Italian eatery, a sushi and teriyaki bar, an outdoor barbecue, a Casa da Cachaça, where you can sample native spirits, and an a la carte restaurant with different cuisine nightly. An outdoor amphitheater holds concerts during high season, and special children's activities are offered during the summer. There's no shuttle bus to the city, but a 24-hour car service runs about $6, and public transportation runs close to the hotel. Completing the sense of a self-sufficient city is a bevy of outrageously priced souvenir and clothes shops. 617 apts. *Expensive. All cards.*

4-Star Hotels

Califórnia Othon
Av. Atlântica, 2616 (Copacabana);
☎ *(21) 257-1900.*
Computer–organized efficiency vies with the old-world charm of this comfortable 4-star hotel. The building is narrow, sandwiched between other apartment buildings on Copacabana's main beach drag. Standards are large, but lack any view worth opening the drapes for; superiors have a small view. Furniture is somewhat dated, but bathrooms were attractively remodeled in 1988. Antique light fixtures add a smidgen of style. All rooms have safes. The colonial restaurant has established a good rep for quality, comfort,

and large plates of pasta. There is no pool, but next door is a typical pizzeria and a sidewalk cafe. 110 apts. *Moderate. All cards.*

★ **Copa D' Or**
Rua Figueiredo Magalhães, 875 (Copacabana); ☎ *(21) 235-6610; FAX 235-6664.*
Management at this three-year-old hotel claims the Copa D'Or is a 4-star hotel with 5–star service, and I saw nothing to dispute this claim. The hotel's only drawback is that it's located 5 blocks from the beach, but a free shuttle service will transport you to the beach and to shopping. A medium-sized pool provides a wraparound view of the city —remember, you are too far from the beach to see any waves. Special handicap showers are available in the top-class executive suites, which also have two TVs, two bathrooms, shower/tubs, safes, and Spanish TV. Deluxe rooms can hold three single beds tightly; there are no standards. Windows are double-glazed to mute the sound of the city street. A special culinary floor holds a sushi bar, an elegant French restaurant, and a salmon-colored breakfast room with wood-paneled floors and floor-to-ceiling mirrors. Excellent lunch buffets are served, with one hot dish, lavish desserts, and plenty of salads for vegetarians. Guests may indulge in sauna and massage; the minimal gym contains a mechanical bike and one weight machine. Best of all, Fielding readers receive a 30 percent discount. 198 apts. *Moderate–expensive. All cards.*

Leme Othon Palace
Av. Atlântica, 656 (Leme);
☎ *(21) 275-8080; FAX 275-8080.*
The philosophy of the Othon hotels is fast evolving from large groups to more personalized individual attention, but structural changes at the Leme Othon have taken more time to develop. A friendly doorman in full dress attire greets you, but a strange sculptured wood wall in the lobby dampens the charm. And the lobby lounge seems impossibly small for such a big hotel. In general, however, rooms are large; deluxe rooms are enclosed by a glassed–in veranda, but furniture is often no more than utilitarian. Standards have the same veranda, but sadly show only a slice of ocean view. All rooms have safes, and baths with separate showers. The hotel seems unusually popular with Italian tourists, which perhaps explains the frequency of polenta and carpaccio on the menus. La Forchette restaurant serves typical and international cuisine, as well as *feijoada* on Sat. The coffee shop is good for fast food, drinks, and omelettes until midnight. The Leme Pub, with a small dance area and intimate leather banquettes, has a citywide reputation for ambience and good live music on Thurs., Fri., and Sat. nights. 193 apts. *Moderate– expensive. All cards.*

Luxor Copacabana
Av. Atlântica, 2554 (Copacabana);
☎ *235-2245; FAX 255-1858.*
The Luxor chain in Rio (three hotels) continues to uphold its reputation for fine service and efficiency. Standards of upkeep are impeccable at the Luxor Copacabana, whose furnishings and architecture suggest the feel of a cottage inn. Renovated in 1991, the hotel, which is ideally located on the beach drag, is usually full. Standard rooms are cheerful and attractive, though not particularly spacious, and lack any view worth looking at. Superior rooms offer a lateral view of the ocean with a veranda on which you must stand in order to see the waves. The best bet is the super–deluxe suite, with queen-size bed and a veranda with a garden. The lobby lounge is situated away from the street in the back of the hotel in order to maintain peace and calm. Breakfast is taken in a charming tea room facing Av. Atlântica. There is no pool. 120 apts. *Moderate–expensive. All cards.*

★ **Luxor Regente**
Av. Atlântica, 3716 (Copacabana);
☎ *(21) 287-4212; FAX 267-7693.*
The relatively substantial size of Luxor's largest hotel belies the intimate feel that characterizes this elite 4-star. Rooms are situated among towers and annexes in a maze-like fashion, and can accommodate beachgoers who want a beautiful (if noisy) view of Copacabana, as well as tourists looking for calmer hideaways in the hotel's interior. The friendly and efficient service is

among the best in Rio. The noted restaurant Forno e Fogão offers hearty cuisine at moderate prices—a good bet even if you aren't staying at the hotel. Even during low season the premises may become home to groups of lively Latin teenagers on vacation, so be prepared for some boisterous activity. 250 apts. *Expensive. All cards.*

Luxor Continental
Rua Gustavo Sampaio, 320 (Leme);
☎ *(21) 275-5252; FAX 541-1946.*
Tucked away on a leafy back street of Leme, this Luxor is situated a tiny block away from the hubbub of the beach drag. As such, its prime location can take full advantage of the hominess of Leme, with a pizzeria on every block, as well as drugstores, ice cream parlors, stationery stores, and travel agencies in abundance. Having spent 10 days here, I grew to feel at home in this smallish hotel, whose staff is excellent and whose restaurant serves a great chicken soup. Corner rooms offer the best view of the beach; otherwise, you will be looking out onto the picturesque side streets and hills of Leme. All rooms come with color TV and minibar. The bar serves drinks until the wee hours. 282 apts. *Expensive. All cards.*

Marina Rio Hotel
Av. Delfim Moreira, 696 (Leblon);
☎ *(21) 239-8844*
Next door to the Marina Palace, the Marina Rio is the former's kid sister—a pint-size version with 69 rooms and one of the prettiest restaurants in the city. The large bedrooms are elegantly appointed, with fine wood headboards and lush brocaded spreads. Unfortunately, all rooms are perfumed to disguise smoke smells, and although I was assured Johnson & Johnson anti-allergic spray is used, the effect is intense. There are no nonsmoking floors. Room service is available 24 hours a day, and guests may use the pool, hairdresser, and sauna at the Marina Palace. Fielding readers receive 20 percent discount. 69 apts. *Moderate–expensive. All cards.*

Olinda Othon
Av. Atlântica, 2230 (Copacabana);
☎ *(21) 257-1890.*
Sculptured beams and antique chandeliers give the lobby of this Othon its *Belle Époque* beauty. Thought it's now 43 years old, the Olinda has managed to stay both current and traditional; even the well-kept corridors exude an old-world charm. Standards are comfortably sized, with an extended area for dressing; however, the views are so nonexistent it's best to keep the drapes closed. Deluxe rooms, with attractive tapestry bedspreads, have excellent views of the ocean, though no verandas. Unfortunately, rooms with views tend to absorb the traffic noise down below. Suites, excellent for New Year's Eve, include an extra sitting room with a veranda overlooking the beach. Electronic keys provide extra security, and all rooms are supplied with safes. The one restaurant offers an Italian menu, and a pianist can be heard nightly in the lobby and bar. A hairdresser is available. 96 apts. *Moderate–expensive. All cards.*

★ Ouro Verde
Av. Atlântica, 1456 (Copacabana);
☎ *(21) 542-1887; FAX 239-6889.*
The Swiss–owned Ouro Verde has long been known as an elite exec hotel, but tourists interested only in pleasure will discover it as one of the most charming traditional-style hotels in Rio. Built in 1951, the Ouro Verde sports the kind of spacious architecture that was possible only in years past, with much of the original sculptured moldings still intact. From the moment you're welcomed through the large brass gates by the formal doorman, you feel as if you've entered an elegant Swiss inn. The huge bedrooms are beautifully furnished, with deep blue carpets, floral spreads, antique desks, and colonial-style couches. The deluxes face the ocean with a huge veranda; an extra sitting room can also be connected. Standards face Corcovado and the rooftops of Rio. Bathrooms are light and bright, with tub/showers. Intriguing are the massive walk-in closets, originally built to accommodate immigrant families who arrived with their sailor trunks. Execs will like the secretarial services, including fax, telex, and multilingual typewriters. A wood-and-leather bar illuminated with an-

tique street lamps opens onto a plant-strewn terrace. A lovely reading room with fresh flowers and publications in French, German, English, and Portuguese looks out onto a flowering atrium. The Ouro Verde restaurant overlooking Copacabana Beach serves top-class French cuisine. Fielding readers receive a 10% discount—and they should grab it. 66 apts. *Moderate–expensive. All cards.*

Savoy Othon
Av. N.S. de Copacabana, 995 (Copacabana); ☎ *(21) 521-8282;*
This choice Othon hotel is perfectly situated for sugar addicts: On one side is Babuska, the best ice cream parlor in Rio; on the other is Kopenhagen, the city's finest chocolate store. Perhaps to assuage the guilty, the lobby is steeped with antique religious paintings and pious folkloric art. The hotel's ambience, however, is all smiles; many employees have worked here over 20 years, so a family feeling abounds. Because it's two blocks from the beach, no ocean views are available, but rooms are attractive, with a Scottish plaid feel. The deluxe rooms, with a couch bed and two singles, give a grand feeling of space; standards are a bit tighter. Don't be surprised if a neighbor's bathroom noises resound through thin walls. All rooms have safes and tub/showers. The Savoy Grill, now open to the public, serves typical Brazilian food for lunch and dinner. Room service is available 24 hours a day, and the bar is open from 4 p.m. to midnight. One disadvantage: the hotel is situated on a busy commercial street where homeless families sometimes camp out. A bevy of souvenir shops, movie theaters, and restaurants are also right around the corner. 15 apts. *Moderate–expensive. All cards.*

3–Star

Bandeirantes Othon
Rua Barata Ribeiro, 548 (Copacabana); ☎ *(21) 255-6252.*
Located on a busy street two blocks from the shoreline, the Bandeirantes is a serviceable hotel, though not especially dripping in charm. Although the lobby is minuscule, rooms are not particularly cramped, but they are rather featureless. Standards, although the same size as deluxes, are quieter and overlook the rooftops of Rio. Some apartments have a tiny but very dear view of Corcovado. One restaurant doubles as a coffee shop, which is good for omelettes, sandwiches, and desserts. Room service lasts till midnight. There is no pool, but a pizzeria is right next door, and there's a nightclub across the street. 90 apts. *Moderate. All cards.*

Castro Alves Othon
Av. N.S. de Copacabana, 552 (Copacabana); ☎ *(21) 255-8815.*
Built in the boom following the end of World War II, the Castro Alves is situated on a very busy commercial street a few blocks back from the beach. As such, you may have to stumble over small dogs and frantic shoppers just to get to the front door. Fortunately, the lounge, with a minuscule bar, has been placed in the back of the hotel for a more relaxed ambience. In 1989 all rooms were renovated; today antique furniture and mauve motifs add a little oomph. Standards boast huge salmon drapes that open onto a small veranda with an excellent, though distant, view of Corcovado. Deluxe rooms, with sitting verandas, look onto a leafy park called the Praça Serzeldo Correia. All rooms have safes and extremely old color TVs. Breakfast is served in La Mole, a connecting restaurant under separate ownership, which has proved a popular medium-priced lunch and dinner spot. A beauty salon is located in the adjacent building. Children up to age eight stay free. 72 apts. *Moderate. All cards.*

Excelsior Copacabana
Av. Atlântica, 1800 (Copacabana); ☎ *(21) 257-1950; FAX 256-2037.*
This charming off-white, colonial-style edifice, part of the Horsa chain, is superbly situated right in the middle of Copacabana's beach drag, surrounded by popular restaurants and souvenir shops. Next door is an apartment building filled with the country's top actors and socialites. Friendly receptionists speak good English and a special concierge will arrange all excursions and entertainment reservations. Halls and doorways are paneled in maple wood, lending a

whiff of old-world sophistication. Claustrophobia-prone guests should opt for the superior and deluxe rooms. The super-deluxes come with a balcony facing the sea, as do suites. Safes are available only at the reception. There is no pool. A lounge area doubles as an art gallery, and the American bar is open until midnight. The restaurant serves international and typical Brazilian food, with a *feijoada* buffet on Sat. 220 apts. *Moderate. All cards.*

Lancaster Othon
Av. Atlântica, 1470 (Copacabana);
☎ *(21) 541-1887.*
A doorman waits under the canopied facade of this Othon built with the generosity of space characteristic of the 1950s. A voluptuous marble staircase winding upwards from the lobby recalls another era, although elevators are available for the faint of heart. Deluxe rooms are actually suite-size, with a veranda facing the ocean and sliding glass-and-wood doors that open to a second room. Standards are equally spacious, though minus the ocean view. However, some may be put off by some carpet stains as well as scratched furniture. All three meals are served in a restaurant that is a strange mixture of quiet elegance and screeching TV. In warm weather, you may sit on the front patio overlooking Copacabana Beach and drink fabulous tropical cocktails. Just watch out for the cars that pull up on the sidewalk. 67 apts. *Moderate. All cards.*

Mar Ipanema
Rua Visconde de Pirajá, 539 (Ipanema);
☎ *(21) 274-9922.*
Five years old, the Mar Ipanema boasts a privileged location down the street from Giorgio Armani on Ipanema's main shopping drag. For a 3-star hotel it is remarkably well kept. Argentines, who seem to have the knack of discovering good budget hotels, make up the majority of the clientele, but Americans are welcome. All rooms are carpeted, with modern furniture and color TV with videocassette and CNN. The only difference between the standard and superior is the floor level, but the view of downtown Ipanema is not worth the extra bucks. The restaurant, small but spunky, serves three meals, and the lobby bar remains open till midnight. 81 apts. *Moderate. All cards.*

★ **Rio Copa Hotel**
Av. Princesa Isabel, 370;
☎ *(21) 275-6644; FAX 275-5545.*
Located down the street from the Meridien Hotel on a busy avenue leading to Rio Sul Shopping Center, the Rio Copa is a comfortable, attractive hotel only 2 blocks from the beach. Attention to details, such as the cool gray tones of the elevator, has helped make the hotel an oasis of calm in contrast to the city street outside. Those looking for excellent living space will be rewarded here. Standards are a lovely mix of cool grays and blues and comfortable furniture. Deluxes come with an extra room that holds a sofa bed. Double-glass windows and heavy drapes keep street noise to an absolute minimum. A pool and sauna should be installed soon. One restaurant serves all three meals. Room service and the small bar is open till midnight. Checkout time quickly fills the tiny lobby with fast-talking Venezuelans and Paraguayans, but consider that part of the local color. 110 apts. *Moderate. All cards.*

Trocadero Othon
Av. Atlântica, 2064 (Copacabana);
☎ *(21) 257-1834.*
Brazilians, Argentines, Chileans, and Italians seem to favor this Othon much more than more northern Americans. Upkeep leaves a little to be desired: The windows are a bit greasy and the lobby has retained a slight mustiness. The deluxes and suites have full ocean views; the standards, somewhat tight for space, look out onto the side and back of the hotel. If you insist on the budget route, however, make sure you ask for a lateral standard. Only a few deluxe rooms have tubs. All rooms have safes. A hair salon is available to guests. There is no pool. The Trocadero's trump card is the Moenda Restaurant, known throughout the city for its Bahian cuisine. Whether you are a guest or not, travelers who aren't heading for the northeast shouldn't miss the opportunity to try this unforgettable cuisine. 116 apts. *Moderate. All cards.*

2–Star

Hotel Carlton
Rua João Lira, 68 (Leblon);
☎ (21) 259-1932.
For a 2-star hotel, the Carlton gives seedy a good name. So the couches are a little tattered and the bedroom lights hang strangely from the ceiling. At least the bathrooms are clean and cheerfully tiled, and the suites are an excellent budget idea for four people. Standards have no view; superiors look out onto a leafy back street of Leblon. Rooms usually come with two single beds; double beds must be requested. All rooms have safes, minibars, and air-conditioning. 45 apts. *Inexpensive. All cards.*

★ **Ipanema Inn**
Rua Maria Quitéria, 27 (Ipanema);
☎ (21) 287-6092
Pleasant carpeted rooms with colorful drapes and marble-topped tables makes this small hotel seem like a neighborhood home. Clean and upbeat, the hotel attracts many Argentines and Americans. Bathrooms are attractively tiled and there is ample closet space. TVs are optional for a small fee. Beach service includes umbrellas and towels. The restaurant serves only breakfast and snacks. 54 apts. *Inexpensive. All cards.*

Predia/Leme
Av. Princesa Isabel, 7, loja 14/15;
☎ (21) 275-5449.
Unsuspecting tourists without a reservation are often brought here by crafty taxi drivers, who profess they know a great deal. And surprisingly, they're right. One of the best–kept secrets in Rio, the Predia/Leme is neither luxurious nor elite, but it is cheap with double rooms, with air–conditioning, TV, and minibar, starting at $20 and going up to $70. For about $38 you can wing two beds, with tile floor, a small kitchen with microwave, an adequately clean bathroom, and only a tiny fragrance of gas. Clients who stay a week might receive a 10 percent discount. Some rooms even have full views of the sea, and the money you save on accommodations can go toward fancy dinners at the Meridien Hotel next door. *Inexpensive. No cards.*

Hotel Praia Leme
Av. Atlântica, 866 (Leme);
☎ (21) 275-3322.
With only two floors, the Praia Leme looks like it's about to be delicately squashed between towering buildings on Copacabana's main beach drag. Guests will nearly feel as if they are staying at a private residence. Internal rooms face side streets; splurge the extra couple of dollars for a room that faces the sea. The fully carpeted rooms include a couch that folds out into an extra bed. Bathrooms are tiled, though only showers are available. There are no elevators, but the friendly staff will carry your luggage. The restaurant serves only breakfast, which you may take in your room. The lobby is comfortable, but faintly musty. You can contemplate the sea at night from the tiny bar. Children under six stay free. 22 apts. *Inexpensive. No cards.*

Hotel San Marco
Rua Visconde de Pirajá, 524 (Ipanema);
☎ (21) 239-5032.
A 2–star hotel in chic Ipanema seems an anomaly, and well, the San Marco is. Standard rooms are similar to those at the Carlton—simple, with two single beds, Formica table, safe, TV, and air-cooling units. Light bulbs here hang strangely from the ceiling. Some of the wood paneling has been scratched, and I found water standing inexplicably in a pool in one bathroom. Deluxe rooms are the size of standards, but furniture appears to be new. Snack bar and room service available only between 7 a.m. and 4:20 p.m., at which time the kitchen staff apparently leaves in a hurry. The staff is friendly, but the ambience is claustrophobic. 49 apts. *Inexpensive. All cards.*

★ **Toledo**
Rua Domingos Ferreira, 71 (Copacabana);
☎ (21) 257-1990
Anyone looking for the best cheap hotel in Rio should stop right here. Of course, don't expect many amenities: There is no restaurant, only minimal room service, and few TVs. But the Toledo, located behind the Luxor Copacabana, is impeccably clean and even has a certain *je ne sais quoi*. The small

hallways are tiled, suggesting the ambience of a guesthouse. The *mini-solteiro* is a Tom Thumb-sized single, with a tiny desk, a small wardrobe, and an extremely space-efficient bathroom. Standards, a surprise with dark blue carpeting and colorful wallpaper, can easily fit three single beds. The *beliche*, with two bunks beds and a doorless mini-bathroom, is perfect for two undemanding children. Not all rooms have windows, but all rooms are air-conditioned. The forgettable breakfast room is a two-flight walk-up, although breakfast may be served in your room. No pool, but the beach is only a block away. The receptionist speaks English more or less, and even the brick-floor lobby isn't the least bit depressing. There is no service charge. 96 apts. *Inexpensive. All cards.*

Apart-hotels

Apart-hotels are residences that are run like hotels, but are actually private, completely stocked apartments that may be rented daily. They usually run half the price of hotels and often are more fashionably decorated. Breakfast and maid service are included, although the kitchen is fully equipped for all cooking. These accommodations are especially good for families or large groups of singles wanting to budget; the quality of some aparts is so superb that sometimes you can't believe the price. A medium rate is about $50 for a 2-bedroom apartment.

Rio Flat Service

Rua Almirante Guilherme, 332 (Leblon); ☎ *(21) 274-7222; FAX 239-8792 .*

This network of apartments with privileged sites in Rio, Copacabana, Leblon, and Lagoa/Humaitá offers 1-and 2-bedroom apartments with fully equipped kitchens, air-conditioning, and color TV. Sauna, pool, playground, and maid service are also available, as well as a video center and a laundry room. Breakfast is included in the daily rate; children under five stay free.

Ipanema Sweet

Rua Visconde de Pirajá, 161; ☎ *(21) 239-1819/267-7015*

A block from the beach, these air-conditioned apartments include a bedroom, living room, kitchen, and veranda. All rooms have color TV, and duplexes with 2 bedrooms are available. There's also a garage, a sauna, and a swimming pool.

BARRA DA TIJUCA

The in-place to hunker down for a spell is in Barra, one of the best beaches now in Rio. In the last seven years, apart-hotels have sprung up like wildfire here, many of excellent quality. The spaciousness of these facilities, as well as the safety and cleanliness of the beaches, make these accommodations ideal for families.

Barrabella Hotel

Av. Sernambetiba, 4700 (Barra da Tijuca); ☎ *(21) 385-2000.*

Largest apart-hotel complex in Rio, located in Barra da Tijuca. Fine swimming pool, good food, and a hot nightclub. The 1-, 2-, and 3-bedroom apartments are popular among singles and the newly divorced.

Barra Beach Rio

Av. Sernambetiba, 1120; ☎ *(21) 389-6333.*

Youth Hostels

For information regarding youth hostels in Rio, write or call:

Associação de Albuergues da Juventude do Estado do Rio de Janeiro (Association of Youth Hostels for the State of Rio de Janeiro)

Rua da Assembléia, 10, room 1616 (downtown); ☎ *(21) 222-0301.*

CULINARY RIO

Rio is a city of indulgence, and food is no exception. *Cariocas* adore eating, and thanks to the syncretic mix of cultures that has richly characterized Brazilian culture since its inception, Rio's culinary scene offers a huge array of international delights that should satisfy even the most discerning gourmet. From romantic Italian grottoes to elegant French salons, from casual seaside bars to rip-roaring barbecue houses, Rio has a restaurant for every mood, every flavor, and every pocketbook. You can spend a couple of dollars on open-grilled chicken or up to $30 for fine haute cuisine. You can nibble a "natural" sandwich walking down the beach or settle into fine-crusted pizza loaded with eggplant, anchovies, and tuna. But dining in Rio is much more than the eternal search for good food. For *cariocas*, it's a time to meet friends, make new ones, show off new clothes, and flirt outrageously. Dress may be casual, even in the most expensive restaurants, but *cariocas* will spend hours preparing to look good for a night on the town.

Cariocas not only love to eat—they love to eat a lot, and the amount of food on your plate will astonish you. Even in small, unassuming restaurants, a main course of beef, for example, with the accompanying platters of rice and beans, can often serve two. The *couvert* usually includes bread, butter, and a plate of olives, but in the finest restaurants, like Satíricon, the fabulous spread of hors d'oeuvres is often as good as the meal. *Couverts* are automatically placed on your table the minute you sit down, so if you don't want it, refuse it. It can add an extra $1-3 to your bill.

Anyone with a yen for **red meat** should head for a *churrascaria*—a Brazilian-style steak house where some of the finest cuts of beef in South America are served. You can either eat à la carte, at restaurants like Baby Beef or Copacabana *Churrascaria*, or brave the more boisterous *rodízio* scene, such as at Mariu's. *Rodízio* means "rotation," referring not to the style of cooking but to the quality of service. For a set price, you stay chained to your seat while a troop of waiters, rhythmically timed to your appetite, stab the middle of your plate with metal skewers, then slice off choice pieces of beef, chicken, and pork with a flourish. This decidedly macho form of dining can go on for hours until you call it quits, or until you decide to move on to dessert. Vegetarians who can at least endure looking at meat shouldn't be deterred, because the salad bars (inclusive in the set price) are full of great salads and fresh vegetables. For some reasons, Brazilians talk louder at *rodízios* than anywhere else, so expect a kind of boisterous elegance. And don't be surprised if your plate is exchanged in the middle of the meal for a clean one. The first time it happened, I thought the meal was over, but it's just one of those many gracious gestures of Brazilian service—they want you to eat off clean plates.

Fish is superbly fresh in Rio. Because of the cholera scare, however, skip the sushi and head for the imaginatively designed kitchens of Sol e Mar, Grottamare, and Satíricon, where you can indulge in enormous *peixadas* (a potpourri of seafood in a delicate broth) or succulently grilled sea bass, squid, calamari, and lobsters. Along the beach in Barra da Tijuca are dozens of simple rustic eateries that serve a hearty plate of just–caught fried fish for about five bucks. Frequenters of Copacabana Beach need only to cross Avenida Atlântica to dine at Príncipe, a tradition in the neighborhood for moderately priced seafood.

As for **European cuisine**, it's still a symbol of status in Rio. A glimpse at the Louis XVI architecture in downtown will prove just how long Brazilians have mimicked French culture in an attempt to become stylish. Recent imports to the French culinary scene, such as Claude Troisgrois, Rio's reigning French chef, and the masterful Paul Bocuse at Saint Honoré, have designed imaginative menus that they reinvent daily. Yet some of the most creative kitchens, like the Italian–styled Ettore's, have been fashioned by third–generation immigrants using the culinary secrets learned at their grandmother's knee.

Home-styled **Brazilian food**, however, is not to be missed in Rio—though it's not exactly easy to find. Dishes like *galinha ao molho pardo* (chicken cooked in its own blood) tastes much better than it sounds, as does *feijoada*, the Brazilian national dish made from the not-so-popular parts of the pig. (See the chapter entitled *Cuisine*.) More an event than a meal, *feijoada* is best eaten at home in the company of friends (who have spent all day to prepare it), but barring any invitations, head for the Caesar Park Hotel on Saturday, which is considered the best spread in Rio. And don't forget the motherland—Portuguese food specializes in codfish, and one of the warmest and most authentic places to find it is at the colorful cantina called Adega do Valentim.

Vegetarians, on the other hand, do get some respect in Brazil, and shouldn't at all feel deprived. Beyond the salad bars at *churrascarias,* there are numerous vegetarian and health-style restaurants downtown that serve hearty plates of veggies and grains. Pasta is readily available in Italian restaurants and you can always order rice, beans, and steamed vegetables, as well as omelettes in any moderate–priced restaurant. Actually, eating vegetarian is one of the cheapest ways to dine in Rio, and you'll even be able to find brown rice (called *arroz integral)* at special places.

Taking **afternoon tea** in Rio is not just a luxurious leftover from colonial days; it's a very reasonable way to stave off starvation until you eat dinner at 9 or 10 p.m. (the normal time for supping in Brazil). Hotels like the Meridien, the Copacabana Palace, and the Caesar Park boast superb buffets of cakes, puddings, breads, and salty pastries that rate as full meals in themselves. For decor that takes you back to the fin de siècle, stop by the Confeitaria Colombo downtown, and don't forget to bring back a box of sweets for your room.

Of course, **noshing** has to be part of a culture that loves to sit at a sidewalk café and watch the girl from Ipanema, Barra, or Leblon walk by. There's no better way to cool down geared–up nerves than with a plate of **frango à passarinha** (fried chicken bits), some good company, and a cold glass of beer. The restaurant/bars I've listed under "*Grazing*" needed only three requirements to make the grade: They had to be well situated, well attended, and serve great *chopp*. Add a little sunshine, and that's really all you need for a great time in Rio. Restaurants are listed according to the type of food and are sometimes cross–referenced. A service charge of 10 percent is usually added to the bill, and you may feel free to add another 5 percent, though it's not expected.

WHERE TO EAT IN RIO

Rates:
Very Expensive -------- over $20
Expensive -------------- $15–$20
Moderate --------------- $8–$15
Inexpensive ------------ $4–$8
Cheap under ----------- $4

Brazilian

Bar do Arnaudo
Rua Almirante Alexandrino, 316, store B, Santa Teresa; ☎ *232-6570. Tues.–Sun. noon–10 p.m.*
Located in the colonial hillside neighborhood of Santa Teresa, this is the place to go if you've braved the streetcar to visit the Chácara do Céu Museum, one of the finest modern art collections in Rio. (Better you should take a taxi.) Family run, Arnaudo's is as homespun as you get here, cooking up the salty dried meats characteristic of Northeastern cuisine (*carne-de-sol* may look like leather, but tastes fantastic). Local artwork enlivens the walls, and you might even run into a few artists who are dying to sell. *Moderate. No cards.*

Escondidinho
Beco dos Barbeiros, 12-A and B (Downtown); ☎ *242-2234. Mon.–Fri. 11 a.m.–4 p.m.*
For four decades chef/owner Maria de Lourdes has folded her motherly warmth into some of the best home-style cooking in Rio. The former president, Juscelino Kubitschek, credited with building Brasília, fueled his political battles on her *feijoada*. *Galinha ao molho pardo*—chicken cooked in its own blood—is a sumptuous native dish that should be tried at least once. *Moderate. No cards.*

Marmita
Rua Jardim Botánico, 6081; ☎ *274-0572. Daily 11:30 a.m.–10 p.m., Sun. until 5 p.m.*
Home–cooked food the way the "aunts" or *tias*—the culinary grand dames of Minas— do it. This food was originally targeted for the stomachs of 18th-century gold-diggers, so expect it to sit heavy. Chicken with okra is a native specialty, as is the baked pork with black beans. At night, the climate of the two–story house leans toward *torresmos* (easily addictive fried pork chunks), black bean soup, and *tira-gostos*—tasty tidbits best downed with a cold glass of *cerveja*. *Inexpensive. No cards.*

★ Macondo
Rua Conde de Irajá, 85 (Botafogo); ☎ *226-9485. Daily 11 a.m.–midnight, Fri. and Sat. until 3 a.m.*
Agnaldo, the owner of this beautiful residential home, hails from the state of Sergipe, and much of his menu boasts native Northeast delicacies such as *carne-seca* and *carne-de-sol*—hearty cuts of dried salty meat, accompanied by pumpkin purée and black bean stews. International influences aren't forgotten, especially in the tournedos he named after himself—finely grilled beef served with a tart mustard sauce, peas, Prussian potatoes, and palm hearts. *Inexpensive. No cards.*

Moenda
Av. Atlântica, 2064 (Copacabana); ☎ *257-1834. Daily noon-midnight*
For those not heading to Salvador, Moenda offers the best Bahian cuisine to be found in Rio. Waitresses in folkloric costumes sport huge smiles and foster the graciousness that's synonymous with Bahia. Health-savvy tourists will appreciate the light touch to a normally heavy cuisine—less oil and fewer spices. Start off with the *acarajé com dois molhos*—a type of bean roll with fried shrimps you buy on Bahia's streets—followed by a variety of fish: the *file de namorado à Moenda* with coconut milk and palm oil sauce is delectable. For dessert the *cocada baiana com quiejo*—a coconut dish with cheese—is a sugar rush. The restaurant, at the Hotel Trocadero, looks out onto the beach with a wonderful view, but don't be surprised if the windows read dirty. *Expensive. All cards.*

Siri Mole & Cia
Rua Francisco Otaviano, 50 (Copacabana); ☎ 267-0894. Tues.–Sun. noon–2 a.m., Mon. only dinner 7 p.m.–2 a.m.

The owner of Bargaço's in Salvador inspired his friend Agda Pereira to open this excellent restaurant for Bahian specialties. With a light touch to the normally oil-laden cuisine, the menu excels in fish stews, and the *siri mole* (soft crabs) are as refined as caviar. The gentle decor enlivened by ficus trees is pretty without pretension, and the chef manages an exact balance between spice and restraint. For starters, try the *acarajé de pilar*, a helping of *vatapá* with dried baby shrimps, then indulge in the house glory, *Sinfonia de Crustaceos*—a delirious symphony of several varieties of fish doused in coconut milk and African palm oil. If you're downtown, try Dona Agda's other restaurant for lunch only, **Pier One** Av. Rio Branco, 1; ☎ 233-1201 A fancier version of the same.

Churrascarias
Baby Beef—Paes Mendonça
Av. das Américas, 1510; ☎ 399-2187. Daily 11:30 a.m.–1 a.m.

This excellent *churrascaria* is right next to a super-size supermarket, the Paes Mendonça, so big the clerks have to travel on roller skates. Shop first, then feast next door on fine beef à la carte. The *picanha*—huge, juicy, and very tender—is my favorite cut. *Moderate. All cards.*

Barra Grill
Av. Min. Ivan Lins, 314;
☎ 399-6060/399-40031. Daily 11 a.m.–2 a.m.

This relatively new *churrascaria* is reaping a fine reputation, particularly among couples who patronize the love motels in Barra. Perhaps that explains the added élan: side plates served individually by waiters (rather than thrown on your table like Frisbees). Eighteen cuts of meat, 24 salads, a hot buffet including lasagna and stroganoff—all for less than $15. The salad and dessert buffet can be bought separately. Always make reservations, especially on Sun., when the lovers head out. *Moderate. All cards.*

Copacabana Churrascaria
Av. N.S. de Copacabana, 1144; ☎ 267-1497. Daily Noon–2 a.m.

Located on Copacabana's main shopping drag, this is the macho man's *churrascaria*, where the chefs dress like Brazilian cowboys and toss slabs of beef over an open fire. Served à la carte, specialties include *picanha* and *maminha* (the soft thigh of the cow). Some dishes, like the *brochette de filet*, serve two. Pizzas and pastas are also available. Tables are close set, but an atrium of tropical trees warms the brick walls. Next door is Vinícius Bar, a darkly lit dance floor with a good dance band. Reserve for Sun. lunch. *Moderate. All cards.*

Esplanada Grill
Rua Barão da Torre, 600 (Ipanema); ☎ 239-6028.

One of Rio's chichi places for à la carte beef (even the napkins come with black bow ties), Esplanada is more expensive than a good *churrascaria*, and in my mind, not worth it ($45 for two, with side dishes like fries and onion rings, is just too steep for this city). Still, *cariocas* cough up the cruzeiros just to be seen in this slender wraparound salon near the Lagoa, especially on weekends, when it's packed. *Expensive. V, MC.*

Estrela do Sul
Av. Reporter Nestor Moreira (Botafogo); ☎ 254-0630. Daily 11 a.m.–3 p.m., 6 p.m.–midnight.

Located near Canecão and Rio Sul Shopping Center, this *rodízio* is generous in its endless stream of meats and at least half a dozen accompaniments. Demand the big crunchy onion rings (*cebola à milanesa*)—they tend to hide in the kitchen. The coconut ice cream was the best I had in Brazil. Unfortunately, the sometimes-on, sometimes-off disco next door can feel like an earthquake erupting, so inquire in advance. *Moderate. All cards.*

★ Mariu's
Av. Atlântica, 290 B (Leme);
☎ 542-2393.

More typical of the barbecue houses of Rio Grande do Sul—Brazil's cowboy country in the south—this is my favorite *rodízio*-style *churrascaria* for ambience, quality, and location, right in Leme overlooking the beach. Menus, in English and Portuguese, are little slips of paper you fill out—just like grade school. Best to check everything off, including the french fries, the onion rings, and dozens of salads. You can even specify rare (*mal passado*), medium (*médio*), or well done (*ao ponto*). In 1993, a "light" menu was introduced, which even lists the number of calories you're consuming and suggests alternatives. Desserts served in huge crystal goblets are exquisite, like the chocolate mousse and the avocado ice cream drenched in liqueur, and especially the chocolate eclairs, called *profiteroles*. Tell somebody it's your birthday and you'll get a cake with sparklers and a chorus of singing waiters. The owner, the young scion of a rich Brazilian family, is the Armani-suited ponytail who's bussing the clients. *Expensive. All cards.*

Porcão
Rua Barão da Torre, 171 (Ipanema); ☎ *521-0999; Av. Armando Lombardi, 591 (Barra da Tijuca);* ☎ *(21) 399-3157.*
The name means big pig and probably refers to the meat; unfortunately, the mascot over the door is too reminiscent of Porky. A chichi address in Ipanema, it's *rodízio*-style service—meaning all you can eat as fast as you can eat it. *Moderate. All cards.*

Continental

Café do Teatro
Av. Rio Branco; ☎ *262-4164. 11 a.m.– 4 p.m. Closed on weekends.*
The official restaurant of the Municipal Theatre skips the *fin-de-siècle* allure and effects the kind of underground cave Moses might have loved. Huge tableaux of Assyrian slaves adorn the walls, and two sculptured sphinxes stand guard at the entrance. The fine food, funky ambience, and relaxing music can cure rainy–day blues. *Moderate-expensive. All cards.*

★ **Clube Gourmet**
Rua General Polidoro, 186 (Botafogo); ☎ *295-3494.*
This salmon–colored, turn–of–the–century house attracts *cariocas* who love to kvetch about the taxes they pay on their Parisian chateaux. Tourists, however, will enjoy the down-home *savoir faire*, the female bartenders and waitresses (very *avant* in Brazil), and an excellent lunch buffet that includes 15 salads, pasta, meat, and entrée. Dinner is more gourmet: for a fixed price you choose from 3 starters, 2 fishes and 1 pasta, 3 meats, and 3 desserts. For the last 12 years, owner/supervisory chef José Hugo Celidônio, a former food critic for Brazilian *Vogue* and *Gourmet*, has been developing an eclectic but highly praised menu with the help of his friends—some of the best chefs in Europe, who also teach at his amateur cooking school. Fresh products, such as butter, cream, and oranges, are daily trucked from his farm, and he boasts the best wine cellar in Brazil. "My tradition was to eat and cook with my friends," he told me, and you can still taste the good vibes in his meals. *Very expensive. No cards; traveler's checks and dollars accepted.*

PAX
Rua Maria Quitéria, 99 (Ipanema); ☎ *247-4191. Daily noon–2 a.m., closed Tues.*
Only two months old when I visited in 1993, Pax is absolutely the newest hotspot in Rio, tucked into a pretty corner off Ipanema's Praça da Paz. Yellow walls, pink orchids, and white-and-tan tables read Santa Monica, but the Spanish chef brings a Latin flair to fish, like the *Peixe Wanda* with an almondine sauce and rice with raisins. The *Filet Pax,* thinly sliced grilled filet mignon, comes with a fine herbed sauce. I had time to try only the desserts, but some, like the chocolate mousse, chocolate crocante, and the maracujá torte are, unquestionably, the best in town. Many people just come for afternoon tea. No reservations, but between 1-3 p.m. and after 9 p.m., expect to wait. *Moderate. No cards.*

Rio's
Pq. do Flamengo (Flamengo); ☎ *551-1131. Daily noon–3 a.m.*
The glorious views of Guanabara Bay and Sugar Loaf may be lost on the businessmen and politicos who eat at this restaurant built by the city for its official guests, but at night,

with the twinkling stars, it's the peak of romance, especially if you retreat to the plushy piano bar after *cafezinho*. Dinner runs about $50 per couple, with user-friendly menus in English and personable first-class waiters. Start with baked crabs or excellent crab pancakes, then move on to Spanish-style octopus, grilled seabass with creamed spinach, or the memorable chateaubriand. Dramatic tableside productions are made for flambés. *Expensive. All cards.*

Fast Food
★ Chaika's
Rua Visconde de Pirajá, 321 (Ipanema); ☎ *247-7974.*
Chocolate-swirled meringues and pastries a mile high greet you on your way into Chaika's, set in the middle of Ipanema's prime shopping drag. My favorite place for non-junk fast food and desserts, Chaika's makes pizzas for 1, 2, or more folks, and its ice cream sundaes are not to be missed —complete with tropical umbrellas and unusual toppings. Service is lively, as is the young clientele, some of whom become obsessed with the video games next door. *Inexpensive-cheap. No cards.*

Bob's
Av. N.S. de Copacabana, 129 (Copacabana); ☎ *275-7045.*
So why shouldn't a burger joint boast an American name? At least the meat is thicker and less papery than at Brazilian McDonald's, and the chocolate milk shakes are definitely healing. *Cheap. No cards.*

Salpicante
Rua Anibal de Mendonça, 55 (Ipanema) ☎ *274-9996*
A clean airy place to lunch a few blocks from the beach. Make your own salad from the bar or get more complicated with grilled chicken (less than $3) or cold roast beef. *Inexpensive. No cards.*

Feijoadas
★ Caesar Park Hotel
Av. Vieira Souto, 460 (Ipanema); ☎ *287-3122. Wed. and Sat.*
Nearly everyone's choice for the best *feijoada* in Rio, the Tiberius restaurant is an elegant surrounding for the country's most famous folkloric dish (see the chapter called *Cuisine.*) The huge black pots containing dried meats, bacon, salted pork, sausage, and odd parts of pig are set up buffet-style, while traditional singers in folkloric costumes serenade the diners. Don't eat for 24 hours beforehand and don't miss the coconut *batidas*—an intoxicating combination of *creme de coco* and *cachaça. Moderate. All cards.*

Rio Othon Palace Hotel
Av. Atlântica, 3264, 3rd floor; ☎ *521-5522*
Children up to age spell eat free at the Othon's *feijoada* buffet every Sat. *Moderate. All cards.*

Fish
Cândido's
Rua Barros de Alarcão, 352 (Pedra de Guaratiba); ☎ *395-1630. Mon.–Fri. and Sun. noon–7 p.m., Sat. noon–11 p.m.*
Long given the crown by visiting French chef Paul Bocuse, who dubbed it his favorite restaurant in Rio, Cândido's looks like a dump on the beach. But *cariocas* drive an hour out to this seaside suburb to sample the fresh fish caught daily. Owner Carmen Sampaio bought the building 21 years ago when the area was only a fishermen's village, but it wasn't until her grilled *lula* (squid) started appearing in the social columns that she took off. Now clients wait up to an hour for a table. Two can dine on grilled seafood for about $35 with wine, while they soak up the sun and bat off mosquitoes. Paul Bocuse claims Carmen makes the best rice in the world. After dining, stop next door at Chez Janine, a popular nightclub. Reservations at the restaurant are absolutely necessary. *Expensive-very expensive. No cards.*

Príncipe
Av. Atlântica, 514 (Leme); ☎ *275-3996. Daily noon–1 a.m.*
One of the better, moderate-priced fish eateries on the beach in Leme. The maitre d' hangs out at the door, sometimes looking a bit like Mafia, but don't let that deter you. *Moderate. All cards.*

★ **Sol e Mar**
Av. Reporter Nestor Moreira, 11 (Botafogo); ☎ *295-1997.*
Don't be turned off by the phrase "tourist complex": here you'll find the best view of Guanabara Bay and Sugar Loaf, first-rate service, and fine fresh fish cooked Spanish style. A good place to come after you've visited Sugar Loaf, Sol e Mar definitely serves the best fruit cocktail drinks in the city. *Camarão no coco* arrives in a big pineapple boat covered with coconut cream sauce, but the best bet is the *Festival de Pescador Mariscos*—a groaning plate of fresh grilled seafood for about $10—enough for two. The desserts are extravagant—from coconut pie and chocolate mousse to tartuffe—the latter, a chocolate ice cream ball drenched in chocolate sauce. Many *cariocas* with big wallets have their weddings and bar mitzvahs upstairs in the glass-enclosed ballroom; a plush disco features live music nightly. *Moderate–expensive. All cards.*

French

Le Bec Fin
Av. N.S. de Copacabana, 178 (Copacabana); ☎ *542-4097. 7 p.m.–3 a.m.*
Only 42 seats, but this classic French restaurant has remained a top-class tradition in Rio for over 40 years. The menu never budges, nor do the kiss-kiss clients who never worry about prices. Romance abounds; with its fabulous marble-and-mahogany bar, flowered chairs, and red brocaded walls, the intimate room resembles a high-class madam's salon. But generosity reigns—the philosophy is to serve sumptuous portions so that nobody leaves hungry. Lots of lobster and rabbit in champagne are commonly run. Reservations required on Thurs. and weekends, when patrons might get to glimpse singing star Roberto Carlos, who is said to dine weekly. *Very expensive. No cards.*

Cafe Un, Deux, Trois
Rua Bartolomeu Mitre, 123 (Leblon); ☎ *239-0198. Mon.–Sat. 7 p.m.–3 a.m., Sun. noon-3 a.m.*
Superchic for *cariocas*, this two-in-one restaurant includes a fine French-style eatery and a chichi nightclub with flashing lights and romantic banquettes. Live shows around 1:30 a.m. are likely to feature stars, such as Martinho da Vila and Sandra Sá. The restaurant, reformed in 1991, may now labor under a different name, but the menu probably still boasts blinis with caviar, *tournedor Rossine* (huge filet mignon with paté and petits pois), as well as delicious crepes and fondues. The owner, Francisco Recarey, a very rich businessman, started out as a waiter and accumulated on his nights off an array of Rio's best niteries, including El Pescador, Babilônia, Help, Scala, Circus, Castelo da Lagoa, and Chiko's Bar. Reservations are a must on weekends. *Expensive. All cards.*

★ **Claude Troisgros**
Rua Custódio Serrão, 62 (Jardim Botânico); ☎ *226-4542. Mon.–Sat. 7:30–midnight.*
Tucked into a leafy side street of Jardim Botânico, this cozy, flamingo-pink chalet is the brainchild of 38-year-old master chef Claude Troisgros, son of one of the great chefs of Roanne, France. Only a few years ago, Claude started out with a tiny 6-table bistro and one waiter (his Brazilian wife was cashier), but he quickly carved a reputation for *la cuisine française pour les tropiques* (French food for the tropics) that few have ever matched in Rio. If you're a true gourmet, money will never be wasted here; in fact, only deep concentration while eating did justice to the unusual herbs, daring combinations, and artistic design of every magnificent plate I consumed. Best to go for the fixed menu (changed weekly). And the kitchen, led by well-trained António Costa when Claude is absent, isn't at all stuffy. Once a client brought a *jacaré* (crocodile) he had just caught and they baked it without blinking. The climax of any meal should be the *panaché des desserts*, which gives you an opportunity to taste a little of everything, including the miraculous chocolate mousse. *Un petit mort*, I guarantee, will follow. *Expensive. All cards.*

Ouro Verde
Av. Atlântica, 1456; ☎ *542-1887. Daily noon-midnight.*

Tucked into the first floor of the Ouro Verde Hotel, this romantic, top-class restaurant does justice to its French-and Swiss-inspired menu. Cuts of beef are excellent, and the desserts leave nothing to the imagination. A window seat gives you a fine expanse of Copacabana beach. *Expensive. All cards.*

Petronius
Caesar Park Hotel, Av. Vieira Souto, 460 (Ipanema); ☎ *287-3122.*
The newly revamped French restaurant of Rio's classiest hotel is, oddly, the best place to see the Tuesday night bikers as they race next to Ipanema's shore. With ivories tinkling in the background and candles illuminating the plush room, white-gloved waiters serve on silver plates with particular grace. Start with the *carpaccio de filet*—a wonder of thinly sliced raw meat, followed by an excellent grilled sole with a devastating crunchy cashew sauce (portions are immense). The Bandeja *Imperial do Pescador* is a stupendous potpourri of fish, shrimp, and lobster for two (a bit steep at $75, but you needn't eat for days prior). The *maracajú batidas* are spectacular. For dessert, a Brazilian friend urged me to try the chocolate mousse with a side dish of soft meringues—an interesting combo. *Cafezinho*, made tableside in a glass globe, is a wonder of heat and gravity. On the way out, don't miss the live fish in the foyer: one has the face of a kitten, and the other, a lion fish, looks extraterrestrial. *Very expensive. All cards.*

★ **Le Saint Honoré**
Av. Atlântica, 1020 (Hotel Meridien, 37th floor, Leme). Daily noon–3 p.m. and 8 p.m.–1 a.m.
Not only has this classic French kitchen been voted number one by the city's best critics, but the wraparound view of Copacabana Beach is one of the most romantic vistas at night. Designed by Chico Gouveia, the famous Brazilian decorator, the salon is a classy study in black, yellow, and white, with a sumptuous piano bar that suggests Cole Porter's ghost might be hanging about. Chef Michel Angier masterfully improvises on the cuisine of Paul Bocuse, offering a different weekly fixed price, as well as à la carte selections. As an appetizer, caviar wrapped in salmon with tartar sauce is the most in demand, followed by female frog's legs and filet of beef in a fine bordelaise sauce. Hot goat cheese usually precedes a cavalcade of exquisite chocolates. Service is elegant, in fact nearly obsequious: when I asked for a doggie-bag, nobody batted an eye. Reservations a must. *Very expensive. All cards.*

Galetos

An American girlfriend who works in Rio claimed she was too scared to walk up to these sometimes murky-looking, open-air counters, but she's missing out on some of the best grilled chicken around. And the price is unbeatable. Salads and fries are extra; other cuts of beef can be grilled. The *couvert*, for a few cents, will get you fresh French bread and a condiment of diced onions and tomato—practically a meal in itself. The service is fast, the ambience casual, and the natives quite friendly. A good option for takeout.

★ **O Crack dos Galetos**
Av. Prado Junior, 63, loja C (Copacabana). 11 a.m.–4 a.m. daily
A block from the beach, a block from the Meridien Hotel, next to a self-service laundromat called Lav e Lev. There's even an erotic nightclub next door. *Cheap. No cards.*

Quick Galetos
Rua Duvivier, 284 (Copacabana)
Open-air counter near the Hotel Internacional Rio. *Cheap. No cards.*

O Crack dos Galetos
Rua Domingos Ferreira, 197;
☎ *236-7001. Inexpensive. No cards.*

German

Bar Luiz
Rua Carioca, 39; (Downtown);
☎ *626-9600. Mon.–Sat. 11 a.m.–11:30 p.m.*
The smoke is thick, the tables tight, and the noise meter rambunctious, but this lovable joint in the publishing district is *the* meeting place for the Woodwards and Bernsteins of Rio. More than a century old, the German-style restaurant remains packed nightly after

8:30 p.m., while guests fiercely devour the famous knockwursts, sauerkraut, smoked chicken, potato salad, and pickles. Even the waiters seem straight out of a brusque Jewish deli, but the *chopp*, ice-cold draft served in generous pitchers, is pure *brasileiro*. Nearby is the Cine Iris, a 200-year-old building that shows porn flicks, but the terrain, I was told, is rough. *Inexpensive. Cards: DC only.*

Gimmicks, Goofballs and Games
★ **Torre de Babel**
Rua Visconde de Pirajá, 128 A, Ipanema; ☎ *267-9136. Mon.–Sat. noon–4 p.m. and 8 p.m.–2 a.m.*
The name means Tower of Babel, and the hodgepodge of artists, painters, and actors who own it wanted a joint to indulge their individual whims. Consequently, the windows are filled with Brazilian kitsch; opera videos play on a huge screen at lunch; nights and weekends alternate between live concerts, video premieres, poetry readings, and fashion shows. Just come for hors' d'oeuvres and the interesting people, or dig into the eclectic, health-savvy menu: grilled vegetables with curry, chicken with chutney, and stone-baked codfish. Worth babbling over is the *Negão de Bebel* (Portuguese for big, black man), which is a wicked slab of fudge that will adhere to the roof of your mouth. The humor-studded restaurant, hidden behind a jungle of plants on Ipanema's main shopping drag, may be hard to find, but look for the topless mannequin with a menu pasted on her chest. *Inexpensive. No cards.*

Mostarda
Av. Epitácio Pessoa, 990 (Lagoa); ☎ *287-7629. Daily 7 p.m.–4 a.m.*
The restaurant started with a group of Portuguese and Spanish owners and an obsession. So successful was the menu, made almost entirely with mustard, that a gorgeous new branch was built overlooking the Lagoa, complete with a disco upstairs. Sit on the veranda outside, or ask for a window seat on the second story, then start off with an explosive cocktail that comes with sparklers. Meats are often as big as their plates. After 9:30 p.m., the tables upstairs are taken. A huge line for the disco starts around 10:45 p.m. *Sun.–Thurs;* if you are having dinner, you are invited to dance free. *Moderate. Cards: AE only.*

★ **La Tour**
Rua Santa Luzia, 651; ☎ *240-5795. Noon-midnight daily*
Eat gourmet, tour the city, and never stand up—this revolving restaurant on the 37th floor gives you the best view of downtown Rio, especially during a worker's strike (which seems to happen every other week). Now owned by a young Brazilian who's transforming the once lackluster kitchen, the restaurant is making a comeback, with an excellent executive gourmet lunch for under $8. At night, surrounded by stars, you'll feel like you're sitting in heaven. Among the à la carte dinners, grilled trout with almonds and grapes is delightful; the specialty, La Tour Royale, ambidextrously mixes meat and fish with different sauces. For dessert, the tartuffe was made for chocoholics. *Moderate. All cards, traveler's checks, and dollars.*

Ice Cream
Babuska
Rua Anibal de Mendonça, 55 (Ipanema) and Rua Rainha Guilermina, 90 (Leblon).
Best ice cream parlor in Rio. Banana chocolate chips and coconut are among the top flavors. *Cheap. No cards.*

Mil Frutas
Rua Jardim Botânico, 585.
One of the best flavors is *chocolate com laranja* (chocolate with orange). *Cheap. No cards.*

Italian
L'Arlecchino
Rua Prudente de Moraes, 1387 (Ipanema); ☎ *259-7745 Mon.–Sat. 7 p.m.–2 a.m., Sun. noon–2 a.m., closed Tues.*
The harlequin decor of this two-story, brick-and-wood house recalls the clowns from the 17th–century Commedia del' Arte, but the cuisine is post-modern Italian. A buffet of iced fish greets you in the foyer, so fresh they're still moving. The owners from Northern Italy offer excellent fresh seafood salad, along with specialties like the *pasta bu-*

catini al cartocci (with fish and mushrooms) and the risotto with asparagus and scampi. Service is first class, though a tad snobby, and prices are continually changing. *Expensive. No cards.*

★ Da Brambini
Av. Atlântica, 514. Daily noon–11 a.m.; ☎ *275-4346.*
The newest addition to the beach drag in Copacabana is an absolute delight. Superb Italian cuisine in a tranquil, friendly environ; even the pasta sauces come piping hot. For less than $9, the *penne alla boscaiola*, with white sauce and mushrooms was such a joy, we still dream about it. *Moderate. All cards.*

★ Ettore
Av. Armando Lombardi, 800, loja D; ☎ *399-5611. Sun.–Thurs. noon–1 a.m., Fri.-Sat. noon–2 a.m.*
Natural rock walls and wooden pews make this famed Italian eatery seem like a peasant's grotto, but the antipastos, pizzas, and pastas are fit for a king. Owner Ettore Sinalschi learned to cook from his Italian grandmother, who inspired such creations as *tagliatelle modo mio* (pasta with thin strips of filet mignon and dry mushrooms) and the *gamberotti* (7 pillowlike pastas filled with shrimp and ricotta). Pizzas arrive with a very refined crust, and desserts, like the chocolate eclair, manage to be silky and firm simultaneously. The takeout counter is to die for. Reservations recommended. *Moderate. No cards.*

Florentina
Av. Atlântica, 458 (Leme); ☎ *275-7698.*
No reservations needed for this user–friendly cantina across the street from Leme beach. Pizza, ice cream sundaes, and pastas for reasonable prices in a boisterous setting. *Inexpensive. All cards.*

Gattopardo
Av. Borges de Medeiros, 1426 (Lagoa); ☎ *274-7748. Noon–5 p.m. daily, Sun. until 4 p.m.*
A great place for elite pizza with fine, crunchy crust. Socialites and theater people adore the Amaral, with tomatoes, eggplant, green and yellow peppers, anchovies, tuna, and olives. Extremely fine pastas with lots of cheese, basil, and tomatoes. *Moderate. No cards.*

★★★★ Grottamare
Rua Gomes Carneiro, 132 (Ipanema); ☎ *227-3186. Daily 7 a.m.–last client*
Wood–beam structures and exotic bouquets give this noted 11-year-old restaurant its tropical élan. Intimate seating is found behind the magnificent bar made out of a boat or in the main dining room, where the service is formal, but exceedingly friendly. The cuisine is Adriatic, meaning from the sea, and the Italian chef/owner, Paolo Neroni, goes to great extremes to please the most subtle palates. So good was our first appetizer—*pizza branca* sprayed with butter and rosemary—that we could have eaten it all night. Specialties are fish grilled *na brasa* (barbecue style); but my favorite was the *peixada* (for two), a glorious black pot of lobster, shrimp, squid, and filets seeped in a broth light enough to preserve flavor. Desserts, like the *torrone*—Italian ice cream with crystallized fruits—are intense. *Expensive. All cards.*

★ Satíricon
Rua Barão da Torre, 192 (Ipanema); ☎ *521-0627. Daily 7 a.m.–1 a.m., Sun. and holidays noon-midnight.*
Rock in Rio graduates like Paul Simon and Sting swear by this elite eatery, which offers the best fish in Rio, not to mention celebrity sightings on a good night. The Roman owner, Miro Leopardi, is the biggest fresh fish exporter in Brazil—hence the still wiggling fresh–water display when you enter. For starters try the *Gran Piatto di Mare*, a cornucopia of 6 types of fresh seafood in natural shells. For entrées, pick your own fish from swordfish to seabass to *tamboril* (a very white fish), as well as the accompanying sauce, or go for the Italian-made pasta and home-cooked fettucine. *Pasta all'Aragosta*, with lobster, champagne, basil, and tomato is stylish perfection. The salmon-colored walls, avant-garde art, tropical plants, and Roman arches may seem a bit faux-Californian, but Brazilians call it classy. Some gastronomics come just for the extravagant dessert menu or to hang out at the bar. Reserve on weekends. *Expensive. All cards.*

Le Streghe
Rua Prudente de Moraes, 129, Ipanema; ☎ 287-1369. 8 p.m.–2 a.m.
This restaurant, disco, and piano bar is popular with the rich, 30-plus set, as well as tourists who want to splurge and dress up. The piano bar is brocaded in mauve and dominated by a huge grand piano; the upstairs restaurant is more tropical, with flowered tablecloths and bamboo beams. The kitchen, under the baton of Stefano Monti, the Italian owner, has a thing for fresh white truffles. And the 13 desserts are infamous, particularly the pineapple flambé. Don't forget to visit the neighboring disco Calígola, run by the same owner. *Very expensive. No cards.*

Mexican
Lagoa Charlie's
Rua Maria Quitéria, 136; ☎ 287-0335.
The best Mexican food in Rio, accompanied by very loud mariachis. *Moderate–expensive. All cards.*

Oriental
Nova China
Av. Epitácio Pessoa, 1164;
☎ 287-3947. Mon.–Fri. 7 p.m.–2 a.m., Sat. noon–2 a.m., Sun. noon–midnight
Nothing surprising on the Chinese menu here, but the servings are honest and the environ unquestionably pleasant—a renovated colonial–style home overlooking the Lagoa. *Moderate. No cards.*

Kioto
Rua Ministro Tavare de Lyra, 105, 3rd floor (Flamengo); ☎ 205-9197.
Sequestered at the top of a snooker salon, in a street everyone passes but nobody knows by name, the Kioto casually mixes Japanese with Chinese. If you can't decide on sushi, sashimi or tempura, there's always sweet and sour pork. *Inexpensive. All cards.*

Chinese Palace
Av. Atlântica, 1212-A (Copacabana);
☎ 275-0145. Daily noon–3 p.m., 6 p.m.–midnight.
Chinese food in Brazil usually doesn't come cheap, nor is the quality spectacular. What the Palace has going for it is its location—on the beach—and a plate of unusually crispy and spicy spare ribs. And the spring rolls are at least recognizable. *Inexpensive–moderate. All cards.*

Take D'Or
Hotel Copa D'Or, Rua Figueiredo Magalhães, 875 (Copacabana); ☎ 235-6610.
A sushi bar for executives, prepared by Nobu San, a recent import from Japan. The real thing. But think twice about cholera. *Expensive. All cards.*

Pizza
Caravella
Rua Domingo Ferreira at the corner of Rua Bolivar. Postal 5-1/2 (Copacabana).
Best pizza in Rio. Period. *Moderate. No cards.*

Also see *Gattopardo* under "Italian."

Portuguese
★ Adega do Valentim
Rua da Passagem, 178 (Botafogo);
☎ 541-1138. Wed.–Mon. noon–2 a.m.; Fri.–Sat. noon–2 a.m.
With the salamis and garlic hanging from the ceiling and the Portuguese guitar trickling down from upstairs, all you need is Columbus to feel like you've landed in Lisbon. The classiest Portuguese food in Rio, Valentim's always guarantees a great spread. The owner, Valentim, with his Telly Savalas face, is one of those rare people at peace with his lot, and every corner of his restaurant exudes his warmth. Ask him to suggest an appetizer, called *petiscos*—all of them sumptuous and filling. Codfish—a Portuguese delicacy—has a million versions here, but I preferred the salmon *na brasa*, barbecue grilled, with almond-spiked rice. Portions are huge and can often serve two. The way they make coffee at your table will make you want to buy the pot. Alvarinho, a wonderful 1948 Portuguese wine, can run you about $200. *Expensive. No cards. Traveler's checks and dollars accepted.*

Antiquarius
Rua Aristides Espindola, 19 (Leblon);
☎ 294-1049. Daily noon–2 a.m.
One of the most chichi restaurants in Rio, Antiquarius has that kind of ineffable reputation that sometimes it can't match. Portu-

guese-inspired inventions with codfish are popular, as is the grilled octopus. Desserts are spectacular but usually steeped in an egg base that might require developed taste buds. Surrounded by such beautiful antiques and people, you might as well get dressed to kill. Reservations recommended. *Very expensive. No cards.*

Vegetarian/Natural
Natural
Rua Barão da Torre, 171 (Ipanema); ☎ 267-7799. *Daily 11:30 a.m.–midnight*
A homey brick house with good vegetarian and health-oriented food. Lunch only served at the location in Botafogo: *Rua 19 de Fevereiro, 118 (Botafogo). Cheap. All cards.*

Sabor Saúde
Rua Ataúlfo de Paiva, 630-A (Leblon); ☎ 239-4396. *Daily 9 a.m.–10:30 p.m.*
One of Rio's best health-restaurants, where the owner claims the vegetables are cultivated in tiny groups without toxins. For those addicted to brown rice, green vegetables, and fresh fruit, enjoy. *Cheap. All cards.*

Downtown is full of vegetarian and health-oriented restaurants open for lunch—popular among working girls and guys. Among the better ones are:

Cheio de Vida
Av. Treze de Maio, 33, sala 403; ☎ 232-6645. *Mon.–Fri. 11:30 a.m.–4 p.m. for lunch, and till 6:30 p.m.*
Difficult to locate (take the escalator up), but feast on the brown rice, green vegetables, and yam torts with soybean hamburgers. *Cheap. No cards.*

Greeness
Rua Sacadura Cabral, 233; ☎ 263-8016. *Daily 11 a.m.–3 p.m.*
Eight salads, vegetable soups, whole wheat bread, and a hot dish with 4 side orders. *Cheap. No cards.*

Teatime, Snacks, Sweet Tooths
Biscuit
Rua Carvalho de Mendonça at the corner of Rua Rodolfo Dantas (Copacabana); ☎ 541-8648.
In the heart of Copacabana, here's a good place to snatch a fast tea with luscious waffles, croissants, *pão de queijo*, and coffee with cream. Try the crepes suzettes. *Inexpensive. No cards.*

Casa do Pão de Queijo
Av. N.S. de Copacabana, 336 (Copacabana); ☎ 235-6424.
A treasure box for the best *pão de queijo* in Rio—tiny, delicate rolls of cheese bread that melt in your mouth and can easily become addictive. *Cheap. All cards.*

★ Confeitaria Colombo
Rua Gonçalves Dias, 32/36; ☎ 232-2300.
Established almost 100 years ago, this traditional pastry shop cum restaurant in the nervous heart of downtown still feels fin-de-siècle, with its fabulous sculptured walls and rinky piano. So a little seediness has set in—the pastry show is still impressive and the slow service just adds to the old–world charm. Waffles are excellent, and if you ask for a plate of *salgados*, you'll be served an array of salty biscuits and torts. For afternoon tea, try the *chá completo*—a dazzling service of cakes, toast, biscuits, sweets, and beverage. A visual must-see for architecture buffs —even the organ music sounds like a 19th-century horror show. There's also a smaller version in Copacabana at *Avenida N.S. de Copacabana, 890;* ☎ *257-8960. Moderate. No cards.*

Cervantes
Av. Prado Junior, 335 (Copacabana); ☎ 275-6147.
Artists and TV stars crowd in here after midnight for snacks and sandwiches. Inexpensive and filling. *No cards.*

Doce Delicia
Rua Anibal de Mendonça, 55, lojas C and D (Ipanema): ☎ 259-0239. *Mon–Fri. 11 a.m.–midnight, weekends 11 a.m.–8 p.m.*
An extension of the Pax restaurant, this delectable tea house two blocks from the beach is a perfect place to escape the heat. The desserts, like the maracujá pie, come straight from one of the best chefs in the city, and the salad bar looks clean.

La Thé Lautrec
Av. Atlântica, 1020 (Hotel Meridien, 3rd floor, Leme); ☎ 275-9922. *Daily noon–2 a.m.*

This fin-de-siècle café, with frosted glass and antique lamps, recalls teatime with Toulouse Lautrec. The 4–6:30 p.m. cavalcade of sweets, breads, and salty delights is a tradition among society ladies who arrive with their just-coiffed hair and cellular phones, but the fabulous spread will delight anyone with a late-afternoon craving. The iced chocolate drinks are perfect for relieving sunstroke, and the chocolate cake is superb. *Moderate. All cards.*

Pérgula
(Copacabana Palace Hotel) Av. Atlântica, 1702; for reservations: ☎ *255-7070, ext. 497. Mon.–Fri. 4 p.m.–7 p.m.*
Newly installed by Brit-born Annie Phillips, a former stewardess and graduate of the Cordon Bleu, afternoon tea at the Copacabana Palace is a hoot. In a cheery salon overlooking the wickedly large pool, Annie personally serves you hot chocolate or at least a dozen kinds of foreign teas from huge silver urns; then the formal waiters bring on Scottish pancakes, scones, and muffins; *then* you are invited to feast from a buffet of assorted finger sandwiches, Brazilian hot canapés, and a feast of sweets, cakes, and ice cream, including the most delicious fresh blackberries I've ever tasted. You'll find all sorts here: Brazilian socialites in Chanel suits, students from the American School, elite birthday parties, and just a few tourists. Sweet flute and guitar add to the luxurious calm. For a fixed price of $10, you could eat enough for lunch and dinner combined. *Moderate. All cards.*

Bars for Grazing and Cruising

Academia da Cachaça
Rua Conde Bernadote, 26, loja C.
A sidewalk café situated between Leblon and Gávea, famous for every kind of *batida* under the sun. The recipe is sugar-cane brandy, lemon, sugar, or honey, and a variety of flavors from chocolate to strawberry. *Inexpensive. No cards.*

Bar Lagoa
Av. Epitácio Pessoa, 1674.
The waiters are a little dense at this seaside bar (the most-oft-heard phrase is "*Garcon, pelo amor de Deus,*" or "Waiter, for the love of God"). But the *chopp* is honest, and the place is always packed. *Inexpensive. No cards.*

Restaurante Meia Pataca
Copacabana Beach.
Probably the most frequented street-side café bar on Av. Atlântica—famous for its *chopp* and for the prostitutes who might sidle up for some business. If you don't find the action amusing, or if you have children in tow, it's best not to linger.

Alberico's Bar
Av. Vieira Souto, 236 (Ipanema). Daily 11 a.m.–3 a.m.
Big, sprawling, and socially adept, Alberico's is the corner address in Ipanema for beachside grazing. Outside, the sidewalk is packed with small tables; inside, the 2nd floor has big picture windows for perusing bikinis. Those in the know skip dinner and order *chopp* and a plate of *petiscos* (or nosheries), such as the *manjubinha frita* (tiny fried fish), *frango à passarinho* (crispy chunks of chicken), or the provolone à *milanesa* (fried cheese strips.) Even the french fries are good. *Inexpensive-moderate. All cards.*

Banana Café
Rua Barão da Torre, 368; ☎ *262-7638. Daily 9 a.m.–3 a.m.*
You may have to flirt with the staff to jump the Palladium-style line, but if you're looking for the in-spot for Rio's tall, tan, and handsome, this is it. Sit outside under the veranda or brave the rock music inside the air-conditioned jungle to sample drinks like "Sex on the Beach" and 19 kinds of pizza. Add to that stylish hamburgers, upwardly mobile hot dogs, and even shrimp flambéed in cognac. Portions tend to be smaller than those at the average Brazilian restaurant, but how else can the clientele keep their figures? To get a good view, come around 8:30 p.m., but the steam doesn't rise until after 11. During the day, families can take advantage of the park and playground across the street. *Moderate. No cards.*

Caneco 70
Av. Delfim Moreira, 1026 (Leblon); ☎ *294-1180/ 10 a.m.–4 a.m.*
On the Tuesday night of the city bike run,

you'll find hordes of cyclists hanging here for a *chopinho regenerador* (a little rejuvenating beer!). The majority chow down on pizza *cortadinha à francesa* and the *bolinhos de bacalhau* for a quick pick-me-up. *Inexpensive. No cards.*

Bar Garota de Ipanema
Rua Vinícius de Moraes, 49 (Ipanema);
☎ *267-8787.*

It was here in 1960 that Tom Jobim and Vinícius de Moraes wrote the song "The Girl from Ipanema" and never looked back. Just two crazy guys who fell for a blonde passing their barstools every day without ever saying *alô*. Of course, she sure sidled up after they got famous, but that's another story. That's about all this bar has going for it, but nostalgia runs deep. During Carnaval this corner of Ipanema, a few blocks from the beach, attracts the most flamboyant personalities, usually in drag. *Inexpensive. No cards.*

Dining in Barra
Giannetto
Av. Sernambetiba, 5800 (Barra da Tijuca);
☎ *433-2429.*

A former mechanical engineer with a gift for cooking has opened one of the most honest Italian restaurants in Rio. Unusual offerings like squid salad, vegetarian antipastos, and eggplant marinated in white wine set the menu apart, and the array of rigatonis, macaronis, and etceteronis are all winners. The pesto sauce is considered perfect. *Moderate. All cards.*

Lokau
Av. Sernambetiba 13500 (Barra da Tijuca); ☎ *433-1418.*

One of plastic surgeon Ivo Pitanguy's favorite spots, Lokau is an informal but pricey eatery on its own dock facing Lagoa de Marapindi—a lake full of baby alligators that are being preserved. Families with children love to come here since free-ranging ducks, swans, chickens, and toucans are all part of the open-air decor, but it can also be very romantic. Grass-hut tables add to the tropical allure, and kids can spend hours on the tire swings. Fish runs about $18, lobster about $25. *Muqueca*—a Bahian fish stew with palm oil—is especially good. Despite the formidable prices, the joint is packed on weekends. *Expensive. No cards.*

★ **Nau Catarineta**
Av. Sernambetiba, 760 (Barra da Tijuca)

One of the most romantic spots in Rio, this cavernlike, candlelit joint about 40 min. from Copacabana is a secret among lovers, who go for the dark lights, the hors d'oeuvres, and the sexy drinks called *batidas afrodisíacas* (the *ostra virgem*, or virgin oyster, with vodka, cream of coconut, and pineapple juice, is particularly fine). Fondues are also a turn-on. Go early, since the place gets packed after 8 p.m., and there are no reservations. *Moderate. All cards.*

Peixe Frito
Av. Fernando Matos, 371; ☎ *492-9494. Daily noon-midnight, Sunday noon-10 p.m.*

The fish lover's version of a *churrascaria*: an all-you-can-eat buffet of grilled fish, fish-inflected salads, and shrimp-defined stews; then the waiter serves you fried shrimps, stuffed crabs, and fried squid till you drop. Families come from the beach, but the high–beamed wood ceilings keep the noise currents circulating. About $12 per person, but sometimes women receive a 20 percent discount. Reservations a plus. *Moderate. No cards.*

Cervejaria Biruta
Av. Sernambetiba, 6470 (Barra da Tijuca); ☎ *433-2769.*

The place to drink forever in Barra—a restaurant with a decor complex featuring at least 9 different environs, from a Texas saloon to a Roman café to the old Rio train station. Go before dinner for excellent *cerveja* and a plate of thinly sliced cold cuts called *gamela de linguiças variedas*, or pig out on the many hors d'oeuvres. *Inexpensive. No cards.*

In São Conrado
Guimas Restaurant
São Conrado Fashion Mall

Frequented by celebs and musicians, this light, airy bistro makes a perfect lunch stop for shoppers at São Conrado Fashion Mall. Menus in English offer chicken breast with blue cheese and fish filet cooked with slices of papaya and covered with Gorgonzola cheese. The salad with warm mushrooms is excellent. While you wait for your food, feel free to doodle on the white paper tablecloths with crayons. *Moderate. All cards.*

Álvaro's
São Conrado Fashion Mall.
Famous for its *chopp* and huge portions of excellent fish. Shrimp omelettes (out of season) run about $20, filet mignon about $7. *Moderate. All cards.*

Lagostão
São Conrado Fashion Mall, Estrada da Gávea, 899, loja 206–A; ☎ *322-0269.*
Excellent seafood. *Moderate. No cards.*

★ Valentino's Il Ristorante
Av. Niemeyer, 121; ☎ *274-1122.*
Top-class Italian cuisine located at the Sheraton Rio Hotel & Towers. Go for lunch and spend the day poolside or at the stunning secluded beach, then finish off with dinner at the hotel's outdoor barbecue grill. *Expensive. No cards.*

RIO BY NIGHT

Cariocas party hard and they party late, and you may find yourself asking, "Don't these people ever have to get up for work in the morning?" That's when you'll probably realize it's not a good idea to do business before noon in Rio. Truly, *cariocas* seem to have limitless energy for late-night fun, and even during the weekdays, you'll find popular restaurants packed from 10 p.m. on. For a tourist, however, there's only one way to survive the nightlife in Rio, and that's by taking a nap between 6 and 8 p.m. every night. By 9 p.m. you'll be ready to dine at a fashionable hour, and by 11 you can start cruising the scene.

There are two faces of nightlife in Rio—one touristic and the other pure *carioca*. First-time visitors will probably feel compelled to witness at least one samba extravaganza, featuring near-naked *mulatas* (cream-colored gals) who flick off their bras, samba to rapid-fire drum licks, and parade around like the Folies Bergère on uppers. The real musical culture, however, is better found in the small piano bars and jazz clubs, where you can settle back and groove on the sensual sounds of *música popular brasileira* (or MPB, a term that refers to the music of bossa nova, Milton Nascimento, Gilberto Gil, Caetano Veloso, and many others). The country's most famous singers can often be found performing at large venues like Canecão or the Imperador, where you can nosh and drink at small tables. Check the newspapers or ask your concierge who is playing.

Discos don't get hot until after midnight, when *cariocas* take to the floor to do what they've done naturally since birth—sing and dance their hearts out. You may be surprised by all the American and Brit rock that the DJs play, not to mention reggae and funk, but there's a joy that exists in Brazilian nightclubs that seems absent in the overly pretentious clubs of, say, New York. Simply, in Rio, people love to express themselves, and the enthusiasm is contagious. Some clubs have special drug-free matinee parties for teens, and some discos even hold roller-skating sessions—with instruction! Single women may go to most discos alone, though rest assured you will be stared at and probably hit upon. And men should be careful about exactly who is picking them up. Transvestite prostitutes are rampant in Rio (and often violent), and some seduction scenes are just foreplay for wallet-snatching or more. (One way to discern gender, I've been told, is to check out the size of the feet and the wrists!)

For the more regionally minded, a stop at a *gafieira* or *forró* hall is essential. Here you'll find some of the best ballroom dancers in South America, or as in the case of the latter, high-spirited native dancing propelled by a Northeastern beat. Big bands often play in these clubs, and the action remains hot until 4 a.m. These dance halls are rarely situated in fashionable neighborhoods, but decent common folk attend them, and there are rarely outbreaks of trouble.

The samba shows may not be enough to satisfy everyone's erotica quotient. In this section, I've included an agenda of clubs that offer live sex shows and striptease, but they should be investigated with caution. One of the recent rages in Rio, however, has been the wildly successful Os Leopardos, which features good-natured male striptease for women only on one night, and presentations for mixed couples and gays on others. The show is tasteful but not tame, and *carioca* girls have been flocking to hold their engagement parties there.

Romantic

One of the best ways to wind up a night of great partying is at one of the plushly romantic hotel bars, like the Meridien or the Caesar Park. Top-class hotels such as these usually feature the city's best local musicians, always gracious enough to take personal requests. And after-hours jam sessions at clubs like Jazzmania and People Down are often better than the regular shows, with famous friends of the soloists sitting in.

And as the night prowling winds down, there's nothing better than breakfast-at-dawn—that is, before you hit the sheets to get back to the beach by noon. If you're not staying at a hotel with a fabulous breakfast buffet, head for the Rio Palace Hotel, where you can indulge in the freshest croissants, cakes, fruits, and omelettes while you watch a glorious sun rise over Copacabana.

A few words of caution for all kinds of night revelers. Don't get so intoxicated that you forget who you are, and remember to take taxis to and from your destination. Carry only the amount of money you will need to get you through the night. And if you can help it, stay away from darkly lit areas.

WHERE TO FIND NIGHTLIFE IN RIO

Piano Bars

★ **Chico's Bar**
Av. Epitácio Pessoa, 1560 (Lagoa); ☎287-3514.
Where Brazilian musicians and out-of-town colleagues come to jam until the wee hours—plush, dark, and sexy. *Moderate. All cards.*

Rio's
Pq. do Flamengo (Flamengo); ☎ 551-1131. Noon–3 a.m.
Part of the restaurant called Rio's, this made-for-romance piano bar is a dark, cushy den with mood-making music—one of the sexiest places in Rio. *Moderate. All cards.*

★ **Saint Honoré**
Av. Atlântica, 1020 (Hotel Meridien, 37th floor, Leme). Daily noon–3 p.m. and 8 p.m.–1 a.m.
A plush piano bar adjacent to the even plusher French restaurant in the Hotel Meridien. *Moderate–expensive. All cards.*

Vinícius Bar
Av. N.S. de Copacabana, 1144; ☎ 267-1497. Daily 8 p.m. Live music weekdays 9 p.m.–2 a.m.; weekends 9 p.m.–4 a.m.
One of the best attended, 30–something bars for live music and dancing, Vinícius is located right next to a good steak house in a prime area of Copacabana. A tradition among *cariocas*, it seats about 350 persons, who come to soak up the solid bands and rip up the dance floor. Tourists will feel welcome—the tables are close and the natives friendly. The joint is named after one of the most beloved lyricists and poets in Brazil—Vinícius de Moraes—though when I was there, nary a Brazilian tune or lyric was heard. Cover charge runs between $6-7. *Moderate. All cards.*

Zeppelin
Estrado do Vidigal, 471; ☎ 274-1549. Thurs. and Sun. 8 p.m.–1:30 a.m., and weekends 8 p.m.–3 a.m.
With the sea in the horizon and a *caipivodca de lima e tangerina* in hand (that's a caipirinha made with vodka and lime and tangerine juices), it's easy enough to fall in love at this popular bar as the lone guitarist plays Djavan, Caetano Veloso and Lulu Santos. Do try the buffalo cheese (*mussarela de búfala*), a Brazilian delicacy. *Inexpensive. No cards.*

Alberto's
Av. Copacabana, 7 (Leme); ☎ 275-4099.
Just two blocks from Leme beach, here's that tiny musical bar that only the locals know about. So maybe the record companies aren't knocking down their door (the house guitar/singers are a bit *desafinado* and even the guest performers sometimes sound like they're braying), but everyone's soul is in the right place and you might even rub knees with an ex-soccer player. The sexy Latin owner (he loves boleros) sometimes plays keyboards, especially on Tango nights (Tues., Thurs., and Sat.) when a young Argentine duo twirls center-stage. By the time you arrive, the club may have hopped to another corner, so have your concierge check the address. Bahian specialties and typical meats are served for a moderate price; music cover is about $2. Weekends you'll need a reservation—there's only ten tables.

Jazz Clubs

Au Bar
Av. Epitácio Pessoa, 864 (Lagoa); ☎ 259-1041. Mon.–Sat. 6 p.m.–2 a.m.
The newest success story in Rio, this 2-year-old-bar has become the place to listen to Brazilian music—romantic, dark and cave–like, with Spanish arches and a view of the twinkling Lagoa. Live Brazilian music (usually piano, bass, guitar, and voice) runs from 5 p.m.–11:00 p.m.; starting at 11:00 p.m., there's a 1-1/2 hour show with well-known national singers, like jazz great Leny Andrade. Sundays feature classical music. Music cover runs about $4; add an extra $8 per person if you eat dinner. There's no cover after 12:30 a.m. Reservations for shows should be made about 2 days in advance. *Moderate. No cards.*

★ **Jazzmania**
Av. Rainha Elizabeth, 769 (Ipanema);
☎ 227-2447. Daily opens 9 p.m., shows at 9:30 p.m., two shows in summer

This jazz club for people who love good music (especially Brazilian jazz) was opened about 10 years ago and was recently reinaugurated with a fabulous sound system. Come early to catch the wraparound vista of Ipanema Beach, stay for dinner, then listen to such greats as Egberto Gismonti, Edu Lobo, and Leila Pinheiro. The Blues Project runs Feb.-April, featuring international stars like John Hammond, Hy Rodgers, and Sugar Blues. Dinner can run around $30, but the entrance fee, $4 on Mon. and Tues., and $5-6 Wed.-Sun., is incredible. During the Free Jazz Festival at the Nacional Hotel, the soloists come here for late-night jam sessions. *Moderate. No cards.*

Le Rond–Point
Av. Atlântica, 10020 (Copacabana);
☎ 275-9922.

A plush chrome-and-glass bar at the Meridien Hotel, with real Magrittes on the wall and a fiery house band that excels in MPB. *Moderate. All cards.*

Mistura Fina
Rua Garcia D'Avila, 15 (Ipanema);
☎ 259-9394.

This casual restaurant with outdoor tables attracts young upper-crust *cariocas* who dig the live band that cooks until 2 a.m. Until 10 p.m., it's a great place to enjoy soft guitar and piano. *Inexpensive. No cards.*

★ **People Down**
Av. Bartolomeu Mitre, 370-A;
☎ 294-0547.

The upstairs club called People is private, but People Down (downstairs) offers some of the best sounds from Brazil and abroad in an intimate setting. Frequenters of the famous Blue Note in Manhattan will be reminded of that haunt. Insider Tip: Excellent bars with live music can be also found at the Meridien, Rio Sheraton, Rio Othon, Rio Palace, and the Caesar Park hotels.

Samba Shows

Oba Oba
Rua Humaitá, 110 (Botafogo);
☎ 296-9848. One show a night at 10:30 p.m.

Although the show Oba Oba that tours the States is enormous fun, this one, based for years in Rio, panders to the lowest common denominator. The music is too loud, the topless dancers bored, and the master of ceremonies seems like he's making fun of a lounge lizard (unfortunately, he's serious). The variety show consists of singers, *destaques* (girls who pose in Carnaval costumes), folkloric dancers, and pathetic group participation—at least the *capoeira* artists, performing martial-art acrobatics, are excellent. If you're a man, be prepared to be pulled up to play choo-choo with near-naked *mulatas*.

★ **Plataforma I**
Rua Adalberto Ferreira, 31;
☎ 274-4022.

Featuring one of the city's best parades of Brazilian beauties, this popular variety show has a new twist these days—*mulato* boys, who waggle their booties on a platform that extends far into the audience. Here, you'll get a more authentic sense of the samba parade: The costumes are better than Oba Oba and the spirit more earthy than Scala. Like a variety show in Harlem during the '20s, the show includes a sultry *mulata* singer with an operatic range and a chorus of gorgeous coffee–colored girls with figures big to small. There's also a very sexy *gaúcho* dancer who does a flaming rope trick that's out of this world. Extremely dramatic, a tribute to Bahia and *candomblé* features drummers who nearly fall into trance. And the gravity-defying acrobatics of the *capoeiristas* are terrific. Seats are close together, and the maitre d' always asks each country to get up and sing. Better learn "New York, New York."

Scala I/Scala II
Av. Afrânio de Melo Franco, 296;
☎ 239-4448. 8 p.m.–4 a.m.

The most sophisticated show in Rio, Scala is more like the Folies Bergère—rich and snazzy, with an international flair, although some cariocas prefer the more folkloric spirit of Plataforma. Fine international cuisine is also served in a luxurious setting, with crystal chandeliers and black marble stairs. Most recommended is the *Tournedos à la Scala*, with mushroom sauce, sautéed potatoes, and *risotto alla Piemontese*. Shows start at 9 p.m., but you can stay and dance until 5 a.m.

Candomblé

Any organized macumba or candomblé for tourists is sure to be less than the real thing. The trance religion, a syncretism of African and Catholic images, is an extremely private affair, replete with powerful drumming, incense, and congregants falling into unconscious trances. Hence, finding a good *terreiro* (the equivalent of a church service) in Rio is not the easiest task, nor would you want to wander there alone, as they are sometimes located in poor neighborhoods not exactly hospitable to strangers. Ask your concierge if he can arrange something for you, usually on a Sat. night. Reserve a private car to take you and pick you up, or better yet, have the car wait for you. If all else fails, **Fenician Tur** *Av. N.S. de Copacabana, 335, loja B;* ☎ *235-3843* conducts a macumba tour on Wed. nights starting at 7 p.m. for about $45, but the authenticity cannot be vouched for. Theatrical presentations of macumba distilled for the general public are held at the club **Terreiro–Um** *Av. Borges Medeiros, 3192;* ☎ *226-0577*. Call for times.

Musical Theaters

Canecão
Av. Wenceslau Bráz, 215; ☎ *295-3044*
The major venue for the city's largest acts, Canecão resembles the smaller clubs in Atlantic City. Check in the newspaper to see who's playing—you might get Tom Jobim, Gal Costa, or Simone. Large screens amplify the stage performance—I once saw Roberto Carlos singing with his own image 30 years younger—eerie. If you sit at a table, order some drinks and a plate of *petiscos*, but if you pay by card, it will take forever to leave. Tickets, about $25, usually go on sale a week before performances and must be bought at the box office. You can also sit on cheaper, bleacher-type seats on the sidelines, but the view isn't great.

Imperador
Rua Dias da Cruz, 170 (Méier); ☎ *592-7733.*
This newer venue for musical shows of international status offers large shows by performers like Tom Jobim and Gal Costa; Shirley MacLaine made a huge hit here. Tickets should be purchased in advance at the box office or at Fiorucci in the Rio Sul Shopping Center.

Rock and Video

Show Point
Rua Maria Quitéria, 42 (Ipanema);
☎ *521-5393. Tues.–Sun. 6 p.m. and 9 p.m. shows*
A coffeehouse Americana-style with a Broadway obsession. Videos of musicals are played upstairs; downstairs you'll find the newest rock groups during the week, and more famous ones on the weekends. Dinner runs about $10, with a $3 cover for live music. *Moderate. No cards.*

Discoteques

Hippopotamus
Rua Barão da Torre, 354; ☎ *247-0351.*
Cariocas will swoon if you say you're going to Hippopotamus, Rio's most exclusive private club. If you're staying at a 5-star hotel (and some 4-stars), you need only show your hotel ID card, but check first. Weekends are packed with chichi Brazilians, but dining in the small but charming salon is possible for a $20 minimum. *Expensive. No cards.*

Stop Night
Av. Atlântica, 1910; ☎ *255-7583. Daily 11:30 p.m.*
Located on the beach in Copacabana, this disco caters to the 25-and-under set, who can understand why there's a coffin in the middle of the dance floor. Upstairs, under a planetarium of lights, a small circular dance floor gloriously looks out on the beach. On weekends, live music starts at 11 p.m., and sometimes up to 1000 people cram in to dance under the tropical plants and rock

walls. During the week, the fee is about $4, $6 on weekends. Dress glitter.

Babilônia
Av. Afrânio de Melo Franco, 296;
☎ *239-4448*
Thurs. and Sun. are a blast at Babilônia, with roller-skating (including instruction) starting at 9 p.m. At 10:30 p.m., the place transforms into a hot disco. Afternoon sessions from 4–8 p.m. on the weekends cater only to teens.

★ **Resumo da Opera**
Av. Borges Medeiros, 1426. Thurs.–Sun., from 10 p.m. Sat. and Sun. 4–10 p.m. (for 14–18-year-olds)
Next to Gattopardo Cafe and Teatro Lagoa, this is the latest trend-setting club owned by Ricardo Amaral, a businessman who understands Rio's night pulse. Special matinee sessions for teens on Sat. and Sun. are drug-free.

Help
Av. Atlântica, 3432; ☎ *521-1269*
Usually only tourists stumble into this neon-blaring disco located on Av. Atlântica—most *cariocas* wouldn't be caught dead there. On the other hand, it seems to be a good disco for single men on the prowl, but beware of prostitutes. You might be charged for your affections.

Zoom
Largo de São Conrado, 20 (São Conrado);
☎ *322-4179*
Hip young couples frequent this glitzy disco in São Conrado, with its razzmatazz light show and excellent sound system. Six bars keep the social interaction hot.

Insider Tip:

The best hotel disco is the Palace Club at the Rio Othon.

Dancing/Gafieiras

Ballroom dancing Fred-and-Ginger style holds a powerful sway over *cariocas*, with special clubs called *gafieiras* allocated for exactly that style. Even if you don't dance, the sight of world-class performers, as well as experienced commoners doing the cha–cha, the samba, and the Brazilian tango should make your heart flutter. A code of behavior dominates the scene, however. A woman cannot refuse an offer to dance, and there may be no "indecent" gestures made between dancing couples. There's even a security man watching to ensure that the unwritten rules are obeyed.

Asa Branca
Av. Mem de Sá, 17; ☎ *252-4428.*
A fabulous New Orleans–style mansion more than 100 years old houses the most sophisticated dance hall in Rio. Even Prince Charles passed through its ornate portals, where well-known Brazilian artists perform live. The house band is infectious. *Moderate. No cards.*

Estudantina
Pr. Tiradentes 79/1st floor (Centro);
☎ *232-1149. Thurs., Fri., and Sat. 10:30 p.m.-4 a.m.*
Here's the best *gafieira* in town, where you'll find serious dancers who know how to have fun. You'll have to brave a rough part of town to get there, but the clientele is respectable. Be on the safe side and take a taxi to the 2nd-story flat. Once inside, you'll be impressed by the tight band and skillful feet. Best day to go is *Thurs. Inexpensive. No cards.*

Elite
Rua Frei Caneca, 4/1st floor (Centro);
☎ *232-2317. Sat. 11 p.m.–4 a.m., Sun. 10 p.m.–3 a.m. Fri. 5–11 p.m.*
Another version of Estudantina, where there's a variety of live bands and the women usually pay half price. *Inexpensive. No cards.*

Sassaricando
Estrada do Joá, 151 (São Conrado);
☎ *322-3911. Thurs.–Sun. 10 p.m.–4 a.m. and Sun. 8 p.m.–2 a.m.*
A post-modern *gafieira* with neon ambience, colored mirrors, and full orchestra playing the hits of Frank Sinatra and Ary Barroso. Tango is the passion on Thurs. nights, and Sun. is dominated by Latin rhythms. Timid singles are helped by a card system that lets the waiters deliver your name and number to a prospective date.

Samba

Dancing samba well is an art, so think about taking a few lively lessons. Classes are held at the **Só Arte Escola de Dança** *Rua Assunção, 207 (Botafogo);* ☎ *286-6522* but check their schedule in advance. Then head for a samba rehearsal at a samba school (see *index*), or the following "**samba clubs**," where simple folks dance couples–samba thigh to thigh. The music might get screechy, but that's the point. (Call in advance to check times.)

Olímpico Clube
Rua Pompeu Loureiro, 116 (Copacabana): ☎ *235-2909.*

Nega Fulô
Rua Conde de Irajá, 132 (Botafogo); ☎ *266-6294.*

Try the following for **forró**, that nearly manic, upbeat dance of the Northeast. These clubs are often fly-by-nights, so ask your concierge to confirm.

Forró do Leblon
Rua Bartolomeu Mitre, 630 (Leblon).
Forró do Copacabana Av. N.S. de Copacabana, 435.

Insider Tip

In 1993 Roberto de Regina, a medical doctor, Renaissance scholar, and director of the Camerata Antique de Curitiba, began giving fabulous harpsichord recitals on his massive estate in Guaratiba, inside a medieval chapel he refurbished himself. Following the performance in full Middle Ages regalia, the guests are treated to a chicken curry dinner, then transported home. A little anachronistic for Brazil (since the Middle Ages never occurred here), but the music and the environs are reportedly charming. Price is about $50 with transportation. Only Fri-Sun.

For more information, call: **Super Fly**, *Av. Epitácio Pessoa, 3624, room 201;* ☎ *322-2286.*

THE MOST ROMANTIC THINGS TO DO IN RIO

- Take a night drive around the Lagoa with the golden-lit Christ marking your way, stopping off for Mexican food at Lagoa Charlie's or chop suey at Nova China.

- Settle into the cozy piano bar at Mariu's in Leme, where there's no cover and the bar opens at 5 p.m. Alcoholic tropical concoctions are delicious, as well as the virgin fruit cocktails with *creme de leite,* orange juice, and strawberries.

- Take a moonlit stroll around the Marina da Glória, topped off by a cocktail or dinner cruise on the Albacora Yacht. Night cruises with dinner on board are held on Thurs., Fri., and Sat. from 9 p.m. to 1 a.m. During the week, dinner only aboard the anchored ship. For reservations, ☎ *205-6496.*

- Take a cab to the elite motels where *cariocas* do their love business (by the hour) surrounded by private saunas, room service, and mirrored ceilings. Best one is VIP's *Av. Niemeyer, 418;* ☎ *322-1662.*

- Snuggle up in the piano bar at Rio's Parque do Flamengo; ☎ *551-1131* and groove on the soft jazz until 2 a.m.

- Ride a horsedrawn carriage through the colonial streets of Ilha da Paquetá (Paquetá Island). Get there by ferry, leaving from Praça Quinze daily. Stay the day and eat a twilight dinner in a typical village restaurant.

- Catch the sunset from any of the following places: Corcovado, Sugar Loaf, Fishermen's Walk in Leme, Urca facing the Rio–Nitéroi Bridge, São Conrado facing Gávea Mountain, and from any point around the lagoon.

- Bathe under a waterfall in Tijuca Forest, followed by a picnic lunch at the Emperor's Table.

- Dance cheek-to-cheek at Asa Branca.

EROTIC RIO

The real eroticism in Rio is free—it's in the waves, in the music, in the lilt of a walk, or the smile of a beautiful woman or man. There is, however, a subculture of porn to be had in Rio, though it doesn't come highly recommended. As there's no law prohibiting live sex on stage, erotic clubs in Rio have gained a rep among world travelers, especially Germans, but to tell the truth, most people find these shows unartistic, animalistic, and violent. On the other hand, that may be exactly what you're looking for. Many of the clubs, located near the Meridien, are often fly-by-nights, with names and addresses changing quickly for whatever reasons your imagination can supply. A good source for information is your concierge, who may have already approached you if you are a single man traveling alone. While I can't be an arbiter of morality in this guide, I do feel obligated to pass on a few warnings: Fights break out often at these clubs, and assaults on tourists are not uncommon. Some taxi drivers won't even take you to them. If you do go, leave all your jewelry, credit cards, and passport in your hotel safe; take only enough money to last you the night, and hide a little extra cash in your shoe.

WHERE TO FIND EROTICA IN RIO

Barbarela Boite
Show Av. Princesa Isabel, 263 A;
☎ 275-7348
Considered to have the most beautiful women performing striptease. Some explicit sex. Located near the Meridien Hotel, in front of the Hotel Plaza Copacabana. Call for show times. Card: MC only.

New Scotch Boite
Av. Princesa Isabel, 7; ☎ 275-5499. Daily 4 p.m.7 a.m.
The erotic show is amplified by the presence of a discotheque, samba show, and striptease with a bevy of *mulatas* with prodigious figures. Located directly across the street from the Meridien, with 6 shows nightly; an opportunity to party. *No cover, no minimum.*

La Cicciolina
Av. Princesa Isabel, at the corner of Rua Viveiro de Castro 15-A; ☎ 275-8949
Named after the Italian porn star turned politician turned artist, Jeff Koons' ex-wife, this bar offers two erotic shows per night. Cover charge plus 2-drink minimum. Call for times.

The Exception to the Rule: Erotica for all Seasons

Os Leopardos
Teatro Alaska, Av. Copacabana, loja Hotel. ☎ 247-9842. Fri. and Sat. at midnight, Thurs. and Sun. at 9:30 p.m. You can't blame this one on the bossa nova, but the latest trend in Brazilian big cities is male strip tease—that is to say, artistic male strip tease! A racier, and more serious version of Chippendales in the States, the original show was called "Night of the Leopards," which made its way around the club scene until it

landed these days at the Teatro Alaska, once a seedy gay theater now resurrected into funkydom. These days, lots of girls hold their engagement parties here, with the bride pouring champagne on the "leopard" of her choice. For the strip finale, which includes some of the most beautiful men in Rio, the participants must come onstage with a hard-on—an effect that looked to these rather inexperienced eyes like Birnam Wood advancing. The show is enlivened by several transvestite MC's, the best of which is Rogéria, an international star with glowing blonde hair and a great singing voice that deserves kudos. Do slink down in your chair if you don't want to be dragged up on stage at the end to give baths (yes!). Obviously, you have to be in the mood for this kind of show, but the night I went, the theater was equally divided between gays, couples, straight men, and single women, all having a good-natured hoot.

Women should also look for spin-offs at other clubs, sometimes called "Casa das Mulheres" (Women's House), which present ladies-only shows.

Do note: The **Teatro Alaska,** located in a shopping mall off of *Av. Atlântica in Copacabana* (near the Rio Palace Hotel), is today better illuminated and secured so that it is safe to attend. Next door, you might note the evangelical church, which always seems to hold loud services just at the time of the show!

Sex Stores
Complement Sex Shop
Av. Nossa Senhora de Copacabana, 581, loja 306 (Copacabana); ☎ *255-9348*
Accoutrements of the sport, including lingerie, aphrodisiacs, videos, and appliances. A discreet shop (3rd floor) on the main shopping drag of Copacabana, but I wouldn't suggest that a single woman go alone.

Escort Services
Escort services that provide more than massage or mere company abound in Rio, and advertisements can be found in tourist brochures and newspapers—using the tag words *Massagem* or *Relax.* The concierge of your hotel will not even blink an eye if you ask for his assistance. However, do note: Although prostitution is not against the law in Brazil, there are few, if any, regulations concerning health, so consider it a dangerous pastime. The services of a more elite class of women are supplied by Scort Girls, which serves businessmen needing anything from a chic companion for a night on the town to a traveling secretary and more.

GAY RIO

Gay life in Brazil has played a colorful if somewhat veiled role in Brazilian culture ever since colonial days. A riveting book on the subject is *Perverts in Paradise,* written by one of the founders of the gay movement in Brazil, who has made a fascinating, if controversial analysis of the gay influence on politics, religion, and the arts. Today, a number of Brazil's most beloved musicians are openly gay and/or bisexual, but it has never colored their popularity. In fact, the most flamboyantly gay performer, Ney Matogrosso, numbers among his fans a lot of older women who adore his campy clothes and outrageous behavior. Carnaval seems to bring out latent transvestitism in a number of men, many of whom are not gay, yet revel in the opportunity to blur social distinctions and indulge in sexual fantasy. All this is not to say that the gay lifestyle is readily accepted in Brazil. Gay bashing is not uncommon, and the fact that a number of transvestite prostitutes have murdered unsuspecting clients has not gone over well in the community. The AIDS epidemic has severely dampened blatant sexual license as well, especially during Carnaval, and anyone traveling to Brazil to live out sexual fantasies should think twice—if not three or four times. It cannot bear repeating enough: No sexually active person, gay or straight, should ever travel to Brazil without condoms. (For more information, see "Disease" in the *Directory.*)

The Scene

Rio is the gay capital of South America. Since Argentina forbids transvestism, international devotees of the art eventually find their way here, particularly during Carnaval. Cinelândia downtown and other places in Lapa have long been traditional gay hangouts, but they remain unsavory, even by carioca standards. It's common knowledge that rich, foreign gays tend to stay at the **Copacabana Palace;** as such, a thin strip of beach in front of the hotel, called "The Bolsa," attracts a lot of *movimento.* Another gathering place is the monthly club called **Turma Okay** *Rua do Rezende, 43* located at Rua Gomes Freire downtown. Other points of interest are:

Maxim's Bar/Restaurant *Av. Atlântica, 1850-A (Copacabana);* ☎ *255-7444* Located in front of the Hotel Excelsior, this bar/restaurant attracts the same clientele as the Copacabana Palace. *Feijoada* is served on Sat., and the fish is considered outstanding. *Moderate. All cards.*

Le Boy *Poste 6, Rua Raul Pompeia*, near the *Stúdio* Copacabana movie house. Owned by a Frenchman, this disco attracts a sophisticated gay crowd.

Basement *Av. N.S. de Copacabana, 1241 LJ I* A new disco in Copacabana caters to all types, with an emphasis on gay.

Underground *Prado Junior, 36* A disco in the red-light district.

Carnaval

The main gay ball, called the Grande Gala G, is usually held at Scala Av. Afrânio de Melo Franco, 296 (Leblon); ☎ 239-4448. All kinds of guests and tourists may attend, though the final roll call tends to be predominantly gay. In 1991, the Sugar Loaf Ball ended up all gay. Trends change with the years, so inquire when you arrive.

Insider Tip:

Warning: Prado Junior–the red-light district, along with the Lido Square near the Meridien, are very dangerous areas to walk through at night.

HANDS-ON RIO

An A-B-C Guide

AIRLINES

See also *Directory*.

Varig Airlines offers direct flights to Rio leaving from New York, Los Angeles, Chicago, and Miami. (*Toll-free* ☎ *800-468-2744.*)

United Airlines flies Miami–Rio and New York–Rio daily.
(*Toll-free* ☎ *800-241-6522.*)

American Airlines flies New York–Miami–Rio daily. (*Toll-free* ☎ *800-433-7300.*)

Japan Airlines flies Tokyo–Rio (with a stop in L.A.) once on Sat. (*Toll-free* ☎ *800-525-3663.*)

Varig and British Airways are the only airlines that fly to Rio from London.

Discounts on flights to Rio are available to members of the **Brazilian American Cultural Center** *20 W. 46th St., New York, NY 10036;* ☎ *212-242-7838 or toll-free 800-222-2746.* For more information see "Package Deals" under *Directory*.

Bas–Brazil Travel Agency offers an excellent 5-night package in Rio, including airfare out of Miami, hotel, transfers from airport, and a half–day city tour for about $986 (about $250 more than a budget-class airfare). For more information contact **Brazil Bas–Brazil** *551 Fifth Ave. New York, NY 10017;* ☎ *212-682-5310.*

ARRIVALS BY AIR

All international flights and some domestic ones use the **Galeão International Airport** (pronounced Gah–ley–ow) *Praça Salgado Filho (Ponte Aérea);* ☎ *(21) 220-7728;* ☎ *(21) 210-2457.* New facilities allow for international passengers who are flying on to other parts of Brazil to check in on the same level, so you won't have to schlep your luggage all over the terminal. In general, however, Setor A is for domestic flights, Setor B for international. Upon arrival, follow the crowds to customs, where you must present your passport, visa, and the card of embarkation you filled out on the airplane. (Remember to keep this card of embarkation because you must present it on departure.) Then follow the signs to pick up your luggage. Located about 45 minutes from Copacabana, Galeão is a modern multitiered structure with a post office, bank, exchange houses, restaurants and bars, and boutiques selling crystals, bikinis, T-shirts, and souvenirs. On your way home, arrive early and browse for any last-minute shopping, although rest assured, prices may be double that which you'll find in the city.

For tourist information, ask for directions to the Rio Tur information booth ☎ *398-4073*, where English–speaking guides will provide you with brochures, maps, and general assistance.

Aeroporto Santos Dumont *Praça Salgado Filho Ponte Aérea;* ☎ *220-7728;* ☎ *210-2457* is a 20-minute drive from the South Zone, just on the edge of downtown. A few air-taxi firms and the Rio– São Paulo shuttle are serviced here.

Insider Tip:

Most Varig flights to other parts of the country leave from the international airport. However, always verify which airport you will be using when you purchase your ticket. I myself had a crazed moment of confusion (not to mention driving my cabbie crazy) after I'd already piled in and didn't know where I was headed. The ticket itself gives no clue.

Airport Transportation

A new road from the international airport was built for Eco '92, cutting travel time to the South Zone down to about 1/2 hour. The easiest way to reach your hotel from the airport is to pre-arrange a transfer with your hotel. Five- and four-star hotels and resorts sometimes provide a tourist bus free of charge; others will add a fee. But considering you will be stumbling off the all-night flight weary-eyed and loaded down with luggage, there is nothing like being met in a foreign country by a friendly face holding a sign with your name.

Whatever you do, don't be bamboozled by young boys offering to carry your luggage or yellow–cab drivers who will try to charm you with a smattering of English. They're notorious for taking tourists "way out of the way"—your final bill could reach into the hundreds of dollars.

Safest bets are the special air-conditioned airport taxis operated by two firms: **Transcoopass** (☎ *270-4888*) and **Cootramo** (☎ *270-1442*), both of whom have booths in the foyer outside the baggage pickup area. Fares to various parts of the city are posted at the booths. A ride to the South Zone, where most of the hotels are located, runs about, paid in advance, $16–17 (20 percent discount for roundtrip). Keep the receipt, because if you leave something behind, it will be easy to retrieve.

White radio taxis, if you can find them, are generally reliable and charge about 20 percent less than the special cabs.

The cheapest way to the city is by special air-conditioned airport buses that stop along the beach drags, as well as all the major hotels. The fee is about $1, and buses leave every half hour from 5:20 a.m.–11 p.m. The bus, which takes about an hour one way, is often the easiest way to return to the airport; ask your concierge what time it will arrive at your hotel. Remember, you must be at the airport for international flights two hours in advance, so leave at least three hours early.

Whatever you do, do not take a normal city bus loaded with luggage. You will probably be relieved of it quick.

Insider Tip:

Have the name, address, and telephone number of your hotel or accommodation written on a piece of paper and ready to show the taxi booth and/or driver. Even if you speak Portuguese, basic facts like these often slip a traveler's mind just when they're most needed.

AIRLINE TICKETS

All tickets must be confirmed 24 hours in advance for domestic flights and 48 hours before international ones; otherwise, your ticket may be sold to someone else. Confirmations can be handled over the phone, but any flight changes must be made in person.

Varig
offices are located throughout the city. The most centrally located is *Rua Rodolfo Dantas 16*, near the Copacabana Palace Hotel in Copacabana, and *Rua Visconde de Pirajá, 351*; ☎ *(21) 287-0440*, on the main shopping drag in Ipanema. The downtown office is located at *Avenida Rio Branco 227*; ☎ *(21) 220-3821*.
Other airlines flying internationally to Rio are:

American Airlines
Av. Pres. Wilson, 165, 5th floor (downtown); ☎ *210-3126*.

British Airways
Av. Rio Branco, 108, 21st floor (downtown); ☎ *242-6020/221-0922*.

Canadian Airlines International
Rua da Ajuda, 35, 29th floor; ☎ *220-5343*.

United Airlines
Av. Pres. Antônio Carlos, 51, 5th floor (downtown); ☎ *532-1212*.

Other popular airlines serving the interior of Brazil are:

VASP
Rua Santa Luzia, 735 (downtown); ☎ *(21) 292-2080*;

TAP Air Portugal
Av. Rio Branco, 311–D (downtown); ☎ *(21) 210-2414*, and

Transbrasil
Av. Calógeras, 30 (downtown); ☎ *(21) 297-4422*.

BANK HOURS

Money may be exchanged at banks, but rates are usually better at private *câmbios*. Hours are *10 a.m.–4:30 p.m.*

BEAUTY SALONS

Most 5-star hotels have good beauty salons, with manicurists on hand. I can't recommend getting your hair colored in Brazil as products tend to run much harsher than in the States, and the tropical sun will eventually bleach any blonde to white. The best hair salons in the city are listed below:

Jambert Haute Coiffeur
Av. Gal San Martin, 1010; ☎ *259-7198*
French and high-class cuts for women of all ages.

Nonato
Rua Visconde de Pirajá, 414 (Leblon); ☎ *287-6297/521-3938*
Rio's most famous stylist for both men and women. Nonato cuts the hair of actors and musicians.

Pauletti
Copacabana Palace Hotel, Av. Atlântica 1702; ☎ *255-7070*
Reliable, inexpensive cuts for men only; about $10 for short hair.

Lynda Hartley
Rua Siqueira Campos, 85C (Copacabana); ☎ *236-0595/257-5192*
A full-service unisex salon with manicures, facials, electrolysis, and ultra-extraordinary beauty treatments.

CITY TRANSPORTATION

See also "Private Cars/Private Guides", below.

Taxis

The easiest way to get around Rio is by taxi. Carioca taxi drivers, however, are infamous throughout Brazil for both their crazy driving and their wily ways, though in the face of such outlandish inflation, who can blame them? To get the best deal for your money, consult the "Taxis" section in the Directory. In Rio, the common house variety—yellow cabs—can be hailed throughout the South Zone on main avenues, and cabs often line up outside tourist attractions and nightclubs. The concierges of upper–class hotels, however, tend to steer guests into the special air-conditioned taxis lined up in their front driveway; these cabs are definitely safer and are controlled by the hotel, but they cost twice as much. You can also ask the concierge to call a radio taxi for you, which will be reliable and cost only 20 percent more than yellow cabs.

> **Insider Tip:**
>
> Returning to the South Zone from the Rio Sul Shopping Center is tricky. If you take the yellow taxis right outside the main entrance, the drivers must make a necessary detour that will run your bill up at least $2, if they are honest. Better to cross the highway and hail a cab going back toward Copacabana.

Cootramo ☎ *270-1442* and **Transcoopass** ☎ *270-4888* are special taxis that can be hired to tour the city. The advantage is that the driver will wait while you shop and dine, and follow you as you stroll. The going rate is a minimum of three hours for $90, plus $30 for each extra hour.

Buses

Hot, crowded, and bumpy, city buses in Rio are only for the experienced native or the die-hard adventurer who can look Jonah's whale in the eye and not flinch. During high season, the chance of getting your pocket picked or purse snatched is more than probable, particularly if you wear loud tropical shirts or lug lots of shopping bags. Sad to say, there are numerous stories about buses being held up in Rio—though not without humor. (One time a bus bandit requested only *ouro* (gold) from his passengers, then politely returned a silver watch to a rider who had coughed up everything, just in case.) Avoid carrying any valuables on you, wear a money belt inside your shirt, hug your purse and backpack to your chest, don't even think about flashing your camera, and try not to look like a tourist. Since most fares are about 10 cents, have your change ready as you board the back of the bus, pay the cashier, then push through the turnstile to your seat.

If you want to travel along the beach drags, flag down a special air-conditioned bus called a *frescão*, which is specifically designed for tourists and stops at the hotels, the two airports, and downtown. The comparably high prices, ranging from 50¢ to $1, significantly cut down on petty thieves.

The main bus station for city and state is the **Rodoviária Novo Rio**
Av. Francisco Bicalho, 1 in São Christóvão; ☎ *291-5151*.

If you are traveling to the neighboring tourist cities of Petrópolis and Teresópolis, a more centrally located terminal is **Menezes Cortes Rodoviária**
Rua São José; ☎ *224-7577*.

Metro

The subway in Rio is nothing like New York's. That is to say, it's clean, bright, and one of the cheeriest places in Rio. Unfortunately, it's very short. Started in 1979, it's still not finished, with only two lines: Line 1 goes from Botafogo Station to the Saens Pena Station in Tijuca and Line 2 from Estacio Station to the Engenho da Painha Station. Combination subway-bus tickets allow you to ride special buses called *integração* to and from Botafogo Station. The M-21 goes to Leblon via Jardim Botânico and Jóquei, while line M-22 goes via Copacabana as far as Leblon. During Carnaval, the subway is the best way to reach the Sambadrome, as the streets are choked with revelers and legendary traffic jams. During most of the year, the subway operates Mon.-Sat. 6 a.m.–11 p.m., except Sun. A single ticket costs about 20 cents; round trips run about 35 cents. All tickets can be bought inside the stations; the ticket is inserted into the slot at the turnstile. For bus and subway routes, check the **Official Guide** handed out by *Rio Tur*, available at the airport and at the main office, *Rua da Assembléia, 10 (8th and 9th floors) in downtown;* ☎ *242-8000; weekdays 9 a.m.–6 p.m.*

Car Rentals

Unless you're a Formula One driver, I wouldn't suggest renting a car in Rio. (See "Driving" in the *Directory*.) Streets are hard to find, and the names are hard to spell and even harder to pronounce; carioca drivers are fanatics. If you must, however, the following companies offer good rates:

Avis
Av. Princesa Isabel, 150 (Copacabana);
☎ 542-4249;
Hertz
Av. Princesa Isabel, 334 (Copacabana);
☎ 275-3245;
Nobre
Av. Princesa Isabel 150; ☎ 541-4646.
Cars may also be rented at the international airport, as you exit from customs.

CLIMATE

Depending on the season (remember, they are backwards below the Equator), I have at times wilted from Rio's heat or shivered from its ocean wind. Generally, though, Rio's weather is beach-perfect—warm and humid, with averages between 75° and 96° F. During the Brazilian summer (**Dec.– Mar.**), temperatures can rise as high as 104° F, but frequent downpours tend to cool the air. The month of **May** usually is rainy. Temperatures from **July to September** can plummet to 62° F, but usually average around 72°. The best month to go in off-season is **September**—before it gets too hot for comfort. Nearly all hotels and good restaurants have air-conditioning.

CONSULATES

The consulate of your own country is your friend away from home. For any emergencies regarding diplomatic issues, including theft, personal assault, lost passports, or life-threatening illness, contact the office immediately. If you are planning to travel to neighboring countries, contact that country's consulate to obtain a visa, as well as travel and health advisories.
U.S.
Av. Pres. Wilson (downtown);
☎ 292-7117.
Canada
Rua Lauro Mueller, 116 (Botafogo);
☎ 275-2137.
Argentina
Praia de Botafogo, 228/room 201 (Botafogo);
☎ 551-9439.
Chile
Praia de Botafogo, 382, room 401 (Flamengo);
☎ 552-5349
Costa Rica
Av. N.S. de Copacabana, loja 309; (Copacabana);
☎ 255-1832.
Germany
Rua Pres. Carlos de Campos (Laranjeiras);
☎ 553-6777.
Great Britain
Praia do Flamengo, 284, 2nd floor (Flamengo);
☎ 552-1422.
Ireland
Av. Princesa Isabel, loja 1205; (Copacabana)
☎ 275-0196.
Paraguay
Av. N.S. Copacabana, loja 404; (Copacabana)
☎ 255-7572.
Peru
Av. Rui Barbosa, 314, 2nd floor (Flamengo);
☎ 551-6296.
Uruguay
Rua Artur Bernades, 30 (Caete);
☎ 225-0084.

CREDIT CARDS

Due to catastrophic inflation, businesses in Brazil are constantly changing their policies toward credit cards. Most hotels accept cards, but a discount is usually offered if you pay in cash (cruzeiros or dollars). Restaurants and stores have similar policies, but many do not accept **American Express** at all (due to the high interest rates), and some businesses may suddenly decide to accept no cards overnight. *Consequently, always check before you eat or buy anything.*

The **American Express** office is located at Praia de Botafogo, 228 Suite 514; ☎ (21) 522-3854 and at *Kontik Franstur Avenida Presidente Vargas, 309/4th floor;* ☎ (21) 296-3131. For card carriers, here's a veritable oasis: services include emergency check cashing, card replacement, and foreign currency exchange. You can even have your mail sent care of the office and they will hold it for you—a good idea if you're going to be on the road a lot. There's also a 24-hour telephone service for any kind of assistance: ☎ 800-5050. The office will, at no extra charge also confirm airline tickets, reroute tickets, and arrange hotel and car reservations, as well as all sightseeing excursions.

EXCHANGING MONEY

See also "Money" in *Directory*.

Most 5-star and 4-star hotels in Rio will exchange money, but the rates are usually lower than in travel agencies or official exchange offices. Banks usually give lower rates than **câmbios**, but higher rates than hotels. Most travel agencies will exchange money, but check the newspaper in advance for the official daily tourist rate. Whatever you do, don't exchange money on the street unless it is with friends you know and trust well. I've heard lots of con stories about a "new-found friend" who was never heard from again. Reliable exchanges can be made at the following:

In Copacabana:
Câmbio
Rua Santa Clara, 50; Fenician Tur Av. N.S. de Copacabana, 335. loja B;
☎ *235-3843;*
Banco do Brasil
Av. N.S. de Copacabana 335, loja B,
☎ *25-8992.*

In Ipanema:
Casa Piano
Rua Visconde de Pirajá, 365;
☎ *267-4615.*

Downtown:
Banco do Brasil
Av. Presidente Vargas, 328;
☎ *271-7413;*
Casa Piano
Av. Rio Branco, 88;
Citibank
Rua da Assembléia, 100; ☎ *276-3636.*
At the International Airport: On departure level.

MAPS

Maps of the city (and the country) can be found in most bookstores, as well as at newspaper kiosks, where you may find a wandering vendor willing to part with good Brazil maps for about $3 (bargain!). Also check at the hippie fairs along *Avenida Atlântica* in Copacabana.

MEDICAL EMERGENCIES

It's not a wise idea to get sick in Rio. Many doctors don't speak English, and health care, to put it politely, is generally not as advanced in Brazil as it is in the States. Your best bet is to contact your concierge, who can recommend you to the hotel's doctor or another physician who speaks English. For serious illnesses or death, do not hesitate to call your consulate immediately (see "Consulates," above).

For names of doctors and dentists who speak English, call the
Rio Health Collective
Av. das Américas 4430, room 303;
☎ *325-9300, ext. 44. Hours: 9 a.m.–2 p.m.*

For sunburns, low-grade fevers, colds, and tourist trots, pharmacists excel in suggesting appropriate reliefs. (For 24-hour pharmacies, see "Pharmacies" under *Shopping*.) The following hospitals have 24-hour emergency service and doctors who speak English and welcome tourists. *Anything you can do to avoid going there, however, would be beneficial to your health.*

Miguel Couto
Rua Mario Ribeiro, 117 (Gávea);
☎ *274-2121;* and
Souza Aguiar
Praça da República, 111 (downtown);
☎ *296-4114 and 242-4539.*

NEWSPAPERS AND MAGAZINES

Rio has two daily papers. **O Jornal do Brasil** is the serious one; **O Globo** is the fun one with the color photos. Both have excellent listings of music, film, and theater events, as well as special exhibitions and children's events. **Veja** is the *Newsweek* of Brazil, with a special "This Week in Rio" insert. Available at international newsstands (such as the one located near the Meridien Hotel on *Rua Princesa Isabel*) are current issues of the *International Herald Tribune, Wall Street*

Journal, Miami Herald, and USA Today, which are flown in daily and distributed by noon.

Before you leave on your trip, write for a free copy of **Rio Life,** a British–edited newsletter catering to the English-speaking community in Rio. You'll probably want to skip fraternizing with compatriots, but you may discover tips on lifestyle, events, and private housing opportunities. You might even think about advertising for an apartment switch. Contact **Rio Life** *Caixa Postal 38025 (Gávea) CEP 22452, Rio de Janeiro, BRASIL;* ☎ *(21) 252-0741; FAX (21) 222-7904.*

POINTS BEYOND RIO
By bus:
Buses to all state capitals of Brazil leave 24 hours a day from:
Rodoviária Novo Rio
Av. Francisco Bicalho, 1; ☎ *291-5151.*
Tickets may be purchased at the station (in advance) or at various travel agencies.
Guanatur Turismo
Rua Dias da Rocha, 16A; ☎ *286-5563*
Located in Copacabana—handles all bus reservations, but don't expect much English or excessive friendliness.
Menezes Cortes
Rua São José, 35 (downtown);
☎ *224-7577*
serves all buses to the outskirts of Rio, as well as to the cities of Petrópolis and Teresópolis. You can also find air-conditioned buses to the Zona Sul from here.

By ferry:
From the docks at Praça Quinze de Novembro, ferry boats and launches cross the bay every 10 minutes to Niterói (a 20 to 30-minute trip) for under a dollar. Boats also leave for Paquetá Island every 10 minutes.

By rail:
Trains for São Paulo and Belo Horizonte leave from **Dom Pedro II station** in *Praça Cristiano Otoni, downtown.* ☎ *233-4090 or 233-3390.*

POST OFFICE
The easiest way to mail a letter is to hand it to your concierge, who will mail it for you or sell you stamps at a small increase in price. Postcards normally run about $1, as do letters up to 20 grams. Post offices are generally open *weekdays 8 a.m.–5 p.m., and Sat. 8 a.m.–noon;* however, the post office in *Praça Serzedelo Correia* in Copacabana is open *Mon.–Fri. 8 a.m.–7 p.m., Sat. 8 a.m.-5 p.m., and Sun. and holidays from 8 a.m.-noon.*

Most offices will deliver express post, registered mail, and parcel service both domestically and internationally.

The **Main Post Office** is located at *Rua Primeiro de Março, 64 (corner of Rua Rosário in downtown);* other offices are *Av. N.S. de Copacabana, 540* in Copacabana; *Av. Princesa Isabel, 323A* in Leme; *Rua Visconde de Pirajá, 452* in Ipanema; and *Av. Ataúlfo de Paiva, 822* in Leblon.

PRIVATE CARS/PRIVATE GUIDES
If you want something different from the run-of-the-herd tours from big agencies, do hire a private guide and driver to spin you around town. Good English-speaking guides and drivers are hard to come by, but I can highly recommend the following for their reliability, expertise, and charm.
Professor Carlos Roquette
☎ *322-4872*
A relic from another century, this highly personable, if slightly eccentric 40-year-old art historian brings old Rio to life like no one I've ever met. For groups of any size, he offers walking tours of the old city, art museums, opera house, and "interiors" of buildings, blending philosophy, sociology and architectural trends into a seamless whole. He's also the source for any hard-to-find object or fact concerning Rio.
Vera Lucia Régis
☎ *541-6701*
Régis is an older, well-educated guide who works only daytime hours. In a private car with driver, she escorts clients to most tourist sites in Rio, as well as on day trips to Petrópolis, Teresópolis, and Parati. She can also arrange boat trips for up to 5 people around Guanabara Bay.

Paulo Cézar
Rua Souza Franco, 783 (Vila Isabel), casa 3, apt. 201; ☎ 268-8499.
Cézar is a hip, up–and–coming painter who excels in art and historical tours and can introduce you to the best galleries in the city. You may also ask to see his private studio; many people walk away with purchases.

Rubéms Topelem
☎ 256-8297, 236-6400
Topelem gives individual and group tours only in jeeps; his main destinations are anything ecological, including the rain forest (see under Tijuca Forest and favela tours). His company is called Bicho Solto, which means a "free animal, one that's difficult to catch."

Maurício Basseres
Av. Epitácio Pessoa, 3624/201;
☎ 226-5207; home: ☎ 286-0666.
Charismatic with big groups and probably stimulating alone, Maurício will take you nearly anywhere for about $100 per 8 hours, including Petrópolis, Búzios, Angra dos Reis, and Rio by Night. Three people will fit in his own car, or he can arrange larger buses through the agency he works for.

José Wanderley
Rua Camarista Meier, 636, B1, apt. 306 (Meier); ☎ 594-3336, 593-7519
This older Brazilian gentleman must be the most honest and decent driver in Rio. For about $50 for 8 hours (it may be higher by now), you can go anywhere, accompanied by his humorous commentary; excursions outside the city usually run more. He can usually be found in front of the Hotel Glória, but he can also be reached at his home number at night (see above). José speaks Japanese, Italian, Spanish, and English with gusto. He will also take you to Itacuruça for a wonderful day trip that includes a schooner trip and buffet in the islands of Angra dos Reis.

Lúcio Cardoso
☎ 322-0747
is a sensitive driver with an air-conditioned car who can usually be found at the Hotel Nacional, car 22. He often works in tandem with Vera Régis (above), through whom you may make contact.

STREET TRAFFIC

Here are some tips for staying safe as a pedestrian. (For more information, see *Beach Blanket Survival Guide*.) Carioca drivers have been known to run red lights, cut the curbs, and even pull up on the sidewalk and park, so don't stand close to curbs, even if you're getting ready to cross. Also, look both ways when you cross, because you never know when the traffic has been officially redirected. Note that even the police advise nighttime motorists, to avoid thefts, not stopping at red lights.

TELEPHONES

See also *Telephones in the Directory*.
Most hotel operators can place long-distance calls for you, but it will be enormously cheaper to dial direct yourself or to go to the public telephone company located at various offices throughout the city: *Av. N.S. de Copacabana, 462 in Copacabana (open 24 hours); Rua Visconde de Pirajá, 111 in Ipanema (open 6:30 a.m.–midnight); downtown at Praça Tiradentes 41 (open 24 hours); Galeão International Airport (open 24 hours); Santos Dumont Airport (open 5:30 a.m.–11 p.m.); the main bus terminal Rodoviária Novo Rio (24 hours), and the Menezes Cortes Bus Station, Rua São José (open weekdays 6:30 a.m.–10 p.m.).*

Local pay phones on the street are bright orange affairs. You must buy tokens called *fichas*, available at any newsstand. To make long–distance calls on the street, look for the blue-colored **DDD phones,** which require special tokens.

Emergency Numbers
Operator .... ☎ *100;*
Police .... ☎ *190;*
Ambulance ...... ☎ *192;*
Fire station ..... ☎ *193.*

TOURIST OFFICE

The main office of Rio Tur, the tourist board of the city of Rio, is located at *Rua da Assembléia, 10 (8th and 9th floors;*
☎ *242-8000).* There is a large tourist lounge where the receptionist speaks French,

Spanish, and English and can ply you with brochures, maps, posters, and other information. It's open Mon.–Fri. 9 a.m.–6 p.m. Other information booths may be found at the **international airport**, at **Sugar Loaf Mountain** Av. Pasteur, 520 (Urca); open 8 a.m.–8 p.m.; **Marinha da Glória** Aterro do Flamengo, Glória; ☎ 205-6447; open 8 a.m.–5 p.m.; and the **Rodoviária Novo Rio** Av. Francisco Bicalho 1 (São Cristóvão); ☎ 291-5151, ext. 143; open 6 a.m.–midnight. **Turis Rio** Rua Assembléia, 10 (7th and 8th floors) is the official tourist organ of the state of Rio de Janeiro. For information and travel assistance, call 252-4512, weekdays 9 a.m.–6 p.m. A second information booth can be found at the international airport.

TRAVEL AGENCIES

There are numerous travel agencies in Rio which offer half-day and full-day tours of various touristic sites. The most popular tours are the Sugar Loaf-Corcovado combo, Tijuca Forest, Rio by Night, and schooner trips around the islands in Angra. The following agencies work with highly personable guides who speak excellent English and are exceedingly reliable.

Turistur
Rua Araujo Porto Alegre, 36; ☎ (21) 240-0173/240-0560; FAX (21) 240-0560

One of the finest travel/tourist agencies in the country, Turistur works with a large European clientele who appreciate the personalized service. However, feel free to walk in off the street and arrange a guide for the day, or make arrangements for travel throughout Brazil.

Diana Turismo
Av. N.S. de Copacabana 330 / Co. 01; ☎ 255-2296

A well–run travel agency set up to serve European and American clientele with class, Diana Turismo will make all your hotel and transportation reservations, including picking you up at the airport. They also offer excellent package tours, including a special Carnaval, deal as well as wonderful excursions outside Rio, like horsebackriding in the Serra da Bocaina (see Greener Rio). In Rio, half-day tours (4-1/2 hours) run about $26 and include a guide, pickup at hotel, city tour, and a stop at Corcovado or Sugar Loaf. All rates are given in dollars, with special discounts for families of four. Package tours of the Amazon and the Pantanal are also available. Write for their itineraries.

Expeditours
Rua Visconde de Pirajá, 414, loja 1120 (11th floor); ☎ (21) 287-9697, FAX 521-4388

is the leading eco-tour agency in Brazil. If you want to do more than just stroll along the sidewalk in Copacabana, a trip to their office is a must to peruse the dozens of options for hiking, trekking, boating, scuba, and sailing throughout Brazil. Owner André von Thuranyi can custom-design sojourns into the Amazon forest, float you through the Pantanal, or introduce you to some of the most secluded islands along the eastern coast. Expeditour guides are hearty guys who love to be outdoors, and they will take you to the max of your energy, if that's what you want. Specialists in botany, bird-watching, and other scientific studies can easily be arranged. For more information, see the chapters on the Amazon and the Pantanal.

VACCINATIONS

See also Directory.

Considering the possibility of unknown syringes and dubious vaccines, I would heartily recommend getting all vaccinations before you arrive in Brazil. Gammaglobulin shots, purchased over the counter, can be administered by pharmacists in the hip behind closed curtains.

If you are desperate for other vaccinations before you go into the jungle, try the following government center for vaccinations:

Posto de Vacinacão do Ministerio da Saúde
Praça Marechal Ancora, Praça XV de Novembro; ☎ 240-8628.

WHAT TO WEAR

Rio is the most casual city in the world. No one bats an eye if you walk to the beaches in the South Zone dressed only in your bathing suit, but it's best to wear a coverup and sandals. Most restaurants (except sidewalk cafés) will expect you to wear a shirt, but ties are declassé, except in the fanciest restaurants, like St. Honoré. Shorts, light summer dresses, cotton and linen slacks, jeans, and T-shirts will get you through the day. At night, *cariocas* dress to kill, in tight, sexy dresses and fashionable slacks. Anyone planning to walk around the city should wear walking shoes or tennies because the pavements are uneven and full of holes.

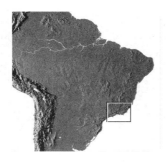

GREENER RIO

National Forest of Serra da Bocaina

No one should ever get stuck in Copacabana for their entire Brazilian vacation. Only kilometers away from the hustle and bustle of Rio is what I call **"Greener Rio"**—*an eco-traveler's paradise of challenging mountain peaks, furious river rapids, fabulous deserted islands, and 19th-century historical villages right out of a movie set.* Options such as the **Costa do Sol** (north of Rio), the **Costa Verde** (south of Rio), and the **Serras** (the mountain chain above Rio) are now part of travel packages that offer something more than the touristic run-of-the-mill. *Cariocas* and *Paulistanos* have long been familiar with these spots, fleeing to their second homes during summer and holidays, but now foreign tourists can fully enjoy these offbeat pleasures with a minimum of effort. One of the easiest trips to make is to the historical city of **Petrópolis,** where the imperial government had its summer home during the 19th century. And just 50 miles west of Rio is the village of Itacuruçá, a departure point for some of the best schooner excursions in the area. Not to mention that some of the best resorts in the country, such as **Nas Rocas** in Búzios and **Pousada do Vale dos Veados** in the National Forest of Serra da Bocaina, are only one to three hours away from Rio by bus. Their unusual environs, added security, and full range of activities are perfect for both families and honeymooners.

NORTH OF RIO

PETRÓPOLIS

Dom Pedro had a good idea when he bought a farm in this cool, mountainous area 41 miles from Rio. In 1843, his son also fell in love with the verdant greenery and fresh air and designated the area the summer home of the imperial government. From 1889-99, Petrópolis was even the full-time seat of the government. As German immigrants found the stunning scenery not only reminiscent of home but a welcome refuge from the heat and disease of Rio, a thriving community developed, with a decided Gothic flavor and a nobleman's attitude. Today many large colonial homes and mansions remain from the empire period (all pink, a curiosity scholars can't explain), as well as romantic cobblestone streets and extravagant gardens. Most tourists come to visit the Imperial Museum and royal churches, as well as to indulge in wholesale shopping along Rua Teresa. Eco-treks across the mountainous plains are also attracting some hardy adventurers.

Insider Tip:

The entire city can be seen in a couple of hours, but the museum, churches, and some restaurants and stores are closed on Mon., so don't even think about going then.

Getting There

A new four-lane highway wraps around a spectacular roller coaster vista between Rio and Petrópolis. The trip takes only an hour as you pass through forested hills, tropical forests, and banana plantations. Take the time to investigate the waterfalls along the highway and revel in the increasingly cooler temperatures. However, don't go on foggy days or if the roads are slick—it's extremely dangerous, although the view of the misty clouds settling into the mountains can be fantastically mystical.

Private guides like **Lúcio Cardoso** and **Vera Régis** ☎ *(21) 541-6701* are the easiest way to get to and around Petrópolis. **Buses** also leave daily from Rio's Menezes Cortes terminal *Rua São José, 35 (Downtown);* ☎ *(21) 224-7577* on the **Fácil** and **Unica** lines every 15 minutes, but the buses fill up fast. Numerous Rio-based agencies, like **Diana Turismo** ☎ *(21) 255-2296* and **Turistur** ☎ *(21) 240-0173* offer day–trips to Petrópolis. For eco-travelers, **Expeditours** ☎ *(21)*

208-5559 conducts trekking expeditions around the mountains, with guides specializing in botany, bird-watching, and geology.

Along the Way

Twenty minutes from Petrópolis on the highway from Rio is a *Terraço*—a wonderful *mirante* (view) marked by a large stone cross.

Florália *Rua Octávio Maul, 1700 (Samambaia);* ☎ *(242) 420-4340. Daily 9 a.m.-6 p.m.* Twenty minutes from Petrópolis proper is this exquisite greenhouse with more than 100 green plants and flowers. Of course, you won't get any through Customs, but at least revel in the fresh air and the beautiful specimens of rare orchids. Next door, a German-style restaurant replete with country-baked smells offers a *chá completo* (something between breakfast, tea, and a pig-out dessert) with a buffet of breads, jellies, brownies, paté, and chocolates for about $6. Buses from downtown stop at its doorstep.

A must-do for the way home is the chocolate store:

Patrones *Rua Coronel Veiga, 1321. Daily 9 a.m.-6 p.m., closed Mon.,* where all kinds of chocolates are made on the premises. No public demonstrations. *All cards.*

Events

During the entire month of June, the

Festa do Colono Alemão (Festival of German Immigrants) erupts into wild street parties, beer-drinking contests, and oompah bands. For more information, write the official tourist board SECTUR *Pr. Mariano Procópio, Petrópolis, RJ CEP 25286;* ☎ *(242) 42-0316.*

Sights

Museu Imperial *Rua da Imperatriz, 220 (Centro);* ☎ *(242) 427-1023. Small fee. Tues.-Sun. noon-5:30 p.m.* Why are they playing *Rhapsody in Blue*? you might ask as you wander through Dom Pedro's 44-room summer palace, but somehow Gershwin's music does manage to throw into dramatic relief the extraordinary paintings, costumes, and furniture of Brazil's imperial era. With luck, by the time you arrive, the royal crown, with 639 diamonds and 77 pearls, will have been put back on display, but just as remarkable are the 19th-century paintings of Rio, as well as the various musical instruments used in the era. The museum is arranged so that you'll feel as if you are actually visiting the palace, with its many rooms and salons. You'll love schussing through the highly polished wood floors on felt slippers, but all coats, cameras, packs, and umbrellas must be left at the door.

Insider Tip:

The horses-and-carriages in front of the museum will take you on to the Cathedral, the Santos Dumont house, and past the imperial mansions.

Cathedral de São Pedro de Alcântara *Av. Tiradentes.* This imposing Gothic cathedral is where Dom Pedro II, his wife, Empress Dona Teresa Cristina, and his daughter, Princesa Isabel (now immortalized in a famous street in Rio), are entombed in sepulchres sculpted with their life-size figures in imperial regalia. Note the large painting of Pedro and his family being led unhappily to exile in Portugal in 1889. Mass on Sun. is offered at 8:30 a.m., 10 a.m., 11:30 a.m., and 6 p.m. (weekdays 8 a.m.). The church is open for visits Mon.-Fri. 8 a.m.-noon and Sun. 8 a.m.-6 p.m. *Free of charge.*

Palácio de Cristal (Crystal Palace) *Pr. da Confluência, Rua Alfredo Pacha. Admission free. Tues.-Sun. 9 a.m.-5 p.m.* This cast-iron and stained-glass construction with stunning French chandeliers was a wedding present for Princesa Isabel, whose own pink-and-white house was but a 2-minute walk away. As the first prefabricated house in France, the pavilion was shipped and then reassembled here in 1884, a wonder for the time. How easy it is to imagine magnificent balls held inside the glass walls while guests strolled in the gardens outside. In fact, it was here that Princesa Isabel danced the night away in celebration of the slaves' emancipation on April 1, 1888.

Casa de Santos Dumont *Rua do Encanto, 124. Tues.-Sun. 9 a.m.-5 p.m.* Brazilians cherish the idea that it was their compatriot, Santos Dumont (not the Wright brothers), who flew the first airplane in the world. A famous inventor, Dumont started in a balloon around the Eiffel Tower, then graduated to a paper plane. A debonair-looking chap of slight stature, he built a house to his own measurements, which stands today as an eccentric homage to his life.

SPORTS
Hang-gliding takes off from the **Rampa da Simeria** in the district of Simeriand and the **Rampa do Parque São Vicente**, in Quitandinha.

SHOPPING
Rua Theresa *Cariocas* descend on this meandering street to snatch up the incredibly cheap buys on shirts, jeans, knitwear, and sportswear. Prices are cheaper here than in Rio, but the style and quality might strike you as old-fashioned.

Sandiges *Estrada da Cascatinha, 46–Galpão 1;* ☎ *42-5868. Open daily 9 a.m.-6 p.m.* Expect all souvenirs to be overpriced in this city; at least at this store, next door to the house of Santos Dumont, the stock is interesting. Crystal birds, sandstone sculptures, and a large collection of sculptured saints, including *candomblé* divinities, are available. Check out the tiny replica of the imperial crown for about $16. *All cards.*

In Tempore *Rua Barão de Amazonas, 35;* ☎ *43-6100.* Nice for a look-see, this antique store features 19th-century Brazilian colonial furniture and English stoneware, silver, and jewelry.

WHERE TO STAY

Pousada de Alcobaça *Rua Agostinho Goulão, 298 (Correas, RJ 25730-050);* ☎ *21-1240.* Located in Correas, a town north of Petrópolis in the Valley of the Gourmets (so–named for its fine restaurants), this once-summer estate has been charmingly transformed into a 10-room bed and breakfast. The treasure here is the excellent cooking of Dona Laura, whose fine pasta sauces are spiked with herbs from her own garden. No leisure program here, but at the very least stop for a meal or tea overlooking the gardens, an exquisite blend of Italian villa, English countryside, and Brazilian forest, with wildflower beds, trellises, and statuary. Rooms run about $70-$80 (breakfast only). *Moderate. All cards.*

WHERE TO EAT

★ **Bauernstube** *Rua João Pessoa, 297;* ☎ *42-1097. Daily 11 a.m.-midnight, except Mon.* Three minutes by car from the museum, this typical German restaurant with log-cabin walls offers a roaring fire throughout winter. Antique gas lamps lend romance to the already comforting lentil soup with sausage (about $6). Hungarian goulash, bratwurst, smoked tongue, and kassler with sauerkraut are also authentically delicious, but do try the *pato* Baden Baden—sliced duck roasted with cabbage. Apfelstrudel with some schnapps for dessert is *de rigeur*. *Moderate. All cards.*

Domenica Restaurante e Churrascaria *Pr. Rui Barbosa, 185;* ☎ *42-6574. Tues.-Thurs. noon-4 p.m., 8 p.m.-midnight. Fri. and Sat. noon-midnight, Sun. noon-6 p.m.* This quiet, sedate colonial-style house facing flowering parks offers excellent specialties such as trout with kiwi and carpaccio with haddock. Fondue bourguignonne for two runs about $16. In back is a *churrascaria* and *rodízio* by the same owners—about $8 per person with salad bar. *Moderate. All cards.*

TERESÓPOLIS

Fifty-six miles from Rio, within proximity to the city of Teresópolis, lies the **Parque Nacional Serra dos Órgãos** —a national park replete with rugged, mountainous climbs, unusual rock formations, and unforgettable vistas. Visitors can roam the 27,170 acres of wild forest, waterfalls, and streams, reveling in the tropical flora and fauna that abound. Also located inside the park is the **Museu von Matius**, specializing in natural history. From the top of **Mirante do Soberno,** Guanabara Bay in Rio can be seen in full, as well as the city of Cabo Frio. Legends have come to be associated with the unusual rock formations, poetically called **Dedo de Nossa Senhora** (Finger of Our Lady), **Dedo de Deus** (Finger of God), and the **Agulha do Diabo** (Devil's Needle). It takes about four hours to climb the park's highest peak, **Pedra do Sino** (Rock of the Bell), towering at 7,422 feet. **Expeditours** in Rio ☎ *(21) 287-9697* excels in planning climbing expeditions here.

THE ESSENTIAL NORTH OF RIO

WHERE TO STAY

Hotel Fazenda Rosa dos Ventos
Estrada Teresópolis-Friburgo, C.P. 92967 (Teresópolis, RJ); ☎ *(21) 742-8833, FAX 741-1157.*
The only Brazilian hotel in the French Relais et Châteaux chain is so adult-oriented it won't accept children under 16 (not even the owner's grandchildren). As such, exquisite peace and calm prevail over these three chalet-style buildings set in the midst of a mountainous 250-acre private park. Spend hours on horseback following forest trails replete with bamboo or pine, swim in two hotel pools or a fresh-water lake, indulge in dry and wet saunas, or play tennis on a lakeside court flowering with bougainvillea. The food is committed Brazilian, with fresh cheeses, fruits, and vegetables from the farm next door. For about $120-$185 a couple, the room includes breakfast, lunch and occasional dinner. Reserve horses on arrival. 41 rooms. *Expensive. All cards.*

Le Canton
Estrada Teresópolis-Friburgo, 12.5 kilometers, Vargem Grande, RJ 25958; ☎ *and FAX (21) 742-6887*
The activities feel like Club Med, but the architecture is all Swiss, in this fantasy maze of turrets, towers, market buildings, and town hall that comprise Le Canton, a Brazilian resort that handles children through disappearing acts (the kiddie recreation programs last from mid-morning to dinner at 8 p.m.). Spend the day hiking to a waterfall, skiing on grass, or playing group volleyball. Three pools offer good swimming, including one heated one. The package, including breakfast and lunch, runs $75-$100, and an extra fee of $20 per child. The horse club offer four extensive tours through the mountains (about $15 per person). *Moderate. All cards.*

WHERE TO EAT

Taverna Alpina
Rua Duque de Caxias, 131
The alternative to a picnic basket in the mountains, this German beer hall proffers excellent sausage, sauerkraut, and potato salad, a tribute to the ancestors of many of the area's residents. *Moderate. No cards.*

Insider Tip:

Best time to stay overnight in Petrópolis or Teresópolis is during the week to avoid the weekend carioca crush, when reservations are hard to come by and rates usually higher. Also, remember to dress for cool climes (sweater, light jacket, and hiking boots).

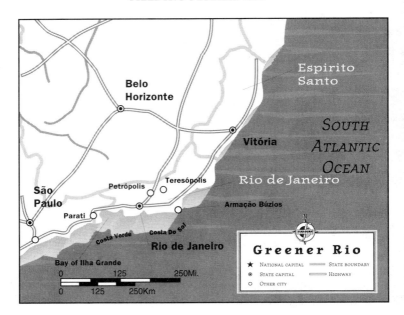

COSTA DO SOL

This stretch of coastline north of Rio belongs to the glitter-and-be-gay set of Rio—an international hotspot that draws celebs and tourists alike. Despite the overload of pleasure-seekers, the area, which is dominated by the city of Búzios, has not yet lost its primitive charm. Easily accessible by bus or taxi, the Costa do Sol nevertheless requires a car to navigate its more remote beaches. Without wheels, foreign travelers would be best suited to the glorious resort of Nas Rocas, especially those in search of that castaway island.

BÚZIOS

Ever since **Brigitte Bardot** did her "I vant to be alone" number here in 1964 (thus magnetizing thousands of paparazzi), the seaside village of Búzios has steadily grown to become the hippest watering hole of the Brazilian elite. On any day of the week, particularly in summer, it's possible to glimpse famous actors, musicians, and artists strolling its quaint cobblestone streets and possibly bathing in the nude at one of the 23 beaches. Although some call the area Brazil's French Riviera, the village of **Armação Búzios** (as it's technically known) has nevertheless retained its paradisaical ambience, though it is no longer a sleepy village. During summer weekends (Dec.-Mar.), the 12,000-strong population swells to more than four times that amount. These days chic, expensive stores line the main avenue, charming pousadas dot the shoreline, and some of the best restaurants in Rio sport branches here.

The magical weather in **Búzios** perhaps accounts for some of its attraction. It's called *Sol e Chuva*—because it can rain at the same time the sun is clearly shining. Though often dramatic, the showers are brief, and they happily cool the air.

Some say the ghosts of 19th-century slaves still roam the peninsula where Búzios is located, about 105 miles north of Rio. In the early 1800s, the largest banana plantation in the state of Rio de Janeiro was situated here, although it was tragically destroyed by fire following a mutinous quarrel between workers and owner. Today, mystically minded Brazilians still consider the area haunted and claim they can "feel" the souls of these slaves moaning in the wind, particularly on **Rasa Island,** which was a refuge for runaway slaves. Such mysticism, however, doesn't seem to dampen any of the active nightlife for which Búzios is noted. Clubs stay open till 5 or 6 a.m., with a number of discos overlooking the shimmering seas.

THE ESSENTIAL BÚZIOS

Getting There

Bus
Take the bus to Cabo Frio from the Rodoviária Novo Rio in Rio. *Av. Francisco Bicalho 1;* ☎ *(21) 291-5151* then catch another bus (or taxi) to Búzios. The bus stops in the center of town at the City Squire, where there is a fresh market on Sat.

Air
Costair Taxi offers 40-minute flights from the Santos Dumont Airport to Rasa Airfield in Búzios. The benefits are magnificent views of Rio on takeoff and an exciting landing in the middle of a marsh. *For reservations in Rio,* ☎ *(21) 220-9052; in Búzios* ☎ *(246) 623-1303.*

Taxi
Your hotel may be able to provide you with a private car and driver (the trip takes 2-1/2 hours direct) or you can hire a radio cab. Fine private drivers are recommended in *Hands-on Rio*. This mode of transport will run up bucks, however, since you will have to pay for the car's return.

Boat
You can sail to Búzios from the Marina da Glória in Rio. Rentals of schooners, sailboats, and large motorboats for fishing are handled by
Escola de Vela ☎ *(246) 205-8646.*

Tours
Ekoda Travel Agency *Av. José Bento Ribeiro Dantas, 222;* ☎ *(246) 23-1490; Rio:* ☎ *(21) 240-7067* can handle requests for tours of the village, as well as hotel accommodations and car rentals. In Rio, ☎ (21) 240-7067.

Getting Around
If you want to do more than stick to your beachside pousada (if it is, indeed, beachside), you will most likely need some sort of wheels. The "in" choice and your best bet, considering the uneven roads and sandy paths, is a dune buggy, which may be rented for a whole day with full tank for about $55. For rentals, contact
Rua Rui Barbosa
51, casa 3; ☎ *(246) 23-1285.*

For car rentals:
Locarauto Sun Side Rent a Car
Rua Celeste A. Costa, 38 (Manguinhos); ☎ *(246) 23-2193.*

THE BÚZIOS SCENE

The philosophy on Búzios is beach, more beach, and boogie all night. The residents of Búzios are extremely laid-back and infamous for their unshakable calm. Whatever you do, don't go to the center of Búzios in the morning, because nothing is open. Everyone, including the shopkeepers, is nursing a hangover, having stayed out to party on **Rua das Pedras** until 5 or 6 a.m. Instead, come around midday, when folks are just beginning to rub the sleep from their eyes. During the summer, **Rua das Pedras** (also known as Rua José Bento Ribeiro Dantas) is transformed into a colorful street fair. A popular meeting place day and night is **Chez Micou**, with a huge open bar and enormous TV screens. Nightlife centers around **Estralagem**, a small, charming pub with live jazz filling the outdoor courtyard, and **St. Trop**, an outdoor reggae-flavored disco overlooking the sea. Dress at night is aimed to kill.

BEACHES

Búzios has 23 beaches, with all kinds of shapes and sizes. **João Fernandes** is perfect for swimming, **João Fernandinho** is excellent for diving, **Ferradura** is known for jetskiing. **Praia Brava** is the nude beach. **Azedo Beach**, an easy walk from Centro, is where Brigitte Bardot's house was located.

SPORTS

You can rent jet skis on Ferradura Beach from the company **My Car**. It's the only rental company in Brazil that imports Yamaha jet skis for one or two persons. Kayak, scuba, schooners ($15 for 4 hours), and surfing are also available.

SHOPPING

Shopping in Búzios is for browsing; everything can be bought cheaper in Rio. However, there are some unusual finds, such as the elegant batik clothes at **Patrick Juvenelle** (in a small mall called Shopping de Búzios, off *Rua das Pedras*) and the secondhand clothing at **Bisa Bizar** *Rua das Pedras, 71* where you can also take tea in the back room overlooking the sea. A video arcade is located next to the Babuska ice cream parlor on Rua das Pedras.

WHERE TO STAY

★ Nas Rocas

Ilha Rasa 7.5 kilometers; ☎ *(247) 23-1303. Reservations:* ☎ *(21) 253-0001.*

One of the most popular resorts in Brazil, Nas Rocas occupies its own Robinson Crusoe-island off the peninsula of Búzios. The late owner, Umberto Modiano, was a Jewish immigrant during the '40s who started exporting coffee and was offered the land on this island (called Rasa) for dirt-cheap prices. Eight years ago, his son, an architect, designed 70 chalets to meld in gracefully with the luxurious natural resources. Exotic flowers and cactus bloom year-round, and huge boulders dot the shore—at night you can sit on the rocks and watch the moon turn the sea silver. Toucans and parrots freely roam the grounds; the latter have mastered the art of stealing cherries off tropical drinks. Schooners leave daily to transport guests to all the beaches of Búzios free of charge—you can even cruise all day, with a lunch stop for barbecue shrimp on Tartaruga Island. Kayaking and windsurfing are also free, and joggers will love the one-mile-perimeter path around the island. The philosophy here is more laid-back than Club Med: children love to come here and parents will find a safe refuge from the traffic and chaos of Rio proper. The suites are perfect for honeymooners; in low season singles might find the going rough—unless you head into Búzios for your nightlife. To get to Búzios, you can either take a 15-minute boat from the hotel's marina, or hire a taxi or jeep. Rustically appointed standards with air conditioning and minibar (no TV!) run about $130, doubles $180, suites around $220. Thurs. and Sun., clients may be picked up at the airport for $25 per person (round trip), or the hotel can arrange a bus pickup at your hotel in Rio. Breakfast is included, but lunch and dinner are extremely overpriced. Reservations can also be made through **F&H Consulting** *4545 Baseline Ave., Santa Ynez, CA 93463;* ☎ *(800) 544-5503. Very expensive.*

Pousada do Martim Pescador

Estrada da Ponta da Sapata, lote 15–A (Praia da Manguinhos), 2.5 kilometers; ☎ *(246) 23-1449.*

Leather, glass and wood furniture transform this 13-room pousada into a home away from home. Your best bet is the two-room suite, which looks out on the fabulous beach of Manguinhos. Squash courts are available, as are pool, sauna, and swings. Rooms run about $90 and include breakfast. *Expensive.*

Barracuda Pousada

Ponta da Sapata; ☎ *(246) 23-1314. Reservations:* ☎ *(21) 262-2013.*

Purple bougainvillea contrasting against the orange dirt road and vibrant green shrubs transform this modest pousada into a luscious tropical estate. A bit isolated, the pousada is located about seven minutes from Centro down a scenic winding road; you must have a car or hire one. Unfortunately, the 23 individual apartments are less impressive than the grounds, but they are functional. Amenities include a pool with a bar, an indoor restaurant, and a game room with a gorgeous wood boat bar. The beach is a five-minute walk away. *Moderate-expensive.*

Lagostim Pousada

Estrada de Geribá, 70; ☎ *(246) 275-2018.*

Located 300 meters from Ferrudinha Beach (considered one of the most beautiful in Brazil), this colonial-style pousada has charm, intimacy, and comfort. Two regal suites are blessed with awesome panoramic views; the nine more rustically appointed apartments and two other suites are fully air-conditioned, with color TV and phone. Guests will enjoy the homey living room, pool room, dry sauna, and full-service restaurant. Nearby you can rent equipment for tennis, watersports, scuba, squash, and surfing. Doubles range from $40-120, and include breakfast. *Moderate-expensive.*

Pousada Portal de Búzios
Estrada José Bento Ribeiro Dantas (Portal da Ferradura); ☎ *(21) 231-1100 for reservations. Phone in Búzios* ☎ *(246) 23-2283.*
The cheap option in Búzios, where rustic takes on new dimensions with these simple rooms with no air-conditioning, located about five minutes from downtown. You'll be surprised to find a pool, but you can actually see the ocean with a good pair of binoculars. Breakfast is served at the three-table dining area. Rates run about $30 per room —a steal in overpriced Búzios. Next door, the simple eatery, **Fernando's Point**, offers some of the best seafood in the village. *Inexpensive. No cards.*

WHERE TO EAT

Most of Búzios' restaurants are located on *Rua das Pedras in Centro.* There are also *barracas* (counters) on the beach for snacks and drinks. Off-season from May to Dec., and especially in Aug., you may find some restaurants closed, particularly at lunchtime during the week.

★ **Satíricon**
Av. José Bento Ribeiro Dantas, 412; ☎ *(246) 23-1595.*
This is the original Satíricon, opened by an Italian immigrant who now manages its sister in Rio—considered one of the finest kitchens in Brazil. The *couvert* appetizer is a meal in itself—an extraordinary helping of two salads, marinated eggplant, mussels, and assorted fish that defies the definition of generous. But do choose from a full Italian-style menu of pastas and seafood, including grilled lobster, fried squid, and superbly cooked shrimp. The bill will take a bite out of your wallet, but it's worth it. *Expensive. All cards.*

Adamastor
Av. José Bento Ribeiro Dantas, 712 (Armação); ☎ *23-1162. 6 p.m.-midnight; noon-midnight Nov.-Mar.; closed Mon.*
One of the most expensive eateries in Búzios, Adamastor specializes in seafood, with grilled lobster and shrimp in cream sauce considered winners. Pasta is also popular. Dinners run between $15-$20. *Expensive. Cards: AE only.*

Kingyô
Av. José Bento Ribeiro Dantas, 1204; ☎ *23-1202. 6 p.m.-midnight, Sat. and Sun. noon-midnight. Closed Wed.*
How can you turn down a female sushi chef? Specialties include sushi, sashimi, sukiyaki, and teriyaki. Live music at the bar. (If there's a cholera scare, run.)

Le Streghe Búzios
Av. José Bento Ribeiro Dantas, 201 (Armação Beach). 8 p.m.-2 a.m. Sat., Sun., and holidays 2 p.m.-2 a.m. Closed Mon.
This high-class Italian kitchen lately gave birth to its branch by the same name in Rio —both famous for their homemade pasta and a light touch on the oil. The ocean view adds a tropical élan and the desserts, such as pears sautéed in white wine and smothered in ice cream, shouldn't be missed. Reserve. *Expensive. Cards: AE only.*

Au Cheval Blanc
Av. José Bento Ribeiro Dantas, 181 (Praia da Armação); ☎ *23-1445. Daily 7 p.m.-midnight; Sat., Sun., and holidays 2 p.m.-midnight. Closed Tues.*
Good French restaurant specializing in seafood. The ocean view enhances the casual ambience. *Moderate. No cards.*

★ **Takatakatá**
Rua das Pedras
According to the owner, the name of this luncheonette is the sound of two skeletons making love on the roof. You'll find the best sandwiches in Búzios here; the Famous Texas Cheeseburger, with ham, eggs, bacon, tomatoes, lettuce, and raw onions, runs about $3, as does the roast beef. The owner, a blond, blue-eyed Dutchman, must be the original Indiana Jones, a lively adventurer

who has millions of wild stories to tell. *Inexpensive. No cards.*

Pensão da Sônia
Rua das Pedras, next to Hotel Pousada and the Redby clothing store.
Basic *pratos feitos* (ready-made plates) make a filling and cheap option—about $3-$4. *Inexpensive. No cards.*

Pizza Na Pedra e Massas
Travessa Oscar L. Campos, 63, near Rua das Pedras
60 (!) kinds of pizza baked in a stone oven. *Inexpensive. No cards.*

COSTA VERDE

The famous Brazilian essayist Rubem Braga said this about the **Costa Verde** (Green Coast): "Nowhere in Brazil is there such intimacy between land and sea." Indeed, this coastal stretch south of Rio, containing more than 100 islands, is one of the most remarkable natural resources of Brazil. A stay at one of the major resorts in Angra dos Reis, or even a day-trip to the historical city of Parati, is considered a special vacation by *carioca*s, who themselves long to escape the city and be pampered by well-organized facilities. Fabulous day-trips to the islands, including a three-hour schooner cruise and lunch at a nearby resort, can be easily arranged through many travel agencies or through private guides (see *Hands-on Rio*) who can drive you up and down the coast, including a stop at the historical city of Parati. Or you can settle in at a resort such as **Portobello** in **Angra dos Reis,** cruise in the morning, and visit **Parati** in the afternoon.

Along the Way

If you ever needed to be reassured of the fertility of God's earth, the drive along the Costa Verde shouldn't be missed. Located south of Rio on BR 101, *the highways are so overgrown with exotic plantlife that you'll feel as if you're traversing a jungle.* Five minutes from **Club Med,** a nearly overgrown path winds through tangled roots and rocks, leading you to a waterfall of uncommon beauty—usually, a small boy along the highway will escort you there. Few will be able to forget the spicy smell of this forest, or the dozens of pink, gold, and purple flowers in ecstatic bloom. Tucked into the rock coves you'll also see bottles and flowers representing macumba shrines, and an armadillo may even cross your path. From the excellent two-way highway that curves around the **Bay of Ilha Grande,** you'll see barefoot boys pushing wheelbarrows along the road and old women strolling home with their heads piled with packages. From this perspective, Angra looks like a storybook cluster of white houses and orange-tiled roofs creeping up the hillside and surrounded by a sensuously snaking sea. Unfortunately, the only things that mar the paradisaical view are the large orange cranes of a nuclear power plant, which continues to be a point of controversy in the country.

Fazenda Nova Graiaú, near the Hotel do Frade, is an antiquated farm of storybook proportions. A former coconut plantation, it boasts an awesome windmill, wild ducks and geese, and superbly landscaped grounds. It can be seen from the highway and is at times open to the public.

Mambucaba, a tiny beachside village halfway between Angra dos Reis and Parati, is a lovely place to do nothing. A port during the 17th century, and once the center of the thriving coffee trade, Mambucaba used to be the favorite of whales, who came to eat the numerous small fish swimming out of the river's mouth. Due to the agricultural crises at the end of the Empire, the city fell into an irretrievable decadence from which it never recovered, but that is exactly why it has retained its antiquated charm. An impressively adorned church, **Igreja de Nossa Senhora do Rosário**, contrasts starkly with the more modest squat houses. The black bees (or *mambucas*), from which the city gets its name, still buzz around the area, particularly next to the bikini–clad girls who make sugarcane drinks from raw stalks. Seaside cafés offer a refuge from the sun, and if you linger long enough, you just may be asked to join in on some sambas.

CRUISES

A day schooner cruise around the tropical islands in the Costa Verde is an excellent idea for anyone on a tight schedule. Clients are picked up at their hotels in Rio and delivered back at the end of the day. A lunch and swim is usually included. Reservations can be made through your hotel or through full-service agencies in Rio, such as **Diana Turismo** ☎ *(21) 255-2296* or **Turistur** ☎ *(21) 240-0560 in Rio.* Or you can contact agencies who specialize in these tours directly, such as:

Saveiros Tour *Pr. Macilio Dias, 2;* ☎ *(21) 780-1003* One of the most experienced operators offering day-trips, including lunch, with stops at Itacuruça island and Jaguanum.

Tropical Angra Tur *Cais de Santa Luzia, 231;* ☎ *(24) 365-0402* This agency offers tours of Angra dos Reis and the Bay of Ilha Grande. Included is a buffet lunch on one of the islands.

Insider Tip:

Snorkeling is often fantastic on these cruises, so ask about available equipment in advance. There will be occasions when you'll have to wade to shore through knee-high water, so dress appropriately. You can get extremely sunburned on these open-sea cruises, even on overcast days, so don't forget sunscreen, sunhat, coverup, and shades. And do be careful about swallowing bay water.

RESORTS IN ANGRA DOS REIS

Portobello
BR–101, kilometer 47 (highway to Angra dos Reis), 9 kilometer; ☎ 789-1495. Rio (21) 267-7375

This 5-star resort, part of the Frade chain (which has three other hotels in the area), is perfect for children. Situated on a hill overlooking the bay, the hotel transports its guests on a ski-lift from the pool area to the beach below. Jetski, kayak, and surfing are all available, as are schooner trips to Guaíba Island. The hotel will also transport you free of charge to the neighboring village of Mangaratiba, the docking-off point for hundreds of island-hopping possibilities. You may also rent a car (and/or private driver) and make the fabulous drive along the coast to the historical town of Parati. Across the street from Portobello is a buffalo farm, which you can visit either by tractor, by horse-and-carriage, or on horseback—a truly enjoyable sojourn. Once a month Ligia Azevedo, the famous Brazilian cosmetician, conducts a spa for guests. Tile-floored rooms, along the lines of Caribbean resorts, run about $106 for deluxe singles, $116 for doubles. Third persons pay $35. Breakfast is included, and lunch and dinner run $3-15 (payable on the bead system). Sauna and tennis are included in the rate; all watersports are extra; 2-1/2–hour schooner trips run about $12, or you can rent a motorboat for about $50. Transfer from Rio is supplied by the hotel in a special air-conditioned bus. Reservations can be made in the U.S. through **F & H Consulting** ☎ *(800) 544-5503*. 86 apts. *All cards and traveler's checks.*

Portogalo
0 BR 101 Norte, kilometer 71 (Itapinhoacanga); ☎ 65-1022

Also part of the Frade chain, Portogalo resort is smaller, but at times livelier. Profusions of hibiscus adorn the tropical bar, the white leather furniture lends a light elegance to the lobby, and the rooms are appointed in tropical chic. The water is clearer than in Portobello because there is no river that falls into the sea. All watersport activities are available, as are schooner trips. Rates run about $99 for singles, and $120 for doubles. Air–conditioned buses from the hotel supply transfers from all the hotels in Rio. Reservations can be made in the U.S. through **F & H Consulting** *(800) 544-5503. All cards.*

Hotel do Frade
BR 101 Sul, highway to Ubatuba, kilometer 123; ☎ 65-1212

Located 2–1/2 hours from Rio, this enormous beach resort enjoys a prime location right on the beach, within walking distance of the Pico de Frade Mountain. Of the three Frade hotels along the southern coast, only this one sports an 18-hole golf course. An excellent infrastructure supports all watersports, as well as horseback riding, cycling, and schooner cruises to the neighboring islands. Single rooms start at $124; doubles run $138, including breakfast. An air-conditioned bus picks up all guests at the hotels in Rio. Reservation can be made in the U.S. through **F & H Consulting** *(800) 544-5503. All cards.*

Club Mediteraneé
Villa das Pedras (beach), BR–101, kilometer 55 (highway to Angra dos Reis), 16 kilometer.; ☎ 789-1635

A fantastically landscaped resort geared on the infamous Club Med philosophy of non-stop excitement, this new colonial-style village enjoys its own crescent-shaped beach between the mountains and the bay. Sports facilities include 9 tennis courts, squash courts, fitness center, soccer, pool, waterskiing, windsurfing, and sailing, and more. Children under 4 years old are not accepted, but singles may find more families here than they're used to. A Mini–Club program keeps kids from ages 6 to 10 entertained. Meals and drinks are conducted on the bead system. In the States, ☎ *(800) CLUB MED for reservations. 324 apts. All cards.*

ILHA GRANDE

It's incredible to think you can still find near-virgin beaches in the coastal stretch between Rio and São Paulo, but on Ilha Grande, they're commonplace. This 122-square-mile island of mountainous jungle, with more than 100 beaches, is a perfect place to take long, picturesque hikes, particularly to the far side of the island, where the beaches are extremely primitive. On the western shores is an ecological reserve, where you can enjoy the island's rich variety of exotic birds, butterflies, and primates.

Ilha Grande was discovered in the early 16th century when Amerigo Vespucci first roamed the coast, but it was long inhabited by Indians who fought fiercely to defend their territory. Later, the island became known as a pirate's cove. Legend has it that one wily *pirata* named José Grego was on his way to the Straits of Magellan when he and his two daughters were shipwrecked on the isle. After he became a successful trader, one of his slaves (who, by soap-operatic coincidence, happened to be his fellow ex-pirate) began to fall in love with one of his daughters. Infuriated, the jealous father killed the slave and took his own daughter as his lover. Afterwards, a curse passed over the island, sweeping away all its inhabitants in a tidal wave, except for José, who managed to bury his lifelong treasures before he died a crazed man.

Looking for José's treasure will no doubt unearth some spectacular natural resources. The tiny hamlet of **Abraão,** where the ferry from Mangaratiba lands, boasts good skindiving about 15 minutes from shore. Beautifully unspoiled beaches, such as **Canto** and **Crena,** are about an hour away by foot. Nearby is **Freguesia Island,** a fishermen's village with an 18th–century cemetery, a colonial green and white church, and 4 separate beaches around the island's perimeter. There's also one restaurant on the far shore. Paradise on earth would be to rent the one beach home here—a 4-bedroom affair with hardwood floors, white canvas furniture, and a glassed-in living room facing the ocean. For more information, call in Rio ☎ *(21) 65–1545.*

Getting There

The village of **Mangaratiba** is less a touristic site than a way station to catch the daily **ferries** to **Abraão,** the main hamlet of **Ilha Grande.** Boats leave from the dock 8:30 a.m.–4:30 p.m. (with expanded summer schedules); the trip takes about 90 minutes. The dock is located about 10 minutes from the Hotel Portobello, and buses run daily from Rio.

Getting Around

Lots of small boats docked in the harbor of Abraão are willing and able to take passengers around the islands. If you're alone, you'll probably need substantial Portuguese to negotiate a price. Ask around for the boatman named **Fifi**, who can take up to 10 people in his flat–bottomed wood fishing boat. (Rates run about $6 per person, or $60 per boat for the day.) A professional certified diver, Fifi also has a *golfo* boat that seats 50 people and is especially equipped for divers. He can be reached *c/o Pousada Mar da Tranquilidade,* ☎ *(243) 288-4162.*

Expeditours in Rio has developed extraordinary 2- and 3-day tours of the islands that include treks to Enseada das Palmas, bathing at the beach at Lopes Mendes, and schooner trips to Saco do Céu and Freguesia. Contact **Expeditours** *Rua Visconde de Pirajá, 414 (Ipanema);* ☎ *(21) 208-5559.*

When to Go

Summer is best—November through March. Expect it to rain a little every night, but days are hot and bright. Winters are cooler and cloudier and often too cold for swimming.

Insider Tip:

Due to the stagnant waters in rivers, watch out for mosquitoes in summer at sunrise and sunset. There's no risk of disease, but you may get covered with bites if you don't use repellant.

THE ESSENTIAL ILHA GRANDE

WHERE TO STAY

Weekend rates on the island run about $40 more than weekdays. Weekends are considered to run from Sat. morning to Sun. afternoon. Few rooms, if any, have air-conditioning, and most are more primitive than rustic. Better accommodations can be found 90 minutes away in Parati, or across the bay at the Portobello Hotel.

Pousada Mar da Tranquïlidade
☎ *(243) 288-4162*
A 2-minute walk from where the ferry docks in Abraão, this stone and wood-beam inn is rustic hominess personified, with hanging green plants and antique wood benches. The rooms are fan-cooled, with no TV or phone; some have minibars. The newer rooms are more congenial, but all doubles on the weekends go for $55 (includes breakfast and lunch Sat.-Sun.); weekday rates are about $10-15 cheaper. Check with the reception about their various island-hopping options for 1- or 2-day trips, including hiking and skindiving. Expeditours Travel Agency in Rio can also arrange a trip to this area. Tents may be rented at
Camping Renato
Av. Getúlio Vargas, 17
a few minutes' walk from the ferry. Outdoor showers with no curtains (you shower in your swimsuit) are available, and the $4-a-night rate includes breakfast. For about $10 a night, the nearby **Pousada da Penha** adds a roof to the bare essentials. Large groups on a budget will enjoy the fan-cooled chalets at
Hotel Alpino
Rua Getúlio Vargas; ☎ *780-1861*
with clean, modern baths and breakfast served on an open patio.

WHERE TO EAT

Dining on **Ilha Grande** is mostly situated in **Abrãao**.
Flor da Ilha Restaurante (*Av. Beira Mar, 20*) is considered the choicest place to eat, complete with a nightclub and a menu of steaks and pizza for $6- $8. Most likely you'll want to plop down beachside at one of **Casarão da Ilha's** stone tables and eat a plate of fried squid *(lula frita)* with squeeze of lime.
Nightlife is as spontaneous as the waves, but do catch the *forró* parties, featuring regional dancing from the Northeast, at **Nilzo** (end of the beach) on Fri., Sat., and Sun.

PARATI

With its cobblestone streets, antique lamps, and 19th-century homes so beautifully preserved, **Parati** might easily be a scene out of a Jorge Amado novel—indeed, the classic film *Gabriela*, based on his novel, was masterfully filmed here. Since it was confirmed as a village in 1667, Parati and its port have witnessed an incredible history of growth, owed in great part to the rich deposits of gold discovered in **Minas Gerais.** By the 18th century, as it became the major port for gold destined for Portugal, the very name Parati rang with a certain magic throughout the colony. Deserting soldiers, runaway slaves, gypsies, convicts, noblemen, and gold diggers all converged on the town, creating a freewheeling population that made its day-to-day doings a veritable soap opera. Even as the gold rush diminished, sugar mills smoked day and night during the 19th century, while countless coffee plantations and cattle farms sprang up in the countryside. Unfortunately, when the Rio-São Paulo road was constructed, Parati fell victim to rerouted traffic and was only later re-discovered as an authentic, nearly untouched historical gem in the 20th century. After a new road to Angra was completed in the 1950s, artists and bohemians flooded the area and instituted new traditions of craftsware. Today, *UNESCO has cited the city's six square blocks as part of the World Heritage List, and Brazil itself has named the city a national monument.*

Located 149 miles from Rio (and 60 miles from Angra), Parati remains one of the country's major tourist attractions at the same time its 26,000 residents continue to thrive on fishing and farming. Bicycles fill the streets, small shirtless boys play in the sand; everywhere there are the kinds of small-town businesses that all but get lost in larger metropolises. Walk to the waterfront and look back on a magnificent scene—the time-warped vista of colonial Brazil.

More tourist information can be picked up at **City Hall** ☎ *(243) 71-1266, ext. 50.* You can pick up a map with the layout of streets.

Getting There

Buses from the main bus terminal in Rio (**Rodoviária Novo Rio**) leave daily (every 3 hours) for Parati on the Eval line and make the trip in 3-1/2 hours. The bus station is located at **Praça N.S. de Guia** ☎ *789-1495* where you can also catch buses to Angra dos Reis, Itacuruçá, Itaguai, Muriqui, and Rio de Janeiro. Private cars may also be hired in Rio (See *Hands-on Rio* under "Private Cars.") As you approach Parati, tune into FM Parati 88.9 to hear advertisements for all kinds of hotels, restaurants, etc. (alas, in Portuguese).

Getting Around

Parati can be seen on foot in a matter of hours, as all the historically appointed streets are cut off to traffic. Roam at will or pick up a map at City Hall. During the day, the town gleams like a treasure box, but at night the antique lamps lend an air of romance unsurpassed in Brazil. A fabulous night vision is the illuminated belfry and white cross of the Santa Rita church against the dark, star–crossed sky. Stores are usually open till late at night.

If you haven't chartered a boat around the islands of Angra, here's your chance for a spectacular schooner cruise. Contact **Soberano da Costa** ☎ *in Rio (21) 267–7794; in Parati (243) 71-1114*. Schooner trips are also available through **Turbo I** from noon to 5 p.m. Inquire at the store called **Papelaria Disque**, across from Café Parati on Rua do Comércio.

SIGHTS

Four churches dominate the 6-block historical center, perfectly exemplifying how even the Church in colonial Brazil catered to a powerful segregation according to class. Located on the Travessa do Gargoata is the

Igreja Matriz Nossa Senhora dos Remédios (1789-1873), built for the middle class—its leafy courtyard, turquoise–and–white altar, and enormously high arches affecting a certain bourgeois élan. Climb the stairs and see the little gallery of paintings and photos of both modern and antique styles by local artists. The antique bells, which are enclosed in colonial arches, are rung every day at 6 p.m. Following the river to the bay, you will reach the

Igreja das Dores, a 19th–century church used by the noble class. Head 3 blocks down Rua Fresca and turn right on Rua Doutor Samuel Costa, where you will find the

Igreja do Rosário, an 18th–century church built for the city's slaves. Turn left on Rua Tenente Francisco Antônio and walk 2 blocks to Rua Maria Jacome de Melo, where you will find the

Sobrado dos Bonecos, one of Parati's finest examples of colonial architecture. On the same street is the city's oldest church, **Santa Rita,** built in 1722 for the city's mulattos. On Rua Santa Rita, the

Museu de Arte Sacre *Tues.-Sun. 9 a.m.-5 p.m.* holds the city's depository of sacred art. The outdoor vegetable market is just down the street. From here, you may be lucky enough to glimpse the city's fishermen lugging in the catch of the day.

The sweetest route to take in Parati, however, is without objective. One of my finest memories is walking along the city's cobblestones, listening to a flutist play "Greensleeves" while we nibbled on coconut candy bought from a street vendor.

EXCURSIONS

★ **Fazenda Bananal** *(Also known as Engenho da Murycana) Estrada para Cunha;* ☎ *(243) 71-1153* Children will adore this 17th-century colonial farm located off a dirt road about 15 minutes from Parati. During centuries past, it was used by the muleteers and pioneers as a trading post for the precious stones unearthed in Minas Gerais and São Paulo; at times, the royal family visited to fiscalize the imperial taxes imposed on the traders. Included in the grounds today is a zoo featuring animals from the Amazon, Pantanal, and Serrado Goiano, with wonderful specimens of *lions, pumas, leopards, tigers, monkeys, pacas, and rare toucans and parrots.* There are two swimming pools for bathing and you can even rent horses to follow the miner's trails through the forest to refreshing waterfalls. The **Restaurante da Murycana,** using many products cultivated on the farm, serves typical farm foods from that era, such as *galinha ao molho pardo, frango à passarinho,* and *bisteca de porco.* On Sat. and Sun. *feijoada* is served. Delicious desserts, made from colonial recipes, may also be bought as takeout. The 48-hectare farm produces some of the best sugar cane in the area—an accomplishment since Parati has long been known as the *cachaça* capital of Brazil. In the small marketplace, *be sure to taste the various samples before you buy—flavors include tangerine, cinnamon, cherry, and various exotic fruits you've probably never heard of.* There's also a **museum** where you can view many of the typical objects used in the past century, such as guns and furniture.

THE ESSENTIAL PARATI

WHERE TO STAY

★ Pousada Frade Parati
Rua do Comércio; ☎ (243) 71-1114
Located on the historical square on the Rua do Comércio, this pousada rates as one of the most charming in a city of charming pousadas. Built like a tropical home, the fully air-conditioned 44 rooms are cozily appointed in rustic woods, and all contain color TV and video, safe, minibar, and phone. An attractive swimming pool is shaded by a tropical garden. A fine restaurant serves all three meals, and breakfast is included in the rate. Singles run around $75, doubles $88. Transfer in an air-conditioned bus from hotels in Rio is provided by the pousada, for about $66 per person round-trip. For reservations, contact in the States, **F & H Consulting** ☎ (800) 544-5503.

Pousada das Canoas
Av. Roberto Silveira, 279;
☎ (243) 71-1133
Two-story, colonial-style house with color TV, minibar, and air-conditioning. The pool is surrounded by a favorably landscaped courtyard, with rooms appointed in a blend of modern comfort and traditional wood. *Moderate. All cards.*

Pousada do Forte
Alameda Princesa Isabel, 33 (Centro);
☎ (243) 71-1462
The motto here is history and leisure, the only pousada in town where all the apartments face the sea. Nearby is the Ecological Reserve do Forte. The attractive pool area is served by a grass-hut bar. *Moderate. All cards.*

WHERE TO EAT

Most of the restaurants in Parati are colonial-style or open-air houses. Go for the fish in this town, most likely just pulled off the docks. In general, all prices are moderate ($10-15 per person).

Ancoradouro
Rua Da Geralda, 345; ☎ 71-1394. Daily 11 a.m.-11 p.m., closed Tues. from April to Dec.
Typical Brazilian food. *Moderate. All cards.*

Corto Maltese
Rua Ten. Francisco Antônio, 130. Closed Tues. April-Dec.
Italian cantina. Restaurant Dona Ondina Rua do Comércio, 2 (Centro); ☎ 71-1584. Daily 11 a.m.-5 p.m.; 7 p.m.-11:30 p.m. International cuisine in a colonial house complete with sunny veranda. *Moderate. All cards.*

Fazenda Bananal
Estrada para Cunha; ☎ 71-1153 (See listing under "*Excursions*").

★ Restaurante Galeria do Engenho
Rua Maria Jácome de Mello, 18;
☎ 71-1349. Daily 11 a.m.-11 p.m.
This cool restaurant with two strong ceiling fans is situated on a side street and features fine seafood. There are 15 kinds of shrimp dishes, including grilled shrimp with such big head and eyes that you have to have a lot of courage to eat them. Excellent is the Camarão Ivan Lins, Milanese-style and fried with cheese (about $13). The calamaris stuffed with cheese and shrimp were also delicious, but they may have been the cause of a few days of delirious belly-aches.

★ Restaurante do Hiltinho
Rua Marechal Deodoro, 233 (Centro);
☎ 71-1432. Daily 11 a.m.-midnight
Creative blends of fish and seafood can be had at this well-received eatery, especially the *caldeirada*—a lightly simmering stew of seafood. Schooner trips can also be arranged here. *Moderate. No cards.*

NIGHTLIFE

If you have a chance, catch **Mansamente**, the famous Brazilian puppet company that's been acclaimed by *The New York Times* for its avant-garde creativity with foot-high puppets and antique doll furniture.

SERRA DA BOCAINA

The **National Park of Serra da Bocaina** is simply one of the most beautiful landscapes in all of Brazil. Situated between the states of São Paulo and Rio, the ecological park contains what little remains of the Atlantic rain forest chain. But more than an eco reserve, it's also a receptacle for the history of colonial Brazil—it holds the old 18th-century gold route from Minas to Parati, as well as the last vestiges of the 19th-century coffee plantations. The park is a welcome vacation spot for adventuresome *Paulistas* (the city of São Paulo is only 167 miles away), and for *carioca*s, who may easily stop in Parati on their way home. Getting to the park takes guts, however. The only way to reach it is through SP–221, an extremely precarious road that requires expert 4-wheel-drive control. And the only authorized vehicles inside the park are those on their way to **Pousada do Vale dos Veados** (see below).

The natural wonders of the park are seemingly endless, though signs of a burning forest are sadly in evidence. The **Mambucaba River** makes dramatic dips and tucks over rocks, creating a spectacular 2,600-ft. waterfall called **Cachoeira São Isidro**. Bromelias and orchids of rare species dot the landscape, as do profusions of Brazilian pines, cedars, *samambaias*, and others. The nearly extinct black monkey roams at will, as do mountain lions, *capivaris*, deer, anteaters, sloths, and wild pigs. Even bird-watching is excellent, with more than 90 rare species, including toucans and parrots. A little before the entrance of the park is one of the most popular hang-gliding points in the country (veterans claim you can stay in the air for 10 hours). The area called **Sertão da Bocaina** is brimming with fishable trout. And hardy trekkers will adore scaling the **Pico do Gavião,** at the top of which awaits a superlative vista of the **Bay of Parati.**

A surprise to those who have been bearing the tropical heat, the park boasts low temperatures the whole year-round. Winter clothes are essential, as are trekking and horseback-riding gear. Also, don't forget some light clothes for skindiving and for bathing in waterfalls and natural lakes.

Along the Way

The Rio–São Paulo road to Bocaina can be read as a documentary of what has happened to the Brazilian Atlantic rainforest. European nationalists who came in the last century talked about the tallest trees they had ever seen; today, the land is sadly flattened, with only the mountainous regions having escaped the slashing and burning that prepared the land for sugar cane, coffee, and, finally, cattle. Today, the Rio–São Paulo highway is one of the most dangerous in Brazil (along with the São Paulo-Curitiba highway), thanks to maniacal truck drivers. Nevertheless, signs of country life still abound. Dozens of highway stands sell papayas and coconuts, as well as enormous clusters of bright yellow bananas. Eighteenth-century towns such as São José do Barreiro, with their grilled verandas and traditional roofs, still languish in another era, especially during the festival of St. Peter at the end of June, when the cobblestone streets overflow with people dancing *forró*.

THE ESSENTIAL SERRA DA BOCAINA

WHERE TO STAY

★ Pousada do Vale dos Veados

kilometer 42 da Estrada da Bocaina;
☎ *(21) 322-4849. For reservations in Rio,*
☎ *(11) 253-0660*

In the heart of the National Park, this must be the coziest, homiest pousada in all Brazil. Because nothing can be constructed in the park that does not conform to the pre-1971 style, the 50-year-old original construction has been preserved, though it's more reminiscent of frontier life. The main building, with dining rooms, living rooms, and 4 bedrooms, is made of wood logs and rock walls, with a traditional Brazilian tile roof. The inn is 17 kilometers from the park's entrance on a wildly bumpy road, and upon arrival you will immediately want to collapse in front of the roaring fire or sink into the soft colonial beds, with the deepest quilts imaginable. Since no electricity is used, the candle-lit rooms and wood-burning stoves immediately take one back centuries. Superb country-style food, grown on the farm, is served buffet-style and warmed under gas heaters. Although it's possible to lie in a hammock all day (the view of the lake from the porch is gorgeous), you can make outstanding climbs up Gavião Peak, follow the Mambucaba

Gold trek from the 18th century on foot, horseback ride to a glorious waterfall, or canoe up and down rivers. Honeymooners can set their beds together overlooking fabulous trees and be woken to the call of roosters. No one speaks English here, but the small staff is so friendly you may never want to leave. Doubles start at $100 with shared bath, $115 with private bath; new, chalet-type rooms with living room are about $135. All rates include full board, transfer from the city of São José do Barreiro, and all activities. Don't leave without taking home a huge loaf of homemade cheese.

Getting There

Expeditours
☎ *(21) 287-9697, FAX 521-438*

in Rio offers a package deal that includes a 6 a.m. pickup in Rio and optional visits to Parati and Fazenda Pau d'Alho, once the largest coffee plantation in Brazil and now seemingly haunted by ghosts. The pousada will also pick you up in the city of São José do Barreiro (at the Catete Hotel), which you can reach by bus from Rio. If you drive yourself (which is not recommended), you'll have to request permission from IBAMA (Brazilian Institute of Environment Preservation) to trek or camp in the park.

Getting Out

The trip out of the park is a bucking bronco ride around a mountainous valley so bumpy you'll have to hold on to the top of the Jeep. I was wrecked for days after this trip (make sure your driver is sober!), but the charm and beauty of the pousada was worth every bruise. The environs are unforgettable, and the country folk in the area are so *simpático*, they even let me use their bathroom at midnight.

HOT FLASH FOR 1994

Master fishermen David Finkelstein and Evelyn Letfuss of *Marlin* magazine write that big-game anglers should steer their rods immediately in the direction of Vitória, in the state of **Espírito Santo** (300 miles north of Rio), where **record-breaking blue marlins**, over 1,040 lbs., are being snared by unexpecting mere mortals. The waters, Finkelstein reports from experience, are also rich in white marlins, as well as tuna, wahoo, and sailfish, and best of all, the beaches and scenery remain untrampled by tourists. Do look for more in-depth coverage of this spectacular area in the 1995 version!

Getting There:

Varig has connecting flights from Rio de Janeiro to Vitória.
Where to Stay: Contact Claudio Hec kilometer ann, **Brazil Travel Service** *2441 Janin Way, Solvang, CA 93463;* ☎ *(800) 544-5503, FAX (805) 688-1021.*

Insider Tip:

Farther north, near Comandutuba Island (Transamérica Hotel) in the state of Bahia, fishing fanatics such as Arkansas "Chicken King" Don Tyson have been easily landing enormous blue marlins, many of them well over 600 lb. A newly installed fishing program at the resort is run by Rogério Nobrega, who works out of two 30-foot boats that make the run to Royal Charlotte Bank, the richest waters for blue marlins, in about 3 hours. For more information, see Getting There.

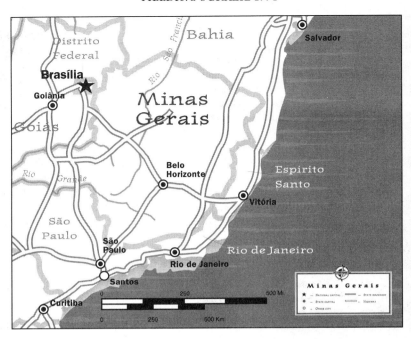

MINAS GERAIS

The Luxurious Fountains of the Spa Park in Caxambú, Minas Gerais

For many people, the true soul of Brazil is to be found in the state of **Minas Gerais**. Sequestered from the coast, embraced on all sides by 5 different states, Minas has developed a profound culture all its own. Throughout its tumultuous history, the state has given rise to painters, sculptors, musicians, politicians, and psychics who have not only enriched the national personality, but have found international fame far beyond their small hometowns and dusty villages. Since the late 1600s, the land itself has delivered some of the world's greatest supplies of gold, silver, iron, and other precious and semiprecious stones and metals. Yet, despite its richness, there is something ineffable about Minas, something in the color of the rust-orange soil and the voluptuous mountains, something in the air, that can never quite be exploited or explained. The best glimpse you can get, beyond visiting in person, is to listen to the early albums of **Milton Nascimento**—a music that is at once sensual yet elusive. As musician Gilberto Gil once told me, explaining the difference between Salvador and Minas: "In Bahia, everything is sun and celebration and joy, but in Minas, everything is hidden—the mountains, the people, even the next curve on the highway is hidden away."

In the final years of the 17th century, the name Minas Gerais (or General Mines) became synonymous with El Dorado as rumors of emerald highways and diamond-studded bushes filtered through the Empire. Men, women, rich, poor, bandits, noblemen, even monks and priests descended upon the mines from every direction, fast giving rise to a feverish society of boom towns and lawless disorder. Although 18th-century Brazil, with the help of Minas, would produce nearly 80 percent of the world's gold supply, most of it slipped through the fingers of the Brazilians and Portuguese into the hands of Northern Europeans. A few, however, struck it rich, settling in towns like **Mariana** and **Ouro Preto**, where they constructed cathedrals of such decorative wealth that no one dare contested their spiritual devotion. Others found more secular ways to indulge their fancies: One young diamond contractor was so entranced with his seductive *mulata* mistress (an ex-slave) that he first built her a lake large enough to navigate a full-sized sailing ship—then he built her the ship.

Today, Mineiros (people from Minas) are deeply tied to their past. You will find more people here who can retell their own state's history than anywhere else in the country, and, indeed, many feel a direct living lineage to it. Some of the most beloved heroes in Brazilian history hail from Minas: the rebel **Tiradentes**, the artist **Aleijadinho**, the politician **Juscelino Kubitschek** (who built Brasília) and **Tancredo Neves**, the first president of the new democracy, who died shortly before taking office. Deeply sensitive to matters of justice, Mineiros have often evinced great force as a group—though sometimes to paradoxical effect. It was troops from Minas who eventually quelled the São Paulo revolt against Getúlio Vargas' regime in 1932's brief civil war, but it was also Mineiro divisions that moved against Rio in 1964 to ensure the success of the military coup.

Today, the tourist possibilities in Minas are so diverse that you could spend an entire 2- or 3-week vacation just exploring the state.

If you have any sense of adventure, you must retrace the steps of the original *bandeirantes* on horseback around the rugged mountainous plains—a trip I have rated as *the* best eco-trek in Brazil. After that, leisurely browse through the towns of **Ouro Preto**, **Mariana**, **São João del Rei**, **Tiradentes**, and **Congonhas**, five beautifully preserved historical towns considered World Heritage treasures. Following that, replenish your energies at the spa towns in the south, where you can "take the waters" in elegant 19th-century style. Finally, anyone with a yen for UFO sightings should head for **São Tomé das Letras**, where it's difficult to tell the humans from the otherworldly creatures who walk the dusty, rockstrewn streets.

Minas Gerais is most famous for its hospitality. In fact, a term for the Mineiro personality has even been coined—*Mineiridade*—a gestalt of behavior forged on self-sufficiency and tempered by a profoundly sensative nature. Stereotyped as slightly suspicious, Mineiros take a long time to make a friend, but once they open up, they stay your friend for life. Mineiros prefer to listen than talk; it's an easy bet that at a table of raucous Brazilians, the one quietly observing the others is probably from Minas. Even Mineiro composers sing about love in a different way. As local composer Tadeu Franco explained it to me, "A love song from Minas isn't just about romance; it's really universal."

BELO HORIZONTE

Despite being the third largest city in Brazil, **Belo Horizonte** preserves the sentiment of an intimate town. The capital of Minas Gerais, it's often considered by the media as one of the best cities in South America to live in. It's nicknamed "Garden City" for good reason—no other metropolis in Brazil boasts streets so strewn with greenery. The unique Mineiro personality can be felt everywhere here: taxi drivers are more than occasionally honest, citizens are concerned and even helpful, and the cultural life, particularly the music scene, is more profound than flamboyant. The most famous dance group in Brazil, **Grupo Corpor**, is based in Belo Horizonte, and musicians like singer **Tadeu Franco**, songwriter **Beto Guedes**, and guitarist **Toninho Horta** lend a sophisticated lining to the contemporary pop scene. Don't forget that **Milton Nascimento's** famous *Clube da Esquina,* the "corner" where his childhood friends hung out to make music, was located here in Belo Horizonte.

While there are a few sites to see in Belo Horizonte, most people use the city as a trampoline to visit the historical towns and spa circuit. But given the availability of some fabulous, moderately priced apart-hotels, a stay in Belo Horizonte for more than a few days could be exceedingly enjoyable. Some of the best restaurants for regional food are located here, as well as an active nightlife that features both solid jazz, and *sertaneja* (country music). Shopping, particularly in the chic **Savassi** neighborhood, is superb, and fashionable clothes are often less expensive than in Rio. New Age adherents and healers who are interested in buying large amounts of crystals (as well as jewelry) should head directly for one of the best shops in the country—**IRFFI**—where bulk purchasers can often maneuver large discounts. As for romance: statistic hounds may appreciate knowing there are 10 women per each man in Belo Horizonte (as opposed to São Paulo, where there are 10 men per every woman).

PAST GLORIES

Belo Horizonte is a new city, a mere hundred years old. At the beginning of the 18th century, it was initially settled by the São Paulo explorer **João Leite da Silva Ortiz**, whose farm, **Curral del Rey**, became the core of the first hamlet. On December 17, 1893, the fertile undulating landscape was chosen among 5 potential areas as the site for a new town. Finally, after numerous political crises in Ouro Preto, the governor of Minas, **Augusto de Lima**, initiated a project to build the political, cultural, and economic center of the state. With architects and engineers arriving from Rio, it took 4 years for the country's first planned city to be constructed. Based on Washington, D.C. and La Plata in Argentina, Belo Horizonte looks like a huge chessboard of crisscrossing streets, broken up diagonally by wide avenues. Though it was built for 200,000 people, it now holds over 2.5 million.

SIGHTS

In 1980, Pope John celebrated mass in what has now become known as the **Pope's Square**. The **Monumento à Paz**, dominating the plaza, represents a testimony to world peace. Of the two triangles forming the monument, one symbolizes the energy sent to heaven through man's faith; the other triangle represents the energy mankind receives from God. Together they form a square representing the synergistic balance that peace brings to the world. The sculptor is **Ricardo Carvão Levy**. Unfortunately, graffiti has defiled much of the monument. Behind the mountains surrounding the city is the deepest gold mine in Brazil, now producing over 600 kilos of gold and 300 kilos of silver per month.

PAMPULHA

Anyone wanting to understand the construction of Brasília should first look at Belo Horizonte, particularly in the northern district of **Pampulha**, where all the principal characters in the architectural drama were situated 20 years earlier. In 1940, Mayor **Juscelino Kubitschek** (who as President would later oversee Brasília) asked architect **Oscar Niemeyer** and landscape designer **Roberto Burle Marx** to help construct **Pampulha** as a neighborhood designed to attract the elite of the city. Following his signature modernist style, Niemeyer created an artificial lake, casino, restaurant, museum, and church. While the museum no longer holds permanent exhibitions (due to lack of funds), it is notable for its onyx ramp in the entranceway, a rich reminder of Minas' natural wealth. The restaurant, **Casa do Baile**, is still open for business, with a wonderful view overlooking the lake; weekends feature the well-known keyboardist Célio Balona. From this side of the lake, Niemeyer's church, known today as the **Igreja de São Francisco**, looks like an unfortunate mistake. Up close, it is more intriguing than ugly, but like everything else Niemeyer constructed in Belo Horizonte (including the downtown public library and the Benge Bank), the church was done in a disturbing series of curved angles that didn't sit well with the conservatives of the 1940s. In fact, the Archbishop refused to consecrate the church because Niemeyer, a member of the Communist party, had seemingly constructed a symbol of the sickle and hammer (the curved church and the unattached tower, respectively), though the architect vigorously denied it. Not until 10 years later would a new archbishop finally open the church's doors. The *azulejo* tiles and murals, by **Cândido Portinari**, one of the most famous of Brazilian artists, are stunning and lend a warmth to an otherwise cool, avant-garde facade. Mass is held at 10:30 a.m. and 6:00 p.m. on Sunday, when you're sure to find it open.

CATHEDRAL

The main cathedral of the city, **Nossa Senhora da Boa Viagem**, is characteristic of the city's temperament: homey, engulfed in greenery, with a touch of Art Nouveau in the colorful stained-glass windows. At any time of the day or night, you'll find Mineiros quietly praying on their knees as candles twinkle on the altar. The rotunda is impressively high, but it is the grounds that are most memorable. Surrounded by flamboyant and ficus trees, you'll feel as if you're sitting in the middle of a forest.

QUIRKS AND CURVES

It's better to show than tell ahead of time, but **Rua Amendoim**, perhaps the most famous street in Belo Horizonte, will astound you. As the street inclines upward, your car will strangely roll forward (instead of backwards). No joke. Today some people try to explain the phenomenon away by saying it's just an optical illusion (not true) or that the soil is so rich it pushes the car forward (also not true). Why the street was named Amendoim is also a mystery. (Some claim that *amendoims*, or peanuts, are great aphrodisiacs.)

GREEN BELO

To get a glimpse of the Atlantic forest, as well as a magnificent view of the city from its highest peak, head for the 1,500-acre natural reserve called **Parque Florestal das Mangabeiras** *Wednesday–Sunday 8:00 a.m.–5:00 p.m.* designed by Roberto Burle Marx. For an initial orientation of the massive acreage, hop on one of the park's internal buses available every half-hour at the entrance. As you descend into the forest you will instantly feel the humidity become stronger and the air cooler; the profusion of plant and tree life will delight any horticulturalist. Eco trails are well marked, but you can also engage in roller-skating, watersports, and canoeing over two artificial lakes. The park's highest point, **Mirante da Mata**, a 20-minute walk from the entrance, is *the* place to contemplate the sprawl of the city. Free eco-oriented painting programs for children take place on Sat. The park must be ecologically acceptable since an entire flock of wild geese arrived unexpectedly one day and hasn't budged since. For a spectacular nighttime view, stop by **Mirante das Mangabeiras**, outside the park.

Getting There

Take a taxi or the blue #2001-A or #2001-C buses marked "*Aparecida*" from Avenida Afonso Pena.

MUSEUMS

Museu Histórico Abílio Barreto *Rua Benardo Mascarenhas; Wednesday–Monday 10:00 a.m.–5:00 p.m.* is the best historical museum in the city. It's situated in a preserved *fazenda* (farmhouse) in Cidade Jardim, now fast burgeoning into a fashionable district. A photographic gallery reveals the mules, mud huts, and oxcarts of Belo's early days, as well as the Art Deco buildings from the 1930s and 1940s. Much more gruesome is the display of slave shackles, called "Little Angels," so-named because the masters felt the restrainers made their slaves act like "angels." In the last century, travelers from the west on their way to the coast would stop in Belo Horizonte to pray at the chapel of Nossa Senhora da Boa Viagem (Lady of the Good Trip); you can see the remains of the original altar here.

Museu de Mineralogia Djalma Guimarães *Rua da Bahia, 1149 (Centro);* ☎ *212–1400, extension 359. Daily 8:30 a.m.– 5:30 p.m., except holidays* Installed in a neo-Gothic building dating back to 1910, this museum was founded in 1974 to honor the great gemologist Djalma Guimarães and displays the mineral wealth of Minas. Among over 5,000 exhibits, the most distinguished piece is "The Patriarch," a 5-1/2 ton quartz discovered in Teófilo Otoni.

The Historical Cities

There is no other place where a visitor can so steep himself in the richness of Brazil's historical past than in the *cidades históricas* near Belo Horizonte. Originally colonized in the late 17th century by the *bandeirantes* (those rough-and-rugged pioneers who heeded the cries of gold emanating from the Mineiro hills), these satellite villages quickly developed from rambunctious mining camps into gracefully constructed towns replete with beautiful 2-story mansions, cobblestone roads, and most importantly, scores of gilt-laden churches that became showcases for Minas' astounding wealth. Spurred by so much precious ore extracted in so short a time, the cities of **Ouro Preto**, **Mariana**, **São João del Rei**, **Tiradentes**, and **Congonhas** soon became rampant with plots of political intrigue and piracy, but this nucleus of colonial communities also gave rise to some of the country's finest artists and artisans—among them, the sculptor and the painter **Manoel da Costa Athaíde**, whose works remain as living masterpieces of the baroque colonial era. During the 18th century, gold-leaf became the rage, and the churches of Ouro Preto, in particular, transformed the colonialists' experience of worship. One 18th-century observer remarked that praying in Ouro Preto's Church of Pilar was like talking to God inside a great golden urn.

Tropical "Fast Food"

Four hundred years ago, just getting to the hills of Minas from Rio de Janeiro was a daunting task; the path led through dense tropical forests, twisting *precipices*, and barbarous mountains. Along with the *bandeirantes* and adventuresome priests also came thousands of newly arrived African slaves, forced to make the arduous 15-day journey from the coast in shackles. It was from these peripatetic beginnings, however, that the Mineiro cuisine was developed—a kind of tropical "fast food" with African undertones that could be made on the highway. *Feijão tropeiro,* a mixture of beans, vegetables, and wild herbs was superlative for travelers since it didn't spoil easily (*tropeiro* refers to the man who takes care of the mules). Since okra could found along the highway, *frango com quiabo* fast became a regional delicacy. *Frango ao molho pardo* (chicken cooked in its own blood) was also developed as a food of convenience. And because cows, pigs, and corn were omnipresent, *bamba de couve* could be whipped up at a moment's notice—a delicious hot porridge of cornmeal spiked with finely chopped kale and tiny pieces of pork.

A Conspiracy

Beyond their artistic treasures and culinary delights, these historical cities are held dear by modern Brazilians for another reason. It was here that the infamous **Inconfidência Mineiro**, a conspiracy spearheaded by Mineiros in the late 18th century, was first initiated against Portuguese rule. Although a failure in its own time, the rebellion became the ultimate symbol of Brazilian independence, later inspiring the colony's successful break with the motherland nearly a century later. Today, it is a rare schoolchild who cannot recite the exciting tale of Tiradentes, the conspiracy's martyred hero. Two hundred years have passed since the heydays of these colonial cities, yet the economic decline of Ouro Preto and Mariana at the end of the mining cycle was actually their architectural salvation. As migrant workers moved onto other areas, it became impracticable to replace the old buildings with more modern examples, as happened in Rio. The decisive act for preserving the two cities was the creation in 1937 of what is now known as the **Department of the Ministry of Culture**. Thirty-nine edifices in Ouro Preto and thirteen in Mariana, including religious and civil buildings, bridges, fountains, and private houses were registered as national monuments in the Department's record books, thus providing legal protection and a permanent guarantee of technical assistance for their conservation. In 1980, UNESCO bestowed the title of "**Cultural Heritage of Mankind**" upon the city of Ouro Preto.

Insider Tip:

A substantial tour of the historical cities should take about 3–4 days, including one to two days in Ouro Preto and Mariana, and 2 days in São João del Rei, Tiradentes, and Congonhas. Add extra time if you like to stroll or if you will be using the public bus as transportation, or taking the train ride from São João del Rei to Tiradentes.

EXCURSION

IN THE SADDLE OF THE BANDEIRANTES

*The sky from our hotel window in Belo Horizonte had looked threatening all morning, but bad weather has never daunted **Túlio Marques Lopes**, who offers the best eco trek in Brazil. At noon Túlio picks us up in a jeep and roars off to his hitching post a half-hour away. By the time the sixteen of us are saddled, the mist has turned to gentle rain and we bundle up in huge yellow ponchos that graze the legs of our horses. Riding a marvelous Argentine horse, Túlio begins to lead us through a cobblestone village to the mountains behind, when suddenly a magnificent rainbow breaks in the sky, setting a new mood. Soon, civilization is forgotten as we wind around granite mountains and grassy valleys, the sky so dramatic in color it nearly sings. The going at times is rough as our horses step gingerly around fallen boulders*

and mudslides, but Túlio is indefatigable, keeping us in line and shouting "Coragem" (or courage in Portuguese). Thoughts of gold rushes and wagon trains fill our minds as we teeter up the rocky embankments, and even the most uncoordinated soul starts to feel macho as the faithful horses sludge onward. Even after the moon rises we keep marching forward, able only to see the faint image of a swishing tail in front of us. Somewhere between exhausted and starving, we find our way to an isolated ranch house, where an elderly backwoods couple prepares a hearty meal over a wood-stove fire (a chicken dish so traditional that the claws are left on the feet!). As we polish off our last beers scrawny farmhands wail out drunken renditions of country tunes. But it's another 2 hours until we finally collapse in the most rustic of pousadas. In the morning we discover we've landed our sore rumps in the quaint village of **São Sebastião das Águas Claras**, a dusty, one-road town where we greet the country folk and peer into old churches. After an ice-cold dip in a nearby waterfall, we head to Dona Dica's for lunch, hitching up our horses and settling into a fabulous feast, with vegetables grown right outside her back door. A few extra beers fortify for us the long trek home; this time we traverse fast-running streams, race over flat plains, and generally feel the soul of the moon. By the time we arrive back home—muddy, scraped, and nearly paraplegic—most of us have come to feel at one with our horses.

What makes this trip so spectacular is the charm of Túlio Marques Lopes, the owner, whose friends were so entranced with his weekend excursions that they forced him to go public. A former film director, lawyer, and *bon vivant,* Túlio has developed a deep feel for the terrain of Minas, able to convince you that you're retracing the steps of the early immigrants. Perhaps by 1993, all his horses will be Manga-Larga Marchadors, an Argentinian breed whose lambada-like trots make long journeys a breeze. Due to the terrain, the pace is so slow that anybody who can stay upright on a saddle can do it, though rainy days provide extra thrills. Full-day ($26) and overnight trips with hotel ($53) for up to 16 people are available (and includes 1 meal a day). More daring adventurers may arrange a special 4-day trek from Belo Horizonte to Ouro Preto! In general, children under 9 are not allowed, but senior citizens in good shape are welcome.

For more information call:
Tropa Serrana c/o **Túlio Marques Lopes** *Rua Gentios 5050/1041 (Belo Horizonte);* ☎ *344-8986, 273-3213, 225-6922.*

THE ESSENTIAL BELO HORIZONTE

WHERE TO STAY

The best accommodations in Belo Horizonte are apart-hotels, some so fashionably decorated you may want to move in forever. Since the city is a business center, weekend discounts are often phenomenal. Any hotel in Savassi will situate you within walking distance of the city's best shopping; you'll also be close to excellent neighborhood restaurants and bars. Downtown hotels tend to be noisy and slightly rambunctious.

Expensive -------------- **Over $60**

Moderate --------------- **$30–$60**

Inexpensive ------------ **Under $20**

Le Flamboyant
Rua Rio Grande do Norte, 1007 (Savassi);
☎ *(31) 273-5233*

A perfect hotel with an unbelievable rate, this 13-floor high-rise in chic Savassi offers rooms that are more like apartments with a kitchen, living room, and bedroom, complete with color TV and video, hydromassage, and central air-conditioning and heat. An exquisitely decorated bar is lined with paintings, and the lobby must have the world's most comfortable leather couches. Breakfast is taken next to the pool, and the finely decorated restaurant serves lunch and dinner. A small pool is enhanced by a private sun deck. The same management intends to open a similar property, the Metropolitan Flat, some 5 blocks away with futuristic gold furnishings, a gym and sauna, pool, and 2 exec salons, plus an auditorium. Businessmen at both properties receive a 10 percent discount, 30 percent discount on weekends. Reserve at least 10 days in advance. All apartments run $65. 40 apartments. *Expensive. All Cards.*

Del Rey Hotel
Praça Afonso Arinos, 60 (centro); ☎ *(31) 273-2211*

Elegant simplicity in this 4-star high-rise downtown is marred only by the inevitable sounds of traffic. The location is central: across the street from the Mineral Museum and close to the park, the handicraft fair, and the Palácio des Artes. Standards, all air-conditioned, come equipped with minibar and TV. The restaurant serves buffet-style. There is no pool. Standard singles run $77, doubles $86, suites $176. 213 apartments, *12 suites. Expensive. All cards.*

Othon Palace
Avenida Afonso Pena, 1050 (centro);
☎ *(31) 273-3844*

Shaped like a huge curve, this 25-floor high-rise is a friendly, inviting hotel located near the beginning of the handicraft fair downtown. All the 5-star services are here: sauna, hair salon, boutiques, jewelry stores, and 24-hour room service. VIP services include a private check-in, separate breakfast, and office salons. Standards and deluxes are nearly the same, except that the latter is located on higher floors. Tastefully appointed, all rooms include 2 separate spaces delineated by a divider; all are equipped with color TV, safe, minibar, tub, and central air-conditioning. The outdoor roof pool boasts a spectacular view of the city, and the restaurant Venezia is known for its pasta. Live music on the roof bar nightly. In front of the hotel is a popcorn man who sells fried pieces of coconut—the most delicious junk food I have ever tasted. Singles run $72, doubles $94; 50 percent discount on weekends. *Expensive–Moderate.* 302 apartments. *All Cards.*

Luxor Savassi Suite Hotel
Rua Antonio de Albuquerque, 335 (Savassi),
☎ *(31) 223-9000*

One of the city's best deals, this elite apart hotel tucked into a leafy street of Savassi is chic, luxurious, and comfortable. Each apartment comes with a bedroom, living room, and kitchen, decorated like a plush private residence. Room service is not available in the hotel but can be ordered from the restaurant down the street. On premises is a pool, sauna, luncheonette, restaurant, and a high-class bar. Good discount for travel agents.

Superiors run $53. *Moderate. Cards: AE, DC.*

Boulevard Plaza
Avenida Getúlio Vargas, 1640 (Savassi); ☎ *(31) 223–9000*
Well situated, this property is more like an apart hotel, with spacious, extremely ample apartments overlooking the shopping district, including a small second room in front of the bedroom. All apartments come with air-conditioning, color TV, and phone. There is no pool. A casual restaurant is open 24 hours, and a bar features live music. 44 apartments. *Moderate. All cards.*

Real Palace
Rua Espírito Santo, 901 (centro); ☎ *(31) 273-3111. Reservations (31) 800–2334*
This 20-floor hotel downtown is filled with men in business suits; families tend to congregate on weekends. A chintzy ballroom effect prevails in the lobby, with furniture that is more boring than tasteless. Standards are large, with a well-stocked minibar and walk-in closets; electronic keys provide more security. Deluxe rooms are not worth the extra bucks. Other services include a beauty parlor, 2 saunas, solarium, tea salon, bar, and nightclub. The tiny outdoor pool is good for 4 strokes. The receptionists speak some English. Standards run $52, doubles $58. 256 apartments. *Moderate. All cards.*

Wembley Palace Hotel
Rua Espírito Santo, 01; ☎ *(31) 201–6966, FAX 224–9946*
Near the train and bus stations and 15 minutes from the airport, this impressive 3-star budget hotel has compact but attractive apartments equipped with fully stocked minibars, bathroom phones, and color TVs. Safes are at the reception. In the late 1980s, the restaurant received an award for the best restaurant in a 3-star hotel. An intimate bar opens daily at 6 p.m. Singles start at $31, doubles $48.105 apartments, 2 suites. *Moderate. All cards.*

Pousada das Aguas Claras
Rua São Sebastião, 10 (São Sebastião das Águas Claras), Reservations: ☎ *(31) 283–2457*
A 6-room pousada that's more like a rustic ranch house is situated in this miniscule village a half-hour by car from Belo Horizonte. Two rooms come with private bath; breakfast is served outside on the small patio surrounded by lush gardens. Communal bathrooms are a few steps down the hallway. From here, you can hike, visit a waterfall, enjoy the country life, and eat at Dona Dica's down the road (see below). The owner, Dr. Fausto Fróes, usually spends his weekends here. 6 apartments. *Inexpensive. No cards.*

Hotel BH Centro
Rua Espírito Santo, 284; ☎ *(31) 222–3390*
This is a tolerable budget hotel in front of downtown's crowded lower-class streets, but the location is relatively safe. You may have to suffer a slight musty smell in the apartments, but breakfast is taken in a high-beamed salon with attractive wood floors. Cheapest room is a *quarto,* with a phone, sink, but no TV; the communal bathroom is down the hall. *Apartamentos* have private bathrooms, TV, phone, but nonexistent decoration. A popular Arabic restaurant with reasonable prices is down the street.*Quartos $5–$9, apartamentos $9–$15.* 27 apartments. *Inexpensive. Cards: MC, DC.*

Albergue da Juventude Pousada Beagá
Rua Timbiras, 2330 (Centro); ☎ *(31) 275–3592*
A youth hostel that is clean, friendly, and well situated downtown. *Inexpensive. No cards.*

WHERE TO EAT

Atmosphere—from romantic to homey—is as important as the quality of cuisine in Belo Horizonte. Locals leave home around 10:00 p.m. to go for dinner; go any earlier, and you will probably find the dining rooms empty. Some of the best regional food in the state can be enjoyed here; listed below are also hangouts where you may run into the city's most famous musicians and poets. For dessert, at least once try *queijo mineiro,* a local sour cheese usually served with a sweet slice of *goiabada* (guava jam) to cut the taste. *Doce de leite,* a caramel-like pudding sometimes topped with shreds of coconut, is also scrumptious.

Expensive -------------- Above $15
Moderate --------------- $5–$15
Inexpensive ------------ Under $5

Churrascaria

Mr. Beef
Rua Gonçalves Dias, 2600; ☎ *337–4255. Daily 6:00 p.m. on*
Maybe you didn't come this far to hear Simon & Garfunkel and Dire Straits, but this Far West saloon also offers some of the best steaks in town. Live music Tuesday–Saturday. *Moderate. All cards.*

Eclectic Funk

★ **Era Um Vez um Chalezinho**
Rua Paraíba, 1455; ☎ *221–2170. Daily 5:00 p.m.–3:00 a.m., only closed Christmas and New Year's*
A Swiss chalet with a pyramid roof (for energy!) may seem a bit anachronistic in Brazil, but this is one of Belo's most romantic eateries. Come for drinks and *petiscos*, which include cheese, salamis, *pastéis*, and *torta de galinha* (chicken pie), or indulge in 6 kinds of fondues. You can even concoct your own salad plate with options that include cabbage, eggs, potatoes, and beets. The coffee drinks are unbelievably good, like the *"Era um Vez"* ("Once upon a Time"), with coffee, coffee liquor, banana, chocolate, sugar, ice cream, whipped cream, and cherries. For dessert, don't miss the *Torta dos Sete Anões* (7 Dwarfs Pie) or the exquisite *Pavê da Vovó* with layers of biscuits, creme, peanuts, and whipped cream drenched in chocolate. Guests can choose between dining outdoors on a porch, downstairs with a rinky-dink piano, upstairs with jazz, or in the tiny attic-like cove. A small music cover is charged. Another branch in Santa Teresa near the old cinema serves only a pasta buffet, but offers a magic show and live bands. *Moderate. All cards.*

French

★ **Chez Dadette**
Rua Coelho de Souza, 70; ☎ *275–1400. Daily noon–3:00 p.m., dinner 7:30 p.m.–last client, closed Sunday*
One of the most respected chef/owners in Brazil, Bernadette (Dadette) Bahia Mascarenhas studied with Pierre Troigros and trained at Lutéce in New York. But the menu she's created in this upscale but homey French bistro is the result of her worldwide travels and crosses everything from Japanese to Indian to French. Catering to heads of state and prime ministers, she confesses that President Collor's favorite dish was the *Rigatoni Chez Dadette*—a light, tropical pasta of prosciutto and dry mushrooms. The filet mignon arrives with caviar and the breast of duck with a caramel sauce of her own invention. Desserts are highly creative like the crepes with passion fruit mousse (the seeds of the passion fruit are roasted for a crunchy topping). Dinners run about $30 per person, or up to $100 if you order Petrossian caviar and truffles. Dadette loves to schmooze tableside when she's not supervising the kitchen; in her spare time she also restores Persian rugs for export. Unfortunately, she's still crying about the time architect Oscar Niemeyer painted the entire map of Brasília on her wall and the cleaning lady washed it off by mistake. *Expensive. Cards MC.*

Regional

★ **Dona Lucinha**
Rua Pe. Odorico, 38 (Savassi); ☎ *227–0562. Daily noon–4:00 p.m., 7:00 p.m.–2:00 a.m.*
Owner of one of the best typical kitchens here, Dona Lucinha serves the kind of traditional food they used to eat on the grand plantations. Eighteenth-century prints on the walls take you back in time, but it's the huge self-service buffet (for an unbelievable $4) that will truly delight gourmands, as well as gourmets. Feast on *feijão tropeiro*, sinfully juicy short ribs, and the best *doce de leite* (a kind of caramel pudding) that I've ever tasted. *Moderate. All cards.*

★ **Mala e Cuia**
Avenida Raja Gabaglia, 1617 (São Bento); ☎ *342–1421. Tuesday–Saturday 11:00 a.m.–midnight. Live music at 9:00 p.m., Friday, Saturday, and Sunday at 1:00 p.m*
Wonderful is the panoramic view of the city's

green hills and skyline seen from the open windows of this pink farmhouse. The cuisine is typically Mineiro, made the old-fashioned way (if you peek inside the kitchen, you'll see the roaring fire). Onions hang from the ceiling; the sweet jams, cheese, marinated peppers, and *cachaças* hugging the wall are all for sale. Specialties are *frango ao molho pardo* (chicken cooked in its own blood). Some of the vegetables are fresh since they're pulled right from the garden. A minimal charge on the weekend covers the live country-style music—a great opportunity to hear regional artists. *Moderate. No cards.*

Pier 32
Avenida Afonso Pena, 3328; ☎ *225-0782. Noon–3:00 p.m. daily for lunch; Monday–Friday 7:00 p.m.–1:00 a.m., Friday and Saturday, bar open til 2:00 a.m., Sunday 11:30 a.m.–5:00 p.m. only*

The kitchen is in the middle of this casual, nautically inspired restaurant alive with talk. At lunch, it's more a business crowd, but at night, the 25–30 set settles in for the typical Mineiro buffet of *feijão tropeiro,* fried manioc, sausage, *farofa,* and stews. Fish and pastas are also available, and a chef in top hat cooks nicely grilled *picanha.* The menu changes daily (only the *picanha* is constant); sometimes there's even rabbit. About $6 per person. *Moderate. No cards.*

Spanish
La Tabernas Bar & Restaurante
Rua Sergipe, 499 (Funcionários); ☎ *26-3490*

Excellent Spanish food and live flamenco music and dance. *Moderate. No cards.*

Varied
★ Cervejaria Brasil
Rua Aimorés, 78; ☎ *225-1099. Daily 11:00 a.m.–1:00 a.m., weekends til 2:00 a.m.*

As tropical a restaurant as you can get this far inland, this open-air eatery with its grass-hut roof is a magnet for the artists and intellectuals of the city. Argentine *picanha,* a juicy chunk of beef, comes simmering on a grill with a sleeve of fat, but that's part of the wonderful taste. You can also choose among 18 other kinds of meat, including kassler with sauerkraut. The smoked fish is delicious. For noshing, try the *tábua de frios* —a wooden tray laden with cheese and meats. Take time here to become acquainted with that special cheese from Minas called *queijo Minas. Moderate. No cards.*

Taste Vin
Rua Curitiba, 2105; ☎ *335-5423. Sunday–Thursday. 7:30 p.m.–midnight, weekends 6:30 p.m.–1:00 a.m.*

If you're dragged out late by a Brazilian friend, or find yourself lost after the theater, head here for the best soufflés in Belo Horizonte—the *queijo-gruyère* (*gruyere cheese*) is superlative. Top it off with a *profiterole,* a delicious cream puff filled with ice cream and drizzled with chocolate sauce. On weekends, the place is packed by midnight. *Moderate. All cards.*

Casa dos Contos
Rua Rio Grande do Norte, 1065;
☎ *222-1070. Daily 11:30 p.m.–2:00 a.m.*
A hangout for the literati, Casa dos Contos is one of the few houses in the city where you can terminate the night guaranteed with good food and excellent service. Try the *medalhão à moda,* medallions of beef prepared with white wine, rice, broccoli, and mushroom. Good pastas, beef, and pizza. *Inexpensive. Cards: AE, MC.*

Restaurante Dona Dica
Rua São Sebastião, 315, access from BR-040 Sul (São Sebastião das Aguas Claras). 11:00 a.m.–8:00 p.m.

The motorbikers who race around the mountain edges discovered this simple abode 20 years ago. Today, superstars like Milton Nascimento and Elba Ramalho make the half-hour drive from Belo Horizonte for the home-cooked food of Dona Dica, owner, chef, and mother superior of this mud-floor eatery for over 40 years. Horses may get hitched up right next to your table while their riders sit down for some grub, but that's part of the charm. While your food's cooking, ask to visit the kitchen where a clay furnace bakes delicious breads and biscuits. The *refeição,* or main meal, consists of rice, beans, meat, salad, and couvert for $6. A typical Mineiro dish— *frango ao molho pardo* (chicken cooked in its own blood) runs about $6.50. Since 1986, Dona Dica has received a top rating in *Quatro Rodas*, the official Brazilian travel guide, and her weather-beaten face proves just how hard she's worked all her life. Still, her hospitality never dims and she loves to show off her back garden, where tomorrow's chicken and pork dinners are scurrying about. On holidays and weekends, the food is always ready; any other time, Dona Dica will whip up something on the spot. While you're in the area, check out the little village with a small wood church. *Inexpensive. No Cards.*

NIGHTLIFE

Bars with Music

After Belo-ites leave work, they head straight for neighborhood bars to relax, flirt, and negotiate their dinner dates. The best bars are in Savassi—casual, often open-air, surrounded by lush trees and vegetation. You'll find the best local musicians performing here.

★ Bar Brasil

Rua Aimorés, 1008; ☎ *225-1099. Monday–Friday 6:00 p.m.–midnight, Saturday and Sunday 11:00 a.m.–midnight*

This bar, the little sister to the Cervejaria Brasil restaurant next door, is one of the hottest joints in town. Singer Tadeu Franco and composer Beto Guedes can usually be found here, wrapped around the stone tables, as well as anyone who's smart and sexy between 20 and 30. Whoever can't fit inside the small woodbeam structure park themselves on the sidewalk. *Inexpensive. No cards.*

Ness

Rua Sergipe, 1331 (Savassi); ☎ *227-0171 Monday–Saturday 6:00 p.m.–last client*

Considered a class-A bar, this English-style pub features all kinds of music (Monday–Wednesday at 9:00 p.m. and Thursday–Saturday at 9:30 p.m.), specializing in fine jazz singers. Cover is about $4. The menu is basic: chicken, steak, appetizers, *chopp*, and fine whiskeys. *Moderate. No Cards.*

Ninho de Cobras

Rua Rio de Janeiro, 2720; ☎ *225-8088.* *Daily 7:00 p.m. on, closed Sunday*

Down some *chopp* and stuffed crabs while listening to fine country music (Sat. only). *Moderate. No Cards.*

A Canga & Candeia

Avenida Contorno, 6342; ☎ *223-9512*

A comfortable, well-attended club with a dance floor. Shows of *música sertaneja* start at 9:30 p.m. Tuesday–Saturday. *Moderate. No Cards.*

Theater

Palácio das Artes

Avenida Afonso Pena, 1537 (Centro); ☎ *210-8900*

Check the newspaper for listings of performances at this grand theater—opera, choral concerts, ballet, and others. *Moderate. No Cards.*

Nightclubs

★ Cabaré Mineiro

Rua Gonçalves Dias, 54; ☎ *227-5860*

Owned by Wagner Tiso, Milton Nascimento's first keyboardist and now a star in his own right, Cabaré Mineiro is the city's primary nightclub, with a different live show—rock, lambada, gafieira, bossa—every night. For major Brazilian acts, it's best to buy tickets 2–3 days in advance. Shows never start before 10:00 p.m.; the age group depends on the act. Sometimes you get lucky and Tiso himself will play. Across the street is a typical regional restaurant called **Cozinha de Minas**.

Boate Tom Marrom

Rua Inconfidentes, 1141; ☎ *224-3728*

A good nightclub, with a great bar and different jazz nightly.

New Sagitarius Night Club

Rua Alfenas, 27 (Mangabeiras);
☎ *221-9304. Monday–Saturday 9:00 p.m. on.*

For men (executive-style) only—considered to be the best in Brazilian striptease.

GAY BELO HORIZONTE

Best bar/disco for gays is:

Le Troisième

Rua Paraíba, 1049 (Savassi). Thursday–Sunday starting at midnight.

SHOPPING

The district of **Savassi** is the home of most of the best restaurants, apart-hotels, cinemas, and shopping malls in the city. Located south of the Municipal Park and the Palácio das Artes, the fashionable neighborhood is bounded on the east by Avenida do Contorno, the south by Rua Congonhas, and Rua Rio de Janeiro on the west. The magazine *Tudo Aqui—Savassi*, sold at newsstands, will give you an excellent map, as well a 64-page booklet of stores, eateries, and services. One of the finest mini-malls in the area is **BHZ Fashion Mall** *Rua Paraíba, 1132* offering some of the most elegant fashions for men and women in Brazil.

Arts and Crafts Fairs

On Sunday at **Praça Liberdade** 3,000 artists show and sell works of ceramic, wood, weaving, metal, glass-cutting, painting, graphics, and drawings.

The **Flower Market** at the Municipal Market on Friday, with 110 stalls, offers a huge variety of plants and flowers. Many vendors grow their own plants and give good advice. **Mercado Central,** downtown, is a farmer's market in the style of a Turkish bazaar, where you must master saying *"um desconto?"* (a discount?) with an irresistible smile. Espadrilles made out of buffalo hide are a swell deal for about $6. Medicinal herbs in their raw state are also for sale, though you must know what you're looking for. And if you're in the market for live animals, you won't be disappointed, though the stench can be awesome (many families, or, rather, their maids, buy their own "very fresh" turkeys and chickens here). There's also a natural food store and stalls of luscious-looking fruit, though remember to wash and peel anything you buy here.

Crystals

IRFFI
Avenida Barbacena, 700-A; ☎ *335-7211*
Those in the know head to this huge store for the some of the best crystals in Belo Horizonte, and maybe in Minas. Leave plenty of time in your schedule to browse through the hundreds of rings, necklaces, pendants, crystals (raw and polished), semi-precious stones, crystal pyramids, soapstone sculptures, and chess sets, etc. You'll also see rocks you didn't know existed, all marked with their supposed healing properties; in fact, if you want to meet some of the area's best healers, you may run into them here. Discounts can be finagled by groups or anyone purchasing in bulk.

Gem Center

Rua Paraíba, 330, 5th floor (Centro) Central Shopping; ☎ *226-3900. Monday–Saturday 9:00 a.m.–7:00 p.m., Saturday 9:00 a.m.–1:00 p.m.*
Extensive collection of gems, jewelry, and precious stones from Minas. Not the place to buy crystals, but good for jewelry. With 15–20 stores, you should browse, compare, and bargain. The tourist board BELOTUR is located upstairs in the same building.

Native Crafts

Serjô
Rua Antônio de Albuquerque, 749 (Savassi). Monday–Saturday 9:00 a.m.–10:00 p.m.
A chic craft stores with the best native handiwork from all over Brazil, including miniature clay nativity scenes, lacework, tapestries, and paintings. Prices are steep, but the store is worth visiting just to see the inventive stock.

Natural Food Store

Homeopatia Vitae *Rua Orange, 67;* ☎ *225-7380 sells Bach Flower Remedies.*

Photo Lab

Foto Retes *Rua dos Inconfidentes, 926 (Savassi);* ☎ *273-3299 Good quick service.*

SPORTS

Soccer is played March–July and August–November on Wednesday, Saturday, and Sunday at the **Estádio Governador Magalhães Pinto**, nicknamed Mineirão. Outside, there's a monument to **Pelé**, Brazil's greatest soccer player, who just may end up president of the country one day (though retired, he's still that popular). A bronze model of the sports hero's feet allows you to step into his arches. Next door is **Mineirinho**, the biggest sports gym in South America.

Healers

José F. de Andrade Gil ☎ *344–2819, 342–3690* Shiatzu and acupuncture.

Ana Magalhães *Rua Chicago, 176, (Sion);* ☎ *255–0457, 285–1565* Massage.

HANDS-ON BELO HORIZONTE

Arrival

Most flights into Belo Horizonte arrive at the modern **Aeroporto Tancredo Neves**, about 18 miles from the center of the city. Avoid taking the red taxis (they cost more). The white taxis are just as good, and will take you to the center of town for about $20–$25 (be prepared for a long drive). Frequent buses will take you to the **Rodoviária** (bus station) or the **Terminal Turístico JK**. Buses to the airport leave from both the Terminal Turístico JK and the Rodoviária; you'll need a full hour for the trip. Air-conditioned *executivo* buses are your best bet (for about $4), leaving from the Terminal Turístico; they take only about 20 minutes. A second airport, **Pampulha**, usually only receives shuttle flights, but check your ticket to make sure. Airlines flying to Belo Horizonte are:

Varig
Rua Espirito Santo, 643; ☎ *273–6060;*
VASP
Rua Carijós, 279 (Centro); ☎ *335–9888;*
Transbrasil
Rua Tamoios, 86 (Centro); ☎ *226–3433.*

Car Rental

Localisa National *Avenida Bernardo Monteiro, 1567;* ☎ *(31) 800–2121.*

City Transportation

City buses are excellent, color-coded for destination: yellow buses have circular routes, red buses serve the center, and blue buses run diagonally. The easiest place to catch a bus is on *Avenida Afonso Pena*, especially if you're downtown.

Taxis are generally cheap, and much more reliable than in other big cities.
Rádio Táxi ☎ *225–5588;*
Coomotáxi ☎ *464–5577.*

Consulates

U.S.A. *Rua Osvaldo Cruz, 165;* ☎ *223–0800.*

Great Britain *Rua Gaspar Viana, 490;* ☎ *224–4822.*

Money Exchange

Banco do Brasil *Rua Rio de Janeiro, 750.*
American Express Kontik-Franstur *Rua Espírito Santo, 1204;* ☎ *273–1288.*

Points Beyond

Daily buses run from the **Rodoviária** ☎ *201–8111* to Brasília, Rio, Salvador, São Paulo, Caxambú, Congonhas, Diamantina, Lapinha, Mariana, Ouro Preto, Poços de Caldas, Sabará, São João del Rei, and São Lourenço. Tickets to towns of tourist interest should be bought as soon as possible in advance, including the round trip (especially on weekends and holidays).

Tourist Information

Special tourist information in English can be found by calling **Alô Belô** ☎ *220–1310*, as well as at centers in the bus station, Praça Sete, and at the airport. The official tourist board of the city is located at **BELOTUR** *Rua Paraíba, 330, 19th floor (Centro);* ☎ *222–5500.*

Travel Agency

Unitour
Rua Tupis, 171; ☎ *(31) 201–7144*
An excellent travel agency with a helpful English-speaking staff offers tours of the historical towns, as well as a 5-day steamboat journey down the São Francisco River. Half-day tours of Congonhas run about $78, one-day tour of Ouro Preto and Mariana about $140 (rates for two are considerably cheaper). A tour of Congonhas, Sao João del Rei, and Tiradentes runs about $200. Airport transfers can also be arranged.

What to Wear

Businessmen tend to wear suits, but general tourists will feel comfortable wearing jeans and a neat T-shirt during the day. Dress at night is casual chic.

OURO PRETO

Minas' premier historical city, **Ouro Preto**, is a treasure of details—gorgeous mansions, curved windows with wrought-iron panes, grilled baroque balconies, antique street lanterns, and cobblestone streets that meander up and down the steep hillsides. What is so surprising is that such a small town should boast 13 baroque churches—from more modest chapels to grand cathedrals washed in a dazzling gold leaf. Today, the city (pop. 67,000) is a real university town with the bohemian flair that students always bring. Crime is low, and it is perfectly safe to stroll around after dark, but on weekend nights and holidays, it's not uncommon to see young scholars and backpackers strung out drunk on the plazas.

The name "Ouro Preto," or black gold, refers to the color of ore first discovered in the area: gold mixed with a dark-tinted palladium. If you are interested in buying precious and semiprecious gems, excellent deals can be found in Ouro Preto and are often one-third the cost of prices at the big–name jewelry stores in Rio. The best (and the most expensive) is **imperial topaz**, mining deposits of which can be found near **Saramenha**, less than 2 kilometers from the city's center, as well as in the districts of **Rodrigo Silva** and **Antônio Pereira**, about 20 kilometers away. An extremely rare stone, imperial topaz can only be found elsewhere in the Ural Mountains in what is today the former Soviet Union. Colors range from yellow to champagne to an intense rose tone.

The city has had its share of historical characters, not the least which has been the more recent *figura* **Dona Olímpia**, made famous by Milton Nascimento in the song of the same name. Once a young woman renowned for her beauty, she was reputed to have lost her first and only love due to her family's financial demise, then later turned eccentric in old age and greeted tour buses dressed in old-style clothes, muttering about the golden days of Ouro Preto. Some locals claimed she was crazy; others called her brilliant; eventually, a Carnaval School was named after her. Alas, she died in the last few years, but shopkeepers still remember her, and you can discover more information about her in local crafts stores.

One eccentric addendum for scientists: The **peripatus**, a prehistoric insect that can be found nowhere else on the planet, has been discovered in the forests surrounding Ouro Preto. A program of conservation has been initiated to protect it.

When to Go:

January 1 *Feast of Our Lady of the Rosary*, celebrated at the Church of N.S. da Conceição, features a rare exhibition of *congado,* a ceremonial 18th-century dance introduced by slaves from the Congo.

February *Carnaval* takes place down the atmospheric streets and squares, with pageants, samba schools, and displays of the traditional figure of Sé Pereira by the Ouro Preto Jockey Club, the oldest Carnaval society in Brazil (1867).

March *Holy Week* is particularly beautiful, with processions and ceremonies reenacting Christ's martyrdom.

April 16–20 *Inconfidência Week*, with various artistic programs, culminates on April 21, *Tiradentes Day*, when the state capital is symbolically transferred to Ouro Preto.

May 2–4 *Feast of the Holy Cross* is an old Minas tradition held on the bridge of Antônio Dias, also known as Marília's Bridge, with fairs, band concerts, fireworks, and free distribution of fried peanuts.

July 1–7 *Anniversary of Ouro Preto.*

August 15–22 *Folklore Week*, with dance and music groups, typical foods, and handicrafts.

September 7 *Independence Day* (and the preceding week) is celebrated with popular shows and fireworks on the main square.

September 17–23 *Horsemanship Jousts.*

November 14–21 *Aleijadinho* Week.

> **Insider Tip:**
>
> *Avoid Mondays, when churches are closed for cleaning.*

PAST GLORIES

It's no wonder that the fever for Brazilian independence was first ignited among the **Inconfidentes** in **Ouro Preto**. Ever since its start as a mining camp in the early 18th century, Ouro Preto has witnessed a fever pitch of emotions. Immediately after a Paulista adventurer named **Antônio Dias** discovered "black gold" while panning near the Itacolomi Peak, thousands flooded the area, setting up makeshift camps along the Riberão and Carmo streams. By 1711, spurred by the appearance of a now prosperous hamlet, the Portuguese government officially founded the village of **Vila Rica de Nossa Senhora do Pilar**, the first to be recognized in Minas. The stunning outpouring of gold, the overburgeoning population, and a frightening lack of food supplies soon erupted in a series of tumultuous rebellions. Ten years later the **Vila Rica Rebellion** broke out, protesting the exorbitant taxes exacted by the Portuguese. The result was the establishment of the Capitania of Minas Gerais, independent of São Paulo, with its official headquarters housed in Vila Rica.

Between 1735 and 1763, gold production peaked and many of Ouro Preto's fine buildings were built, including the **Governor's Palace** and numerous bridges and fountains. By 1780, the city was a spider's web of paved, winding streets and elegant 2-story houses with terraced gardens ebullient with flowers. Inspired by Iberian counter-reformist ideals, the new settlers began to build magnificent baroque churches at the end of nearly every great road.

National Freedom

The political movement considered by historians to have most profoundly influenced colonial Brazil was the **Inconfidência Mineira** (1788–1792). On its face a protest against royal taxes, it was really a muffled cry for national freedom, modeled after the 1776 rebellion of the North American British colonies. Though the conspiracy was a collusion of many social classes, the only name Brazilians remember today is that of **Tiradentes** (The Tooth-puller) whose real name was **Joaquim José da Silva Xavier**, a part-time dentist, mineralogist, low-level militia officer, and engineer whose "loner" personality earmarked him for martyrdom. Enflamed with republican ideals, Tiradentes was able to inspire a nucleus of supporters. But before action could be taken, one of the participants renounced the others, hoping to have his personal debts rescinded, and the cause was immediately lost. At the conspirators' trial, which became a circus of denials and betrayals, Tiradentes alone admitted full responsibility, even though his defense lawyer tried to prove him insane. While the sentences of his colleagues were commuted to exile, Tiradentes' punishment resounded with Iberian revenge: he was to be hung, drawn, and quartered in public, his salted head posted in Vila Rica "till it rotted" and the other members of his body posted in the neighboring cities where he had preached rebellion. (Fortunately for the townspeople, the skull was stolen by compatriots after a few days and was rumored to have been buried in the hills near the city, supposedly filled with gold dust.) It took a hundred years to redeem Tiradentes' name, but now the Brazilian flag bears the motto of his rebellion: "Freedom—Even Late," a phrase originally from Virgil. In Ouro Preto, the central square today bears not only Tiradentes' name but his statue.

ARCHITECTURAL HISTORY

Religious buildings proliferated in Minas ever since the early days of colonization. At first they were rough little chapels raised alongside the paths leading to the mining zones, where a statue of the patron saint of the expedition was placed. Later, as a group settled into a particular area, a full-fledged chapel was built, with bells hung in eccentric coves. As civil authorities founded the village, another kind of church began to appear—the mother church, a true sign of attained prosperity. Meant to hold large congregations of (white) worshippers, churches like Conceição and Pilar, with their monumental frontispieces, were impressive calls to worship, framed by two bell towers and filled with an opulent explosion of baroque decor. In Pilar, in particular, the refinement of gilt carving is purposefully organized, resulting in one of the most remarkable baroque interiors to be found in Brazil.

A BIRD'S EYE VIEW

Ouro Preto is situated in the area of the **Espinhaço** mountain range in the metallurgic zone known as the **Ferrous Quadrangle**, one of the most important iron ore sites in the world. It lies 98 kilometers (about 60 miles) from Belo Horizonte and has approximately 45,000 people. The climate is characteristic of mountain localities, with temperatures ranging from 25°F–82°F (Leather jackets are good for late fall and winter.) The city's highest point is the **Itacolomi Peak** at 5,600 ft.

SIGHTS

Ouro Preto is a bit difficult to navigate on foot. The following tour is best done with a driver. (See under "Private Guides" in Hands-On.)

Start your tour of Ouro Preto at its birthplace—the **Capela do Padre Faria Church**, built in 1701 by the first *bandeirantes* and the expedition's priest named Padre Faria, who upon seeing the first flow of golden ore immediately opened his own mines. When the Portuguese authorities in Lisbon soon imposed a new tax (called the **Royal**

Fifth, requiring all gold dust to be minted into bars and 20 percent taxed), Padre Faria decided he wasn't about to pay it. Instead, he petitioned the Vatican to receive his church under direct subordination, and from that point on, never paid one cent to the royal coffers. Nor did he stick around to manage his flock; when the mines ran dry, Father Faria mysteriously disappeared—obviously, with gold—for the rest of his life.

The church's unpretentious facade in Jesuit style contrasts strongly with the gold-leaf decor inside, though not all the gold ended up on the walls or in Padre Faria's pockets. (During a recent restoration project twelve gold bars were found hidden in a wall.) Although initially built only for whites, the church today welcomes all worshippers, in particular, pregnant women who come to pray before the images of **Our Lady of the Rosary** and **Our Lady of the Good Deliverance**. Especially characteristic of the region is the image of Christ as **Our Lord of the Green Cane**, a red-caped Saviour holding a stalk of sugar cane—a sacred symbol of the state. If you look closely at some of the frescoes, the foyer's fountain, and the columns over the door, you'll discover Indian motifs—a sign that the priests working with Padre Faria had probably been in contact with Indian missions. During the inauguration of Brasília, the church's bell was taken to the new capital to be rung at the first solemn mass. *Mass is held every Sunday at 6:00 p.m. Visiting hours: 8:00 a.m.–noon daily.*

Poorer in decor but certainly not in spirit is the **Igreja de Nossa Senhora do Rosário dos Pretos** (Our Lady of the Rosary of the Blacks), also called St. Efigênia. During the 17th and 18th centuries, the Portuguese engaged in rabid slave trade with the countries of Angola and Guinea, sometimes buying entire conquered tribes from African chiefs. In the early 1730s, the Portuguese sold one such tribe, including their chief, to gold miners in Ouro Preto, but his subjects eventually bought back his freedom by hiding bits of stolen gold dust in their hair. Once freed, the chief, Chico Rei, fortuitously discovered the richest gold mine in Ouro Preto, and started buying back his tribe one by one, eventually founding the first black community. Constructed between 1738–1745, this church remains a symbol of the tribe's African unity; note the non-Brazilian, very African elephant on one of the frescoes. Over the main altar the ceiling painting features not only a black pope but also two black saints—Benedictine and Antônio Donato (though their features appear white). The Madonna atop the front portal is attributed to Aleijadinho. The door's red panes of glass are all new, except the dark tinted portion, which is original (notice how crystal clear it is.) *Visiting hours: noon–5:00 p.m.*

Bandits

Nearby on **Rua Santa Efigênia** is the house of **Pirata Vira-e-saia**, now reputed to be haunted. During the 18th century it was owned by a rich Portuguese merchant, whose undercover troop of bandits continually ambushed the Portuguese convoys laden with gold. Vira-e-saia managed to infiltrate the mint house with one of his agents, who conveyed which ship was holding the real cargo by turning the image of **Our Lady** in the nearby oratory to the right direction. After some major coups, the agent was eventually discovered and tortured, the pirate's daughters violated in front of their father, and the entire family killed. It's said the nearby church was built at the end of the 18th century to ward off lingering bad spirits. Across the street from the house, the oratory with the cross can still be seen, but the image of Our Lady has been destroyed.

The nearby **Praça de Marília** is also laden with romantic intrigue. The poetically inclined **Thomás Antônio Gonzaga**, one of the leaders of the Inconfidentes (and also Chief Justice in Ouro Preto) used to meet his betrothed **Marília do Dirceu** at the fountain in this square (now called **Fonte de Marília**). Whether young Marília had been involved in the conspiracy was never determined, but after her lover was arrested, she chose never to marry. The poetry he wrote to her is now considered some of the best literary examples of the colonial period.

Located on the other side of the fountain, **Matriz de Nossa Senhora da Conceição de Antônio Dias (Museu Aleijadinho)** is the largest church in Ouro Preto, with 8 lateral altars crammed with fat-cheeked cherubs, suspended gold grapes, and winged angels. The architecture of the church is attributed to Aleijadinho's father; his famous son lies buried at the feet of the altar of Our Lady of Good Death, shown lying in her white robes in the sculpted sepulchre. Down some rickety stairs (in what used to be the crypt) is the **Aleijadinho Museum** (you'll have to stash cameras and bags in the provided lockers; entrance fee is about 50 cents). In the first room are precious objects taken from the old church, such an ornate incense burners, bells, and pure gold chalices of inestimable value. A 17th-century crucified Christ in ivory is considered to be a perfect example of anatomical perfection. Attributed to Aleijadinho is the sculpted figure of São Francisco de Paula and also the crucified Christ on the Cross, the latter a curious historical commentary. A friend of Tiradentes, Aleijadinho carved the sign of a rope and blood on Christ's neck to commemorate Tiradentes' martyred death through hanging. *Visiting hours: 8:00 a.m.–11:30 p.m. and 1:30 p.m.–5:00 p.m.*

Aleijadinho's Greatest Achievement

The church of **São Francisco de Assis Church** (1765) is a tribute to the fortitude and artistic determination of Aleijadinho, whose body by that time had become so debilitated that his slave assistants had to tie his instruments to his hands and carry him on their backs. The church, which he designed himself, was his last and greatest achievement. All the carvings on the main altar, including the angel on the ceiling supporting a huge crystal candelabra, are his; the figures of Saint Louis and Saint Francis he actually sculpted on the ceiling, which is why they are so precious. In the back room is a magnificent fountain that took him three years to complete. The ceiling painting (1802–1812) is the work of **Manoel da Costa Athaíde** —a *trompe l'oeil* effect showing Our Lady of the Assumption. *Visiting hours: 8:00 a.m.–11:30 a.m and 1:30 p.m.–5:00 p.m. The fee is 50 cents, but you may use the ticket from the Aleijadinho Museum.*

Matriz de Nossa Senhor do Pilar is the second richest church in Brazil, with over 1,000 pounds of gold (the first is São Francisco in Salvador). Constructed in 1728–1733, it was inaugurated with a month of magnificent processions, led by nobles and their slaves masquerading in Greek costumes. The main artists responsible were the Portuguese **Antônio Francisco Pombal** (to whom the general idea of the church's decoration is attributed) and the sculptor **Francisco Xavier de Brito**, considered one of the possible teachers of Aleijadinho. The 4 cherubs with their feet dangling over the altar are the zenith of baroque art; their very cellulite seems to be made out of solid gold. The ceiling looks curved but is actually an optical illusion achieved through artistry. Look high up on the balcony in front of the altar and you'll see the carved feet of a human being dangling over the edge. During Holy Week, the statue of the Lady with a dagger in her heart is taken in procession to Our Lady of Mercy church while the figure of Christ is carried on Thursday to the main square in replication of the Via Cruxis. In the back room, the sacristy boasts an amazing chest of drawers made entirely from one piece of jacaranda wood. *Visiting hours: noon–5:00 p.m.*

> **Insider Tip:**
> Beside the church is the **Nativa Photo de Época**, where the photographer **Renato Castelfranchi** will take photos of you in an atmospheric courtyard dressed in historical costumes. A bit overpriced, but entertaining for those trying to recapture past lives.

The Mint

Taking a right, turn up **Rua Rodolfo Bretos** and around into **Rua São José** (also called Rua Tiradentes), where you'll find lots of bars and restaurants for a needed breather. Cross the small stone bridge to the **Casa de Fundição** (The Mint), also known as the **Casa dos Contos**, which was used in the 18th century as a government bureau for collecting the royal tax. Constructed in 1787, it was one of the most luxurious manor houses of its time, originally the private residence of **João Rodrigues de Macedo**, a senior official of the Portuguese administration and one of the richest men in Brazil. Later, it was used as a guesthouse for VIPs; notice the refinement of its upper rooms whose ceilings are decorated with rococo paintings.

Inaugurated in 1769, the **Teatro Municipal de Ouro Preto (Casa da Opera)** is the oldest public theater in Latin America to remain in continual use. Both emperors, Peter I and II, attended performances here, sitting in the royal box, surrounded by nobles. The acoustics are wonderful, and if you can manage to hop on stage, you'll get an intimate perspective from the performer's eye. Check out the stone floor dressing rooms downstairs. *Visiting hours: 1:00 p.m.–5:00 p.m.*

PRAÇA TIRADENTES

Adorning the **Praça Tiradentes** is the statue of Minas' first and premier martyr, Tiradentes. On one side of the square is the **Museu da Inconfidência** (Museum of the Inconfidentes), which was once both the former jail (1st floor) and the municipal chamber (2nd floor). All the remains of the exiled conspirators were brought back and buried here (some were collected from as far away as Africa). Also in the museum are fine examples of sacred art, systems of illuminations, vehicles of transport, and artisanry. The backroom shows documents from the conspiracy, including the original death sentence of

Tiradentes by the Queen of Portugal. Also here are two of the original pieces of wood from his gallows, as well as some of his dental equipment. On your way out, notice the green iron door and double grills of the former prison windows—no one ever escaped.

Next door to the museum is one of the finest churches in Ouro Preto, the **Igreja de Nossa Senhora do Carmo**, designed by **Antônio Francisco Lisboa**, the father of Aleijadinho, who took over supervision after the former died in 1766. For over 40 years, Aleijadinho fiddled with the decoration, some of which, like the baptismal font in the sacristy, rate as baroque masterpieces. Attached to the church is an impressively displayed museum of sacred art, housed in a recently restored mansion. *Visiting hours: 8:00 a.m.–11:30 a.m. and 1:00 p.m.–5 p.m.*

On the other side of Praça Tiradentes is the former Governor's Palace, now the **School of Mines and Metallurgy** of the University of Ouro Preto—an impressive building, with the appearance of a fort. Young people from all over Brazil come here to study; you'll see motorbikes leaning against the walls, one of the many icons of modern Mineiro culture. Adjacent to the university is the **Museu de Mineralogia da Escola de Minas** *Noon–5:00 p.m., fee: about 50 cents* • not just for mineralogists, but anyone interested in precious and semi-precious stones, crystals, and rare rock formations. Tours usually visit only the first floor, but scientific-minded persons should also head for the second floor, which has over 23,000 samples of minerals, including imperial topaz.

GOLD MINE

Opened in 1702, this gold mine called **Boca da Mina** formerly belonged to two Portuguese brothers who had no relationship to Chico Rei; nevertheless, it's often referred to today as **Mina do Chico Rei**. In 100 years of exploration, more than 6,000 tons of gold have been extracted. Today you can walk through some of the remains, then take a bit of lunch or early dinner at the adjacent restaurant. The present owner of the complex is a feisty 78-year-old local named **Dona Marazinha**, who has lived in the adjacent house for over 50 years. *Visiting hours: The mine is opened 7:00 a.m.–6:00 p.m., restaurant noon–5:00 p.m. A small boutique of crystals and pottery is also on premises.*

THE ESSENTIAL OURO PRETO

WHERE TO STAY

Accommodations in Ouro Preto run from colonial elegance to the bare-bones room of a fraternity house. Moderate-priced pousadas, surrounded by tropical vegetation and forests, can be so inviting that you might want to stay for a few extra days. Good discounts can be found in low season, particularly at family-run pousadas.

Expensive -------------- Over $60

Moderate --------------- $30–$58

Inexpensive ------------ $10–$25

Cheap Under ----------- $10

★ Solar do Rosário
Rua Getúlio Vargas, 270;
☎ *(31) 551-1032*

I saw this new hotel in its last construction stage, but it promises to be one of the most luxurious accommodations in Ouro Preto. As per the city's strict building regulations, this 100-year-old building has retained its baroque colonial facade while the interior has been transformed into a 5-star property. All the finishing material has been extracted from the area, such as the pink quartzite floors that appear gold when polished. Individual apartments have retained the original ironwork balconies, and one suite even has a heartbreaking view of the Igreja do Rosário right next door. You can sip drinks in an outdoor garden and contemplate the bell tower, or walk 12–15 meters inside an adjoining mine that was discovered during construction. A roof pool and sauna is on the drawing board, and guests will have special privileges to use the nearby private golf course. All rooms have central air-conditioning and heat, and some suites have fireplaces. A sauna and tea salon are also planned, as are 2 top-notch restaurants, one with a typical wood stove. 37 apartments. *Expensive. All cards.*

Pousada do Mondega
Largo de Coimbra, 38; ☎ *(31) 551-2040, FAX 551-3094*

This charming 2-story pousada manages to be historical, attractive, and comfortable all at the same time, and the location can't be beat—right off Praça Tiradentes, overlooking the São Francisco church. A smell of pine wafts through the small, but inviting lobby; a restaurant is being built in the lobby. The rooms, immaculately clean, are filled with colonial-style furniture; fine art adorns the corridors. Best to ask for rooms with a balcony; the attic apartment with its triangular roof is quirky, but good for three short people who don't need a view. Rooms, all of which have color TV and minibar, run from $68 to $81. 18 apartments. 2 suites. *Expensive. All cards.*

Estrada Real
Rod. dos Inconfidentes, kilometer 87 (Road to Belo Horizonte); ☎ *(31) 551-2122*

Long the most elaborate resort complex in the city, this hotel combines *caseira* charm with top-notch efficiency. The only problem is that it's located about 5 miles outside Ouro Preto, on a hill overlooking the city. Little difference between the deluxe and standard—all are spacious, with color TV, minibar, but no heat. Gardens are lovely to stroll through, the pool is enormous, the tennis courts playable, and the wood-beamed dining room extremely attractive. Chalets are great buys for families of 3 or 4; some come with jacuzzi and fireplace. Lining the hotel's hallways are local paintings and sculptures for sale. Handicapped facilities available. Doubles start around $70. 30 apartments, 12 chalets. *Expensive. All cards.*

★ Pousada Solar das Lajes
Rua Conselheiro Quintiliano, 604; ☎ *(31) 551-3388*

Nationally acclaimed sculptor Pedro Correia de Araújo has reconstructed this rustic pousada around the original colonial walls of an 18th-century estate; the result is an unusual blend of nature and natural resources that provides a calm, quiet retreat from the tourist hubbub. An easy 10-minute walk from *centro*, the hotel is located down a stone path and surrounded by overgrown gardens and at least 80 different kinds of fruit trees. Some of the rooms are old slave quarters; some even have their stone window seats intact, from where you can contemplate verdant fields. An outdoor pool, which Pedro made himself, overlooks the city. Many of the rooms sport antique beds and old lanterns; Pedro's fascinating sculptures adorn the grounds. Just meeting the owner is a trip, an innovative genius who speaks heavily accented English and is constantly puttering with the house. Doubles run $30–$35, singles receive a 10 percent discount. 13 apartments. *Moderate. No cards.*

★ Quinta dos Barões
Rua Pandiá Calógeras, 474 (Barra);
☎ *(31) 551–1056. To reserve: Rua Eng. Vicente Assunção, 66 Pampulha, Belo Horizonte;* ☎ *(31) 441–1623*

Formerly the first German consulate, this 300-year-old house has had a long and sensational past. The present owner, descended from one of the Inconfidentes, will eagerly show you photos and prints from the Second Empire; just one look at his enormous antique keys and original door latches will send you reeling back in time. Much of the furniture is original–antique headboards, wood-carved desks, shuttered windows; in fact, the bathrooms were originally used as alcoves to lock up the master's virgin daughters. The view from the 4-star rooms, across grassy knolls, is spectacular; from the lobby you can see the ruins of the original stone house. A fireplace is being constructed in the cave-like dining room, but apartments do not have heat or air-conditioning. Walking to the city will be difficult from here, but across the street is a handmade bedspread factory. Standards start at $45, deluxe $54. 7 apartments. *Moderate. All cards.*

Hotel Priskar da Barra
Rua Antônio Martins, 98;
☎ *(31) 551–2666*

Brightly polished wood floors add to the attractiveness of the apartments in this two-story hotel about a 15-minute walk uphill from the city. Families will particularly enjoy the enormous pool and the children's pool. A romantic option is the wedding suite with chiffon curtains and a lace-covered table and couch in an extra room. All rooms come with a color TV, great minibar, and radio, but no heat or air-conditioning; some rooms have fans. Singles run $32, doubles $39. 17 apartments, 4 suites. *Moderate. No cards.*

Grande Hotel
Rua Sen. Rocha Lagoa, 164;
☎ *(31) 551–1488*

When the state government ceremonially transfers to Ouro Preto on April 21, the governor stays at this traditional hotel, whose glass-enclosed lobby looks out over the city's rooftops. Unfortunately, the Niemeyer-designed facade, the only modern one in the city, is a real blight in contrast to the truly glorious colonial houses down the street. The restaurant, however, is excellent, supervised by the oldest and most famous chef in the city. The furniture in the small standards is more old than old-fashioned, but the bathrooms are clean. Suites with balconies overlooking the most preserved part of Ouro Preto are exceedingly desirable. Before gambling was banned, the hotel labored as a casino and still exudes a little of that swashbuckling environ. The lush grounds were designed by Burle Marx; there is no pool. Across the street is the Old Mint House, where gold was melted down for taxes and where one of the Inconfidentes committed suicide. Single standards start at $29, double $37, suites at $50. Children under 5 are free. 35 apartments. *Moderate. All cards.*

Luxor Pousada
Praça Antônio Dias/ Rua Dr. Alfredo Baeta, 16; ☎ *(31) 551–2244*

This 16-room pousada occupies an old colonial mansion, with an inner courtyard that nearly suggests a monastery. The location, across the street from the glorious Matriz de Nossa Senhora da Conceição, is prime, and you can safely walk home from the center at all hours. Rooms are colonial style and extraordinarily comfortable; the only quirk the strange paintings chalked on the wall that suggest a strange hippiness. The most wonderful rooms are the suites, particularly the "A" suites with two rooms, hardwood floors, huge antique beds, and snug comforters. A fireplace in the salon makes a cozy nook, and the gourmet restaurant is considered one of the best in the city. Singles start at $51, suites $74. 16 rooms. *Moderate–Expensive. All cards.*

Hospedaria Antiga
Rua Xavier da Veiga, 13; ☎ *(31) 551-2203*

Young people with backpacks tend to stay at this former public archive, still owned by the original family. The style reminds me of an old highway chalet, with rough red stucco walls matched by even rougher furniture. Bathrooms are minimal, and not always clean, but huge shuttered windows overlook verdant gardens. Rooms can hold 1, 2, or 3 beds; there are no TVs, but some rooms have minibars. Singles and doubles run about $24, which seems high for the quality. 16 apartments. *Inexpensive. All cards.*

Pousada e Galeria Panorama Barroco
Rua Conselheiro Quintiliano, 722; ☎ *(31) 551-3366*

Located next door to the Solar, this could be your home away from home, especially if you're into New Age, No Nukes, Eco Treks, Crystals, and Doing Your Own Laundry. The very personable David Peterkin (an American) and his Brazilian wife, Lucia, runs this traditional-style pousada where every room has its own homemade motif. The 2 bathrooms are shared. The lobby, jam-packed with crystals, jewelry, and objets d'art from all over the world, does nothing to dispel the hippie feel, and Lucia even grinds her own coffee, which she buys south of Minas. David, who is an anthropologist and archeologist, leads excursions to Congonhas, the Imperial Topaz Mine, and any destination you can concoct outside the city limits (for about $6 per hour, divided among the riders in his 4-wheel jeep, or $50 per day plus his expenses). At night he pulls out videos for the guests and even sets up a telescope for night watching. From among the international set that descends here, you're sure to make some lifelong friends. Daily rate is $7–$8, including breakfast. *Cheap. No cards.*

WHERE TO EAT

Expensive	-------------	**Over $10**
Moderate	--------------	**$5–$10**
Inexpensive	------------	**Under $5**

★ Casa do Ouvidor
Rua Direita, 42; ☎ *551-2141. Daily 11:00 a.m.–3:00 p.m., 7:00 p.m.–10:00 p.m*

Considered the best kitchen in Ouro Preto, the Ouvidor exudes colonial simplicity, with leather-tooled lampshades and shutters open to the fresh breeze. The menu in English and Portuguese features typical dishes like *tutu à Mineira* (roasted pork loin with mashed beans, boiled eggs, and pork sausage), *feijão tropeiro* (beans mixed with manioc flour, fried egg, pork loin, and sausage), and *frango com quiabo* (chicken with okra). The soups are excellent and the filets are simple but well cooked. Desserts include homemade sweets and preserves, and especially ice cream. Entrees about $5. *Moderate. All cards.*

Grande Hotel Restaurant
Rua Sen. Rocha Lagoa, 164; ☎ *551-1488*

The restaurant of this old-fashioned hotel is all modern elegance in a cool salmon-and-gray decor. The chef, the oldest in the city, is famous for his typical dishes, especially the *bambá de couve*, a delicious cornmeal porridge with finely chopped kale and pieces of pork loin. Another delicacy rarely offered is the *macarronada mineira*, macaroni served with baked sausage. For dessert try the *goiabada com quiejo*, an intensely sweet jelly-like paste of guava served with a wedge of sour Mineiro cheese. Dishes run between $4–$5. *Moderate. All cards.*

Calabouco
Rua Cidade de Bobadela, 132;
☎ *551-1222. Daily 11:00 a.m.–3:30 p.m., 7:00 p.m.–10:30 p.m., Sunday 11:00 a.m.–3:30 p.m*

Located off Praça Tiradentes, this atmospheric eatery looks like an underground cave, with its rough brick walls and wood tables; an interesting record collection from avant-garde jazz to Elis Regina plays all night. The simple menu features well-seasoned steaks, but the joint's greatest virtue is that it serves dinner starting at 7:00 p.m.—a *pecado* in Brazil. Omelettes run $4, main entrees $5–$9. *Moderate. No cards.*

★ Taberna Luxor
Rua Dr. Alfredo Baeta, 10 (Praça Antônio Dias) ☎ *551-2244. Noon–3:00 p.m., 7:00 p.m.–10:00 p.m*
A lushly decorated restaurant, undergoing renovation when I was there, but previously beloved for the flambées prepared tableside, such as the Siberian steak with vodka, cream, mushrooms, and rice, and Steak Diana, flambéed with brandy. Dishes about $7. *Moderate. All cards.*

Relicário 1800
Praça Tiradentes, 64; ☎ *551-2855*
The owner, a private French teacher in Ouro Preto, has ebulliently decorated this centrally located eatery with cedar sculptures and local artwork (the name means the place where you keep relics). For some reason not yet understood, guests receive a surprise wooden spoon. A 20-year-tradition on the square, the menu features typical dishes and beef and chicken. During vacations and weekends, call for reservations. *Moderate. All cards.*

Restaurante & Pizzeria Casa Nova
Praça Tiradentes, 84. Daily 11:00 a.m.–3:00 p.m., 6:30 p.m.–12:30 p.m.
Not just 14 kinds of pizza, but steaks and typical dishes here at this informal eatery off the main square. Saturday night features live classical guitar starting at 8:30 p.m. English spoken. Dishes run about $7. *Moderate. No cards.*

Taverna do Chafariz
Rua São José, 167, ☎ *551-2828. Daily 11:00 a.m.–3:00 p.m., 6:30 p.m.–11:00 p.m., closed Monday*
Located on a charming narrow street (which is actually the main commercial way), this quiet and elegant eatery, a tradition since 1929, offers excellent typical dishes, like *frango ao molho pardo*, as well as imaginatively cooked chicken and steaks. The house is where the famous poet Alphonsus de Guimarães died in 1930. During holidays, you'll need reservations. *Moderate. No cards.*

NIGHTLIFE

Shows, theater plays, and musical performances occur frequently. A schedule of these events always appear posted on the billboard of the **Tourist Information Office** at the bus station and the **Central Reception Office** *Praça Tiradentes, 41.*
There are numerous bars where you might stumble on an improvised chorus with guitar accompaniment. Best bar in Ouro Preto is the small and cozy **Acas 91** *Praça do Rosário. Wednesday–Sunday 8:00 p.m. on; live music on Saturday nights.*

SHOPPING

Jewelry
Ouro Preto is full of jewelry stores, and if you have time, you might run around comparing prices, but I've found the most reliable in price and quality to be **Brasil Gemas** *Praça Tiradentes, 74;* ☎ *551-2976. Daily 9:00 a.m.–8:00 p.m.* The specialty of house is Imperial Topaz at $10–$600 per carat. Rings are set in 18-karat gold and take about 2 hours to custom-make. Raw amethysts are excellent as are the emeralds, which run $100–$2,000 per karat. Prices are about one-third the price of H. Stern in Rio. *All cards.*

Sweets
Toca *Rua Direita, 131. Daily: 10:00 a.m.–9:00 p.m.* A must for stocking up on local goodies, such as homemade liquors, *pão de queijo* (cheese bread), and a dazzling array of *salgadinhos* (small salty appetizers). The chocolate mousse and cheesecake will fit nicely into minibars.
Licor Caseiro de Jabuticaba *Rua São José, 165;* ☎ *551-1011. Daily: 10:00 a.m.–6:00 p.m.* Liqueurs, jellies, and homemade condiments by a talented local, Milton Trópia—all free of chemicals.

Crafts and Clothes
Crafts and souvenirs can be found around Praça Tiradentes, Rua Direita, Rua São José, Largo de Coímbra, and Rua Cláudio Manoel. Among the best shops:
Seleiro *Rua Direita, 191;* ☎ *551-1774. Daily: 9:00 a.m.–7:00 p.m.* Craftwork in

soapstone and ceramics. Articles in pewter. Oil paintings.
Jirau *Rua Direita, 122;* ☎ *551-3135.* Monday–Saturday 8:00 a.m.–6:00 p.m. Brazilian fashion and exclusive T-shirts with images of Ouro Preto.

HANDS-ON OURO PRETO

Arrivals
Rodoviária
Rua Pe. Rolim, 661; ☎ *551-1544*
Eleven buses leave daily from Belo Horizonte for Ouro Preto about every two hours. Traffic is heavy, so book your return ticket as early as possible, especially weekends and holidays.

Money Exchange
Banco do Brasil
Rua São José, 195; ☎ *551-2663, extension 31*
Rates are poor; better to exchange in Belo Horizonte.

Points Beyond
Direct buses from Ouro Preto to Congonhas are available at 2:00 p.m. and 3:30 p.m. daily, as well as to Mariana (every half-hour). Hitchhiking is relatively safe in this part of the country, and you may find a college student who doesn't mind a rider on the back of his moped.

Post Office
The post office is located across from the Hotel Miranda, on Rua Direita.

Private Guides
Official English-speaking guides may be hired through the **Tourist Information Office** *Praça Tiradentes, 41;* ☎ *551-2655* One reliable guide is **Cássio A. Antunes.** Guides without a car run about $25 for full day (8:00 a.m.–6:00 p.m.); it's considered polite to provide lunch for the guide. A private guide with taxi runs about $7 per hour. You might also consider hiring a taxi without a guide. The entire city by car can be seen in about 2–3 hours, but leave time for leisurely strolling.

Tourist Information Office
Tourist Information Office is located at *Praça Tiradentes, 41.* Here, you can obtain information in English about sites, guides, hotels, pousadas, and alternative accommodations like the college fraternities called *repúblicas*.

Travel Agency
Dall'tour *Praça Tiradentes, 116;* ☎ *551-3164.*

MARIANA

Ouro Preto, the political capital of colonial Brazil, and **Mariana**, the religious capital—these two sister cities are situated only 7-1/2 miles from each other, so close that 18th-century power-brokers thought they might end up merging their futures together. While the cities remain separate entities today, they did reach an interchange of roles in centuries past, when Portuguese governors installed their headquarters in the less tumultuous Mariana during political rebellions. In reverse, the 18th-century bishop **Dom Frei Domingos** often chose to flee to Ouro Preto to escape the political pressures of his own chapter, returning to Mariana only for important religious festivals.

While Ouro Preto is extremely hilly and uneven, basically situated on three hills separated by valleys, Mariana is built on smoothly sloping land suitable for building squares and gardens. Discovered July 16, 1696 by *bandeirantes* from São Paulo searching for gold along the banks of the **Riberão do Carmo**, the villa was officially dubbed **Nossa Senhora do Carmo** in 1711. In 1743, the king of Portugal dispatched his architect **José Fernandes Pinto de Alpoim** to plan the urban design of the first official episcopal headquarters and capital of Minas. Two years later the name was changed to Mariana, after the queen **Dona Maria Ana** of Austria, wife of Dom João V.

Historical Town

Today, time seems to have stopped in this historical town where little has changed since the colonial era. Even the cobblestone streets, a model of straightness, dates back to the 18th century. Two hundred years ago, horses came to refuel at what is now the principal plaza, **Praça Gomes Freire**. (Note the iron gate around the pond, which is in the shape of a horseshoe.) It's a lovely place to watch the town walk by and listen to local music groups during festivals. The fountains around the city were also built in the 18th century (prior to indoor sinks!) and served as a meeting point for townswomen; legend has it that slaves often hid gold in their hair and washed it out at these fountains.

Mariana's quiet charm and historical grace has attracted a subculture of artists, musicians, and poets who lend a bohemian flair to the city. Much of their craftwork, particularly wood-carved doors and furniture, approach the mastery of ages past. Among the most famous artists who welcome visitors to their studios are the sculptor

Alvaro Madeira, the painter **Zizi Sapateiro,** and the portraitist **Elias Layon.** A must-hear are the organ performances of **Elisa Freixo,** artist-in-residence at the Cathedral. Nothing can bring alive colonial history more than hearing the marvelous architectonic strains of Bach or Buxtehude played in this gold-washed baroque cathedral.

> **Insider Tip:**
>
> With such flat streets, Mariana can be easily navigated on foot, but you will need a car to visit the gold mine, **Minas da Passagem**, and the arts center of **Vila Brumado** (see below).

SIGHTS

Igreja de São Pedro dos Clérigos *Colina de São Pedro. Tuesday–Sunday noon–6:00 p.m.* Rumors of ghosts and demons so abounded during the construction of this 18th-century church that the workers refused to finish it, despite its daring curvilinear architecture. Some say a priest was mysteriously assassinated during the construction; others believe that ghosts were stealing the building material. Only in the last 4–5 years has it begun to function as a church. Constructed around 1780, the magnificent jacaranda altar is worth a look. From here, you can see the cross planted on the nearby hill, put there to destroy the demons that were felt to be present.

Seminário de São José was constructed in 1935 for Dom Helvécio and his secular students. In the steps leading to the front door, you'll see bits of imperial topaz that were embedded in the bricks. (Sadly, they have no real value!) Inside, the chapel boasts an extraordinary portrait by **Pedro Gentillo** of Dom Helvécio in the "Big Brother" style; no matter where you go, Dom Pedro's eyes will follow you around. Imagine how the painting must have inspired terror in his young impressionable scholars.

Considered the most important plaza in Minas,

Praça João Pinheiro dates back to the 18th century, when it housed the public prison; now it's the mayor's office. The clock under the bell tower always rests at 9:00 a.m. because that's the time the councilmen open up their doors for business. It was also here that slaves who escaped from their masters were severely punished in public.

In Mariana during the 18th century, the *irmandades* (or brotherhoods who venerated a certain saint) nearly went mad with competitive fervor, going so far as to build two churches directly across from each other. The first, the green-doored

Igreja de São Francisco de Assis *Daily 8:00 a.m.–noon, 1:00 p.m.–4:00 p.m.* was built from 1763–1794. Aleijadinho was contracted to do the sculptures on the door, but his true masterpiece inside consists of the vestry's two ceiling panels, which illustrate in exact chronological order two different moments of the same vision of St. Francis. The church is most notable for the suspended St. Francis above the multi-tiered altar ascending on red ribbons up to Christ, but the ceiling painting is just as riveting—a tumultuous depiction of Noah's Flood. In the sacristan on the right, notice the painting of St. Francis holding the Cross; the eyes of the skull next to him will follow you around the room. The hair on the Christ statue is natural, symbolizing that the hair and nails of a human being never disintegrate. Across the grassy square, the

Igreja Nossa Senhora do Carmo *8:00 a.m.–5:00 p.m.* was constructed in 1784 to display an even more powerful facade to the public. Aleijadinho was commissioned to sculpt the cherubs over the door, considered one of the most beautiful portals in Mariana. The towers in the form of a medieval castle and the balconies with lacework sculpted in soapstone all add to the church's charm.

Museu Arquidiocesano de Arte Sacra de Mariana *Rua Frei Durão, 49. Tuesday–Sunday 9:00 a.m.–4:45 p.m. Fee is about 50 cents.* This is the second most complete sacred art museum in Brazil (the first is the Museu do Carmo in Salvador). A salon of extremely fine paintings features works by Aleijadinho and his contemporaries; an extraordinary rendering of the Madonna in her purest essence has an unforgettable face. The second floor features sculptures by Aleijadinho, many completed after he lost the use of most of his fingers. Sacred music manuscripts, mostly performed by black slaves, are also on display. The Fonte de Samaritana in the foyer is a soapstone sculpture by Aleijadinho. Tradition has it that you must close your eyes, turn your back to the fountain, make a wish, then throw a coin. If the coin goes in the fountain, you'll get your wish.

Across the street from the museum is the

Igreja de Nossa Senhora da Assunção, the largest and oldest cathedral in Minas, as well as the richest in artwork. It's also called **Sé,** or just **Cathedral.** Constructed in 1709–1750, the church was the beloved labor of Aleijadinho's father and José Pereira Arouca, who fashioned one of the most beautiful *paraventos* in the state (the door in front of the real door, which keeps the wind out). Unfortunately, the church is left dark most of the time to preserve the art, but if you stand at the altar and look back to the front door, you'll notice how the columns incline on either side, representing the structure of Noah's Ark. The 1701 Schnitger-made organ is spectacular, a gift to the bishop of Mariana from Dom João V, and thrilling concerts are given on request by the artist-in-residence **Elisa Freixo.** Hopefully, you will be lucky enough to at least hear her practice, usually in the afternoons. Lights come on from 6:00 p.m. to 8:30 p.m. for mass.

The time to hang out on the **Praça Claudio Manoel** in front of the church is around 4:00 p.m. when school lets out and school children of all ages fill up the square.

To the left of the church is **Rua Direita** (usually to the right of a cathedral but inverse in Mariana), the main street of the city. At No. 50, a former residence of the governor of Minas has been transformed into a museum featuring furnishings from the 18th century. The balconies are the only ones in the world made out of soapstone.

EXCURSIONS

Mina da Passagem *On the way to Mariana. Daily 9:00 a.m.–6:00 p.m. Fee is about $7 for adults, about $5.50 for children.* Some have called it a tourist trap, but I thoroughly enjoyed my visit to Mina da Passagem, the oldest gold mine in Brazil. Begun in 1779, the mine was first owned by a German baron; up to 1880, slaves worked here under strenuous conditions, many of them dying while underground. (In fact, many psychics in deep meditation have witnessed spirits here.) After producing over 35,000 kilograms of gold, the mine became defunct and is now open only to tourists. A trolley without seat belts (hang on!) slowly takes you down the 11-kilometer tunnel to the main gallery where you can witness different layers of quartz, black tourmaline, graphite, and pyrite (the latter looks like false gold). The shrine you will see is for **Santa Barbara,** the patroness of all mines—an ironic statement, since women, considered the epitome of bad luck, were never allowed underground. Before you leave, it's traditional to leave the saint a few coins, or even some lipstick, which she adores. The mine is said to have a relation to Chico Rei, the tribal chief whose freedom was bought by his former subjects working as slaves in this mine. It's most likely that some of the gold extracted from this mine can be found today in the Efigênia Church in Ouro Preto.

Insider Tip:

The 40-minute trip is not strenuous, and the atmosphere is cool and humid, but those prone to claustrophobia might be advised to skip it. However, anyone into crystals and the power of rocks will find the atmosphere delightful. Visitors are even allowed to take a piece of quartz home, but be careful not to cut yourself. Happily, there are no bats here, since they only like naturally made grottoes. Make sure you wear tennis shoes.

Getting There

The mine is located on the outskirts of Mariana, 20 minutes from Ouro Preto. Local buses go there, or ask your private driver to stop there.

VILA BRUMADO

About 25 minutes from Mariana, over a rocky dirt road, lies **Vila Brumado,** a primitive, near-magical village, whose 8,000 residents are nearly all artists. Children learn the craftwork from their fathers starting at the age of 5 or 6; among their artisanry skills are sculpting, straw work, embroidery, and pottery. A small but feisty waterfall may be visited, alongside which is a makeshift restaurant (weekends only); better to take your own picnic lunch. If you hire a car in Mariana (or Ouro Preto), you'll be able to visit the private homes of individual artists and view their simple life-styles up close. This is a village where horses are still hitched in front of houses and most children run around barefoot. Some families even use water to make electricity.

Adão de Lourdes Cassiano *Rua Firminho Ulhôa, 233;* ☎ *557–2052* Forty-eight years old, Adão has been working 21 years as a sculptor, and his specialty is stunning 2-tiered nativity scenes carved out of single cedar tree trunks. A rare tranquility and joy exudes from the eyes of this extraordinarily simple man whose work sells well in Germany. He and his nephews work day and night to finish pieces that run about $1,200 each.

Artur Pereira *Rua das Flores, 139* One of the best known wood sculptors in the region, Artur lives in a simple home that defies his international success. His specialties are strong animal figures—quartets of birds and large lions that serve as chairs.

THE ESSENTIAL MARIANA

WHERE TO STAY

★ Pousada Typographia
Praça Gomes Freire, 220;
☎ *(31) 557-1577*
Across from Praça Gomes Freire, this is the prettiest pousada in town, in a restored 18th-century mansion. The owners were the first family to own a printing firm in Mariana, and their 1730 printing machine adorns the lobby. Guests eat off silver inherited through generations and many of the family's porcelain and pottery are displayed. Simple, but elegant, wood furniture enhances the apartments, all of which look out onto the square or historical back streets. Bathrooms are impeccable. Doubles run $48, singles $36. Best to reserve. 20 apartments. *Moderate. No cards.*

Hotel Central
Rua Frei Durão, 8; ☎ *(31) 557-1630*
Cheapest rooms in the city, but only a last-ditch option. Singles run $5, doubles $9; you can use the bath for an extra $2. TV's go for an extra $2.50. No breakfast, but coffee is served from 7:15 a.m. to 9:00 a.m. *Inexpensive. All cards.*

WHERE TO EAT

Tambaú
Tr. São Francisco, 26; ☎ *557-1399. Daily 11:00 a.m.–3:00 p.m., 7:00 p.m.–11:00 p.m., closed Wednesday*
One of Mariana's best restaurants, off Praça Gomes Freire, this house was the first palace of the governor of Minas in 1720. *Frango com quiabo* (chicken with okra) is good as are all the typical plates, about $5.50. *Moderate. No cards.*

Alvorada
Rua Jorge Marques, 101; ☎ *557-1300*
Three minutes by car from *centro*, this *churrascaria* is hardly homey with its aluminum roof, but it's the only one in town. Best bets are the typical plates. Specialties include banana splits. Plates run $3–$5. *Inexpensive. No cards.*

Portão da Praça
Off the Praça Gomes Freire
Twelve tables and a waterfall (!) makes this former 18th-century gold house a cozy lunch spot. *Moderate. No cards.*

Free Lanches
Rua Frei Durão, 108
Ice creams, sweets, fresh tropical juices, all homemade. Near the Museum. *Inexpensive. No cards.*

NIGHTLIFE

Minas Adega & Bar
Rua Direita, 92
Live music, cheese, wine, and cocktails.

SHOPPING

Artist Studios Atelier Gamarano
Travessa São Francisco, 22; ☎ *557-1835*
Here, the artist Ladim shows his wood sculptures, doors, bureaus, and furniture. Mailing to the U.S. is possible. Magnificent carved doors run about $300 (plus $200 to ship). American Express is accepted.

Atelier Alvaro
Praça da Sé, 164; ☎ *557-2093*
Doors, panels, wood carvings, and sculptures.

Zizi Sapateiro
Rua Santana, 52; ☎ *557-1139*
A former shoemaker is one of Mariana's true *figuras*. After a lifetime cobbling, he started painting local scenes in a primitive style and became an overnight success; today he's one of the most important artists in Minas. Paintings run from $300 to $500, up to $3,000. His son also paints and sells under the name Tumão.

Layon
Rua Direita, across the street from artisan ato Tia Maria. Daily 9:00 a.m.–6:00 p.m
The city's best classically-trained artist, Elias Layon is famous for his near-Rembrandt portraits, which take about a month to complete (each about $1,500). Of Jewish descent, Layon has a stellar sense of humor about living in such a Catholic-dominated region. Ask for his calling card—hand-paint-

ed on the spot.

Crafts

Artesanato Tia Maria
Rua Direita, 8; ☎ 557–1716
The house for homemade liqueurs; the specialty is Pétalas de Rosas, topped with a little knit hat. Ask to taste—the *jabuticaba* is superb.

HANDS-ON MARIANA

Arrivals
Cars (with guides) may be hired in Ouro Preto through the Tourist Information Center.
Buses for Mariana leave from Praça Tiradentes in Ouro Preto every half hour. The name of the bus is ADJUR, which also leaves every half-hour from the Terminal Turístico in Mariana for Ouro Preto. Buses from Belo Horizonte to Mariana take about 2-1/4 hours.
Taxis from Ouro Preto run about $8–$10, but do try bargaining.

Climate
Only 15 minutes from Ouro Preto, Mariana is nevertheless slightly warmer. Your ears will pop as you descend to the valley.

City Transportation
Taxis can be found at *Praça JFK*, ☎ 557–1355 and *Praça Tancredo Neves*, ☎ 557–1872.

Private Guide
An excellent guide in Mariana, although he does not speak English, is **João Orestes** Rua Anibal Walter, 105; ☎ 557–1533 Other guides may be hired through the Tourist Information Center.

Tourist Information
The bus from Ouro Preto makes its first stop in Mariana at the Tourist Center called **Deturce** (Terminal Turístico Manoel da Costa Athaíde) *Praça Tancredo Neves;* ☎ 557–1533 where you can pick up brochures and information in English. The office has a bar, restroom, and artisan store where you can buy interesting T-shirts with Mineiro themes. A great buy are the records of Elisa Freixo, the organist of the Cathedral.

Private tours can also be arranged here, running about $11 with guide and car (2 hours), or $26 for guide plus small bus for 4 people (2-1/2 hours).

Travel Agency
CMP Turismo Ltd. Rua Eugênio Eduardo Rapallo; ☎ 557–1255 can make arrangements for tours to other cities.

When to Go
July 16 *Birthday of the city and state*, celebrated by numerous singing groups.
March–April *Holy Week* is celebrated with dramatic theatrical processions led by the bishop in historical clothes and special organ recitals.

> **Insider Tip:**
> Avoid Mondays when all churches are closed for cleaning (in Ouro Preto as well).

SÃO JOÃO DEL REI

Of all the historical cities, **São João del Rei** is the one that lives and breathes a sincere religiosity all year round. From dawn till dusk, the air is marked by the "language of the bells," an 18th-century tradition that announces the birth and death of its citizens through the pealing of the church carillons. (Through the number of tolls, the town learns the sex of a newly born baby or whether the deceased was a man, woman, priest or nun.) Holy Week is particularly special in São João, with solemn high masses held in every church, and full orchestras performing traditional baroque music. Throughout the holy season, processions of saints file through the streets, accompanied by the clamoring of church bells and the swinging incense of the priests.

São João del Rei is also the birthplace of two of Brazil's most important heroes— **Tiradentes**, who died a martyr's death as leader of the Inconfidência Mineira, and **Tancredo Neves**, who died in 1985 shortly after winning the country's first civilian presidential election after twenty years of military rule. A savvy politician, Neves (who was called Tancredo by his constituents) was also a visionary, and his sudden death affected Brazilians as deeply as did the loss of JFK in the United States. In 1986, a memorial museum was established by his widow to convey the deep strain of humanitarianism that ran through his personal and professional life. Since Tiradentes and Tancredo died on the same day (a fact replete with mystical symbolism), **Tiradentes Day** in São João del Rei is a heavy-laden commemoration, with a high mass held in the Igreja de São Francisco and a special service at Tancredo's graveside.

The best time to visit São João is on Friday, Saturday, and Sunday, when you can ride the **Maria Fumaça**, an authentic steam engine that travels to Tiradentes. Secular festivities throughout the year also have a particular São João flair. **Festa Junina** (most often held in June and sometimes July) is a country-style party when everyone dresses up like yokels and celebrates a mock wedding with a pregnant bride. **Carnaval** lasts for 4 days, with 4 samba schools and *blocos* making their way through the colonial streets, capped by a uniquely provincial climax: At 5:00 a.m. on the last day, everyone piles out to the street in their bedclothes and revels till the sun rises.

PAST GLORIES

Bandeirantes from São Paulo first discovered gold in the hills that surround São João del Rei in 1705. The village was first known as **Nossa Senhora do Pilar**, later gaining its present name in 1713, in honor of Dom João V of Portugal. Through the development of the gold industry as well as *agropecuária* (the combination of agriculture and stock-raising), the village was transformed into a bustling market city, thriving to this day. The city became more famous after the death of Tancredo Neves; on the day of his burial, so many wanted to attend that the "doors" of the city finally had to be closed because the streets couldn't hold any more people.

A BIRD'S EYE VIEW

With its present population of over 80,000, São João del Rei has been able to expand into urban modernity without encroaching on its colonial area. Cut in half by the **São João River**, the two parts of the city are joined by two 18th-century stone bridges, the **Ponte da Cadeia**, in front of the Hotel Porto Real, and the **Ponte do Rosário**. The latter leads into the commercial zone where cars vie with horse drawn carts arriving laden with goods from the countryside. Behind this commercial zone is the main colonial nucleus full of finely-wrought baroque churches, flowering courtyards, and winding cobblestone streets. While **Rua Arthur Bernardes** is the main street of the old city, Rua Santo Antônio is one of the most picturesque, with each house a different colonial color. Some parts of the street are so narrow that you'll often see cars backing up to let the other one through. Building regulations are so strict that when the new owner of a house with an inclined wall wanted to destroy it, the patrimony committee made him rebuild it. In front of **FUNREI,** the city's university, you can see a fine example of a *pau brasil* tree, running with the red sap that was used as paint in baroque churches.

Insider Tip:

*Driving into São João del Rei from Belo Horizonte, all sweet fanatics must stop in the city of Lagoa Dourada at the **Fabricado pela Glória** for the freshest rocambole in Minas. A specialty of the state, rocambole is a type of orange-loaf cake filled with the finest layer of creme de leite. It can be bought in slices at restaurants, but at this bakery, it comes so fresh it truly melts in your mouth.*

SIGHTS

Overlooking a wide square with towering palms, the **Igreja de São Francisco** *Tuesday–Sunday 8:00 a.m.–noon and 1:30 p.m.–8:00 p.m.* is one of the town's most attractive churches, a true feat of architectural design. One only needs to see the main sanctuary from the choir loft to appreciate the extraordinary engineering it took to create such wide arches. While Aleijadinho carved some intricate decorations on the side chapels, it was one of his students who was responsible for the glorious carvings of the main interior. Although they look alike, the altars are masterpieces of subtlety; in fact, you must look closely to appreciate the fine differences, each one telling a different story. Originally, all the carvings were intended to be covered in gold leaf, but the mines ran dry before the task could be completed; after some time, even the original white base coat was removed to show the raw wood. On either side of the front door are fantastic sculptures; lean against the front door and look up into the eyes of Christ. Supported fiercely by the **Third Order of São Francisco,** a lay community, the church is now in the throes of controversy as the order fights against modernists who want to change the traditional baroque music and ritual. (The order has a good idea: I had the privilege of attending mass on Tiradentes Day, a baroque-influenced ritual so rich in theater, crashing organ chords, and incense that it left me in tears.)

In the cemetery behind the church lies the graveside of **Tancredo Neves,** a point of homage among some Brazilians who view him as a saint. (Notice the various ex-votos and plaques thanking him for "graces granted.") On the black marble tombstone reads the epitaph, taken from one of his speeches, *"My beloved land, you have my bones which shall be the last identification of my being to this blessed place,"* indicating his total, near-religious dedication to his country. On Tiradentes Day, a special service is held graveside, attended by local politicians, his wife Risoleta, and their many children and grandchildren.

Memorial Tancredo Neves *Rua Padre José Maria Xavier. 9:00 a.m.–5:00 p.m. Saturday, Sunday, and holidays. Entrance fee about 30 cents.* Anyone interested in the heart and soul of Brazilian history must visit this memorial museum commemorating the private life and professional career of Tancredo Neves through photos, newspaper clippings, and personal effects. Most moving is the room memorializing Neves' death, accompanied by the voice of Milton Nascimento singing *"Coração de Estudante"* (Student Heart), his song that became synonymous with the death of Tancredo by rallying the nation's spirit. A film in Portuguese shows thousands crowding the streets of

São Paulo as Tancredo's body was flown to Brasília for burial, then carried in procession through São João to its final resting place. When the country first learned of the politician's untimely demise, many went into shock (some were even felled by fatal heart attacks), forcing Tancredo's wife, Risoleta, to address the nation and urge them to calm down. Captured on film, her incredible courage and extension of love to the nation produced an amazing reversal in the nation's mood, helping the new regime under Sarney to take root.

Museu Regional do SPHAN *Largo do Tamandaré. Tuesday–Sunday 12:30 p.m.–5:30 p.m. Fee is about 30 cents.* Housed in a rare colonial-style mansion, this fine museum features treasures from the region, such as antique carriages, exquisite wood-carved headboards, and a strange collection of life-sized Greek muses in the garden. An 18th-century ceiling painting with people in typical clothes of the time is extraordinary—it was found by accident when the house was being destroyed. Don't miss the gramophones that actually recorded and played music in the 19th century.

From the museum, walk down

Beco da Rameira and turn left to **Praça Embaixador Gastão da Cunha.** Catty-corner lies the **Igreja de Nossa Senhora do Rosário.** Although small, the church boasts marvelous white walls and columns strewn with colorful angels peeping over the altar; the altar itself looks like a huge wedding cake. Next door is situated **Solar dos Neves,** the family residence of the Neves clan for over two hundred years, and Tancredo's birthplace. Visitors aren't allowed inside, but you can enjoy from the outside the lovely blue and white shutters dripping with red flowers. Across the street is

Doces Caseiros *Praça Embaixador Gastão da Cunha, 71.* a necessary pit stop, to stock up on Mineiro sweets home-made by a local couple. A jam made from the black *jabuticaba* fruit is decidedly special, as are the homemade tropical fruit liqueurs. But don't walk out without trying the *cajuzinho*, a kind of peanut butter roll made from cashews.

Down the same street as the church is the

Museu de Arte Sacra *Praça Embaixador Gastão da Cunha, 8;* ☎ *371-4742. Tuesday–Saturday 9:00 a.m.–5:00 p.m., fee about 30 cents.* Also housed in a finely restored mansion, this collection of sacred art is small, but interesting, with music manuscripts dating back to the 18th century, when liturgical orchestras were mostly peopled by slaves. Elaborate raiments, oratorios, and sculptures are here, but the most riveting is the nearly life-sized mannequin of Senhor dos Passos com Cruz (Lord of the Steps with the Cross); if you look under his robes, you'll see that only his hands, face, and feet are sculpted. Nearly next door is the

Igreja de Nossa Senhora de Pilar *Tuesday–Sunday 7:00 a.m.–11:00 a.m., 2:00 p.m.–4:00 p.m.*, which was closed for repairs when I visited, but if you have a moment, step in. Some have called this gold-engulfed church one of the most beautiful in Brazil. Of lesser interest across the Largo do Rosário is the **Igreja de Nossa Senhora do Carmo.** In the nave are statues, particularly the ones with long flowing hair, that appear startlingly real. Inside the church, note the little painted cherub faces popping out of the ornately baroque wall.

> **Insider Tip:**
>
> A tour around the city can be made on a little train called **Trenzinho da Alegria**, which looks just like the Maria Fumaça. Pick it up at the train station, only on weekends and holidays.

EXCURSIONS

MARIA FUMAÇA TRAIN TO TIRADENTES

The chic way to reach Tiradentes from São João del Rei is to hop a ride on the 19th-century steam train **Maria Fumaça**, or Smoky Maria. Inaugurated in 1881 by Dom Pedro II, this spit-and-polish *trenzinho* (little train) is entirely authentic, all the way down to its hissing stack, wood pew seats, and friendly conductor who loves to blow the whistle. The 30-minute scenic trip winds around some of the most exquisite pastoral landscapes in Minas—golden fields, sparkling lakes, and the fits and starts of the Rio Grande River as it snakes along the gentle slopes of the **Serra de Tiradentes**. If you sit close to the front on the left side of the train (coming from São João), you'll be able to look behind you on the curves and see the end of the train (a particular regional thrill suggested by my guide). Even more fun is to hang out the window and wave at all the locals who come to greet the train from their porches four times a day. One of the first railroad lines in Brazil, built to accommodate the burgeoning textile industry, the route lost its commercial value when the highway was completed, but it was later revived as a tourist attraction and cultural patrimony. Unfortunately, ex-President Collor gave little priority to the preservation of culture and continually threatened to close down the train. Ride it while you can.

Before you leave, arrive early at the **Estação Ferroviária** in São João, to browse through the museum of transport in the lobby. Besides great old steam engines, there are fascinating photos of the interiors of the original cars.

The train from São João leaves for Tiradentes at 10:00 a.m. and 2:15 p.m., and returns 1:00 p.m. and 5:00 p.m. on Friday, Saturday, Sunday, and holidays only. (From December–February and the month of July, the train runs daily.) For more information, ☎ 371–2888. If you want to stay longer in Tiradentes, note that local buses leave regularly for São João.

PEWTER FACTORY

John Somers *Avenida Leite de Castro, 1150;* ☎ *371–4422. Monday–Saturday 9:00 a.m.–6:00 p.m., Sunday 10:00 a.m.–6:00 p.m.* In 1981 the wreckage of the *Utrecht*, a 17th-century Dutch frigate in the service of the West Indies Company, was found off the island of Itaparica in Salvador, Bahia. Sunk during a battle with Portuguese fleets, the 300-year-old ship was laden with goods, all of which had rotted away with the exception of nonorganic and nonferrous items, such as brass, bronze, stone, and above all, pewter. The recovered goods represent the largest collection of pewter from a datable source, including table and kitchen utensils, officer tools, and an entire surgeon's kit. John Somers spent nearly 5 years cataloguing, restoring, and reproducing these designs, many of which are now offered for sale in finely wrought copies. Candlesticks, tea services, trays, picture frames, utensils, and goblets make excellent gifts that are so sturdy they will definitely outlive you. A museum attached to the store displays some of the original items, as well as modern designs inspired by the booty.

MINERAL SPRINGS AND SPA

Ten kilometers from the city is **Agua Santa** *Avenida Pres. Castelo Branco;* ☎ *371–3855. Tuesday–Sunday 8:00 a.m.–5:00 p.m.* a health complex with a mineral-water springs run by the owners of the Cantina do Italo in São João. Guests can dive into two swimming pools full of mineral water, enjoy exercise classes out of doors, or indulge in water massage. The water, which comes straight from the *serra*, is highly recommended for good health. It's about $1.50 to enter; you can drink all the water you want free.

THE ESSENTIAL SÃO JOÃO DEL REI

WHERE TO STAY

Porto Real
Avenida Eduardo Magalhães, 254; ☎ (32) 371-1201

The city's main hotel, with rooms of simple elegance and corridors that have the air of a monastery. Restaurant serves *feijoada* on Saturday. Doubles run $49, suites $54. 32 apartments. *Moderate. All cards.*

Pousada Casarão
Rua Ribeiro Bastos, 94; ☎ (32) 371-1224

A charming estate in typical colonial style, this 15-room pousada is the height of hominess. Rooms feature antique furniture and carved headboards; hammocks hang in the courtyard. From the front door, there's a spectacular view of São Francisco Church. There's also an outdoor pool. The husband of the gregarious owner is a doctor, so if you get sick, you're safe. Restaurant serves only breakfast, but during Holy Week and Carnaval, dinner is also available. Reserve three months before holidays. Singles $11, doubles $21, suite $25. 15 apartments. *Inexpensive. No cards.*

WHERE TO EAT

Quinta do Ouro
Praça Severiano de Resende, 4; ☎ 371-2176. Daily 11:00 a.m.–11:00 p.m.

Packed on Sundays after church, this colonial-style restaurant overlooking the city's river, Córrego do Lenheiro, is situated on the side of the Historical Museum. Not surprising, then, that the best dish is the *Medalhão à Inconfidentes* (steak, bacon, sauce, mushrooms, and fries) for about $7—named in honor of the Mineiro rebels who tried to defeat the Portuguese. Steak *au poivre* is large and tender, and pastas are interesting, but leave room for the *Abóbora com coco*, a delicious caramel-like pudding topped with shredded coconut. After dining, stroll through the surrounding narrow streets full of antique grillwork and traditional wood shutters. *Moderate. No cards.*

Trattorio Conca d'Oro
Tuesday–Thursday 11:00 a.m.–10:00 p.m., weekends 11:00 a.m.–last client

Blue-and-white trattoria with matching tablecloths and a full line of lasagna, cannelone, fettucine, gnocchi, and pizzas. Most popular *prato* is fettucine with 4 cheeses, for about $5. *Inexpensive. No cards.*

Cantina Do Italo
Praça Severiano de Resende, 4; ☎ 371-2862. Daily 11:00 a.m.–11:00 p.m.

Typical Italian cantina with pastas, pizzas, and excellent fried trout. Don't pass up the pizza topped with chicken and a creamy catupiry cheese.

Sinhazinha
Praça São Francisco, 38; ☎ 371-1754. Weekdays 1:00 p.m.–6:00 p.m., weekends 8:00 a.m.–10:00 p.m.

A warm, cozy mini-tea house right in front of the São Francisco Church, with 5 tables and loads of homemade *doces* and *salgadinhos*.

HANDS-ON SÃO JOÃO DEL REI

Arrival

Buses to São João del Rei run regularly from Belo Horizonte. Friday and Sunday tend to fill quickly, so buy your ticket in advance. Buses also go to Congonhas from Ouro Preto, from where you can catch an evening connection to São João del Rei.

From the Rodoviária, take a local bus to the **Terminal Turístico** Praça Dr. Antônio Viegas; ☎ 371-2438 in the center of town. The stop is located on the opposite side of the street from the main entrance. At the terminal, you'll find a free brochure with a map of the city.

Exchange

It's best to exchange money in a larger city, like Belo Horizonte or Rio, before arriving.

When to Go

September 7 *Independence Day,* celebrating Brazil's freedom from Portugal with parades.
February *Carnaval.*
June 24 *Festa Juninas.*
March–April *Holy Week.*
April 21 *Tiradentes Day.*

TIRADENTES

Cut through by the São José River, **Tiradentes** is a sleepy village with no major attractions, except for a universe of great photo ops at every corner. Less preserved than Parati and boasting a population of only about 7,000, Tiradentes, nevertheless, has more natural charm: flowers falling nonchalantly over doorways, dilapidated shutters, narrow cobblestone alleyways that lead to one perfect antique street lamp. Even the Church of São Antônio seems to magically transform itself when seen from different angles and in different lights. Founded around 1702, the community was soon outpaced by São João del Rei, but today remains a weekend escape for *cariocas*, in particular, who love to come and shiver in June and July. Many soap operas and movies are filmed here, and you're likely to stumble across some famous actors and *artistas* dining in the local restaurants. As you walk through the town, notice the wave-like roofs called *eiras* on many houses; the number of waves used to indicate how rich the owners were. The separated cobblestone bricks in the street were known as *solteironas* (or spinsters)—certainly a commentary on the social status of unmarried colonial women. Around the **Praça das Mercês** are numerous silver shops, featuring craftwork made in Tiradentes. Though I can't vouch for the authenticity, I did see "real silver" necklaces being offered for about $7.

An ecological preserve, the **Serra de Tiradentes** can best be seen from the Maria Fumaça train that runs between Tiradentes and São João del Rei (see under "São João del Rei") Wild orchids grow profusely in the gently rolling hills, and numerous waterfalls attract bathers in the summer. If you look closely, you may even be able to see wild monkeys roaming around.

A mandatory pilgrimage must be made to the city's famous soapstone, Chafariz de São José, or Fountain of Saint Joseph, dating back to 1749. Two centuries ago, women and slaves brought their ceramic bowls here to fill up with water that came from the hill above, flowing through 540 meters of natural stone tubing. Since then, the fountains have given birth to many legends. For instance, if you want to get married, drink from the middle one. If you want to stay single, drink from the one on the left, and if you want to get divorced, head for the left one. Today, women still come to wash their clothes in the natural spring water and dry them on the grassy knoll above.

Up the hill is the **Igreja de São Antônio,** the second richest church in Brazil with over 482 kilograms of gold. Built in 1710, the riotously golden church was mostly funded by local residents who were promised a great seat in heaven by the parish's priests. The Arabic-styled ceiling over the altar features female angels on the left and male angels on the right, indicating to the congregation where the sexes should sit. One of the church's greatest treasures is the German-slide organ that dates back to 1798, an instrument that few can play; there are only two like it in Brazil. The red paint used in the structure is taken from the *pau brasil* tree (the red sap is mixed with egg white). Note the mystical figures sitting in front of the choir loft, supporting so many things that they look exhausted and sad. The intriguing sundial in the courtyard was built between 1710–1730. The adjacent cemetery was certainly built after the 18th century, because prior to that time, people were buried under the floor of churches, marked here by numbers on the stone tablets.

On the right of the church is the **Museu Padre Toledo,** established on the site where Tiradentes lived between the ages of 9 and 11. The present building was the former residence of Padre Toledo, a participant in the Inconfidentes Conspiracy, who also housed daughters of important families, ostensibly to protect their virtue. (Brazilian history is rampant with stories of wayward priests who indoctrinated their young charges into the ways of the world, unbeknownst to their parents.) The richly decorated house seems to suggest that the priest was well paid for his services; on display are antique beds, porcelain collections, and excellent artwork, including ceiling paintings whose religious content is hard to detect.

Insider Tip:

There are two orchestras here that play only locally composed repertoires, from the colonial era to the present. Ask around about any scheduled performances.

THE ESSENTIAL TIRADENTES

WHERE TO STAY

Many residents rent out rooms in their private homes or pousadas, which line the road leading to the village from the train station. Take your pick.

★ Solar da Ponte
Praça das Mercês; ☎ *(32) 355-1255*
This unusual pousada is nearly a shrine to the lost arts and crafts that once made São João a thriving community. The owner, John Francis Parson (a Brit), and his Brazilian wife, Ana Maria, a university art professor, deeply researched 18th- and 19th-century techniques to recreate as authentically as possible original Mineiro designs, even down to the door handles. All the ironwork was made by local craftsmen, and even the nails were especially forged for the hotel. None of the rooms have TV, phone, or minibar, but they are masterpieces of rustic elegance—part of a living museum where even the flower pots are carefully crafted. Instead of a garden, a natural forest surrounds the outdoor pool; afternoon tea (included in the rate with breakfast) may be taken in a special salon with exquisitely carved tables. The owner's two horses may be used on the weekends, but if you stay here, you'll need to rent a car. Rumor is, Brazilians who don't have a "connection" don't get a reservation, but I can't imagine that applies to us foreigners. Best to call in advance. Singles run $36, doubles $43. 12 apartments. *Moderate. No cards.*

WHERE TO EAT

Taberna do Padre Toledo
Rua Direita, 202; ☎ *355-1222. Daily 11:00 a.m.–10:00 p.m.*
Chairbacks are in the shape of baroque pineapples at this eatery near the Museu Padre Toledo. Specialty is *frango ao molho pardo* and *frango com quiabo* for about $10. *Moderate. No cards.*

Donatello
Rua Direita, 202. Tuesday–Friday 11:30 a.m.–11:00 p.m., Saturday, Sunday 11:30 a.m.–12:00 a.m., closed Monday
Whenever they're filming in the area, artists and actors descend on this special Italian cantina—maybe it's the handpainted ceiling typical of the city's style before the Neo-classics washed everything over. Or maybe it's the sensuous cuisine, like the *Agnolotti 1790* —green and white pasta filled with ricotta, raisins, and walnuts, and drowned in white cream and bubbling hot cheese. Two can eat a big plate of lasagna for $6, and pizzas arrive with a graceful light crust. The *tábua de quiejo* —a plate of local cheeses—is a steal. *Inexpensive. Cards: AE, V.*

Bar Aluarte
Largo do O, 1; ☎ *355-1314*
Owners Pedro and Marci Roos met in Tiradentes as tourists and threw their lot together in this bar, where every nook and cranny reflects their warm personalities. They designed everything here, from the lights to the wood tables to the woven rugs on the ceiling. Thirty-something Marci makes the whole wheat pizzas while Pedro tends drinks like the *vaca profana* (profane cow) with vodka, grapes, and condensed milk. Drifting from their excellent sound system are international tapes they've picked up on their world travels; live music happens on holidays and special weekends. Next door, they also own the Aluarte restaurant, and behind, a little hotel with 4 bedrooms, each with their own garden and fireplace.

SHOPPING

Casa da Prata
Largo das Forras, 4, ☎ *355-1343*
Silver shop.

Richard's Antiques
Located near the Aluarte Bar, this antique store features fine colonial furniture in Mineiro, English, and European styles. The owner is a tall, chic, black man who inherited the store from his adopted white family.

HANDS-ON TIRADENTES

City Tour
The best way to see the city is to rent a horse for $4 an hour or a horse-and-carriage for $7

when you arrive at the train station.

Climate
In June and July it gets cold here, about 35°F–38°F.

Tourist Information
Departamento de Tiradentese Turismo da Prefeitura Municipal *Rua Resende Costa, 71;* ☎ *335-1212.*

CONGONHAS

Reposing tranquilly on the hillside as though swept up by the gold rush, then brutally abandoned once the adventure was over, is the small town of **Congonhas do Campo** would have long been forgotten if not for a series of mystical and artistic events that transformed it into one of the greatest showcases of baroque art. Here, on this quiet, hidden hill, the tortured soul of Aleijadinho was able to find the peace he needed to create what would become his last and most impressive achievement—the twelve soapstone **Prophets** and the Six Stations of the Cross that adorn the courtyard of the **Basílica do Senhor Bom Jesus de Matosinhos**. For the previous 38 years Aleijadinho had worked on numerous and varied projects throughout Minas; finally, at the age of 58 he accepted the commission that would not only become his deepest labor of love but testimony to his Christ-like suffering. Today, pilgrims from all over Brazil converge on the site, particularly during Holy Week, when highly theatrical reenactments of the Calvary are performed with over 200 characters dressed in Biblical costume. During the rest of the year, most tourists visit Congonhas in a day trip from Belo Horizonte or Ouro Preto.

PAST GLORIES

The mysticism that surrounds Aleijadinho's masterworks in Congonhas dates as far back as the origins of the church—the site of which even today inspires numerous miraculous healings. The church itself began as the answer to a prayer of a Portuguese settler, **Feliciano Mendes**, who had journeyed to Minas in the early 18th century in hopes of fortune. Befelled by a seemingly fatal illness, he was spared from death by fervent prayer and vowed to devote his life to **Senhor Bom Jesus**, collecting alms as a beggar for a small oratory. Later, he begged the ecclesiastical authorities to allow him to convert his mere cross into a chapel. Hearing of his miracle, pilgrims from all over Minas journeyed to the site, donating their pigs, cows, horses, and dowries for the construction. By the time Mendes was dead and long forgotten, the church in 1777 had become a reality.

Accepting the commission 20 years later, **Aleijadinho**, aided by numerous slave assistants, completed the 66 cedar-wood images of the **Six Stations of the Cross** between August 1, 1796 and December 31, 1799; it would take another five years to finish the 12 life-sized

Prophets. Much of the initial work of carving down the huge slabs of soapstone and wood was taken care of by assistants; Aleijadinho was said to have applied himself only to the general vision and the details: quirks of design that can be seen throughout his life's work, such as the large, nearly Oriental eyelids, the elongated fingers with square nails, the cleft chins divided into two sections, the high eyebrows connecting in a continuous line with the nose, and the sinuously curving liplines. Despite the fact that Aleijadinho's illness by the time of this project had almost completely debilitated him, the artistic excellence displayed in these works cannot be faulted.

A BIRD'S EYE VIEW

As a rather unattractive industrial city, Congonhas itself has little to offer in the way of attractions, besides Aleijadinho's masterworks and a waterfall park. About 84 percent of the city's 65,000 residents work in the iron industry. The name Congonhas comes from a plant found in the countryside that makes a tea similar to *maté herva*, and can be used also as a tranquilizer. Photos of Congonhas from the 1930s can be seen inside the **Cultural Office** near the church, along with pictures of Congonhas' sister city, **Matosinhos**, in Portugal. A famous **Festival of Song** is held annually in the city, with stars as big as Milton Nascimento performing outdoors to thousands of fans. Many theater, dance, and sacred choir groups also present programs.

ALEIJADINHO:
The Artist's Life

Much of the personal history of perhaps Brazil's greatest artist lies in obscurity, as much a victim of hyperbole as rumor. What has never been contested is the artistry and devotion of **Antônio Francisco Lisboa**, *nicknamed* **Aleijadinho** *(the Little Cripple). The mulato, Brazilian-born sculptor was able to claim direct ties to the Baroque Iberian tradition; his father,* **Manuel Francisco Lisboa**, *a well-trained carpenter, had come to Brazil straight from Portugal during the heady days of the gold rush and had quickly developed into a master builder and architect. The young Antônio, the result of an illegitimate liaison with a Negro slave, was fortunate enough to be accepted and raised by his father; indeed, most of his skills were absorbed through osmosis as he hung about his father's projects. Although Aleijadinho received no formal education, he was fiercely dedicated to the Bible and to the study of anatomy, both of which deeply influenced his artistry. Up to the time he was 39, he lived a bonvivant life, until he was struck with a crippling disease (some say leprosy, others venereal disease) that progressively deteriorated his body and tortured his spir-*

it—a particularly gruesome fate for one so compelled to create with his hands. As Aleijadinho lost fingers and toes, he was reduced to working on his knees, and as self-hatred and self-consciousness festered, he started to work behind tarpaulins, arising for work before dawn and returning late at night to avoid being seen by curious crowds. Like Beethoven, who was felled by deafness late in life, Aleijadinho developed a fanatic's commitment to his art that increased in the same increments that his body inhibited it. His three talented slaves, whom he had trained as assistants, were the only human beings allowed near him, carrying him on their backs and weathering his foul temper. It was rumored that he even asked them to break his fingers with his own mallets when the pain became too much to bear. Although Aleijadinho showed a preference to soapstone from his very first work, the **Church of St. Francis** in Ouro Preto, he remained loyal to this soft bluish variety of stealite until his death, possibly because, like his favored cedar, it was the easiest to manipulate in his condition. At the age of 58, he began what would be considered his greatest ensemble, the **Stations of the Cross** and **The Prophets**, which he was able to complete only by having his assistants strap his tools to his wrists. At the age of 76, so debilitated that he could not rise from bed, he retired to the house of his daughter-in-law in Ouro Preto, having been abandoned by his last disciple and extremely bitter over unpaid commissions. He died nearly forgotten.

SIGHTS

THE STEPS OF THE CROSS

The best way to visit Aleijadinho's shrine is with the reverence of an 18th-century pilgrim, starting at the base of the hill and passing through the **Stations of the Cross** on the way up to the **Basílica**. Due to defilers, studying the tableaus at extremely close range will be difficult as grills keep the public from entering or touching the figures. Although Aleijadinho remained loyal to the Baroque tradition, his figures are all infused with a vivid physicality that is at times almost frightening. The Roman soldiers, especially, boast markedly ferocious features, in contrast to the stiff jointless bodies of the Jewish disciples and the always reverentially carved figure of Christ. After being shaped by Aleijadinho and his assistants, all the figures were painted by **Manoel da Costa Athaíde**, one of the period's greatest artists, who used natural paints mixed from ox blood, egg whites, crushed flowers, and vegetable dyes.

As displayed in these tableaus, Aleijadinho's genius lay not only in his technical skill but in his ability to infuse the Calvary's saga with his own political views (decidedly pro-independence) through the minute manipulation of details.

Tableau #1 reenacts the **Last Supper**, with a decidedly Oriental-lidded Jesus (an influence from the Portuguese colony in Macau, China). Remarkable are the passionate gestures of the figures, infused with the contorted energy of real-life devotees—a religious fervor that is not to be underestimated in Brazil. In fact, during a festival in recent years, fanatics actually shot the figure of Judas with a gun, hence his pockmarked face.

Tableau #2 shows Jesus in the **Garden of Gethsemane** with the sleeping apostles; that's the angel Gabriel hanging in suspension.

Tableau #3, **Judas betrays Jesus** to the Romans. Most notable is Jesus' bloody ear, and the hand cut off a Roman soldier by Peter.

Tableau #4 shows the **Flagellation** and the moment the crown of thorns was placed on Jesus' head. A remarkable detail are the ankle boots worn by all the Roman soldiers (a style fashionable with the Portuguese authorities at the time); note that the apostles always appear barefoot (a subtle commentary on the impoverished status of the Brazilian colonists). In this scene, particularly, the flowing movement created by Aleijadinho out of solid wood is truly stunning.

Tableau #5, symbolizing the **Calvary**, shows Jesus carrying an enormous cross surrounded by Romans and the jester of the court. Here again, Aleijadinho has placed the mark of Tiradentes on Jesus' throat (the trickle of blood represents the Mineiro's death by hanging), not a small hint of where the artist's true political sentiments lay.

Tableau #6, the **Romans hammer the nails** into Jesus' body, surrounded by other thieves. Most interesting is the fact that Mary Magdalene is dressed as a typical Portuguese woman, much older and stockier than the traditional lithe representations.

THE PROPHETS

As you climb the soapstone-brick path up the hill, Aleijadinho's **Twelve Prophets** in the courtyard of the church seem to be engaged in a slow-motion ballet, their stone beards so expertly carved they appear to waft in the wind. Meant to be viewed from afar, the statues look life-sized from the street, but in reality are much smaller and short-legged. Despite their fragility, they stand pondering man's condition with a remarkable robustness; the poet **Carlos Drummond de Andrade** once remarked that they even seem to be expressing the epitome of the Mineiro personality—moody, taciturn, melancholy, and messianic. Though they stand with great dignity as separate beings, from a distance there seems to be a mystical unity tying them together. A researcher recently discovered that the impassioned ensemble, made some years after the conspiracy, actually corresponds to the rebels of Tiradentes' **Inconfidência** conspiracy. **Jonas**, with his heavy expression of death—vacant eyes and slack-jawed mouth—is thought to be Tiradentes; **Amos,** the artist's representation of himself. Critics consider the statue of **Daniel**, carved from one piece of stone, to be the best. Sadly, a few of the statues have had their hands cut off by defilers, and now it is expressly forbidden to touch them.

THE BASILICA

After seeing these riveting pieces of art, you may find the **Basílica** slightly less impressive. A Greek influence may be seen in the columns, while an Oriental flair characterizes the dragons from whose mouths hang chandeliers. The stained-glass windows are particularly beautiful for the shadows they cast on the altar and pews. Only four of the reliquaries on the altar are by Aleijadinho. Housed in a glass on the altar is the original effigy of the dead Christ that Mendes brought from his hometown town of Braga, Portugal, on whose basilica this church was based.

Of particular human interest is the **Milagro Room,** next to the church, full of very old ex-votos and offerings from those who have received healings and miracles. The collection is a kind of living answer to the power of Aleijadinho's art to inspire faith and personal resolve among devotees. Most intriguing are the many photos of weddings; the couples shown either resolved their problems through marrying or were at least saved from divorce. You'll see lots of wax heads and arm casts; many of the really old **ex-votos**, dating back to the early 18th century, record dramatic escapes from fires, raging bulls, and coach crashes. If the room isn't open, the guards will be happy to open it for you, if they aren't at lunch.

> **Insider Tip:**
>
> Many marriages take place in the church; hopefully, you'll be lucky enough to catch one. If you want to walk downtown, it's only about 15 minutes away.

PARQUE DA CACHOEIRA

An ecological park of over 250,000 meters, this "waterfall resort" about 15 minutes from the city features a variety of kiosks to make your own barbecue, hiking trails, sports fields, and a decent restaurant and snack bar. On Saturdays, special eco programs are held for children. A natural swimming pool is available, and camping areas may be rented for about 50 cents.

THE ESSENTIAL CONGONHAS

WHERE TO STAY

Colonial Hotel
Praça da Basílica, 76; ☎ *(31) 731-1834*
Located across from the Prophet's Rooms, this tiny 2-star features antique furniture and bedspreads. An outdoor pool and children's pool overlooks the city. Doubles run $24. 12 apartments. *Moderate. No cards.*

Newton Hotel
Avenida Júlia Kubitschek, 54,
☎ *(31) 731-1352*
Located downtown on the main street, the rooms here are very simple, but clean, with TV, but no minibar, heat, or air-conditioning. Most tourists prefer to stay closer to the church. Singles go for $8, doubles $20. 39 apartments. *Inexpensive. No cards.*

WHERE TO EAT

Cova do Daniel
Hotel Colonial, Praça da Basílica, 54; ☎ *731-1834. Daily 11:00 a.m.–6:00 p.m.*
Located next to Bom Jesus, this blue-and-white colonial house serves solid typical dishes like *Tutu à Mineira*. There are several private coves for lingering, including one completely strange optical illusion. *Moderate. No cards.*

Tio Panga Churrascaria
Rua Doutor Mario Rodrigues Pereira, 96; ☎ *731-1534*
Connected to the Hotel Casarão, this is a decent steakhouse with 12 cold dishes, 8 hot plates, and desserts for about $5. *Inexpensive. No cards.*

SHOPPING

Bel-Artes
Praça da Basílica, 27; ☎ *731-1832*
Of the several souvenir shops near the church, this one has some of the best collections. Statues of the Madonna in soapstone are particularly lovely, but be careful packing them; they are extraordinarily fragile. Crochet and embroidered linen make fine gifts, and there are some good choices on clear quartz crystals. Film and batteries are also available, though usually more expensive than in the larger cities.

HANDS-ON CONGONHAS

Arrivals and Departures
Buses from Belo Horizonte run 6 times a day; best to buy your return tickets as soon as possible. From São João del Rei, take the São João del Rei-Belo Horizonte bus and get off at Muritinho; from there, you take a local bus (about every half hour) into Congonhas. To reach Ouro Preto from Congonhas, either go via Belo Horizonte, or take the local bus to Muritinho or Conselheiro Lafaiete and change to a bus for Ouro Preto via Itabirito.

Climate
Temperatures range from 61°F to 74°F, plummeting as low as 46°F in winter.

Tourist Information
The **Cultural Office,** located across from the Church, will provide you with a few brochures. Guides always seem to be hanging about to explain the Steps and the Prophets of Aleijadinho, but don't count on superlative English. It's easy enough to escort yourself through the area, but you need to go to the Cultural Center to ask permission to enter the chapel surrounding the Basílica. A policeman will accompany you.

Travel Agency
Unitour *Rua Tupis, 171;* ☎ *201-7144* located in Belo Horizonte, can arrange day trips to Congonhas with transportation originating in a variety of historical cities.

When to Go
September 7–14 *Jubilee of Bom Jesus de Matosinhos.*
October *Song Festival.*
Holy Week reenacts the Via Cruxis in an emotional, dramatic procession, supported by 200 local actors dressed in Biblical costumes.
Carnaval is celebrated in the center of the city with 4 schools.
June *Congado festival* with folkloric groups, African dances, and typical foods.
August *Cultural Week* commemorates the life and death of Aleijadinho.
December 17 *City's birthday.*

THE SPA TOWNS

A collection of towns, collectively known as *Circuito das Águas* (or Water Circuit) lends an aura of mysticism to the south of Minas. Tucked into hilly countryside favored by cool temperatures and dry air, the best of these spa towns, including **São Lourenço**, **Caxambú**, and **Poços de Caldas**, have been constructed around mineral water springs that are reputed to have healing qualities. In high season, activity at the hydromineral parks resembles something between a Catskills resort and *Death in Venice,* as visitors, both young and old, faithfully fill up their tin cups at various fountains. A stay in these peaceful, crime-free towns is a relaxing, if not possibly miraculous, way to experience the interior of the state.

Also remarkable about this region is that it has attracted all sorts of spiritual groups convinced that the end of the world is near; many believe that this area will be one of the few to withstand the rages of Judgment Day. One such town, **São Tomé das Letras**, has also become known nationwide as a major landing area for UFOs. About a half-hour away, in **Carmo da Cachoeira**, is the **Fazenda Figueira**, a devoted spiritual community founded by **Trigueirinho**, a famous author and former film director who is well known for his contact with extraterrestrials.

SÃO LOURENÇO

SIGHTS

PARQUE DOS FONTES

São Lourenço's **Parque** could pass as something straight out of Albert Brooks' version of Heaven. Built around a gleaming lake, the landscaped acres are flanked by woody hillsides and dominated by elaborate Art Deco fountains bursting with 6 different kinds of mineral water. The green-and-white Hydrotherapy Center called the **Balneário** looks like a huge sacred temple, hosting some 500,000 people a year who take advantage of the special mineral baths, energetic water massages, and body therapies. It's open from 8:30 a.m. to noon and 2:30 p.m. to 4:50 p.m. daily (Sunday mornings only) and has separate facilities for men and women. During high season, you should make an appointment for a private bath or massage as soon as you arrive.

Getting Your Fill of Water

Anyone may drink from the individual fountains, but if you are going to do it seriously, you should probably have a medical consultation available through the park's clinic. There are 6 types of waters: **bicarbonatadas sódicas** for kidney problems, gastrointestinal disturbances, hepatitis, arthritis, and gout; **magnesiana** for ulcers and hepatitis; **alcalina** for peptic ulcers and stimulation of the nervous system; **ferruginosa** for anorexia and anemia; **carbo-gasosa** for digestion and renal problems; and **sulfurosa laxativa** for chronic ulcers, diabetes, and allergies. To get the full effect, you should drink the water for 21–30 days. What you shouldn't do is drink too much at one time or mix too many different waters on the same day. (Otherwise, you'll find your body "cleansing" itself at a turbulent rate!) Inside the park you can only take home 2–3 liters (after 2 days it loses its potency), but you can fill up free outside the park at the fount at Vila Ramon.

After getting your fill of water, stop by the grotto of **Nossa Senhora dos Remedios,** strewn with plaques and flowers and even plastic limbs, to thank her for your healing. Near the grotto is a magnificent example of a *pau brasil* tree. If you're feeling energetic, you can jog around the perimeter of the park or rent paddleboats, kayaks, or canoes to traverse the lake. There are boutiques, crystal stores, and metaphysical bookstores, as well as a restaurant and luncheonette. In

Parque II (adjacent to the main park), you can rent bikes and take baths in mineral water. There's also two tubes of mineral gas, which you bend down and breathe in (it's reported to be good for colds).

A half-block from the park is a series of chalets called **Aldeia Vela Verde**, with all kinds of artisanry for sale, such as crocheted clothes, straw purses, and handmade sweaters. If you're paying in cash, ask for a discount.

> **Insider Tip:**
>
> *Bring your own cup to the park, or pay about 75 cents for a plastic one. The fee to enter the park is about 50 cents (children up to the age of 8 are free). For more information call* ☎ **331-1940**.

ALSO TO SEE

Templo da Euboise *Avenida Getúlio Vargas, 481. Sunday 4:00 p.m.–6:00 p.m.* Founded in 1949 by the spiritualists Henrique José de Souza and his wife, Helena, this Greek-style temple is the center for an interfaith organization dedicated to universal wisdom. Around the turn of the century, the founder, during travels in India at the age of 16, became initiated into a Buddhist monastery in Ladakh, hidden in the Himalayas. The essence of Euboise is the search for perfection according to the triad *bem-bom-belo*, and the sublimation of imperfections through yoga. The temple's adepts participate in an ongoing spiritual practice, closed to visitors except on Sundays, when they are received between 2:00 p.m.–4:00 p.m. In front of the temple is a plaza that visitors are invited to circle upon arrival and departure to "receive the energy." It's been said that when President John F. Kennedy died, a group at the temple held a seance and claimed his bust appeared. Members of the organization feel that the land in this region is sacred and will survive the end of the world. On February 20–25, the temple receives thousands of adepts and curiosity-seekers for cultural events, theaters, debates, and conferences.

THE ESSENTIAL SÃO LOURENÇO

WHERE TO STAY

Hotel Brasil
Al. João Lage, 87; ☎ (35) 331-1422
The town's luxury hotel, though not on the scale of a 5-star. The presidential suite has a fantastic veranda overlooking the park, and handicap facilities are also available. Some suites even have hydromassage. There is an indoor pool as well as a fountain and bath of mineral water outdoors. Singles start at about $60. 145 apartments. *Expensive. All Cards.*

Hotel Primus
Rua Cel. José Justino, 681;
☎ (35) 331-1244
Standards are clean and spacious, deluxe rooms are even larger with an anterior room. An octagonal, indoor heated pool and an outdoor pool and sauna add to the diversions. Nice buffets with fresh vegetables are good for dieters. Standards run $47, doubles $63. 129 apartments. *Moderate. All Cards.*

Fazenda Emboabas
Rua Cel. Jorge Amado, 350 (Solar dos Lagos); ☎ (35) 331-1833
This country estate, constructed around beautiful rolling hills outside the city, is a remarkable place to relax into nature. Extremely spacious rooms with burnt-orange jacaranda furniture and glass doors look out onto beautiful vistas; ask for the ones with wood floors. An elegant lobby with grand piano and oriental rugs add allure to the rustic charm. Pigs and cows roam the grounds (you're invited to milk them!) and horses are available for riding. A separate building holds a theater, screening room, and convention salons. There are also outdoor tennis courts, soccer fields, luxuriant gardens, sauna, massage, and discounts for group. Cars are provided to the mineral park or you may walk the route in 20 minutes. Doubles start at $54. 20 apartments. *Moderate. All Cards.*

WHERE TO EAT

Chalé
Avenida Comendador Costa, 589;
☎ 331-2058. Daily 11:00 a.m.–midnight
This open-air eatery with a high-beam roof is the city's best—made cozy in winter by a roaring fireplace. Fondues, pizzas, and typical plates run about $3–$10. *Moderate. No cards.*

Mamma Mia
Avenida Cel. José Justino, 674;
☎ 331-3242. Monday–Friday 6:00 p.m.–midnight, 11:00 a.m.–3:00 p.m. and 6:00 p.m.–midnight on Saturday and Sunday
Famous for pizzas.

SHOPPING

Crafts
Try the mini-shopping mall called **Centro de Artesanato** on **Rua Wenceslau Bráz** for handmade baskets of *palha* (straw) and crochet bedspreads and sweaters.

Chocolates
Chocarte Rua Wenceslau Bráz, 71. Daily 8:00 a.m.–9:00 p.m. Stock up on locally made chocolates and fruit-flavored liqueurs. A regional favorite is *pé de moleque*, a type of peanut brittle.

HANDS-ON SÃO LOURENÇO

Arrival
São Lourenço is 3 hours from *Rio* by car (5 by bus); 5 hours from *Belo Horizonte* (8 by bus) and 4 hours from *São Paulo* (6 by bus). The *Rodoviária* is located half a block from the main street, *Avenida Dom Pedro II*, where you'll find lots of hotels, bars, and restaurants. Buses to *Caxambú* leave at 7:00 a.m., 10:00 a.m., 2:00 p.m., 3:50 p.m. and 6:00 p.m.

City Transportation
Taxi Brasil ☎ 331-2650 for visiting nearby cities.
City Taxis ☎ 331-1354.

Climate
Temperatures range from 55°F to 71°F— a typical European climate conducive to deep breathing and relaxation.

Goat Ride

Children will adore riding around the park on a goat near Praça Brasil for about $1.50. Look for the goatherd near the tourism kiosk.

Horses

City tours in a horse-and-buggy (for 3 persons) can be hired at the corner of *Avenida Getúlio Vargas* and *Avenida Comendador Costa* for about $3 per hour.

Tourist Information

Brochures and folders can be picked up at the tourism kiosk on **Praça Brasil** *8:00 a.m.–11:00 a.m., 1:00 p.m.–6 p.m.* in the center of the city.

CAXAMBÚ

Although slightly smaller than São Lourenço, **Caxambú** is a much more interesting spa town to settle into (although the two cities, a mere 19 miles apart, are so close, you might as well pay a visit to both). The first spring was founded in 1814, attracting hordes of 19th-century visitors who believed the water had powers to cure. The reputation of the springs soared when **Princesa Isabel**, daughter of the emperor **Dom Pedro II**, cured her sterility from the font now bearing her name (a combination of alkaline gas and iron, also indicated for anemia). In gratitude, she built a small gothic chapel, **Igreja de Santa Isabel de Hungria**, which still stands today, overlooking the springs. Today **O Parque das Águas** is owned by the mayor's office, although the water is made available through the Superágua company, responsible for the bottling and commercialization of over 200,000 liters of mineral water daily. The park itself is a Victorian oasis of tranquility, a veritable paradise where you can stroll and sip water at leisure, indulge in hydrotherapy baths, or engage in more invigorating exercise around the shimmering lakes.

Situated on the plateau of Mantiqueira, Caxambú is reachable over good asphalted roads, about 222 miles from Belo Horizonte, 144 miles from Rio, and 167 miles from São Paulo. The area, built on several hills (the highest which holds a commanding figure of Christ), is dominated by coffee plantations and cattle ranches; among the unusual animals bred here is the Manga-Larga Marchador, a trotting horse excellent for long rides. A visit to nearby **fazendas** (farms) is an excellent way to experience the countryside. In September, fishermen can head for a city-subsidized **trout farm** and fish by the kilo. Like all the cities of the interior of Minas, the people of Caxambú get up early and go to bed early. After dinner, before sleeping, it's become traditional to take a turn around the principal plaza, close to the park, where there is Belgian-style bandstand dating back to the last century. If gambling is reinstated in Brazil, Caxambú might reclaim some of its past glories, when the city was a magnet for high rollers and politicians who filled the hotel's ornamental salons. Today, the city is as peaceful as they come in Brazil; violence is unheard of and the street cleaners still sweep the roads with huge tree branches.

SIGHTS

PARQUE DAS AGUAS

The "Waters" Park in Caxambú is not just a plot of land for consuming mineral water; it's an entire entertainment complex designed to heal the body, mind, and spirit. Just strolling about the immaculately tended grounds and breathing in the fresh air rich with the scent of pines and flowers is enough to reinvigorate one's soul. Built at the turn of the century, the 11 fountains with various kinds of mineral water are constructed in attractively designed Art Nouveau pavilions with steps leading up to the fount; the dramatic effect leaves you with the impression that you are drinking from the lips of the gods. If you are using the waters medicinally, however, you should request a medical consultation (not free) that will direct you to the proper founts. In truth, a few of the names of the waters can be misleading. Many people imagine that **Fonte Beleza** is for beauty treatments, but the name actually came about because so many people gasped "*Que beleza*" (how beautiful) upon seeing the lovely fountain. The **Ernestina Guedes** fountain must have a good story behind it, but I don't know it; today it's used for hemorrhoids. Particularly impressive is the **Dom Pedro**, with its replica of the crown of the monarch.

The **Balneário** *8:30 a.m.–5:00 p.m.* with its magnificent painted tile floor, will take you back centuries—that is, if you ever were a royal receiving a bath from your servants. The *ducha* I opted for involved a very muscular lady shooting a heavy stream of warm water at my naked body for 10 very long minutes (at least I had remembered to request "*não frio*" or *not cold*). Fortunately, that torture was followed by a relaxing, warm bubble bath with exotic minerals. Many other kinds of water therapies are also available. Men and women are separated in the bathhouse, but don't expect anyone to understand English. (In fact, make sure you have the phrases *muito frio* (too cold) and *muito quente* (too hot) down pat before you start.) There is also a beauty salon for women, where you can buy special shampoos and cleansers.

If getting douched like a duchess starts to get boring, you can always choose to **paddleboat** around the manmade lake or ride the newly installed **ski-lift**—an exciting feet-dangling jaunt over verdant hills. Don't miss an inspection of the unusual children's **playground**, built by the ingenious architect **José Tabacow**, whose outdoor learning games are gargantuan-sized, like the slide in the shape of a sundial and an iron musical scale that you can actually play. A major attraction that everyone seems to love is the **natural geyser**, which explodes every 3 hours. The hilltop restaurant, with its castle-like turrets and a huge Coke bottle, is the epitome of Brazilian kitsch, but the food is passable. Water fanatics can also take a look at the **Superágua Factory**, where the famous Caxambú water is bottled.

On the side of the park, you can rent horses at **Ponto de Animais** for about $3 an hour.

> **Insider Tip:**
> The hours of the park are 7:00 a.m.–6:00 p.m. The entrance fee is about 50 cents, a little more on the weekends. Bring your own cup or buy a plastic one for about 75 cents.

TROUT FARM

Owned by the *prefeitura* (mayor's office), this **Criação de Trutas**, in front of a rich forested reserve, was established to breed trout. In February, up to 20,000 trouts are spawned; in September, there is the **Festival of Trouts**, when you may come at dawn to fish. Visitors pay by the kilos caught, and the money is given to a fund for poor children. This dam used to be a water reservoir for the city, but was turned into an ecological preserve with a social vision. On the nearby hillsides, you can see strange orange mounds that resemble the stone formations at Stonehenge, but are actually the dirt homes of **cupim**, a kind of termite local to the region.

TREE FARM

At **Horta Florestal**, a conservation program funded by the government outside the city, trees are grown for city dwellers who would like to replant them in front of their homes. About five people a day come to take home free saplings. Anyone interested in Brazilian greenery will appreciate the 50 types of trees. Unfortunately, U.S. customs prohibits the transport of live plants. (A horse-and-buggy ride in front of the Hotel Glória will transport you there and back.)

EXCURSIONS

Many horse trails lead out to *fazendas*, or country farms, like **Fazenda Santa Helena**, the most famous. Call the Secretary of Tourism for more information, ☎ *341–1136*.

THE ESSENTIAL CAXAMBU

WHERE TO STAY

Hotel Glória
Avenida Camilio Soares, 590;
☎ *(35) 341–1233*

One of the city's premier hotels, primely situated across from the park, the Glória was inaugurated in 1946. A massive dining hall with antique chandeliers serves 3 meals a day on real silver plates and fine crystal goblets. Dark wood furniture and enormous old-style lounges give the feel of an old-country hunting lodge. Bathrooms have been reformed in marble. All rooms have color TVs, some have air-conditioning, some suites have hydromassage. The property is perfect for those who want the feel of a pousada with the efficiency of a hotel. Doubles run $91 ($71 in low season), singles $46. 119 apartments. *Expensive. All cards.*

Palace Hotel
Rua Dr. Viotti, 567; ☎ *(35) 341–1044*

This comfortable, old-fashioned hotel is not unlike a Catskills resort (actually inaugurated in 1894), with an upright piano played from the balcony during meals. Multi-course meals are excellent here; *à la carte* menus include a cold buffet of chicken, roast beef, and fresh vegetables every night. A charming antique sink graces the dining room for washing your hands before eating. During high season, the Katacumba nightclub is one of the few places to swing in town; a screening room also is available. The rooms are graced with antique bureaus and headboards, complementing the original Art Deco light fixtures in the hall. Outside, a horse and buggy awaits riders. *Expensive. All cards.*

Hotel Marques
Rua Oliveira Mafra, 223; ☎ *(35) 341–1013*

Something between a funky rooming house and an old folks' home, the Marques actually has a perfectly respectable clientele, and some of the lowest rates in town. The reception area has two TVs, and the food is reputed to be good (all 3 meals included). All rooms have tubs. Doubles run $29, singles $16. 46 apartments. *Inexpensive. No cards.*

WHERE TO EAT

Most hotels offer three meals included in the room rate, so dining out is usually partaken of only by residents. However, the restaurant listed below is so good it's worth wasting your meal ticket at least once, if not a couple of times.

★ **La Forelle**
Rua Dr. Viotto, 190; ☎ *341–1249*

Danish cuisine at its heartiest—and with an authentic bloodline. Owner Antônio Godtfredsen's father, an early immigrant in the 1920s, was the first to make blue cheese in South America. Only about 30 Scandinavians are left of this once-thriving community of milk farmers and cheesemakers, but some of their secrets can still be tasted here, like the filet mignon with roquefort—the best I have *ever* tasted. The menu is colossal, from smoked salmon with mushroom-spiked scrambled eggs to delicious pâtés with homemade bread and all kinds of fondues. The specialty is smoked trout with almond sauce, but unforgettable is the *peito de frango empanado* in curry sauce. The homemade apple pie is tender, crispy, and creamy, all at once. Reservations are absolutely necessary; make sure you sit Senhor Antônio down for some stories from the old days. Dishes run between $5–$14. *Moderate. All Cards.*

> **Insider Tip:**
>
> *Scandinavian cheeses, gruyere, roquefort, and parmesan, can be bought at* **Sobradino Laticínio** *Avenida Gabriel Fernandes. The label "Skandia" is the best from the area.*

NIGHTLIFE

During high season check out the Katacumba nightclub in the **Palace Hotel,** the nightclub in **Hotel Glória,** and **Overnight** on *Praça 15 de Setembro.*

La Nave 307 *Rua João Pinheiro, 307* is a young hangout for pizza and beer from 7:30 p.m. onward.

SHOPPING

Among souvenirs to buy in the center of the city are handmade crochet objects, handmade rugs, intriguing T-shirts, bamboo purses, and homemade liqueurs.

On the way back from the trout farm, stop at **Doces Imperial** *Rod. BR 354, kilometer 92;* ☎ *341–2691* for sweets, *balas de leite com mel* (juicy caramels), *doce de leite,* canned fruits, and fruit liqueurs. Prices are a little cheaper here because this is the factory. For stylish sweats and T-shirts, try **W. R. Confecções** *Avenida Dom Pedro II, 538;* ☎ *331-2784.*

HANDS-ON CAXAMBÚ

Arrival

Buses from Rio run on the **Viação Cidade do Aço** line twice a day, 4 times on Friday. From Belo Horizonte, buses on the **Viação ENSA** line run 2 times a day, 4 on Friday and Saturday. From São Paulo, the **Resen Sense** line runs 5 times a day. Buses to and from São Lourenço run 6 times a day. During high season and holidays, you should buy your tickets for the big cities 10 days in advance (December–February and July). Other times, buy 1–3 days in advance.

City Tour

Horse-drawn carriages can be hired in front of the Hotel Glória to go to Horta Florestal for about $6 ($5 around the city).

Tourist Information

Visit the **Secretary of Tourism office** at the white kiosk on *Praça 16 de Setembro* Monday–Friday *9:00 am.–noon, 2:00 p.m.–6:00 p.m.*

When to Go:

January *National Motorbike Competition.*
July *Rock na Rua* (Street Rock) festival features new Brazilian bands on the third weekend.
May *Video festival* featuring new works.

An Old Woman Stubbornly awaits the Coming of Extraterrestrials

SÃO TOMÉ DAS LETRAS

São Tomé das Letras must be *the* strangest town in the whole world. Isolated in the middle of a granite mountain, the village is about 150 meters above sea level, yet a strange smell of sea pervades the air. Just getting to the town, over an incredibly rocky road, may prove daunting, but the moment you approach, you'll begin to feel an unmistakable shift in the atmosphere—a kind of eerie timelessness promoted by its glassy-eyed inhabitants who look like they've just been defrosted from Woodstock. Most of the 7,500 residents live in eccentric stone houses they have made themselves, though many of the dwellings look to be somewhere between half-constructed and fully abandoned. Despite its primitive lifestyle, São Tomé has received enormous Brazilian TV coverage since it is considered one of the prime locations for the sighting of *discos voadores,* or flying saucers. In fact, an apparently sane gentlemen named Tatá, the owner of a small pousada, claimed in an interview with me that he has seen *and* talked to arriving extraterrestrials for the last 30 years. In general, the residents of São Tomé, many of whom have been mystically guided to settle here, believe that the civilization of a new world will be founded in the area in the year 2005. Located in the sand-based village are over 30 holes, one of which is believed to lead directly to a thriving civilization located at the center of the earth. (My one travel precaution: think twice if anyone tries to sell you a ride on a space ship.)

Mysticism has been a part of the city since its origins. According to one legend, a runaway slave from a baron's farm in Campo Grande had been hiding in a cave when he discovered an image of São Tomé. The saint then appeared to the slave, asking him to return to his master, present the image, then build a chapel close to the cave. With great courage, the slave did as he was asked and was not only *not* punished, but freed as promised. The phrase *das letras* or "of the letters," refers to the indecipherable hieroglyphics that were discovered on the cave wall. Some say ancient Phoenicians wrote them; others claim it was descendants of Atlantis, who lived in a subterranean city of the cave called **Gruta do Carimbado**. Another popular legend claims there's an underground tunnel that runs between São Tomé, Brasília, and Machu Picchu in Peru, forming a sacred triangle. In more recent years, hippies, healers, and psychics have moved here, as well as some very strange creatures who actually look like extraterrestrials getting accustomed to human forms (seriously). A few handicrafts are sold, particularly miniatures of the locals' stone houses, all which resemble some kind of architecture from outer space.

The quartzite sites are fascinating to see (some people still chip away at them for a modest livelihood), and anyone sensitive to rock formations and crystals will find their energy both invigorating and strangely unsettling.

Despite (or because of) its oddities, the city lives mostly on tourism, though the infrastructure is minute. There are only 35 telephones, a first aid center with a doctor once a week, 1 bank, 1 pharmacy, 1 supermarket, 2 small inns, 5 restaurants, and 12 bars. If you're game, you might be able to rent a hammock in a private home.

Getting There

São Tomé is located 195 miles from Belo Horizonte, and 20 miles from Tres Corações. If driving, take the road that links Caxambú to Juiz de Fora. About 10 kilometers after you leave Caxambú, turn left and take a gravel road about 50 kilometers, or about 1 hour. Pay attention, because there is only one very small sign on the road. Buses arrive and depart about 3 times a week.

Pousada *Praça do Rosário, 25* Owner Oriental Luiz Noronha, otherwise known as Tatá, calls himself an *arqueologia mística*, mystic archeologist. He owns the simplest of pousadas (only 2 rooms) and an even simpler restaurant, whose walls are plastered with his media coverage over the years. One room runs about $3. To contact him, call the São Tomé operator (area code 201) and leave a message.

Pedra Mística Atelier *Praça Central* sells crystals and sweets.

Vendinha das Gnomos offers an excellent bag of natural homemade granola.

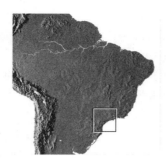

SÃO PAULO

São Paulo Business District

Think of the city of São Paulo as the Brazilian Big Apple, only sweeter. With 15 million people, **São Paulo** rates as the *third largest city in the world,* complete with all the problems of a still-burgeoning metropolis—traffic jams, pollution, slums, and noise. But there is a charm in the residents of the city (called *Paulistanos*) that somehow makes all these problems seem a bit smaller. Taxi drivers are honest *(mais ou menos)*, waiters gracious, and shopgirls irrepressibly helpful.

Whatever is modern in Brazil can be found in São Paulo. A dominant political force, *Paulistanos* like to say they work for the rest of Brazil. And they love to talk in industrial percentages. The state of São Paulo (of which the city is capital) produces 62 percent of the country's sugar, 33 percent of coffee, and 50 percent of fruit exports, all the while utilizing 60 percent of the available electrical energy. Its 64,000 industries correspond to 50 percent of the country's total industrial output; 70 percent of the country's wealth passes through Avenida Paulista, the banking center of the country. For all its hard-driving activity, São Paulo almost seems like its own country.

But there is much more to the city than skyscrapers and industry. Over 1,600 events are held here daily. The São Paulo Convention and Visitors Bureau actively competes on the international market to host conventions, seminars, and exhibitions from fields as diverse as medicine, arts, science, and commerce. Whatever intellectual currents occur in Brazil are often forged first in São Paulo; the hearts of the theater, film, and literary worlds are here. Certainly the best medical care is here, as are the country's finest museums. As one Paulistano said to this transplanted New Yorker (and without a trace of irony!), "If you can make it here, you can make it anywhere in Brazil."

One of the major attractions of the city is its diverse ethnicity. During the 19th century, as slavery was abolished, immigrants from Italy, Germany, France, and Japan, among others, converged on the area, forming strong communities and forging distinctive cultures. Today, the Italian neighborhood of Bexiga, the Japanese Liberdade, and various Arab, Jewish, and Korean communities provide colorful backdrops in a city that hardly seems to belong to a tropical country.

3,000 Restaurants and 3,500 Bars

If you need one good reason to go to São Paulo, go to eat. The syncretic mix of cultures has produced some of the most cosmopolitan menus in Brazil, as well as masterful chefs. With its 3,000 restaurants and 3,500 bars, São Paulo is a city where you can find an excellent dinner at 4:00 a.m. While *Paulistanos* flee the city on the weekend, 70 percent of other states come here just for the nightlife. Friday is the hub of the weekend; clubs and bars often stay open till the last client leaves.

Of course, being located about 43 miles inland, São Paulo can hardly compare to Rio in terms of natural wonders. Yet, in its own way the city benefits from a privileged location. At least one beach resort, **Guarujá,** is located a mere hour away. And if *Paulistanos* want to shiver in a foresty highland, they can head to **Campos do Jordão,** the Aspen of Brazil's eastern coast (with ski-lifts, alas, but no snow).

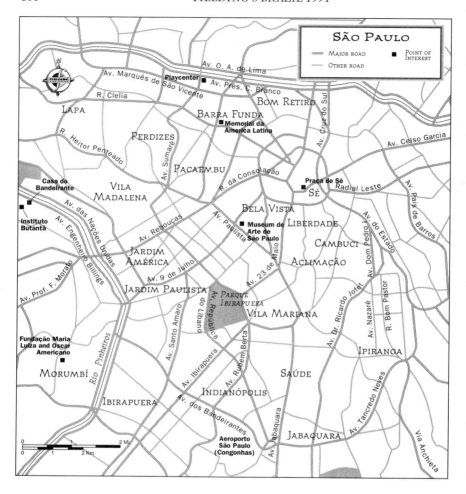

SÃO PAULO (CITY)

PAST GLORIES

The sprawling metropolis of São Paulo began in 1555 as a tiny Jesuit mission established along the Tietê River to convert the Tupí-Guaraní Indians. Eventually, the modest station grew into a trading post, around which a new settlement was founded. The true heroes of colonial expansion in São Paulo state, however, were the daring bands of expeditioners, called *bandeirantes*, who plunged into the interior seeking wealth and power, runaway slaves, precious metals, and new territory in the name of the crown. These *bandeirantes* were romantic figures, traveling immense distances by foot and canoe as they opened new routes of communication and became wealthy landowners themselves. Though not a few of them were rogues and runaway criminals, their single-minded determination and hard-driving persistence became traits that were forged deeply in the personality of the modern *Paulistanos*—if stereotypes are to be believed.

In 1711, São Paulo officially became a city. The sleepy provincial town was jolted into prominence at the end of the 19th century as the coffee cycle took hold and railway expansion throughout the **Paulista Plateau** transformed the city into the most important center of the province. Enormous coffee plantations, called *fazendas*, swept over the area, creating power and wealth for its owners and scores of job opportunities for the lower-class. **Dumont**, the most famous coffee farm at the end of the 19th century, was practically a city in itself, with 13,000 acres of coffee fields and 5,000 live-in employees. When slavery was abolished in 1881, waves of immigrants descended on the plantations, offering a cheap form of labor. Italians were the first to arrive, followed by a boatload of 781 Japanese in 1808. Dreaming of making a little money, then returning to their homeland, the Japanese were spurred on by agricultural conquests; by the second generation, they had progressed from working the fields to selling produce. Today, some of the largest industries in Brazil are owned by Japanese descendants.

São Paulo's industrial boom began in the 20th century, gaining extraordinary proportions after World War II. Factories cropped up, invading the lowlands and attracting more immigrants, who began to change the economic and cultural face of the city. Jews of Eastern European origin came to Brazil as itinerant peddlars and flocked to Bom Retiro, a *bairro* near the Luz train station. As they gathered economic power they moved the limits of the city even farther south, while Koreans—São Paulo's latest immigrants—moved in behind them. Arabs also started arriving in the early 20th century from Syria and Lebanon, bringing with them strong religious ties (divided equally between Muslims and Christians), as well as a penchant for excellent sweets and spicy cuisines (all of which can be found in the *bairro* around Rua 25 de Marco).

A BIRD'S EYE VIEW

Paulistanos have recently adopted the slogan "São Paulo cannot stop"—for good reason. At present, the city covers over 2,000 square kilometers, an area 3 times the size of Paris, but its outskirts are still snaking southward. The traditional heart of the city lies around **Praça da Sé,** an enormous concrete plaza throbbing with activity during the day and dominated by the **Catedral Metropolitana,** a towering neo-Gothic structure completed in 1954. Opposite the cathedral along Rua Boa Vista is the **Pátio do Colégio,** one of the few historical sites left in São Paulo, housing the first college and chapel of the Jesuit mission. Also located here is the home of the infamous **Marquesa de Santos,** mistress of Emperor Pedro I. North of Praça da Sé on Avenida Tiradentes 676 is the **Igreja e Convento da Luz,** an 18th-century Franciscan monastery that today houses the **Museu de Arte Sacra.**

The hub of the commercial district is **Avenida Paulista**, home to scores of companies and banks, including Bank of Tokyo, Bradesco, and Banco do Brasil. South of the commercial district, straddling Rua 13 de Maio, is **Bela Vista,** also known as **Bexiga** (São Paulo's Little Italy), where you can find hundreds of Italian cantinas and excellent pizzerias. South of Praça da Sé is the Japanese district of **Liberdade,** through which runs its main street, **Rua Galvão Bueno.** In the north of the city, **Bom Retiro** received the first Arab immigrants, though it is in the *bairro* of **Pacaembu** that Arabs and Jews continue to live together in harmony as they have for years. A number of the finer hotels, like the Maksoud Plaza and the Crown Plaza, are located in **Cerqueira César,** to the west of Bela Vista. Going south from Cerqueira César, you'll find the **Parque Ibirapuera. Jardins,** an elite neighborhood where magnates of industry live, is full of fine bars and shops; the area between Estados Unidos and Faria Lima streets are now being zoned to ensure that only houses will be built. One of the nicest neighborhoods to browse through by car is Morumbí, the site of fabulous mansions and an extravagant shopping mall by the same name.

SIGHTS

LIBERDADE: JAPAN TOWN

The home of the Japanese community in São Paulo, **Liberdade** is a colorful neighborhood full of wonderful sushi bars, native boutiques, and narrow cobblestone streets. A symbol of the neighborhood, the red oriental arches overhanging the main street, **Rua Galvão Bueno,** add an exotic flavor. The best time to visit is during one of the 4 Japanese festivals. On December 31, during the **New Year's Festival,** riceballs, eaten for good will, are distributed free of charge to all visitors during the street fair. The celebration of the **Buddha's Birthday** in January includes a procession of a statue of the Buddha carried by children dressed in ceremonial robes. During the **Festival of the Stars** (second Saturday in June), personal wishes are written on a piece of paper and attached to a stick of bamboo. Perhaps the most colorful event is the **Oriental Festival** (first Saturday in December), when the streets fill with people singing and dancing folkloric tunes in traditional costumes.

Every Sunday throughout the year, an **Oriental Fair** is held in the main square from 10:00 a.m. to 7:00 p.m., with vendors hawking plants, ceramics, crafts, and typical sweets.

The **Nikkey Palace Hotel** also organizes Japanese events throughout the year. Located on Rua Tomáz Gonzaga, **Maruyama** is the largest folklore and jewelry store in the neighborhood, with precious stones considerably cheaper than at H. Stern. For the area's best Japanese restaurants, see under *Restaurants*. For shopping in Liberdade, see under *Shopping*.

OTHER OUTINGS

Butantã Institute *Avenida Vital Brasil, 1500 Butantã);* ☎ *211–8211. Daily 8:00 a.m.-5:00 p.m., closed Monday. Fee about $2* Snake buffs will love the numerous displays of Amazon serpents, spiders, and scorpions at this research center, famous for the anti-venom serums it produces for domestic and international markets. The bus "Butantã" runs from Praça da República.

Exotiquarium *Morumbí Shopping Mall. 10:00 a.m.–10:00 p.m.* Rumored to be the largest aquarium in South America, it is, at the very least, the most exotic for a shopping mall. It even boasts a pink river dolphin. Once in the mall, you can eat, bowl, ice-skate, or shop.

Zoological Gardens *Avenida Miguel Stéfano, 4241 (Água Funda);* ☎ *276-0811. Daily 9:00 a.m.–5:00 p.m.* Ranking among the 10 largest and best equipped in the world, this zoo boasts over 2,500 animals and 130 species from lions, tigers, and monkeys to waterfowl and a nest of leaf-cutting ants in their natural environ. The gardens are well cultivated, and there are numerous snack bars.

Playcenter *Rua Dr. Rubens Meirelles, 380 Barra Funda);* ☎ *826-9511. Tuesday–Friday 2:00 p.m.–10:00 p.m., Saturday 2:00 p.m.–11:00 p.m., Sunday 10:00 a.m.–10:00 p.m.* Even *Paulistanos* in business suits talk wistfully about the largest amusement park in South America, and many adults play hooky to enjoy the dozens of rides scattered over the 180,000 square meters. The park also includes restaurants, snack bars, a 180-degree movie screen, and a cable car.

Jaraguá Peak *Via Anhaguera, kilometer 18* Located in the State Park of Jaraguá in 5 million square meters of green forest, the peak is 1,135 square meters high and offers an excellent panoramic view of the city. Easy treks can be made around a paved track, and there are numerous lakes for scenic picknicking.

Simba Safari *Avenida do Cursinho, 6338 (V. Morães);* ☎ *846-6249. Tuesday–Friday 10:00 a.m.–4:45 p.m., Saturday, Sunday, and holidays 9:00 a.m.–5:00 p.m.* A strange sight in a cosmopolitan city, but wild lions, camels, zebras, and monkeys do roam this 100,000-square-meter park, at peace in their natural habitats. Visitors are admitted for the safari-like tours in their own cars, or they may rent one. A cafeteria and playground are also available.

The Waves *Avenida Guido Caloi, 25;* ☎ *521-8666* Landscaped by Roberto Burle Marx, the first aquatic park in São Paulo was inaugurated in 1991 and is geared for irresistible fun. The main attractions are the swimming pools (with waves à la Wet 'n' Wild), as well as illuminated fountains, jet-streams, and water slides. There's also a sauna and an artificial solarium.

Ibirapuera Park Joggers should head straight for S.P.'s biggest park, designed by Oscar Niemeyer and landscape artist Roberto Burle Marx. Dominating the grounds are 4 lakes, a plant nursery, and a Japanese pavilion with a replica of the Kyoto Imperial Palace. The Museum of Contemporary Art is also located here, as is the Museum of Modern Art (MAM), the Aeronáutica Museum featuring the Santos Dumont airplane), and the Folklore Museum. The Planetarium presents shows at 4:00 p.m. and 6:00 p.m. weekends and holidays. To get here, take the Monções bus 675-C from the Ana Rosa metro station to the park.

MUSEUMS

São Paulo has scores of museums. Here are a few of the most interesting.

Museum de Arte de São Paulo *Avenida Paulista, 1578. Tuesday–Friday 1:00 p.m.–6:00 p.m., Saturday and Sunday 2:00 p.m.–6:00 p.m.* One of the finest art collections in Brazil, MASP has an impressive exhibition of masterpieces, including works by Rembrandt, Rubens, Renoir, Toulouse-Lautrec, and Raphael. The foremost Brazilian artists and sculptors are also represented. The building itself—a unique elevated rectangle supported by two bright-red panels split through the middle—has been cited often for architectural achievement.

Fundação Maria Luiza and Oscar Americano *Avenida Morumbí, 3700;* ☎ *842-0077. Tuesday–Sunday 10:00 a.m.–5:00 p.m.* Opposite the Palácio dos Bandeirantes (the seat of the State government), this museum is the former home of the industrialist Oscar Americano and shows just how the elite of Brazil have spent their riches. Important works of the famous Brazilian painters Di Calvacanti and Portinari are on display, as well as fine furnishings and memorabilia of the Brazilian royal family.

Casa do Bandeirante (Pioneer House) *Praça Monteiro Lobato;* ☎ *211-0920. Tuesday– Friday 10:30 a.m.–5:00 p.m., Saturday and Sunday 9:00 a.m.–5:00 p.m.* This living museum recreates the traditionally rustic homestead of 18th-century pioneers called *bandeirantes*, by whose courageous efforts the interior of São Paulo was settled.

Casa do Sertanista *Avenida Prof. Francisco Morato, 2200 (Caxingui);* ☎ *211-5341* Exhibitions of Indian folklore and handicrafts under the direction of the famed Indian researcher Orlando Villas Boas.

Museu da Imagem e do Som *Avenida Europa, 158. Tuesday–Sunday 2:00 p.m.–10:00 p.m.* Ongoing photo exhibitions and a back archive of Brazilian film, video, and music, which can be rented by the public.

Memorial da América Latina *Avenida Mário de Andrade, 664, next to the Barra Funda metro station. 9:00 a.m.–9:00 p.m.* Designed by Oscar Niemeyer to commemorate the solidarity of Latin America, this oddly shaped memorial resembles three lumps of chocolate ice cream with a splash of whipped cream on top. In the nearby museum complex is a spectacular array of Latin American crafts, a photo library, books, magazines, films from the continent, and a restaurant. During the weekends, drop by for free concerts by Brazilian and Latin musicians.

THE ESSENTIAL SÃO PAULO

WHERE TO STAY

São Paulo hotels are primarily geared for executives. The high and low season in São Paulo is nearly the opposite from that of Rio. Low season runs from December to February, (including the month of July which is school vacation). Active months, when rates are usually the highest, are August–November. Rates given here are usually the highest charged; negotiate for good deals during periods of low activity.

Best bets are the luxurious apart-hotels, whose rooms resemble high-class apartments, equipped with fully stocked kitchens and marvelous decor. Rates are usually much cheaper than comparable 5-star hotels, and all you forego are the bevy of restaurants, hair salons, and boutiques that crowd the lobbies of the larger hotels.

Very Expensive -------- **Over $140**

Expensive ------------- **$80–140**

Moderate -------------- **$40–80**

Inexpensive ----------- **Under $40**

5-Star ★

Maksoud Plaza
Al. Campinas, 150 (Bela Vista);
☎ *(11) 251–2233; FAX 251–4202; reservations: toll free 22) 800–1155*

A marvelous oasis from the city snarls, the Maksoud is one of the best-run hotels in São Paulo. The vine-entwined lobby, which has been compared to the Contemporary Hotel in Walt Disney World, is an extravaganza of dining areas and elite shops, calmed by the ever-constant rush of waterfalls. Not a place for screaming kids, the hotel attracts guests like David Rockefeller and Henry Kissinger, who enjoy the $1,200-a-day Presidential Suite. Rooms are built in circular fashion around an open lobby; management has been known to drop watermelons from the 21st floor just to test security's reactions.

Music seems to be everywhere. At the 150 Club, jazz greats like Earl Hines and Carmen McRae perform regularly to packed houses; *chorinhos* can be heard in the Batidas e Petiscos Bar, soft jazz with a renowned trumpeter in the Trianon Bar, and classical concerts Wednesday–Sunday in the theater. The 5 restaurants are all top class: a Scandinavian buffet, a Japanese sushi bar, a barbecue grill, a gourmet pizzeria, and a 5-star French gourmet. Society ladies take afternoon tea in the atrium, serenaded by chamber music, and cultural events, seminars, and sneak previews are held in the theater. Standards, attractively appointed with modern art, boast electronic controls, blackout curtains, minibar, makeup mirror, bathroom phone, and tubs. Special Trinitron TVs offer 120 channels with in-house video. Japanese breakfast is available, as are special secretarial services. Most important, the management is intimately involved with the personal needs of each client; a computerized system records all personal requests in case of return visits. In its relentless pursuit of novel entertainment, the hotel has even hosted cow-milking contests in the lobby. 416 apartments. *Very expensive. All cards.*

★ **Caesar Park**
Rua Augusta, 1508 (Cerqueira César);
☎ *(11) 285–6622; FAX 288–6146*

One block from Paulistano Avenida, the commercial heart of downtown, the Caesar Park caters to captains of industry and top-level execs with special needs. Long a favorite among Japanese clientele who appreciate the exquisite decor, the 17-year-old hotel is now actively seeking the American market, particularly women traveling alone. Like its sister hotel in Rio, the Caesar Park is now part of the Weston chain. Every nook and cranny of the hotel is impeccably appointed, including the walnut-walled, British-style pub with live music nightly. Special gastronomic festivals add excitement; *feijoada* is served Wednesday, and the Japanese restaurant is considered one of the best in the city. Bedrooms all have scales, hairdryers, makeup mirrors, and safes. Japanese-style apartments, equipped with futons, low tables, and bamboo screens, have become the rage among honeymooners. A renowned hairdresser, Jacques Janine, is on premises, as well as a sauna, outdoor pool, and masseur. 177 apartments. *Very expensive. All cards.*

Sheraton Mofarrej & Towers
Al. Santos, 1437 (Cerqueira César);
☎ *(11) 284–5544; FAX 289–8670*
From the gold sculptures to the gold elevators to the black marble floors, covered in priceless Oriental rugs, the Sheraton's lobby looks like an Arabian palace. A veritable wonder, the Presidential suite takes up the entire 22nd floor. The Vivaldi restaurant boasts a stunning wraparound view of the city. The coffee shop is a study in waterfalls. All bedrooms come equipped with hairdryers, scales, special mirrors, and safes. The outdoor pool is decorated like a tropical jungle, and the indoor pool is bordered by fine wood-plank floors. Equipped with a masseur, the health club also offers weight-training and dry sauna. 244 apartments. *Very expensive. All cards.*

Grand Hotel Ca' d'Oro
Rua Augusta, (129 Centro);
☎ *(11) 256–8011; FAX 231–0359*
This hotel oozes with old-world charm, the kind appreciated by clients like the King of Spain. Owned by a traditional Italian family for the last 38 years, the hotel actually resembles a small village, with a maze of corridors that connect the original building to the newer annex. Standards in the old building must rate as the largest in São Paulo, but the tradeoff is out-of-date furniture, which leaves a heavy impression. Lunch buffets look out onto the pool, with its barbecue area and playground. A second pool is located rooftop. To complete the patriarchal touch, there's a snooker room, a reading room, and the top-class Ca D'Oro restaurant, one of the few city niteries where a tie is important. Sauna, gym, and hair salon are available for guests, but the most-favored meeting place is the lounge, where guests have been known to fight for space in front of the wood-burning fireplace. 290 apartments. *Expensive. All cards.*

★ São Paulo Hilton
Avenida Ipiranga, (165 Centro);
☎ *(11) 256–0033; FAX 257–3137*
This circular, 33-story high-rise boasts the fine service and attractive decor of Hiltons worldwide. Many execs come just to breakfast in the attractive coffee shop, which serves a groaning buffet. The top 3 executive floors require a special key, and VIP guests may take their breakfast and cocktails in a private lounge serviced by bilingual receptionists from 7:00 a.m.–10:00 p.m. A full array of gourmet restaurants and intimate bars make socializing pleasant, and an adjacent shopping arcade serves all needs. Individual rooms are spacious, with extremely comfortable beds. There's also a steam room and pool. The only drawback is the hotel's location in the old section of downtown, now a magnet for sleazy characters, prostitutes, and transvestites who stroll the surrounding streets after the sun goes down. To be safe, don't walk around the area at night and always take taxis. 380 apartments. *Very expensive. All cards.*

Crowne Plaza
Rua Frei Caneca, (1360 Cerqueira César);
☎ *(11) 284–1144; FAX 251–3121*
Only 5 years old, the Crowne Plaza boasts the highest occupancy factor in the city. The American Airlines crew on the São Paulo–Miami flight stays here, and for good reason—the gym is excellent, the rooms spacious, and the lunch buffet, with its huge grill of shrimp, fish, and paella, looks inviting. Located 50 meters from Paulistano Avenida, the hotel is also within sneezing distance of 10 international banks. The lobby sports a fantastic view of the garden, which creates a haunting optical illusion. Friday nights, a jam session with visiting musicians draws crowds in the hotel's new cultural center. On Wednesday and Saturday *feijoada* buffets are served. Most standards have queen-size beds; all have tubs, large

mirrors, hairdryers, and safes. An extensive gym is equipped with free weights, bikes, saunas, and a small Jacuzzi. A concierge floor serves private breakfast for VIP clients, as well as a free bar and secretarial service. Non-smoking floor. 223 apartments. *Expensive. All cards.*

4-Star

Nikkey Palace

Rua Galvão Bueno, 425; ☎ *(11) 270-8511; FAX 270-6614*

In the heart of the Japanese district, this hotel is the place to be during the Japanese festivals (including New Year's Eve and Buddha's birthday), when the neighboring streets are filled with parades and festivities. About 70 percent of the clientele are Japanese, who enjoy the optional Japanese breakfast of rice, soy sauce, soup, and fish. The furniture also suits Japanese needs—low, sedate furniture (although some pieces look a bit worn). Best bets are junior suites, about twice as large as a 5-star double, for about the same price. The Japanese restaurant in the basement is the largest in the city. The men-only sauna, frequented by yuppies and a variety of artists, was ranked the best in São Paulo by *Playboy* magazine. Shiatzu for both men and women is available Tuesday–Saturday. Recent renovations intended to extend the capacity of the hotel. 95 apartments. *Moderate–expensive. All cards.*

Eldorado Boulevard

Avenida São Luis, 234 (Centro);
☎ *(11) 256-8833; FAX 222-7194*

International execs, mostly from the U.S. and Argentina, populate the Eldorado, located downtown. The 24-hour coffee shop is frequented by TV and theater actors, usually after midnight. Rooms are more serviceable than luscious, with color TV and minibar; some rooms have tubs. The exec floor is not substantially nicer, but VIP service does include fruit bowls, shoeshines, and robes. Suites have a living room, dressing room, and a large bath, plus an outdoor veranda; 11th floor is nonsmoking. An international restaurant and self-service buffet, plus a bar, round out the culinary needs. 157 apartments. *Expensive. All cards.*

Fortune Residence and Executive Service

Rua Haddock Lobo, 804 (Jardins); ☎ *(11) 282-8697; FAX 815-5323*

This apart-hotel is considered the best in São Paulo. Though the 2-room apartments are owned by individual investors, an excellent management supervises the 42 apartments and provides security and maid service. The living room is extremely classy, though the bedroom is small. A balcony provides additional space. Complimentary breakfast is served in the coffee shop, as well as light meals and snacks. There is also a pool, gym, and sauna. A full set of kitchen utensils is available on request. Other services include: 110 volts, central air-conditioning, and convention room. Apartments start at $131, children up to 12 are free. *Very expensive. All cards.*

3-Star

Excelsior Hotel

Avenida Ipiranga, 770; ☎ *(11) 222-7377; FAX 222-8369*

A complex of 180 simple apartments with phone, air-conditioning, and TV. There's also a coffee shop, bar, and barbershop. Singles run about $41, doubles $52. 180 apartments. *Moderate. All cards.*

Fuji Palace

Largo da Pólvora, 120; ☎ *(11) 278-7466; FAX 279-9041*

This adequate hotel is located in the Japanese district, where you can enjoy the streetside atmosphere and the excellent cuisine. Rooms include minibar, TV, phone, and air-conditioning. Singles run about $45, doubles $56. 77 apartments. *Moderate. No cards.*

2-Star

Esplanada Hotel

Largo do Arouche, 414; ☎ *(11) 220-5711*

Modest but clean apartments located downtown with minibar, air-conditioning, and TV. Singles run $17, doubles $24. 48 apartments. *Inexpensive. No cards.*

Regência

Avenida São João, 1523; ☎ *(11) 220-9611*

As simple as they come without getting

seedy. Rooms have phone, radio, TV, and minibar. Singles run $18, doubles $23. 49 apartments. *Inexpensive. No cards.*

WHERE TO EAT

São Paulo is the culinary capital of South America. Eating well is the way *Paulistanos* like to spend their hard-earned paychecks, and they do it in fabulous surroundings; this is a town where the bathrooms of some 5-star restaurants are as beautiful as the dining rooms. Quality, not quantity, is the rage here, as well as an endless list of possibilities: from Scandinavian buffets to *wienerschnitzel* to the tiniest portions of *nouvelle cuisine*, with every ethnic group represented. Like clothes and music, restaurants in São Paulo are subject to the cruel winds of trendiness (*Paulistanos* are known to be incredibly fickle), but the restaurants I've listed here tend to make the best lists every year. Dinner service starts no earlier than 8:00 p.m., but restaurants don't reach their peak service till after 11:00 p.m. Dress can be surprisingly casual; the only night businessmen don't need to wear a tie is Saturday. (You must, however, always wear one at the Jockey Club and the restaurant Cuisine du Soleil at the Maksoud Plaza.) Restaurant rows include Rua Haddock Lobo and Rua 13 de Maio in the Italian district. Arab restaurants are located along Rua 25 de Março.

Expensive -------------- **$30 up**

Moderate -------------- **$10–$25**

Inexpensive ------------ **Under $10**

Brazilian/Portuguese
Abril em Portugal
Rua Caio Prado, 47 (Consolação);
☎ *256–5160. Daily 8:00 p.m.–last client, closed Sunday*
Portugal in April (as the name says) is what this restaurant recreates—from the Portuguese-inspired panels and ceramic tiles to the Iberian cuisine. Add strolling guitarists and some of the best *fado* singers in the city. *Moderate. No cards.*
Bacalhau do Rei
Avenida Moaci, 279 (Moema);
☎ *533–4318. Daily 11:00 a.m.–midnight, Sunday 11:00 a.m.–5:00 p.m., closed Monday*
Near the Central Market, this is the leading eatery for Portuguese-style codfish. Stained-glass windows from the '30s adorn the walls. *Moderate. Cards: D, MC.*
Bolinha
Avenida Cid Jardim, 53 (Jardim Europa);
☎ *852–9526. Daily 11:00 a.m.–1:00 a.m.*
Best *feijoada* in São Paulo in a modest environ. *Moderate. All cards.*
O Profeta
Rua dos Aicás, 40 (Indianópolis);
☎ *549–5311. Daily 11:45 a.m.–1:00 a.m.*
Typical Brazilian food with a Mineiro swing—that heavy but delicious fare from the state of Minas Gerais. The waiters dress as monks, hence the name The Prophet, but live music cuts through any signs of encroaching piety. *Moderate. All cards.*

Churrascaria
Baby Beef Paes Mendonça
Avenida Nações Unidas, 16741 (Morumbí);
☎ *843–7829. Daily 11:30 a.m.–1:00 a.m*
Always a reliable, if not excellent steakhouse situated near the Morumbí Shopping Center, next to Carrefour, a gargantuan-sized supermarket where the clerks wear rollerskates and very short skirts. *Moderate. All cards.*
Esplanada Grill
Rua Haddock Lobo, 1682 (Cerqueira César); ☎ *881–3199. Daily noon–3:00 p.m., 7:00 p.m.–1:30 a.m.*
The young, hip, and restless attend this steakery right next to the classy Fasano. That means who's who at the next table is more important than what's on your plate. *Moderate. Cards: MC, D.*
★ **The Place**
Rua Haddock Lobo, 1550 (Cerqueira César); ☎ *282–5800. Daily 11:30 a.m.– 1:30 a.m.*
The place you *must* visit at least 3 times: once for drinks, once for dinner, and once for dessert. Start with complimentary hors d'oeuvres in the plush, carriagehouse bar—a tiny feast of mini-pizzas, nuts, and cro-

quettes. Dinners (including a huge self-serve salad buffet) are prepared tableside; don't miss the house rice, sauteed with onions, crispy sliced potatoes, and oven-fried eggs. Fish like the *truta à jardineira* (trout) is favorably seasoned, but the grilled beefs are also superb, and the *carpaccio* with cheese strips, onions, and toast is out of this world. Desserts like the papaya and chocolate mousses are worth their own trip. Damage for two without wine is about $40. Reserve. *Expensive. All cards.*

French

★ La Casserole

Largo do Arouche, 346; ☎ *220–6283. Daily noon–3:00 p.m., 7:00 p.m.–midnight, closed Tuesday*

French peasant cooking as cozy as a warm iron pot. Walnut-carved chandeliers and blowups of Notre Dame enhance the continental ambiance of this very old, very established restaurant, once featured in *Gourmet* magazine. *Inexpensive–Moderate. All cards.*

Le Bistingo

Al. Franca, 580 (Cerqueira César), ☎ *289–3010. Tuesday–Friday noon–3:00 p.m., 7:00 p.m.–midnight; Saturday 7:00 p.m.–1:00 a.m.; Sunday noon–4:00 p.m., 7:00 p.m.–11:00 p.m., closed Monday*

One of the city's best French restaurants, Bistingo is patterned after the original in Paris—candlelit elegance and private banquettes. Specialties are fish, particularly poached haddock with roquefort, and grilled shrimp with apples. Lunch is usually packed, and you'll also need a reservation on weekends, when the wait can be at least a half hour. Two, with wine, runs about $100. *Expensive. No cards.*

German

Arnold's Naschbar

Rua Pereira Leite, 98; ☎ *256–5648. Monday–Saturday 6:00 p.m.–midnight*

One of the best German eateries in the city, with a romantic ambiance and generous portions of trout, *picanha*, and stuffed chicken breasts. *Moderate. No cards.*

International

★ Ouro Velho Jardins

Al. Jaú, 1617 (Cerqueira César); ☎ *881–0271. Daily noon–3:00 p.m., 7:00 p.m.–midnight*

For the last 27 years, Senhor Bené and his family have been dedicated to quality at this elegant French-style bistro (the name means "Old Gold"). The menu is small but finely executed, with the house chateaubriand a clear winner. *Feijoada* is served on Saturday. The flurry of waiters around each table makes you feel you're at a private party, and the clientele is always upper-crust. *Expensive. All cards.*

Moraes

Praça Júlio de Mesquita, 175; ☎ *221–8066. Daily 11:00 a.m.–2:00 a.m.*

A favorite dive of chef Massimo Ferrari who raves about the fabulous steak grilled in garlic and oil. You may have to shoo away the pimps and prostitutes, but that's part of the scene. *Inexpensive. Cards: MC, D.*

Italian

Ca' D'Oro

(Grande Hotel Ca' D'Oro) Rua Augusta, 129; ☎ *256–8011. Daily noon-2:30 p.m., 7:00 p.m.–10:30 p.m.*

The John Houseman of restaurants: where the waiters are humorless, but the service is faultless and the Northern Italian cuisine favored by heads of state is exceptional. Pasta melted with four cheeses is a sensual explosion, as is the traditional *casconcelli bergamasca*, sweet-and-sour ravioli plumped with various meats, raisins, and a splash of amaretto. The best dessert is the *torroncina*, ice cream loaded with peanuts and caramel. Two can eat for about $40 (minus wine), surrounded by century–old chandeliers, antique serving tables, and a kitchen so clean they insisted on showing me. Reserve. *Expensive–very expensive. All cards.*

Cantina Balilla

Rua do Gasômetro, 332 (Brás); ☎ *228–8282. Daily 11:00 a.m.–2:00 a.m.*

Small, old-fashioned, and humble with superb Italian food and moderate prices. Live music. *Moderate. All cards.*

Fasano
Rua Haddock Lobo, 1644 (Cerqueira César); ☎ *852–4000. Daily 8:00 p.m.–1:30 a.m., closed Sunday*

The late Italian-born Victor Fasano served Eisenhower and Dietrich. Forty years later in 1991, his grandchildren revived his top-class eatery in a spectacularly remodeled mansion. Service is something from an MGM movie: waiters love to remove silver covers with a musical flourish. Unfortunately, the portions, though beautifully arranged, are so *small* they are almost laughable. Still, the *tortelloni di zucca* is impressive as is the tangy passion fruit mousse with a blueberry sauce. Ask to tour the wine cellar, one of the best in the city. No ties necessary, but the ambiance is classy. Reserve. *Expensive–very expensive. All cards.*

★ Mássimo
Al. Santos, 1826 (Cerqueira César); ☎ *284–0311. Daily 11:30 a.m.–3:00 p.m., 7:00 a.m.–midnight*

If Mássimo was the only reason to come to São Paulo, it would be enough. Everything about Mássimo Ferrari's top-class restaurant bespeaks his personality—passionate, tender, and full of great humor. An Italian-Brazilian, Mássimo learned to cook from his mother when he was 9; today, his repertoire of over 800 dishes has brought him a world-class rep. If he has any philosophy, it is to mine the simplicity of food by exploiting its natural sensuality. Even the restaurant is sensuous, from the enormous poinsettias to the luxurious table settings and the Versailles-like bathrooms. The feast Mássimo cooked me was a dream: velvety cream-filled gnocchis, perfectly grilled goatlegs and *picanha*, exquisitely baked trout with shrimp sauce, finely herbed wild rice and ratatouille—every dish, accompanied by its own special wine, was a wonder of subtle flavors and spices. The *couvert* alone—plates of freshly baked croissants, breads, sweet butters, and paté—was an embarrassment of riches. Only a small percentage of Brazilians can afford the stiff prices, about $30 per person), but no traveling gourmet should ever pass up the opportunity to dine here or just come for drinks and dessert—the Brazilian guitarist in the plush bar is superb. The night isn't over, however, until Mássimo bounds out of the kitchen, pulls up his suspenders, and shrugs, "Simple, very simple."

Mezzaluna
Rua Bela Cintra, 2231 (Jd. Paulista); ☎ *881–8633. Daily noon–3:30 p.m., 7:00 p.m.–2:00 a.m.*

Live music and good Italian food at affordable prices. *Moderate. No cards.*

Japanese

The best Japanese restaurants with the most reasonable prices are located on Rua Tomás Gonzaga in Liberdade, the Japanese district. Service is friendly, if inscrutable; you'll be lucky to find waiters who speak Portuguese, let alone English. The street action in Liberdade, alone, is worth the trek, especially at night, when Japanese lanterns illuminate the atmospheric sidewalks.

Gombe
Rua Tomás Gonzaga, 22A (Liberdade); ☎ *279–8499. Daily 11:30 a.m.–2:00 p.m., 6:00 p.m.–midnight, closed Sunday*

The menu is in Japanese, but the waiters understand "sushi," "sashimi" and "yakitori" in any accent. Noodles run about $3.50, raw fish dishes about $7. Look for the rustic Japanese country design next to the Casa Ono bookstore.

Sushi Yassu
Rua Tomás Gonzaga, 110 A (Liberdade); ☎ *279–6622. Daily 11:30 a.m.–2:30 p.m. and 6:30 a.m.–12:30 a.m.*

Sushi bar plus private rooms, next door to Maruyama, with Japanese music and air-conditioned comfort.

Mariko
(Caesar Park Hotel) Rua Augusta, 1508; ☎ *285–6622*

Superlative cuisine at top-dollar prices, in one of the most elegant hotels in the city.

Hidetaka Kanazawa
Rua Galvão Bueno, 378; ☎ *270–1801*

Not a restaurant, but a takeout counter, selling all kinds of Japanese sweets and confections.

Jewish

Z Deli
Al. Santos, 1518 (Cerqueira César); ☎ 285–6509. Daily 7:00 a.m.–7:00 p.m., Saturday 6:00 p.m.–midnight, closed Sunday
Kosher food and deli-style goodies, herring with *creme de leite*, and quiches stuffed with cheese, salmon, mushrooms, and leeks. *Inexpensive. No cards.*

★ **Cecília**
Rua dos Bandeirantes, 112 (Bom Retiro); ☎ 228–9174. Daily 11:30 a.m.–3:30 p.m., closed Monday
Cecília Judkowitz had to move after seven years to accommodate the growing bevy of fans who clamor for her gefilte fish, kreplach, and marinated herring with homemade mayonnaise and onions. Delicious desserts include fruit compotes and ricotta and apple tarts. The surrounding neighborhood is known for its wholesale houses.

Pizza

La Brasserie
(Maksoud Plaza Hotel) Al. Campinas, 150; ☎ 251–2233
A late-night hangout open around the clock, with irresistible gourmet pizzas (try the one with escargot).

Cristal
Rua Arthur Ramos, 551; ☎ 210–2767. Daily 7:00 p.m.–1:30 a.m., Fri. and Sat. till 2 a.m.
The pizzeria most frequented by famous people, who adore the fine crusts and salad bar. You can also order grilled meats. *Moderate. No cards.*

Michelluccio
Rua da Consolação, 2396; ☎ 256–5477 and Avenida Pompéia, 600. Daily 5:00 p.m.–1:00 a.m.; Friday, Saturday and Sunday until 3:00 a.m.
An unabashed favorite in the city, for its thick-crusted pizzas and creative toppings. *Inexpensive. Cards: DC, MC.*

Rm With a Vu

Terraço Itália
Avenida Ipiranga, 344 (Edifício Itália, across from the Hilton Hotel); ☎ 257–6888. Daily noon–2:00 a.m., dinner at 8:30 p.m., dancing at 9:30 p.m.
São Paulo from the 41st floor is the place to which rich *Paulistanos* drag out-of-towners whom they want to impress. The view is awesome; unfortunately, the international cuisine is somewhat lackluster. Better to nurse a cocktail in the wonderful leather-and-wood bar, or boogie on the dance floor to a live band. If you do choose to eat, you'll find the waiters impeccable, and your dinner can be prepared by the time you are seated. Filet mignon comes with herbs and madeira sauce; the trout with a serviceable cream sauce. I was here in a brilliant rain-and-lightning storm, which, despite not one square inch of view, was still wildly exciting. Reserve. *Expensive–very expensive. All cards.*

Sandwiches

La Cave
Rua Clodomiro Amazonas, 77 (Itaim Bibi); ☎ 829–0859. Daily 10:00 a.m.–midnight, closed Sunday
Excellent for sandwiches, with 15 types of rolls, 12 kinds of Italian breads, and a cornucopia of fillings. Try a La Cave: ham, buffalo cheese, and artichoke hearts on a baguette. *Inexpensive. No cards.*

Scandinavian

Viking
(Maksoud Plaza Hotel) Al. Campinas, 150; ☎ 251–2233
This fabulous Scandinavian buffet (for lunch only) offers smoked salmon, cold salads, liver paté, and steak tartare for about $15. *Moderate. All cards.*

Vegetarian

Salad's
Avenida Brig. Faria Lima, 1191 (Shopping Center Iguatemí); ☎ 210–2277. Monday–Friday noon–3:30 p.m., Saturday and Sunday noon–5:00 p.m.
Flowered wallpaper, wicker dividers, and faux blue skies make a light and airy environ for chic salad eaters. A different buffet of 12 salads is offered daily—Wednesdays is devoted to fish salads. A special baker makes stunning desserts in big tulip glasses: the *Torta*

de Belmont, topped with whipped icream and fudge sauce, is superb, but the coconut ice cream is the best in the city. Saturdays are packed with shoppers from Iguatemí Mall next door, so make a reservation. *Expensive. No cards.*

Cheiro Verde

Rua Peixoto Gomide, 1413 (Cerqueira César); ☎ 289–6853. *Monday–Friday noon–3:00 p.m.; Saturday and Sunday noon–3:00 p.m., 7:00 p.m.–10:30 p.m. (later on Saturday)*

Vegetarians should love the natural wood tables in this tiny house where salads run under $4. Excellent is the Primavera, a brown-rice casserole with *castanhas*, raisins, and cooked vegetables for under $5. A bulletin board with holistic and spiritually oriented activities adorns the front hallway. *Inexpensive–moderate. No cards.*

(Cheap) Vegetarian

Here are some inexpensive vegetarian restaurants where you can get fresh cooked veggies, salad, hot entrée, and dessert for under $4.

Cachoeira Tropical

Rua João Cachoeira, 275

Next door to a homeopathy store.

DA Dieta Alimentos Dietético

Rua Clodomiro Amazonas, loja 4; ☎ 820–4534

Diet foods and products.

Associação Macrobiótica

Rua Bela Cintra, 1235 (Cerqueira César); ☎ 282–8831. *Daily 11:00 a.m.–2:30 p.m., 5:30 p.m.–7:45 p.m., closed Saturday and Sunday*

A fixed menu of brown rice, cereals, vegetables, and fish.

Tea Houses

As Noviças

Avenida Cotovia, 205 (Moema); ☎ 533–0692. *Daily 3:00 p.m.–11:00 p.m.*

Take tea in this convent-styled teahouse with piped-in Gregorian chants and handsome waiters dressed like friars. A fixed price (about $8) includes 63 kinds of delicacies, plus excellent hot chocolate, tea, or *café com leite*. *Moderate. All cards.*

Twenty-four Hours

Café Brasserie Belavista

Alameda Campinas, 150; ☎ 251–2233

A great place to collapse, this café, located in the gorgeous Maksoud Plaza Hotel, is sometimes busier at 4:00 a.m. than it is all day. You'll find fast-cooked food and pizzas, as well as an excellent tea served daily from 3:00 p.m.–6:00 p.m.

Fran's Café

Avenida Ipiranga, 354, Edificio Itália

This little bar serves coffee, cakes, and cookies day or night. *Inexpensive. No cards.*

With Music

Café Piu-Piu

Rua Treze de Maio, 134; ☎ 258–8066. *Daily 8:30 p.m.–3:00 a.m., closed Monday*

One of the busiest bars in Bexiga, with good shows of jazz, country, and rock. Cover runs about $3. *Inexpensive. No cards.*

Café Teatro Opus 2004

Rua Pamplona, 1187; ☎ 884–9086. *Daily 8:00 p.m.–last client, closed Sunday, Monday and Wednesday*

One of the best clubs for all kinds of music. Tuesday is blues night, Thursday jazz, Friday and Saturday are covered by excellent house bands. Shows start at 10:00 p.m., cover runs about $4. *Inexpensive. All cards.*

Cauã

Rua Alvaro Anes, 43 (Pinheiros); ☎ 815–1326. *Daily noon–last client*

Eat Latin (*empanadas* and Argentine chicken) listening to folkloric Latin American music. Cover runs about $3, and sometimes includes a flamenco show or set by famous Latin percussionists. *Moderate. Cards: AE.*

NIGHTLIFE

Hotel Bars

Chariot

(Caesar Park Hotel) Rua Augusta, 1508; ☎ 285–6622

Daily 11:30 a.m.–2:00 a.m. The best hotel bar in S.P.—elegant, calm, with the feel of a plush English pub. From Mon.–Sat. 8 p.m.–midnight, a fine local pianist plays classical American music, jazz, and MPB. *Moderate. All cards.*

Nightclubs

Nightclub hopping in São Paulo can be as easy as strolling down **Rua Franz Schubert**. During the day this tiny 200-meter street doesn't look like much, but at night, it transforms into Party Alley, with six major nightclubs lined up along the left side of the street. Like *cariocas*, *Paulistanos* start partying late and don't go home til dawn. The dress code aims towards the provocative; for women, short skirts are *de rigueur*. One tip: some clubs require loads of attitude, others just a penchant for down-home fun.

Gallery
Rua Haddock Lobo, 1626; ☎ *881–8833. Tuesday–Saturday 8:00 p.m.-2:00 a.m.*
The ultimate in snobbery, with a reception desk manned by David Bowie–like androids. The restaurant/nightclub belongs to Victor Olivia and the decorator Uza da Pau, who has pitted real Italian sculptures against Aubusson tapestries and baroque candelabras. Clients of 5-star hotels receive special passes to grace the hallowed halls. Dinner for 2 (specialties include duck) runs about $100; live jazz in the lush piano bar, drinks included, runs about $30. Best to go on Tuesday and Wednesday when the disco is free, and the piano bar drops its minimum. A block away is The Place restaurant. *Very expensive. All cards.*

Up and Down
Rua Pamplona, 1418; ☎ *285–1081*
The disco of São Paulo, where everyone gives everyone the twice lookover. Great Latin dance music, American rock, voluble DJs, and huge TV screens showing old movies. This is neon flash-and-dash at its best. *Moderate. No cards.*

Cotton Club
Rua Franz Schubert, 59; ☎ *814–0515. Tuesday–Saturday 9:30 p.m.–last client, peaks after 11:30 p.m.*
With rustic wood pews downstairs and a flashdance disco upstairs, this cavernlike club caters to the 25–35 crowd and offers the best blues, jazz, and rock in the city. Three different types of bands play nightly. Tuesday night's Chippendale-type striptease for women only attracts the elite of São Paulo (tickets, about $25, must be bought two weeks in advance). Cover for the club is $7, drink minimum $13. *Moderate. All cards.*

Stardust
Rua Franz Schubert, 135; ☎ *210–5283. Daily 9:30 p.m.–4:00 a.m.*
Some tourists might find this dinner and dancing club corny, but owner Alan Gordon's joie de vivre can't be faulted. Russian Jewish by way of Shanghai, Gordon fronts an indefatigable New Orleans-style band and shmoozes with customers between sets. Clients can dance Charlestons until four in the morning. *Moderate. All cards.*

Tramp
Rua Franz Schubert, 159; ☎ *210–9093. Daily 8:00 p.m.–last client*
Since Brazilians go to clubs as prelude to more intimate doings, this elite private club for the 25–40 set rates as perfect foreplay. Prospective members are scrutinized, but tourists, if they call ahead, are welcome inside for a drink. The piano bar is pink, mauve, and cushy; the dance floor hot. *Moderate. All cards.*

Crowne Plaza Theatre
Crowne Plaza Hotel) Rua Frei Caneca, 1360 (Cerqueira César); ☎ *284–1144. Daily midnight–4:00 a.m.*
Friday night jam sessions are held here, in the hotel's new cultural center, where the week's featured musicians invite their friends for a *canja* (the word actually means chicken soup, but refers to the time when musicians played just for their soup). Cover is $10. Reserve. *Moderate. All cards.*

Samba Shows

Palladium
(Shopping Center Eldorado, 3rd fl.) Avenida Rebouças, 3970; ☎ *814–9461*
Carnaval-based extravangas featuring *mulatas* dancing fast-moving sambas. *Moderate. All cards.*

Plataforma I
Avenida Paulista, 412 (Cerqueira César); ☎ *289–5238*
Mulatas in string bikinis, *capoeira* artists, folkloric music, and cheeky masters of ceremonies offer this samba extravaganza com-

SÃO PAULO (CITY)

plete with elaborate Carnaval costumes. *Moderate. All cards.*

GAY SÃO PAULO

Gays tend to frequent the sauna in the **Hilton**. Other gay bars and shows include:
Corintho
Al. dos Imarés, 64; ☎ *530-9780*
Live shows from Thursday–Sunday, with singers and dancers.
Homo Sapiens
Rua Marquês de Itú, 182; ☎ *221-4540*
Live shows starting at 11:00 p.m., Thursday–Sunday.

> **Insider Tip:**
>
> *Transvestites tend to hang around the Hilton Hotel and have tricked a lot of tourists and Formula 1 drivers looking for women.*

SHOPPING

The main shopping streets are Rua Augusta (once the most chic area in S.P.), Rua Doutor Mario Ferraz, and Rua João Cachoeira (cheap). Rua Maracatins is full of stores and boutiques selling clothes and shoes at wholesale prices. Best buys are leather goods.

Native Handicrafts

Artíndia
Rua Augusta, 1371, #119 (Cerqueira César); ☎ *883-2102*
Here, you can buy native indigenous crafts made out of feathers, wood, and ceramics.
Casa do Amazonas
Avenida São Luis, 187, store 14; ☎ *258-9727*
A large variety of authentic indigenous art, specializing in *arte plumária*—extravagant headdresses and sculptures made out of exotic bird feathers.
Galeria de Arte Brasileira
Rua Al. Lorna, 2163; ☎ *853-8769*
A one-stop souvenir store sells Bahian and *candomblé* dolls, Indian baskets, *carajá* (fertility dolls), hand-carved wooden necklaces, T-shirts, native lace crafts, and *balangandãs* (traditional silver bracelets worn by slaves).

Stones

Park-Pedras
Rua Augusta, 1523; ☎ *288-0819*
Large selection of precious and semi-precious stones from the mines of Minas, with an adjoining factory that makes jewelry.

Street Fairs

Arte e Artesanato
(Art and Handicraft) Praça da República. Sunday 8:00 a.m.–1:00 p.m.
A grand open-air bazaar of sweets, music, and crafts.
Artesanato Oriental
Praça da Liberdade. Sunday 8:00 a.m.–6:00 p.m.
Oriental handicrafts fair.
Antiguidade do MASP
Avenida Paulista, 1578. Sunday 10:00 a.m.–5:00 p.m.
The MASP antique fair.
Flower Market
Praça Charles Miller. Sunday.
A wonderful profusion of exotic and common flowers.
Embu
Sun. 9 a.m.–6 p.m.
Located 27 kilometers from the city, this colonial town has been transformed into an arts and crafts center—a kind of artistic Woodstock. Sundays feature a renown fair. Take bus #056 from the Conceição metro station or #179-S from the Tietê Rodoviária; the trip takes about an hour one way.

Shopping in Liberdade

Minikimono
Rua Galvão Bueno, 22 (Liberdade); ☎ *278-0322*
Liberdade is filled with antique and jewelry stores. This is one of the better clothes stores, with silk robes for about $50 and complete Ninja outfits for kids for about $35.

Shopping Malls

Shopping Center Iguatemí
Avenida Brigadeiro Faria Lima, 1191; ☎ *210-1333*
This is considered the best shopping mall in S.P. and a hangout for teens on the week-

ends. There are 5 cinemas, bank, and post office. At Lojas Americanas you can find Woolworth's-type items. Also Bruno Minelli (men's), Hi-Fi (records), Petistil (stylish children's wear), Joge (lingerie), Victor Hugo (leather), Bichodaseda (chic linen suits), Boat (punk), Sidewalk (teen's), Maria Bonita (best for chic women's clothes), and Rose Benedetti (internationally known for costume jewelry). The third floor is a food pavilion with pizzas, hot dogs, burgers, ice cream, and exquisite cakes.

Shopping Center Morumbí
Avenida Roque Petroni Jr., 1089;
☎ *533-2444*
One of the most exotic malls in Brazil, with an ice-skating rink, exotic aquarium, video game room, bowling, gourmet foods center, and even a lost-and-found center for kids. The most stylish stores in Brazil have branches here.

HANDS-ON SÃO PAULO

Arrival
International Varig flights from the States usually fly into São Paulo's International Airport (also called Guarulhos) after arriving direct in Rio. American Airlines also flies direct from New York's Kennedy Airport to São Paulo daily.
Domestic As the center of Brazilian industry, São Paulo can be easily reached from most major cities in the country. From Rio, take the air shuttle Ponte Aérea from the Santos Dumont Airport to the Congonhas Airport in São Paulo. Flights leave on the half hour from 6:30 a.m. to 10:30 p.m.; the fare is about $70 each way. Reservations are recommended, especially on the weekends. Taxis are available at both airports into the city for about $35. Cheaper is the airport bus, which runs between the International Airport and Congonhas and the downtown terminal at Praça da República at about half-hour intervals (45 minutes at night). A separate bus line can also take you to the Tietê Rodoviária, the city's main bus terminal. Fares run about $3.
Bus São Paulo can be reached by bus from Rio. The trip takes about 7 hours, with rest stops at about 2-hour intervals. The scenic route along the seashore on the Rio-Santos Highway is a lovely, relaxing way to see the coastline and backroad villages, but the buses are not air-conditioned. Express buses, which are air-conditioned, also run frequently between Rio and São Paulo.
Train The *Santa Cruz* passenger train runs between Rio and São Paulo and makes the 170-mile trek in about 9 hours. The train usually leaves at 11:30 p.m., with sleeper fare available.

Climate
From December to February, temperatures can reach 90°F. Between June and August, cold waves can plummet temperatures as low as freezing, but only for a few days. Lots of rainfall is received between January and March, when it's quite hot and humid. July days are beautiful.

City Transportation
Unless you're becoming a native, forgo the bus system and splurge on taxis. They're safer, faster, and a lot less taxing on the nerves. Bus service to the airport, however, can save you up to $30 one way.
Taxi Most hotels offer luxury taxis, paged by your concierge. Cheaper rates can be had from radio taxis, ☎ *251-1733*. White and blue taxis serve Guarulhos only; ☎ *940-7070*. For service to Santos and Guarujá, call Expresso Luxo ☎ *223-5161*.
Bus For bus service to the International Airport, ☎ *221-9103*. The major bus station is the Terminal Rodoviário do Tietê *Avenida Cruzeiro do Sul 1800;* ☎ *235-0322*. A second terminal is located at Terminal Rodoviário do Jabaquara *Rua Jequitibá;* ☎ *577-0872*.

Consulates
American Consulate General *Rua Padre João Manuel 933;* ☎ *881-6511*.
Canadian Consulate General *Avenida Paulista 854, 5th floor;* ☎ *287-2122*.
British Consulate General *Avenida Paulista 1938, 7th floor;* ☎ *287-7722*.

Emergencies
Police ☎ *190*.

Special police headquarters for foreign visitors ☎ 251-1733.
Drugstores on duty ☎ 136.

English
English is spoken at all 5-star hotels, better restaurants, at a few downtown shops, and in some shopping malls.

Hair Salons
The best hair salons are the Colonial, L'Officel, and Beka.

Medical Emergencies
Two excellent Oriental doctors are Mestre Liu Pai Lin ☎ 852-2258 for Tai-chi and healing teas and Jojima ☎ 852-2476 for acupuncture and teas.

Money Exchange
Currency can be exchanged at the São Paulo International Airport (Guarulhos) and at banks throughout the city. Look for travel agencies marked *câmbio* along Avenida São Luiz (downtown), near the Praça da República, on Avenida Paulista (Jardins area), and in the Iguatemí shopping center. Major hotels will exchange money and traveler's checks, but beware: The rate you will receive for the dollar at a hotel will probably be lower than the tourist dollar.

Newspapers
The major newspapers are *O Estado de São Paulo* and *A Folha da Tarde*. Hotel newsstands usually sell international editions of *Time* and *Newsweek*, as well as the *International Herald Tribune*.

Points Beyond
Direct flights are available to other Brazilian cities from Guarulhos: Manaus (4 hours); Salvador (2 hours); Brasília (90 minutes); Belo Horizonte (90 minutes); Iguaçu Falls (90 minutes).

Safety
Among the 500,000 foreigners living in São Paulo you'll be less conspicuous as a tourist than in Rio. Most *Paulistanos*, even if they don't speak English, will try to be helpful, though do take the common precautions of securing your wallet and purse and leaving the jewelry at home. A team of 50 elite police speak English and have lessened the force of *trombadinhas* (kids who snatch purses). Areas to avoid: downtown, particularly at night.

Tourist Information
Ample information in English is available at tourist information booths located at Praça da República, Teatro Municipal, Praça da Sé, Praça da Liberdade (downtown), and the Ibirapuera, Morumbí, and Iguatemí shopping malls. For weekly events, shows, and trendy clubs, pick up a copy of *Veja São Paulo*, part of the weekly magazine *Veja*. The English publications *Where* and *São Paulo This Month* also give good tips and are available at most hotels.

The **São Paulo Convention and Visitors Bureau** *Rua Alameda Campinas, 646, 5th floor;* ☎ *289-9397* offers a wealth of booklets, brochures, and maps. Make sure you ask for their publication *The Best Restaurants in São Paulo*. The post office is **Correio Central** *Praça do Correio;* ☎ *831-5222.*

Travel Agencies
The **American Express** office is located in the **Hotel Sheraton Mofarrej** *Rua Al. Santos, 1437;* ☎ *284-6622.*
Receptur *Avenida Ipiranga, 104 Downtown);* ☎ *259-4066.*

What to Wear
São Paulo is a serious business town. *Paulistanos* wear suits on most occasions; for men, ties are common, and even women tend to wear suits, though they are usually short, sexy, and brightly colored. Outside the business environment, casual wear should be directed toward the season. A jacket (leather is good) is needed during the winter months, but shorts are fine for casual excursions during the summer. Always take an umbrella, especially between December and March.

GUARUJÁ

When the pollution and the summer sun get too intense, *Paulistanos* head for the seaside resort of **Guarujá,** only an hour away. Like *carioca*s, the residents of Guarajá are sunworshippers, and not especially work-oriented. For years, high-class *Paulistanos* have enjoyed beautiful beachside homes in private neighborhoods called *condomínios*. In 1989, a new highway from Anchieta Isle made the two cities more accessible, opening up the resort to an even greater stream of vacationers. During high season (December–Carnaval and July, when the population of 200,000 nearly doubles), it's almost impossible to find a room without a reservation.

A few beaches in Guarujá have been officially declared polluted. **Asturias Beach,** however, is good for swimming. **Tombo Beach** is excellent for surfing. The **Jequiti-mar Beach** (where the resort of the same is located) is considered the safest. Two kilometers north of the resort is a beach where fishing boats land with the day's catch; the best seafood restaurants are located here.

The city's main beach is **Pitangueiras,** full of sidewalk cafes, bars, and luncheonettes. Like most of Guarujá's beaches, however, the undertow here is strong and bathers must take care. A dramatic view of the shoreline can be seen from in front of the **Gávea Hotel,** where you can enjoy a tropical drink and watch the sun set. **Terraço,** next to Escat Video on Pitangueiras Beach, is also an in-spot for a cool drink. For about $5, you can rent a horse-and-carriage and mosey through the town.

Somewhat gloomy in low season, (not to mention cold and windy), Guarujá is valiantly trying to make the island profitable year-round. In August, 1991, the city sponsored the **International Folklore Festival,** an event that may become annual. In order to avoid the seasonal crunch, the best time to come is during the month of May.

A blue-and-white ferry to the city of Santos (the most important port in Brazil and another holiday resort) looks a bit scrappy but is actually very safe. The trip takes only 5 minutes.

Getting There

Buses run continuously throughout the day to Guarujá from São Paulo.

THE ESSENTIAL GUARUJÁ

WHERE TO STAY

Casa Grande
Avenida Miguel Stefano, 999 (praia da Enseada); ☎ (132) 86–2223. Reservations: S.P. (11) 282–4277
Cannons in the lobby of this 5-star white fazenda recall a 19th-century plantation. The magnificent glass lobby is built around tropical gardens that tower toward the heavens; in fact, the entire grounds are exquisitely landscaped. The arrangement of the inner courtyard and pool resembles a Caribbean resort. Music continually wafts through the grounds, vying with the crashing sound of waves. A full pleasure center includes the circular pool, day and night tennis courts, a sauna, an exercise bike, racquet games, and weight equipment. A festive American-style snack bar and an international restaurant offer fine cuisine; you can even nosh on oysters and crab claws inside the pool. Suites, some of which have verandas, are stunningly decorated, with two double white beds, large bath, and living room. Standards are small, with no view; most worthwhile are the deluxe rooms, overlooking the garden courtyard, with an extra small room holding a couch and table. Rates, including breakfast, start at $110 for singles, $135 for doubles; for lunch and dinner, add another $15 per person. 162 apartments. *Expensive. All cards.*

Delphin
Avenida Miguel Stefano, 1295 (praia da Enseada), ☎ (132) 86–2111, FAX 87–2382. Reservations: SP (11) 259–6100
The Delphin has been called the camping club for Argentines, who tend to travel in large, noisy groups. A leather-and-walnut decor offsets the nautical antiques in the lobby. The pool is not particularly pretty, but guests can saunter to the beach, where they will be plied with drinks, natural straw umbrellas, and plastic chairs. Double deluxe rooms have no view; standards have no real window. The best bet, particularly for four, is the garden suite, with its own balcony, looking out on a wondrous tropical view. A nightclub rocks during summer. Rooms range from $50-$160. 114 apartments. *Moderate. All cards.*

Strand Hotel
Avenida Prestes Maia, 385 (praia do Tombo); ☎ (132) 86–6734
This three-floor hotel doesn't believe in frills, let alone exciting decoration, but it is spacious, breezy, and a good budget option, especially for families. There is no air-conditioning, but well-placed fans and large open windows set up a breeze, if the door is left open. The large pool and tennis courts are unusual for a small hotel; unfortunately, the TV room looks like an old folk's home and the corridors have a dark, waddly feel. Children up to 5 are free; if you stay at least 7 days, you'll receive a 40 percent discount. Apartments start at $50, breakfast not included. 42 apartments. *Moderate. All cards.*

Jequitimar Hotel and Spa Ala Szerman
Avenida Marjory Prado, 1100 (praia de Pernambuco); ☎ (132) 53–3111
Eight kilometers from Guarujá, on the road to Bertioga, is this extremely attractive resort right on its own beach. The swimming and boating are excellent and fishing grounds are available. Accommodations are chalets of varying size. Many rich Brazilians come to take advantage of the spa facilities, which include aerobics, water sports, and cellulite and massage treatments. A gourmet diet menu is served to spa participants in a salon separate from the main dining room. Two nightclubs keep the after-dark action hot. 68 apartments. *Very expensive. All cards.*

WHERE TO EAT

Expensive -------------- $25 up
Moderate -------------- $10–$25
Inexpensive ------------ Below $10

Il Faro
(Il Faro Hotel) Rua Iracema, 38 Enseada; ☎ 53–1980. Daily noon-1:00 a.m.
Paulistanos love this homey Italian cantina

with its white stucco arches and pictures of Venice. Over 50 pastas are available. Fish cooked in red tiles (the ones on the roof!) are specialties, and the *camarões Afrikana* in garlic sauce is excellent. For dessert, *torta da casa* is a chocolate brownie-like cake dotted through with almonds and splashed with whiskey. The owner, an Italian immigrant, loves to shmooze, and even the head waiter speaks English, French, and Spanish. *Moderate. All cards.*

Strand
Avenida Prestes Maia, 385; ☎ *86-6734*
Best *chopp* in town at this German bierhouse at the Strand Hotel, where the presidents of Volkswagen and Hertz hang out. The menu is in German and Portuguese. The best bet is sausage with sauerkraut, wienerschnitzel, and bratwurst, each about $5. *Moderate. All cards.*

Picanha's
Avenida Santos Dumont, 825, ☎ *552-947. Daily noon–2:00 a.m.*
Four blocks from downtown, this *churrascaria/rodízio* across from the bus station looks like a cross between a ranch and a cathedral, but the *cachaça* is free and the price is reasonable at $8 per person. If you have to wait for a table, you even get free drinks and hors d'oeuvres. A self-service salad bar is included; dessert is extra. Live music nightly. *Moderate. All cards.*

★ **Alcide's**
Avenida Dom Pedro 1, 398
Every dish at this boisterous ranchhouse looks superb. Alcide, the owner, names his creations after his friends; even his wife Matilda got a shrimp dish laden with apples and cream. Big enough for two, Mignon Alcide's looks like a huge corn dog, but is actually a superb steak stuffed with cheese and bacon and wrapped in a hot crust. During summer, up to 50 people wait a half hour to eat, so avoid peak hours between 2:00 p.m.–4:30 p.m. and after 8 p.m. Local artists show on the walls. *Moderate. All cards.*

Restaurante do Joca
Estrada de Bertioga, kilometer 12
This open-air eatery near the pier serves the best stuffed crabs in the city. The fried bananas are perfect. *Moderate. No cards.*

Churrascaria OK
Avenida Santos Domont, 825; ☎ *55-2947*
Excellent steak house.

NIGHTLIFE

Young adults and teens head for **Terraço**, at the corner of Rua Petrópolis and Avenida Marechal, for *chopp*, milkshakes, burgers, and pizzas. Near the Gávea Hotel, **Aquarius Boite**, is the city's disco, where the average age is 25. Be prepared for strobes, deafening volume, and a DJ who keeps the American rock, samba, and reggae loud. From the parking lot is a magnificent view of Enseada Beach.

SHOPPING

Guarujá Center Shopping, off of Pitangueiras Beach, is an indoor mini-mall, with merchandise at least 15 percent more expensive than in São Paulo. For souvenirs, flowers, crystals, and local artisanry, try **Le Petit Triann** *Rua Petrópolis, 15 Pitangueiras Beach.* **Centro Cultural de Guarujá** *Rua Petrópolis, 7,* upstairs from Escot Video is owned by the artist Ortega, whose work mostly lines the walls. He also excels in Miró and Picasso replicas. The city's only **cinema** is located on *Rua Mario Ribeiro,* across the street from the shopping center. The drugstore **Droga Raia** is located next door to the cinema.

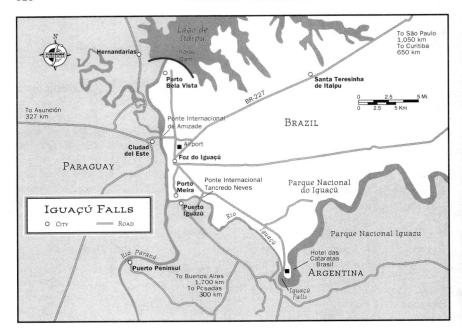

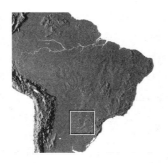

FOZ DO IGUAÇU

Iguaçu Falls

Niagara Falls has been called a "trickle in God's mind" compared to the torrential thunder of **Iguaçu Falls**, the second most important tourist site in Brazil. Rising from a modest stream that originates near Curitiba (the capital of Paraná state), the **Iguaçu River** inches its way westward over a 745-mile journey, slowly coalescing its tributaries and small streams until—just before it merges with the great Paraná River—it plunges passionately over an 2,624-ft. high cliff. What makes such a spectacular view is not just one cataract, but 275 interlinking ones that form a horseshoe torrent around the semi-circular cliff. Throughout the day, rainbows explode over the shimmering torrents, tropical birds fly overhead, and fish can be glimpsed struggling against the white crashing foam. Given its near-mystical beauty, it's no wonder that recent "spiritual-discovery tours" of South America have included the Falls as a "power spot" destination.

The Falls were first discovered in 1525 by the Spanish explorer **Alvaro Nunes Cabeza de Vaca**, who had fallen into disgrace at the court for not having brought back substantial riches from his Mississippi River treks. Appointed the Royal Overseer for the Jesuit-founded colonies along the Paraguay River, he quickly became bored and set off to explore the mouth of the Iguaçu River. When he first heard the terrifying roar of the currents, he immediately disembarked and set off on foot to confront the vision face to face. Unfortunately, Vaca was in such disrepute back home that no one at the Spanish court cared to hear of his marvelous discovery.

Numerous legends of the Falls are now part of the folkloric tradition. In general, they have to do with a young boy and girl from the Caigangue tribe, who once inhabited this region. The most romantic story involves **Tarobá**, a beautiful, but sightless young girl who inspires her lover Naipí to sacrifice himself to the gods so that she might see. As the story goes, **Naipí** is swallowed up by the crashing of rocks at the very moment Tarobá regains her vision, thus making her the first person to catch sight of the newly created falls. Of course, Tarobá's regained eyesight was hardly recompense for her lost love, but it's said you can still hear her dead lover crying "Tarobá, Tarobá" under the sound of the Falls.

THE FALLS: THE BRAZILIAN SIDE

Part of a National Park ostensibly protected by environmental guidelines, the Falls are located near the towns of **Foz do Iguaçu** in Brazil, Puerto Iguazú in Argentina, and **Ciudad Presidente Stroessner** in Paraguay. With a population of 200,000, Foz do Iguaçu has enjoyed a major expansion following the construction of the **Itaipu Dam**, the world's largest hydroelectric station. Beyond visiting the waterfalls, many Brazilians come to the tri-city area to take advantage of the cheap shopping in Paraguay; American travelers, however, usually find the quality of merchandise suspicious, if not outright damaged.

The Falls can be viewed both from the Brazilian side and from the Argentine side—a combination that provides both a panoramic and more detailed perspective. Just from the Brazilian side, there are at least three ways to experience the Falls, and if you can accomplish all three in your visit, you'll have had a holographic view of one of nature's most fantastic accomplishments. For a leisurely visit, plan two days; otherwise you can get a cursory view by arriving early in the morning and departing at night.

BY FOOT

The easiest (and cheapest) way to see the Falls is to walk on foot around the visitor's walkway. The lovely stone path that snakes around the side of a woody cliff gives you various platforms to view the Falls at different angles. You may be lucky enough to receive a visit from the park's resident *coatis*—racoon-like fellows who are smarter than cats and will even eat seeds right out of your hand. But be careful: I once witnessed an exciting *coati* catfight (over some candy) that inspired packs of them to come squealing angrily out of the woods. The shimmering noise you may hear under the roar of the Falls is the rhythmic beating of hundreds of *cigarra* wings—a grasshopper-like insect that fills the air with its powerful song, then dies.

At the end of the walkway, a small elevator will take you to the top level, where there is a souvenir shop and an observation point to view the top plateau of the Iguaçu River. It's from here that you can get close enough to the Falls to get sprayed. In cold weather, a light raincoat may be helpful, but in hot weather, why not wear a bathing suit and a pair of shorts and enjoy it?

BY AIR

Helicopter rides *over* the Falls give you a spectacular view of the rocky plateaus from above—a kind of geological tour seen from an astronaut's eyes. The price is steep: $40 for 5–7 minutes, and $150 for 25 minutes (the latter includes the city, the dam, and the Falls), but the trip is worth it and not unduly discomforting. Ecologists, however, have been complaining that the noise of the helicopters is seriously disturbing the forest animals, who have sought refuge deeper inside the woods. **Helisul Taxi Aereo** *Rodoviária Cataratas, kilometer 6.5;* ☎ *74-2414, 74-1786* can be found outside on the roadway; no reservations are necessary, though there may be a slight wait. Also, try **Edra Helicópteros** *Avenida Cataratas, kilometer 18;* ☎ *74-5022* The cost is $40 for ten minutes, $150 for 40 minutes.

BY WATER

The **Macuco Boat Safari**, located inside the National Park, is the brainchild of a native Chicagoan, Peter George, who discovered this eco-trek only 6 years ago and has been delighting unsuspecting tourists ever since. A rocky 10-minute jeep ride carries you through a tropical forest where you may see (only in the very early morning) monkeys, pumas, javelins, and pigs. The trail leads past the beautiful waterfall of the São José River (a hearty trek over narrow trails and log bridges) to the dock, where hundreds of multicolored butterflies will swarm over you, lighting on your face and hands, as you wait for the boat to arrive. Shortly, you'll pile into an aluminum motorized canoe, complete with life-jackets, and head for the series of falls called "The Three Musketeers." What starts out as a peaceful float suddenly turns wildly exciting as the rapids churn faster and the magnificent view of the Falls come into focus—a voluminous spray of steam and foam falling like pure energy from the azure-blue heavens. In June and July, when the river is higher, you can even go an extra 5 meters closer to the Falls, but no matter the proximity, the trip will make you feel like one of those 17th-Century *bandeirantes* who scoured the jungles of Brazil looking for treasure. At the same time, it's not difficult to sense the fragility of these natural resources and how necessary it is to preserve them as we head for the 21st Century. On the way back, the guide will no doubt point out the various kinds of jungle trees, particularly the palm, from where the delicious *palmitos* (palm hearts) are obtained. (It was here that I first learned that palm trees, which take 15 years to mature, die when the *palmito* is cut—enough to make me boycott my own consumption of them.)

Between November and December, you will be blessed with the sight of thousands of butterflies being born; during September and October, white and yellow wild orchids burst into bloom.

Other fascinating eco-tours are offered by this same company, including alligator hunting, dourado fishing (best in October and November), and vigorous half-day walking tours. Boats can also be rented by the hour or day and outfitted with scientific equipment and specialized guides. For more information contact Ilha do Sol Turismo e Navegação *Rua Lima, 509 (Beverly Falls Parque);* ☎ *74–4244.*

Getting There

If you are staying at the Hotel das Cataratas, all you need do to reach the Falls is cross the street and walk down the paved stairway to a mile-long cliffside path leading to the waterfalls. Other hotels may supply a transfer to the entrance, but a private guide on the Brazilian side is not really necessary. Buses from the local bus terminal downtown *(Avenida Juscelino Kubitschek)* run every half-hour from 8:00 a.m.–6:00 p.m., including holidays and Sundays, and drop you off at the road above the stairway. The fee is under 50 cents. Cars may also be rented at the airport from three agencies.

THE FALLS: THE ARGENTINE SIDE

For many, the Argentine side of the Falls is the most impressive; the maze of catwalks and footpaths go so close to the waterfall you will feel as if you're about to be avalanched. Getting there takes a little more effort, though. The easiest way is to join an organized tour. Or you can take a bus to **Puerto Iguazú**, which departs from the main bus terminal every half-hour from 7:00 a.m.–9:00 p.m. daily. Entering the park will cost about $1; ask for a map. A trail called **Circuito Inferior**, which starts at the Visitor's Center, will allow you to revel in the beauty of the Falls for about two hours. The most impressive sight is the **Garganta del Diablo** (Devil's Throat) at **Puerto Canoas**, a conjunction of 14 separate falls that combine to form the world's most voluminous single waterfall in terms of flow per second.

If you do not stay longer than the day, you will not need a visa, but check with the Argentine consulate to be certain. In any case, it's a good idea to take your passport as identification.

OTHER SIGHTS

ITAIPU DAM

If Iguaçu Falls is a natural-born beauty, **Itaipu Dam** is a facelift. A manmade harness of water power that cost over 9 billion U.S. dollars (plus another $15 billion in financial charges), Itaipu is considered by the Brazilian government as one of their greatest industrial achievements. Indeed, its 18 turbines, now fully operating, provide the country with one-third of its electrical power, but at an ecological cost that is only now being truly fathomed. The name Itaipu means "Singing Rock" in the language of the Guarani, an Indian tribe who would have been appalled to have witnessed the climatic changes and fauna redistribution resulting from the dam's razing of over 869 miles of tropical forest. Ironically, Itaipu was also the name of a small island that has long since disappeared due to the dam's construction. Destroyed as well was **Sete Quedas** (Seven Falls), a magnificent waterfall once rated by the *Guinness Book of World Records* as the greatest in the world.

Eager to offset controversy, the Visitor's Center presents a slick, pro-dam documentary that obscures these issues and instead shows the immense challenges faced by the construction team (*Daily 8:00 a.m., 9:00 a.m., 10:00 a.m., 2:00 p.m., 3:00 p.m., 4:00 p.m.*). Free guided tours, which leave from the Visitor's Center at 8:30 a.m., 10:30 a.m., 2:30 p.m., and 4:30 p.m. from Monday to Saturday, are diverting, though not as enjoyable as spending more time in the forest or at the Falls. Technical visits by scientists and engineers may be arranged 2–3 days in advance, and are much more interesting than the group tours, including a guided tour of the plant and the impressive spillways. This kind of tour, however, is not recommended for children, who might push an important button and shut down electricity from here to Rio de Janeiro.

Getting There

To get to the Visitor's Center of Itaipu Dam, take a bus from the main bus terminal; they leave hourly.

ECOMUSEUM

Inaugurated in 1987, this ecologically oriented museum gives homage to the region's flora and fauna in artistically mounted displays. Indigenous crafts and tools from the pre-Columbian and colonial eras are also represented. This museum is usually included on the tour of Itaipu Dam. The museum is located by Rodovia Tancredo Neves, near the Itaipu Binacional Gate.

THE ESSENTIAL FOZ DO IGUAÇU

WHERE TO STAY

Expensive -------------- $80

Moderate --------------- $40–$80

Inexpensive ------------ Under $40

★ Hotel Bourbon

Rodovia das Cataratas, kilometer 2.5; ☎ *(456) 76–1313, toll free (11) 800–8181*

The Bourbon is a full-scale resort hotel with enough diversions to convince you to stay longer than the usual one day. The sweet smell of tropical flowers and the calming rush of a tiny waterfall pervade the lobby. The sprawling grounds still retain the feel of an intimate estate or tropical country club; most attractive is the large circular pool surrounded by exquisitely landscaped gardens. Organized leisure activities include gymnastics, walking, tennis, soccer, and leisure programs for children who cavort around with Mickey Ratão (Mickey Mouse). A mini-spa with dry and wet sauna, jacuzzi, and massage are available. An elegant à la carte dining room overlooks the pool; lunch and dinner buffets are served daily, with a poolside barbecue on Saturdays. Room are plush, with views of the landscaped garden; the only difference between the deluxe and standard is the makeup mirror in the bathroom. The Bourbon is also walking distance to the Rafain Churrascaria, 2 kilometers from downtown. Rates start at $80 for single, $94 for doubles. 180 apartments. *Expensive. All cards.*

Hotel das Cataratas

Rodovia das Cataratas, kilometer 28; ☎ *(456) 74–2666*

The impressive, colonial-style Das Cataratas has gained a popular reputation since it is the only Brazilian hotel that offers a view of the Falls. Unfortunately, this reputation is misleading. Even though the Falls are an easy walk across the street, the view from the apartments is some distance away and often obscured by trees. Moreover, you cannot confirm a room with a view in advance, and must accept whatever you receive on arrival. The alternative view, of the tropically–landscaped backyard, may actually be preferable, since a variety of animals, including ostriches and emas, stroll around at will. Rooms are spacious, furnished in the rich carved woodwork of the colonial period. Breakfast is served from 4:00 a.m.–10:00 a.m. to accommodate guests departing on early-morning flights. A barbecue buffet is served poolside for lunch and dinner, with music nightly. Tennis courts and game room round out the sports. Varig handles all reservations for the hotel, since it is full owner. If you are interested in an apartment with a view of the Falls, book a luxe room and take your chances. Standards start at $48, deluxe $67. 206 apartments. *Moderate. All cards.*

Hotel Carimã

Rodovia das Cataratas, kilometer 10; ☎ *(456) 74–3377. FAX 74–3531*

Located on the Rodovia das Cataratas, this 4-star hacienda-style hotel is a mere 10 minutes from the airport. Modern sculptures dominate the large lobby, as well as a travel agency that can arrange tours of the area. A huge, unusually–shaped pool is accompanied by a children's pool. Two restaurants include a *churrascaria* and a coffee shop for sandwiches and drinks. Simply furnished, standards differ from the superior and deluxe only in size, and the amount of food in the minibar. Children in the same room as their parents are half-price. Standard singles start at $43, doubles $48. 421 apartments. *Moderate–Expensive. All cards.*

Continental Inn

Avenida Paraná, 485; ☎ *(456) 74–4122*

Teenagers, Argentines, and engineers from Itaipu Dam stay at this nicely appointed 3-star with an outdoor pool overlooking the city. No restaurant, just a coffee shop that serves breakfast. Six blocks from the center of downtown, the hotel prides itself on its calm atmosphere. Tropical drinks may be nursed on a circular outdoor veranda. 66 apartments. *Moderate All cards.*

Cisne

Avenida Brasil, 144; ☎ *74-2488*

Located across the street from the Centro Gastronômico in the hubbub of downtown, this 2-star has minimally decorated rooms and a simple, but dear coffee shop. All rooms are air-conditioned with small desks, tiny bathrooms, and even tinier closets. Only the deluxe have TVs. There's no elevator. Singles run $24, doubles $30, triples $32. 27 apartments. *Inexpensive. All cards.*

Recanto Park Hotel

Avenida Costa e Silva, 3500; ☎ *(456) 73-4144*

The best option for a medium-priced accommodation, the soothing Recanto Park opened in 1991. Perfect for families, it's a favorite among Argentines, Uruguayans, and Germans. Pleasantly furnished apartments are all air-conditioned and come with small verandas. No real difference exists between standards and deluxes except for some minor decorations. Suites, with a couch bed, can accommodate up to 5 persons. Presently, there is a path for walking and jogging, and a gym is planned for the future. The restaurant serves only breakfast. Doubles run around $42, suites $64. Children up to 5 are free. 72 apartments. *Moderate. All cards.*

WHERE TO EAT

Since most tourists rarely stay longer than a day or two in Foz, the city has not developed into a culinary oasis. The Arabian community has contributed some provocative cuisine, and there is at least one fine steak house, Búfalo Branco. Noshers should head for the Gastronomic Center downtown. Excellent meals can also be found at the Bourbon and San Rafael hotels.

Expensive -------------- Above $10

Moderate --------------- $5–$10

Inexpensive ------------ Under $5

Rafain

Rodovia das Cataratas, kilometer 6.5, ☎ *74-2720. Daily 11:00 a.m.–4:00 p.m., 6:00 p.m.–midnight*

Built as a huge barn seating 1,200, this *churrascaria* has no air-conditioning, so pray for a cool wind. The buffet, which runs between $4–$5, includes a self-serve salad bar, dessert buffet, and all the meat you can eat. A musical presentation of Latin American music starts at 9:00 p.m.; by 9:30 p.m., a Paraguayan troupe of women are dancing with bottles. Not the greatest cuts of beef, but you can go up to the grill and choose what you want. During high season, come early (by 8:00 p.m.), to avoid the rush. *Inexpensive. No cards.*

Centro Gastronômico Rafain

Avenida Brasil, 157, ☎ *74-5050*

There aren't any 24-hour restaurants in Foz, but this gastronomic complex downtown is a fun place to hang until 3:00 a.m. or 4:00 a.m. Owned by the Rafain family, one of the cities' most powerful hoteliers, the outdoor bazaar features pizza, pastries, ice cream, and meat pies at individual stalls; indoors, a charming air-conditioned teahouse serves more sophisticated fare. The lunch buffet ($4) is downtown's best bet, with 7 cold salads, 2 cold meats, lasagna, fish, and pasta, as well as the ubiquitous rice and beans. In high season, samba shows erupt in the outdoor plaza around 9:00 p.m.; while you're watching try out the incredible sweet called a "Balloon." *Moderate. No cards.*

★ Churrascaria Búfalo Branco

Rua Rebouças, 550;
☎ *74-5115. Noon–11:00 p.m.*

Head here for the best steaks in Foz—an elegant eatery situated in one of the ritzier districts. Waiters wear tuxes (though you don't need a tie), and the chefs cook your order from scratch. A cold buffet of salads includes Arabian kibe, eggplant, and potato salad. The dessert cart is spectacular. Dinners run about $10. *Moderate. All cards.*

Abaeté

Rua Almirante Barroso, 893 (Galeria Viela), ☎ *74-3084. Daily 11:00 a.m.–3:00 p.m., 7:30 p.m.–midnight*

Next door to Al Manara restaurant in the same shopping gallery, Abaeté offers international cuisine at candlelit tables. Codfish, paella, and a full array of chicken and steak are cooked with an Arabian flair. *Moderate. No cards.*

Du Cheff Restaurante

Rua Almirante Barroso, 683; ☎ *74–3311*
Situated in the San Rafael Hotel in the downtown district, this international eatery serves a full menu of chicken, beef, and pasta, with specialties like the *pato ao vino* (duck in wine sauce) for a reasonable $6 and fish dishes like *surubi ao tartare* for $5. From the road you can see Ciudad del Este and the skyscrapers of Paraguay. *Moderate. All cards.*

Al Manara

Rua Almirante Barroso, 893 (Galeria Viela); ☎ *72–1112. Daily 11:00 a.m.–3:00 p.m., 7:00 p.m.–11:30 p.m.*
Drawing on the substantial Arabic population in Foz, this small but homey Arabian restaurant serves Middle Eastern delicacies *rodízio*-style. For about $7 you can dine on 13 dishes, including kibe, hummus, babaganoush, falafa, kafta (meat), yogurt, and sweet desserts. *Moderate. No cards.*

Pizza D'Oro

Avenida Jorge Schmmepfeng, 500; ☎ *72–1961. Daily 7:00 p.m.–5:00 a.m.*
When the last bus from the National Park leaves at 7:00 p.m., head for this pizzeria where the waiters dress in tuxes and you can dance til 5:00 a.m. Two to three people can fill up on 13 kinds of pizza for under $4. Beef, chicken, pasta, salads, fish, and desserts are also available. The artistic cover (under a dollar) includes the live rock, blues, and Brazilian folk. *Inexpensive. No cards.*

NIGHTLIFE

Oba Oba Samba Rio Rafain Samba Foz Nightclub

Rodovia das Cataratas, kilometer 6.5; ☎ *74–2720. Daily 10:30 p.m.*
on Iguaçu's version of the typical Rio samba extravaganza, with beautiful *mulata* showgirls in glittery bikinis and over 40 folkloric singers and dancers. Visitors are encouraged to join in. *Moderate. No cards.*
A folkloric show is also held at the **Rafain Churrascaria** (see above). Disco dancing can be found at **Whiskadão** *Rua Almirante Barroso, 763,* which turns frisky on the weekends. On a clear night, hang outside the **Gastronomic Center,** where samba bands start blasting around 10:00 p.m.

SHOPPING

Artesanato Chocolates *Três Fronteiras, kilometer 11* If you're traveling by car, stop by this enormous souvenir shop with trays of jewelry, machetes in leather cases, leather gun holsters *gaúcho*-style, and a chocolate shop that must be inhaled to be believed. Also available is *Café Iguaçu,* a coffee exported throughout the country and famous for its *cafezinho* blend.

HANDS-ON FOZ DO IGUAÇU

Arrival

Many people arrive in Iguaçu in the morning and leave the same night. This makes for a full-packed day and can be strenuous, particularly if you are city-hopping on a 3-week air pass. On the other hand, nightlife is slim, and anything more than a handful of good restaurants is hard to find. You could extend your trip by crossing the border to shop in Paraguay, visiting the Argentine side of the Falls, or taking a more involved eco-trip.
Air Varig/Cruzeiro *Avenida Brasil, 821;* ☎ *74–3344;* **VASP** • ☎ *74–2999;* and **Transbrasil** ☎ *272–4669* all fly into the city's international airport, with good connections to and from all major Brazilian cities. The airport is located 18 kilometers from downtown (about $15 by taxi). The bus from the airport to town ("Dois Irmãos") does not accommodate large bags of luggage.

Bus

The bus station is located at *Avenida Brazil, 99, behind the Hotel Foz do Iguaçu;* ☎ *73–1525.* If you're prepared for long bus rides, you can embark from Curitiba (9–11 hours), Porto Alegre (16 hours) or São Paulo (15 hours). Direct buses from Rio take about 22 hours. Air–conditioned express buses on the Pluma line are suitable for sleeping and cost twice as much.

Consulates

If you plan to spend the night in either Argentine or Paraguay, you will need a visa and must pass through immigration procedures on either side of the Ponte Presidente Tan-

credo Neves, the bridge that spans the Iguaçu River between the two countries.
Argentina
Rua Dom Pedro, I, 28; ☎ 74–2877.
Paraguay
Rua Bartolomeo de Gusmão, 777; ☎ 72–1169.

Money Exchange

Good rates can be found at the airport exchange house. In the city, try Casa Jerusalem *Avenida Brasil, 1055*. If you're planning to visit Argentina, it's a good idea to have a handful of Argentine currency for bus fare, food, and park fees (*cruzeiros* are accepted but at a low rate).

Travel Agencies

Most good hotels will arrange tours of the Falls and special excursions. A good travel agency that also exchanges money is **Bomcâmbio** *Avenida Juscelino Kubitschek, 565;* ☎ 74–1100.
Rafain Turismo
Avenida Olimpio Rafagnin, BR 227; ☎ 73–3434 is the city's leading travel agency (the family owns a nightclub, 3 hotels, and a gastronomic center).

Tourist Information

Paranatur
Rua Almirante Barroso, 485 is the official tourist board and can supply information in English. For information by phone, dial 139.
Tourist booths
are also at the airport. In Puerto Iguazú, Argentina, an information booth is located at *Praça Almirante Tamandaré, 64*.

When to Go (Season)

Between **April and July**, the rainy season plumps the volume of the Falls to their full peak, but the sky is often overcast and you will surely need a jacket to protect against the chilly air.

In **March**, at the end of the dry season when the Falls reach their lowest ebb, the weather can approach the uncomfortably humid, and mosquitos abound. In years past, due to drought, the Falls have been known to dry up altogether, or, as in 1983, flood the area to such an extent that several spectator catwalks were destroyed. Whatever the time of year, do check the water conditions in advance, or you may be sorely disappointed.

When to Go (Time of Day)

It's difficult to suggest the best time of day to see the Falls. In early morning, the mist in the air rises mysteriously to meet the tumultuous waters, and at sunset the play of orange and pink lights over the water is magical. It's under a bright sun, however, that the full majesty and volume of the Falls can be experienced, especially if you want to take clear photographs. Entrance to the park on the Brazilian side is about $2, best during the week when the crowds are less.

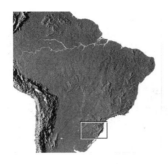

SANTA CATARINA

The Most Traditonal Band in Blumenau Plays German Oom-Pah Music

Santa Catarina is both the name of a state in southern Brazil and the name of a connecting island on which is situated the state capital, **Florianópolis** (which is also at times the name of the island—a point of continuing confusion even for Brazilians). Like other parts of southern Brazil, Santa Catarina boasts a decided European flair, thanks to the millions of immigrants since the 18th century who have been attracted by the cool temperatures and the fertile hills. Today, Santa Catarina's population is made up of three distinct ethnic groups: **Germans**, the first to settle, who contributed both their intellectual and industrial acumen; **Italians**, who still toil the land as farmers, and **Azoreans** (from the isle of Azores in Portugal), who populate quaint fishing villages that haven't changed in centuries. Interestingly, this syncretic mix of European cultures has created one of the most hospitable social structures in Brazil; foreigners constantly remark about the warm welcomes received in this region. Cities such as **Blumenau** and **Joinville** have hung onto their cultural traditions mostly through large German folk festivals and historical renovations, but in smaller towns, like the isolated **Pomerode** (30 kilometers north of Blumenau), 80 percent of the population still speaks German fluently, and tiny Treze Tilias (descended from the Austrians and recently delivered from obscurity by a TV soap opera) still looks as if it had been transplanted from an Alpine village.

The coastal drive from Blumenau to Florianópolis is one of the most beautiful in the country, lined with rolling green hills, grazing cattle, and quaint colorful houses in *einxaimel* (German) style. The main highway **BR 101** is uncommonly hazardous because crazy drivers tend to crisscross in front of each other with a vengeance, but the view of the primitive, undeveloped beaches is superb.

So many mystical legends surround the history of Santa Catarina island that it has been dubbed *Ilha das Bruxas* (Island of the Witches). Most of the prevailing myths have something to do with beautiful women (i.e., witches!) who lure "innocent" fishermen to their doom. Many say that the old Azorean women who spend their days making lacework in the northern fishing villages are "full of power." In any case, Florianópolis has recently been hosting an annual New Age convention, which brings together the best astrologers, Tarot readers, crystal vendors, and healers from all over Brazil during the month of August.

SANTA CATARINA 341

FLORIANÓPOLIS

Florianópolis is the perfect place to escape from the social-climbing pressures and high prices of more upwardly mobile beaches like Ipanema and Copacabana. Joined to the mainland by 2 bridges, Florianópolis doesn't stand out as a city in itself; instead, tourists head straight for the 42 beaches that dot the 25-mile long island. Since it has not been subjected to industrial development, the city has little, if any, pollution, and the beaches remain pristine. The island and mainland is served by excellent bus service, but a car will be necessary if you want to investigate the more remote beaches and fishing villages.

BEACHES

The northwestern side of the island, with its relatively calm seas, is best for swimming. The best restaurants and hotels are located at **Praia Canasvieiras**, but during high season it's sure to be packed with fashionable beachcombers, many from the neighboring countries of Uruguay and Argentina. **Praia Juerê** beach, which attracts families to its calm waters, is usually full of sailboats. Between **Jurerê** and **Daniela** beaches, a series of coves tucked under the road is well worth investigating. Around the **Lagoa da Conceição**, a large saltwater lagoon, you'll find many simple restaurants specializing in seafood, with open-air verandas looking out onto the sea. Here you can rent canoes labeled "*Barco para Passeio*" to row around the lake with a guide ($6 per half-hour). At the entrance to the lagoon, **Barra da Lagoa** remains a colony of Azorean fishermen who continue their daily seawork oblivious to the onslaught of tourists piling into the tiny bars and restaurants. It's here you might see fish hanging from an iron pole for sale. Unfortunately, several years ago, an eco disaster occurred here when millions of sardines suddenly died. An eco park near Barra is called **Parque da Florestal Rio Vermelho**.

Unless you are an expert swimmer, avoid the eastern shore since the rough undercurrents can be deadly. **Praia da Joaquina**, however, makes an excellent beach for surfing (the national championships are held each January). The road to this beach, filled with hilly green areas and small quaint houses, is as *exotic* as the shoreline itself; cows graze near *peixarias*, or makeshift stalls selling fresh fish. For strolling, **Praia do Campeche** (which connects to **Joaquina**) has the rep for being the most beautiful beach, but be careful with the torturous undertow.

> **Insider Tip:**
>
> *Wait to do your shopping till you get to the airport. There is an excellent mall of shops there, especially a great T-shirt store called Textil & Cia, where you can buy an Ilha das Bruxas T-shirt (one of my favorites from the hundreds I brought back from Brazil). Also, if you love seeing planes take off, get to the airport early and watch from under an outdoor shelter.*

THE ESSENTIAL FLORIANÓPOLIS

WHERE TO STAY

If you're coming for beach time, avoid staying in the city of Florianópolis and head for the chalets and pousadas along the various beaches of Santa Catarina island. Note that many hotels close for low season (April–November) as do some restaurants.

Hotel Diplomata
Avenida Dr. Paulo Fontes, 800 (Centro); ☎ *(482) 23–4455*
The best executive hotel located downtown is, unfortunately, a half-hour from the beach. The 4-star supplies its own transfer to the beach, however, as well as private cabanas and shower facilities. Noise from the highway down below can be difficult at night, so ask for a room on the side without traffic. Service is top class; an elegant dining room for dinner and a 3-course breakfast is luxurious. 90 rooms. *Expensive. All cards.*

Jurerê Praia Hotel
Al. 1 (Praia de Jurerê), 25 kilometer; ☎ *(482) 66–0108*
These black-and-white, avant-garde-looking chalets might look better in Brasília, but the complex on a well-preserved beach is excellent for families. The smallest cabana for $40 holds 2 persons; the large (at $70) fits 4 nicely, and the best at $92 suits 5. The apartment-like houses hold a bedroom, dining room, patio with grill, and full kitchen, and guests can take advantage of the pool and resort-like grounds: a perfect environ for total relaxation. Reserve 30 days in advance, special weekly rates available. 58 chalets. *Moderate–expensive. All cards.*

Ponta das Canas Praia
Rua da Praia, Estrada Geral de Ponta das Canas, 33 kilometer.; ☎ *(482) 66–0311, 66–0680*
This low-key, 3-star resort with a tropical backyard is packed with grass huts for dining and relaxing. A modest spa from November–April offers eco-walks, tennis, volleyball, scuba, windsurfing, and bicycling. Boat trips can also be taken to the nearby ruins. The homey restaurant overlooking the sea serves wonderful grilled shrimp. Other native restaurants and bars are within walking distance. Ask for a room with a view. Singles run $42, doubles $54. 55 apartments. *Moderate. All cards.*

Cris Hotel
Praia da Joaquina, 17 kilometer; ☎ *(482) 32–0380*
A decent budget hotel on the beach of Joaquina, with air-conditioning and minibars. Singles start at $33, doubles $37. 757 apartments. *Inexpensive. No cards.*

> **Insider Tip**
>
> For a list of houses to rent ($15–$20 a day!), write the mayor's office, c/o the **Secretary of Tourism** (Portal Turístico de Florianópolis, SETUR) Praça 15 de Novembro (Centro); ☎ (482) 22-9200, or **Ilhatur** (a travel agency) Rua Felipe Schmidt, 27; ☎ (482) 23-6333. If you rent for a whole month in low season, it's even cheaper!

WHERE TO EAT

The most sophisticated restaurants are located downtown, but if you're beachside, go for fish, particularly steamed or grilled just off the boat. In the area of Beira-Mar Norte (in the north of the city near the Hercílio Luz Bridge), you'll find several notable restaurants, such as Moçambique (seafood), Pizzaria Don Pepe (pizza), and Restaurante Kaffa (Lebanese).

Maurílio
Praia da Joaquina; ☎ 32–0172. Daily 11:00 a.m.–11:00 p.m.
Stuffed crabs *(siri recheado)* go great with beer as does the *camarão ao bofo* (steamed shrimp) at this casual seaside eatery. *Inexpensive. No cards.*

Andrinus
Rua Geral da Lagoa da Conceição; ☎ 32–0153
This simple seaside, adorned with paintings of local fishermen, serves a shrimp buffet: 14 dishes for $15 (you'll pay twice as much in São Paulo!). A veritable steal. *Moderate. No cards.*

Meneghini
Avenida Beira-Mar Norte, 400 (downtown); ☎ 22–7546. Daily noon-3:00 p.m., 6:30 p.m.–midnight, closed Monday
Good steak house. *Moderate. All cards.*

Armação Ilimitada
SC-406 (Praia da Armação). Daily 10:30 a.m.–1:00 a.m.
Interesting pizza with live music and wine located on Armação beach. *Inexpensive. No cards.*

NIGHTLIFE

Most bars on the island feature live music. Bar do Erico, near Mole and Joaquina beaches, is a hotspot bar with live MPB (Brazilian popular music).

HANDS-ON FLORIANÓPOLIS

Arrival

Flights run daily from Porto Alegre and São Paulo. Buses are available from Porto Alegre, São Paulo, Brasília, Curitiba, Blumenau, and Joinville. Check the following airlines:
Varig/Cruzeiro/Rio Sul
☎ 24–2811.
VASP
☎ 36–3033.
Transbrasil
☎ 36–1380, 23–7777.

Car Rental

Avis
☎ 36–1309, 22–5099.

Hitching

Hitching is probably safer here than anywhere else in Brazil. Locals are so friendly that you won't have to wait long for a pick-up.

Money Exchange

Banco do Brasil
Rua dos Ilhéus and
Lovetur
Avenida Osmar Cunha, 15.

Taxis

Air Taxis
☎ 36–1311.
Taxi
☎ 197.

When to Go

December–May is the best time for the beach (though foreigners may enjoy the less crowded strands during November, March, April and May). June–November is colder, with a delightful wind, but you will need a jacket, and the beachcombing might be chilly.

The **Festival of Shrimp** is held in January,

National Surfing Championships the last week in January. *Semana de Florianópolis*, a weeklong festival of folkoric music and dance, is held during the last week of March. The **Rodeio Crioulo** (rodeo) is held in July.

JOINVILLE

Joinville and **Blumenau** carry on a good-natured competition over which city is more hospitable to tourists. Located in the valley, **Joinville** (population: 343,000) welcomes guests with large bouquets of flowers, but the German-descended residents of both cities seem to party equally hard, downing about the same amount of beer. The land on which Joinville was settled was originally given as a dowry to the **Prince of Joinville** upon his marriage to the daughter of the Portuguese emperor Pedro I and his consort **Dona Leopoldina** of Austria. In 1851, under a deal with Hamburg lumber companies, nearly 200 German, Swiss, and Norwegians descended on the 43-square miles of virgin forest. Attracting more immigrants throughout the century, the city grew into the state's foremost industrial center. Today, Joinville, known as **Cidade das Flores** (City of Flowers), is a city to browse through. Streets are impeccably clean and filled with bicycles, a citywide pastime. And much of the architecture remains staunchly German; according to a recent law, new banks and shops do not have to pay taxes if they build in the *einxaimel* style. The well-kept parks are all maintained individually through the patronship of various industries, who take active interest in maintaining the city. Enjoying an enviable location, Joinville is a half-hour both from the beach and the *serra*.

In July, the city is transformed by the biggest **dance festival** in Latin America (fourth in the world), attended by international teachers and graced by performances (from flamenco to ballet) in open plazas, factories, and theaters. One local *figura* who can be enjoyed throughout the year is **Alberto Holdereger**, a lawyer turned singer, whose near-Pavarotti voice and girth nightly turns up at local restaurants, bars, and festivals.

SIGHTS

The majority of German-style houses are concentrated along the cobblestone street **Rua 15 de Novembro**. Artisan and produce stores line the main street **Rua Princesa Isabel**, which runs parallel to Rua 15 de Novembro and Rua 9 de Março. The most interesting historical stop is the **Museu Nacional de Imigração e Colonização** *Rua Rio Branco, 229;* ☎ *22-4485. Tuesday–Friday 9:00 a.m.–6:00 p.m.; Saturday and Sunday 9:00 a.m.–noon, 2:00 p.m.–6:00 p.m.* Once the palace of the

Prince of Joinville, who never returned to Brazil to inhabit it, the building has since been turned into a museum honoring the history of the German immigrants in the region. The excellent exhibition displays 19th-century sewing machines, old Victrolas, clocks, military uniforms, and complete furnished salons from the Imperial era. Most compelling is a 19th-century barnhouse complete with period equipment. The palm trees lining the courtyard in front of the museum were actually grown from seedlings taken from the royal palms in Rio's Botanical Gardens.

Also worth a glimpse are the Indian artifacts at the **Museu Arquelógico de Sambaqui** *Rua Dona Francisca, 600;* ☎ *22–0144. Tuesday–Friday 9:00 a.m.–noon; Saturday and Sunday 9:00 a.m.–noon, 2:00 p.m.–6:00 p.m.* Donated by an amateur archaeologist, this display includes ceramics from the Tupí-Guaraní Indians, 4,000-year-old sculptures of whales, and special arrows developed only by Indians in this area to kill animals without drawing blood. The staff speaks English and will even let you try to carve a tiny indenture Indian-style into a stone with a mere piece of flint. (You could be there all day.) The 15-year-old **Catedral São Francisco Xavier** on *Rua do Principe* is ultramodern with circular stained-glass windows depicting the history of Joinville. One of the best examples of German architecture is the old train station (1910), with its steepled orange brick roof and chocolate-brown windows. Perched on a hillside with a panoramic view of the city, the **Cemitério do Imigrante** (the immigrant's cemetery) is interesting as a walk through its ancient tombstones; it has now been preserved as a national patrimony.

THE ESSENTIAL JOINVILLE

WHERE TO STAY

Tannenhof
Rua Visconde de Taunay, 340; ☎ *(474) 22–8011, FAX 22–8011*
The town pride, this pretty, German-style high-rise is a homey, but elegant meeting place for the town's elite. The German-print curtains in the bright, white apartments and the folkloric tile in the bathroom lend a touch of the motherland. Standards have no heat, but all rooms have air-conditioning and color TV (deluxes have heat). Almost all rooms have grilled verandas. A panoramic restaurant serves excellent buffets and offers live music nightly. Standard singles start at $24, doubles $28. 103 apartments. *Moderate. All cards.*

Anthurium Parque Hotel
Rua São José, 226; ☎ *(474) 22–6299, FAX 22–6299*
This small German-style guesthouse boasts old-world furniture and blue-and-white shutters, but the beds feel like bricks. An eggplant-shaped pool is offset by landscaped gardens and swings. Breakfast includes sumptuous chocolate cakes and strudels. Suites run $53, deluxe singles $30, and doubles $40. 49 apartments. *Moderate. All cards.*

WHERE TO EAT

Tannenhof
Rua Visconde de Taunay, 340; ☎ *22–8011. Daily noon–3:00 p.m., 7:00–10:00 p.m., closed Sunday. Live music.*
A substantial buffet runs about $4, but specialties (about $13) are renowned, such as shrimps flambéed with cherries and typical plates of duck and sausage. *Moderate. No cards.*

Brunkow
9 de Março, 607 (Centro). Daily 11:30 a.m.–2:00 a.m., on Sunday only the bakery.
The oldest and most traditional *confeitaria* (sweet shop) in the city, famous for its sweets, homemade bread, and banana cake. *Moderate. No cards.*

Bierkeller
Rua 15 de Novembro, 497; ☎ *22–1360. Daily 11:00 a.m.–3:00 p.m., 6:00 p.m.–11:00 p.m.*
Sit on wood benches under antelope horns and savor the typical German plates like *marreco com repolho roxo* (goose with purple lettuce) and bratwurst with sauerkraut. Oom-pah music and dark beer round out the picture. *Moderate. No cards.*

Churrascaria Ataliba
15 de Novembro/BR 101 (Expoville). Daily 11:00 a.m.–4:00 p.m., 6:00 p.m.–midnight, closed Sunday p.m.
Ataliba is always a good name in the South for *rodízio*-style beef. One price (about $6) also includes hot dishes, 42 salads, and 10 desserts—enough for any vegetarian. Children can fish in the nearby lake. *Moderate. No cards.*

> **Insider Tip:**
>
> Visitors shouldn't miss **Joinvilândia**, a entertainment complex with a restaurant, chocolate factory, and artisan shop, 10 minutes from the city on BR-101. At the restaurant, **Moinho da Oma**, you can feast on colorful dishes like purple cabbage, bright yellow sauerkraut, green lettuce, and golden brown sausage. (The loud music might be insufferable, but where else could you hear Bizet's "Toreador Song" played by an oom-pah band?) After dining, take a scrumptious tour of the chocolate factory (they give out free samples!) and check out the sculptured erotic chocolates for sale. The creative entrepreneur, Laércio Beckhauser, started the factory as a small kitchen and watched it grow into one of the best success stories in Brazil. Ask if his **Oma Farm** has opened, a private estate he is transforming into an ecological farm.

NIGHTLIFE

The most beautiful pub is **Chopperia Sop**. Or try **Escotilha** (open only at night), where the waiters are dressed as sailors.

SHOPPING

Centro Commercial is a shopping mall selling local products, such as lace at **Lepper** and procelain at **Porzellanhaus**. Also try **Artesanato da Terra**, where you can buy your very own Fritz and Frieda dolls (symbols of the German influence), as well as unusually attractive carved-wood cars. At **Chocolate Caseiro Germânico**, you'll find a variety of homemade chocolates, German hats, and *cachaça* in porcelain bottles. The **Crafts Fair** is held the second Saturday of each month at *Praça Nereu Ramos*.

Travel Agency

Adinco Turismo
Rua 9 de Marco, 857; ☎ *22-1115.*
Tivoli Agência de Viagens
Rua Princesa Isabel, 374; ☎ *22-3244.*

When To Go

Orchid-lovers will adore the 10-day **Festa das Flores**, held during the second half of November to the accompaniment of German folk music, dance, food, and *bier*. **Semana de Joinville** is a weeklong festival in March featuring typical foods, folkloric dance, and music. **Oktoberfest** in nearby Blumenau takes place in October.

Insider Tip:

Antartica cerveja (beer) made in Joinville is considered the best in Brazil due to the city's high quality of water. Ask for it throughout the country.

HANDS-ON JOINVILLE

Arrival

Seven flights run daily from São Paulo and Rio. Bus service from neighboring cities is excellent with hourly departures to Blumenau (2 hours), Florianópolis (3 hours), Curitiba (2-1/2 hours). Seven buses daily to S.P. (9 hours), one bus daily to Rio (15 hours), and two to Porto Alegre (10 hours).

Car Rental

Localiza National
☎ *22-6510.*

Taxi

Taxi
☎ *22-6426.*

Tourist Information

Secretary of Tourism
Praça Nereu Ramos, 372; ☎ *22-1437. Monday–Saturday 8:00 a.m.–6:00 p.m.*

BLUMENAU

Oom-pah music, blonde hair, and blue eyes fill the sparkling clean streets of **Blumenau**, a city of proud German origin picturesquely perched on the banks of the **Itajaí River**. The city of approximately 213,000 was founded in 1859 by Dr. Hermann Blumenau, whose descendants still live in the area and run a charming pousada. Scores of German immigrants followed Dr. Blumenau, as did a wave of Italians; it was only well into this century that the residents even felt compelled to learn Portuguese, so isolated were they by poor river connections.

Today, in Blumenau, whatever German traditions remain are as much a touristic device as true nostalgia for roots, but the locals are so cheerful they make the *gemütlichkeit* work. Local German bands perform nightly at the Biergarten, the city's main entertainment complex in the **Praça Hercilio Luz**, and numerous restaurants offer choice German cuisine. However, the main German event is the **Oktoberfest**, which attracts over a million visitors each year.

Nearly destroyed by several tragic floods, the city began the Oktoberfest festival on a citywide basis in 1984 to recoup financial losses and reinvigorate the people. The first festival, 17 days long, was a smashing success, and now visitors from all over Latin American come to swill beer, eat wienerschnitzel and spätzle, and cart home German crafts and crystal. Called the "second party in Brazil next to Carnaval," Oktoberfest is actually a much more organized event, even suitable for children. As part of a long-running tradition, local seamstresses sew costumes free of charge for visitors and shoemakers cobble traditional footwear. Beer-swigging contests from large glass tubes are a continuous day-to-night diversion, and when a reveler gets too drunk, the police just graciously escorts him or her home. During the week, 2 parades are held down the main street and a food fair takes place in the pavilion. To make liquid consumption easy on the revelers, *chopp* is distributed by bierwagens free of charge throughout the downtown area. Hotel reservations must be made at least 6 months in advance. If you want to stay with a German family write: **Secretaria de Turismo de Blumenau**, *Rua Alberto Stein, s/no. Bairro da Velha, Blumenau, Santa Catarina, Brasil.*

> **Insider Trivia:**
>
> *Fritz and Frieda are the official mascots of the city—a short, dumpy German man with wire-rim glasses and his much taller, blonde, pig-tailed girlfriend. Also, during Oktoberfest, the custom is to pin as many medallions, broaches, and feathers on your green-felt Alps cap as you can. The height of Oktoberfest chic, however, is a drinking cap that involves a ridiculous contraption of two cups with connecting tubes that run straight into your mouth. Perhaps the most oft-repeated phrase during the festival is: "Wir trinken unser Bier" (We drink our beer)—in German!*

SIGHTS

Fundação Casa Doutor Blumenau *Alameda Duque de Caxias, 64 Closed weekends.* This library and museum catalogues the history of Blumenau; the display of clothes worn by the first immigrants is worth the visit. An ecological park named Spitzkopf, adorned with picturesque waterfalls and walking trails, is a lovely place to stroll through. The chic street of the city, **Alameda Rio Branco**, is full of German-styled mansions and restaurants teeming with people, especially on the weekends.

THE ESSENTIAL BLUMENAU

WHERE TO STAY

★ Viena Park Hotel
Rua Hermann Huscher, 670 (V. Formosa);
☎ *(473) 22-4633*
Almost resort-like, this moderate-sized 5-star has the feel of a privileged private home. The incredible suite has two jacuzzis, one of which is situated on an outdoor veranda. An elegant restaurant serves German specialties, and the bar is well known for its fruit cocktails. Guests completely fill the hotel during Oktoberfest and December–February, taking advantage of the tennis courts, saunas, and poolside *churrascaria*. Single deluxes start at $71, doubles, $76, suite $142. 90 apartments. *Expensive. All cards.*

Hotel Cristina Blumenau
Rua Paraíba, 380, (473) 22-1198
A German-style house owned by Cristina Blumenau, the daughter of the city's founder Herr Otto Blumenau, conveniently located near the Oktoberfest Pavilion. Breakfast (included) is served in a charming salon with white curtains and bright tablecloths. Rooms come with air-conditioning and TV; there's also a homey living room with TV, and guests may use the kitchen. Ask for a larger room in the old house. Reservations required. Doubles run about $17. 20 apartments, 2 floors, no elevator. *Inexpensive. No cards.*

WHERE TO EAT

German delicacies are everywhere here—from Hungarian goulash to pig knuckles *(eisbein)* and sauerkraut. Do try the *café colonial*, a southern traditional tea served from noon to 5:00 p.m. It includes a luscious buffet of cakes, breads, sausages, applestrudel, cheese, and jellies that can pass as your one meal of the day. An excellent one is held at the Himmelblau Palace Hotel.

Frohsinn
Morro do Aipim, 1 kilometer (acesso pela Rua Itajaí); ☎ *22–2137. Daily 11:00 a.m.–2:30 p.m., 6:00 p.m.–11 p.m., closed Sunday*

Tucked on a hillside, this large wood-beam chalet looks out onto the River-Itajaí-Açu. Long lines of patrons wait patiently for the excellent Hungarian goulash with spätzle, smoked salmon, and Viennese sausage. Excellent fondue with salad runs under $9. *Moderate. No cards.*

★ Cavalinho Branco
Alameda Rio Branco, 165; ☎ *22–4300. Daily 11:00 a.m.–last client*

At the city's best German restaurant, housed in a stunning mansion, fill up on pig knuckles and sauerkraut, roast duck à la Hamburg ($5), applestrudel, and schnitzel. *Inexpensive. Cards: AE.*

Le Bon Gourmet
Rua 7 de Setembro, 818; ☎ *22–1277. Daily 11:30 a.m.–2:00 p.m., 7:00 p.m.–11:00 p.m.*

Blumenau's top-class French eatery happily esconced at the Plaza Hering Hotel. *Moderate–expensive. All cards.*

★ Confeitaria Cafehaus Glória
(Hotel Glória) Rua 7 de Setembro, 934; ☎ *22–6942. Daily 7:00 a.m.-8:00 p.m.*

Stained-glass windows, German tableaus, and a fabulous spread make *café colonial* (tea) at this coffee house a must. For under $4 you can gorge on bread, paté, cheese, sweets, sausage, and even omelettes. *Inexpensive. No cards.*

Ataliba
Rua Alberto Stein (Proeb); ☎ *22–5088. Daily 11:00 a.m.–3:00 p.m., 7:00 p.m.–midnight; Sunday 11:00 a.m.–4:00 p.m.*

Best *rodízio*-style steak house in town, with live music. *Moderate. No cards.*

Himmelblau Palace
(Hotel) Rua 7 de Setembro, 1415; ☎ *22–5800. Daily 4:00 p.m.–8:00 p.m., closed December–February*

Breakfast is excellent, with hearty German cakes, quiche, scrambled eggs, ham and sausage, and fried bananas with cinnamon. Excellent *café colonial. Moderate. No cards.*

NIGHTLIFE

Blumenau Biergarten Restaurante
Tuesday–Sunday 11:00 a.m.–last client is an entertainment complex located in a woody park, complete with restaurant, beer garden, shops, and loud German bands on Sunday at 5:00 p.m.

Check to see if the **Orquestra de Câmara de Blumenau**, a big success in Europe, is playing at the **Teatro Carlos Gomes**. There are also frequent performances of ballet and theatre.

Nighttime activity centers along **Avenida Beira Rio**, where 3 adjacent *chopparias*—**Tunza**, **Casinha**, and **Bude** —play loud Brazilian rock and serve *chopp* in German mugs. **Bude** is the most famous.

Live Brazilian music can be heard nightly at **Bar Kriado** *Rua Alwin Schraeder, 137. Monday–Friday, starting at 5:00 p.m.* On the outside wall, you can see how high the floods came in 1983 and 1984.

Across the street from Cavalinho Branco restaurant on *Avenida Alameda Rio Branco* is the **Baturité** disco, *which opens at 11:00 p.m. but doesn't start rolling until 1:00 a.m., Friday, Saturday and Sunday.*

SHOPPING

Blumenau is famous for its hand-blown **crystal**. Two excellent labels are **Cristal Blumenau** and **Hering**, all available at **Moellman** (on the main street), a white-and-brown German house that looks like a carved piece of chocolate. Other excellent buys are the porcelain and china made by **Porcelana Schmidt**. Delicious homemade honey breads *(honigschnitten)* can be found at **Adega Montenegro** *Rua Dr. Amadeu da Luz, 226* where you can also stock up on Bavarian chocolates (Blumenaier Scholoade is the best) and 100 percent pure **malt whiskey** called *Barrilete* in beautifully designed cases. Also available are **German wines** made in the region; the best is Richburg Riesling 1989, a dry white wine.

The biggest department store is **Lojas Hering**, where you can buy German-dressed dolls, special drinking helmets, green felt hats, and red suspenders for Oktoberfest. Homemade jams are also special buys as are unusual handmade Christmas tree decorations. A cheap lunch can be found upstairs.

> **Insider Tip:**
>
> *The most traditional band in the city, **Banda Cavalinho Branco** plays oom-pah music every Saturday outside the garden in front of Moellman's. Find a seat at the nearby chopparia and enjoy.*

HANDS-ON BLUMENAU

Arrival

You will have to fly to Floriánopolis and take a bus to Blumenau. Hourly bus service is available from Floriánópolis, Joinville, and Itajaí, plus frequent service to Curitiba, São Paulo, Foz do Iguaçu, and western Santa Catarina. The Rodoviária (bus station) is about 5 miles from the center of town; take the Cidade Jardim bus from downtown.

Money Exchange
Vale do Hajaí Turismo e Câmbio
Avenida Beira Rio, 167.

Tourist Office

The tourist office is located at *Rua 15 de Novembro, 420.* Brochures, maps and friendly assistance. Some English.

When to Go

Besides **Oktoberfest**, other reasons to go to Blumenau are: **Festa do Cavalo**, a rodeo held April 1–14; **Semana de Blumenau** starting September 2, with typical foods, dance, and music; and the **Blumenau Marathon** in the last Sunday of July.

CAMBORIÚ

Once called the Copacabana of southern Brazil, **Camboriú** has lost its ultra-elite rep as the South's best beach spa, but thousands of tourists still descend on the high-rise hotels, high-gear nightclubs, and 8 mini-beaches where cows still graze. Good hotel rates can be found when the value of Argentine currency drops in relation to the *cruzeiro*, since the city is a destination for Argentine vacationers. The first nude beach in the South is here at Praia do Pino, and around Camboriú Bay you can swim 100 meters in waist-level water. Along the main beach drag, **Avenida Brasil**, you'll find special truck-like buses to transport you along the strand. Two or three times a day, fishermen pull in their nets, and fish can be bought right off their boats. International surfing competitions are held once a year. **Barra de Camboriú**, a small fishing village across the bay, can be visited by canoe or car, and schooners may be rented at **Praia Laranjeiras**.

SIGHTS

The drive from Blumenau to Florianópolis, which passes through Camboriú, is one of the most beautiful farm countries in Brazil. In Gaspar, about 1-1/2 hours from Florianópolis, is an immense cathedral that looks like a story-book palace from the highway.

Parque da Santur *BR-101, kilometer 137;* ☎ *66-0033* is a major tourist complex with a mini-zoo, mini-farm, train rides, aquarium, and *tartarugário* (turtle farm), bird and reptile museum, and restaurants with typical Italian and German foods.

THE ESSENTIAL CAMBORIÚ

WHERE TO STAY

Marambaia Cassino Hotel
Avenida Atlântica, 300; ☎ *(473) 66-4099*
This 4-star is the city's principal luxury hotel. The adult and children's pool is surrounded by tropical gardens, and rooms are sleekly furnished. The circular floors open onto a plant-strewn lobby. 111 apartments. *Expensive. All cards.*

Rieger Apart Hotel Residence
Rua 701 N, 162/188; ☎ *(473) 66-2807.* *FAX 66-2807*
Something between a hotel and a private apartment complex, this residence offers attractively appointed 1, 2 and 3 bedroom apartments equipped with full kitchens. A thermal pool is being constructed, and guests may also enjoy a wet and dry sauna, a spa, and convention facilities. The location is prime, a block from the morning market where food are fruits are sold. Make reservation in July for January. 108 apartments. *Moderate. All cards.*

WHERE TO EAT

Moenda Calamares
Avenida Atlântica, 5340; ☎ 66–2587. Daily 11:00 a.m.–2:00 a.m.
Good seafood and *picanha na brasa* (steak served on a grill) for about $6-$7. *Moderate*. No cards.

Macarronada Italiana
Rua Dom Alfonso, 160; ☎ 66–0788. Daily 11:00a.m.–4:00 p.m., 6:30 p.m.–11:30 p.m.
Lasagna, pizza, and pastas.

Insider Tip:

A Camboriú tradition is to eat grilled corn on the beach.

HANDS-ON CAMBORIÚ

Arrival

Daily flights from Rio, São Paulo, Curitiba and Porto Alegre. The airport is located 12 kilometers from the city on BR-101. Daily bus connections are available to all surrounding cities.

Car Rental

LocaSul
Rua 15 de Novembro; ☎ 44–0411.

When to Go

September–April is the prime beach time.

NIGHTLIFE

All the best nightclubs are located on the South Bay. Try **Whiskadão** (Big Whiskey), and **Mario's,** a magnificent show of samba and transvestites on Rua Florianópolis.

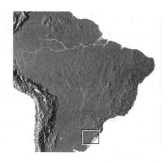

RIO GRANDE DO SUL

The Craggy Coast and Raging Ocean of Torres

Consider **Rio Grande do Sul** the Texas of Brazil. The southernmost state in the country, bordered by Argentina in the west and Uruguay in the south, **Rio Grande do Sul** is steeped in a powerful cowboy culture shared by the *pampas* of all 3 countries—that vast territory of cattle-grazing grasslands that provide the best beef in South America. Like Texans, natives of Rio Grande do Sul (called *gaúchos*) have throughout their history evinced a fierce pride in their culture and region, forced as they were to defend their borders without the help of the central government, who tended to ignore them for centuries. When **Getúlio Vargas**, the state's most famous resident, seized national power in 1930 through a coup d'etat, the country perked up to Rio

Grande's existence; since then it has developed into one of the most educated regions in the country, and definitely the most picturesque.

gaúcho

The term **gaúcho** (gow-oo-shoo) also refers to the figure of the macho Brazilian cowboy, a colorfully dressed character who still survives authentically in the smaller towns of the extreme south. In the larger cities, *gaúcho* dress is often worn at festivals or at special parties; the suede chaps, red kerchief, and black baggy pants tucked into knee-high boots usually require a large-shouldered frame to look appropriately virile, but these days girls and young women have appropriated the voluminous pants as street fashion, wearing them with form-fitting turtlenecks. Recently, the South's version of country music, particularly accordion-propelled folk tunes, has peaked the interest of youths, who are now returning to their roots for inspiration. Recent TV soap operas have further helped to revitalize the culture already replete with colorful aphorisms and romantic traditions.

chimarrão

At least once during your stay in Rio Grande, you must partake of *chimarrão*, an herbal tea that substitutes for *cafezinho* as the daily caffeine fix. A communal ritual, the making of *chimarrão* from *erva maté* (the raw leaves of a bitter-tasting plant) takes time not only to prepare properly but to sip gracefully; in 1991 the state government passed a law prohibiting the use of *chimarrão* in public offices because workers were wasting too much time drinking it (in contrast to *cafezinho*, which takes only a few seconds to down). Traditions die hard, however; I once saw a fashionable woman in the Porto Alegre airport stroll toward her plane, nonchalantly sipping from her *cuia*, the traditional cup made from a gourd. Today, many hotels and inns have *chimarrão* salons, rustically appointed with antique stoves and saddles, where you may experiment in private. Beware, however, that the taste is strong and often impossibly bitter.

Today, in Rio Grande do Sul, the traditions of German and Italian immigrants have blended with the stauncher *gaúcho* traditions to create a variety of earthy, European-flavored communities. Picturesque towns like **Gramado** and **Canela**, with their German-styled chalets and mountainous vistas, offer unusual options for the vacationer wanting to escape hot tropical climes. In the interior of the state, you will find Brazil's best **wine-producing regions**, where visitors may pick grapes at family-run vineyards and stock up on the country's finest vintages. Finally, the shoreline, dominated by the resort city of **Torres**, is unique for its craggy rock formations and the mysterious legends they have inspired.

Method for Making Chimarrão

*Chimarrão, a traditional **gaúcho** tea that originated in Paraguay on the Paraná border, is a sign of hospitality among friends, family, and business partners. If you spend any time in this region, it's almost certain you will be offered some in the form of a communal cup. (Although it's considered impolite to refuse, gaúchos claim that the hot water kills any germs.)*

To make *chimarrão*, follow these instructions:

1. Fill a *cuia* (traditional cup) two-thirds full with *erva maté* (tea leaves).
2. Pack the tea to one side and pour water (warm or cold) up to the slant.
3. Let the *cuia* rest from 5–10 minutes till water is absorbed.
4. Close the tip of the *bomba* (silver spoon-like straw) and put it in the empty space of the *cuia*.
5. Keep the *cuia* in the support, with the *bomba* closed as you pour in hot water. Then start serving.

FIELDING'S BRAZIL 1994

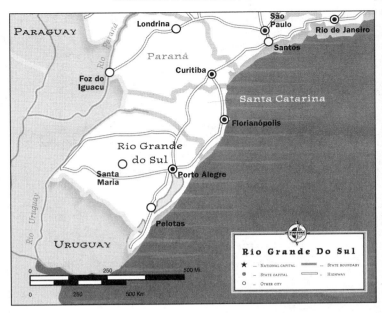

PORTO ALEGRE

Despite more than 1 million people (3 million in the suburbs), **Porto Alegre**, the capital of Rio Grande do Sul, still retains its small-town feel. Maybe it's the 19th-century balconies with antique facades that labor next to the towering skyscrapers or the vendors in horse-drawn carts who collect bottles and garbage in the old sector of downtown. Lying on the eastern bank of the Guaíba River, where 5 rivers converge to form a freshwater lagoon, the city dates back to 1755, when it was founded as a Portuguese garrison to guard against Spanish invasion. The city did not reach prominence, however, until it became Brazil's largest exporter of commercial meat. Today the commercial sector is situated on a hill overlooking the residential levels down below.

Most tourists use Porto Alegre as a jumping-off stop to tour the more picturesque cities of Gramado and Canela. However, the **Mercado Público,** near **Praça XV,** does hold some interest as a replica of Lisbon's Mercado da Figueira, its maze of stalls offering everything from *gaúcho* tea (*erva mate*) to food and handicrafts. On the left is the Neo-classical **Palácio Municipal**, the former mayor's office, built between 1898–1904. **Avenida Otavio Rocha** is a sidewalk mall where you'll be able to find *gaúcho* music in the discount bins of record stores.

Residents of Porto Alegre are soccer fanatics; their soccer club won the world championships in 1983. One or two games a week throughout the year are held at **Estádio Beira-Rio** (except for January and February). **Praia Ipanema** is polluted, but at night the drag is a major hangout for teens, who fill the street with their motorcycles, short skirts, and confident stares.

THE ESSENTIAL PORTO ALEGRE

WHERE TO STAY

★ ★ ★ **Plaza São Rafael Hotel**
Avenida Alberto Bins, 514 (Centro);
☎ *(512) 21-6100*

As elegant as you get in Porto Alegre, this 5-star is a full-service hotel with outdoor pool, sauna, beauty salon, Varig office, *churrascaria*, gift shop, and *salão de chá* (tea salon). The impressive lobby bustles with execs and famous guests. Ask for an apartment with a view of the water; you'll be able to look down into other people's backyards. The live music in the bar is renown. Exec apartments start at $58, deluxe rooms $77, 10 percent discount if you pay in cash. 284 apartments. *Moderate–Expensive. All cards.*

Porto Alegre Ritter
Lg. Vespasiano Júlio Veppo, 55 (Rodoviária, Centro); ☎ (512) 21-4044
Across the street from the bus station, and within walking distance of downtown, this 3-star offers the service of a 4-star, since you can use the pool, sauna, and restaurants at the hotel next door. Suites are comfortable, though even deluxes have no real decoration. A *chimarrão* salon serves tea. An executive buffet is a pleasant spot to catch a quick, decent lunch for about $5. 107 apartments. *Moderate. All cards.*

Terminal Tur
Lg. Vespasiano Júlio Veppo, 125 (downtown); ☎ (512) 27-1656
Well situated across from the bus station, this modest 2-star offers reasonably adequate rooms for excellent prices. 60 apartments. *Inexpensive. No cards.*

WHERE TO EAT

★ Churrascaria Galpão Crioulo
Avenida Loureiro da Silva (Parque da Harmonia) (Cidade Baixa); ☎ 26-8194. Daily 11:30 a.m.-3:00 p.m., 7:30 p.m.-1:00 a.m.), shows start at 10:00 p.m., 10:30 p.m., 11:15 p.m.
Rio Grande's most typical barbecue house (*rodízio*-style) housed in a big rowdy barn with a gift shop for *gaúcho* supplies. The 15 rounds of beef (including chicken hearts) are excellent, the folkloric show featuring 8 dancers is lively, and the band, with accordion, traps, and electric guitars, booms. *Moderate. All cards.*

★ Recanto do Tio Flor
Avenida Getúlio Vargas, 1700 (Menino Deus); ☎ 33-6512. Daily 11:00 a.m.-2:00 p.m., 6:00 p.m.-1:00 a.m.
Owner Alceri Garcia Flores, lovingly nicknamed Uncle Tio, has served the best regional food in Rio Grande for the last 10 years. Every plate is a macho delight, from the *matambre enrolado* (tasty slabs of rib beef with Texas-style sauce) to the *espinha* (juicy backbones that skid around the plate). The home-style joint can get rowdy when the clients start to sing, but the real floor show is wonderful: an attractive quartet who perform everything from elegant salon dances to flamenco-type stomping. The spur-and heel competition between the men is thrilling. Dishes run between $3-$4, (cover $1.50) and a self-service buffet is available at lunch. *Inexpensive. No cards.*

Ilha Natural
Rua Andrade Neves, 42, 1st floor; ☎ 25-0214. Daily 11:00 a.m.-2:30 p.m.
Vegetarian cuisine in this meat-oriented culture is difficult to find, but not impossible. Try the buffet of salads, hot dishes, and a variety of desserts. *Inexpensive. No cards.*

NIGHTLIFE

Gruta Azul
Rua Farrapos, 1274; ☎ 22-9380
Designed like a dark tropical grotto, this "high-class" dance club is the Brazilian version of "Ten Cents a Dance." Couples and single men come to watch semi-attractive girls without much talent gyrate in leotards and hula skirts to the strains of a live band; afterwards, the clients are invited to flirt. Dinner and drinks are also available. Exactly why I found this famous joint so depressing became crystal-clear when I asked my companion what these girls actually *do*. "Everything," he said. *Moderate. All cards.*

Sala Jazz Tom Jobim
Rua Santo Antônio, 421; ☎ 25-1229
offers the best jazz in the city.

Avalon
Rua 24 de Outubro, 1320. Tuesday-Sunday 8:00 p.m.-2:00 a.m.
is known for its live MPB and cool bossa nova.

HANDS-ON PORTO ALEGRE

Arrivals
Varig, Transbrasil, VASP, and Rio Sul all fly into Porto Alegre. The **Salgado Filho International Airport** is located 8 kilometers from downtown. A modern sophisticated subway system offers service from the airport to the Mercado Público (Public Market).

Car Rental
Aureo Sul
Rua Ouro Preto, 964, Esq. Sertório; ☎ 41-9017.

Climate

Very hot summer (temperatures can soar to 91°F), with winters averaging about 42°F.

Consulates

U.S.A.
Rua Cel. Genuino, 421/9th floor; ☎ 26-4288 (downtown).
Great Britain
Rua Pedro Chaves Barcelos, 3091; ☎ 32-2745.

Folklore

To gather more folkloric information, contact the **Gaúcho Tradition Centers**, CTG 35 Avenida Ipiranga, 5200; ☎ 36-0035.

Money Exchange

Banco do Brasil
Rua Uruguai, 185, 10th floor.
Exprinter
Sen. Salgado Filho, 247.

Taxi

Radio Taxis
☎ 23-1122.
Special air-conditioned cabs with pre-established fares for long and short trips are available through **COOTAERO** ☎ 42-6673.

Travel Agency

Mercatur
Avenida Salgado Filho, 97; ☎ 25-8055
Excursions to the 5-city area, wine country tours, and money exchange.

Tourist Information

CRTUR
(the official state tourist board) is located at Rua dos Andradas, 1137, 6th floor; ☎ 28-7377.
Information booths also are located at the airport and the train station.
EPATUR
is the tourist board for Porto Alegre, located at Travessa do Carmo, 84; ☎ 25-4744.
Information booths are also located at Praça 15 de Novembro; ☎ 21-0220.

When to Go

During the **Festa dos Navegantes** on February 2, the image of the Nossa Senhora dos Navegantes is carried through the streets from the Igreja do Rosário to the Igreja Nossa Senhora dos Navegantes, accompanied by a boat procession through the harbor and displays of barbecue and typical dances. **Semana Farroupilha,** on September 20, celebrates *gaúcho* traditions.

SHOPPING

Porto Alegre is a fount of *gaúcho* artifacts, though most goods can be bought cheaper in Gramado and Canela. One of the best traditional stores is **Invernada Grande** Rua Senhor dos Passos, 166, Praça Otávio Rocha; ☎ 27-2961, where a cowgirl or boy could go crazy over the knee-high boots, leather capes, voluminous *gaúcho* pants, silver spurs, and finely engraved saddles. **Alchieri** Rua Voluntários da Pátria, 777; ☎ 25-0473 also features typical arts and crafts. The best shopping mall is **Iguatemí Shopping** in Zona Norte.

Igreja Sao Pedro in Gramada is famous for the 71,000 stones that comprise its structure

GRAMADO AND CANELA

A mere 54 miles from Porto Alegre, these two picturesque towns situated high up in the **Serra Gaúcha** are a favorite among mountain climbers and anyone in need of a good box of chocolates. The Bavarian-styled towns (nearly villas) date back to 1875 when the first Italian and German immigrants settled to pursue farming. Today, the *einxaimel* architecture and impeccably kept gardens are as much touristic attractions as ancestral homage, but the quaint beauty of the area can't be denied. Horses are still tied up in front of traditionally tiled homes, and residents resemble Rip Van Winkle as they walk through the cobblestoned streets sipping tea from traditional *cuias*. During the summer months, the air is fragrant with rose-colored hydrangeas (from which the region, known as *Região das Hortências*, gets its name), and during the winter, the cool (if not freezing) air is a refreshing change to tropical heat.

A rivalry used to exist between these two mini-cities; these days they've found it more advantageous to unite forces. Gramado still boasts the better hotels, the coziest restaurants, and easier access to shopping, but Canela offers the finest in natural wonders, like the **Parque Estadual do Caracól**. After trekking to some of the country's most fabulous waterfalls, make sure you find a table at a *café colonial*, a traditional tea house that serves a glorious spread of cakes, cookies, jams, breads, cheeses, hot chocolate, and tea.

SIGHTS

In Canela

Located 4-1/2 miles from Canela, the **Parque Cascata do Caracól** is a 25-hectare park full of mountainous vegetation with a 131-meter waterfall that cascades dramatically down a forested cliff. Within the park there is also a restaurant, crafts fair, and playground, as well as camping facilities. Hardy trekkers can walk down a path to the foot of the waterfall, or travel an additional 5 miles beyond the park to the **Vale da Ferradura**, with its 400-meter canyon, around which the Rio Santa Cruz forms a horseshoe; the vista is particularly lovely at sunset. Don't miss a side trek to the **Araucária Multissecular,** a 150-foot-tall pine tree rumored to be between 500 and 700 years old. It takes about 8 persons to fully embrace the trunk.

In the city of Canela is the **Igreja Nossa Senhora de Lourdes**, also known as the **Catedral de Pedra** (Cathedral of Stones), because it's made entirely of basalt rock.

In Gramado

With access from Rua das Hortênsias, the **Cascata Véu de Noiva** is a 21-meter waterfall in the middle of dense vegetation, said to resemble a bride's veil.

Lago Negro, on *Rua 25 de Julho 175*, is a beautiful lake surrounded by pines, where you can rent rowboats. Constructed by Oscar Knorr, the **Parque Knorr** is considered to be the heart of the city, a picturesque park where you can stroll at leisure, smell the flowers, and take photos of the *alegria do jardim* (profuse bushes of red flowers).

In the center of the city is the **Igreja São Pedro** (1943), notable for its richly colored stained-glass windows and the 71,000 stones that create the structure.

Mini Mundo *Rua Horácio Cardoso*; ☎ *286–1334. Tuesday–Sunday 1:00 p.m.–6:00 p.m.* Not just for children, this 800-square meter miniature replica of Frankfurt, Germany, was created by Otto Hopper and his son, Heino, incorporating details from their favorite fairy tales. The marvelous work of art comes replete with a Bavarian-style cathedral, tiny waterfalls, and a real train that choo-choos around the perimeter.

Gaúcho Culture

Gramado's only museum is owned by a colorful local, **Lúcio Petersen,** who has spent his life collecting *gaúcho* paraphernalia. Saddles with silver stirrups, stuffed armadillos, and animal-teeth necklaces fill his 2-room display house; in the back is a *galpão crioulo*, a rustic room with an antique stove where traditional tea is served. Ask to see Senhor Lúcio's two horses ("You can't be a real *gaúcho* without horses," he told me), as well as his homemade *cachaça* collection, some bottles of which he just might sell to you. To see the museum, contact the Tourist Office.

Centro Municipal de Cultura *Rua São Pedro, 369;* ☎ *(54) 286–2522, ramal 25* holds *gaúcho* dance classes every Tuesday night from 7:30 p.m.–8:30 p.m.

THE ESSENTIAL GRAMADO AND CANELA

SPAS

Instituto Balneo e Lodoterápico
Avenida Borges de Medeiros, 3550 (Gramado); ☎ (54) 286-1027
This spa offers mud therapies rumored to be excellent for such disorders as rheumatism, infections of the skin, obesity, and impotence, all under medical supervision.

Kur Hotel
(Parque/clínica) Rua das Nações Unidas, 533 (Gramado); ☎ (54) 286-2133
A glorious place to rest, this famous health spa with hotel accommodations features minimum stays of one week. Not just for weight control, the clinic deals under medical supervision with all kinds of illnesses. Lectures on nutrition and psychology accompany 25 types of physical therapy, including herb baths, massage, compresses, and sauna. Aerobic classes are available, as is a special walking pool. The hotel's store sells excellent herbal shampoos and herbs, as well as *guaraná*, a natural Brazilian stimulant. The Chinese shiatzu I tested was authentic but brutal. 19 apartments. *Expensive. All cards.*

WHERE TO STAY

★ Hotel Serra Azul
Rua Garibaldi, 152 (Gramado);
☎ (54) 286-1082
Exposed wood-beam ceilings, roaring fireplaces, and excellent service make this 5-star hotel both elegant and rustic. Rooms are spacious and equipped with electronic controls, heat, and color TVs. The *Roda de Chimarrão* is a typical *gaúcho* salon for drinking traditional tea and *cachaça*. The excellent location offers easy access to sweater shops and crafts stores. Guests may play at the Gramado Golf Club. Singles start at $54, doubles $66. 152 apartments. *Expensive. All cards.*

★ Laje de Pedra
Avenida Presidente Kennedy (Canela);
☎ (54) 282-1530. Reservations in Rio: (21) 224-4798
Even if you don't stay at this fabulous mountain resort, do stop by the lobby to catch one of the region's best vistas: a paradise valley around which snakes the River Caí. The hotel even has its own backyard park, including a heated pool set amidst the greenery. A *chimarrão* salon is an inviting environ to experiment with *gaúcho* tea, or you can spend the evening indulging in wine and cheese in the cavelike restaurant. The hotel's disco is one of the few nightspots in a city where most everyone curls up early before a fireplace. Rooms are rustically appointed, but only the ones with a view of the valley are worth it. Singles start at $85, with discounts in off-season. 250 apartments. *Expensive. All cards.*

Hotel Serrano
(Parque) Avenida das Hortênsias, 1160 (Gramado) ☎ (54) 286-1332
One hundred meters from the center of town, this 4-star is also located on its own extensive backyard park. Rustic wood doors recall the forest outside; rooms are well-equipped with color TV, video, heat (no air-conditioning), and a huge minibar. Heated pool and sauna are also available; babysitters can be hired for about $3. December–February special activities are arranged for children. Since there are no elevators, guests will have to walk up and down stairs. The hotel's clothes store is excellent. Deluxe rooms start at $80, suites $110. 84 apartments. *Expensive. All cards.*

Hotel das Hortênsias
Rua Bela Vista, 83 (Gramado)
☎ (54) 286-1057
Situated on its own forested estate near the center of town, this exclusive Swiss-style chalet is decorated in fine wood furniture. Ferns drip from the balconies, and the lobby is the picture of hominess with a roaring fireplace; rooms are spacious. An indoor pool and sauna complement the rustic feel, but the restaurant only serves breakfast. Standard doubles $55, deluxe doubles $66. No children under 2 years of age. 16 apartments. *Moderate. No cards.*

Hotel Pousada das Flores
Avenida das Hortênsias (road to Canela),
☎ *(54) 286-1841*
Log wood walls decorate this Bavarian-style chalet with spacious, though austere rooms (heat, but no air-conditioning). The small lobby sports a fireplace and the lovely wood furniture of the region. Across the street is the Café Colonial Bela Vista, where you can find a scrumptious afternoon tea; down the road is a fascinating furniture factory. Doubles run $31, suites with bathtub $36. 16 apartments. *Moderate. No cards.*

Hosperdaria Andrade
Avenida Borges de Medeiros, 3585 (Gramado); ☎ *(54) 286-3356*
Located 10 minutes from downtown, this newly built 2-person hotel boasts simple but clean furnishings. All apartments have color TV, minibar, and shower, but no heat or air-conditioning. Breakfast in a tiny salon is included. Doubles run $23. 8 apartments. *Inexpensive. No cards.*

Hotel Cavalo Branco
Rua Reinaldo Sperb, 108 (Gramado);
☎ *(54) 286-1254*
This is a good option for low-budget families. Apartments are not air-conditioned, but contain color TV. Suites can sleep 5. A heated pool is located on the balcony and there is also a small playground. The restaurant serves only breakfast and snacks at night. Singles run $24, double $26. 27 apartments. *Inexpensive. No cards.*

WHERE TO EAT

Churrascaria Três Reis
Avenida Borges de Medeiros, 2713 (Gramado); ☎ *286-1874. Daily 11:30 a.m.–5:00 p.m., 6:30 p.m.–midnight*
Next door to where the Film Festival is held, this intimate *rodízio*, with a fine salad bar, even serves popcorn with their *cafezinho*. Try the soup "Ainho Lini." *Moderate. All cards.*

★ St. Hubertus
Rua da Carriere, 974 (Lago Negro);
☎ *286-1273. Daily 11:30 a.m.–2:30 p.m., 6:30 p.m.–11:00 p.m. Closed Tuesday, March–May, and August to November*
This Swiss-style restaurant is considered the best in Gramado, with a bar worth waiting in, covered with wine labels. The lace tablecloths and panoramic forested scenery makes the $9 fondues (including shrimp and chocolate) taste even better. Try some regional wines like Almaden, Garibaldi, and Adega Aurora. The hotel of the same name has a different owner, but its 20 apartments are also exceedingly pretty. *Moderate. All cards.*

Torre
Avenida das Hortênsias, 3845 (Gramado);
☎ *286-1921. Daily 2:00 p.m.–9:30 p.m. December–February opens at 10:00 a.m.*
Old photos of immigrants and *gaúchos* from the early 1930s line the walls of this traditional tea house where the waitresses dress like German *fräuleins*. For about $4, you'll receive 7 plates of sweets, sausage, chicken, polenta, cold cuts, vegetables, jams, and steaming pots of coffee, tea, and chocolate. Downstairs is **Lucirene**, an excellent knitwear store, and **Artesanato**, a good crafts store for leather, iron crafts, and wine and cheese. *Inexpensive. No cards.*

★ Café Colonial Bela Vista
Avenida Cel. Diniz, 2155 (Gramado);
☎ *286-1608. Daily 8:30 a.m.–11:00 p.m.*
Considered the best *café colonial* in Gramado, with over 60 types of food. *Moderate. No cards.*

Churrascaria Garfo e Bombacha
Estrada do Caracól, kilometer 5 (Canela);
☎ *282-1829. Daily 1:00 p.m.–10:00 p.m.*
An excellent *churrascaria* with a *gaúcho* folkloric show. *Moderate. No cards.*

> **Insider Tip:**
> *Make sure you try the delicious quentão, hot wine and cinnamon with a touch of lime.*

SHOPPING

You'll find over 30 sweater stores in this region; two of the best are **Malharia Vovó Anita** *Avenida Borges de Medeiros, 2717*, next to the **Gramado cinema,** and **Knitmaage** downtown. Cashmere sweaters from Argentine wool can be found at *Avenida Osvaldo Aranha, 235;* ☎ *282-2223.*

The best *gaúcho* clothes can be found at **Dan Mathi Nativa.** Leather jackets, hot pants, and vests direct from the factory are sold at **Kouro Arte** *Avenida das Hortênsias, 3021/1438 and 1835 (Gramado).*

The largest gift store (with a large variety of *chimarrão* sets and *gaúcho* hats) is **Artesenato Martini** *Avenida das Hortênsias, 5480.*

For local wines and cheese, try **Casa di Vinho Jolimont** *Avenida Osvaldo Aranha, 370;* ☎ *282-1232 (Canela, across from the cinema).*

High-quality *gaúcho* boots are sold at **Casa da Bota** *Rua Henrique Muxfeldt, 67.*

If you have time, visit the fascinating handmade furniture factory **Moveis Serrano Fabrika** *Avenida das Hortênsias, 4070.* The sawdust is knee-deep, but the designs are outrageously inventive, like the chair that folds into a ladder and another that turns into an ironing board. An agent in Texas delivers orders to the U.S.

Chocolate

The region excels in chocolate. Seventy varieties can be found at **Chocolate Caracol** *Avenida Dom Guanella, 1638/ RS 236;* ☎ *282-1829.* **Chocolate Caseiro Gramado da Prawer** *Avenida de Hortênsias, 4100* is located near the Pousada das Flores. **Chocolate Cogumelo** *Rua Dona Carlinda, 554;* ☎ *282-2422* is best known for its truffles and fruit-filled chocolates in the best European style.

NOVA PETRÓPOLIS

A half-hour drive from Gramado on the northeast mountain ridges lies Nova Petrópolis, one of the sleepiest, safest cities in all Brazil (the residents don't even lock their car doors!). In the 19th century, **Nova Petrópolis** was established by German immigrants from the Austro-Hungarian Empire, as well as by Prussians and Bavarians who maintained their own customs while adopting the *gaúcho* traditions. Because the land so resembled Petrópolis (where the Emperor summered near Rio de Janeiro), the immigrants called their territory "New Petrópolis." Today the area is considered a model of development for a small landed estate. At 6:00 a.m., carillon bells start ringing, with a hundred tolls at 6:30 a.m., making it impossible for any normal person to remain sleeping, although the residents claim they don't even hear it anymore. Most children speak German at home, and many groups seriously study folkloric dances, particularly for Oktoberfest. Noted for its atmosphere of "nothing going on," the town is a perfect place to rest. Horse-drawn carts still mosey down the avenues and cattle graze contentedly in the tall grassy fields.

> **Insider Tip:**
>
> Do be careful of mosquitoes—once considered, a widespread problem, but now only frisky at night in hot weather.

SIGHTS

The main tourist attraction in Nova Petrópolis is the **Parque Aldeia do Imigrante** (Park of the Immigrant), a sprawling forested park that features a reconstructed immigrant village brought from different parts of the region. Peacocks and chickens wander freely around the picturesque lake, where you can swim and rent paddleboats; a beer garden hosts winter and summer festivals. The park is perfect for long, idyllic walks, as well as offering a shopping complex for local crafts.

You'll need a guide and jeep to take you over the long rocky road that goes to **Ninho das Águas,** one of the best hang-gliding drops in the country. At the platform, you'll find a fantastic view of the countryside. To see the variety of plants grown in the region, visit the nursery **Floricultura Ursula,** which supplies flowers to the region's hotels.

Don't miss *café colonial* at **Recanto Suíço,** an 8-table German-style eatery where the owner herself serves the generous tea beneath antique cuckoo clocks and all sorts of knickkacks. *Nata*, a cream-like substance, is exceedingly wonderful on toast with jam; even the butter here comes shaped like flowers.

THE ESSENTIAL NOVA PETRÓPOLIS

WHERE TO STAY

Veraneio Recanto Suíço
Avenida 15 de Novembro, 2195;
☎ *(54) 281-1229*
German hominess at this tiny estate-like hotel, where you'll feel like you're living with the owners. The apartments attached to the main house are cozy, some even have their own chalets. Doubles run about $19. 4 suites, 4 chalets, 2 cabanas. *Inexpensive. All cards.*

Hotel Petrópolis
Rua Cel. Alfredo Steglich, 81;
☎ *(54) 281-1091*
A simple chalet house with a tiny pool, overlooking a mountain view on a picturesque estate. Singles run $17, doubles $23. 21 apartments. 9 chalets. *Inexpensive. No cards.*

WHERE TO EAT

Chopp Colonial
Avenida 15 de Novembro, 2087;
☎ *281-1499*
Simple recognizable food at this German-style building; the plate of the day ($5) usually includes chicken, noodles, rice, polenta, slaw, and beets. Try the Malzbier—a black sweet beer. *Inexpensive. No cards.*

Colina Verde
BR 116, kilometer 185.5 (Vila Olinda);
☎ *281-1388. Tuesday–Sunday 11:30 a.m.–1:30 a.m., café colonial 4:00 p.m.–7:00 p.m. Sunday and holidays.*
Well-cooked dishes for about $4 include soup, cheese, salad, potatoes, chicken, and sauerkraut. *Inexpensive. No cards.*

Cantina Príncipe di Napoli
Avenida 15 de Novembro, 832;
☎ *281-1202*
This brightly colored Italian cantina is strewn with party streamers and graffiti. Try the hearty plates of lasagna. *Inexpensive. No cards.*

Insider Tip:

Don't buy cachaça in the supermarket. The best is homemade; try the Velho Barreiro sold at specialty stores.

SHOPPING

The main street of Nova Petrópolis is full of shops that sell sweaters—which is a major product of the region—both handmade and factory-made. One of the best stores is **Christian Malha**. Also try **Art' Elis** for leather briefcases and lace handiwork; **Malharia Beatriz** for needlepoint and sweaters; **Arte & Manha** for interesting children's sweaters; **Salão do Artesanato** for excellent *cachaça* in fruit-filled glass bottles. At **Folklorica**, owner Gessy Deppe makes wonderful German-style clothes, dolls, and dancing shoes; you can even order custom-made dresses.

HANDS-ON NOVA PETRÓPOLIS

Arrival

Buses run regularly from Porto Alegre and Gramado.

Climate
Summers are hot and humid in the valley, up to 85°F; during winter, temperatures can fall to 10°F. Frost is an annual phenomenon and snow can occur now and then. Best months to go are April–May, September–October, and January–February.

Tourist Information
Secretaria Municipal de Turismo
Rua Cel. Alfredo Steglich, 95;
☎ (54) 281-1088.

Travel Agency
Turisflor
Avenida 15 de Novembro, 1936;
☎ (54) 281-1107
offers one-day tours of Canela and Gramado, as well as Caxias do Sul.

When to Go
In the last weeks of July, the **Festival de Folclore** features dance groups from all over the world. In the last week of January, **Festival de Verão** features German-style bands and typical foods.

TORRES

Rio Grando do Sul is not particularly noted for its coastal resorts, despite the unbroken 310-mile-long coast visited frequently by Uruguayan tourists. Torres is the one exception; with its mountainous cliffs and raging ocean, it's a dramatic point to visit even in off-season. Getting there is half the beauty: The rolling green hills on the road from Porto Alegre are strangely reminiscent of Texas, except for the white *garças* (tiny white birds), who love to perch on the backs of friendly cows. The beach resort is considered one of the cleanest in Brazil, since the waste of the city is not permitted to drain there. The dynamic coastline has given birth to hundreds of legends, and once you glimpse the mysterious rock formations off the cliff, you will understand why the boatmen are inspired to spin such magical yarns. One popular legend tells of a beautiful mermaid who appeared to a fishermen, asked for a comb, then pointed out a fabulous treasure. (Another version claims the fisherman went mad just from the sight of the mermaid and never retrieved the treasure.) In summer the main beaches, like Praia Grande, teem with colorful cabanas and bathers; better to go in March or November.

The main street of Torres has the feel of a small rural town. Along the beach drag, however, are houses of such architectural interest that students from all over the country come to Torres just to study them.

BEACHES

Praia da Guarita, the main beach in Torres, is a gathering for elite bathers. Take a walk up over the rocks and stone steps to see a magnificent view of the beach and the sand dunes. You are not permitted to touch the vegetation, which is part of a microsystem under the supervision of landscaper Roberto Burle Marx, but do walk down to the **Furnas do Diamante,** one of the most dramatic and raging seas in Brazil. With great care, descend into the grotto and stay all day, particularly if you've packed a lunch bag. Full of mist mixing with foam, the cave has given birth to myriads of legends; it's particularly mysterious at full moons. As you walk north along the edge of the cliff the green fields might remind you of Druid country in England. The last descent, **Ponte da Portão,** sports a cliff with totemlike faces carved naturally into the rock. Photo ops abound everywhere.

On the other side of **Rio Mampituba** is Santa Catarina, where you can see fishermen throw their nets after leaping dolphins have pointed out the schools of fish.

Parque Estadual de Guarita is an ecological park that you can drive through and contemplate the massive beige sand dunes.

EXCURSIONS

Região dos Alambiques, an area outside the city where horses still graze in front of houses, is well known for its *cachaças*. Tucked into the nearby hillside is a grotto (*Gruta*) famous for its miraculous healings, as well as scads of magnolia trees that lend a delicate feel to the air. Built in 1950 by the parish, the tiny altar at the top of a steep stone stairway still attracts thousands of pilgrims, many of whom climb the stairs on their knees and report miraculous healings.

On the same dirt road is **Sitio Nirvana Produtos Naturais**, the brainchild of "immigrants" from the more industrial city of Caxias do Sul, who have become committed to living off the land. Owners Spalding Rover, a New Age painter, and his wife, Mirtes, run this ecologically minded store, which sells fantastic honey bread, honey drops, natural oatmeal, and tropical-flavored liqueurs packaged in beautiful gift kits. Upstairs is a perfect view of the grotto, as well as their own paradisiacal backyard. Ask to see Spalding's inspirational paintings.

Delicious cheese and wines can be bought at **Adega Don Cido** on Beira 101.

THE ESSENTIAL TORRES

WHERE TO STAY

Continental Torres
Rua Plinio Kroeff, 465; ☎ *(532) 664–1811*
A five-star hotel offers efficient service and a substantial restaurant. 132 apartments. *Expensive. All cards.*

Dunas Praia Hotel
Rua 15 de Novembro, 48;
☎ *(532) 664–1011*
This 3-star hotel is made for the beach, located steps away. Breeze from the sea cools the rooms without air-conditioning and you can always escape to the verandas. All rooms come with phone, minibar, and color TV. Deluxe rooms start at $52. The hotel is most likely open only between December and March. 59 apartments. *Inexpensive. All cards.*

De Rose Palace Hotel
Avenida Rio Branco, 429;
☎ *(532) 664–1087*
Super deluxe rooms (for $33) are nearly suite-like in this moderate-priced hotel, where a rooftop restaurant offers a pleasant

diversion. All rooms include color TV, phone, and minibar, but only some have air-conditioning. The smallest doubles start at $21. *Inexpensive.* 51 apartments. *All cards.*

> **Insider Tip:**
>
> *Homes can be rented for 30 days during the summer for about $2,000; apartments near the beach run about $500. Contact the **Secretary of Tourism** Avenida Rio Branco;* ☎ *664-1219.*

WHERE TO EAT

Restaurante Mirador Praia
(Dunas Praia Hotel) Praça Mal. Deodoro, 48; ☎ *66-4101. Noon–3:00 p.m., 8:00 p.m.-11:00 p.m.*

The restaurant at this 3-star hotel far exceeds the quality of the accommodations. Shrimps are a good deal; the *camarão tropical* (about $6) is a steamy shrimp stew served in a sweet pineapple. *Moderate. All cards.*

★ **Café Colonial Tia Zilma**
BR-101, kilometer 11, Porto Colônia. Daily 8:00 a.m.–9:00 p.m.

A country-style inn located outside the city near Lagoa Itapeva is shaded by fig trees dripping with moss—a symbol of Rio Grando do Sul. Through the wood-shuttered windows you can gaze upon grazing cows as you munch on grilled ham and cheese sandwiches, deli buffets, and the *torta mesclada*—a thrillingly light coconut cake topped with chocolate sauce. *Moderate. No cards.*

Restaurante Molhes
Avenida Cristóvão Colombo, 30; ☎ *664-2229. Daily 11:00 a.m.–3:00 p.m., 7:00 p.m.–midnight*

A short walk from the Continental Hotel, this restaurant features huge black beetles dive-bombing through the open windows. Nobody offered an explanation, but the fish specialties, like the grilled shrimp, were excellent. *Moderate. All cards.*

★ **Restaurante Parque da Guarita**
Parque da Guarita; ☎ *664-1390. Daily March–November noon–6:00 p.m.*

The fantastic park surrounding this grass-roofed eatery transforms its simple decorations into casual elegance. In summer the house is teeming with clients clamoring for local *mariscos* (shellfish) or the *casca de siri* (stuffed crabs). *Tainha* is a large fish from the region, serving 2. Dishes run $4–$6. Afterwards, take a walk around the rocky coves where crashing waves and provocative rock formations create one of the most beautiful vistas in southern Brazil. *Moderate. No cards.*

Ravenna
Avenida Br. do Rio Branco, 117; ☎ *664-1031. Daily 11:00 a.m.–3:00 p.m., 7:00 p.m.–3:00 a.m., March–November 7:00 p.m.–3:00 a.m.*

Best pizzeria in town *rodízio*-style, with live music. *Moderate. No cards.*

> **Insider Tip:**
>
> *Near the Continental Hotel, there's a bridge that takes you to the state of Santa Catarina on the other shore. You'll find lots of simple eateries there.*

SHOPPING

For custom handmade boots try **Artesanato Ávila** *Avenida José Bonifácio, 491;* ☎ *664-1446* Knee-high buffalo suedes go for about $54.

HANDS-ON TORRES

Arrival
Buses run daily from Porto Alegre, and frequently, Florianópolis.

Climate
Summer temperatures (December–March) average around 75°F and 68°F in winter, making the area the most temperate in the state. May–August is too cold to bathe in the ocean.

Money Exchange
Money can be exchanged at Banco do Brasil and at the bus station.

Tourist Information
Secretaria de Turismo
Avenida Rio Branco; ☎ *664–1219.*

When to Go
Festival do Mar in November features all kinds of sports competitions, kite-flying, sand sculptures, poetry readings, and musical shows.

Annual **balloon festivals** occur the first week in May.

WINE COUNTRY

North of Gramado and Canela on BR-116 lies the cradle of Italian immigration in Brazil. Wine-making dominates the yearly calendar here, immigrants having discovered extraordinary conditions of soil and climate as far back as the 19th century. The region can be considered a 5-city community: **Caxias do Sul**, **Farroupilha**, **Garibaldi**, **Carlos Barbosa**, and **Bento Gonçalves**, all of which can be visited leisurely in a couple of days (or, at least the major sites, including winetasting, crammed into a 1-day tour). For the most part, the picturesque roads, lined with rolling hills and fertile valleys, are good, except when they're bad and then they're awful.

Customs of the area are extremely conservative. Italian is still spoken at home, Catholic traditions remain strong, and family life is a high priority (women tend to marry young, though they have just recently begun to work outside the home). Accommodations can be found throughout the region, but one of the best (for its central location and park-like estate) is the Samuara Alfred (see below).

CAXIAS DO SUL

Following BR-116, via São Vendelino, you'll come upon **Caxias do Sul**, one of the most industrialized cities in the region. Save your wine-tasting for Garibaldi, but most worthy of a stop here is the **Igreja de São Pelegrino** *Avenida Itália, 50 (Caxias do Sul)*, which houses an excellent replica of Michelangelo's Pietá, as well as 14 magnificent paintings of the Via Sacra by the Italian master Aldo Locatelli. As life-like as cinema, Locatelli's style uses immaculate detail to express the torment and despair of Jesus' life. The padre of the church, Father Mario B. Pedrotti, is a world-class spirit who loves to show off his church; ask him to show you his neon-lit cross and sepulchre, which electronically rise from the church floor to an electronic recording of "Taps." Also visit **Ana Rech**, a chic suburb of Caxias, full of excellent Italian cantinas and interesting shops.

THE ESSENTIAL CAXIAS DO SUL

WHERE TO STAY

★ Samuara Alfred
RS-122, kilometer 69 (Highway to Farroupilha); ☎ (54) 225-2222. Reservations in Porto Alegre (512) 26-2555
About an hour from Porto Alegre and 40 minutes from Bento Gonçalves, this resort hotel is perfectly situated for visits to the 5-city area. Rooms are large, and mine happened to look out onto one of the most beautiful scenes in Brazil—wooded mountains foreshadowing a duck-filled lake. Massively forested grounds are excellent for strolling, and families can take full advantage of the large, indoor heated pool, sauna, tennis courts, and soccer field. Small animals seem to be always scurrying about, and one morning there was even a large white rabbit hopping through the breakfast room. A large TV room features wide screens and a roaring fireplace. An interesting game played here is *bocha*, the Latin version of 10-pins. Single deluxe rooms run about $73, doubles $90. 81 apartments. *Moderate. All cards.*

Bela Vista Parque Hotel
Avenida Rio Branco, 1965;
☎ (54) 283-1177
Old-world charm at this 50-year-old renovated hotel on its own forested grounds in Ana Rech, a suburb of 10,000 near Caxias. A cozy bar, heated pool, and living room with roaring fireplace add to the country-style warmth. Spacious doubles with exposed brick-and-wood walls look out onto the forest. A Saturday buffet serves typical Italian foods for about $6. Standards $72, doubles $61. 51 apartments. *Moderate. No cards.*

WHERE TO EAT

Cantina do Waldemar
Rua Antônio Ribeiro Mendes, 3054 (Via Veneto);☎ 224-1520. Daily 11:30 a.m.-2:00 p.m., 7:00 p.m.-midnight. No evening hours April-November
This typical Italian cantina with wood benches and exposed brick walls offers a simple menu, but dinners come with a feast of side dishes, including antipasto, *sopa de capeletti* (chicken soup), salad, and pasta—all for about $4. Try a hearty regional wine like Granja União. *Inexpensive. All cards.*

Roda Pizza Giordani
Rua Governador R. Silveira, 1268;
☎ 223-2703. Daily Tuesday-Sunday 7:00 p.m.-11:00 p.m.
Best pizza in Caxias, *rodízio* style, including 28 different kinds. The chocolate pizza with *creme de leite* is to die for. A $4 set price includes salad. After 9:00 p.m., the joint starts hopping. *Inexpensive. No cards.*

Alvorada
Rua Os 18 do Forte, 200; ☎ 222-4637
Excellent grilled chicken. *Inexpensive. No cards.*

SHOPPING

Fine quality sweaters can be found at **Malhas Celli** Rua Visconde de Pelotas, 2473; ☎ (54) 221-3555.

HANDS-ON CAXIAS DO SUL

Arrival
Buses arrive daily from Porto Alegre.

Climate
Temperatures average around 60°F.

Tourist Information
For the 5-city area, contact **Semtur** Rua Alfredo Chaves; ☎ 222-3344 Booths and info at Praça do Centro Administrativo and at the kiosk at Praça Rui Barbosa.

FARROUPILHA

Considered the heart of Italian immigration, **Farroupilha** is most noted today as the wholesale capital for shoes and sweaters. You'll probably need a car and guide to make the factory visits, but you can make a steal on well-crafted boots and department-store quality sweaters. (One excellent sweater store is **Malharia Farroupilha** *Rua Treze de Maio, 275;* ☎ *543–765.*)

Also notable is the **Sanctuário de Nossa Senhora do Caravaggio**, located 6 kilometers from downtown. For the last 100 years, at least 500,000 faithfuls have made pilgrimages here during the month of May. On the perimeter of the city is **Parque dos Pinheiros**, 22 hectares of virgin forest sporting a fine restaurant, lake, pools, and sports courts. During the last days of October, a traditional *gaúcho* festival called FEGART is held.

GARIBALDI

Located in the middle of an exquisite valley, **Garibaldi** is the champagne capital of the region, responsible for over 96 percent of the country's production. The city is also the skiing capital of the country (one of the few places where it snows in Brazil, although not consistently). The city takes its name from **Guiseppe Garibaldi**, an Italian hero who took part in the **Farroupilha Revolution**, a provincial revolt against the Empire that failed. This is the best place to visit wineries, stroll through vineyards, and indulge in wine-tastings, as listed below.

THE ESSENTIAL GARIBALDI

WINE-TASTING

Coop. Vinícola Garibaldi, LTDA
Avenida Rio Branco, 833;
☎ *(54) 262-1100. Daily 8:00 a.m.–11:00 a.m., 1:15 p.m.–5:00 p.m., Sunday 8:00 a.m.–11:00 a.m., 1:15 p.m.–5:15 p.m.*
This winery is notable because it's the only cooperative in the area: 1,650 families of the region make up the ownership and more than 60 million kilograms of grapes are harvested yearly. Best buys are the rosé and white wines.

Maison Forestier
RS 470, kilometer 62.2; ☎ *262-1811. Monday–Friday 8:30 a.m.–4:40 p.m., Saturday and Sunday 9:00 a.m.–4:00 p.m.*
A classic name, this winery was the first in Brazil to possess its own land. Enter through the long forested driveway reminiscent of "*Les Liaisons Dangereuses*," and ask for the guided tour, which includes a fascinating film about the wine-making process. The best labels are the Reserve Forestier and the limited Cabernet Sauvignon (about $5); also try Gewürstraminer for $5. Most expensive is the Porte Forestier (about $9), which you can only buy here.

Granja Piccoli
Rua Lodovico Cavinatto, 1127;
☎ *221-7744.*
A medium-sized vineyard owned by a single family, where you can walk through the orchards and pluck off the grapes when they're in season (January–March). Don't forget to walk through the vat room with its overpowering aroma of wine. Beside 9 types of wine, you can buy excellent grape juice and dried apples.

Peterlongo
Rua Manoel Peterlongo Filho, 216; ☎ *262-1355. Monday–Friday 8:00 a.m.–11:00 a.m., 2:00 p.m.–5:00 p.m. (3rd weekend of the month 9:00 a.m.–4:00 p.m.)*
Since 1912, when the Peterlongo family developed the first Brazilian champagne, the sector has represented 70 percent of the municipal's economy. Guides in typical costumes escort you through the underground vats; don't miss the Cave de Bacco, where you can taste samples under the illumination of electronically lit grapes. Ask for the English brochure.

WHERE TO STAY

★ **Hotel Cascacurta**
Rua Luis Rogério Casacurta, 510 (Garibaldi)
☎ *(54) 262-2166*
Folks from Porto Alegre and São Paulo come to Garibaldi to buy good wines at excellent prices, breathe in the fresh air, and settle into the comfort of this beautifully renovated 12-room chateau. Tastefully decorated apartments with a view to the rolling hills are

a mere $20; the elegant restaurant is the best in the region, with a great lasagna for $3. Downstairs is a cavelike eatery that opens onto landscaped grounds. Reservations are needed 1 week in advance. *Inexpensive. No cards.*

BENTO GONÇALVES

In the heart of the colonial Italian region lies **Bento Gonçalves**, situated a little more than a hour by car from Gramado and Canela. The main annual event is the **Festa Nacional do Vinho** held in the last weeks of July. **Museu Histôrico Casa do Imigrante** *Rua Erny Hugo Dreher* located in the high part of the city, is one of the most complete museums in the area, with an archive that includes over 3,000 photos of Italian immigrants. Complete with a skating rink and antiquated trains, the forested **Parque da Fenavinho** sponsors major expositions. Don't miss the **Igreja São Bento**, the second church in the world to be shaped as a wine vat. Built in 1982, the church was constructed during a drought year when the parishioners built the church as a petition for rain. As things tend to happen in Brazil, rain poured the minute the church was completed. At the **Igreja do Christo Rei**, enjoy the 100 varieties of roses that are in full bloom January–March.

THE ESSENTIAL GONÇALVES

WINE-TASTING

★ **Casa Valduga**
Access from RS-470 (68.5 kilometer); ☎ *252-4338. Office located at Travessa Guaíba, 89;* ☎ *252-2709*
The French chef Paul Bocuse chose Casa Valduga as the best Cabernet in Brazil in 1989. The house also gets my vote as the most charming winery in the region, owned by a first-generation Italian and his 2 sons. (Their gnarled and grape-stained hands should alone prove the extent of their labors.) Combining old-world wisdom with high-tech Brazilian schooling, the family has come to produce over 120 varieties of grapes that they leave in homemade vats until they mature. Between January and March, visitors may collect grapes and eat them free of charge, then sit down to a fabulous Italian buffet lovingly cooked by Mother Valduga, whose homemade cheeses and salamis are delicious. Having started with nothing, the Valduga family now sells in bulk only to 5-star properties, like the Meridien Hotel in Rio, as well as Mássimo's (the restaurant) in São Paulo, who also orders an exclusive vinegar. Guests are welcome throughout the week, but should make reservations in advance for the weekends. Contact the Secretary of Tourism for a map since the rocky path is often difficult to find.

WHERE TO STAY

★ **Hotel Dall'Onder**
Rua Erny Hugo Dreher, 197 (Bento Gonçalves) ☎ *(54) 252-3555*
The principal 4-star in the area boasts 7 suites with jacuzzis. Deluxe apartments are tight, but well appointed, and include color TV, minibars, central heat, and electronic controls. The heated pool and sauna opens onto gardens, and the wine cavern with fireplace is a cozy place to sample the best vintages. Deluxe singles run about $30, doubles $36. 150 apartments. *Moderate. All cards.*

WHERE TO EAT

Casa de Pão, Queijo e Vinho
RS-470, kilometer 68; ☎ *252-2250. Daily*

11:00 a.m.–2:00 p.m., 6:30 p.m.–11:00 p.m., closed Monday
The simplest of bodegas, but the Italian house plate is an embarassment of riches: salami, cheese, pasta, chicken polenta, fried sausage, and salad for a mere $5. Downstairs, pick up regional salamis, homemade breads, cheese, and wines. *Inexpensive. No cards.*

Onder
Rua Erny Hugo Dreher, 197; ☎ *252–3555*
Large Italo-Brazilian families love the hearty plates at this semi-sophisticated restaurant in the Dall'Onder hotel. A *gaúcho* show is offered every Friday, Saturday, and Sunday, and during the week you may be lucky enough to catch a hilarious choir of senior citizens who act out old Italian songs and tell jokes. *Inexpensive. All cards.*

CARLOS BARBOSA

The only reason to stop in this tiny town between Garibaldi and Bento Gonçalves is the **Tramontina** store, known worldwide for its cutlery, tableware, and garden tools. The factory down the highway sports sheep grazing in front, but the quality of its utensils is excellent. And the prices are excellent.

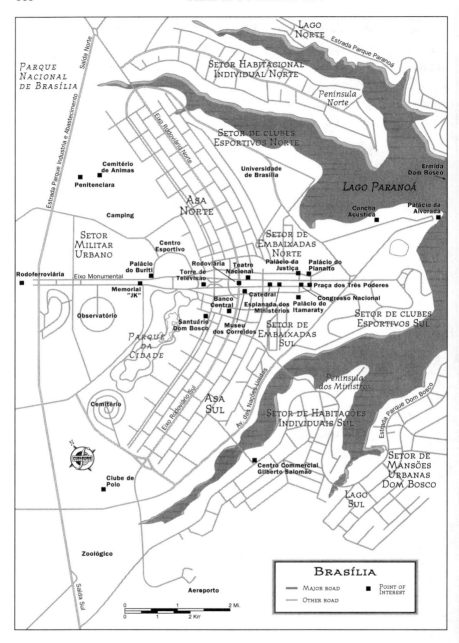

BRASÍLIA

Cathedral Metropolitana Nossa Senhora

Oscar Niemeyer, the architect responsible for the construction of **Brasília**, keenly described the ultramodern capital of Brazil as "the city Juscelino Kubitschek made with unlimited audacity and confidence." Truly, it *was* overweening *chutzpah* and daring imagination that built this wildly futuristic city literally in the middle of nowhere. Located on the desolate plateaus of Central Brazil, one thousand miles from the coast in the state of **Goiás**, Brasília sits among the dry arthritic shrubs of the *cerrado*, looking, for all its circular, pyramidal, and polygonal buildings, just like desert sculpture. Although most visitors arrive by airplane, the oddity of Brasília's location can only truly be appreciated by land. As you drive across the lonely plains of the Central Plateau, you will go hundreds of miles without ever sighting a human—until suddenly, the highway widens, billboards blare out, gigantic modern sculptures pop up like mirages, and at one carefully choreographed moment a 14-lane speedway rears into view. You have arrived in Brasília.

Despite the fact that Brasília has evolved into an efficient city complex since its construction in the late 1950s, it still remains for many a powerful metaphor. For some, it symbolizes Brazil's arrival into the industrial era. For others, it's considered an architectural disaster, a monumental descent into conspicuous consumption, and the *megalomania* of a populist politician hell-bent on posterity. To a third, underground minority, Brasília is beloved as the capital of the Third Millenium—the focus of mystical and mysterious vibrations that are set to usher in the next one thousand years. As such, I suggest you visit Brasília with three sets of eyes: political, aesthetic, and spiritual. If you only see concrete, you will side on the opinion of Simone Beauvoir who in 1963 called the city "an elegant monotony." But if you are keen to another sense, you can be inspired not only by the architecture, which seems to thrust into space with a passionate burst, but you'll be able to "grok" the enormous spiritual energy generated by a subculture of religious practitioners. In truth, the architectural meaning of Brasília is as much about space as it is about form. If the steel-and-glass structures seem at first cold to you, stop for a moment and contemplate their edges against the gorgeous ever-changing sky: the blue of day, the pinks and oranges of dusk, the twilight firmament at night. It's been said that 80 percent of all visitors to Brasília leave wanting to fly, and that's because the majority of Brasília is an awesome expanse of sky.

PAST GLORIES

When you consider the mystical origins of Brasília, it's no wonder that an astronaut was moved to say that the city is "the prettiest sight on Earth from space." Ever since the middle of the 18th century, the idea of transferring the capital from the coast to the center of this uninhabited interior has been the dream of numerous visionaries. Politicians first talked about the idea of a Brazilian inland capital in 1789, and in fact the plan was written into the constitution in 1891. On August 30, 1883, an Italian priest, named **Dom João Bosco** had a truly remarkable dream in which he found himself traveling across the Andes to Rio in the company of a celestial guide. In his dream, he noticed mountains, plains, and rich deposits of metals, coal, and oil between the 15 and 16 degree latitude, as well as a wide stretch of land at whose point a lake had formed. As he later related, a voice in his dream repeatedly told him that when people came to excavate the mines hidden in the mountains, there would appear a Promised Land, "flowing with milk and honey." Quite intriguing is the fact that the topography in the dream exactly corresponds to that of Brasília, which was constructed between the 15 and 16 degree latitude (the lake referred to is the manmade **Lagoa Paranoá**, which was built to temper the low humidity). Indeed, it was about 75 years later (or three generations, as Dom João Bosco had predicted) that the vision of a "Promised Land" was realized. Today a cathedral in homage to Dom João Bosco is one of Brasília's most beautiful churches.

The Project Of JK's Career

It wasn't until the presidency of **Juscelino Kubitschek**, who fueled his campaign with the fiery promise to build a new capital, that the energy to build Brasília finally connected with the vision. The project became the central, if not all-consuming, project of JK's career. Many were skeptical of the government's ability to build in the middle of a wasteland, but Kubitschek rallied the nation with seductive political goals: By focalizing the power of the federal government in Brasília, he claimed that the population of the interior would be stimulated, the capital cleansed of the "negative" international influences it felt in Rio, the federal budget empowered to deter inflation, and the country endowed with a living symbol of modernism. In essence, what the former physician-turned-politician was offering the country was 50 years of economic progress in 5—a chance to make leaps of innovation in every area, from housing to transportation, education, commerce, and the social sciences.

The Plan

At the insistence of Oscar Niemeyer, who had already been selected as the principal architect for the project, the federal government in 1957 held a national competition to select a city plan. At first, many thought the winning submission by **Lúcio Costa** was a joke. In contrast to the hundreds of elaborate designs submitted by other contestants, Costa's entry consisted only of 5 medium-sized cards, some of which were mere sketches of crosses, or two axes on which was superimposed an equilateral triangle. In fact, Costa claimed he had not even planned on entering the competition, but after a long deliberation of the problem, the sign of a cross had popped unbidden into his head. Although some have called the shape of Brasília a plane, a bird, or a dragonfly, Costa described it as the kind of "X" mark you would make in the sand if you were locating a treasure. Despite (or because of) its simplicity, the jury, which included Niemeyer, saw in Costa's plan the thrust and unity required to meet the growth of a capital city. Mystics like to point out that the simple design also has roots in ancient sacred symbols, especially Egyptian hieroglyphics. As Costa envisioned, one axis, called the **Eixo Monumental**, would constitute the fuselage of the city—the official political and administrative offices—while the other axis would comprise the residential sector.

Hopes For A New Life

Fueled by paper money and international loans and grants, Brasília was built in an extraordinarily short time, pressured by JK's desire to inaugurate the city before he left office. A gold rush atmosphere prevailed. Bulldozers, food, and cement were dropped in by helicopters; migrants from all over Brazil came in hopes of a new life. As architects, administrators, and workers shared the same makeshift houses, bars, and restaurants, a frontier democracy was momentarily enjoyed, what Niemeyer called "a climate of fraternization resulting from identical discomforts." Kubitschek himself came to visit often, staying in a wooden building built in 10 days, called **Catetinho**, or Little Catete (after the Presidential Palace in Rio). To the delight of the *candangos* (or workers), Kubitschek walked around the site without police protection, threw barbecues for the workers, and even sent each employee of the federal construction company a signed letter of thanks upon leaving the Presidency.

In April 1960, exactly 3 years, 1 month, and 5 days after the master plan was revealed, Brasília was inaugurated with 150,000 guests in attendance, including President Eisenhower and Queen Elizabeth. Unfortunately, the 38-ton fireworks salute proved a bit premature. Many of the buildings had to be redone when they collapsed after too-hasty construction; road junctions still had to be eliminated; landscaping in the residential sector was a dream away. The enormous debt—2 billion dollars worth—was left in the hands of Kubitschek's successor, **Jânio Quadros**. Most disturbing of all was the fact that the planners had failed to account for the homes of the migrant workers who chose to remain once their jobs were completed. As a result, satellite cities sprung up around the Federal District to house the overflow—some of them miserable shanty towns little different from Rio's *favelas*.

THE ARCHITECT

Much of the fun of touring Brasília is trying to guess what shape Niemeyer had in mind when he created various buildings. Although the architect was known for jesting with interviewers, he once claimed that he liked to throw a wadded piece of paper up in the air and used whatever shape it landed in. In truth, Niemeyer had been the leading student of Le Corbusier, founder of the modern planned city, whose designs were profoundly based on social philosophy. For his services, Niemeyer accepted only minimal pay (the equivalent of U.S. $300 a month), and like the other workers, he lived in the most makeshift of accommodations until the project was completed. Because the workload was monumental, he often sketched the basic ideas and left the details to a team of architects and engineers. Politically, Niemeyer had the most socialist of intentions in constructing apartment complexes that were identical and, therefore, classless, but one of his great disappointments regarding Brasília was to discover that utopian societies cannot spring spontaneously from utopian architecture unless the necessary social changes are first initiated.

A BIRD'S EYE VIEW

Although getting around a city that uses only a series of codes and numbers for street names might seem daunting at first, the system is perfectly logical, if hardly poetic. The city is carved into sectors—the residential sector, the hotel sector, the banking and commerce sector, etc.—and their addresses represent the proximity north and south of the **Eixo Monumental**, or east and west of the other main axis called **Eixo Rodoviário**. For example, SCN 310 means Setor Commercial North (from the Eixo Monumental) at # 310. Fortunately for the tourist, all the major architecture of Niemeyer (the political buildings) are located within walking distance along the Eixo Monumental.

It was Costa's genius that placed the **Rodoviária** (bus station) at its most logical point—at the center of the city where the Eixo Monumental and the Eixo Rodoviário meet. Within easy walking distance from the bus station is the **Cathedral** and the **National Theater**. About a half-hour walk away are the towers and dome of the **National Congress**. The **Hotel Nacional** is also just a stone's throw away as are two of the biggest shopping centers, on either side of the Rodoviária. For a quick overview of the city, there's a circular bus route (bus #106) that gives you a long outer city tour (leaving and departing from the bus station; just be careful to keep your wallet close at hand). Taxis are also plentiful, though they tend not to be cheap in Brasília. The easiest way to see the city is to arrange a professional tour offered by one of the many travel agencies, which may even pick you up at the airport and deliver you back the same day for late-night flights. To see the city during the day and again at night, with the monuments fantastically illuminated against the dark sky, is like seeing two different faces of the moon; if you have the money, you won't be disappointed. A daring way to see Brasília is from the sky—in an **ultraleve**; for more information contact the owner **Moacei** at his office ☎ *223-5506 or at home* ☎ *248-6136.*

Most people live in apartment complexes called **Superquadras** —nearly identical blocks of apartments based on the fundamentally utopian premise that the architectural design of Brasília would inspire the development of a classless society. The layout, however, never quite prevented the proliferation of political bribes to obtain choice locations (closer to the center), nor did it keep residents from decorating their apartments with individual style. At least, residential addresses are fairly easy to decipher. For example, SQS 510, bl. 4-209 means Superquadra South (of the Eixo Monumental), *bloco* (block) 4, apartment 209. Sometimes, signs on the street are not clear, so if you're visiting a private apartment, don't feel daunted. Each apartment block has a porter who will be happy to direct you; they're used to even long-time residents getting lost. (My local friends continually dropped me off at the wrong address, particularly at night, when the *superquadras* really do look alike.)

> **INSIDER TIP:**
>
> Traditionally, many tourists fly into Brasília in the early morning, spend the day sightseeing, and fly out in the evening. Frankly, this is a hectic way to experience a city that needs to be absorbed in a contemplative fashion. Especially, if you're interested in the more esoteric aspects of the area, you'll need a few more days. Hours can be spent at the **Templo da Boa Vontade**, and if you're seriously interested in receiving healings at the spiritual community **Vale do Amanhecer**, you should plan at least an extra half-day. Excursions through travel agencies can also be made to natural parks and waterfalls about 100–150 kilometers from the city; one of the most beautiful is **Salto de Itiquira**, replete with 4 waterfalls, a canyon, and 36 streams of mineral water.

DAILY LIFE

What is it like to live in Brasília? The term *Brasilite* (Brasilia-itis) was coined by the first generation of migrants to refer to the boredom of living in anonymous, identical apartment houses. Added to that was a deep longing for the hustle and bustle of city life—a tradition in most Brazilian cities, where much of the social and commercial life is played out on the street corner. In fact, it was the *people* who insisted that shops be put back on the street in contact with the curb. In frustration, many upper-echelon bureaucrats—hungry to display their individuality by negating the modern aesthetic—moved out of the apartment complexes and into their own houses on the other side of the city. If you have time, take a drive around to check out some of the more extraordinary houses: I even saw an igloo-type construction that had been handmade by a Japanese-descended scientist.

Brasilite does have its positive side. Despite the impoverished status of such satellite towns like Sobradinho and Planaltina, the standard of life in the Federal District is high and the crime rate extremely low. For every 4 superblocks, there is a church, movie house, police, post, school, gym, art center, and gas station, and every superblock is walking distance to a small shopping center full of food stores, restaurants, and boutiques. It is expensive to live here (since 60 percent of what is consumed must be imported), but there is no lack of urban services. Though nightlife is palpable (after all, the city is full of ambitious young politicians), the real activity seems to take place behind closed doors (in Brasília, it's said, everyone's in bed by ten, then goes home at six in the morning). From personal experience, I can say that there is a certain buzz of peacefulness that prevails in the city. Given the opportunity to stay several weeks in a private apartment, I discovered the layman's life here can have a slow, unthreatening rhythm all its own.

> **Insider Tip:**
>
> *Due to an incredibly low humidity (under 12 percent), it is very easy to become dehydrated in Brasília without knowing it. This is of particular concern for infants and the elderly. If you are staying for only a day, you probably won't have to worry about dry hair and chapped lips, but do drink as much water as you can—up to 3 liters. Long-term residents fight a continual battle against the dryness through the ubiquitous use of lotions, hair tonics, lozenges, etc. One of the most serious problems caused by the dryness is spontaneous fires, which you might see along the highway's dry, desert-like vegetation. As such, please don't carelessly throw cigarettes on the ground.*

SIGHTS

Many people claim there are two powers in Brasília—one political, the other spiritual. (In fact, a popular joke runs: If there really is so much spiritual power in Brasília, why isn't the government doing a better job? The answer: Imagine what it would be like without it!) In any case, the following tour has been divided into two sectors—to respect the traditional separation of church and state—though, in Brazil that line is often finely drawn. (For more information about the Collor family's intimate relationship with psychics, see the chapter *Traveler's Guide to Brazilian Spirits*.)

POLITICAL BRASÍLIA

As envisioned by designer Lúcio Costa, the main political and administrative buildings are located along the horizontal axis of the city. On the eastern tip is the area known as the **Power Plaza Complex**, comprising the **National Congress**, the **Palace of Justice**, the **Itamarati Palace**, the **Planalto Palace**, the **Historical Museum**, and the **Supreme Court**. Dominating the center of this complex is the **Praça dos Três Poderes** (Square of the Three Powers), representing the forces of the Executive, Legislative, and Judicial branches.

The **Congresso Nacional** *Monday–Friday 8:00 a.m.–noon and 2:00 p.m.–5:00 p.m., Saturday and Sunday 9:00 a.m.–noon and 2:00* *p.m.–5:30 p.m.* is one of the most well-known landmarks of Brasília. Though Niemeyer would never admit it, many people feel that his downward-turned dome (seating 120) symbolizes the elitist views of the **Senate**, while the up-raised bowl of the **House of Representatives** points to its openness to the views of the people. Others claim that the bowl receives inspiration from the heavens while the dome keeps it contained. On April 21, the anniversary of the city, the sun rises exactly in the middle of the office buildings between the dome and the bowl, which house the offices of the Congressmen. These two towers, both 28 stories, were constructed to be the highest buildings in Brasília by mandate of JK. (The law normally permits only seventeen stories). You'll probably see people climbing over the dome, which is entirely permitted. Less exhausting tours can be made of the interior of the Congress, but must be scheduled in advance at the **Department of Public Relations** ☎ *31–5107* English-speaking guides are available.

Bountiful Flow Of Justice

Also designed by Niemeyer, the **Justice Palace**, the seat of the Ministry of Justice, is famous for its facade of suspended curved platforms from which falls a curtain of water—perhaps, as some say (though sometimes sarcastically), a symbol of the "bountiful flow of justice" in the country. A fine view of the building can be seen from the balcony of the **Itamarati Palace**, designed by Niemeyer, with gardens and pool by Roberto Burle Marx. Here, at the President's palace, heads of state are formally received, first passing by the front courtyard's sculptures of extremely large-hipped women—perhaps a symbol of another kind of Brazilian justice. In the foyer, the first sculpture you'll see is the "Polivolume," by Ana Maria Vieira, made entirely from aluminum; that the artist invites you to push and pull the movable sculpture into any shape you wish is considered a symbol of the people's power to effect political change. The indoor gardens are full of plants from the Amazon and do well because of the shadowed light. Upstairs are galleries and salons full of 18th-century furniture and modern and classical art: one particularly intriguing piece is the "Namoradeira"—a three-cushion love seat for a girl, her boyfriend, and her mother. In front of the building, the sculpture entitled "Meteors," by Bruno Giorgi, represents the continents of the planet; it's made from interlocking pieces of marble and at night makes a marvelous reflection in the dark pools. Note that visitors to the palace may not wear short pants. Group tours are given free of charge Monday–Friday at 4:00 p.m. if no foreign heads of state are visiting. No photos are allowed.

Changing Of The Guard

Behind the National Congress, on the north side, the **Palácio do Planalto** *Monday–Friday 9:00 a.m.–10:30 a.m., 3:00 p.m.–5:00 p.m.* houses the president's office, not always open to the public. You can, however, enjoy the changing of the guard at 8:30 a.m. and 5:30 p.m. daily. When the President is in town, he ascends the ramp of the Planalto in a ceremonial procession (complete with a band playing the National Anthem) every Tuesday at 8:30 a.m. and descends Friday at 5:30 p.m. Most people don't go inside the **Panteão da Pátria**, or National Pantheon, but its external view is riveting; the shape of two doves in flight suggests the sense of unlimited freedom. The building was constructed in honor of former President Tancredo Neves and all the nation's heroes. In 1961, at the request of Kubitschek's wife, the First Lady, Niemeyer built a pigeon house across from the Pantheon. The 250 pigeons that were shipped in are affectionately known as the Brazilian Air Force, roosting during the day on top of the dove-like building. Nearby are the impressive sculptures of two warriors (by the same artist who made the "Meteors" at Itamarati Palace). Constructed in 1985 during the military regime to symbolize the sovereignty of Brazil, the warriors stand 105 meters high; the flag, which flies continuously, is particularly evocative against the dark sky. The changing of the flag, accompanied by a military band, occurs at 9:00 a.m. the first Sunday of each month.

Final Resting Place

The **Memorial JK**, erected by Niemeyer to honor Juscelino Kubitschek, looks like a submarine emerging out of water. A statue of Kubitschek sits atop a 28-meter pedestal on the roof; inside, his body is retained in a red-lit crypt that makes a dramatic, if avant garde final resting place. The museum inside boasts a fascinating display of his personal and political life, told through photographs, ceremonial costumes, medals, and documents pertaining to the construction of the city. Born September 12, 1902, in Minas Gerais, Kubitschek studied to be a doctor, but found himself succeeding in politics. After he passed the next presidency to Jânio Quadros on January 1, 1961, he became a senator, but in July 1964, his political rights were suspended for ten years by the military dictatorship, during which time he took exile in Europe. When JK returned, he met his final demise in a suspicious car accident. Although he certainly went to his death with the badge of Brasília, many claim he was responsible for beginning the gargantuan foreign debt, which today still threatens to choke the country to death. In the museum, there is also a library, art gallery, and small snack bar. The entrance fee is about a dollar. A short walk north from the JK Memorial is the **Pálacio do Buriti**, seat of the local government, set in its own square dominated by a Buriti palm tree. It's also nicknamed Sweetheart's Square because of all the parked cars that congregate at night. If you have time, take a drive down **Avenida das Nações**, where all the embassies have constructed residences following the architectural style of their own country.

> INSIDER TIP:
>
> JK was savvy in picking the date April 21 for the inauguration of Brasília. Rome commemorates its founding on April 21, and Tiradentes was killed on April 21, 1792. Since the conspirators of Tiradentes' Inconfidencia dreamed of moving the capital to the interior, JK, a born Mineiro, was happy to accommodate them.

SPIRITUAL BRASÍLIA

Santuário Dom João Bosco *Avenida W-3 Sul, Q 702. Mass: Monday–Saturday 1:00 p.m. and 6:00 p.m., Sunday 8:00 a.m., 11:00 a.m., 6:00 p.m., 7:30 p.m.* This Gothic-style church dedicated to the Italian visionary who dreamed up Brasília is appropriately ethereal; the wash of color from the blue-stained glass (12 different shades) gives the effect of sitting in heaven. Designed by the architect Carlos Alberto Neves with gardens by Roberto Burle Marx, the church was founded in 1964 and the first mass was held March 23, 1970. The sculpted bronze doors hold the story of Dom Bosco's dream; above is the life of Jesus carved in stone. Above the altar is an 8-meter high crucifix with the image of Christ carved from a single block of wood by Gotfredo Thaler. To the left of the altar is a statue of Dom Bosco. The most striking feature is the awesome chandelier, weighing over 1-1/2 tons, with 74,000 pieces of glass.

Igreja de N.S. de Fátima *107/108 South* Built by Oscar Niemeyer with gardens by Roberto Burle Marx, this small, modest chapel was the first church in Brasília, erected in 1958 at the request of JK's wife,

Sara Kubitschek, in honor of the Virgin of Fatima. Some have said the roof's flying triangle resembles a nun's habit. The street in front is the only one in the city that has a name, called **Rua da Igrejinha** (Street of the Small Church).

Catedral Metropolitana Nossa Senhora Aparecida *Esplanada dos Ministérios. Mass: Monday–Friday 6:12 p.m., Saturday 5:30 p.m., Sunday 8:30 a.m., 10:30 a.m.* Oscar Niemeyer once claimed to a journalist that he designed Brasília's cathedral in thirty minutes, trying to make something that did not remind people of their sins. In fact, his futuristic circular temple, with sculptures by Ceschiatti suspended from the roof, more resembles an inverted chalice and crown of thorns, though at night it looked to me just like a space center for ETs. In any case, the upward-thrusting movement seems to carry the eye and soul straight to heaven while the pill-like Baptistry to the right grounds one back to earth. After the church was completed on May 3, 1957, the stained-glass windows were taken out to reduce the heat, and Niemeyer spent the next two years trying to make the structure look more like a church. As you enter the cathedral the dark corridor he called the Meditation Zone prepares you for the bright illumination of the sanctuary. The bells atop the candelabra were donated by Spain and are engraved with the names of Cabral's boats. The acoustics are so good that if you stand at one curve of the wall, you can perfectly hear the person at the next curve. The wooden cross on the left was used in the first mass of Brasília. Next to the church, a flower stand sells dried flowers typical of the *cerrado*. Note: Shorts and bermudas are not permitted.

★ **Templo do Boa Vontade** *SGAS 915, LT 75/76;* ☎ *245-1070* The heartchild of José Paiva, a well-known writer and broadcaster, this interfaith temple, opened October 21, 1989, is the most inspiring chapel in Brazil. Built through local and international donations, the temple is dedicated to the idea that the "altar preferred by God for His Worship is the human heart." As such, every detail is geared towards instilling a meditative state of mind in order that the visitor may open up to greater energies. At the inauguration, the stunning jacaranda doors were knocked on 17 times, and since then have remained opened. (As the chapel is open to the public 24 hours a day, many people come to visit in the dead of night.) Every detail in the chapel involves the number 7 (considered the number of perfection); even the sides make a seven-sided pyramid, the first in the world. In the Nave, the tradition is to walk slowly around the 7 rings of black marble, meditating on releasing your negative energy, until you reach the center, over which presides the largest purest crystal in the world. Then you slowly return on the white marble rings, absorbing positive energy, until you reach the front of the altar. (My guide claimed that Russian Kirlian photography has proven that those returning on the white lane have clearer auras than when they began.) There is also a "Sala do Silêncio" (Room of Silence), where you are requested not to speak, as well as an art gallery of Brazilian and international artists. (Look for the German artist Ula Haensell, who makes healing mandala plates corresponding to each *chakra*.) Also, walk past the natural font of water that flows from the earth below and is filtered in a spiral to receive energy from the crystal. Downstairs is a memorial room, considered the heart of the temple, where you are encouraged to pray according to your own path. A brilliant, multicolored tile panel represents yin and yang energies, the chakras, and the spirit's awakening to God. In the inner room, the violet-lit suspended coffin symbolizes the spirit's transcendance over death. Near the exit is a souvenir shop, where you may purchase literature by Paiva Netto in English as well as a variety of crystals.

VIEW OF THE CITY

The best view can be seen from the 218-meter high **TV Tower**, which looms like a steel skeleton over the city. Designed by Lúcio Costa, it's located by the Eixo Monumental, Setor Oeste (West), and can be reached easily from the Rodoviária (bus #131) or on foot. There's an acceptable restaurant, a bar, and gift shop. On weekends and holidays, a crafts fair is held at the base.

GREEN BRASÍLIA

If the concrete and steel of Brasília becomes overwhelming, there are several well-designed parks and gardens to escape to. Located on the South Lake, the **Botanical Gardens** cover 600 hectares, loaded with different environments representative of the region, and 8 kilometers from the north of the city is the **Brasília National Park**, a reserve of 32,800 hectares, where flora and fauna of the region are preserved. Open to the general public are mineral springs, two natural swimming pools, natural woodland, orchidarium, and tourist facilities. For tourists, it's best visited during the week.

Located at the heart of the city is the **City Park**, designed by Costa and Niemeyer, with landscaping by Roberto Burle Marx. Over the 40 acres is spread an artificial lake with a boat dock, ridges, waterfalls, and islands, where you can pedal-boat, fish, and kayak, as well as dine in an adequate restaurant. Other attractions include a swimming pool with waves, playground, and outdoor barbecue.

Along the banks of the **Paranoá Lake** and surrounded by a wooded area of eucalyptus trees is the **South Lake Recreation Area**, with a boat dock, restaurant, playground, and fishing pier. At the time of the construction of Brasília, Lago Sul had been a very small river that was damned and expanded to provide more humidity. On a nice night, it's a lovely place for drinks or dinner overlooking the lake. From a plane, you can see the chic homes of the area, each one boasting a swimming pool.

ESOTERIC EXCURSION

Vale do Amanhecer *(just 45 minutes out of Brasília)* is a community of 3,000 "channelers" or psychic mediums, totally dedicated to the healing of others. (For more information, see the chapter *Traveler's Guide to Brazilian Spirits.*) Visitors may attend healing sessions in the eclectic-designed temple on Wednesday and Sunday afternoons, when clients are received individually for psychic counseling and the "laying-on of hands." To arrange a visit, you may arrive without a reservation (there is a simple restaurant on the grounds), or you may arrange an English-speaking guide and transportation through the tourist agency **Prestheza** ☎ *226–6224*.

NIGHTLIFE

Two excellent bars, usually with live music are **Bar Academia** *308 Norte;* ☎ *274–8828* and **Chorão** *302 Norte;* ☎ *226–0891*. Many people tend to head for the entertainment complex **Gilberto Salomão**, where they can pick from a variety of bars, discos, and fine restaurants. The environment is dynamic and ever-changing to reflect trends. One of the most active clubs in the complex is **Hippus** *SHIS QI 5 Conj. Gilberto Salamão;* ☎ *248–2890. Nightly 10:00 p.m. on Tuesday and Thursday nights features '60s music, Wednesday Afro-Caribbean, Friday and Saturday pop; Sunday from 4:00 p.m. to 8:00 p.m. is reserved for teens 12–16 years old. A cover is only charged on the weekends ($9 for men, $8 for women, with free drinks).* Another hot club is **New York New York** *SHIS QI 9. Nightly 10:00 p.m.–5:00 a.m., closed Sunday and Monday.* Music is changed according to the clientele; after 3:00 a.m. the DJ "lets the animal go," as he says. The small disco floor is tinged in blinking red lights, and the cushy banquettes are inviting. Cover is about $6–$7, including one free national drink. The young and terminally hip patronize **Zum** *SHIS QI 5 Conj. Gilberto Salomão;* ☎ *248–2890*.

Older singles (especially women 30–40) frequent **Flash** *Setor Hoteleiro Norte;* ☎ *225–3393.*

> INSIDER TIP:
>
> *I was told there is no high-class place for meeting "party girls" in Brasília because they are usually called by phone–a very high-class service arranged through your concierge.*

THE ESSENTIAL BRASÍLIA

When To Go
Once a year at Easter, a great reenactment of the **Passion of Christ** takes place on the mountains of the **Planaltina**. As one local guide told me, "They really put Him upon the Cross and nail Him." Hundreds of locals dress up in Biblical costumes, and there are even Roman-like constructions erected along the way.

During the week, when the **President** is in town, he ascends up the ramp at the Palacio do Planalto, accompanied by a military guard and band, and descends on Friday at 5:30 p.m.

What to Wear
Brasília is a formal city, where most official political business is conducted in suits. Female visitors to government buildings should wear a dress or tailored pants, men, a sports jacket. Some churches do not allow Bermudas or shorts.

GAY BRASÍLIA
Since this is a political town, the gay scene is mostly underground, but I was informed by reliable sources that the town is full of transvestites (draw your own conclusions). **Aquarius** is one of the few "official" hangouts, but it's considered sleazy. Gays (and prostitutes) tend to hang out at the **Edifício Eldorado**, a shopping complex, after 8:00 p.m.

SHOPPING
Brasília raises convenience shopping to an art, with a shopping complex for every 4 superblocks. The major shopping centers are **Conjunto Nacional** and **Park Shopping**. Located across from the National Theater, Conjunto Nacional can be recognized by its vertical ad panels as brightly lit as Times Square. A tourist guide (steep at $9) can be found at the **Livraria Sodiler** on the first floor. Near this bookstore, a bulletin board called **Mural Comunitário** lists different cultural events happening throughout the city. **Park Shopping**, with 8 movie houses, is much more modern, and features a large playground and lots of restaurants. The best place to buy precious and semi-precious gems is **Gemas do Brasil** *SQS 303 in the commercial district.* An excellent esoteric bookstore, **Thot Livraria**, is located in the **Edifício Eldorado** shopping complex. A few books are in English, though most are in Portuguese; among the many topics are works of French spiritualist Allan Kardec, who has influenced generations of Brazilian mystics, as well as fascinating tarot decks. The owner, who is also a publisher of esoterica, speaks some English and can direct you to any healer in the city. Also on sale is a video documentary of Brazilian esoterics. Nearby in the same complex is **Cheiro Verde**, a natural-foods buffet luncheonette.

HEALERS
Look for a copy of *Guia Ser Alternativo* (in Portuguese), a guide to the esoteric services in Brasília (available in health food stores, bookstores, etc.).

Forças Ocultas *SCLN 209, bloco D, loja*

21; ☎ 273-5680.
is an esoteric center sponsoring courses and individual sessions in tarot, astrology, practical magic, Bach Flower remedies, hypnosis, and numerology.

Instituto Ser *SHIS Q1 05, Chácara 81 (Lago Sul).*
An alternative spiritual center offering courses in astrology, ayurvedic massage, Tibetan healing, rebirthing, and meditation.

Selma Marga ☎ *248-1695 and 248-1255.*
Excellent masseuse.

WHERE TO STAY

If you decide to stay overnight in Brasília you won't find cheap accommodations easily. Most of the hotels, located in the Hotel Sector (Setor Hoteleiro), run from moderate to expensive. Because Brasília is a Monday–Friday business town, however, great discounts can be found at most hotels from Friday night through Sunday, although you may have to inquire pointedly if a discount is not directly offered. Also, traffic is less hectic on weekends, and if you plan to visit the spiritual community Vale do Amanhecer, note that it is only open to the public on Sunday and Wednesday. Advance reservations are highly recommended at any time, particularly if you want a view (many people prefer to stay on the upper floors of high-rise hotels for the magnificent vistas).

Expensive ------------ **Over $70**

Moderate ------------ **$40–$70**

Inexpensive ----------- **Under $35**

Hotel Nacional
Setor Hoteleiro Sul, lote 1; ☎ *321-7575, FAX 223-9213*
Inaugurated in 1960, the 5-star Nacional was the first hotel built in Brasília and still attracts the big, traditional names, like Queen Elizabeth, as well as Brazil's own top officials who do not live in the city. The stream-lined lobby appears to be permanently time-warped in the 1960s, though it's usually filled with important-looking persons in expensive business suits. Hallways are carpeted in bright square patterns and wood-paneled walls, exuding a sense of decorum and propriety. The impossibly large Alvorada Suite has an impressive view of the Congress, Cathedral and National Theater. Even standards have a touch of chic, though the furniture has not been updated for decades. The egg-shaped pool is the largest in the city and the sauna is especially clean. Guests particularly enjoy the connecting Galeria, owned by the hotel and housing numerous airline agencies, exchange house, car rental, bookstore, and boutiques. During high-priority news events, the hotel is jammed with journalists who hole up in the enormous convention salon and transmit faxes all night. Standard singles run $73, doubles $82. Thirty percent discounts are available in July and December–February Special weekend rates, though the hotel is usually packed with politicians during the week. 346 apartments. *Expensive. All cards*

★ **Naoum Plaza**
Setor Hoteleiro Sul QD 5, bloco H/I; ☎ *226-6494, FAX 225-7007*
The chic lobby of this 5-star high-rise is reminiscent of Rio's Caesar Park—plush oriental rugs and highly polished marble floors. The elegant restaurant looks onto a landscaped garden replete with waterfalls. The top 3 floors, with private entrances, have VIP services. All rooms are appointed with designer-styled spreads, walnut headboards, and electronic controls; all have tubs. Prince Charles and Princess Diana graced the Presidential Suite—a stunning expanse of five rooms, French colonial-style furniture, outdoor jacuzzi, and wraparound verandas. The small, rectangular-shaped pool has an outdoor sun deck, and a health club and Turkish bath are also available. English-style afternoon tea is a tradition here; a jazz bar offers fine music nightly. If you're in the mood, follow Princess Di's habit and go jogging around Parque Cidade (City Park) across the street. Standards singles run about $72, doubles $91. 200 apartments. *Expensive. All cards.*

San Marco Hotel
Setor Hoteleiro Sul QD 5, bloco C; ☎ *321-8484, FAX 224-3935*
From the rooftop pool of this 5-star hotel

can be seen a magnificent view of the TV Tower. Standards, with color TVs and minibars, are fashionably appointed with gold carpets and peach spreads. Suites are gracefully appointed with leather couches and a glass-top dining table in the adjoining room. All rooms have verandas. There's also a gallery of small shops, including a car rental and a travel agency. The rooftop restaurant is a bit functional but does offer a wraparound view of the city. A piano bar offers live music nightly. Standard singles run about $89, doubles $112. *256 apartments. Expensive. All cards.*

Eron Brasília
Setor Hoteleiro Norte, QD 5, lote A,
☎ *321–1777, FAX 226–2698*
Pelé and Michael Forbes have stayed at this 4-star high-rise with its white marble lobby dominated by a modernized painting of Jesus. Corridors are well kept and exceedingly clean; apartment doors are painted in blue-and-white colonial style. Rooms are adequately furnished, though on the smallish side; the only difference between standard and deluxe is that the latter has a better stocked minibar and electronic controls. On Wednesday, the restaurant serves a special buffet with delicacies traditional to the state of Pernambuco, for about $11. Clients may use the prestigious Golf Club, with whom the hotel has an arrangement. Forty percent discount on weekends. Standard singles run about $93, doubles $118. *180 apartments. Expensive. All cards.*

★ Bristol Hotel
Setor Hoteleiro Sul QD, 4, bloco F;
☎ *321–6162, FAX 321–2690*
 The Bristol has the quality of a 4-star hotel, but the management claims it gets more business masquerading as a 3-star. It's also the only 3-star hotel in Brasília that has a pool. Standards, with gold satin bedspreads, are quite acceptable spaces with large glass sliding windows. Deluxe rooms have verandas. An indoor pool with a glass rooftop offers a fabulous view of the city, particularly at night. The restaurant, which also doubles as a coffee shop, serves international food both *a la carte* and buffet. The hotel's one jarring detail is the salesmen allowed to stand at the entrance of the hotel hawking jewelry and crystals. Singles run $48, doubles $62. Thirty percent discounts are available on weekends. *141 apartments. Moderate. All cards.*

Hotel das Nações
Setor Hoteleiro Sul, QD 4, bloco I,
☎ *225–8050, FAX 225–7722*
The lobby of this 3-star lacks even a pretense of luxury, but at least the brown-and-white marble floor matches the couches. The air-conditioned apartments are adequate, if a bit kitschy, with old-time phones, electronic controls, a small desk, and a minibar. The restaurant called Panela o Brasil offers a large buffet with cold and hot dishes good for vegetarians and an a la carte menu that specializes in *carne de rã* (frog meat!). A tiny bar has four tables. Doubles start at $55. Weekend discounts up to 20 percent are available. *129 apartments. Moderate. All cards.*

Mirage Hotel
SHN QO 02. bloco N; ☎ *225–7150*
The lobby of this 2-star has got more oomph than others in the same inexpensive category. Apartments are clean, and come with color TV, phone, but no minibar; the bathrooms are small but acceptable. Breakfast is served in a cheerful salon with plastic-covered tablecloths and a snack grill for hamburgers and omelettes. Alcohol isn't served after 11:00 p.m., and silence is required after 10:00 p.m. The hotel is located in a complex with several other similar properties. Management does not accept credit cards, and a sign at the reception reads "Don't insist." Doubles run $26, singles $20. *69 apartments. Inexpensive. No cards.*

CAMPING

Those wanting to feel the "vibes" in Brasília might do well camping. The most centrally located site is **Camping de Brasília** in **Setor Áreas Isoladas Norte**, behind the Kubitschek Monument and the Buriti Palace. The #100 bus gets you there from the Rodoviária downtown. Fees are about $2–$4 a night. About 46 kilometers out of town on Estrada da Ponte Alta/Estrada da Marila are the **Bela Vista** campgrounds ☎ 226-2663.

WHERE TO EAT

Though hardly the culinary capital of Brazil, Brasília does not lack for good meals. All hotels, even 3-stars, have decent restaurants and fair prices. Execs tend to go out for drinks between 6:30 p.m. and 7:30 p.m., then return home and dress for dinner, which starts no earlier than 9:00 p.m. Most restaurants are hard put to serve decent fare at 7:00 p.m. On Saturday you can find *feijoada* everywhere except in *churrascarias*.

Expensive	Over $15
Moderate	$5–$15
Inexpensive	Under $5

Churrascaria

★ **Spettus**

Setor Hoteleiro Sul, QD 5, bloco E; ☎ *223–9635. Daily 11:30 a.m.–1:00 a.m.*
Near the TV Tower and across the street from the São Marco Hotel, this is one of the best all-you-can-eat steakhouses in Brasília. The extravagant options of 22 cold salads, 14 hot plates, and 18 types of Argentine meat will set you back about $13. But, as the manager says, "If you don't have good service, you don't have to pay." Happy hour takes place on a small veranda overlooking the highway, but that's Brasília. *Moderate. All cards, dollars accepted.*

Easy Lunch

Coisas da Terra

Avenida W-3, North, QD 703, bloco D, loja 41, subsolo; ☎ *226–6748. Daily 11:30 a.m.–4:00 p.m.*
Eat lunch on the covered patio or inside this airy restaurant trimmed with greenery, where the casual-chic buffet of salad, vegetables, fish, and chicken is filling. Sandwiches run about $3; the grilled chicken on French bread is excellent. Women traveling alone will feel welcome. *Moderate. No cards.*

Eclectic Funk

★ **Carpe Diem**

SCLS 104, bloco D, loja 1; ☎ *225–8883. Monday–Wednesday noon–4:00 p.m., 7:00 p.m.–midnight; Thursday–Friday noon–4:00 p.m., 7:00 p.m.–dawn, Saturday noon–dawn, Sunday noon–midnight. Beer garden open Monday-Wednesday noon–2:00 a.m., Thursday–Friday noon–dawn, Sunday 8:00 a.m.–midnight. Breakfast Saturday–Sunday 8:00 a.m.–11:00 a.m.*
A waggish menu full of elaborate explanations and a bevy of tall, beautiful women (actually mannequins) set the tone for this eclectic eatery owned by 2 journalists, 2 architects, and 1 engineer. The chef is Swiss, but the cuisine is funky Portuguese, with specialties like *feijoada com lirismo* (with lyricism), *peixe em alcaparras*, fish prepared in a vinegar base with capers and hot butter, and the *filé com 4 pimentas* (steak grilled with red, green, black, and white pepper). Friendly and breezy, the joint breaks open at midnight with the young and terminally hip, who gravitate between the outdoor beer garden, the restaurant, the piano bar, and a small import shop that sells Sidney Sheldon, Bulgarian jam, and Grey Poupon for outrageous prices. *Moderate. All cards.*

French-Brazilian

Gaf

SHIS QI 05, bl. C, ljs. 16/24 in the Centro Comercial Gilberto Salomão; ☎ *248–1754*
Dark, cushy, and chi-chi, Gaf attracts the haute couture of Brasília, namely politicos with their mistresses. An excellent jazz singer adorns the marvelous bar area, enhancing the romance. The menu is a French-Brazilian mix, specializing in seafood shipped from the Northeast and Santa Catarina. The house shrimp is flambéed in cognac; also intriguing is the *Filet à Sauce d'Escargots* with garlic. Since Gaf fills up fast after 11:00 p.m., make reservations for late-night dining, but also consider just coming for drinks and dessert after a night tour of the city. *Expensive. All cards.*

French/International

Florentino Grill

Comércio Local Sul, QD 405, loja 1; ☎ *242–9901. Daily: 11:30 a.m.-2:00 a.m.*
Top of the politicos' A-list, Florentino is, with the exception of Cachopa, the closest restaurant to the hotel sector. Outside is a

lovely covered garden veranda; inside, a high-class, English-style pub with mahogany-paneled walls and tartan carpets. The French-style menu features *mini-lagosta* (small but tasty lobster for about $21), *paillard* with fettucine, and grilled chicken with asparagus for a reasonable $9. Despite the French menu, however, the chef will cook anything on demand—even cheeseburgers. At noon, the street in front of the restaurant is filled with chauffered limos.

Natural
A Caminho do Natural
Comércio Local Norte, QD 302, bloco B, loja 7; ☎ *226-6733. Noon–3:00 p.m. and 5:00 p.m.–9:00 p.m., closed Sunday.*

Just a small stool and tabletop, but the vegetarian self-service is hearty, including all kinds of beans, vegetables, and brown rice for about $3. Also, the place to stock up on beans, whole wheat bread, granola, delicious oatmeal cookies, and sugarless sweets. A bulletin board details all the New Age activities of the city. *Inexpensive. No cards.*

Vivalavanca
HIGS 707, boulevard L, Casa 48; ☎ *244-2127. Noon–2:30 p.m., 6:00 p.m.–2:00 a.m.*

Located in a private home in the residential sector, this small, but airy restaurant (and organization) promoting macrobiotics is my favorite lunch spot. Simple, but well-cooked plates of brown rice, salad, beans, and a little cake run about $2.50; add another 50 cents for soup. You'll have to endure eating on wood stools, but you're sure to find like-minded souls, especially if you're interested in healers. Honey, beans, whole wheat breads, etc., are also on sale; classes and courses are periodically given. The organization promotes the work of Tomiko Kikuchi, who brought macrobiotics to Brazil. *Inexpensive. No cards.*

Portuguese
★ Cachopa Restaurante
South Sector QD 5, (Galeria Nova Ouvidor), subsolo 1, loja 127; ☎ *224-9192. Noon–4:00 p.m., 7:00 p.m.–last client about 2:00 a.m., Sunday only for lunch.*

The name of this Portuguese-style *adega* means "menina" or "girl," but there's nothing childish about the menu, except perhaps for the *Ovos Moles de Veiro*, a kicky-sweet concoction of egg yolk, sugar, and cinnamon that mothers traditionally serve their children. Gypsy shawls cover the rough-hewn walls of this traditional spot in Brasília for the last 25 years; specialties include *Bacalhau na Brasa* (codfish grilled in the Portuguese style) for about $15, as well as chicken for about $10. Even diet plates are available with vegetables grilled without oil. Downstairs, a special lunch buffet charges $6 per kilo. The music charge for about $2 covers the solo singer from Sunday–Thursday and multi-stylistic house bands on the weekends; movement starts after 9:30 p.m. A special buy is the Portuguese clothes and wines on sale in the lobby. *Moderate–Expensive. All cards.*

With a View
Pontão
45 SHIS QL 10/12 (Ponte Costa e Silva). Noon–3:00 a.m.

This outdoor/indoor restaurant overlooking the lake is a lovely place to contemplate the reflection of the city lights (though chilly in July). After 6:00 p.m. a fine local singer with guitar provides serenades. Pizza, pasta, and chicken are specialties, but it's best to come just for hors d'ouevres and beer. Music cover runs $2, minimum consumption $3.50 during show. *Inexpensive. No cards.*

HANDS ON BRAZÍLIA

Arrivals
The international airport is located 13 kilometers from the center of the city. Taxis run about $10–$12. Bus #102 also runs to and from the airport, originating in the Rodoviária. If you plan to fly into Brasília in the morning, sight-see, and fly out at night, you can leave luggage at the airport in secure lockers. (Also see *Points Beyond*, below).

City Transportation
The bus system in Brasília is excellent, with the Rodoviária located at the center of the city—walking distance from the cathedral.

Climate

From November–February, the countryside in Brasília is intensely green. In the winter months (June–August), the land is very dry and often parched brown. Brush fires can easily occur. The month of March receives the most rain. Temperatures are generally moderate, and cooler during the evening.

Consulates

U.S.A. *SES Avenida das Nações, lote 1;* ☎ *223-5143.*
Great Britain *SES Avenida das Nações Q 801, cj. K, lote 8;* ☎ *225-2710.*
Canada SES *Avenida das Nações Q, 803, lote 16;* ☎ *223-7515.*
Australia *CP 11-1256, SHIS QI-09, Conj. 16, casa 1;* ☎ *248-5569.*

Money Exchange

Money may be exchanged at the airport, as well as in hotels. Also, some tour guides will change money—generally a safe thing to do here. Good rates can be found at the following banks:

Banco do Brasil *SDS Q 1, bl. A; Ed. Sede 1;* ☎ *212-2230.*
Banco Econômico *SCS Q 1, bl. 1. Ed. Central Loja 15/16;* ☎ *225-8783.*

Tourist Information

The local tourist board is **DETUR** ☎ *321-3318* Brochures may be picked up at the airport (international side) and at the bus station. For any kind of information, dial 156. For information about movies, dial 139.

Points Beyond

Air:

Varig offers regular shuttle services daily to Rio and São Paulo, regular service to other major cities, and special regional services to the interior of Goiás, São Paulo, Pará, and others. VASP flies to Corumbá and Cuiabá daily. **Transbrasil** offers reduced-fare night-flights to Manaus.
Varig/Cruzeiro *CLS 306 bl. B, loja 20;* ☎ *242-4111.*
VASP *SCLS 304 Bl. E, loja 9;* ☎ *244-2020.*
Transbrasil *CLS 305, bl. C, loja 30;* ☎ *248-6433.*
TAM (Transportes Aéreos Regionais) ☎ *248-6978.*
TAP-Air *Galeria Hotel Nacional;* ☎ *223-7138.*

Bus:

Both regular buses and *leitos* (air-conditioned, with food service) are available to Rio (20 hrs); São Paulo (16 hours), and Belo Horizonte (12 hours). Also, less comfortable buses go to Goiâna, Cuiabá, Campo Grande, Porto Alegre, Fortaleza, Natal, Salvador, and Recife. At the new bus terminal, you can leave luggage secured in lockers.

Train:

The *O Bandeirante* train, opened in 1981, leaves Brasília only on Friday night for São Paulo (about 24 hours), with a connection made in Campinas. The station is located past the TV tower, on the far side of the Eixo Monumental.

Private Tour Guides

An historically oriented guide who speaks excellent English is **James Roll** *SQS 404-F-306;* ☎ *(61) 226-8855.*

Sports

There is free Tai Chi every morning between super block 104 and 105 at 6:00 a.m.

Travel Agency

Prestheza *Hotel San Marco, Setor Hoteleiro Sul QD 5, bl. C,* ☎ *226-6224.* Excellent agency with a variety of touristic options, owned by a Japanese-descended Brazilian named Shiro. Guides are good English speakers and informative; special excursions can be arranged to Vale do Amanhecer as well as forests and waterfalls in the surrounding environs.

Presmic Travel Agency *Hotel Nacional, SHS, lote 1,* ☎ *225-5518* Group tours (half and full days) leave twice a day (9:00 a.m. and 2:00 p.m.) from the Nacional Hotel. All guides speak both Portuguese and English. Nighttime tours are also a possible choice.

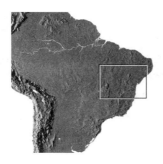

BAHIA

Salvador

The womb of black culture in Brazil—the state of Bahia, and especially, its capital city, Salvador[*] —holds special meaning for Brazilians, no matter what their racial identity. Those who have only heard reports of Bahia's exquisite beaches, fiery cuisine, magnificent colonial churches, and exotic voodoo sessions spend their lives longing to visit; those lucky enough to visit dream immediately of returning. True, many of the treasures of Bahian culture can be sampled in the restaurants and nightclubs of Rio, but there is something in Bahia that must be experienced firsthand—and that is the *heart* of the people. Deeply rooted in a mysticism best expressed through joyous cel-

---

[*]. The city of Salvador is also often referred to as Bahia (Bah-ee-ah), a point of continual confusion among tourists

ebration, the Bahian passion for life arises directly from the profound devotion of the masses, descendants of African slaves who were dragged mercilessly to Brazil over three hundred years ago by Portuguese merchants. Tortured, humiliated, and subjugated to the whims of the sugarcane plantation owners, these black immigrants clung to their African traditions, fiercely preserving their customs behind closed doors until today, when their celebratory festivals, music, and cuisine have fused with the popular life of the people. Today, the name Bahia itself has become synonymous with "soul"; even in Rio's Carnaval, the *alas* of Bahian-dressed women, with their huge hoop skirts and dangling necklaces, brings tears to everyone's eyes—a reminder (unconscious, perhaps) of the strong black maternal figures who were responsible for raising so many generations of Brazilian colonists. But the black culture of Bahia has done more than nurse Brazil; it's given birth to some of the country's greatest poets, musicians, and painters, including songwriter Dorival Caymmi, novelist Jorge Amado, poet Vinícius de Moraes, bossa nova great João Gilberto, and musical superstars Gilberto Gil, Caetano Veloso, Maria Bethânia, and Gal Costa, among others. Without Bahia, one could argue, Brazil might never have been able to transcend the rather conservative, uptight attitudes of its Iberian mother.

Far From Being The Only Attraction

Most travelers are probably familiar already with **Salvador** as the major destination in Bahia—a magical, time-warped city where cows still walk down the highway beneath the shadow of towering skyscrapers. Yet the beachside capital city is far from being the only attraction in the state. Dotting the Bay of All Saints, on whose banks Salvador sits, are over 36 islands, easily reachable by public ferry or day cruises. Only 1-1/2 hours away by bus is the well-preserved colonial town of **Cachoeira**—the site of the most authentic *candomblé terreiro* (church of Afro-Brazilian trance worship) in Bahia. And secluded in the interior, not more than an hour from Salvador, are some of the greatest beach resorts in South America, namely **Comandatuba Island** (Transamérica Hotel) and **Praia do Forte**. Not only are these spectacular estates crime-free, they offer the finest combination of natural beauty and luxury service, including pristine beaches, fascinating excursions, and play-perfect weather.

SALVADOR

"*About 11 o'clock we entered the Bay of All Saints, on the northern side of which it is situated. It would be difficult (to) imagine before seeing this view anything so magnificent . . . If faithfully represented in a picture, a feeling of distrust would be raised in the mind.*"

Charles Darwin (1832)

One of the most beloved destinations in Brazil, Salvador is a city of mystics, magic, and music—a sacred land where intoxication is often considered a prelude, or at least, the postlude, to religious salvation. Even the writer Jorge Amado, whose novels are nearly travelogues of Bahia, advises visitors to Salvador to make their first offering of *cachaça* to Exu, the wily, two-horned African god who guards the thoroughfares of the city. Such gestures are not even considered superstitious in Salvador, where animism is a form of daily life, and Christian saints and African gods are worshipped syncretistically together in a sensual mess of devotion. Only in Salvador do you see the sacred images of Mary as the Nossa Senhora do Leite (Our Lady of the Milk) used to encourage women to breastfeed. And even businessmen and intellectuals tie fetishistic ribbons called *lembranças do Bonfim* around their wrists and wait for their wishes to come true.

For the first-time visitor, Salvador can feel like a barrage of exotic sense perceptions, since everything, from business to love to extreme poverty, is lived out on the street. Even the smell of the city—a mixture of sea and sweat and spices—is enough to send you into a whirl. There are hundreds of magnificent baroque churches to visit, scores of beaches to scavenge, tiny colonial alleyways full of folkloric crafts, and regional foods, but you could discover the heart of Bahia simply by soaking up the many faces of children on the **Praça da Sé** or the **Church of the Bonfim**. Hunger has carved cunning desperation into many of these street children, but you haven't experienced Salvador until you've been suddenly corralled into a corner by a group of them desperate to sell you something—*anything*. Though these young children may irritate you or sometimes scare you, try to remember they are often working to support families of ten or more, if they have not already been abandoned themselves. Simply, one cannot go to Bahia without acknowledging the extreme poverty of a majority of the population. In fact, Salvador is the only Brazilian city where you'll see little boys selling coffee from a cart on the street or even trying to hawk a single cigarette.

Yet for all its despair, Salvador is also a city of rhythm and celebration. Next to Rio, it boasts the biggest Carnaval blowout in Brazil, not an organized parade in a sambadrome or coliseum, but an explosion in the city's streets jam-packed with percussion ensembles, *trio elétricos*, twirling, hoop-skirted women, and neighborhood *blocos*. Many say you haven't experienced the real Brazilian Carnaval until you come to Salvador. During the rest of year, folkloric religious celebrations seem to dot the calendar nearly every week, giving the people ample excuse to drink, eat, and dance until dawn.

City Of Poetry

As one of the great architectonic centers in South America, Salvador is also a city of poetry. Even the street names are lyrical reminders of the colorful life that once teemed on its colonial-wrought cobblestones. Located in front of the Governor's Palace is **Rua do Tira Chapéus** (Street of the Hat-Tipping) where lines of royal subjects had to doff their hats obsequiously whenever the authorities passed by. **Beco da Maria Paz** (Alley of Maria Paz) was named after a prostitute well known for her charms during colonial times. Rebels fighting for independence from the Portuguese had their heads chopped off and displayed on **Rua da Cabeça** (Street of the Head), near Praça Piedade. In Ondina, **Rua Escravo Miguel** (Street of the Slave Michael) was inspired by the story of a farmer whose daughter ran off with his slave named Miguel; when the young girl died, Miguel threw himself, with traditional Latin passion, to his death in the sea.

The Goddess Of The Ocean

Indeed, even today the sea in Salvador retains such mystical power that the captains of the colorful *saveiros* crisscrossing the bay still sing that it's best to die in the foamy green waves thinking of **Iemenjá**. The Goddess of the Ocean, Iemanjá is not a figment of imagination in Bahia, but a living force that even today guides the conscious and subconscious habits of Bahianos. As Jorge Amado wrote, "Wherever there is a fishermen or sailor, there Iemenjá is with her love and seduction." Rumored to have a fondness for combs, mirrors, and bright red lipstick, she's said to live in diverse places—in the ruins of the Forte da Gamboa, in Rio Vermelho, in Barra, in Itapuã, Pituba, and Itaparica—and makeshift shrines to her can be found everywhere, from dark alleys to coves along the beach. On February 2, her feast day, the city is transformed by one of the most beautiful and impassioned celebrations of the year, replete with dancing, singing, and drinking as canoes and sloops laden with presents are pushed far out to her home in the deep dark sea.

PAST GLORIES

Salvador's bay owes its name to Cabral's expeditionaries who first anchored in the harbor on **November 1, 1501**, the Catholic feast day for All Saints. Among the first native people to greet the settlers were the warfaring **Tupinambá** (or Tupí), whose cannibalistic ways did not win them friends. Some less pious settlers—deserters, renegades, and shipwrecked sailors—did manage to commune with a few tribes by teaching them military tactics; in fact **Diogo Alvares**, a shipwrecked Portuguese sailor, eventually married two Indian princesses and sired an entire dynasty of *mestizos*. While the Jesuits tried to missionize the natives, the Portuguese authorities in Bahia preferred bartering labor for goods, but the Indians, unaccustomed to European ways, soon succumbed to disease, exhaustion, and disinterest.

Securing the port of Salvador also did not prove easy. After numerous squabbles with Dutch and French pirates, **Dom João III** established direct royal control by sending a resident governor, **Tomé de Sousa**, to commence construction on Brazil's first capital. Impressed with the fertile lands in the coastal plains surrounding the Bay called the **Recôncavo**, the crown ordered the first sugar plantation built. The problem, however, was labor. When the native Indians quickly proved unreliable, the Portuguese turned to the one foreign labor pool they knew only too well.

In truth, it was precisely the nefarious **African slave trade** that populated colonial Bahia. By the beginning of the 18th century, more than 1.2 million black Africans had already been shipped to Bahia in shackles, many of them dying on the way; by the beginning of the 19th century, one-third of the population was enslaved. Bahian society soon became based on the hierarchy of the plantation, where masters lived a seigneurial life, protecting or abusing their retainers at will. The city of Salvador thus grew up as a complement to the state's agricultural industry—the place where merchants pushed papers and moved the plantations' goods on to other ports. Developing far away from the wharves on the upper city was the religious and governmental life: The first **Jesuit College** was established in 1549, followed by the monasteries of **Franciscans**, **Benedictines**, and **Carmelites** by the close of the 16th century. Later, when the cultivation of tobacco centralized in nearby Cachoeira, a less elite class of merchants began to emerge in Salvador. Still, the entire economy was dependent on slave labor, and although a slave revolt failed in 1835, it sent shivers of fear through the white community. Eventually, even Abolition, in 1888, did little to change plantation politics, which simply moved into a neo-feudal model, indenturing the former slaves to their previous owners through debt.

The enormous inequalities rampant in Bahia (to this day) have not gone unheeded. In 1897, the longing for a better life led to one of the most extraordinary peasant revolts in Brazilian history. Starting in the *sertão*, the uprising consisted of followers of the mystic **Antônio Conselheiro** who refused to submit their rustic settlement of **Canudos** to Portuguese authority. The simple *sertanejos* valiantly fought off not only the local police, but state troopers, until federal troops decimated the entire village shanty by shanty. A marvelous fictional account can be found in Euclides da Cunha's celebrated novel *Os Sertões* (published in English as *Rebellion in the Backlands*).

CULTURE

CANDOMBLÉ

Bahia is considered the heart of *candomblé* worship in Brazil (though it can be freely found throughout the country, particularly in Rio). For more information, see the chapter *Traveler's Guide to Brazilian Spirits*. To seek out and attend authentic sessions of the trance-worship religion, however, takes some private scoping. Any *candomblé* performed in a theater or offered on a group tour by a travel agency is bound to be diluted—usually straw-dog performances that exploit the color, music, and dance of the religion without any genuine feeling. In Salvador proper, there are hundreds of *terreiros* (*candomblé* churches), though the sessions are usually held after midnight on Saturdays in poor black neighborhoods verging on slums. (Don't take much money and don't expect anyone to speak English.) If you tell the concierge of your hotel you would like to attend a "real" *candomblé*, he will most likely be able to arrange it for you—for a tip, that is; the session itself is free. If you do go, take a taxi, and pre-arrange for a pickup; the first time I went, my taxi driver was so surprised I was alone that he insisted on waiting for me—not a bad idea. The session can go on until dawn, though you will most likely be ready to leave in a hour or two—the tiny room gets hot and stuffy fast. Attend with a sense of decorum and utmost respect. (You are there only to witness quietly, not participate.) Do not wear shorts or bermudas (anything white is best). And, under no circumstances should you ever record, videotape, or take photographs. (From experience, I can say that you will either be summarily dismissed from the room or stripped of your film.) If you're offered any food, it's most likely to be fried bean curd; accept it gracefully, though you needn't eat it. Donations are appreciated, but if an adult acting like a child demands money from you, it is most likely a practitioner incorporating the spirit of a childlike divinity; he or she only wants a few coins as a symbolic appeasement. Any donation you care to give for attending should be given directly to the *mãe* or *pai de santo*, the leaders of the *terreiro*. For more information, also contact **Bahiatursa**; ☎ *241-4333*.

> **Insider Tip:**
>
> The best and most beloved terreiro is **Casa Branca**, Avenida Vasco da Gama, 463, founded more than 350 years ago by slaves. Another highly respected terreiro, founded in 1922, is **Menininha do Gantois** Alto do Gantois, 23 (Federação); ☎ 247-3302. Some consider the city of Cachoeira, outside Salvador, to boast the most authentic trance worship sessions in Brazil. (See **Cachoeira**.)

CAPOEIRA

"Nowadays one does not need to feel the cold contact of the straight razor on the skin, to regret the blood of another person on his or her hands . . . to feel goosebumps . . . while walking through dark alleys in order to discover the power of Capoeira . . ."

Bira Almeida (1986)

Capoeira, the uniquely Brazilian martial art that you will see throughout Bahia, has enjoyed a dark and steamy past. Even its historical origins are controversial. Some claim that *capoeira*, born out of a fierce desire for freedom, began as an acrobatic technique developed by slaves who were forced to hide their self-defense practices from their masters. Others claim the techniques derived from an African male puberty rite, or that the name refers to the partridge called a *capoeira*, which fiercely engages in bloody cock fights. Since the 18th century, the Brazilian police have considered *capoeiristas* little more than lowlife, once exiling a particularly scruffy bunch of hooligans to the horrible penal colony on the island of Fernando de Noronha. When restrictions on popular culture were unexpectedly eased under the repressive regime of Getúlio Vargas, *capoeiristas* finally began to enjoy some freedom, facilitated by the teaching of the century's greatest master, **Manoel dos Reis Machado** (known as **Mestre Bimba**), whose school, opened in 1932, is still located near the Pelourinho. As late as the 1950s and 1960s, *capoeiristas*, always poor, still lived a knife-edged existence, populating violent gangs and sharing the narrow *becos* and honky-tonks of old Bahia with prostitutes, drunken sailors, and other nefarious figures.

Gravity-Defying Acrobatic Attacks

Today the martial art has developed from being a paramount fighting technique into a spectacular visual show. The main moves are performed in pairs, in a series of gravity-defying acrobatic attacks that include somersaults, backbends, and head-high kicks. The training for the sport is not only physically but also artistically demanding: A student must learn to play several instruments, though primarily the *berimbau*, a single-stringed gourd whose rhythms demand a keen sense of timing and coordination. Some of the rhythms and chants refer to Catholic saints and African deities; others originated from secret signs that warned the *capoeiristas* of approaching police. Through the ever-changing music, the *capoeirista* creates either a succession of harmonious forms, generates a confrontation of strategies, or engages in slow-motion counterattacks, all best performed by one whose spirit is equal to his or her technical skill. Indeed, true *capoeiristas* strive to attain what in Portuguese is called "Axé," a special energy connected to the universal flow. Those who've undertaken the sport as a martial art form even seek to transcend ordinary states of consciousness and claim that practice of the sport expands their perceptions of time and space.

Unfortunately, most of the professional capoeira you will see in Brazil will be tainted by showmanship, though it is still visually thrilling. Even the lithe, but well-developed bodies of the practitioners, nearly sculpture-like, could themselves be considered art forms. Some of the best performances can be seen at the restaurant **Solar do Unhão** or in front of the **Mercado Modelo** (although the latter performers may turn aggressive if you don't donate some cruzeiros to their supposedly free show). Many of the schools around the Pelourinho are considered rough to visit, though there is an unusual school for small boys located across the street from a good youth hostel **Solar** *Rua Macapá, 461* in Ondina; classes are usually held in the late afternoon. The academy of Mestre Bimba is located at *Rua Francisco Muniz Barreto, 1 (1st floor)* in the Terreiro de Jesus.

A BIRD'S EYE VIEW

Salvador is perched on a privileged sight—a 200-foot bluff overlooking the glimmering **All Saints Bay**. For many Bahianos, the bay itself is nearly a personality; as Jorge Amado writes in his novel *Juiabá*, "the sea gives a peace the city cannot bring." In colonial times, the cliff acted as a perfect natural fortress for the port; today it divides the city into two parts: the **Cidade Baixa** (High City) where the commercial district and wharfs are located, and the **Cidade Alta** (Low City), heart of the historical center. Unless you embark on an island cruise, most of your tourist activity will be centered in the Cidade Alta. The fastest way to travel between the two levels is by the **Elevador Lacerda**, a lift connecting **Praça Cairu** and the **Mercado Modelo** with the **Praça Municipal** (Tomé de Sousa) in the Cidade Alta. Unfortunately, the lift is also the most dangerous way to go—probably the site of more assaults and thefts than any other place in Salvador. (See *Safety in Salvador* on the next page.) Steep hills called *ladeiras* also connect the two levels, but most tourists, especially those carrying anything valuable, would be best advised to take a taxi.

With more than 2 million people, Salvador ranks as the third largest city in Brazil, behind São Paulo and Rio. A large percentage of the working poor are squeezed into the city's middle suburban areas; others—such as the more recent immigrants from Northeastern droughts—inhabit squatters' camps called *invasões* along the outer circle of the city. Even in the historical district, near the Pelourinho, families of ten or more are crammed into tiny apartments and you'll no doubt walk past homeless mothers and children camped out on the street. Most of the hotels and tourist activities are located along the shoreline in middle-to-upper class neighborhoods, such as **Ondina**, where singer Gilberto Gil has a penthouse. Enjoying a recent renaissance, the district **Barra** is one of the choicest places to roost; the city's best hotels, bars, and restaurants are all located here within walking distance of each other, and the beach is superb (see below under *Barra*). If you get a chance, drive around the upper-middle class neighborhood of **Graça**. The compelling geometric high-rises in shades of red, black, white, and orange are the works of **Fernando Peixoto**, whose avant-garde designs are now gracing other cities.

SAFETY IN SALVADOR

Salvador is so full of exotic distractions that your attention may be diverted from your personal safety at just the wrong time. However, the same kind of precautions suggested for Rio should be followed in Salvador—if not more so—since the level of extreme poverty and desperation is even more intense in this Northeastern city. Also, many of the poorer neighborhoods are situated within, or immediately adjacent to, the colonial area, where most of the touristic activity takes pace. *Perspicacious*, rather than paranoid, should be your watchword. In general, don't walk around with much money, and separate your credit cards from your traveler's checks. Lock up your passport, plane tickets, and extra valuables in the safe in your hotel room. Avoid carrying expensive cameras. Don't ever exchange money on the street (there are too many tales of disappearing dollars) and most of all, try to blend in with the vibe of the city. Take taxis when you can or the special tourist bus that goes down the *orla*, and take particular caution at the following locations (all best avoided completely at night):

- **Lacerda Elevator:** Avoid day and night.
- **Praça da Sé:** The old, abandoned buildings on the street across from the Excelsior movie house is a center of crime, drugs, and prostitution.
- **Pelourinho:** At all cost, avoid strolling on foot at night.
- **Convento da Piedade:** outside the Praça da Piedade.
- **Ladeira da Conceição:** an area of prostitution.
- **Any side streets** or back alleyways in the colonial area.

BEACHES

As in most beach towns of Brazil, the *orla*, or shoreline along the Atlantic Ocean, galvanizes most of the touristic activity in the city. Bahia has the longest coastline in Brazil, more than 15 miles. It's here, from **Porto da Barra** northwards to the beach of **Itapoã**, that the best hotels are located, as well as apart–hotels and small pousadas. Due to pollution and some natural characteristics, such as rocky shores and torturous waves, some of the beaches closest to the city are not suitable for swimming and are best utilized as places to walk, talk, and gawk. As in Rio, the best beaches are located farther out—sometimes a real trek—but special and regular buses go down the *orla* regularly. Along almost all the beaches are *barracas* selling food and drink, as well as vendors hawking beer and *acarajé*, fried bean cake.

The shoreline of Salvador actually begins at **Porto da Barra**, the site where Tomé de Souza, the first governor of Bahia and Brazil, arrived in 1549 and where the Dutch landed in 1624. It's now a small port, where the Western telegraph cables come ashore. The **Farol da Barra** is a fortress built in 1583; its lighthouse started to function in 1839. **Barra**, located where the Bay of All Saints meets the Atlantic Ocean, is one of the most active beach scenes, though swimming is not suggested (the only safe place to swim in Barra is near the lighthouse). **Praia do Farol**, near the **Farol Flat Hotel**, has become a family-oriented beach. As a swimming site, **Ondina** is not at all suitable, but it is picturesque, with artificial pools formed by the natural rocky coves. At **Rio Vermelho**, on the far side of **Ondina**, you'll find local native fishermen weaving their fishing nets, which resemble enormous spider webs. Nearby an arts and crafts fair is held every Friday sponsored by SESI. On the second of February, a celebration of *candomblé* offerings is held near the **Casa de Iemenjá**, a tiny house of worship built for such gatherings.

Originally a fishermen's village, **Pituba** has lots of restaurants and bars for flirting, but the sand is not clean and is often full of rubbish; still, lots of teens congregate here, as well as mothers and children. **Jardim de Alá** is a nice place to picnic, but the water is definitely polluted and often exudes an unattractive odor. At night, though, it's a beautiful place to sit at a grass hut bar and contemplate the moonlight.

New Year's Eve

By all accounts, **Piatã** is Salvador's most beautiful beach. On its far side, **Itapoã** has been the subject of a beloved song by Vinícius de Moraes, which you are sure to hear at least once during your stay in Bahia. On New Year's Eve, Itapoã is the place to be, when *candomblé* devotees, dressed in white, place illuminated candles on the beach and offer food, money, and flowers to the sea goddess Iemenjá. As befits his poetic status, Vinícius de Moraes used to live in this neighborhood. Nearby are the dark waters and white sandy hills of the

Abaeté lagoon, as well as an inlet formed by Ruas J and K, which makes for excellent sailing and diving. On the far side of Itapoã's lighthouse, **Stella Maris** attracts lots of surfers. Also known for surfers and lots of beautiful girls is **Jaguaribe Beach**. **Pitau** is where the chic people hang out, particularly by the Casquinha restaurant and the surrounding *barracas*. **Corsário** is the best beach for children, with calm, warm waters and clean sand.

Outside the city settlements, following the north coast along Coconut Road, small settlements between **Arembepe** and **Praia do Forte** still retain their rural simplicity; here, you'll find numerous fishing villages that haven't changed for centuries. The islands dotting the bay are also points of touristic destination. (Also, see Excursions below.)

SIGHTS

ON FOOT

One of Dorival Caymmi's most famous songs extol the 365 churches in Bahia, one for each day of the year; in truth there are only about 165, some of the best ones located in the historical center easily accessible on foot. The best place to start your walking tour of Salvador is the pigeon-strewn **Praça da Câmara Municipal**, where the shimmering magnificence of the All Saint's Bay can embrace you. Dominating the square is the **Palácio do Rio Branco**, the former Governor's Palace, which has been destroyed by war and restored several times; hence, the eclectic Greek columns, baroque windows, and neoclassical eagles. Unfortunately, the sumptuous interior, bedecked with a rococco ceiling and finely restored paintings, is only open to the public in the afternoon (*Monday–Saturday 2:00 p.m.–5:00 p.m.*). Also facing the square is the **Câmara Municipal**, the 17th-century city hall. Walking towards the harbor, you'll glimpse the **Lacerda Municipal Elevador**, which can take you to the lower city, the departing dock for island cruises, and the **Mercado Modelo**. From this privileged view above the harbor, contemplate the red-tiled roofs of the old city and the **Forte de São Marcelo** in the middle of the bay, once a prison but now headed for a new life as a casino, if the law will permit.

Colorful Street Scenes

Next, head down **Rua da Misericórdia** to **Praca da Sé**, keeping to the middle of the street, whenever possible. (Be particularly careful when you pass the street **Ladeira da Misericórdia** because thieves tend to race down this alley after committing a crime.) Before reaching the Praca da Sé, you'll pass by the **Igreja da Misericórdia** (opened only on Sundays), featuring the largest ivory Christ in Brazil, about one meter high. The plaza itself, one of the most colorful street scenes in Salvador, is a crossfire of *figuras* straight out of a Fellini movie—from the snakeoil salesman hawking a magic elixir for eternal youth to Sonia Braga look-alikes sauntering down the narrow alleyways with their (usually foreign) clients.

Crossing the Praca da Sé and heading down **Rua Guedes de Brito**, you'll enter the heart of colonial Salvador—the **Praça Terreiro de Jesus**, the site of the city's original public water supply. Here, shaded by the large leafy branches of almond and poinciana trees, the many faces of Salvador come alive: from the homeless street boys who aggressively hawk souvenirs, to the old shoe-shine men sipping *cafezinho* on chairs made of rags, to the famous white-skirted *Bahiana* who ekes out a living selling *acarajé*—fried bean cake grilled on an open fire. Sunday morning is a lively time to visit, when the square is transformed into a weekly **arts and crafts fair**; you'll find homemade lace, leather goods, traditional musical instruments like the *berimbau* and the *pandeiro*, as well as fine primitive paintings. It's from this plaza that you can directly enter the **Pelourinho**, the cobblestone square where colonial slaves were severely punished in front of their masters. (The actual *pelourinho*, or whipping post, was removed as a humanitarian gesture by the government about twenty years ago.) Shaded by huge trees and lined with colonial mansions, the square has been designated a patrimony, or cultural treasure, by UNESCO since it is considered the site of the most important collection of 17th- and 18th-century colonial architecture in South America. Sadly, it's also become today the site of nefarious scams that take advantage of distracted tourists. (Young boys throwing firecrackers is often a tactic to divert attention.) Also situated on the Largo do Pelourinho is one of the best eateries for regional food, called **SENAC** (see "Where to Eat")—a fine place to stop for lunch or dinner. (If you dine here at night, do take a cab in and out of the Pelourinho.)

Catedral Basílica

Heading for the northwest corner of the Terreiro de Jesus, you'll find the green sculptured doors of the **Catedral Basílica** *Tuesday–Saturday 9:00 a.m.–10:30 a.m. and 2:00 p.m.–5:00 p.m., Sunday 9:00 a.m.–10:00 a.m.* originally a chapel built in 1557 for the Jesuit Seminary. After many restorations, it boasts today an eclectic facade that pits Greek classical columns against the curvaceous designs of the Baroque. Inside are the remains of Mem de Sá, the Portuguese nobleman/soldier who finally expelled the French from Rio de Janeiro in 1567. Next to the cathedral is the **Museu Afro-Brasileiro** *Tuesday–Saturday 9:00 a.m.–5:00 p.m.* housed in what was the first medical school in Brazil during the last century. On the ground floor is a marvelous exhibition heralding the richness of Brazilian black culture—from religion to music to martial arts and artisanry. Fascinating are the imaginative sculptures of *candomblé* divinities dressed in their uniquely personal styles (colors, jewelry, weapons, etc.) and surrounded by their favorite foods. (You can tell which divinity a devotee is dedicated to by checking out the colors of his jewelry and clothes.) While you're here, give a nod to Exu, the protector of the city, a devil-like figure with pitchfork, two horns, and erect genitalia who is featured in many of Jorge Amado's writings. Most inspiring are the blown-up photos of *pais* and *mães de santo*—the formidable priests and priestesses of *candomblé* whose enormous spiritual power was forged in the face of great poverty and despair. In the basement of this building you'll find the **Ethnological and Archeological Museum**, a showcase for Indian ceramics and fossils retrieved from native burial sites.

Architectural Treasure

Crossing the Terreiro de Jesus on **Ladeira do Cruzeiro**, you'll come upon the finest 16th-century architectural treasure on the square, the **Igreja e Convento de São Francisco**. Built by slaves in the 16th century, the church is the essence of Baroque, its cornucopia of winged angels, beatific saints, immaculate virgins, and pious-looking animals adorning every nook and cranny. What is shocking at first sight is that every hand-carved object seems to be covered in gold leaf—an ancient technique that can only be approximated today through using a mixture of yellow, green, orange, and brown paints to give the illusion of gold. Most amazing among the objets d'art are the icons the African slaves managed to slip in from their own cultures: notice the statue of the sea goddess Iemanjá riding the prow of the main pulpit, as well as the bare–breasted, pregnant women perched on the side of the jacaranda balustrades. The altar itself was inspired by Bernini's St. Peter's Altar at the Vatican, and the main statue of Saint Francis grasping Christ follows the painting of Murillo, which now hangs in Madrid's Prado Museum. From the front altar, turn around and look at the back choir loft, where the ceiling is made of wood boxes forming hexagons, stars, trapezoids, and crosses in representation of the Virgin's life. On the right hand side of the church (unfortunately, not illuminated) is one of the most sacred sculptures in Brazil—that of St. Peter of Alcântara, carved from one piece of wood. If you squint hard enough, you may be able to see his perfectly proportioned hands and the finely wrought muscles in his body. Next to him, with babe in arms, is St. Benedictine, the Ethiopian slave who saved a dying baby. In the side entrance hall, painted-tiled panels in sculpted wood frames retell the life of St. Francis de Assisi, whose philosophy of charity and service is still carried out by the church today. If you visit in the morning, you'll no doubt see a long line of Bahia's poor and crippled, who line up daily to receive free bread at 7:00 a.m. and free beans and meat at 11:30 a.m. *The church is open 8:00 a.m.–11:30 a.m. and 2:00 p.m.–5:30 p.m. daily, though you must enter through the side door. When there is a service, you can enter through the front door. Mass is held daily at 7:00 a.m., 8:00 a.m., 6:00 p.m., 7:00 p.m., Tuesday 7:00 a.m., 7:30 a.m., and 6:00 p.m., Sunday 7:30 a.m., 9:30 a.m., and 11:00 a.m. A blessing to St. Anthony is held every Tuesday. Pamplets in Portuguese can be bought for about $2 at the office on the right.*

Third Order Of São Francisco

Next door on the left is the **Igreja da Ordem Terceira de São Francisco** *Monday–Friday 8:00 a.m.–noon, 1:00 p.m.–5:00 p.m. Services are held on the fourth Sunday of each month at 8:30 a.m.; fee about 30 cents.* Built in 1702–3, the secular Third Order of São Francisco exerted a strong cultural and religious influence during the 18th and 19th centuries; today it boasts more than 1,000 brothers and sisters, who support a hospital, an old folk's home, and ongoing social work with the prostitutes, thieves, and addicts who live in the area. Ever since an unsuspecting painter chipped off a chunk of the original facade that had lain hidden for 150 years, the church has been slowly returning to its former glory; the interior, once entirely decimated, was restored to a neoclassical design in the last century. The sculptures of the saints are original, but notice they are all wearing the robes of this order. Most stunning is the image of the Madonna on the altar; her facial expression is one of the purest in Brazilian art. (A better view can be seen from upstairs.) The room to the right of the sanctuary is the eerie Room of the Saints, hosting the nearly life-sized statues that are carried through the streets during religious processions. In the cloister connected to the sacristy is a marvelous tiled mural that could be considered the wedding album of Dom José, the elder son of Dom João V, who married an Austrian princess. It even shows the carriage of the wedding party (not unlike Princess Di's), accompanied by a retinue of bowing and scraping courtiers. High society weddings are still held in this courtyard, and upstairs, the order holds its meetings around an immense antique jacaranda table, surrounded by sacred objects donated by the order's wealthiest families. The view from the shuttered windows upstairs will give you an intimate look on the neighborhood down below, a bevy of back streets and cobblestone alleyways full of tenement homes.

It's an odd stop, I admit, but in front of the church is a store I find endlessly fascinating, the **Funerária Durán**, which sells marvelous wood-carved coffins, equal in artistry to those of the old masters. Souvenirs of a more common variety can be found at the nearby **Olímpia—Múltiplos Artes & Turismo**, where you can purchase interesting local artwork, including miniature sets of *maracatú* bands. Just in case you're tempted, the hotels around the Pelourinho here may look alluring—much of their colonial architecture is still intact—but it's my opinion that you're taking your life in your hands if you hang out here after dark. Even the beautiful Convento do Carmo Hotel, once located here, had to close its doors finally because of assaults on tourists. (For more information, see "Where to Stay.")

Black Congregation

Cross to **Rua Alfredo Brito**, a narrow alleyway next to the **Museu Afro-Brasileiro** until you can see the oriental spires of the **Igreja Rosário dos Pretos**, towering over the Pelourinho. Built by slaves for their own community, the church today still boasts a primarily black congregation. The last scene of the film *Dona Flor and Her Two Husbands* was shot here. Turning right on Rua Ribeiro Santos, you'll come upon the **Igreja do Senhor dos Passos**, where the video for Paul Simon's 1990 album, *Rhythm of the Saints*, was filmed on the steps of the church.

Across the street, stop for a typical tropical fruit drink such as *abacaxi* (pineapple) or an ice-cold *cerveja* at **Dona Chika-ka** *Rua Luiz Viana (Ladeira do Carmo, no. 17)*. The delicious cakes and sweets are all home-made, typical of the region. From here, gear yourself for a steep climb up **Rua Luiz Viana**, past the fantastic delapidated arches of the **Igreja Nossa Senhora do Carmo** *Daily 9:00 a.m.–noon, 2:00 p.m.–6:00 p.m., mass only on Sunday morning,* founded 356 years ago. (A tourist police station is located here.) Inside is an inner courtyard of crafts, through which you'll have to pass to reach the main sanctuary. The church possesses one of the most vulnerable, beseeching images of the Crucified Christ I have ever seen, entitled *Jesus Diante de Pilatos* (Jesus with the Crown of Thorns), positioned against a highly theatrical, red-curtained altar. In the sacristy is a stunning, though terrifying wood carving of the sleeping Christ, made by the same slave who carved the Christ image on the main altar; he accomplished the task in eight years using only two knives. Plant resin was used to get the exact color of skin, but the blood droplets were made from 2,000 rubies imported from India. The slave died immediately after finishing his masterpiece. On Good Friday, the image is placed on a silver platter and carried in procession through the Pelourinho.

Souvenirs

If you have time and energy left, there are numerous stores for jewelry, handicraft, and souvenirs around the Terreiro de Jesus, but be careful to stick to the main streets, avoiding any alleyways that seem particularly spooky. Fine lace stores can be found along Rua Alfredo Brito, and several jewelry stores are located near the São Francisco Church. (Also see "Shopping.")

Insider Tip:

*For a quick, cheap lunch near the Pelourinho, head for the restaurant **Atabaque Ghandi** Rua Gregório de Matos, 53 (Pelourinho);* ☎ *321-7073. Daily noon-2:00 p.m. the headquarters of the **Filhos de Ghandi**. In 1945, the organization Sons of Gandhi was founded during a strike at the harbor; today they head up one of Carnaval's most famous blocos and help the homeless during the rest of the year. Their mascot is a veritable Gandhi double–**Raimundo Queiroz**, a 68-year-old Bahiano, who needs only a little encouragement to put on his white loincloth and staff. The uncanny resemblance will give you chills. From May–Carnaval, the group holds open rehearsals on Sundays from 3:00 p.m.–10:00 p.m. Lunch at their simple luncheonette runs about $1.50 for a hearty plate of beef, fried fish, or one typical dish. Inexpensive. All cards.*

BONFIM

The heart of Bahian religious culture—the fervor, the passion, and the poverty—can best be seen at the **Nosso Senhor do Bonfim**, Salvador's most popular Catholic church, located high up on a hill in the western suburbs. (Take a taxi or visit on a group tour.) No matter the time of year, the scene outside the church always looks frantic, but devoted Bahianos consider a trip to Bonfim a true pilgrimage. As soon as your bus or taxi arrives, a bevy of poor native boys will aggressively descend on you, hawking tiny ribbons called *lembranças*, a symbol of the church. (Warning: if you buy one ribbon from one boy, the whole crowd will attach itself to you.) Leaning against the front doors, with the saddest faces imaginable, are some of the city's most pathetic cripples. Inside the church, which is always at least half full, is a shrine to the promise of a better life. Bahianos from all over the city come here to pray for the health of loved ones, for the healing of a marriage, for the manifestation of a boyfriend or girlfriend, for financial reversals—for anything that touches their everyday lives. And devotion often reaches fanatic heights; you just might see parishioners climbing up the steps on their knees or sunk into a prayer position for hours. Inside the Room of Miracles, plastic arms, heads, legs, and even hearts and lungs eerily hang from the ceiling; they are **ex-votos**, or offerings representing the parts of a devotee's body that have or "will be" miraculously healed. The photos and signed letters adorning the wall tell manifold stories. One photograph even expresses thanks for the release from a kidnapping January 23–February 9, 1991—an increasingly common occurrence among rich Brazilian families. Many of the notes pinned to the wall are requesting healings and include lists of promises the petitioners will fulfill when they receive their healings. The huge and extremely heavy wood crosses stashed in the corner are used by supplicants who promise to carry them during a religious procession if their prayers are answered.

More Than Souvenirs

The *lembranças do Bonfim*, sold by the native boys outside the church, are actually more than souvenirs. Believers pin them to the walls of the church and loop them around candlesticks to remind God that they are asking for help. You'll also see Bahianos from all walks of life walk around with these gnarled ribbons on their wrists. Stemming from a *candomblé* practice, the tradition is to make a wish while the ribbon is tied on your wrist; when it falls off, you throw it away in water and your wish will appear. What tradition doesn't tell you is that after a week the ribbon starts to look really ratty, but for some unknown mystical reason remains indestructible. (After one whole year, I'm still waiting for the stringy mess to fall off!) It's considered terrible luck to rip it off.

On the second Thursday of January, one of the most important Bahian festivals—Lavagem do Bonfim—takes place at the church. Starting at the Igreja de Nossa Senhora Conceição, hundreds of Bahianos, native women dressed in traditional white hooped skirts, embroidered blouses, and turbans, progress along the seafront to the Igreja do Bonfim, where they scrub the steps and square clean and adorn the church with flowers and brightly colored lights. Joyous partying follows in the evening and every night until Sunday, as the square fills up with drunken revelers.

BARRA

Squeezed between the Atlantic Ocean and the Bay of All Saints in the most southwestern nook of Salvador, the district of **Barra** might easily be considered the Ipanema of Bahia, except for the heavy current of bohemianism that runs through it. Once the home of industrialists and plantation owners, the neighborhood has been recently saved from decline by substantial restoration and the subsequent influx of young, beautiful people who stroll the beach day and night. Many good, medium-ranged hotels are located here, as are some of the best restaurants—from casual outdoor eateries featuring Greek, Italian, and fast food cuisines to colonial-style mansions offering typical Bahian delicacies. The beach, while beautiful, is more for strolling than swimming, but that doesn't seem to deter sunworshippers who head for the fried fish and cold *cerveja* in the many *barracas* lining the shore.

One of the major sites in the area is the **Farol da Barra**, the city's lighthouse built in the 19th century and still in use every night. Most city tours stop here; inside are two museums containing various historical maps and centuries-old documents. From this hill, you'll have a good view of Itaparica Island and you may even catch a glimpse of pro-level surfers battling the high waves down below. In general, the beach is considered a family beach, and at 5:00 p.m., hordes of teens converge at the lighthouse to enjoy the fabulous sunset. The **Forte de Antônio** was built in the 17th century as the first fortress to defend the bay.

For Barra's main street action, head for **Rua César Zame**. There you'll find **Tiffany's** restaurant (a new wateringhole featuring moderately priced French dishes) and right next door, the **Cantina Roma**, a favorite Italian pitstop. At the corner with **Rua Barão de Sergipe**, you'll find lots of bars, streets fairs, and a constant crowd during high season. Nearby, **Bar Oceânia** is a traditional meeting place for singles.

Tourists and residents alike often head for Barra just for the shopping. Strewn with greenery, the **Barra Shopping** mall makes an ultrachic statement, with fine clothes stores, professional photo labs, cinemas, and a capuccino stand. One of the best places to buy high-quality Northeastern handicrafts is at the **Instituto Mauá** *Praca Azevedo Fernandes, 02;* ☎ *235–5440. Monday–Friday 8:00 a.m.–6:00 p.m., Saturday 8:00 a.m.–4:00 p.m.* Nearby, the **Banco Econômico** gives a good exchange rate for the dollar.

Insider Tip:

Even Barra is getting more dangerous at night. Keep to illuminated areas, watch your bags, and, if possible, take a taxi.

MUSEUMS

Museu de Arte Sacra *Rua do Sodré, 276;* ☎ *243–6310 Monday–Friday noon–6:00 p.m. Fee is about 30 cents.* Not only is this museum the third largest collection of sacred art in the world, it's a marvelous oasis of peace, particularly on a rainy day when you can sit on a stone window seat and look out onto a tumultuous sea. Interestingly, the building's turbulent past belies its soothing ambiance. In 1665, a brotherhood of Barefoot Carmelites stopped here on their way to convert Indian tribes and asked permission from Portugal to build a church. One hundred and fifty years later, as the rest of Brazil was fighting for independence, the monks tried to persuade parishioners—*during confession!*—to remain Portuguese, but their subterfuge was soon discovered and they were immediately shipped back to Portugal. The original church, finished in 1697, retains elements of the Baroque and *manierista* styles, while the museum, established in 1959, is elegantly arranged to offset the architecture. As you enter the monastery you'll pass through the tiled sitting room off the inner courtyard where the monks' families came once a month to visit them. Marriages are often performed in the glorious Baroque-roccoco sanctuary, where there are tiled pictures of the original monks who arrived barefoot. The pure silver altar, crowned by a statue of St. Theresa of Avila, comes from the Cathedral da Sé, now defunct. Within the museum proper, a series of small galleries overflows with marvelous objects, including a wood sculpture of N.S. de Rosário by the 19th-century sculptor Pereira Baiõ (the robes are so flowing they look blown by the wind). Do note that the painted sculptures of the short-legged São Cosme and São Damião, with their black bowl-haircuts, look incredibly like the musician Paul Simon! (He must have some karmic connection with the city since he recorded with Bahian musicians in the late 1980s.) Also fascinating is the "*Redoma com o Senhor Menino Deus*"—a bell jar of the Baby Jesus surrounded by baby ducks and tiny teacups. On the first floor, the painting of N.S. *Após a Flagelação* from 1796 looks nearly black in closeup but becomes hauntingly clearer as you step farther back. Before leaving, pick up a color booklet of the collection for about $2.

Museu Abelardo Rodrigues *Rua Gregório de Mattos, 45,* ☎ *321–6155. Monday–Friday 1:00 p.m.–7:00 p.m.* Collected by a Recife doctor (who was also a journalist and lawyer), this exhibition of sacred Northeastern art gives a fine perspective of the development of Brazilian styles from the 17th to the 19th centuries. Unfortunately, the collector made no notes, so the researchers can only presume origins. Many of the magnificent pieces of carved wood have been stripped of gold so that you can see the virgin wood. In the 17th-century statues, you'll notice the carved vestments have less movement, rendering a greater sense of peace. During the 18th century, the Baroque style transformed the saints into elaborate figures with flowing robes, wavy hair, and clear facial expressions. As the Baroque was dying in the 19th century, the style regained an elegance of form and a simpler expression. The most treasured part of the collection is the 18th-century "São Miguel Arcanjo" (the Archangel Michael), a perfect representative of Baroque movement and decoration. In the cabinet called "Popular," you can see how amateur artists tried to imitate the styles of the masters. In the lobby of this former colonial mansion, there's a map of the city with major tourist points labeled by pictures.

Museu Carlos Costa Pinto *Avenida 7 de Setembro, 2490. Daily 3:00 p.m.–7:00 p.m., except Tuesday.* Settled in an old colonial house at an easily reachable address in Barra, this museum features jewelry, furniture, crystal, and perhaps the only examples of *balangandãs* in Salvador—the silver chains of fetishes worn by slaves. Modern-day versions of the bracelets can be purchased in the Mercado Modelo.

Museu de Arte da Bahia *Avenida 7 de Setembro, 2340;* ☎ *235-9492. Tuesday–Saturday 2:00 p.m.–6:00 p.m.* A rainy-day option, this collection in a colonial mansion includes diverse paintings, porcelain, and furniture from both Brazil and Europe.

BOAT EXCURSIONS

If you are staying in Salvador for a few days, hop on a schooner to one of the 36 adjacent islands—an excellent way to beat the heat and see the outer reaches of the All Saint's Bay. Numerous travel agencies offer daily schooner excursions that leave about 9:00 a.m., weather permitting, but if you speak decent Portuguese, you might be able to bargain with the owners of the smaller *saveiros* (long, narrow fishing boats) moored near the Mercado Modelo.

Globo Turismo took me for an invigorating cruise on a tri-decker schooner serenaded by local sambistas singing at the top of their lungs. About 15 miles from Salvador, the schooner docked some 100 feet from the **Ilha dos Frades**, one of the largest islands in the bay, and among the most beautiful, with dense coconut groves and primitive settlements that still retain their colonial architecture. To reach the shore, we stepped into canoes, then waded the last few feet in ankle-high water (a few *machões* swam the whole way). Waiting for us on the strand were a hearty band of natives vigorously hawking the crafts of the region—carved knives, handmade jewelry, wood combs, and contraband snakeskins and turtle shells. As the sun reached its zenith, we sat at umbrella-shaded tables for a cold beer and a few bowls of excellent cracked lobster. Time was left for inspecting the colonial church at the top of the hill and climbing gingerly over the craggy reefs. After a few leisurely hours, we took another 45-minute cruise to **Ponta d'Areia**, a bit more inhabited, where a hearty lunch of *siri caranguejo* (stuffed crabs) was served under a grass-hut roof. Afterwards, we strolled over the dirt roads of the traditional village and then stretched out for a glorious afternoon tan. Around 5:00 p.m. the boat made a beeline back for Salvador as the sun set dramatically over the horizon.

Other schooner destinations offered by travel agencies include **Ilha da Maré**, which features the community of **Santana**, known for its handiwork of **bobbin lace**.

Itaparica, the largest island of the bay, is extraordinary for the fauna and flora that have been largely preserved in their state. Only twelve miles from Salvador, it was first inhabited by the Portuguese in 1560; the name itself comes from the Indians and means "stone fence." You can reach Itaparica by the **São Joaquim Ferry**, which leaves several times daily from the dock adjacent to the **São Joaquim**

Market. The crossing takes about 45 minutes (you can sit down below or lean over the railings for a better view), but you must pre-schedule your ticket two to three days in advance (to avoid long lines, especially on weekends). Awaiting you on the other shore of Itaparica will be small buses to the various beaches, or you can rent a private car. Besides a famous **mineral water spa** (the only one located on a beach in Brazil), there are also good hotel accommodations, such as the Hotel Icaraí and the Grande Hotel, as well as numerous *pensões* (boarding houses). Among sites to check out are the **Fort of São Lourenço** and the 18th-century **Church of São Lourenço**. Twelve kilometers from the township of Itaparica is the settlement of **Mar Grande**, where the best beaches are located: **Barra do Gil, Barra Grande, Tairu, Aratuba**, and others. **Club Med** is also located there, as well as a few decent pousadas, such as **Pousada Mar Grande**. (See under "Where to Stay.")

RAINY DAYS

It does rain in Salvador, especially in winter (June–August), when it may get too cold and windy to enjoy the beach. Don't despair. Here are some cloudy day options.

- Take a leisurely stroll (rather than the twenty minutes offered by tours) through the **Mercado Modelo**.
- Hang out in **Barra Shopping** mall, complete with cinema and food complex.
- Visit the **Museum of Sacred Art** and others listed above.

Insider Tip:
Avoid taking a schooner excursion if the sea is choppy.

THE ESSENTIAL SALVADOR

WHERE TO STAY

Accommodations in Salvador and surrounding environs run from the luxury resort to intimate pousadas that still retain their colonial charm. Unfortunately, except for the Quatro Rodas Sofitel, most hotels are not located on beaches conducive to swimming; in most cases, you'll have to take a taxi or cab to a suitable strand. Because of the active nightlife and good shopping, many tourists like to roost in Barra. Although some travelers end up in dirt-cheap hotels near the Praça da Sé, I can't recommend them for safety or cleanliness; if you want to go the bottom-line budget route, you're better off in a youth hostel.

Expensive -------------- **Over $70**

Moderate --------------- **$40–70**

Inexpensive ------------ **Under $40**

Cheap Under ----------- **$10**

★ Bahia Othon Palace

Avenida Pres. Vargas, 2456 (Ondina); ☎ *(71) 247–1044, FAX 245–4877. Reserve in Rio* ☎ *(21) 233–6373, (800) 4877*

With its impressive white stucco facade and wraparound driveway, the 5-star Bahia Othon effects the style of a tropical palace in the middle of suburbia. Its location is dramatic —on a grassy knoll jutting over a rocky coast pummelled by crashing waves. The enormous lobby, complete with Tarot reader in a grass hut, is connected to a split-level mall full of boutiques and jewelry stores. A stunning pool complex offers extensive space for sunning. From June 15–March 15, a leisure team organizes volleyball, aquatic games, walks, and bingo; programs for children above 4, as well as babysitters, are available. The Othon loves to throw minishows and cultural events for conventions; nonparticipants can slip in unnoticed. Business execs who apply for VIP service receive a special breakfast on the 12th floor and free afternoon cocktails. Huge wall-to-floor glass windows in the main restaurant overlook the pool. Fabulous lunch and dinner buffets are offered. Best bets are deluxe rooms, appointed with wicker furniture and tartan spread, with a perfect vista of the sea from the windy verandas. Special cabana-type apartments are available for those who stay at least a month. The Hippopotamus nightclub is a popular hot spot. Doubles range from $70–$120. Fielding's readers receive a 20 percent discount. 277 apartments. *Expensive. All cards.*

Meridien Bahia

Rua Fonte do Boi, 216 (Rio Vermelho); ☎ *(71) 248–8011, FAX 248–8902*

A massive high-rise on the dramatically craggy Rio Vermelho beach, the Meridien attracts chic Europeans who appreciate the cool efficiency of the French-speaking staff. The lobby furniture is sleek rather than tropical, though the carved wood panels behind the reception are of native design. The outdoor/indoor restaurant poolside features a stunning view of the sea and provides a constant soundtrack of crashing waves. Most unusual, the pool boasts a voluptuous image of Iemenjá painted on the bottom. Equipped with small balconies, all rooms face the sea; the only difference between the standard and deluxe is the decoration. St. Honoré restaurant is an oasis of gourmet French cuisine and the nightclub Regine's is elite. The earth-shattering caws of caged *araras* (parrots) and toucans can be heard throughout the lower levels. Although you can't swim at this beach, Barra and Jaguaribe are 15 minutes away, as is Pituba. Doubles start at $91, executive suites (2 rooms) $110, plus 10 percent service charge. 426 apartments. *Expensive. All cards.*

★ Enseada das Lajes

Avenida Oceânica, 511 (Morro da Paciência, Rio Vermelho); ☎ *(71) 237–1027*

The moment you enter this exquisite private residence transformed into a first-class pousada, you'll feel immediately at home. Set high on a hill called Morro da Paciência, it's a perfect place to view the Festival of

Iemanjá on February 2, when a special boat laden with gifts is pushed out to sea. The fabulous living room and veranda, where breakfast is served, looks out onto a raging sea. An inner courtyard, with an antique fountain, is a lovely place to read books and meditate. Each apartment is individually furnished with antique furniture. If the daily rate is too stiff, at least come for lunch or dinner—a rustic, yet elegant, affair for about $11–$15 (reservations required). For special holidays, reserve rooms months in advance. Standard doubles run $160, deluxe $180, and superdeluxe $205, with breakfast included. 9 apartments. *Very expensive. All cards.*

★ Sofitel Quatro Rodas Salvador

Rua Passárgada (Farol de Itapoã), 28 kilometers; ☎ *(71) 249–9611, FAX 249–6946*

As is its style in other cities, the Sofitel Quatro Rodas is the closest thing to an island resort in Salvador. Located on Itapoã Beach, the hotel believes a guest should never be bored. As such, there is a constant stream of parties and leisure activities, as well as a luxurious pool, golf course, tennis courts, mini-spa, hair salon, and nightclub. Shows by Dionne Warwick, Tom Jobim, Júlio Iglesias, and others are presented in the gymnasium. Adorning the lobby is a gargantuan 18th-century sugar mill; the piano bar is filled with the statues and voodoo accoutrements of *candomblé* saints. The coffee shop is an intimate cove with native-dressed waitresses under a bamboo roof. New Year's Eve is famous for its big bash, as well as June 24, the São José festival, when guests dress up in country-style clothes and dance *forró*. Spacious and attractively appointed, the superior rooms laterally face the sea, while deluxes face the sea and the pool (the latter is sometimes noisy). Unfortunately, the floors are carpeted, which, in a seaside resort, often results in a slight musty odor. The closest beach is a 5-minute walk away, but for better swimming, you'll have to walk twice as far. A hotel bus leaves four times a day to the Mercado Modelo, and twice a day to Farol da Barra—about an hour away. Cars make the distance in half the time. Superior doubles, including breakfast, run about $66. 195 apartments. *Moderate–expensive. All cards.*

Hotel da Bahia

Praça 2 de Julho (Campo Grande); ☎ *(71) 321–3699, FAX 321–9725*

The only 5-star hotel downtown, the Hotel da Bahia is a 10-minute drive to Barra, but the walk, down a tree-lined avenue, is extremely scenic. The breakfast room, decorated with lively wall murals, provides a huge breakfast buffet with typical Bahian foods. Buffets are also offered for lunch and dinner, but the menu caters to American tastes as well, including triple-decker sandwiches and banana splits. A second, more elegant restaurant specializes in lobster, filet mignon, and pastas. Pleasantly arranged standards look out onto the avenue; the superiors look onto the pool area with a small veranda. When you buy your ticket at Varig, you can receive a 20 percent discount for the ticket and the room, including transfer from the airport. Doubles run from $50–$70. 292 apartments. *Moderate. All cards.*

Marazul

Avenida Sete de Setembro, 3937 (Barra); ☎ *(71) 235–2121, FAX 235–2121*

A lobby shaded with darkened glass provides a comfortable place to crash in this 4-star hotel in Barra. The coffee shop, which serves breakfast and light meals, opens onto a small, circular pool. A restaurant featuring Brazilian specialties can serve large groups. Rooms are more serviceable than decorative, and run on the small size. Singles go for $59, doubles $66. No extra service charge. 124 apartments. *Moderate. All cards.*

Hotel do Farol

Avenida Presidente Vargas, 68 (Barra); ☎ *(71) 247–7611*

The lobby has little space to mill, but the location is right on the seashore, around the block from Barra's finest restaurants and bars, and across the street from a small shopping mall. Standards, with faux brick walls, are cozy and cheerful, with a veranda opening onto the beach and tiled baths with tubs. A fan-shaped pool gives you a full view of the surfers. And the receptionist should speak English. Singles run about $47, doubles

$52. 80 apartments. *Moderate. All cards.*

Hotel Ondimar
Avenida Presidente Vargas, 1843 (Ondina);
☎ *(71) 245–0366, FAX 245–4834*
This 3-star hotel in Ondina, near the Othon, provides service without frills. Standards are tight with no view; much larger deluxes, with seaside views, are worth the extra bucks. The breakfast room has American-style-banquettes for fast foods, lunch and dinner; there are no other restaurants nearby. A pool will be built. Shopping Barra is a 10-minute walk away. With advance notification, you can arrange a car to pick you up at the airport. Doubles range from $37 to $52 for deluxe. Children up to ten are free. 24 apartments. *Moderate. All cards.*

Farol Barra Flat
Avenida Oceánica, 409 (Barra);
☎ *(71) 237–6722*
The best centrally located apart–hotel in Barra is spacious and colorful, and suited for families. Fully air-conditioned apartments, with a kitchen and bar, are built around a plant-filled inner courtyard. There's also a pool, sauna, and rooftop restaurant. Breakfast is included in the daily rate. Doubles run from $36, and $39 with view. Two-room flats go for $48 and $53. 38 apartments. *Moderate–inexpensive. No cards.*

★ Villa Romana Hotel
Rua Prof. Lemos de Brito, 14 (Barra); ☎ *(71) 247–6522*
One of the most charming options in Salvador, this is a country-style pousada full of antique tapestries and native pottery. Because they were built in phases over the last 20 years, rooms differ dramatically in size; some are tucked into cubby-holes, others are enormous. Make sure you ask for an "amplo" with high-beamed ceilings. Even the corridors here are romantic, rustically appointed with objets d'art collected by the owners on their international travels. Italians tend to stay here for a month, particularly for the Italian-oriented cuisine, a throwback to the owners' ancestry. The restaurant, with pretty waitresses in native costume, is particularly inviting. A very unusual-shaped pool with its own outdoor veranda overlooks the city. Singles are an unbelievable $22, doubles $26, suites $41. Low-season discounts range from 25–30 percent. 49 apartments. *Inexpensive. All cards.*

Ondina Praia Hotel
Avenida Presidente Vargas, 2275 (Ondina);
☎ *(71) 371–0099*
For a 3-star hotel, the Ondina Praia has a decided upper-class feel, with a plant-dominated lobby filled with breezy, pastel furniture. The restaurant is tastefully appointed in shades of maroon; the breakfast room is full of hanging plants. Some rooms have front views to the sea, though they are obscured by large complexes like the Othon. All apartments are air-conditioned and include TV and minibar, but bathrooms are tiny. The outdoor pool is not large. Twenty–thirty percent discounts during low season. Singles run $33, doubles $37. 46 apartments. *Inexpensive. All cards.*

★ Barra Turismo Hotel
Avenida 7 de Setembro, 3691 (Porto da Barra); ☎ *(71) 245–7433*
This is a good budget idea for those who want to take advantage of Barra's social scene. The lobby is dreary, but the rooms have been restored and include a little balcony with a beautiful view of the sea. (Make sure you ask for the view.) City buses to downtown and the beaches stop at the front door. Nearby is a handicrafts market and many bars and luncheonettes. Singles go for $22, doubles $24. 60 apartments. *Inexpensive. All cards.*

Golden Park Hotel
Avenida Manoel Dias da Silva, 979 (Pituba);
☎ *(71) 240–5622*
This serviceable, friendly hotel is situated on the second avenue back from the shoreline. Although the beach here is not good for swimming, the bus stops in front of the hotel, and Itapoá is about 20 minutes away. Some rooms have a tiny view of the beach, but this is not a place to stay locked in your apartment all day. A small rooftop pool is served by a bar. The air-conditioned rooms are opened by electronic keys and include video TV and minibar. A pleasant restaurant serves lunch and dinner. Singles run $33,

doubles $35, no service tax for large groups. 60 apartments. *Inexpensive. All cards.*

Youth Hostel

★ Solar
Rua Macapá, 461 (Ondina);
☎ *(71) 235-2235*

Located a few blocks from the beach on a shady residential street, this youth hostel has a bright, clean aura. Across the street is a *capoeira* studio and next door is a 24-hour luncheonette. Some rooms have 8 bunk beds, with a cabinet that locks and a shared bathroom with hot and cold water. There's also a laundry you can use yourself. All ages, all countries converge here—men and women are separated. About $6–$7 per bed, including breakfast. 54 beds, 3 rooms for women, 2 rooms for men. *Cheap. No cards.*

In the Pelourinho

The historical center near the Pelourinho has a few hotels that are throwbacks to the rooming houses of centuries past. The architecture is delapidated colonial, the atmosphere funky, and the prices unbelievably low, but unless you're looking for swashbuckling adventure, you won't feel safe here. Plenty of tourists get robbed in broad daylight; after dark it's even worse. Single women should forget it. If you're in the habit of braving these kinds of accommodations, I seriously suggest you travel with your own sheets and towels and wear your money strapped to your chest while you sleep.

Hotel Colon
Praça Anchieta, 20, beside the Igreja São Francisco; ☎ *321-1531*

Old men and cats sleep in the hallways, and green fungus grows in the tub, but the original colonial architecture is appealing, particularly the wood-carved doors. An American professor of some obscure subject is reputed to be living here, though I never saw him. Rooms with bathroom run about $6, doubles with shared bath about $5, singles $4. 30 apartments. *Cheap. No cards.*

In Itaparica

Club Mediterranée
Highway to Nazaré, kilometer 13; ☎ *(71) 833-1141*

Located on the island of Itaparica, the Club Med of Bahia proffers that kind of insistently perky service of Club Meds world-wide. The staff is young, sexy, and dedicated to making sure you don't stay cloistered in your air-conditioned, chalet-type apartment. The grounds are luxuriously landscaped with tropical vegetation, wood bridges, and a beach right out the backyard. Most of the social scene centers around the extensive pool area, though there are also horse rides down the beach, hikes to native villages, windsurfing, archery, aerobics, lambada, etc. Guest talent shows include stripteases performed by the guests. Even though 70 percent of the clientele are families (mostly Brazilians and Argentinians with a smattering of French, Americans, and Italians), I've known singles who go home beaming. Children are kept wonderfully entertained all day long. Most remarkable is the quality and quantity of the cuisine—all-you-can-eat buffets of lobsters, prime rib, lamb, pastas, patés, French pastries, ice creams, and crepes every day and night. The best time to go is September-March (December is usually full). You must reserve in advance. 345 apartments. *Expensive. All cards.*

RESORTS IN BAHIA

★ Hotel Transamérica
Highway to Canasvieiras (Ilha de Comandatuba); ☎ *(126) 212-1122, telex: 2474. Reservations: Rua Colômbia, 587 in São Paulo;* ☎ *(11) 282-0999. 251 apartments. Very expensive. All cards.* Located on Commendatuba Island, **Transamérica Hotel** is the most luxurious resort in Brazil. Situated on a 25,000-acre grove of coconut trees, the hotel takes advantage of several islands, all pristinely maintained to ecological perfection. The ride to the hotel is a paradisiacal tour of Bahia's landscapes. An air-conditioned motor coach picks you up in Ilhéus (about 277 miles from Salvador), then follows the fabulous coastline south—past brilliant white beaches hugged by a dense tropical forest. After about 20 minutes, the sandy shore turns into an ocean wilderness, as enormous palm leaves fan the highway

and cattle graze over the high cliffs. Fifty minutes later, you cross the channel in a flat-bottom barge, where on the opposite shore, a cordial receptionist greets you with a tropical drink and leis. (All that's missing is a midget yelling, "The plane! The plane!") The main hotel, with 3 wings, plus a complex of private bungalows, is designed for total indulgence, its wood, rattan, and straw decor reflecting the island's natural but elegant lifestyle. The pool area is a voluptuous complex, enhanced by waterfalls and tropical bridges, yet steps away is a private beach so beautiful that you will never want to budge. All nautical sports from waterskiing, to kayaks, sailboats, motorboats, and hobbie cats, are concentrated along the Rio Doce channel; deep-sea fishermen come back with stories of dolphins, sea bass, red snappers, and others. Eco-minded adventurers will appreciate the mangrove-studded savannas perfect for exotic bird-watching. Four restaurants, including a special kid's club, an outdoor grill, an international buffet, and a special seafood restaurant, serve high-quality cuisine. Rooms in the main complex are luxuriously appointed, though the more rustic bungalows provide more privacy (especially great for honeymooners who are served candlelit dinners in bed). The most fun I had in my too-short stay was a motorboat jaunt to the island of Dona Vida, the resident mystic who even has a straw house made in the shape of a pyramid. This feisty, 70-year-old European became so popular with the hotel's clients that the management gave her her own island, where she receives guests for spiritual counseling and a great shrimp lunch. Rates for the resort depend on the accommodation, but generally start around $180 per person (breakfast and dinner included). For those looking for tropical luxury and security in Brazil, this must be heaven. For more information, contact in the United States **F&H Travel Consulting** ☎ *(800) 544-5503.*

★ **Agua Viva Praia Hotel**

Praia da Fazenda (Bom Jesus dos Pobres, 34 kilometers). Reservations in Salvador ☎ *(71) 359-1132* Three hundred years ago, the government gave this spectacular land with 26 kilometers of prime coast to the family whose descendants still own it. In 1989, they built 12 cabanas to share with the rest of the world, and they are projecting more. Rustic, totally dedicated to beachlife, the "hotel" is a mere step away from the ocean, where you can indulge in all watersports and even horseback ride over the glorious dunes. The owner's wife is an international chef who prepares dishes that surpass even those at Bargaço's, one of Salvador's finest eateries. Tramping through the family's 1,000 acres of rainforest is great fun; a fabulous walk to a waterfall took us through knee-high rushes and rocky streams. Individual bungalows are smallish but air-conditioned, and include minibar and tiled bathrooms; nights can be spent on the porch in a hammock. With doubles only about $40, this is a great budget alternative to a high-class resort, with nary a reduction in beauty. Just coming for the day and eating lunch should be joyous. 12 cabanas. *Moderate. No cards.*

Getting There

The hotel is located about 81 kilometers from Salvador. If you whine, the hotel might pick you up in Salvador, but it's easy enough to take the bus from Salvador to Bom Jesus dos Pobres (4 a day, about $3); it leaves you 30 meters from the hotel. Or drive 4 kilometers on the Santo Amara-Cachoeira Road, turn left, and go to Caubara Cabuçu and Bom Jesus dos Pobres. After Cabuçu, you will see the hotel sign and turn left toward the beach.

WHERE TO EAT

Carybé, a famous Bahian painter, has said that "all Bahian food is holy." Indeed, many of the dishes served today in restaurants originated as offerings to the gods of *candomblé* and still have liturgical rituals attached to their preparation. Although both Portuguese and Indian influences can be tasted in the peppery cuisine, the kitchens of colonial plantations were dominated by African slaves —"usually two or three enormously large women," as historian Gilberto Freyre described them, who flavored their native dishes with a *dendê* palm oil that turned everything reddish-yellow. Added to the pot were also generous doses of malagueta peppers, potent enough to draw tears from its willing victims. Food was so important to the colonialists (little other entertainment did they have) that sometimes great chefs were given their freedom in gratitude for a memorable meal. At the very least, black cooks were often invited into the dining room to be toasted with song in front of the master's guests.

Among the most beloved Bahian dishes of African descent are *carurú* and *vatapá*. Eaten for centuries by slaves and masters alike, *carurú* is a stew made with okra, fish, shrimp, nuts, garlic, onion, and pimenta. An accompaniment to many dishes, *vatapá* is a type of porridge, prepared from rice flour, ground cashews, and peanuts, ginger, mint, and lots of palm oil. Even more exotic is *sarapatel*—a pork dish made with innards and other unmentionables, stewed in the pig's blood. Though the exact recipe varies from chef to chef, *xinxin* is a ragout of chicken prepared with salt, onion, garlic, oil, shrimps, and pumpkin. Enjoyed on Saturdays, Bahian-style *feijoada* is made with red beans, not black. In general, servings of all dishes in Bahia are generous, often accompanied by a series of side dishes, including *farofa de dendê* (manioc flour fried in palm oil).

Delicious desserts have long been the specialty of Bahian cooks, particularly during colonial times when a veritable war was waged between those made on the street and those made at home. Almost all Bahian sweets are made from coconut. *Cocada*—coconut candy boiled in sugar, water, lemon, and ginger—comes either *branco* (white) or *preto* (black), depending on whether light or burnt brown sugar is used. Also delicious is *quindim*, a sticky little pudding cake made from egg yolks and coconut.

Many fine regional restaurants can be found throughout the state of Bahia, especially in Salvador, but one word of caution: be sparing when you first try the traditional dishes and see how they set with your stomach. The heavy use of palm oil and the profligate use of pepper, combined with too much sun and excitement, could easily lay you up in bed for a few days.

Expensive -------------- **Over $15**

Moderate --------------- **$5–$15**

Inexpensive ----------- **Under $5**

Typical Bahian
★ Casa da Gamboa
Rua Newton Prado, 51 (Campo Grande); ☎ *321-9776. Noon–3:00 p.m., 6:00 p.m.–midnight*

Sixty-three-year-old Conceição Reis learned to cook on the farm where she was raised. Now her traditional/international cuisine is famous throughout the country, as is her motherly warmth, which she dispenses tableside. In her charming colonial-style house overlooking the bay, dine on Salvador's best examples of *moqueca* and *vatapá*, as well as native desserts. Start off with *caranguejo na casca*—crab legs fried in a batter of egg, flour, and lemon. Lobsters are especially fresh, caught practically outside the front door as are the many varieties of fish and shrimp. The octopus vinaigrette, a cold salad, is unusual. What is special about Dona Conceição's kitchen is her creative use of condiments. "We spice with love here," she laughs, although she might be referring to the warmth of her folkloric-dressed waitresses whose beautiful faces enhance the almost devotional service. Ask for a table beside the blue-shuttered windows; the view of the moored fishing boats is highly romantic. *Expensive. Cards: AE*

★ SENAC
Largo do Pelourinho, 13/19 (Pelourinho); ☎ *321-5502. Daily 11:30 a.m.–3:30 p.m., 6:30 p.m.–9:30 p.m., closed Sunday Folklore show Wednesday–Saturday at 8:00 p.m. and 8:45 p.m.*

One of the most delightfully civilized experiences in Salvador, SENAC (which stands for Serviço Nacional do Comércio, the state-run restaurant school, which trains young chefs in native Bahian cuisine) is a perfect place to escape the hubbub of the Pelourinho area. The waiters-in-training are young, attractive, and so serious. The massive buffet includes 40 native dishes; the 20 on the right are made with *dendê* (African palm oil) and the 20 on the left are without (take care: an excess of the oil can cause digestive problems). If the traditional food looks daunting, there is also excellent fried chicken and recognizable vegetables. The waiter might take your plate the moment you finish, but feel free to take a clean one and start over. Drinks are not included, but all diners receive a delicious *batida*, which tastes something like peach liqueur. Buffet runs about $6–$7, service not included, so tip the kid well. A light tea is served from 5:00 p.m.-7:00 p.m. If you don't want to eat, just stop to check out the privileged view of Salvador's rooftops from the colonial-style, green-shuttered windows. Cookbooks of the house cuisine run about $3. *Moderate. All cards.*

Filhos de Ghandi

Rua Grefório de Matos, 53 (Pelourinho); ☎ *321-7073. Noon–2:00 p.m.* See under Walking Tour.

Seafood

★ **Bargaço**

Rua P, QD 43, lotes 18/19 (Jd. Armação); ☎ *231-5141. Noon–3:00 a.m., 7:00 p.m.–midnight*

An open-air restaurant with absolutely no ambiance has worked hard to garner acclaim as the best fish restaurant in Bahia. A great meal can be had from ordering a few of the enormous appetizers of shrimp, raw oysters, crab, and lobster. Or try traditional entrées like *mariscadas* and *ensopados*, fish stews simmered in a variety of sauces that arrive bubbling hot. Appetizers run about $9, entrees about $15. *Expensive. All cards.*

Casquinha de Siri

Avenida Otávio Mangabeira (Pietá); ☎ *249-1234*

Dance under the stars at Bahia's best beach (Piatá), where a live band swings to Brazil's golden oldies, and the regulars nosh on *tira gostos* like delicious *siri mole à Milanesa* (fried crabs) and *pitinga ao molho tártaro* (small fried fishbits). At night the ambiance is unabashedly lively, but it's also a good lunchstop if you're sunbathing nearby. Night music cover runs about $3.50. *Moderate. No cards.*

Frutos do Mar

Rua Alm. Marquês de Leão, 415 (Barra); ☎ *245-6479. Noon–4:00 p.m., 6:00 p.m.–1:00 a.m.*

Across from the Farol Flat Hotel, this fish eatery features waitresses in folkloric dress and menus in English. Try the *siri mole* (soft shell crabs) or the *sururu* (little mussels). *Moderate. All cards.*

International

★ **Phelippe Camarão**

Rua Alexandre Gusmão, 104 (Rio Vermelho); ☎ *237-4052. Noon–midnight daily. Happy hour with live music 6:00 p.m.–9:00 p.m.*

Phelippe Camarão was an Indian from Natal who was knighted by Phillipe II, King of Spain, for helping the Spanish throw the Dutch out of colonial Brazil. Now he's the name of this chic restaurant in the former home of Bahiano painter Luiz Jasminute. The decor is a mishmash of kitsch and couture, with objets d'art crammed into every nook; an oriental rug even hangs on the ceiling. Shrimp with flambéed pineapple is scrumptious at $9; one of the most popular dishes is octopus rice, a meal in itself. *Talharim com fruto ao mar* (spaghetti with fish) runs about $6. Desserts in general are good, but the chocolate mousse is exquisite. The "cool" contingent of high society packs the restaurant, especially on weekends, when you'll need a reservation. On a full moon, the candlelit veranda overlooking the city is extremely romantic. *Moderate. All cards.*

Churrascaria

★ **Esplanada Grill**

Rua Anisio Teixeira, 161, sobreloja (Boulevard 161) (Itaigara); ☎ *358-1203. Noon–3:30 p.m. and 7:00 p.m.–1:00 a.m.*

The top name in Salvador for à la carte steaks. Live music nightly. *Moderate. All cards.*

Baby Beef
Avenida Antônio Carlos Magalhães (Next to Paes Mendonça); ☎ 244–0811. Daily 11:30 a.m.–3:00 p.m., 6:00 p.m.–midnight
Excellent steaks à la carte, especially the huge *picanha*. Crispy french fries and excellent *macaxeira frita*. Check out the mammoth supermarket Paes Mendonça next door. A second Baby Beef is also located in the Convention Center in Pituba, *Moderate. All cards.*

Italian
Il Forno
Rua Marques de Leaõ, 77; ☎ 247–7287. Noon–3:00 p.m., 6:00 p.m.–1:00 a.m.
An Italian bistro with American posters offers the best pizza in Salvador, not to mention a snazzy location in Barra. Thirty-four varieties—medium sizes run about $8. Steaks and chicken are also available. Sit outside on the terrace and watch the world go by. *Moderate. All cards.* Across the street is **Baguette e Cia,** a cheerful counterette with long French bread sandwiches and excellent ice cream sundaes. *Inexpensive. No cards.*

La Gula
Avenida Presidente Vargas, 2400 (Ondina) Hotel Ondina Apart; ☎ 203–8314. Noon–3:00 p.m., 7 p.m.–1:00 a.m., closed Monday.
Among locals, this cantina is considered the best for Italian food—pastas, lasagna, and pizzas. *Moderate. Cards: AE.*

Arabian
Aladin
Rua Marques de Leão, 173. Daily 11:00 a.m.–2:00 a.m.
The point ("in-spot") of Barra (at least this year) offers fine Arabic entrées, including stuffed cabbage and lamb. Or go just to nosh on hors d'oeuvres like *baba ganoush*, *kibe*, and *pastel de carne*, and look over the teens (18-19) who hang out here. Weekends are sardinelike. *Inexpensive. No cards.*

Fast Food
McDonald's
(yes, the hamburger joint from up north) gives new meaning to spic and span, conveniently located downtown across the street from the Varig Airline office on Praça Inglaterra. (The American Express office is also nearby, at the corner of Rua Miguel Calmon.) Another McDonald's is located about a 5-minute walk from the Mercado Modelo.

Natural
Cozinha Natural
Rua Belo Horizonte, 124 (Barra); ☎ 237–1012. Daily 11:30 a.m.–8:00 p.m., Saturday–Sunday 11:30 a.m.–4:00 p.m.
Health-oriented menu and natural foods. *Inexpensive. No cards.*

Ice Cream
Perini
Across the street from Barra Shopping Center, offers the city's best ice cream, including a full array of tropical fruit flavors.

Street Food
You may hear their nasal *ê-ê-ê-ê* cry before you see their huge white hoop skirts and colorful turbans, but the **Pretas do Acarajé** are an institution on Salvador's streets. These native women, who make and sell the delicacies called *acarajé*, or fried bean cake, are beloved throughout the city; often their culinary secrets have been passed down through generations. The Preta do Acarajé makes her dish right on the street, grating *fradinho* beans on a stone, and frying the mixture with dendê oil, dried shrimps, onions, and salt in a clay pan that sits on a little rustic stove. Since the exact taste differs slightly from cook to cook, everyone has a different opinion over who makes the best, but the Bahiana who causes the biggest traffic jams is **Dinah** at the **Largo de Santana** in **Rio Vermelho**, in front of the old church of **Sant'Ana**. Between 4:00 p.m.–10:00 p.m., traffic stops and people cram the streets just to buy her soulfully cooked cakes.

> **Insider Tip:**
> *When the cook asks you "Pimenta?" learn to say "Um pouquinho" (oon-poh-kee-nyoo) or your eyes will be streaming with tears from the pepper.*

On Sundays

A fishermen's colony during the week, **Itapagipe Beach** transforms into a weekend party when sunbathers pack the grass-roof *barracas* and chow down on fried fish and cold beer.

Fish Market

The new **fish market** located at **Largo da Mariquita** in **Rio Vermelho** has become an in place to eat typical dishes and drink exotic-flavored *batidas*. Americans living in Salvador tend to eat lunch here; at night the small tables and wood chairs served by various kitchen stalls are crowded with locals. The smell of fish inundates the air, but one *batida* at **Diolino's** (considered the best in Bahia) will cure anything. Insanely delicious is the "Gala Gay" with coconut and guava mix (about 30 cents for a tiny cup); you'll probably want to stock up on bottles. Do take a browse through **Casa das Folhas #20,** a stand selling *candomblé* and medicinal paraphernalia.

WHAT TO DO AT NIGHT

Salvador is a city to savor at night. Cool winds and fresh air make lingering at sidewalk cafés a tropical pleasure. Most tourists will want to spend one night watching a folkloric show; they are much more authentic in Bahia than in Rio. The best show is situated in the atmospheric colonial house of Solar do Unhão (see below under *Folklore Shows*), where you can also partake of a fine buffet of typical foods.

Bars

Bar-hopping in Barra is also a popular activity—easy to do since many of the liveliest pubs are located along Avenida Setembro de 7. Some of the best bars in Barra are: **Bacchus** *Avenida Presidente Vargas, 115, loja 3;* ☎ *245-6749. Monday–Saturday starting at 9:00 p.m.,* **Clube 45** *Rua Barão de Sergy, 196;* ☎ *237-3778. Daily 7:00 p.m.–5:00 a.m., with live music,* **Habeas Corpos** *Rua Marquês de Leão.* Of late, the district of Rio Vermelho has nearly eclipsed Barra in the number of hot spots that offer good music. Among them are: **Cheiro do Mar** *Rua Borges dos Reis, 14;* ☎ *247-1106. Noon–2:00 p.m., 5:00 p.m.–on;* **Graffiti** *Rua Odorico Odilon, 41. Tuesday–Sunday 6:00 p.m. on;* and **Bar 68** *Largo de Santana, 3rd floor; Monday–Friday from 6:00 p.m. on, Saturday from 7:00 p.m. on.*

Discos

There are also plenty of clubs for dancing. My favorite is **Casquinha de Siri** *Avenida Otávia Mangabeira s/no., Praia dos Coqueiro (Piatá);* ☎ *249-1234* with a sprawling open-air dining room and a great dance band that plays Brazilian golden oldies (see *Where to Eat*). The disco **Hippopotamus** at the **Bahia Othon Hotel** is a popular spot for locals and tourists. One of the newest discos is **Zouk Santana** in Rio Vermelho, with a $3 cover and an excellent sound system. Best lambada in the city is found at **Sabor da Terra**, near Boca do Rio (next door is another new disco, **Krypton**). Samba bands heat up at **Cartarerê** in Cardeal da Silva.

Reggae comes alive in the **Cidade Alta** on Tuesday nights (the only relatively safe time to stroll through the historical center after dark); during the rest of the week, shops close up early. Most popular are the **Bar do Reggae** *Rua João de Jesus, 32* and **Bar Baro** *Rua Alfredo Brito.*

> **Insider Tip:**
>
> *A not-to-miss event is the rehearsal of the drummers from* **Olodum**, *the Carnaval* **bateria** *(percussion group) featured on Paul Simon's 1990 album* **Rhythm of the Saints** *but who are stars in their own right in Brazil. The event takes place from 7:00 p.m.–11:00 p.m. behind the* **Teatro Antônio Miguel** *on Rua João de Jesus in an open field called the Quadra, as well as on Sundays in the* **Largo do Pelourinho** *from 6:00 p.m.–11:00 p.m.*

Folklore Shows

Solar do Unhão
Avenida do Contorno (Gamboa); ☎ 245-5551. Noon–midnight. Show starts at 11:00 p.m., closed Monday.
Most consider the folkloric show in this renovated sugarcane mill to be the most artistic in the city. Native dancers in skimpy costumes, virile *capoeira* artists, and a bevy of hot drummers keep the passions flowing; the colonial atmosphere adds even more romance. Enter the restaurant through the corridor of the former mansion, stepping over the railroad tracks that formerly carted products to and from the harbor. Dinner is included—an all-you-can-eat buffet of native delicacies. Most travel agencies (check at your hotel) offer group rates (including transportation), which is the safest way to go to this isolated neighborhood. For the show, make sure your seat is around the stage, but not too close to the drummer! *Expensive. All cards.*

Theater

Teatro Maria Bethânia
Named after the sultry singer and sister of Caetano Veloso, features theater performances and a cinema that shows art films. Check the newspapers for listings.

GAY SALVADOR

Barra
Particularly in front of the lighthouse, has become a popular hangout for gays. Downtown, two clubs are frequented: one mysteriously known as **Holmes 24th** *Rua Gamboa de Cima* (opposite the Rua Banco dos Ingleses near Campo Grande), best reached by taxi, and the **Tropical Nightclub** *Rua Pau da Bandeira*. Also check out the courtyard near **Tiffany**'s restaurant in Barra.

SHOPPING

Native crafts are a true expression of Bahian culture. Artists display their wares in hotel lobbies, outdoors in the main *praças*, in fairs, and at state-operated institutes that assure quality and fixed prices. Principal materials employed by the artisans are wood, silver, gold, leather, lace, ceramics, clay, and sisal (entwined rope). Musical instruments like the *berimbau* are good buys, and most airlines will let you board with the gourd in hand, though you may have to ship the bow (carefully wrapped in cloth or newspaper) with your luggage. If you're heading to the Amazon, it's better to buy a hammock in Belém or Santarem, where they're cheaper.

Mercado Modelo
Monday–Saturday 8:00 a.m.–6:00 p.m., Sunday 8:00 a.m.–noon

Mercado Modelo is located in front of the Lacerda Elevator in the lower city and is usually the last stop on all city tours. First installed in the old customs house in 1915, it's been ravaged by two fires and was rebuilt the last time in 1984. With 190 stalls, this three-story market is like a Turkish bazaar, where the first price is a joke and bargaining is expected (though in Brazil, it should always be done with charm). Primitive Bahian art and sculptures are excellent buys as are the chess sets with traditional figures (located upstairs). You'll also find plenty of musical instruments, as well as fine embroidered and lace tablecloths. Most interesting are the *carrancas*—sculptured miniatures of the monsters with winged ears, grizzly smiles, and red tongues that hang on the front of ships to ward off spirits.

In the front of the market is a round stage where *capoeira* artists perform and will expect money if you take their picture or stand there more than three seconds. (The habit offended me until I learned that *capoeira* artists are usually poor and given no support from the government. But don't be intimidated.) Of the two restaurants in the market, the best is the **Camafeu de Oxóssi** *Daily, open 11:00 a.m.* overlooking the bay, where you can find traditional dishes.

The intriguing sculptures near the Mercado Modelo that look like two big *bundas* are the work of **Mario Cravo**, who innocently claims he just liked the shape. Bahianos insist the shape represents one of two things: 1) the voluptuousness of Bahian woman or 2) things that both the mayor and the governor have.

Institu Mauá
Praça Azevedo Fernandes, 02; ☎ 235-5440. Monday–Friday 8:00 a.m.–6:00 p.m., Saturday 8:00 a.m.–4:00 p.m.
Some of the best Northeastern handicrafts can be found at this tasteful store in Barra, supported by the state government. Quality is high and prices fixed, but numerous items can't be found elsewhere, like corn straw ducks, ocarinas (flutes) made out of pottery, and native paintings. Ceramic *orixás*—statues of *candomblé* divinities—are excellent buys.

SESI
Avenida Sete de Setembro, 261 (Mercês). Monday–Friday 8:00 a.m.–noon, and 1:30 p.m.–6:00 p.m.; ☎ 245-3543 (Two other locations: **Loja Rio Vermelho** Rua Borges dos Reis, 9; and **Loja Porto da Barra** Forte de Santa Maria (Barra).
Walking distance from the Meridien Hotel, this co-op crafts store in a colonial house was founded to support native craftspersons from the interior. Many of the handwork and patchwork items, sold here at fixed prices, can only be found in the countryside. Small postcard paintings from Itaparica are good buys, as are thumb pianos, Indian-made rain sticks (a musical instrument that sounds like rain), and wooden jewelry. Afterwards, walk over to Largo Santana and buy some *acarajé* from Dinah, the famous street vendor (see above under *Street Food*). Across the street is a popular bar **Cheiro de Mar** and around the block is the **Teatro Maria Bethânia**. Nearby, at the corner of Rua João Gomes and Largo da Mariquita is the **Teresa Galerias de Arte**, a gallery featuring posters and painters from well-known Brazilians.

Historical Center

Along the cobblestone streets of **Rua Alfredo Brito** are numerous artisan shops that are fun to peek in. Stores along the Pelourinho include lacework, sculptures, and folkloric paintings. The most beautiful Bahian clothes are at **Artesanato Protasio** Rua Alfredo Brito, 13 where you can find white lace nightgowns, shirts, and dresses. More sophisticated styles and fine tablecloths can be found next door at **Santa Barbara Handcraft**.
Near the São Francisco Church, on Praça Anchieta, there are numerous jewelry stores to which tour guides often steer travelers.

Simon
Praça Anchieta 1, Ed. Derike, lojas A & B, Monday–Saturday 9:00 a.m.–6:00 p.m.; ☎ 242-5218, Sunday 9:00 a.m.–1:00 p.m.
Simon features handmade jewelry and will deliver it to your hotel (an excellent idea). Prices, however, run about 3 times the amount I paid for similar quality in Ouro Preto (Minas Gerais) and may even be higher than prices in Rio. A special product is called "Mask"—the matrix rock of an emerald handmade by communities of Indians near Porto Seguro ($25–$30). Also sold are precious and semi-precious stones made for healing purposes (designed so that the stone of the ring can touch the skin). Also available are Bahian cigars made at Suerdieck, one of the biggest plantations in Bahia. Good English spoken. *All cards and money*.

Nearer the church is **Las Bonfim Gems Jewelers**, the oldest jewelry store in Bahia. If you are buying for business, they will sell wholesale. Specialties are chess sets made of onyx and sodalite, as well as raw amethysts.

Gerson Jewelry Store
has very high prices and has been known to sell blue topaz as the more expensive aquamarine. Beware.

Shopping Malls

Shopping Barra
Avenida Centenário. Monday–Friday 9:00 a.m.–10:00 p.m., Saturday 9:00 a.m.–7:00 p.m., Sunday 3:00 p.m.–9:00 p.m.
This three-floor, ultra-modern mall is a cool, dry place to get out of the heat or rain. A telephone company is on the first floor, as well as fast-food restaurants and cinema. Some of the best stores include **Timberland** shoes, **Cheda** for men, **Gas** for chic children, and **Dimpus** for hip women.

Next to Salvador Praia Hotel is a small shopping mall housing **Itaparica Turismo,** one of the city's best travel agencies. Next door are two important art galleries: **Escritório de**

SALVADOR

Arte da Bahia Avenida Presidente Vargas, 2338 (Ondina); ☎ 245-5033 and **Cavalete** Avenida Presidente Vargas, 2338 (Ondina); ☎ 345-5033. Another excellent gallery is **Limpia** Praça Anchieta, 16; ☎ 321-8896.

On **Rua João Gomes** there are several fine antique shops.

SPORTS

The best high-tech gym in Salvador is located at the **Ondina Apart Hotel** Avenida Presidente Vargas, 68 (Barra); ☎ 247-7611. Daily 6:30 a.m.–12:30 p.m. and 3:00 p.m.–9:00 p.m. A chic meeting place for singles, it's owned by Julião Castello, famous in Bahia for training the Arabian football team. Talk to him for a special tourist rate if you're in Salvador for only a few days.

HANDS-ON SALVADOR

Airport

Aeroporto Internacional Dois de Julho Estrada do Coco, ☎ 204-1010 is a modern airport with various snack bars, restaurant with a fine buffet, souvenir shops, and even a hairdresser. If you are arriving on an international flight, you will have to pass through customs. To reach your hotel, you can take special air-conditioned buses that run from the airport along the shoreline, but the easiest way is to reserve a special taxi by paying in advance at the white booth in the middle of the arrival lounge (where you exit from customs). The clerk will ask the name of your hotel, and you pay according to the neighborhood you are going to. Then you will be directed to hand your receipt to the first special taxi in line. Be careful, however—there are also "regular" taxis waiting for customers, and unless you can firmly express yourself in Portuguese and know how to bargain, you will most likely be taken for a "very long" ride.

Arrivals

Salvador may be reached directly from the States on Varig Airlines, which runs a direct flight from Miami to Salvador once a week on Monday, leaving at 5:00 p.m. and arriving the next day at 3:45 a.m. For a minimum stay of 21 days (maximum 3 months), a round-trip ticket in low season runs about $1,102 (high season $1,202). A 7-day minimum, 30-day maximum ticket is also available. All tickets must be bought 14 days in advance.

Originating in Rio, daily flights to Salvador are handled by **Varig**, **Cruzeiro**, **VASP** and **Transbrasil**. The trip takes about two hours and costs $376 round trip, if you have not previously purchased a Varig Air Pass.

Varig/Cruzeiro Rua Carlos Gomes, 6; ☎ 243-1244.

VASP Rua do Chile, 27 (Cidade Alta); ☎ 243-7277.

Transbrasil Rua Carlos Gomes, 616; ☎ 241-1044.

Bus Station

Rodoviária de Salvador Avenida Antônio Carlos Magalhães (Iguatemí); ☎ 558-0124.

Car Rental

Nobre Avenida Tancredo Neves, 999; ☎ (71) 371-9848.

City Transportation

Conveniently, most of the historical sightseeing in Salvador, concentrated in the Cidade Alta, can be easily done on foot. To get to a favorable beach for swimming, you must either take a taxi or a bus. The Lacerda Lift connects the high and low cities, but it is best to avoid it, due to the high number of assaults.

Buses:

Buses in Salvador tend to be hot, crowded, and unsafe for tourists not used to third-world travel. Best bets are the air-conditioned frescão, an air-conditioned express coach, which you can catch on the sidewalk up from Praça da Sé for about 75 cents. The frescão has two routes: one to the **Iguatemí Shopping Center** (via Barra and Rio Vermelho beaches, stopping near the Rodoviária), and one to the **Airport**, which passes Pituba and Itapoã beaches.

Taxis:

Taxis are plentiful and relatively cheap in Salvador, but drivers here have been known to be as sneaky as they are in Rio. Since the city government implored the *motoristas* to clean up their act in the name of tourism (preceding some important conferences), I have actually noticed a definite accentuation on the positive. If you want to avoid getting "taken" for a ride, however, make sure you know where you're going, how to get there (ask your concierge), and about how much it will cost—in advance. I don't like to say it, but some hotel doormen have been known to be in cahoots with cabdrivers, so stay alert.

Radio Taxi
☎ 243-4333.

COMTAS
(special cabs) ☎ 245-6311.

Ferry:
The islands in All Saint's Bay may be reached by both ferry and tourist excursion boats, which leave from the **Terminal Turístico**, behind the Mercado Modelo. Ferries handling automobiles leave from the **Terminal da Estação Marítima**, past the docks to the right.

Climate

Sunshine is Salvador's greatest free pleasure. Average temperatures range from the mid-70s to the high 80s (25°C-32°C), with a refreshing sea breeze cooling the peak days of summer. The best time to go, climatewise, is September-March. Rainy months are April, May, and June, when you're most likely to run into a nasty ocean squall that will dampen beachdoings for days at a time. However, even in summer, a fast but brief downpour happens about once a day, clearing the hot air for even brighter sunshine.

Consulates

In case of lost passports, stolen merchandise or extreme illness, contact your own consulate immediately.

U.S.A.
Avenida Antônio Carlos Magalhães (Cidadela Center Building); ☎ 358-9195.

Great Britain
Avenida Estados Unidos, 4; ☎ 243-9222.

Credit Cards

American Express office is located at **Kontik Franstur** Praça Inglaterra 2 (1st floor); ☎ (71) 242-0433. Monday-Friday 9:00 a.m.-noon, 2:00 p.m.-4:00 p.m. They are extremely friendly and will process emergency check cashing, card replacement, foreign currency exchange, and client mail for all cardholders. A Telephone Service Center is available on a 24-hour/7-day basis: for lost and stolen cards, ☎ 800-5050; for lost traveler's checks, ☎ (11) 545-5018 or 545-6223 in Salvador.

Money Exchange

As in Rio, it's best to avoid cashing traveler's checks or exchanging dollars at your hotel, where the rate will be somewhat lower than the official tourist rate. Better rates can be found at **Banco do Brasil** Avenida 7 de Setembro, 733 and Avenida Estados Unidos, 561 (Cidade Baixa). Located across from the Ondina Apart Hotel, **Banco Econômico** Avenida Oceânica, 2400. Monday-Friday 10:00 a.m.-4:00 p.m., is good for exchanging traveler's checks and American currency. Rates are substantially better here than at the nearby Bahia Othon Hotel.

Medical Emergencies

Private Clinic Rua Barão de Loretto, 21 (English spoken).

Photo Development

FOTO Lab Shopping Barra, 1st floor; ☎ 247-4004.

Police

For emergencies ☎ 197.

Private Guide

Silvia Vannucci Chiappori Largo do Campo Grande, 124/1202; ☎ 245-3924, or 235-2047, FAX 235-2047, is president of the Guide Association of Salvador and an excellent English-speaking guide herself. If she can't help you, she'll find someone who can. If you're planning to use her services, it's best to call in advance. She is well connected with many travel agencies.

Public Telephones

If you need to make long-distance phone calls away from your hotel, you'll find telephone stations at **Shopping Barra**, the **Mercado Modelo**, the **airport**, the **bus station**, and the **Centro de Convenções** (Convention Center).

Tourist Information

The last governor of Salvador didn't pay much heed to tourism, but the attitude is now changing. College students who speak other languages have been hired to run the tourist information booth at the airport (in the lobby where you pick up taxis). Supplies are sometimes low, but they should have free copies of maps, some English-language brochures, and a copy of the city magazine *Itinerário* (in Portuguese). Inquire about the *Salvador Tourist Guide*, a 61-page book with some English translations published by Emtursa. Other information centers staffed by Bahiatursa, the state's official tourist board, are:

Porto da Barra
Praça Azevedo Fernandes; ☎ *245 –5610. Daily 9:00 a.m.–6:00 p.m.*

Rodoviária
(Bus station) Avenida Antônio Carlos Magalhães (Pituba); ☎ *231–2831. Daily 9:00 a.m.–9:00 p.m.*

Mercado Modelo
Praça Visconde de Cairú; ☎ *241–0242. Monday–Saturday 9:00 a.m.–6:00 p.m.*

Travel Agencies

Travel agencies in Salvador are best used for schooner excursions and general transportation, such as a **Panoramic Tour** of the city, or a trip to **Solar do Unhão**, a folkloric dinner show (it's a hefty taxi ride away from most hotels). Unfortunately, walking tours tend to treat clients as herds, and English-speaking guides don't always sound as if they are speaking your language. Large groups of Argentinians usually dominate these tours, so if you understand Spanish better than Portuguese, you'll be one step ahead.

Itaparica Turismo
Avenida Presidente Vargas, 2338, loja 5; ☎ *245–1455, FAX 245– 8918,* offers historical tours, island excursions, and evening folkloric shows. Airport transfers are also available. Trips to Cachoeira and Praia do Forte can also be arranged; if you are staying at the Praia do Forte Resort, however, the hotel provides its own transfer.

LR Turismo
Avenida Sete de Setembro, 3959; ☎ *247–9211 (Barra)* The leading agency in Salvador conducts up to nine different tours, including a walking tour of historical Bahia, Salvador by night, full day-trips to Cachoeira, island jaunts, and a handicraft and architectural tour. Tours are generally conducted in multilingual groups in comfortable air-conditioned buses. Make sure you request a guide who speaks English well.

When To Go

Bahianos need little impetus to throw a celebration. Between Carnaval, Holy Week, feast days for saints, homages to *candomblé* divinities, and historical remembrances, there seems to be at least one major festival in Salvador per month. All these colorful festivities are public affairs—usually involving street processions, native foods, music, dance, and, more often than not, drunken revelry by the end of the day. If you can make it to any of the following festivals, you'll get a rare glimpse into the "real" Bahia. Just watch your wallet and be prepared for voluminous crowds.

December 31–January 1
Festa de Nosso Senhor dos Navegantes is celebrated by the simple men of the sea who give praise and thanks to the "God of Navigators" for helping them survive the previous year. Festooned with flowers, a vessel containing the image of Bom Jesus is sailed, in the company of hundreds of small boats, from the Igreja da Boa Viagem through All Saint's Bay to the Igreja da Conceição da Praia, where the statue of the Virgin Mary is awaiting it. Later, the festival returns to the Largo da Boa Viagem with fireworks and native music.

January 6
Festa dos Reis Magos The Festival of the Three Kings starts in the early hours in the Square of Lapinha as the Maji and shepherds pass through streets to the Praça da Sé, accompanied by brass bands, honor guards, gypsies, and folkloric characters.

January
(second Thur. for 8 days) Lavagem do Igreja da Bonfim considered the major fetishist festival in Brazil, focuses on the washing of the steps of the Church of Bonfim by local women. As participants chant African hymns little donkeys garlanded with streamers parade single-file from the center of the city to the church, carrying barrels of water on their backs. During the week, bands of musicians play popular and classical music around the square while native-dressed girls sell typical Bahiano dishes. The final night is punctuated by a stunning display of fireworks.

January
(first Monday after Bonfim) Festa da Ribeira is as wild as Bonfim is devoted, with young boys and girls, impervious to race, class, or position, dancing in the streets of Itapagipe, drinking traditional *batidas* and partaking of native foods.

February 2
Festa de Iemanjá is a grand Bahian festival, honoring the protectoress and mother of the sea. It begins a week before, with parades, dances, and special foods. On February 2, fishermen and the *casas de santo* meet at the Largo de Sant'Ana in a simple church. A small stone house filled with presents is then launched out to sea.

February
Carnaval is characterized by enormous crowds following behind blaring *trios elétricos*, motorized open-air trucks carrying a small band. Music star Caetano Veloso traditionally composes a *frevo*. Two weeks before the Carnaval on Sunday is Festa do Rio Vermelho. Fifteen days after Carnaval is the Lavagem da Igreja de Itapoã. (For more information, see the chapter on *Carnaval*.)

March 29
Founding of the city.

May 19
Festa de São Francisco Xavier celebrates the patron saint of the city.

June 13
Festa de Santo Antônio The patron saint of marriage (and Ogum's equivalent in *candomblé*) is celebrated with special dances. During the month of June is also a 12-day *candomblé* festival honoring all the divinities.

June 29
Festa de São Pedro The feast, honoring Saint Peter, patron saint of widows, serves corn in every imaginable form, as well as grilled beef chunks washed down with *quentão* (hot spiced wine).

July 2
The Independence of Bahia is celebrated in the city's main square, Campo Grande.

August
International Fair of Precious Stones Four days of exhibitions for buyers of precious stones, usually held at the Hotel da Bahia. Contact Bahiatursa for more information.

September 7
Independence of Brazil Parades and fanfares celebrating the release from Portuguese domination. Everyone dresses in white and carries green and yellow feathers.

September 27
The whole month of September celebrates São Cosme and São Damião, the most important black Catholic saints. Special masses are held and traditional foods eaten, like *vatapá*, *carurú*, and *efó*.

December 4
Festa de Santa Bárbara The festival of Santa Barbara (or Iansã, in *candomblé*) is celebrated with religious processions, lots of *cachaça*, and *capoeira* demonstrations. A local okra dish is served to all.

November 29–December 8
Festa da Conceição da Praia The protectoress of Bahia (the syncretic parallel to Iemenjá) is honored for a week, with festivities in front of the Cais Cairu. Beer, batidas, typical foods, and samba.

Insider Tip:
Most museums are closed on Monday.

CACHOEIRA

For cultists-in-the-know, the tiny, sleepy market town of **Cachoeira**, about 70 miles from Salvador, buzzes with spiritual fever—it's said to have one of the most authentic *candomblé* centers of worship in Brazil. Daring tourists have been known to make the two-hour trip to attend the Saturday night *terreiro* session in nearby **São Felix**, but getting there itself is a pilgrimage of endurance. About twelve hot, non-airconditioned buses run daily from the main terminal in Salvador, but drivers sometimes drive maniacally over the pockmarked highway (mine almost hit a dog), and they tend to play their scratchy boom boxes at peak volume. You may also have to share bus space with dogs, cats, squawking chickens, and crowing roosters, that often accompany their owners. Survivors of the trip will be rewarded, however, with a colonial village that still sports the fine buildings, churches, and cobblestone streets of its 18th-century heyday. Overnights can even be spent in a restored convent, complete with a bevy of bats that love to swoop down from the high-beamed ceilings.

Located in the **Recôncavo**, the fertile coastal plains surrounding the **Bay of All Saints (Baía de Todos os Santos)**, Cachoeira was once the primary port and trading post for the sugarcane plantations that supplied the state with its fruits and spices. In 1822, the inhabitants of the city gained a feisty reputation when they took on a Portuguese warship docked in the harbor, becoming the first community in the country to claim allegiance to Dom Pedro I. When Dom Pedro visited with his court, Cachoeira was even dubbed the capital of Brazil for a brief 48 hours. Today the Recôncavo is one of the most important agricultural centers of the state (mostly harvesting tobacco, peppers, and cloves), although Cachoeira and its nearby twin town of **São Félix** have never quite advanced to the 20th century. The people still live a primitive life, embraced by religious devotion, farm life, and small-town intrigues. Folklorically, white, black and Indian cultures collide here to produce a rich tradition of song and dance, including **bumba-meu-boi**, **afoxé**, and **samba-de-roda**, all which can been seen and heard during the various festivals held throughout the year. Among the liveliest is the **Festival of São João** on June 22–24.

If you're traveling along BA-026, you'll pass through the town of **Santo Amaro**, the birthplace of Caetano Veloso and Maria Bethânia, two of the most lyrically-inspired musicians of *música popular brasileira* (MPB). Indeed, talent still reigns in this region; the moment I stepped off the bus in Cachoeira, I discovered two young boys (the next Gilberto Gil and Caetano Veloso?) sitting on the dusty curb, working out tunes with their guitar. Offsetting the unpressured life, however, has been a series of disasters over the last few decades that have shaken Cachoeira's confidence. In 1969, a dam broke due to human error and kept the entire city under water for three weeks. Water marks left from the flood can still be seen along some of the old buildings.

SIGHTS

ON FOOT

Starting from the **Pousada do Convento**, turn right on **Rua Inocêncio Boaventura** to see the ruins of the **Convento do Carmo** from the 16th century. Like the São Francisco Church in Salvador, this stone- and-wood structure houses a shocking display of gold-leaf ornamentation. An old custodian with an ancient set of keys will open the church, which is only in use during Easter. Most interesting are the Oriental eyelids of many of the sculpted saints—these all hail from the Portuguese colony of Macau, China. Also startling is the shiny blood droplets on the Christ figures, made from a mixture of cow blood, rubies, and herbs. The lifelike figure of Jesus with a red wig is carried through the streets on Good Friday.

Historical Center

Walk a few yards down to the **Casa da Câmara e Cadeia** (1698–1712) on **Praça da Aclamação**, the historical center of the city during the 18th and 19th centuries. During the fight for Independence in 1822, this yellow-and-white colonial building acted as the prison; now it is the mayor's office. On the Praça da Aclamação is the **Museu do Iphan**, an 18th-century landowner's house, where you can view typical furniture of the era. Notice the bars on the window, which kept the slaves out, and the antique chair in the lobby, used to transport the mayor. The theater in the backyard sponsors musical events and *capoeira* demonstrations.

Next door is the gallery of the 90-year-old artist **Cincinho**, whose primitive, *naif* style is indicative of the region. The next shop houses **Casa Velha Arte**, *daily 8:00 a.m.–6:00 p.m.*, a handicraft store featuring the paintings of João Gonçalves, a sculptor and painter inspired by the rituals of the Nossa Senhora da Boa Morte.

Further up **Rua 13 de Maio** is **Igreja Matriz de Nossa Senhora do Rosário**, dedicated to the patroness of the city. During Pentecost Sunday, when I visited, the entire church was wrapped in white ribbons adorned with white plastic pigeons. An historian has claimed that the church displays the most blue Portuguese tiles in Brazil. The highly treasured sacraments are kept in a pure silver cabinet on the left behind the white-and-gold gates.

Built In 1595

Turn uphill on **Ladeira d'Ajuda** to arrive at the first church in Cachoeira built in 1595, called the **Igreja de N.S. d'Ajuda**. You must ask the priest to open it, so bang loudly on the door. Next door is the **Museu Irmandade N.S. da Boa Morte**, documenting the history of a sisterhood of female slaves who banded together to buy the freedom of other slaves. Today the sisterhood still functions and holds a famous three-part feast in August (usually the last Friday before August 15): on the first day, they commemorate the death of those who died seeking freedom; on the second day they hold a symbolic funeral; and the third day they celebrate the freedom of Nossa Senhora da Boa Morte as she ascends to heaven. The present members of the sisterhood must be black, over 45 years of age, and have had at least 3 years soliciting money for the projects of the organization, which includes social work and care for the homeless. During the festivities all the city's *candomblé* groups turn out in full white regalia, dancing and singing in African dialects.

Next door is the **City Hall** (Prefeitura Municipal). Follow the brick steps of the street to the right of the city hall to the **Praça Doutor Milton**, where there is a bronze fountain (*chafariz*) from 1827; the city's inhabitants used to come here to fill their clay jugs. In front, the yellow church with the belfry is the 18th-century **Santa Casa da Misericórdia**. Turn right on **Rua Ruy Barbosa**, a main shopping street with a drugstore, bar, restaurant, and bookstore. Turning onto **Rua Cons. Virgílio Damazio**, you'll discover a great place to roam. Much of the town here is in evocative ruins, but you can also see the old train station from here and the iron box-girder bridge built by British engineers in 1885, which connects to the city of São Félix.

At **Praça Manoel Vitorino**, in front of the train station, you'll find the city's second best typical restaurant, **Gruta Azul**, filled with cages of tropical birds. After lunch walk along the edge of the **Paraguaçu River** to **Praça Teixeira de Freitas**, where you can rent a canoe and guide to tour the river. A trip to the lighthouse and back (about one hour) will run about $5. It costs about 30 cents to cross the river to São Félix. Nearby in the square on Rua 13 de Maio is the **Atelier de Dory**, the studio of one of the city's best sculptors. If you get desperate for entertainment, the movie house on the *praça* shows films on Friday, Saturday, and Sunday.

CANDOMBLÉ

Candomblé sessions are held at the **Terreiro de Vannuú** on *Varre Estrada* in **São Félix** on Saturday nights. To get there, cross the bridge connecting Cachoeira and São Felix, which starts after the cemetery. The walk is about one hour and is relatively safe if you don't get lost, but it's best to go with a native of the city or with a guide from Salvador who has connections; remember, *candomblé* is a very insular, deeply serious religious practice of trance worship. (Contact Bahiatursa for information regarding attendance. For more explanation about the actual practice, see the chapter *Traveler's Guide to Brazilian Spirits*.) The sessions are held in a small wood cottage, packed to overflowing with the congregants, who arrive around 10:00 p.m. and stay until dawn. Guests are usually ushered to a seated position, but the room can get hot and claustrophobic.

THE ESSENTIAL CACHOEIRA

WHERE TO STAY

Pousada do Convento
Rua Inocêncio Boaventura; ☎ *(71) 724-1716, Reservations in Salvador* ☎ *(71) 235-3949*
The timeless vibes of this old Franciscan monastery make for an atmospheric accommodation—the best in the city. The high-beamed corridors are so wide that at least 10 monks could walk side by side without touching. The rooms, built around an inner courtyard, are large, with the original stone window seats and jacaranda-carved headboards. The antique keyholes don't always work, but even more unsettling are the black fuzzy balls that hang upside down from the high-beamed hallway. Management nonchalantly assured me that these "house bats" weren't harmful and even offered to let me photograph them. Actually, the perpetual guests only add to the medieval allure. The restaurant, which serves all 3 meals, is considered the best in the city. Rooms run between $14-$18; all have minibars, air-conditioning, and modern plumbing. 25 apartments. *No cards.*

Restaurant e Pousada do Pai Thomaz
Rua 25 de Junho, 12; ☎ *(71) 724-1288*
A 2-in-1 pousada with a reputable restaurant near the waterfront. Red-brown jaqueira wood lines the walls of the restaurant, which features *sarapatel*, the viscera of hogs boiled in their own blood (rumor has it, the dish has a strange, "exotic" taste). You'll have to climb steep stairs to reach the simple rooms, which are several notches below the quality of the Convento. Cleanliness is not the best virtue here. Doubles run about $8, including breakfast. 13 apartments. *Inexpensive. No cards.*

WHERE TO EAT

Gruta Azul
Praça Manoel Vitorino, 2; ☎ *725-1295. Daily: 11:00 a.m.–3:00 p.m., no dinner*
Across from the ancient train station, this lively eatery has noisy parrots and excellent native dishes that run about $2–$3. The city's specialty, excellent here, is *maniçoba*—a stew of manioc leaves, okra, and a variety of dried, salty meats; it looks like gruel but is actually tasty. Built around a lovely courtyard, the restaurant also features ceramic handicrafts for sale. *Inexpensive. All cards.*

NIGHTLIFE

Massapé
Rua 25 de Junho; ☎ *724-1319. Daily: 11:00 a.m.–midnight*
The only restaurant where there's action at night. Specialties include *carne de sol com pirão*—dried salty meat with manioc flour boiled in water. *Inexpensive. All cards.*

HANDS-ON CACHOEIRA

Arrival

Bus tickets from Salvador to Cachoeira run about $3 one way. Buses are not air-conditioned, and the ride can be riotous. About 12 buses run a day (the last leaves at 7:00 p.m.), and tickets are best purchased in advance. Bus lines include Viazul and Princesa. Schooners may be hired to traverse the bay and the Rio Paraguaçu to arrive in Cachoeira.

The **Rodoviária** (bus station) office is opened daily 5:00 a.m.–7:00 p.m.

Tourist Information

A tourist post on Rua 13 de Maio will give you a brochure about the town and directions. Don't expect any English. Daily 8:00 a.m.–5:00 p.m., closed weekends.

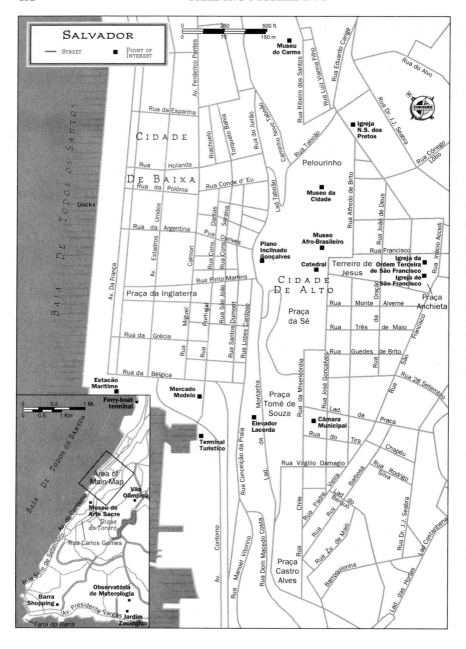

PRAIA DO FORTE

Praia do Forte *is one of the last authentic fishing villages in Brazil—cocooned in a national park, yet featuring some of the best luxury resort options in Brazil.* Eighty-five kilometers north of Salvador, you can walk an hour over pristine beaches without finding another footprint, but you'll also enjoy comfortable lodging, excellent seafood, a turtle reserve, and intriguing wildlife. Most recently, an elite mix of vacationers, from environmentalists and surfers to musicians and movie stars, have descended on this gorgeous stretch of sand, especially during high season, when the sea turns into a veritable fishbowl of windsurfers, sailboats, snorkelers, and divers. During off-season, you'll have more opportunity to get to know the simple folk who populate the sleepy village, which, thanks to strict building regulations, has miraculously retained its unpretentious charm.

The recent revival of Praia do Forte can be taken as a model for eco-preservation. In 1972 **W.H. Klaus Peters,** the German-Brazilian mastermind behind the resort, bought a 25,000-acre coconut plantation that fronted 7-1/2 miles of beach. The purchase gave him title to the fishing village of Praia do Forte, the castle ruins, and the surrounding rain forest. In the following years, he created a foundation to maintain the castle and turned the forest into a reserve administered by Brazil's federal environmental agency. In an unprecedented gesture in Brazilian history, he donated the land title of the village to its inhabitants, but only after the municipality in 1989 adopted a series of strict zoning regulations. Today, within the village of 3,000 inhabitants, no buildings may reach over two stories high, and all must be constructed of native traditional materials, such as *piassava* palm fronds and colonial tiles. Homeowners are required to plant four coconut palm trees for each one they cut down, and houses may only be passed on through families. All the streets, except the main highway, remain unpaved.

Also located at Praia do Forte is the headquarters of **TAMAR**, the national conservation project for *tartarugas marinhas*, or sea turtles—now the symbol of the village since fishermen stopped killing them. Each October, hundreds of sea turtles lay their eggs along the seashore, with the help and protection of the conservationists; in 1992, they expected to release the one millionth turtle hatchling into the sea. The TAMAR complex includes a small museum and water tanks, where you can observe the turtles closehand.

Ecology

The slogan of the eco-minded village says it all: "Enjoy, don't destroy." What is at stake is a marvelous eco-system along the River Timeantube called *mangue* (pronounced *man*-gay), a swamp-like area full of mangroves whose roots have adapted to the twice daily rise and fall of the river (at least 1-1/2 meters). Acting as a breeding ground for microorganisms necessary for marine life, the marsh is stock full of shrimp and crabs that you can nearly catch with your hands. Visitors can take a windsurf board and paddles, and spoon two kilometers down to a lake, keeping watch on the profuse variety of tropical birds that perch near the banks. The best time to see the birds is at dawn, when you will also see *jacarés* (alligators), snakes, and turtles.

> **Insider Tip:**
> *Praia do Forte is one of the safest and most crime-free beaches in Brazil. Of course, no matter where you travel, personal safety precautions should always be followed (locking up valuables, etc.), but incidents here are practically nonexistent.*

SIGHTS

Despite its size, there are scores of things to do in Praia do Forte; in fact, you could spend your entire two-week vacation here and never get bored. Besides the watersports and horseback riding offered by the resort, some other suggestions are:

- A quarter-mile walk from the white-painted lighthouse are the **Papa Gente** natural pools, formed from the rocky reefs that dot the shore. During high tide, these sand-bottomed pools, a favorite among snorkelers, fill chest-high with crystal-clear water and become natural aquariums flush with tropical fish.

- A 20-minute walk down the paradisaical shore takes you to the **village of Praia do Forte**, full of *barracas* that serve fantastic grilled shrimp. Alongside a deserted boat wreck on the shore, you might find the village mystic, his dreadlocks flowing, banging out folkloric tunes on his *berimbau*. There's also a blue-and-white native church, an excellent example of a colonial-style church still in use. From here, a five-minute walk takes you to the **TAMAR** project, where you can view turtles in open tanks and stroll through the small museum. A small gift store features excellent T-shirts with "Save the Turtles" themes (all profits are funneled back to the project). A 20-minute video of the project is available in Portuguese. (For an English version, ask at the Praia do Forte Hotel.)

- Take an energetic ten-mile hike along the isolated beaches to **Imbassaí** —accessible only by foot, boat, or a jeep down a dirt track.

- Across the road from the entrance to the Praia do Forte Resort Hotel is a lagoon and wetlands that contain another natural area, the **Timeantuba Bird Reserve**. Exploring by canoe, the casual naturalist can easily spot alligators and 173 bird species.

- A three-mile hike from the Praia do Forte Resort Hotel are the **hilltop ruins** of a fortified medieval manor house, formerly owned by **Garcia d'Avila**, a mere bailiff to the governor of Salvador. In 1549, the Portuguese monarchy awarded him over 308,000 square miles of prime acreage, upon which he would build the largest secular edifice in colonial Brazil. Exactly how he built it remains a mystery—some claim he dismantled a castle in Portugal and reassembled it here. For over two centuries, the castle and its vast estate has stayed in the hands of the d'Avila family, constituting at the end of the 18th century the largest private property in the world. Today, the ruins, romantically overgrown with flowers and tall grasses, make a fascinating tour.

- At **Barraca Nativa** schooners may be rented for one to four hours for about $100 per group.

EXCURSIONS

Odara Turismo, which maintains its branch office at the **Praia do Forte Resort Hotel**, ☎ *832-2333*, offers half-day and full-day excursions by jeep. For $20 per person, you can make a half-day excursion of the castle ruins, hike through the ecological preserve, visit a traditional manioc flour mill, or a swim under the waterfalls of the Pojuca River. For $60 per person, a full-day excursion includes an outdoor barbecue and a visit to a remote beach with dune formations.

THE ESSENTIAL PRAIA DO FORTE

WHERE TO STAY

Accommodations in Praia do Forte range from the elite and semi-elite to full-fledged primitive; worse comes to worse, you could probably convince someone to let you hang your hammock on their porch. Even if you don't stay at the Praia do Forte Resort Hotel, you can still partake of their excursions, water sports, and restaurants—for a fee, of course.

★ Praia do Forte Resort Hotel
Estrada do Coco (Praia do Forte); ☎ *832-2333, FAX 832-2100*
This luxurious complex, the flagship property of the village, offers tropical accommodations in split-level wings that snake through a 35-acre seafront coconut plantation. The tiled apartments are big enough for a family with 2 children, as an extra area separated by a divider holds additional couches. The rooms are not air-conditioned, but the cooling ocean winds provide comfort; guests might even choose to sleep in hammocks on their own private veranda.

With the accent on the natural, the resort offers windsurfing, sailing, scuba, 2 tennis courts, 2 restaurants, and 4 swimming pools. (Two-hour mini-courses in windsurfing are available for $65.) In November 1991, the Club Mistral was opened by two Germans, featuring the newest equipment in the world. Horseback riding is available every day (warning: what they call "frisky" turned out to be nearly unmanageable), and a different tour is offered daily, such as a hike to the castle, a trek to a waterfall, passage down the river on a floatboat, and a tour of the Vila dos Pescadores on foot. The rate for one apartment (up to four persons) runs $145, including breakfast, taxes, and all sports activities, except for windsurfing and catamaran, which run about $10–$15 an hour. Fielding's readers receive 15 percent discount. *132 apartments. Expensive. All cards.*

About 300 yards down the beach is the more tropical alternative run by the same owner,

Pousada Praia do Forte ☎ *(71)*
835-1410. Facing a reef and the open sea, this rustic inn (only a 15-minute walk from the main hotel) offers 17 igloo-like chalets with straw roofs, and structural beams made from coconut palm trees. Hibiscus flowers invigorate the primitive landscape. Some rooms have fans, though you can sleep in a hammock on the private porches; all have mosquito nets. The expanse of sea seen from the lobby/dining room is awe-inspiring. The pousada is located right next to TAMAR. Guests can use all the services at the main hotel. A cabin for two, with breakfast and dinner, runs $103 during high season. Children under five are free. *Expensive. All cards.*

Pousada Tatuapara
Praça dos Artistas; ☎ *876-1015*
One of the most charming pousadas in the village, and a cheaper alternative to the Praia do Forte properties listed above. Split-level suites feature a bedroom upstairs and downstairs dining room connected by a rustic wood stairs. Standards are one room. All apartments look out onto a flowered courtyard and come with fan and minibar. Standards run $36 for 2 persons, suites for 3 run about $42. *23 apartments. Moderate. No cards.*

Camping Grounds
For about $8 per night, camping grounds are available near Vila dos Pescadores. Contact the Praia do Forte Hotel. For other options, call the **Praia do Forte Resort Hotel** ☎ *832-2333, FAX 832-2100,* who will make reservations for you at any-priced hotel or pousada.

WHERE TO EAT

The buffet and à la carte cuisine at the Praia do Forte Hotel are excellent, but they can become costly if you eat every meal there. A short walk to the village will reveal a number of casual eateries for typical dishes, excellent seafood, and snacks.

Starlight
Praça dos Artistas. Noon–4:00 p.m., 8:30 p.m.–midnight, snacks 4:00 p.m.–8:00 p.m.

This is one of the village's most attractive restaurants, with brick floors, natural wood tables, and a spacious tropical feel. Stop by to check out the specialties of the day. Live music under the stars on Saturday makes a nice place to crash.

A walk down the dirt path to the left is **Boca-Piu** *Al. do Sol. Daily 10:00 a.m.–midnight* with heavy boat chains gracing the doorway of a traditional white stucco house. The front room features lambada; the homey back patio surrounded by enormous trees is for dining. Try the *pitu à milanesa*—large shrimp native to the area, or just slow-sip some tropical drinks with a side plate of *bolinho de peixe* (pastry-stuffed fish appetizers). Work up a free sweat with lambada bands on Friday and Saturday starting at 10:00 p.m. Somehow, the dear waitresses here manage to be tropical without even trying.

For sandwiches and fast typical dishes check out the straw-roofed **Restaurante Casa da Dinda**. *Daily 8:00 a.m.–midnight on the main street.*

Casa Alemã

Located on the main street, is good for German cuisine. Good pizza can be found at **Pizzaria Gastón** on the main street, next to the pharmacy. The neighborhood bar is **Bar do Souza**, also on the main street—a hangout for those who love *moqueca*.

HANDS-ON PRAIA DO FORTE

Arrival

Every Monday afternoon, Varig flies from Miami to Salvador. By special prior arrangement with the Praia do Forte Resort Hotel, a minivan shuttles visitors from the airport to Praia do Forte, 30 miles north (or about 45 minutes) on the newly paved **Estrada do Coco**, or Coconut Road. For 1–3 passengers, the van costs $47 on weekdays, $60 on weekends and at night. Group rates can be arranged.

Taxi Cometas, a 24-hour service at the Salvador airport, also offers car service: $64 on weekdays and $90 on weekends and weekday nights. For cheaper rates, contact Deborah Scott Leitsch, the English-speaking manager of **Odara Turismo** ☎ *(71) 86–1080* to arrange a pickup.

When to Go

Temperatures rarely dip below 76°F or rise above 84°F. During the rainy season March–August, the water loses its placid azure quality and turns choppy. Diving is best December–February, when the water is clearest, though this is high season, when rates are highest and the hotels are packed. From the middle of August–March, the sun is stellar.

458   FIELDING'S BRAZIL 1994

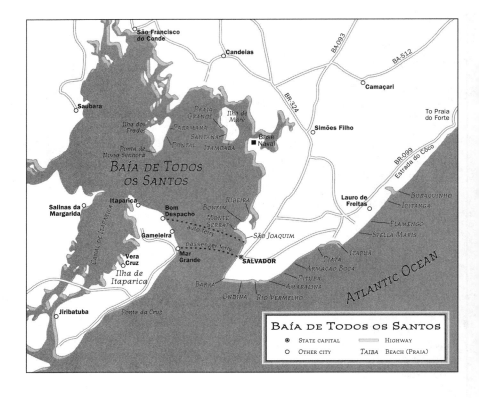

PARTY BAHIA
PORTO SEGURO

The resort town of **Porto Seguro** and its nearby beachfellows **Arraial d'Ajuda** and **Trancoso** lie at the heart of the Brazilian party scene. Come summer (December-February), sun-worshippers descend on this strip of Bahian coast from all over Brazil; many stars like Gilberto Gil and singer Gal Costa own beachside villas here. Porto Seguro is also famous among Brazilian history buffs, for it's here, at longitude 17 degrees south, that **Pedro Alvares Cabral** first discovered Brazil on April 22, 1500. (See the chapter *Historical Roots*.) At the very least, Cabral was lucky: the Indians who met him at shore were reported to be friendly, unlike those a few years later who decimated the first community of settlers, including the first church in Brazil and its two priests. Built on a cliff, the colonial area of the city, called **Cidade Alta**, still houses the reconstructed church, a small fort, and other 16th-century buildings.

Down below, in **Cidade Baixa**, is where the party-time begins. While Porto Seguro's beaches are not wide, they become as packed as Copacabana in December, with the overflow of tourists clogging the narrow cobblestone streets. Building regulations, which prohibit any structure over 7-1/2 meters, have preserved the tropical simplicity of the skyline; in fact, any structure along the beach line must also be made with small mud tiles or grass huts. During Carnaval, which lasts for 3 days, the 56,000 population doubles, and very drunken revelers can be seen traipsing after a *trio elétrico* (an amplified band on the back of a truck). During low season, when the streets seem nearly ghostlike, many writers and poets come here to revel in the silence.

The best beaches are located in Arraial d'Ajuda and Trancoso, along with a most rarefied social scene, one that mixes laid-back locals with gorgeous *carioca* teens, aging hippies, bohemian movie stars, and international jetsetters. A 1-1/2 hour ferry ride gets you there, though you can also take a schooner ride from Porto Seguro. Accommodations in all three towns run toward the *au natural* pousada, and excellent discounts can be found in off-season. Do note that most people spend little time in their rooms.

SIGHTS

History buffs will not want to miss **Cidade Alta**, the Old City, perched on a cliff high above the city. After the first community was burned by the Indians, the next band of daring settlers moved to the top of this cliff, where they could keep a strategic watch on the sea and the Buranhen River. The only image said to have survived the desecration was a statue of St. Francis of Assisi, now considered to be the oldest religious icon in Brazil; it can be seen high above the altar in the **Igreja de Nossa Senhora da Penha**, built in 1535. Unfortunately, the church, as brightly lit as a boardwalk and strewn with plastic roses, appears too kitschy to be real. An even more ancient church is the **Igreja da Misericórdia**, which dates back to 1526. Nearby is the **Museu da Cidade**, a two-room museum that includes images of saints from the 17th and 18th centuries and funeral masks from the Ticuna Indians. Most interesting is a display of the history of the Brazilian flag; the first flag of the republic, used only for four days between November 15–19, looks amazingly like the Stars and Stripes. Also, in the area are a small fort, the remains of a Jesuit College, and the **Marco do Descobrimento**, the two-meter-high column placed by the Portuguese in 1503 to proclaim their sovereignty over the land.

THE ESSENTIAL PORTO SEGURO

BEACH EATERIES

Life along the beaches of Porto Seguro are concentrated at lively *barracas*, open-air bars known for their excellent seaside cuisine and interesting clientele who hang out till all hours along the strand. The following are the most famous:

Porto Fino Bar/Restaurant
Porto Fino Beach, north to Cabrália
Owner Guiseppe is a friendly, blue-eyed Italian Brazilian, whose love for pasta only equals his love for his clients. Indulge in the excellent Italian specialties under his sheltered restaurant or eat outside in your bathing suit under grass huts, where the water can tickle your toes. Guiseppe speaks English and will prove a fine navigator of the scene.

Vira Sol
Taperapuan Praia; ☎ *288-2350. Daily: 8:00 a.m.–5:00 p.m.*

This bar and restaurant, located on Taperapuan beach, features a casual nautical theme and a young crowd that grooves on loud dance music. Children will love the tropical playground, and adults may rent jet-skis. The bar, an upside-down canoe, serves typical foods like *peixe embriagado*, literally, "drunken fish," marinated in wine sauce.

★ Neptunnos Bar and Restaurant
Ponto Grande Beach

boasts a magnificent view of the reefs, where the beach converges at a point. From here, you can see why Cabral chose the area to land, because the bay, surrounded by reefs, makes for gentler waters. Typical foods like *peixe assado* (baked fish) and mussels are considered tops. The best reason to stop by is to pet the house sloths, who look like E.T.'s and hang upside down from their palm-leafed hut. If you look kind enough, the owner may even let you hold them—it's an incredible feeling when this animal, the slowest in the world, puts his paws around your waist and falls asleep.

Barraco do Mutá

Here, you can rent **Voos de Ultraleve,** a 2-seater plane with a small engine and three wings that lands on water. One person goes at a time, accompanied by the pilot—$13 for 10 minutes. A culinary specialty here are the *bolinhos de bacalhau* and *aipim*, which are made hot on the spot.

PARTY SCENE

The main drag beside the shore in Porto Seguro is named **Rua Portugal**, but everyone calls it **Passarela do Alcool** —a local joke that refers to the part-fact/part-fantasy that everyone here is reeling around drunk. At the very least, you'll find lots of tiny bars where you can sit outside and enjoy the cool breeze. If you want to pick up the local brew, head for **Colônia Brasil** *Avenida Portugal, 188;* ☎ *289-2670* which features the highly creative *cachaça* mixes of owner Eduardo Caminha. Pure *cachaça* from Porto Seguro is called Aguardente Verde, and Eduardo has over 200 kinds, many with exotic fruits. For the macho at heart, he even sells a *cachaça* with a snake fermenting inside the bottle, a tradition among fishermen, and reportedly good for the skin and blood as well as being a vaccine against the venom (of course, if the snake is inside the bottle, how can it bite you?). There's also a bottle fermenting with a crab, which is reputed to be a fine aphrodisiac/cold remedy. Another typical drink here is *Pau do Indio*, made of alcohol, *guaraná*, honey, and 32 herbs. The owner is generous about tasting; make sure you try the Gabriela liqueur, a silky-smooth concoction of clove and cinnamon.

WHERE TO STAY

Expensive -------------- Over $45

Moderate --------------- $20–$45

Inexpensive ------------ Under $20

★ **Porto Seguro Praia Hotel**
BR-367; ☎ *(73) 288-2321, FAX 288-2069*
Located across the street from the beach, this 4-star is the city's best—a palm-lined, ranch-style complex replete with tropical ambiance and efficient service. The wood-planked large bedrooms are decorated with mahogany frame beds, and come with mini-bars, spacious bathrooms, color TV, and verandas. The huge, exotically shaped pool and bar makes a relaxing alternative to the shore, as do the tennis courts surrounded by palm trees. There is also a gym, boutique, and 24-hour room service. Singles start at $45, doubles $50, suites $78. During low season, 30 percent discount if paying in cash, 20 percent with cards. *115 apartments. Expensive. All cards.*

Pousada do Descobrimento
Avenida Getúlio Vargas, 330; ☎ *(73) 288-2452/2004*
A clean and perky pousada with a charming breakfast room located 200 meters from the beach. The chalet-like rooms, built around a tropical courtyard, come with verandas, air-conditioning, phone, safes, and hammocks. *16 apartments. Moderate. All cards.*

★ **Pousada Porto Príncipe**
Avenida dos Navegantes, 82; ☎ *(73) 288-272*
Located on the main street, this slightly upscale pousada offers lovely colonial-style rooms with verandas, minibars, phone, modern bathrooms, color TV, and air-conditioning. The beds have nice wood frames offset by matching cabinets. An attractive pool dominates the inner courtyard. High season doubles go for $60, $30 in low. *23 apartments. Expensive. All cards.*

Pousada Casa Azul
Rua 15 de Novembro, 11; ☎ *(73) 288-2180*
Situated in the center of town, this 100-year-old home has now been named an historical patrimony. The blue-and-white exterior is so beautiful that the individual apartments hardly compare, but they are adequate. Housed in a building separate from the main house, the apartments have

private patios, air-conditioning, and minibar; no phones or TV. Clients may use the phone in the reception and there is a small TV room. Nearby is the cultural center, where musical shows and events are often held. *Moderate. No cards.*

WHERE TO EAT

Expensive -------------- Over $15

Moderate --------------- $5–$15

Inexpensive ------------ Under $5

Oskarin
Rua Pedro Alvares Cabral, 145. Daily: 5:30 p.m.–last client, closed Sunday.
Brightly colored eatery with Arabian specialties like hummus, tabouli, and kibe under $3. *Inexpensive. Cards: AE, DC. MC.*

Casa Rústica Avenida
Getúlio Vargas, 348; ☎ *288-2399. Daily 11:00 a.m.–11:00 p.m.*
Best in the city for *parrilhada*, with steaks, chicken, and grilled pork under $5. Picanha comes on a smoking grill at your table. *Inexpensive. Cards: MC, V.*

Grelhados
Avenida 22 de Abril, 212
Fine grilled meats, chicken, and fish in an attractive environ. *Moderate. No cards.*

Três Vinténs
Avenida Portugal, 246. Daily: noon–11:00 p.m.
Stone walls and a dramatic color scheme at this bar/restaurant featuring soulfully cooked Bahian specialties like *moqueca, polvo* (octopus), and *bolo de camarão* (shrimp rolls). *Moderate. Cards: AE.*

Populi
Rua São Braz, 163 (Cidade Histórica)
Boisterous pizzeria on a dirt street lined with coconut trees and flamboyant trees that bloom all summer. *Moderate. No cards.*
Café La Pasarella *Rua Portugal, 224.* An all-purpose snacks hangout: pies, drinks. tea at 5:00 p.m., espresso day and night, and even breakfast. *Inexpensive. No cards.*

NIGHTLIFE

Even if you don't dance lambada yourself, head for the **Boca da Barra** —a huge, brightly lit, open-air grass hut where the best dancers congregate. During the summer it's packed, while on-lookers sit on bleachers. It's free, except for drinks.
Fliperama
Avenida Portugal, 23 is a popular video arcade.

SHOPPING

At the plaza called **Coroa Vermelha** you'll find an Indian crafts market run by a tribe of the Tupí-Guarani. About 1,000 Indians live on a 57-hectare reservation near the city, still preserving their traditions and supplementing government subsidies through fishing and hunting. Life has hardly been idyllic for these natives, as they've become victims of a bureaucratic mess that has allowed industries and farmers to encroach on their borders. In the past few years, an iron company took over the Vale do Rio Doce, which had been previously designated tribal land; fortunately, the company has now been indicted. Among the crafts for sale are headdresses of brightly stained feathers (pink seems to be the favorite color), wood-carved combs, beaded jewelry, and bows and arrows. The chief of the tribe, **Jocana Jiroa Baixu**, is a charming, extremely handsome young man, often stationed at one of the main stalls. If you speak Portuguese, he will give you a rundown of tribal concerns. During the entire month of April, Indian celebrations are held featuring typical foods, dance, music, and body-paintings.
Praça da Bandeira is the main courtyard of Porto Seguro, featuring a nightly hippie market of handicrafts. The streets in the neighboring vicinity are also full of shops.

HANDS-ON PORTO SEGURO

Arrivals
Flights to Porto Seguro leave from Salvador on **Nordeste** airlines daily at 3:30 p.m. Other airlines that fly to Porto Seguro are: **Nordeste** ☎ *288-2108* (airport); **Rio-Sul** *Hotel Seguro Praia, BR-367;* ☎ *288-2321.*

One kilometer from the center of the city, the **Rodoviária** is a stone-and-wood-beamed structure, featuring a snack bar that opens at 5:30 a.m. Two buses run daily from Salvador to Porto Seguro, on the Expresso São Jorge line, as well as direct buses to Rio. The bus trip between Ilhéus and Porto Seguro is one of the most exotic tropical landscapes I have seen in Brazil—one that will make you believe in God's original plan for the planet. With a forest on one side and the gorgeous shoreline on the other, the bus snakes through a primitive landscape that plumbs the depths of poverty but also reveals the heart of interior Brazil: pastel-colored shanties, barefoot boys playing in the sand, and old women carrying heavy loads on their heads.

Buses also run to Belo Horizonte, Ilhéus, Rio, Salvador, and São Paulo.

City Transportation
Taxi
☎ *288–2400.*
Interlocadora (car rental) ☎ *228–2335.*

Money Exchange
As of 1991, there were no *câmbio* in Porto Seguro, but Banco Brasil may have opened one by now. Try **Descobrimento Travel** *Avenida Getúlio Vargas, 330.*

Schooner Rentals
Cia do Mar
Praça dos Pataxós; ☎ *288–2981.* Owner Arthur Priolli has two boats and can charter schooners.

Tourist Information
Bahiatursa
The tourist office is located at *Praça Visconde de Porto Seguro (Casa da Lenha);* ☎ *288–2126. Daily: Monday–Friday 8:00 a.m.–8:00 p.m.*

Travel Agency
Mucugê Exotik Travel Agency
Avenida dos Navegantes, 53, ☎ *(73) 875–1238, FAX 875–1238.* can arrange excursions anywhere throughout Brazil, as well as book rooms for the Mucugê Hotel Village in Arraial d'Ajuda. The owners of the agency are also presently selling prime real estate here that should prove fine investments in the future. English is spoken well.

Descobrimento Turismo
Avenida Getúlio Vargas, 330; ☎ *(73) 288–2452/2004.* can arrange city tours, schooners to Trancoso and the reefs of Coroa Alta, diving tours to Recife de Fora, a coral reef teeming with marine life, and treks through the National Park of Monte Pascoal.

ARRAIAL d'AJUDA

Arraial d'Ajuda is not for the conventional tourist. Sometimes compared to Ibiza in Spain, this tiny fishing village across the river from Porto Seguro wallowed in obscurity for more than 500 years until it suddenly became *the* "Party City" of Brazil a few years back. Some even claim *lambada* was born here (see below). From all accounts, an odd mixture descends on the village in high season—rich singles, movie stars, famous musicians, aging hippies, precocious teens, and anyone who is tall, tan, dark, and handsome. Compared to Porto Seguro, which has only three bars, Arraial has more than *fifteen*— some residents consider the whole city a bar. Certainly a kind of makeshift nightlife happens wherever it's ignited. The main action starts on Broadway, the central drag, sometime after 11:00 p.m. By 7:00 a.m., you don't know if the people you meet on the road are just waking up or on their way to bed.

A green courtyard separates Broadway from the city's one church, **Nossa Senhora d'Ajuda**. It might have been significant that an electric amp and guitar was lying beneath the altar when I checked it out. Built between 1549 and 1551, the church is the second oldest in Brazil. You'll find the "real" Arraial-enses hanging out there.

By all accounts, Carnaval in Arraial is a wild and crazy time. Broadway gets so packed you can't walk through, and revelers generally push the outer limits of the Dionysian celebration. Rumor is, there are ten girls to every two guys. There is no organized parade, but people generally follow after a *trio elétrico*, which fills the streets with high-volume samba. Given the various activities that go on in public, anyone adverse to drug consumption probably won't feel at home. Reservations for any pousada during Carnaval should be made at least two months in advance.

BEACHES

The beaches in Arraial are glorious, primitive, and models for *Swept Away* fantasies. Following **Mucugê** are: **Pitinga** (2 kilometers), **Lagoa Azul** (3 kilometers), **Taipe** (4 kilometers), and **Rio da Barra** (7 kilometers). Pitinga has long been known as a nude beach; these days it's tending toward the completely nude—one of the few places in Brazil.

THE ESSENTIAL ARRAIAL d'AJUDA

WHERE TO STAY

★ Mucugê Hotel
Village Estrada p/Mucugê, 6 kilometer;
☎ *(73) 875-1238*

Twenty years ago, Luiz Claudio Ferreira bought up a lot of land in Arraial when nobody could remember its name. Today he's selling off prime lots (the last was to an Arab sheik) but is still keeping the best for himself—mainly, the Mucugê Hotel. As a world traveler, he wanted to create his own vision of the fantasy pousada, and he has truly succeeded, with the prettiest, cleanest complex in the area, located on a spectacular landscape that includes a river, an ocean, and acres of coconut trees and tropical vegetation. The apartments are built into chalet-like structures, all with verandas; the duplex suites, which come with kitchens, are built on stilts with private patios. A common living room and bar is completely homey, and the staff is so hip you won't know who are guests and who are employees. Decor runs to the rustic, and you can wake up to the roar of the ocean; breakfast is on the other side of a wood bridge, just steps from the sea. Friends of the owner—"only interesting" people—drop in all the time; Robert de Niro stayed a week. During off-season, the pousada is nearly deserted so you're sure to enjoy peace and privacy. Any travel arrangements can be made by the family agency, which can arrange expeditions in the area and throughout Brazil, including the Amazon. Anyone interested in prime real estate (it's tripled in price in the last few years) should take a hike here—fast. Doubles run $50, suites (for 4) $100, 20 percent discount in low season. Make reservation for high season 2 months in advance. 17 apartments. *Expensive.* Cards: AE.

Pousada Fragata
Estr. p/ praia do Mucugê, 5 kilometer ;
☎ *(73) 875-2044. Reservations in São Paulo* ☎ *(21) 264-8569*

This colonial-style pousada, located 300 meters from the beach, is one of the nicest in Arraial, its tropical ambiance preserved in the palm-lined courtyard. Apartments are rustically appointed with wood-frame beds; all come with air-conditioning, color TV, minibar, and very clean bathrooms. Doubles in high season run $40, $20 in low; 8-day package at Carnaval and Christmas/New Year's runs $40. Reserve a month ahead. 8 apartments. *Moderate.* Cards: V, MC.

Pousada Brisas
Saída p/Trancoso; ☎ *(73) 288-2348*

A driveway full of cashew trees that grow horizontally leads to the lobby of this pousada, looking out onto a fabulous panorama of grassy fields and raging ocean. A fantastic jungle is only steps away and the ocean about a 5-minute walk. The apartments, in white stucco chalets with orange-tiled roofs, are simple, with a brick bed stand, mosquito nets, and minibar; no air-conditioning or phone. If you want a fan, you must ask for one. Some rooms have an extra space for children. During high season, 3 meals a day are served (breakfast included in the rate), along with 24-hour service. The owner speaks English. Doubles run $40–$50, half-price in low season. 18 apartments. *Moderate. No cards.*

Pousada da Estrela
Rua do Campo de Aviação; ☎ *(73) 875-1183*

If you decide to stay in town here, head for this good-feel pousada, off a quiet street, across from the police station, and only 800 meters from the beach. The inner courtyard is so packed with plants you might have to slice your way through. The 5 simple rooms come with double beds, mosquito nets, minibar, and extra hammock: no TV, air-conditioning, or phone. Duplos are split-levels, with 2 ceiling fans. Doubles go for $21 (high), $16 (low), duplos $50. *Moderate. No cards.*

Hotel Porto d'Ajuda
☎ *(73) 288-2942*

A rock concert producer named Sergio Pessoa opened this new complex for those who "want the feel of the sea"; in fact, it's the only hotel where the boats practically come up to your door. Located where you cross the ferry (turn left to Coconut Grove), the hotel offers all watersports from skiing and sailing to windsurfing. The restaurant serves Japanese food. All rooms are air-conditioned and come with phone, TV with video, minibar, and an extra living room. Doubles run about $70–$80. 10 apartments. *Expensive. All cards.*

WHERE TO EAT

Alto Astral
Broadway
Located on the main drag, this hangout is so homey that some clients seemed to have grown into the woodwork. *Picanha* for two runs about $7. *Moderate. No cards.*

★ Restaurante São João
Praça Brig. Eduardo Gomes. Daily 11:00 a.m.–9:00 p.m.
Best homemade food in town, at the home of Senhor Manoel. Don't be daunted by the screaming babies in the living room or the laundry in the courtyard; under his aluminum-beamed roof you'll enjoy 6 kinds of *moqueca* ($7–$8 for two), shrimp stroganoff, and *frango ao molho pardo*. Be prepared to bat away flies. *Moderate. No cards.*

Varanda Grill
Rua São Benedito. Daily: 4:00 p.m.–11:00 p.m., closed Monday.
Best joint in town for grilled meats. Portions are for one person; *picanha* runs about $4. The *torresminhos* and french fries are excellent. *Moderate. No cards.*

Mão na Massa
Rua Bela Vista. Daily: 1:00 p.m.–midnight (high season), 3:00 p.m.–11:00 p.m. (low)
This "real-Italian" adega is one of the most romantic spots in town, with creamy lasagna, 10 kinds of pizza, and grilled meats. Start off with the great *pão de alho* (toasted garlic bread). Desserts are memorable. *Moderate. Cards: AE.*

NIGHTLIFE

While others have claimed it was the creation of Madison Avenue, most residents here firmly believe that *lambada* was created at the **Jato Bar**. The official "papa" is **Maroto**, the owner of this wood-floor bar, a gorgeous, young man with flowing dreadlocks and a wild-Jesus look who could easily be Brazil's answer to Patrick Swayze. A natural dancer, Maroto claims to have mixed samba with Northeastern folkloric steps to create the first *lambada*—a fast-twirling dance where the couple literally looks joined at the hips.

Whether or not Maroto actually discovered *lambada*, he at least seems to have well trained the locals, who dance here with a grace and joy rarely seen in grosser commercial demonstrations. During high season, Maroto gives classes that are not to be missed, and during low season, you'll have to negotiate privately with him, but one warning: He is so shy that he actually turned down some Brazilian producers to headline an international *lambada* show. When he finally takes to the tiny dance floor with his wife, however, it's a major event.

HANDS-ON ARRAIAL d'AJUDA

Arrival
Arraial d'Ajuda and Trancoso may be reached from Porto Seguro by taking the ferry, which runs regularly (about every half-hour during high season). If you are coming from the tiny airport in Porto Seguro, you may take a taxi to the ferry (about $3) or all the way to your hotel in Arraial for about $12 (rates depend on the season). If you cross the ferry without a taxi, you'll have to find another one on the other side. It's quite likely that you could hitch a ride anywhere along the route; people are extremely friendly and you'll be relatively safe.

Climate
Hot during the day and refreshingly cool at night, with temperatures averaging 95°F. Rain at night is very common. Watch out for mosquitos—nets are *de rigueur* here.

Rentals
Wind Point Parracho, a 5-minute walk down the beach from Mucugê Hotel, rents kayaks, windsurfing equipment, and horses.

Also contact the Mucugê **Travel Agency** ☎ *875-1238.*

When To Go

Once a month in Arraial, there is a full-moon festival with bonfire and live music—a big free party that starts after midnight. March–April is low season. May–June is the cheapest time to come, but the weather is not reliable and the social scene is *nada*. September–October the village comes back to life in preparation for the summer blitz.

TRANCOSO

Walk about 7 miles down the beach from Mucugê, or traverse a torturous dirt road through the forest (about half-hour by jeep) to reach **Trancoso**, a tiny fishing village seemingly in the middle of nowhere. The road there is full of potholes so you will have to swerve right and left to avoid them, but the scenery is pure folkloric Brazil—native fishing huts, crowds gathered before evangelicals screaming on scratchy mikes, chicken and horses blocking the road. The wind-swept beach is dramatic, flanked by high cliffs and washed by huge waves that send foaming crests to the strand. Inspired by such primitive natural resources, many bathers have been known to strip *totally*—an occurrence, if you can believe it, which is uncommon in Brazil. The most famous meeting point is the **Barraca Itaip,** a grass-hut bar where you can dine on catfish and crabs at tables made out of logs.

The village of Trancoso itself is the smallest I have yet to see in Brazil. High season turns the small football field in front of the church into a den of activity, but even during off-season, locals look for any excuse to have a celebration; once I ran across a group of school children giving a lively musical performance at their graduation. Mostly, you'll find old men playing dominoes in the shade or old ladies resting on their porches. Almost everyone seems to walk around barefoot, maybe because the beach is just down the hill behind the church.

THE ESSENTIAL TRANCOSO

WHERE TO STAY

Hotel da Praça
Reserve in São Paulo ☎ *(11) 813–6011*
Located off the main square, this tiled-roof complex features individual chalets on stilts, surrounded by a woody grove. All apartments come with fan and minibar. No pool, no TV, just a gorgeous tropical landscape with magnificent old trees. $23 for double, $28 for suites. 11 apartments. *Moderate. No cards.*

Pousada Sol da Manhã
C.P. 86
Dutch owner Aart Tlan and his Brazilian wife, Dora, were the first in Trancoso to rent out rooms in their native-style house. He also now owns a pineapple farm, from which his guests eat the fruits. Five simple rooms come with a fan; you share bathrooms. Doubles are $15 in high season, $10 in low. The house has no phone, so leave a message for a reservation at Central Telephone ☎ 867–1115. In off-season, Aart may be the only one in town who speaks English. *Inexpensive. No cards.*

Pousada Hibiscus
Reservations in São Paulo ☎ *(11) 826–4200*

Wood-frame beds with mosquito nets and a ceiling fan in this simple 8-room pousada, with bathrooms cleaner than most. The beach is a 15-minute walk away. Doubles run $15. *Inexpensive. No cards.*

WHERE TO EAT

Rama is considered to be the best restaurant, built in front of a massive tree with elephantine gnarled trunks. Also try the pizzas at **Tucano** and the all-natural sandwiches at **Abacaxi**.

HANDS-ON TRANCOSO

Arrivals

A bus runs between Arraial and Trancoso about every hour. Jeeps can be rented through the **Mucugê Travel Agency** in Arraial. The walk along the beach will take about an hour.

Telephone

The only telephone is at the **Posto Telefônico,** near the bus depot, *open 7:00 a.m.–10:00 p.m.* The number of the central operator is ☎ (73) 867–1115 or ☎ 867–1116.

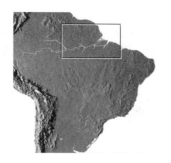

THE NORTHEAST

Jangadas on the Beach

In Brazil, the **Northeast** is synonymous with the hard, hot life. Cactus and dense scrub called *caatinga* dominate the landscape of the region's interior, an unforgiving territory where the heat is fierce and the land is parched brown for most of the year. *Nordestinos*, as the residents are called, are legendary in South America for being survivors, forced by perpetual droughts, famines, and political upheavals to uproot their homes and migrate thousands of miles each year in search of water. Though the states of **Sergipe, Pernambuco, Alagoas, Paraná, Rio Grande do Norte, Ceará, and Maranhão** occupy only 10 percent of the national territory, a fourth of the population resides there, 30 million of them in substandard subsistence. Yet something in the Northeastern character is indefatigable; despite a life that teeters perpetually on the precarious, *nordestinos* always seem to find their way back home. They know that in a moment of rainfall the vast, semiarid backland called the *sertão* can suddenly transform, the cactii burst into bloom, and the parched brown earth return overnight to life.

Pleasure Spots To Indulge

Ironically, the coastal cities of the Northeast are among the finest pleasure spots in all Brazil, where the blue-green ocean water seems limitless and the sunshine a boon to leisure, rather than the bane of an impoverished existence. Some of the best eco-treks in Brazil are located along this northeastern shore—so much fun that you should consider stopping even for a day or two just to indulge. Braving the dunes of Natal in a daredevil dune buggy or charging out in a *jangada* to one of Maceió's mid-ocean parties are adventures not to be missed. For historical buffs, the colonial centers of **Salvador**, **Olinda**, and **São Luis** (the latter just recently restored), stand as impressive monuments to the artistry and craftsmanship of centuries-old Brazil.

While the Northeast was the first part of Brazil to be settled by Europeans, it was, nevertheless, territory hard won by the Portuguese. As early as the 16th century, the Portuguese began to dominate the coastal regions with sugar plantations, giving rise in Olinda and Salvador to a prosperous merchant class often at odds with the noble elite. Beginning in 1624, the Dutch kept the area in constant turmoil through fierce invasions until they were finally expelled 20 years later, retiring to the West Indies, where they beat the Portuguese at their own sugarcane game. It was then that the colonization of the *agreste* and *sertão* accelerated—runaway Indians and escaped slaves mixing with a new breed of frontiersman, the *vaqueiro*, or cattle driver. Today, cattle-raising continues to be a viable industry, though during periods of drought, the paltry ribs of the cows remain acute reminders of Northeastern reality.

Roots and Religion

The racial mix in the Northeast makes a startling contrast to the predominantly white, European ancestry of the South. The largest concentration of blacks in Brazil are located here—descendants of the African slaves imported to work the plantations. But a mixture of Portuguese and Indian influences also predominates, which can be seen in the hard, carved features and short stature of tan-colored *mestiços*. A deep-rooted spirituality also runs through the veins of Northeasterners. It's here, in the *sertão* of Bahia, that the first millenarian revolution took hold, when the mystic **Antônio Conselheiro** led his impoverished followers in a tragic rebellion against the federal government. And then there was the religious fanaticism inspired by the so-called miracles of **Padre Cícero Romão Batista**, which deeply affected the political development of the state of Ceará. Today, almost a century later, Padre Cícero's image in the form of icons still exerts a powerful spiritual force on the people of the backlands.

Off The Beaten Path

The tourist sites covered in this chapter are principally the capital cities of each state (including the desert island of **Fernando de Noronha**)—all major destinations beloved for their beaches, nightlife, historical communities, and folkloric crafts. Any travel *beyond* these capital cities should be considered off the beaten path, though in future editions *I hope to traverse some of the more rugged interior towns*. By staying along the coastal communities, however, you will be blessed with cooling winds that temper the hot, nearly constant sunshine. Note, though, that as you go up the coast from Maceió to São Luis, approaching **Amazônia,** you will feel the temperature rise steadily higher until you think you can't stand it anymore; that's when it's time to head for a tree-shaded jungle. The arts and crafts markets are always a great escape from the heat; there you can find jewelry and decorations made out of bone and leather, straw and lace, as well as fine ceramic sculptures.

As for accommodations, hotel rates are generally cheaper in the Northeast than in the South, and, accordingly, the rooms are rarely as nice. The *maresia*, or the sea wind, is insidious, and sometimes even the best hotels retain a slight musty odor. Primarily, English is spoken only at 4- and 5-star hotels, and even if you speak Portuguese, you may find the hard and fast clip of *nordestinos* difficult to grasp at first. (Even when asked politely to slow down, *nordestinos* seem totally incapable of doing so!) Besides the desert island of **Fernando de Noronha**, which is a scuba diver's dream of a lifetime, one of the best resorts in Brazil is the **Pratagy Resort** in Maceió—a veritable treasure trove of ecosystems that will leave any amateur or professional botanist thrilled.

474 FIELDING'S BRAZIL 1994

MACEIÓ

One of the Northeast's favorite beach resorts, **Maceió** is the capital of **Alagoas**, Brazil's second smallest state. When it was first discovered, the city was dedicated by settlers to São Gonçalves, a Portuguese saint; later, in the 18th century the patron saint was changed to **Nossa Senhora do Prazer** (Our Lady of Pleasure)—a prophetic nomenclature. Today, sunworshipers fill the wide promenade running along the shore where 75 *barracas* (or open-air bars) ply vacationers with food, drink, and live music all night long. Squeezed between the open sea and a lagoon, **Lagoa do Mundaú**, Maceió feels like a small city, although its population of 700,000 certainly cancels out any provincial status.

Sugarcane remains one of the principal industries both in Maceió and in the state; on the drive from the airport, you can spot a sugarcane factory, as well as large plantations along the road to **Marechal**, a nearby colonial town. Unfortunately, the chemical factory Salgema, one of the state's most important enterprises, has become a notorious polluter of the city's lagoon and some surrounding beaches. As a result, tourists should avoid the beach in front of the Luxor Hotel.

The family of ex-President Fernando Collor de Melo has been a traditional name of power and wealth in Maceió for the last 200 years. (The family name is de Melo.) You might in fact meet some of his relatives on the beach, who are still complaining that he didn't tell his uncle or his cousins (or even his own mother!) before he froze the banks in 1990.

The people of Maceió feel a special connection with Americans. During World War II, after Brazil sided with the U.S. following the Nazi decimation of several Brazilian ships, an airport was built here by Americans to control the sea. In **Manuel Duarte Square**, you can still see the miniature Statue of Liberty, which was given to the city as a sign of friendship. The Kennedy family is also popular here. When JFK was President, he gave substantial monetary support to the city and directed the hospital boat *Hope* to dock in the port for a year. Residents deeply felt his death. Downtown, a street near the Gstaad restaurant on Ponta Verde Beach has been named **Avenida Robert Kennedy**.

> **Insider Tip:**
>
> In 1991, Maceió's **jangada** excursions to a natural waist-high pool in the middle of the ocean was rated by the Brazilian travel industry as the #1 tourist adventure in Brazil..

A BIRD'S EYE VIEW

The best place to view the city is from the **Mirador de Santa Teresina**, where you can see the full expanse of the lagoon. Precious little is left of the historical city, mostly situated in the **Praça Marechal Floriano Peixoto**, which is dominated by the neoclassical **Governor's Palace** on one end and the **Igreja Bom Jesus dos Marítiros** on the other. The one art museum worth seeing is the **Fundação Pierre Chalita**, owned by Maceió's greatest painter, who in 1980 created a foundation to house his own fabulous accumulation of 17th- and 18th-century sacred sculptures. One of the most extensive collections in Brazil, it also features French masterpieces, as well as Chalita's own fine works on the top floor. (His 1957 painting of Christ on the Cross created an immense scandal because he left the genitalia showing.) A School of Beaux Arts is also housed on the premises.

BEACH SCENE

Maceió has made its beaches user friendly with the mosaic promenade that runs the length of the major beaches; every few hundred yards, grass-hut cafés offer cool escapes from the sun, excellent seafood, and live music all night long. (The trend after dusk is to bar hop.) The palm-lined **Pajuçara Beach** is the main city beach, excellent for bathing, as is **Jatuíca**. Nicknamed Little Riviera, **Ponta Verde** Beach attracts the "beautiful set" who like to pose on the many rocks jutting out to sea; the fact that you can't swim here makes the beach that much more elite. Although excellent for surfing, the violent waves at **Cruz das Almas** have caused many deaths and have inspired the appointment of lifeguards all week during high season (weekends in low). If you want to escape the crunch of the crowd on the northern beaches, head for **Praia do Francês**, 10 miles to the south, where you'll be greeted by an enormous stretch of pristine white sand, foresty borders, and an energetic surf. To get there, take the bus marked "Deodoro," which runs hourly, from in front of the old train station. Then explore the well-preserved colonial town of **Marechal Deodoro.** (See *Excursions* below.)

The best *barracas* along the beach:

Felline *Praia Ponta Verde* offers candlelit jazz at night (piano, sax, and flute), as well as crepes, *petiscos*, and seafood.

Lampião *Praia Jatuíca* features a hot dance floor propelled by live lambada and *forró* bands under a shady grove of coconut trees.

Ipaneminha *Praia Pajuçara* serves excellent *petiscos*, with music only at night.

Casa do Povo *Jatuíca Beach* attracts a young set who love to *samba*. Single women looking for dates are welcome.

> **Insider Tip:**
> *Be careful of male prostitutes who look like women strolling the orla. There've been stories of assaults.*

EXCURSIONS

MARECHAL DEODORO

About 13-1/2 miles from Maceió lies the quaint village of **Marechal Deodoro**, one of the best-kept colonial towns in Brazil. Once the capital of the *capitânia* in 1817, Marechal was for centuries reachable only by boat through the South Lagoon; 20 years ago a road was built, but the small-town tranquility hasn't been tinkered with. Barefoot children still play in the street (often swarming tourists for cash), women lay their colorful laundry out on the rocks to dry, and fishermen sit in the windowsills of their 19th-century houses repairing fishing nets. The beautifully landscaped **Praça João XXIII** leads to the city's major treasure, the **17th-century Convento de São Francisco,** which has now been transformed into the **Museu de Arte Sagrada.** Inside, rich brown floors of *pau-brasil* (the tropical redwood from which the name "Brasil" is taken) lead to impressive displays of 17th, 18th, and 19th century sacred art—from life-sized, often terrifying wood carvings of Christ to charming miniatures of saints. Nearby is the unassuming birthplace of the **Marechal Deodoro,** the first president of the Republic in 1889; it's now a **museum** housing artifacts of his life. A controversial figure, Deodoro was a general of the Empire who mounted a military coup against the Emperor, ordering him to leave the country within 24 hours. Unfortunately, after assuming the first presidency, Deodoro made a mess when he dissolved Congress and had to resign during a state of siege in 1891. (The **museum,** on *Rua Marechal Deodoro, 25*, is open *Tuesday-Sunday 8:00 a.m.-5:00 p.m.*) Next door to the museum is **Vera Artesanato** *Rua Marechal Deodoro, 2*, an excellent shop for lace, linen, and embroideries made in the area.

JANGADA PARTY

They're called *jangadas*—flat-bottom canoes with droopy masts and enormous sails that create a floating village right in the middle of the ocean. They're easy enough to find. Even if you don't hear the hoarse yells of "jangadas" along Pajuçara Beach in front of the Othon Hotel, you can't miss their blue-and-white sails waving madly in the wind. First you mosey down to the shore and pick your boatman, bargaining him down to the going rate of $5–$6 for a 3-hour excursion. Then you wade to the boat and settle into the wobbly hull as your boatman arranges his sails over your head, nearly whipping you overboard. Suddenly you're sailing off to an undisclosed destination, water raining down on you as the boatman wildly splashes his sails. About 15 minutes later, you'll see 20-some other masts bobbing up ahead. Your boatman pulls up and parks, then suddenly a handsome young man wearing nothing but a bowtie and swim trunks jumps on board. Aghast, you think you're about to be robbed until he smiles and explains he's your waiter. Jumping back in the water, he swims over to a floating kitchen and brings you a cold beer and a plate of spicy lobsters. Soon an enthusiastic young local paddles over to your boat and invites you for a swim; to your surprise, you can actually stand up in this natural "pool" and the water doesn't even reach your waist. You wave back at the next *jangada*, full of sun-tanned Argentines, who catch you doing your best breaststroke on their video camera. A floating samba band bangs out lively tunes as you sip tropical juice straight from a coconut shell. Three hours later you've been invited to two parties, a yacht cruise, and an evening at a beachside *barraca*. By the time you return to the beach, you're so exhausted you convince the boatman to carry you to shore in his arms.

> **Insider Tip:**
>
> If you can only go to Maceió for a day, go for this **jangada** adventure. The sensation of being able to stand up and party in the middle of the ocean will make you feel like a sea god. But go light. Take a towel, enough change for food and drinks, and lots of suntan lotion. If you can, leave your shoes on shore, and wear shorts (or just your swimsuit and a coverup) for wading to and from shore. Note that camera equipment or notebooks can get wet easily. Boatmen prefer not to take singles and often wait for a full boat.

THE ESSENTIAL MACEIÓ

WHERE TO STAY

Expensive -------------- Over $60

Moderate -------------- $35–$60

Inexpensive ----------- Under $30

★ Village Enseada Pratagy

Praia de Pratagy (dist. de Riacho Doce), 20 kilometer ; ☎ *(82) 231-4726, FAX 231-5134*

Located about a half-hour drive from Maceió, the Pratagy is one of Brazil's finest destinations—a fascinating ecological hotel and a romantic resort. The road there is a scenic adventure; the bumpy path takes you past tropical fields, traditional shack like homes, and barefoot boys taking dips in the Riacho Doce river. The lobby is a surprise; marble floors vying with wood logs create the epitome of rustic elegance. The preserved ecosystem (approved by IBAMA) is endlessly intriguing: 150 miles of private pristine beach in combination with *mangue* (swamp), which harbors all sorts of critters like snails and crabs. Room are rustic, but fashionably appointed, with all the leisure comforts, except one. (The hotel hopes the absence of TVs will inspire socializing.) One night a month at full moon, magnificent luas are held poolside with live music and bonfires. A huge breakfast buffet is served in a high-beamed, bamboo eatery that flows out to the innovative pool complex created with mineral water and waterfalls. Organized leisure activities, such as hydrogymnastics, volleyball, soccer, jogging, windsurfing, and kayaking keep guests active. There are even special *lambada* and *forró* classes. Behind the pool flows the Rio Caboclo with its own wood bridge, where guests may fish. A treat is the large number of *peixe-boi* (manatees), a species considered extinct in Brazil. The second phase of construction will include tennis, volleyball, squash courts, and golf course, all probably finished by 1993. The hotel is also planning a spa. Low season rates run $73 per couple. *96 apartments. Expensive. All cards.*

Maceió Mar Hotel

Avenida Alvaro Otacílio, 2991 (Ponta Verde); ☎ *231-8000, FAX 231-7085*

Marble floors and ceramic tile facades lend casual elegance to this new 4-star across Ponta Verde Beach. The pleasant bar and snack shop downstairs is a meeting place for artistic types who often make art expositions around the curvaceous bar. The 127 rooms, all with views, are stylishly decorated in bamboo and wood; deluxes have an extended area that holds a couch bed, desk, and chairs. The pool, strangely shaped like the lagoa, looks nearly unswimmable, but it runs provocatively through the open-air lobby. Upon advance request, airport transfers may be arranged. Seafront standards go for $73, seafront deluxes $76. Twenty percent discount if paid in cash. *121 apartments. Expensive. All cards.*

★ Matsubara Hotel
Avenida Brig. Eduardo Gomes, 1551 (Cruz das Almas); ☎ *231-6178, FAX 235-1660*

Owned by a prominent Japanese family, the Matsubara is one of Maceió's prime 5-stars, with enough luxurious details to be considered a resort. The lobby is a sprawling atrium around which are constructed 5 stories of apartments, overhanging with greenery. The exquisitely landscaped grounds inspire outdoor lounging and offer a viable alternative to beachcombing. The pool complex is massive, with wood bridges and islands of flowers shaded by coconut trees; even the tennis courts drip with flowers. Roaming the grounds are 8 giant turtles, beloved by guests. The suites are lusciously appointed with satin spreads; standards are more sedate, but all rooms have verandas and most have ocean views. Also servicing guests are a hair salon, Turkish bath, boutique, jewelry store, and convention salon. The lushly appointed nightclub, usually opened on weekends, is a hot spot. Superior rooms run $80–$90, deluxes $90–$100. Discount in low season is 30 percent. Fielding's readers receive an additional 15 percent discount. *110 apartments. Expensive. All cards.*

★ Hotel Jatiúca
Rua Lagoa da Anta, 220 (Lagoa da Anta); ☎ *231-2555, FAX 235-2808*

Built around a lagoon and the ocean, and about 20 minutes from town, Jatiúca has the feel of a high-class resort village. The lobby is one of the most beautiful in Maceió, designed by sculptor Fernando Lopes with embroidery artists from Alagoas; the grounds are also artistically landscaped. The two parts of the hotel are connected by a grass-roofed walkway separating the apartments from the leisure activities and beach. Numerous fine restaurants and snack areas dot the grounds, including a romantic beachside bar. The beach, to which the hotel has immediate access, is not private, but tight security keeps anyone who is not a guest from entering the grounds. Apartments are large and tastefully furnished, with verandas looking to the garden or pool. New Year's Eve, which draws elite Brazilians from all over, is an 8–day blowout with a huge bonfire on December 31. In high season (July and November–February), a full set of leisure activities is available, including tennis, volleyball, soccer, and walking. Standards run $89, deluxe doubles $98, suites $163. *95 apartments. Expensive. All cards.*

Hotel Enseada
Avenida Dr. Antônio Gouveia, 171 (Pajuçara); ☎ *231-4726, FAX 231-5134*

This black-and-white hotel looks almost like a cathedral with its angular geometric facade. Formerly an apart-hotel, the 9-story Enseada is built around an indoor pond and atrium of tropical vegetation. The air-conditioned rooms are all enormous, befitting its former status, fashionably styled in red, black, and white decor. Superior rooms are suitelike, with two rooms and a veranda. Guests may be picked up at the airport if requested in advance. Rooms range from $50 for doubles to $62 for superiors. Ten percent discount during low season. *101 apartments. Moderate. All cards.*

Ponta Verde Praia Hotel
Avenida Alvaro Octacilio, 2933 (Ponta Verde); ☎ *231-4040, FAX 231-8080.*

Here's a good middle-range hotel well placed on Ponta Verde, a beach frequented by the young, rich, and chi-chi. The restaurant (all 3 meals) is cheerful with local avant-garde art. The small pool right off the street offers little privacy, but there are also a children's pool, pool bar, and small playground. The seafront room, with a full beach view, is pleasant, with walnut headboards, full-length mirror, and tiled bathroom, but save a few dollars with the lateral sea view, which is sufficient. A panoramic glass elevator gives a magnificent view of the ocean. Fielding's readers receive a 10 percent discount; low season should net an additional 30 percent. *68 apartments. Moderate. All cards.*

Jacarecica Praia Hotel
AL-101-Norte, (Jacarecica); ☎ *231-2591*
Definitely a budget experience, this hotel is located across the street from one of the best beaches for swimming. During low season, the restaurant is not open, but discounts up to 50 percent are offered. An odd, amoeba-shaped pool with grass-hut kiosks adorns the back yard. All apartments are air-conditioned, and have color TV and minibar; deluxe doubles run about $27. Twenty-four-hour room services delivers fast food and sandwiches. *30 apartments. Inexpensive. Cards: AE.*

WHERE TO EAT

Gstaad
Avenida Robert Kennedy, 2167; ☎ *231-1202, 221-2780. Daily 7:00 p.m.–1:00 a.m., closed Sunday.*
The famous come to see and be seen at this elegant Swiss-style eatery, the most expensive in Maceió. Flowered upholstery lends a seaside tropicália; the marble floors and mahogany columns add élan. Dishes are named after the owners' friends; one wonders if the Filet à Senhorzinho Malta, named after ex-First Lady Rosane Collor, is still on the menu. Fondues are specialties. After 10:30 p.m., a soft sax and piano kick in with moody jazz. Women in chic linen suits with short sleeves looked like they were freezing in the strong air conditioning, but ties are not necessary. *Expensive. All cards.*

Fornace
Avenida Robert Kennedy, 2167 (Ponta Verde); ☎ *231-1780. Daily noon–3:00 p.m., 7:00 p.m.–2:00 a.m., Sunday noon–midnight*
The poor man's Gstaad, with the same chef but more reasonably priced pizzas, meat, and fish. A luncheonette-style sprawl, with a tiled floor and air conditioned salon, serves excellent shrimp omelettes for about $6; pizzas start at $3. The outdoor terrace in front is for leisurely loitering. *Inexpensive. All cards.*

O Laçador
Avenida Robert Kennedy, 2750 (Ponta Verde); ☎ *231-5575. Daily 11:00 a.m.–midnight.*
Fine *rodízio*-style steakhouse (all you can eat) with a fascinating gaúcho folkloric show, featuring the cowboy culture, music, and dances of Rio Grande do Sul. *Moderate. All cards.*

Manzuá
Rua Durval Guimarães, 1370, ☎ *231-9787. Daily 11:00 a.m.–3:00 a.m.*
A little less chi-chi than Gstaad but "*gente importante*," nevertheless. Fish, pasta, and excellent service on Ponta Verde Beach. Live music in the piano bar keeps the politicos happy. *Moderate-Expensive. All cards.*

Aroeiras
Rua Mário Nunes Vieira, 240 (Mangabeira); ☎ *232-3059. Daily 11:00 a.m.–3:00 p.m., 6:00 p.m.–2:00 a.m.*
One of the most traditional restaurants in Maceió, featuring Northeastern cuisines like *carne de sol, macaxeira, farofa, feijão tropeiro,* and *manteiga do sertão.* In high season and festivals you should make reservations. *Moderate. All cards.*

Restaurante do Alipio
Avenida Alipio Barbosa, 321 (Ponta da Barra) (Lagoa Mundaú); ☎ *221-5186. Daily 11:00 a.m.–1:00 a.m., Sunday 11:00 a.m.–6:00 p.m.*
Prices have risen since this rock-simple eatery began to pack them in on the banks of the lagoon in Barra do Pontal. Unfortunately, the quality is not what it used to be. Still, fried fish is a good bet, as is *carne de sol.* Waiters have a strange sense of humor here. (One told us our wait would be 20 minutes, then brought the food in a matter of seconds.) Better to go after the sun sets, when live music is played nightly. *Moderate. Cards: AE.*

Bem
Rua João Canuto da Silva, 21 (Praia de Cruz das Almas); ☎ *231-3316. Daily 11:00 a.m.–1:00 a.m.*
This traditional, well-known restaurant on Cruz das Almas beach does wonders with *Peixe à Escabeche,* a regional fish cooked in its own blood, in a kind of stew served with *pirão. Sururu*—a typical mollusk found only in the lagoon—is also a specialty. Lobsters are caught on the high seas, but there are times when it's forbidden to fish for them—

specifically, in April and June, when you'll be served frozen lobster. *Camarão Hawaii*, served in a pineapple, and 10 kinds of *muqueca*, including shrimp, lobster, and oyster, round out the menu. Lunch on the veranda is breezy. *Moderate. No cards.*

Rodízio Lagostão
Avenida Dq. de Caxias, 1384 (Centro); ☎ *221-6211. Daily 6:00 p.m.–midnight, high season noon–midnight*

Seafood *rodízio* (all you can eat) with 19 dishes of shrimp, lobster, muqueca, stuffed crabs, mollusks, etc. If you're a fish lover, how you can go wrong for $10? *Moderate. No cards.*

New Hakata
Rua Dr. Antônio Conceição, 1198 (Ponta Verde). Daily 11:00 a.m.–3:00 p.m., 7:00 p.m.–2:00 a.m.

Casual to the point of unimaginative, this Japanese-inspired fisheria, with an outdoor patio and air-conditioned salon, is well known for its *carapeba*—the most famous typical fish found in Maceió. Specialty is cuisine cooked *na chapa*, served on a sizzling grill. If you look helpless, the waiter will skillfully deliver the head from the tail, but be careful of bones—I almost choked to death. Fish is priced according to size; the $8 variety is sufficient for one, accompanied by sautéed vegetables and rice. Located near the Maceió Mar Hotel, the restaurant sits on an inner street a few blocks from shore. *Moderate. All cards.*

NIGHTLIFE

By Bar Brasil *Rua C, 320 (Jatiúca). Daily 6:00 p.m.–last client daily.*

A star bar in the city, where the garlic bread is as famous as the *chopp*. The *picanha* served with fried *macaxeira* comes in a close second.

Lua Cheia *Rua do Asfalto (Garça Torta). Tuesday–Sunday 11:00 a.m.–midnight.*

Situated on the Litoral Norte (northern beachhead), this bar for the post-hippie generation offers alternative shows for those who prefer to remain far from the chi-chi of the city.

Fellini
at the end of Avenida Robert Kennedy (Ponta Verde). Daily 6:00 p.m.–last client.

Nicknamed the "pianos' mar" (sea of pianos), this is the place to sink down into good local jazz.

> **Insider Tip:**
> To dance samba, head for Casa do Povo on Jatiúca Beach. Female tourists looking for singles are a common sight.

GAY MACEIÓ

There are no exclusively gay bars in Maceió, since the lifestyle here runs toward the discreet. One heterosexual bar frequented by gays, however, is

Off Public Bar
Rua Dr. Silvério Jorge, 1194 (Jaraguá). Friday–Sunday 10:30 p.m.–last client.

The bar is practically the dance floor, and the mechanical music tends to run international.

SHOPPING

Take a hired car or bus out to *Pontal da Barra*, along the shores of the Lagoa do Mundaú, formerly a fishermen's village and now filled with stores of traditional lacemakers. Ask for the house of *Teka*, one of Maceió's most famous lacemakers, who in her youth was considered one of the most beautiful girls in the region. Today, her weather-drawn face tells the story of a hardship existence, but the joy in her eyes when she shows you her artistic designs brings back her former glory. To get to her house, you'll pass the quaint town square and walk through a dirt road past traditional cottages, where barefoot boys play in the mud and old women spend the day on their stoops. Teka learned her craft from her mother at the age of 8, and today can complete a $400 wedding dress in about 10 days. Her designs have been featured in expositions throughout the country. Everyone knows where she lives, but her official address is *Travessa São Sebastião, 56, Pontal de Barra.*

The Mercado de Artesanato
Parque Rio Branco (downtown) Daily 8:00 a.m.–6:00 p.m. offers a good choice of ceramics, wood-carvings, native paintings, and lace embroderies.

HANDS-ON MACEIÓ

Arrival
The airport is located 20 kilometers from downtown. Taxis run $18–$20, or you can take a bus to the train station or near Hotel Beiriz on Rua João Pessoa, 290.

City Transportation
Both the city bus and a special *jardineira* bus make all stops along the *orla* (beach drag). The bus that goes from the center of town down the *orla* is marked Centro Barra Cruz das Almas.

Money Exchange
Aeroturismo *Rua Barão de Penedo, 61.*

Points Beyond
Flights run daily to Brasília, Curitiba, João Pessoa, Natal, Recife, Rio, Salvador, and São Paulo. Buses run to most large cities, such as Salvador, Belém, Fortaleza, Brasília, and São Paulo.

Tourist Information
Ematur *Duque de Caxias, 2014 (downtown);* ☎ *221-8987* Information booths are also located at the airport and the bus station.

When to Go
High season (December–February) is hot and crowded; better to hit the beaches from March–May. Avoid July and August due to heavy rains. From September to December, rain and sun alternate.

RECIFE AND OLINDA

Home of one of the great Carnaval blowouts in the Northeast, **Recife** is the capital of the state of **Pernambuco** and one of the major industrial cities north of Salvador. What draws tourists, besides the pre-Lent festivities that usually last 10 days, is an excellent coastline of natural pools formed by the craggy reefs, or *recifes* (hence its name). Weather is uniformly beach friendly, and there are also glorious stretches of primitive strands north and south of the city. In addition, 4 miles away, the colonial town of **Olinda** remains one of the country's greatest architectural treasures, a perfect city to experience cultural time-warp as you stroll leisurely over the 400-year-old cobblestone streets.

Recife beats to a different *ritmo* than the rest of Brazil. During Carnaval, which mostly descends on the tiny alleyways of Olinda, samba is all but obscured by the more frenzied, high-temper beat of folkloric dances like the *frevo*, the *maracatú*, and the *caboclinho*. Towering *bonecos*—papier-mâché figures of folk heroes and caricatures of local politicians—dominate the *praças,* where it's said people spend more money on beer than on their costumes. *Trios elétricos*—small bands blaring away on the back of trucks—bring the decibel level over the edge. Certainly Olinda has gained the reputation for one of the wildest street Carnavals in Brazil; residents who can't stand the excitement often escape to the local Jesuit Seminary for 4 days of peace and quiet.

HISTORY

Although Olinda is today considered the "bedroom community" of Recife, it was founded before Recife and once overshadowed the harbor city in its colonial greatness. After Olinda was established in the 1530s, the Portuguese proceeded to plow most of the surrounding fields into sugar plantations. By 1630, forces from the Dutch West India Company expelled the settlers, burning down the glorious wrought churches and rebuilding the new capital, Recife, whose swampy lands opened onto a more favorable harbor. Conquering territory from the southern border of Alagoas all the way to Maranhão, the Dutch expanded their monopoly on the sugarcane industry by maintaining tight control on the slave trade, but they also introduced advancements in tropical medicine, weather analysis, and zoology. They erred, however, on the side of politics, ignoring the tensions beginning to explode among the original settlers; by 1654, the Dutch were forced to surrender Recife to the Portuguese, and they never returned.

The mercantile Dutch transformed Recife into the first bourgeois commercial center of Brazil. By the time they left, the village of 100 houses had grown into a bustling port with over 2,000 houses. But they had also created a class struggle. The rural aristocracy based in Olinda began to feel threatened by this growing commercial class and labeled them *mascates*—a derogative word employed by the aristocracy to refer to those who had to work for a living. Tempers erupted, but by the end of 1711, a governor dispatched from Lisbon reconciled the War of the Mascates with a generous pardon for all. However, for two more centuries, the gap between the aristocracy and the bourgeoisie lingered. A conspiracy revolution in 1817, inspired by European enlightenment ideals, not to mention the War of 1812 in the States, abolished all titles of nobility, the brazilwood monopoly, class privileges, and even some taxes. This was considered the principal revolt of the colonial period, but it, too, was eventually quelled and Pernambuco returned to the fold of the new republic within three months.

A BIRD'S EYE VIEW

Perhaps it's more wish fulfillment than reality, but Recife is often called the "Venice of Brazil," since the heart of the city sprawls over 3 islands— **Santo Antônio**, **Boa Vista**, and **Recife** proper, all connected by more than 2 dozen bridges over the Beribe and Capibaribe Rivers. The business district is situated on the island of Santo Antônio and surrounded by a few colonial churches. Most of the middle class crowds into the southern area along the **Boa Viagem** Beach, where the majority of the better hotels are located, as well as hundreds of beachside eateries and clubs. Stay away from the docks on Recife Island at night, a veritable sleaze center.

SIGHTS

IN RECIFE

To get a glimpse of colonial Recife, head for the large square known as

Pátio de São Pedro in the district of Santo Antônio. Reminiscent of Rome with its dozens of flying pigeons, the plaza is lined with bars and artisan stores but is dominated by the

Igreja de São Pedro *Daily 8:00 a.m.–11:30 a.m., 2:00 p.m.–5:00 p.m.* Constructed between 1728 and 1782, the church boasts an impressive facade that nearly resembles an opera house, as do the gold-leafed boxes inside. The ceiling painting in the main sanctuary is a fabulous example of trompe l'oeil and provides an immense sensation of radiating energy. Go up three flights of rickety stairs (the kind out of a horror movie) for a fantastic panoramic view of the city from the church's rooftop. On the corner of the Pátio, you'll find the best sculpture shop in the city—

Livraria Cordel, which features the woodcuts of artists Amaro Francisco and Jota Borges. (Some of the sculptured saints seem so alive they look as if they could perform a miracle any second.) You'll also find excellent native paintings here, and scores of *cordels*—old poems, romances, and biographies in pamplet form that take their name from the cords on which they are hung for sale. Since *cordels* were the primary form by which the natives in the interior passed on their news, their themes (wife abuse, murder, and politics) were always topical, if somewhat tabloidish. Even if you can't read Portuguese, the woodblock-cut designs on the front covers are usually sensational enough to rate as fine souvenirs. At night, the bars around the Pátio teem with Recifenses, especially on the weekends when you can hear excellent live bands. With your purse tucked tightly under your arm or your wallet in an inside pocket, wander around the inner streets surrounding the Pátio to the

Mercado de São José. Packed with stalls hawking everything from herbs and dried fish to jeans and tablecloths, some of the alleyways are barely big enough for two people to pass, but the scene is exciting—definitely the epitome of a frenzied third-world marketplace. If your sandals need fixing, you'll even find shoemakers using sewing machines so ancient they have to be pedaled. Across the esplanade is a fruit and vegetable market open daily.

A taxi ride away, on the shores of the Capibaribe River, is the

Casa da Cultura. By the time you arrive, you'll probably be feeling steamy, so buy a cold Coke and a bag of roasted cashews or boiled Indian corn, then stroll slowly around this former prison now transformed into the city's major arts and crafts market. Good buys are hammocks, lace handiwork, and straw pottery. My favorite purchase were the miniature *maracatú* and *frevo* bands bought at **Kafua Artesanato** (room 116). Just make sure you repack the fragile little sculptures yourself because the newspaper the store uses won't be sufficient. To get a better look at the impressive structure of the ex-prison, cross to the other side of the river. It will take at least an half-hour by car to reach the

Museu do Homem do Nordeste, but it's one of the best museums in Brazil for the study of Northeastern culture and history. Once inside, you'll find that the compulsory guided tour (in English) will give you a quick overview; afterwards, graciously inquire if you can wander around on your own. Several galleries are devoted to such topics as sugar, cattle, popular religion, pagan festivals, and ceramics, and there are also impressive exhibits of native handicrafts. Make sure you check out the **Galeria de Arte Popular,** which features the sculptures of a peasant farmer named **Mestre Vitalino**, who became famous for his nearly lifelike clay portraits of the residents of his small village. To get to the museum, hire a **taxi** for a ride through the leafy residential neighborhoods or take the **bus** *#552 Dois Irmãos Rui Barbosa*. The **museum** is located at *Avenida 17 de Agosto, 2187 (Casa Forte);* ☎ *268-2000. Tuesday, Wednesday and Friday 11:00 a.m.–5:00 p.m., Thursday 8:00 a.m.–5:00 p.m., Saturday, Sunday and holidays 1:00 p.m.–7:00 p.m., closed Monday. Confirm in advance.* **Vitalino's** works can also be found at the

Instituto Joaquim Nabuco *Avenida 17 de Agosto, 2187 (Casa Forte);* ☎ *268-2000. Tuesday, Wednesday and Friday 11:00 a.m.–5:00 p.m., Thursday 8:00 a.m.–5:00 p.m., and Saturday and Sunday 1:00 p.m.–5:00 p.m.* This museum also features some of the best Northeastern folk art in Brazil.

OLINDA ON FOOT

Next to the cities of Parati, Ouro Preto, and São Luis, **Olinda** stands as one of the great architectural treasures still remaining from colonial Brazil. Spread across several small hills and fanning along the shore, Olinda is a mere 4 miles north of Recife—a wonderful maze of cobblestone streets, pastel-colored mansions, baroque churches, and market squares that invite leisurely strolling.

The colonial complex, about 10 square kilometers, is but one-third of a modern metropolis of nearly 400,000 that stretches out behind it, but it's the center of excitement for the Northeast's most frenzied **Carnaval**. During the rest of the year, colonial Olinda acts as a magnet for the bi-cities' bohemians and intelligentsia, who congregate at night in the numerous bars along the shore and in the **Alto da Sé.** Since Olinda was designated a national historical patrimony in 1980 and a world monument by UNESCO in 1982, building regulations have forbidden the construction of any modern architecture unless the lot is totally vacant.

Getting There

To get to Olinda, take bus #902 or #981, both marked *Rio Doce*. From the center of Recife, buses marked *Rio Doce* or *Olinda* will also get you there.

Olinda has over 22 churches and 12 chapels, a few which can be glimpsed on this energetic walking tour. Note that some of the slopes are steep and temperatures can rise sharply, so make sure you take a few rests in the shade. Begin at **Praça do Carmo**, where the first Carmel church built in Brazil is located, the **Igreja do Carmo** (1588). The imposing church may still be closed for restoration, but knock loudly on the door and perhaps the *vigia* (watchman) will let you slip inside for a peek. Walk down *Rua do Vasconcelos* to the **Igreja de São Bento** a monastery founded by the Portuguese in 1736, *Wednesday–Friday 8:00 a.m.–11:30 a.m., 4:00 p.m.–5:30 p.m.* The original site dates back to 1596, but the Dutch decimated this area when they invaded Pernambuco, and it wasn't until 1761 that the Portuguese could rebuild it. São Bento is considered the richest church in Olinda with a cedar wood altar and two gold pulpits (the left one is used by the priests and the right by the richest family); slaves were not even allowed to enter the main sanctuary. The beautifully preserved ceiling was painted with colors made from tropical fruit trees condensed with banana oil. To the left, on Rua 13 de Novembro stands the *São Sebastian Church*, constructed in 1686 when the city was overrun with rats. (São Sebastian is the protector of rats.)

Walk uphill on Rua São Bento over the original stones forged by slaves who used particles from the reefs cemented with whale oil. The black stones are called *cabeça de negros* because the slaves carved portraits of heads into them. On the corner of 15 de Novembro and Rua São Bento stands the 16th-century yellow-and-white façade of the **Mayor's Office**, rebuilt in neoclassical style. Number 182 on Rua São Bento is the home of singer **Alceu Valença**, a popular Northeastern singer who specializes in *frevo* and returns to Olinda every year for Carnaval. Walk back to the *Praça*, then left on Rua 27 de Janeiro. The yellow-and-black house is the **Pitombeira dos Quatros Cantos**, the meeting place of the principal *frevo* club that dances in Carnaval. At night it transforms into a popular bar. During Carnaval, the concrete walls around here are saturated with graffiti, a creative and often highly political outlet of expression that the entire city engages in; after Carnaval, the government keeps the best ones and washes off the rest—until the next Carnaval.

Walking down Rua 27 de Janeiro, you'll reach **Igreja de São Pedro**, founded in the 17th century and rebuilt by the Portuguese in the 18th century in baroque style. During Carnaval, the steps of the church become an outdoor bed for anyone too drunk to go home. Walk around the church to Rua 7 de Setembro, turn right on Rua São Bento, and notice the #301 house with the Portuguese blue-tiled facade. About this time, you might be approached by a street artist like **Jota Caxiado**, who sells fine line drawings. From here, walk straight till you reach the **Mercado da Ribeira**, formerly the site of slave auctions attended by sugar plantation owners, and now a handicraft center; if you go behind the market on the right side, you can peep inside the backyard of some of Olinda's finest artists, restoring wood and plaster saints.

The Principal Corner Of Carnaval

At this point Rua São Bento becomes **Rua Bernado Vieira de Melo**, where the romantic **L'Atelier** restaurant is located. If you're not ready for a full meal, at least stop in for a drink on the back patio overlooking the city or dig into a *Coupe Atelier*—melon, vanilla ice cream, meringue, and cherry liqueur—just the thing for heatstroke. The restaurant is a block from the principal corner of Carnaval—**Quatro Cantos**—the meeting point of all the *frevo* clubs (specifically, the corner of Rua Bernardo Vieira de Melo and Ladeira da Misericórdia and Rua Prudente de Moraes).

The short rest stop will be imperative if you continue up **Misericordia**, the highest slope of Olinda and a killer on the calves. Turn left on **Beco dos Quatros Cantos** and go down the hill. There you'll find a mineral well with natural spring water that's perfectly safe to drink. During Carnaval, revelers come here to both drink and shower at the same time. Walk back up the hill to **Rua do Amparo**, the oldest street in Olinda. Near here, at #91, is the home of **Antônio Cardoso**, who is famous for the *pau do indio* he sells—homemade *pinga*, with 32 ingredients, including herbs and other macrobiotic products that are supposedly good for the health. It's also a hefty shot of intoxication, about $3 for a liter bottle, and the major liquid consumed during Carnaval.

All-Female Choir

Up the steep hill is the **Igreja da Misericórdia,** reconstructed in the 18th century. Between 4:30 p.m.–5:00 p.m. you may be lucky enough to stumble upon the angelic all-female choir rehearsing with a nun who plays a tiny organ. The church is noted for having one of the most tasteful displays of gold in a Brazilian church; notice the Portuguese-tiled mural depicting scenes of Our Lady of Conception. The white inner door in the foyer was originally used to keep slaves from entering. Outside the church you can find some of the best lacework for sale in the Northeast, as well as a magnificent view of the shoreline.

Sacred Art

Walking toward the seashore, you'll pass the **Museu de Arte Sacra** *Rua Bispo Coutinho, 726;* ☎ *429-0036. Daily 9:00 a.m.–noon, closed Monday,* featuring some of the oldest examples of sacred art in the country. Nearby, on the **Praça da Sé**, you can find the lowest prices for native crafts. Sit down on the square and indulge in a tapioca (coconut shreds wrapped in manioc flour), a grilled wonder that needs to be washed down with a cold Coke. Ask for the vendor **Duda**, who sits near the stone cross making probably hundreds of tapiocas a day. The Praça is open around the clock, and it's a nice spot to come for a breakfast of tapioca and coffee. The church on this square, **Igreja da Sé**, is an original from 1537, though the interior has been subjected to numerous reforms throughout the centuries.

From the Praça walk down **Rua Coutinho** pass the **Jesuit Seminary**, built in 1656—the highest point in Olinda. It was here that the first ideas of Brazilian independence sprang. During Carnaval, if you want to avoid the frenzied revelry, you can actually rent a room here for four days, though you must reserve a month or two in advance.

Turn right on **Rua São Francisco** to the **Convento de Nossa Senhora das Neves** (1585), the first Franciscan church in Brazil. Today it remains a monastery for men, with the Sant'Ana Chapel still in use. Just don't walk around here at night because it's not safe due to the lack of traffic.

Insider Tip:

Sobrado 7 *Daily 10:00 a.m.–8:00 p.m., located below the Mourisco restaurant, offers the best native paintings and artisanry in the city. It accepts all cards.*

BEACHES IN RECIFE

Only a few minutes from the city's center lies **Boa Viagem**, Recife's principal beachhead, which, thankfully, remains relatively unpolluted. More than 6 kilometers long, it's graced with fine white sand, leafy grass huts, and colorful *barracas*, not to mention the steady stream of activity day and night. Right offshore, hundreds of natural rock pools are formed by the craggy reefs, making them inviting coves to wade through when the tide is out. Special illumination after hours permits nighttime bathing. Many of the best hotels are located along the beach drag, **Avenida Boa Viagem,** and you can also find quaint pousadas tucked into the many side streets.

Besides bathing and the occasional *jangada* ride, the main activity on the beach seems to be eating. Evidence is the perpetual parade of colorful native vendors down the strand hawking everything from fresh coconut milk to cut pineapples, boiled shrimps, beer, and *batidas*.

Transportation to the beach is exceedingly easy. From Avenida Dantas Barreto, you can pick up *frescões* to Boa Viagem, special air-conditioned buses for about 50 cents.

BEACHES NEAR RECIFE

Beaches north and south of Recife are considered by many to be far superior to Boa Viagem, and certainly the exotic flavor of small villages and fishermen coves adds to the glamour of strands near-deserted during the week and packed on the weekends. These days, forgo the northern beach of **Itamaracá,** now infested with too many tourists, for the sleepier villages of the south. Buses from Recife go down the scenic coastal road, the **PE-60,** or *via litoral*, to **Gaibú**, about 12-1/2 miles from Boa Viagem. (Note you may have to go to Cabu first.) But even the main highway, **BR-101,** will take you past silky stalks of sugar cane waving sensuously in the wind. (Frankly, either trip is a wonderful way to see rural Brazil, with its typical orange-tiled roofs and groves of coconut trees.) More like an obstacle course, the turnoff to Gaibú must be one of the worst roads in Brazil, but you'll be rewarded with a beach as rural as you'll ever find. During the week, the craggy coastline is nearly deserted, but weekends teem with motorcycle couples who pat themselves on the back for having survived the 1-1/2 hour runnerblade trip from Recife. Because there are no reefs to cut the violent waves, be careful swimming. (Surfing, however, is great.) An even worse dirt road winds around the cliff to **Cacheta** —one of the most beautiful primitive beaches around. A rocky promontory juts out to a sea full of lobster boats and native children trying to surf on makeshift boards. You can scamper over the rocks or get out of the shade at **Bar do Artur**. Do meet Artur, the bar's owner, a perpetually cheerful professional beach bum, who will take your photo for his "memories wall" and serve you the specialty—fried needlefish *(agulhas fritas)*, though you'll need about 5 to fill you up. On the weekends, elite Recifenses adore the excellent sound system, not to mention the snorkeling by moonlight.

Porto das Galinhas

From Cabo, buses also head directly to the village of **Porto das Galinhas,** a community that's fast growing as a summer condo resort, although the sea is still full of traditional fishing and lobster boats. If you're looking for peace and quiet, go during the week; action turns steamy come weekends. At low tide, all the reefs appear and create natural pools. At the end of the main street is **Bras Bar**, the principal hangout, where you can find excellent steel fish. A *jangada* trip out to the natural pool runs about $2 (though they looked dangerous to me, and if the sea is rough, you better be a very good swimmer). Snorkeling is also great here, though you should bring your own equipment. Most exciting is just the glorious color of the water, which changes from deep, deep blue in the winter to grayish green in the summer.

Accommodations in **Porto das Galinhas** run from seaside pousadas like **Porto do Sol** *telephone in Recife:* ☎ *(81) 222-0461* to the more elegant rustic charm of the **Hotel Pontal de Ocaporá** ☎ *678-1166. Reservations in Recife:* ☎ *(81) 224-9193.* Júlio Iglesias brought an entourage of Brazilian beauties to this picturesque villa of grass-hut chalets situated on a stunning, but secluded section of Porto das Galinhas. Cobblestone paths lead to tropical bungalows with verandas overlooking the sea; even the 3-pool complex with its own waterfall looks out onto the ocean. All water sports equipment may be rented on premises. Suites run $90–$110. *Expensive. Cards: AE, DC, MC.*

Getting There

You can take a bus in front of the airport to Gaibú, as well as to Porto das Galinhas about twice a day, for less than a dollar.

THE ESSENTIAL RECIFE AND OLINDA

WHERE TO STAY

Expensive -------------	**Over $80**
Moderate -------------	**$35–$65**
Inexpensive ----------	**Under $35**

In Recife

★ Mar Hotel
Rua Br. de Souza Leão, 451 (Boa Viagem); ☎ *341-5443, FAX 341-7002*

The steel-and-aluminum lobby of Recife's principal 5-star ought to read as "cold," but actually it's one of the most attractive foyers in Brazil. Plants and oriental rugs enliven the area that opens onto an exquisite pool complex with gushing waterfalls. The Mont Black restaurant offers fine Swiss-style cuisine, and a Japanese sushi bar and coffee shop will fulfill other palates. "The After Dark" piano bar offers a fine view of the city, and dancing and dinner take place on the roof garden during the weekend. A teahouse serves colonial-style tea every afternoon. Deluxe rooms overlooking the pool are spacious and inviting, and the beds are probably the most comfortable in Brazil. Gal Costa graces the Presidential Suite when she's in town—a veritable wonder of stylish decor, complete with jacuzzi and sacred art sculptures. Double standards start at $95. 207 apartments. *Expensive. All cards.*

★ Hotel Miramar Recife
Rua dos Navegantes, 363 (Boa Viagem), ☎ *326-7422*

Only 5 minutes from the airport, this 5-star doesn't match the ones in Rio, but it's an excellent choice for Recife, especially considering the 50 percent discount given to Fielding's readers. Antique chandeliers adorn the intimate lobby while a fantastic aquarium perks up the restaurant serving international and Brazilian cuisine. Laps can be easily negotiated in the huge pool, and a bevy of boutiques will serve all shopping needs. Standards do not differ radically from other rooms; all come with safes, color TV, minibar, and electronic keys. No rooms have a sea view, though some look out onto the pool. Standard doubles start at $80, but excellent discounts are offered in low season. 173 apartments. *Expensive–Moderate. All cards.*

★ Recife Palace
Avenida Boa Viagem, 4070 (Boa Viagem), ☎ *325-4044, FAX 326-8895*

The dark-speckled lobby of this 5-star is ice-cold (a relief in Recife, where air-conditioning is mandatory). Oriental rugs, tapestries, and a grand piano make you feel luxurious. Standards are very large with an extra sofa bed; only suites and super deluxes have full views. All rooms come with tubs, safes, color TVs, and electronic controls; the white marble in the bathrooms add a rich detail. The Savoir Faire, specializing in seafood crepes, is one of the most sophisticated French eateries in the city, or you can choose to eat on the open-air terrace surrounding the small pool. The Happy Ending nightclub is a hot spot. Standards run about $100, with up to 30 percent discounts in low season. 294 apartments. *Expensive. All cards.*

Fator Palace Hotel
Rua dos Navegantes, 157 (Boa Viagem), ☎ *326-0040, FAX 326-8953*

Formerly an apart-hotel, the Fator is 50 meters from Boa Viagem beach. Though it's rated as a 4-star, the quality is more like three. Antique wood tables and potted plants fill the lobby; live music is offered Monday–Saturday in the pub. The small, oddly shaped pool is surrounded by high-rises, and elevators have been known to be temperamental. Standards and superiors differ only in the view; the latter comes with a balcony. Bedrooms are small, but white-and-beige decors lend lightness. Airport transfers can be arranged. Doubles start at $64, suite $85. 180 apartments. *Moderate–expensive. All cards.*

★ Hotel Casa Grande & Senzala
Avenida Conselheiro Aguiar, 5000 (Boa Viagem); ☎ *341-0366, FAX 341-0366*
A stunning 4-story colonial house with turrets and balconies, this pousada-like hotel offers service in the grand manner of the great sugar plantations. The wood-planked corridors gleam golden-bright under the antique illumination, and you must even use huge antique keys to enter your apartment. Old photos of Recife line the salmon-colored walls of the individual rooms decorated with colonial furniture, while greenery drips from the windows that look out onto an inner courtyard complete with an antique fountain. The suite, with an extra room, is totally charming. The elegant Mucama restaurant is the most atmospheric in the city, with waitresses in folkloric costumes affecting obsequious airs. Fifty meters from the beach, the hotel can also arrange excursions, and clients have use-privilege at the Caxangá Golf Club. Fielding's readers receive a 20 percent discount. *50 apartments. Expensive. All cards.*

Internacional Othon Palace
Avenida Boa Viagem, 3722 (Boa Viagem), ☎ *326-7225*
A beach atmosphere prevails at this downscale Othon, where an Oriental rug and a few green couches pass for the lobby. The tiled-floor apartments all offer a partial view of the beach, though the bathrooms are not impeccable. The restaurant, featuring Italian cuisine, offers all three meals (and *feijoada* on Saturday), and light snacks can be enjoyed on the roof bar, which offers live music on weekends. There is also 24-hour room service. Double standards start at $38. *257 apartments. Moderate. All cards.*

Veleiro Praia
Rua Prof. Osias Ribeiro, 67 (Boa Viagem); ☎ *326-7360*
This simple 3-star is across the street from the beach. To avoid claustrophobia, ask for a view if you plan to spend any time in your room. An arrow-shaped pool provides room for sunning (though within view of the street), and meals can be taken next door at the Choparia Ponte. Standard doubles start at $26. *15 apartments. Inexpensive. All cards.*

Hotel Praiamar
Avenida Boa Viagem, 1660 (Boa Viagem); ☎ *326-6905*
Across the street from the beach, this tiny hotel has the charm of an *albergue*. Antique ceiling lamps hang in the corridors of this former farmhouse; breakfast is taken in a simple but friendly salon with antique grilled windows. Best room is #101, with an original wood-carved closet, sunken tub, and shower. Rooms are air-conditioned; safes at the reception. The pool is the smallest I have ever seen. Doubles start at $25. *14 apartments. Inexpensive. All cards.*

★ Pousada São Francisco
Estrada da Aldeia; ☎ *251-0058*
More modern than the usual pousada, this is one of the best deals in the city, and only a 100-meter-walk to the beach. Rooms are small but cheerfully decorated with native prints and woven bedspreads. Superior and deluxe rooms have verandas to the sea, and all rooms come with air conditioning, phone, and minibar; safes are at the reception. The two parts of the hotel are connected by a grass-roofed corridor. Across the street is one of the most beautiful colonial homes in Recife—now a psychiatric hospital. Doubles run from $14–$26. *40 apartments. Inexpensive. All cards.*

In Olinda
★ Sofitel Quatro Rodas Olinda
Avenida José Augusto Moreira, 2200 (Casa Grande), ☎ *431-2955, FAX 431-0670*
Families, honeymooners, and foreigners head for this 5-star resort hotel designed for leisure about 10 kilometers from the center of Olinda. The philosophy is Club Med without the pressure: from jetskiing and kayaking to tennis, windsurfing, massage, and soccer, you'll be entertained all day long. A

special children's program keep kids out of parents' hair for as long as they like. Nearly every night a special folkloric program (food, music, and dance) is offered, or you can escape to the candlelit arches of the cavelike bar. The coconut-tree grounds lead out to Casa Grande Beach, where a tight security force keeps nonclients from entering the hotel. Apartments are exceedingly attractive, especially for the price (including a 20 percent discount for Fielding's readers—making it much cheaper than the Recife Palace). Special tourist excursions can easily be arranged, but many guests never want to leave the grounds for long. 195 rooms. *Expensive. All cards.*

Pousada dos Quatro Cantos
Rua Prudente de Moraes, 441;
☎ *429-0220*
Funky on the verge of seedy—but a favorite among adventurers, this budget pousada is located on one of the prettiest streets of colonial Olinda; during Carnaval, the best folkloric groups meet at the corner, a sight you can enjoy from the grand colonial veranda. Once a fabulous mansion of interlocking balconies and balustrades, the pousada dates back to the beginning of the century; today it's only 10 minutes from Pau Amarelo Beach. Religious art peps up the wood-floor apartments.; bathrooms are as simple as they come. Some rooms have air-conditioning; the lowest priced rooms have only a fan and share a bathroom; all rooms have color TV and phone. Safes at the reception. For Carnaval stays, you must reserve months in advance. Rooms with air-conditioning run about $12. 14 apartments. *Inexpensive. No cards.*

WHERE TO EAT

In Recife
Marruá Restaurant
Rua Ernesto de Paula Santos, 183 (Boa Viagem); ☎ *326-1656. Daily 11:30 a.m.–1:00 a.m.*
The closest equivalent I could find for *marruá* is "cowpoke"—the guy who throws the lasso around the calf. An oddly suitable name for this pristine *churrascaria* where the walls are so white you'll want to throw paint on them. Elegant service and superb steaks, located in the convention center. *Moderate. Cards: AE.*

★ **Mucama**
Casa Grande Hotel, Avenida Conselaeiro Aguiar, 5000; ☎ *341-0366. Noon–3:00 p.m., 7:00 p.m.–midnight*
The moment you sit down at this gorgeous colonial-style restaurant, a white-turbaned waitress arrives with a silver pitcher and bowl for washing your hands. Candlelight softly illuminates the Art Deco walls full of antique porcelain plates; when excellent live jazz isn't playing, a sophisticated hush prevails. The menu, developed by an Italian-trained chef, is highly imaginative, featuring native fish like *tainha* and *suburim*, as well as *Filé colosso* (steak with caviar and salmon). The tasty *Camarão na Forca* is grilled shrimp skewered to a guillotine-like structure and flanked by pineapple chunks. Even more exquisite than the food is the graceful service, though the obsequious attention may make you feel like a plantation owner. *Expensive. All cards.*

Oficina de Massas
Avenida Boa Viagem, 2232;
☎ *326-0543. Daily 7:30 p.m.–midnight, Sunday noon–midnight*
The oddest troupe of stuffed Italian mannequins flank the foyer of this charming cantina, where you can eat in or take out the city's best pasta. "Slimming" pastas made with whole wheat flour are available, as well as a full line of Italian ice cream desserts. The salad buffet runs about $5, the house pastas only a bit more. *Inexpensive. No cards.*

Porcão
Rua Eng. Domingos Ferreira, 4215 (Boa Viagem), ☎ *326-1656. Daily 11:30 a.m.–12:30 a.m.*
Marble floors and long tables for groups at this fine *churrascaria*, with a salad bar that will please any vegetarian. Children under 5 are free, ages 5–10 pay half. *Moderate. All cards.*

Spettus
Avenida Agamemnon Magalhães, 2132; ☎ *221-3060. Daily 11:30 a.m.–1:30 a.m.*
Excellent *rodízio* with 16 types of meat, plus

10 different vegetables and complements. The gigantic self-service salad bar is included in the price, about $10. Live music at lunch and dinner. *Moderate. All cards.*

★ Restaurante Danado de Bom
Rua Dom José Lopes, 64 (Boa Viagem); ☎ *326-5636*

This tin-roofed, open-air eatery offers some of Recife's finest typical cuisines. Waitresses are adorable in their khaki shorts and gun belts, dressed as *cangaceiras*—bandits who were troopers under the legendary highway robber Lampião. Order lots of different small portions here, like *mandioca* with *charque* (dried meat), *arrumadinho* (with shreds of beef with onions, tomatoes, and parsley), *ovo de codornas* (tiny eggs of a tiny bird), *sarapatel* (interior pig organs boiled in its own blood) and *peixe frito* (fried fish). An excellent seafood plate is the *Marinhada* (with shrimp, lobster, oysters, mussels, and paella). Plates run $4–$8. *Inexpensive–Moderate. No cards.*

In Olinda

★ L'Atelier
(Olinda) Rua Bernardo Vieira de Melo, 91 (Ribeira), ☎ *429-3099. Daily 7:00 p.m.–11:30 p.m., closed Tuesday.*

Swiss owner Michel Barbault salvaged this abandoned Dutch-style mansion and transformed it into one of Olinda's most atmospheric environs. Sit on the porch overlooking the city of Recife for an apertif, then head for one of several small salons to indulge in a multinational menu featuring steak au poivre, duck paté, lobster, and chicken in red wine sauce. The owner and his partner sell the avant-garde tapestries on the walls. Best to make reservations during high season. The restaurant is located 1 block from the principal corner of Carnaval. *Moderate–Expensive. All cards.*

Mourisco
Praça Cons. João Alfredo, 7 (Carmo); ☎ *429-1390. Daily 11:00 a.m.–1:00 a.m., closed Monday.*

Live music and fresh fish. *Moderate. No cards.*

NIGHTLIFE

In Recife

Weekends start on Thursday in Recife. Lots of activity happens around the numerous outdoor bars in the Pátio de São Pedro, especially on the weekends, when excellent live bands and folkloric dance troupes perform.

One of the most romantic spots in the city, Som das Aguas, in the Graças district, features lambada and *forró* Wednesday–Saturday. Eat a typical Northeastern food under straw roofs or smooch in near-total darkness under a palm tree while the neon-lit dance floor rocks. A $2 cover charge after 9:00 p.m.

In Olinda

The **Alto da Sé** teems with activity 24 hours a day, especially on weekend nights. A mishmash of dance music, from *frevo* and merengue to samba and *forró*, breaks out every Friday and Saturday night around 11:00 p.m. at the **Clube Atlântico,** on the Praça do Carmo. (Look for the sign of the couple dancing on a crescent moon.)

SHOPPING

Casa da Cultura
Rua Floriano Peixoto. Monday–Saturday 9:00 a.m.–8:00 p.m., Sunday 3:00 p.m.–8:00 p.m.

Constructed in the 19th century, this former prison was transformed into an arts and crafts market in 1975, now replete with art galleries, artisanry stores, museums, theatres, bars, and snack counters.

Shopping Center Recife
Daily 10:00 a.m.–10:00 p.m.

This modern 2-floor mall is adorned with waterfalls and marble floors, and a select variety of stores. The all-purpose **C&A department store** predominates; there's also a food village on the second floor.

Fundação de Cultura da Cidade de Recife
Pátio de São Pedro, 10

The Cultural Foundation of Recife, where you may buy popular records and Portuguese books. Every Friday, free folkloric dances are held here at 8:00 p.m. Upstairs you can ask for a tourist map.

HANDS-ON RECIFE

Airlines

The following airlines make regular flights to Recife.

Varig
Avenida Guararapes, 110; ☎ 224-9096.
VASP
Avenida Manoel Borba, 488; ☎ 421-3088.
Transbrasil
Avenida Conde da Boa Vista, 1546; ☎ 231-0522.

Arrival

Aeroporto Internacional dos Guararapes
☎ 341-6090 is located 11 kilometers from downtown in Imbiribeira. Taxis to downtown cost about $10; tourist taxis are about twice as much as ordinary red taxis. There's also an airport bus that takes about an hour.

If you're arriving in Recife by bus, you'll find the Rodoviária (bus station) seemingly in the middle of nowhere, but an underground rail called the metro will whisk you to the Estação Central in the center of the city; the hotel district is a short cab ride away.

City Transportation

Buses

The main bus terminal is **Santa Rita Bus Terminal** Cais de Santa Rita (São José); ☎ 224-5499 Located 1 kilometer from downtown, the terminal offers information centers and a luggage storage on the ground floor. Other buses originate on Santo Antônio in Pracinha and along Avenida Guararapes. Buses tend to be crowded and hot; air-conditioned buses called *frescões* that run along the Boa Viagem beach costs about 50 cents and are worth it.

Car Rental

Norte Locadora
Avenida Domingos Ferreira, 232; ☎ 326-9813.
Hertz
Avenida Conselheiro, 4214 (Boa Viagem); also at the airport.

Taxis

Radio-Taxi
☎ 222-0625.
Special Taxis
☎ 325-2643.
Special Airport Taxis
☎ 341-1888.

Climate

Summertime reigns mostly year-round in Recife, with temperatures averaging between 73°F and 85°F.

Consulates

U.S.A.
Rua Gonçalves Maia, 163 (Boa Vista); ☎ 221-1412.
Great Britain
Avenida Marquês de Ilonda, 200, suite 410; ☎ 224-0650.

Money Exchange

Banco do Comércio
Rua Matias de Albuquerque.
Lloyds
Rua do Fogo, 22.

Points Beyond

Transbrasil, Varig, and **VASP** all fly to major cities in Brazil. **Varig** and **Transbrasil** fly direct to Miami. **Air France** flies to Paris.

Tourist Information

Official state tourist posts for **EMPETUR** are located at the airport (24 hours), the main **bus station** 7:00 a.m.–9:00 p.m. *and at the* **Casa da Cultura** Monday–Saturday 9:00 a.m.–8:00 p.m., Sunday 3:00 p.m.–8:00 p.m. The municipal tourist office is located at **Store #10**, in the **Pátio de São Pedro**. Ask for a copy of the *Historical Circuit of the City of Recife*, with an excellent map and tons of facts in English. Also, pick up the small brochure called *Viva Olinda*, which can give you some facts about the historical city.

Travel Agencies

Frevo
Rua Ant. Gomes de Freitas, 131 (Ilha do Leite); ☎ 222-3127.

When to Visit

Carnaval explodes in typical Northeastern fashion in February. Don't miss **Easter**, when the Passion is reenacted at Nova Jerusalém, a city theater surrounded by wooden walls, where 500 actors in 12 plays reenact Christ's Passion on a mobile stage. *Forró* music is featured during festivals in **June**, along with typical foods such as corn. In **July**, "*Vaqueiro*" worship, promoting the Northeastern cowboy culture, is celebrated. **August** has been dubbed Folklore Month, featuring native dances, expositions, ceramics, and poetry festivals.

NATAL

For the last four years, **Natal**, the capital of Rio Grande do Norte, has replaced Salvador and Maceió as the hot-spot resort of the Northeast. Despite years of drought and poverty, the city of more than 500,000 inhabitants is now attracting even São Paulo businessmen who are envisioning a future for the region, one full of exceedingly exotic sand dunes that some say were the inspiration for Antoine de Saint Exupéry's *The Little Prince*. Until 1983, the main beach drag, **Via Costeira**, was virtually empty; today it is the main tourist strip, with immense white sand dunes lining one side and modern hotels on the other. Despite its modernity, Natal still boasts beaches of pristine beauty, particularly those located north and south of the city. And it's here in Natal that you can find the best restaurant of Northeastern cuisine north of Bahia: **Raízes**

Thousands of years ago, Natal was just water and sand. As the African wind called *Vento Alisios* swept through the region, dunes were created and vegetation blew in from the sea. Consequently, *falesias* were formed, those mountainous red-colored cliffs that provide the craggy vistas overlooking the shore. Presently Natal and its surrounding beaches offer over 1,700 hectares of dunes, the veritable inspiration for breathtaking, dune-buggy adventures that are more exciting than roller coasters. Botanists have also identified over 350 kinds of vegetation, mostly *catinga*—forests of knotted dwarf trees and stunted bushes that support the structure of the dunes. Once Natal's largest dune, **Morro da Careca** (or Bald Hill, so named because it didn't have any vegetation) has sadly been degraded by the dune-sliding of teenagers down the slopes; today the sport has been prohibited by law.

Located on the easternmost tip of the South American continent, Natal was founded on Christmas Day, 1599, by the Portuguese, who had to wrestle it first from the Potangi Indians and later from the Dutch who had arrived in search of brazilwood. During World War II, Natal became known as the *"Trampolim da Vitória"* because American soldiers used the area to depressurize before going home. (The city was the site of the largest U.S. Air Force base outside its own territories.) Later, the Kennedys also became vogue. Downtown, a bust of JFK is accompanied by one of his quotes that still speaks so poignantly to Brazil: "If a free society cannot help the many who are poor, it will not be able to save the few who are rich."

A BIRD'S EYE VIEW

The treasures in Natal are the **sun and surf,** and there is little of historical value left in the 400-year-old city. A good place to grasp the expanse of the city's beaches is atop the **Mãe Luiza Lighthouse,** where you can see **Praia do Forte, Praia dos Artistas, and Praia do Meio,** as well as the rocky vista of **Praia da Areia Preta.** Dominating the entrance of the **Rio Potengi,** on whose banks Natal is situated, is the **Forte dos Reis Magos** *Tuesday–Sunday 8:00 a.m.–noon and 2:00 p.m.–5:00 p.m.,* founded in 1598 as a defense against marauding invaders. In the **Cidade Alta,** little remains of colonial times except for the small alleyways and squares, but of some interest is the 18th-century **Igreja de Santo Antônio.** (The bronze cock perched on the church's Moorish tower makes an ironic statement about the patron saint of marriage.) An obligatory stop for newcomers is the **Centro de Turismo,** housed in the old prison and now an enclave of artisan stores.

BEACHES IN NATAL

Natal's fine beaches begin in the city and extend north and south hundreds of kilometers. Even on rainy days, the windswept waves crashing against the reefs make for dramatic vistas. Natural reefs, which begin in front of the Othon Hotel, can be seen at low tide, but never swim beyond the second reef, as the open sea can often turn violent.

One of the first beaches developed in the city was **Praia dos Artistas**, the site of bohemian activity during the 1960s. Today the water is polluted, but surfers still enjoy the high waves, and a large crafts fair is held there from 4:00 p.m.–10:00 p.m. daily.

Six kilometers from downtown, **Praia do Forte** is the best beach for bathing, surrounded by voluptuous dunes and protected by reefs that form natural pools. The city's fortress is also located here. Between Praia dos Artistas and Praia do Forte, **Praia do Meio** is also protected by natural reefs and boasts a vital infrastructure for leisure. Grass-hut kiosks line the strand, and on New Year's Eve, a huge festival of *candomblé* is held around the sculpture of Iemenjá, created by Natal artist Jordão Arimatéia in 1985. On the far side of Praia do

Meio is **Praia Areia Preta**, known for the black rocks that form provocative grottoes and caves. A more residential area, the beach houses numerous bars serving excellent *coquetel de frutas* and *caipirinhas*.

The *in* beach lately is **Praia de Ponta Negra**, 8-1/2 miles from downtown on the southernmost strand within the city limits. Considered one of the Northeast's most beautiful, the strand features a small bay surrounded by tall dunes and palm trees. Luas at full moon are great fun, illuminated by bonfires and serenaded by improvising guitarists; down the strand nightclubs, bars, and restaurants keep the action tight. On Sunday, the streets are packed with young beautiful kids hanging out on their cars. Surfing is best near the **Morro da Careca**.

BEACHES NEAR NATAL

SOUTH

The best way to scope out the beaches south of the city is by boat. Schooner trips leave twice a day in high season near the dock at **Cotovelo beach.** Sailing north, you will pass **Barreira do Inferno** (where a rocket base is located), **Pirangi do Norte** (home to high-powered politicos), **Praia Pirangi do Sul** (a tiny fishing village) and the sophisticated condos of **Búzios.** Most schooner trips stop at *a natural pool, where bathers can jump off the boat and swim to a rocky outcropping in the middle of the ocean.* Due to the high winds of Natal, these trips can be a little lambada-like, with the waves as big and curvaceous as the dunes. (*For schooner information, contact Marina Badauê* ☎ *238-2066.*)

Before or after your schooner trip, stop at **Cotovelo Restaurante** *Praia de Pirangi;* ☎ *237-2020. Daily 10:00 a.m.–5:00 p.m.* for excellent *carne de sol* and grilled lobster. Wadeh Faraj, the hearty Lebanese owner, says he started this open-air restaurant—considered one of the most exotic in the Northeast—as a joke; he just wanted a place to drink with his friends. Today, the locale looks through a forest of palm trees onto a glorious ocean vista, where huge black boulders only add to the beauty. Senhor Wadeh is also building a series of chalets next to the restaurant (some with complete kitchens) that should prove paradisiacal accommodations—especially for families. You'll only need to scramble down a stone stairway or over the rocky cliff to get to the beach. A bus that stops at the restaurant transports guests to the marina, where you can catch an outgoing schooner.

Further Exploration: Don't miss the "**Largest Cashew in the World!**" in the villa of **Pirango do Norte**. The grove is a delicious spot to come after the beach—a mysterious *Secret Garden* of trees growing in the sand. On the ground, the grove's gnarly roots spread out like scary tentacles; up above, the branches have become interlocked into a leafy arbor that whistles in the wind and makes leaflike shadows on the sand below. The "world's largest" cashew tree is big, and information in English concerning its history can be found in the adjacent artisanry shop, where you can also see women making traditional lace. The amusing double-entendre signs adorning the grove have all been posted by the Tahiti Motel (an hourly hideaway for lovers), imploring you not to violate the trees by touching or walking over the roots. Down the road a fantastic view shows you in contrasting colors where the Rio Pirongi and the Atlantic Ocean meet.

NORTH

With access through RN 160, **Genipabú** is 22 miles from downtown, a pit stop for most dune buggy tours. Down the glorious (but these days, crowded) beach, you can either ride horseback, take a *jangada* trip on a flat-bottom boat, or rest in the shade of an open-air restaurant. Three miles north lies **Tabatinga**, reportedly full of jumping porpoises (though I didn't see a one), where you can stop for a drink on a cliff overlooking a magnificent dune-swept beach. The best time to come to the **Mirante** is at full moon, when the sea turns silvery and the grass-hut bars surrounded by coconut trees seem even more romantic. You'll find the **Mirante Turístico Bar** near the sign "Vista Panorâmica dos Golfinhos."

EXCURSION

DUNE BUGGY ADVENTURES

It's a cool windy day in Natal, and at the wheel of our 4-wheel-drive jeep is dune buggy owner **Zenilda Pinheiro**, the kind of bronzed, muscular, long-legged gal who wouldn't dare flinch on a bucking bronco. Zenilda can read the dunes of Natal like the curves of her husband's back, both of them long-time pros who know that the slope and texture of the dunes can shift in an instant. If you want an adventure to remember (and one you'll survive), you need experts like the Pinheiros.

The trip starts sane enough, then slowly gains in momentum. With the wind slicing our faces, we head out of Natal on the highway, crossing the Rio Potengi, bordered by a massive grove of *mangué*, a tropical ecosystem of tall trees rooted in water and chock full of crabs. The river from whose banks you can see the lights of Natal is itself a natural breeding ground for shrimp. (*Potengi* is Tupí-Guarani dialect for shrimp.) Though we're still within the city limits, we begin to pass traditional houses—pastel-colored shacks with orange-tiled roofs. After about 10 minutes, the famous dunes appear in the distance, voluptuous silver-gray mounds that seem almost ghostlike. Passing through the village of Santa Rita on Genipabú Beach, we watch fishermen cast their lines from rocky cliffs. Zenilda races the buggy near the edge of the shoreline, and as we lean out of the windows, we all get drenched.

At Genipabú Beach we pile out for a quick água-de-coco under the shade of the bar. From a native boy I rent a frisky horse and trot down the shoreline, barely staying upright when dune buggies full of drunken beachcombers zoom past me in the opposite direction. A braying burro plops in my path and I swerve to avoid hitting him. Passing up a ride on a *jangada*, we jump back in the jeep for the real rollercoaster ride. Zenilda gives us two choices: "*emocional*" or "*calma*" —referring to the level of thrill our stomachs can take. My friends, all Natal locals, argue for calm. We agree on medium.

Zenilda heads for the dunes outside Genipabú, when suddenly we feel like we're gliding on snow. In a minute, what had seemed like a straight plane quickly turns sideways as Zenilda tilts the buggy left, then right, jumping off cliffs, spiraling up and down the mounds. Screaming, we cling to the bars of the jeep as sand fills our hair, our eyes—and especially our mouths. Suddenly a lone native man appears like a mirage, holding a lassoed burro. For a buck, I ride the critter around for a few minutes. (Take even longer to mount —it's surprisingly easy to barrel over the ears of a burro.) After contemplating the crystal-blue lakes in the valley below, we climb back in the jeep as Zenilda steels her hands on the wheel for one last sensational dive—horizontally down a dune. Luckily, I've sat in the front; my companions in the back look dazed.

Our final stop is **Redinha Beach,** from where we can see the port and the old fort from one of the banks of the Potengi River. Less sensational than Genipabú, Redinha has nevertheless retained the charm of its quaint village life—an atmospheric destination for the urban crowds that pile in on the weekends. Before we take shelter under the roof of O Pedro, an open-air eatery, we make a stop at the tiny local church to say a few thanks for surviving. Then we settle down to enormous plates of *camarões na casca* (garlicky shrimps encased in their shells) and tall, cold glasses of *chopp*. The only thing left to do after celebrating is wash the sand off from every part of our bodies. Luckily, the ocean is a mere step away.

Insider Tip:

The sun in Natal is fierce, and exposure in a dune buggy is maximal. Make sure you generously dowse yourself with suntan lotion, and you should consider taking a hat that ties under your chin. Coverups that you can easily tie around your waist would also be helpful. On these cliff-hanging trips, be careful that your camera equipment doesn't fall out of the buggy.
*To contact the Pinheiros or other professional drivers, call **APCBA (Independent Association of Buggy Owners**) Rua João Pessoa, 267;* ☎ *235-1062. Or contact the state tourist office **EMPROTURN** Avenida Deofore, 249;* ☎ *221-1452.*

THE ESSENTIAL NATAL

WHERE TO STAY

Most of Natal's best hotels are located on the Via Costeira; if you don't have a car, you'll have to take a bus or cab to get to the main beaches. (The beaches along the hotel strip are too rocky to be safe for swimming.) Accommodations run from exceedingly comfortable resorts to less imaginative, but moderate-priced hotels. The most atmospheric properties are outside the city—in pousada-like digs that give you the best feel of tropical living.

Expensive -------------- **Over $80**

Moderate -------------- **$40–$70**

Inexpensive ------------ **Under $40**

★ Hotel Parque da Costeira

Via Costeira, kilometer 7 (Mãe Luísa Beach); ☎ *222-6147, FAX 222-1459*
From the street, the Parque da Costeira looks like a module from Venus. Inside, the white curvaceous columns separating the rooms more resemble the resorts on the Greek island of Mykonos. The pool area is the most spectacular in the city—with two saltwater pools and a double slide kids will adore. Even the tanning area is split into 3 sprawling levels that wrap around the hotel. Wicker furniture enlivens the fully air-conditioned rooms, all which have a fabulous view of the pool and the crashing sea. The owner, from São Paulo, attends constantly to creative details, especially in the indoor and outdoor restaurants, both of which offer fine cuisine. Keeping the feel of a beach resort, the hotel has no elevator for its 3 floors. Rooms range from $80 for doubles to $117 for suites. If you pay in cash during low season, you'll receive a 30 percent discount. 96 apartments. *Expensive. All cards.*

★ Vila do Mar

Via Costeira, 4233; ☎ *222-3755, FAX 222-8422*

Owned by the Secretary of Industry and Commerce, the Vila do Mar on Barreira d'Agua beach is one of Natal's finest resort hotels, gracefully integrating the natural resources of stone, wood, and plant life with the dunes and sea that surround it. Just walking to your room is a tropical adventure, past artificial lakes brimming with flowers. The simple, but stylish apartments have sitting verandas with spectacular views. The restaurant Tuaçu is an elegant dining room in pastel oranges and pinks, and the breakfast buffet is one of the best spreads in Natal—the freshly fried tapioca pancake shouldn't be missed. The large pool and children's pool, surrounded by coconut trees, provide ample space for tanning. A hair salon, sauna, masseur, tennis courts, and travel agency are also on premises. Singles start at $80, doubles $88, suites $161. 210 apartments. *Expensive. No cards.*

Marsol Natal
Via Costeira, 1567 (Parque das Dunas); ☎ *221-2619*

High wood-beam ceilings and traditional tile roofs make this 2-floor hotel a model of tropical comfort. A good-sized pool with a children's pool is surrounded by luscious vegetation, with grass-hut umbrellas for shade. Standards with stone floors are extremely small, with bathrooms barely big enough for essentials. Considerably more spacious, the deluxes, with brown tile floors and wood carvings, are attractive; you can even sleep in a hammock on the veranda. Luxurious suites, with a couch bed in the living room, are tailored for families. An arched-roof structure that takes advantage of the city's strong breezes houses a multipurpose game room; there's also a playground. The restaurant is well known for its typical foods, like *carne de sol* and *galinha à cabidela* (stewed giblets). A veranda inside the grass-roofed bar offers a excellent view of the pool and the ocean. Standard doubles start at $62, deluxe $86. Children up to age 5 free. 90 apartments. *Moderate. Cards: AE.*

Natal Mar
Via Costeira, 8101 (Ponta Negra); ☎ *219-2121, FAX 219-3131*

The first hotel to be built on the Via Costeira (1984), the Natal Mar exudes a friendly seaside ambiance; you'll feel totally surrounded by dunes and sea. Luxes look out onto the ocean, but standards have verandas that give a spectacular view of the sand dunes, especially at sunset. All apartments are air-conditioned, and come with color TV, 2 wicker chairs, and minibar. There is no elevator. A bar inside the circular pool, where you can sip tropical drinks, helps relieve the heat; you can also shade yourself under the grass-roofed umbrellas. The restaurant serves all 3 meals. Two boutiques, a playroom with pool, and a sauna complete the services. Double standards run about $58, deluxes $67. 176 apartments. *Moderate. All cards.*

Barreira Roxa Praia Hotel
Via Costeira, kilometer 5 (Mãe Luîsa); ☎ *222-1093*

Once the governor's house, the Barreira Roxa Praia was later transformed into a school of tourism, but now functions solely as a private hotel. All the apartments are enormous, slightly resembling college dorm rooms, with little decoration. The 42 air-conditioned apartments contain color TV, minibar, and video; safes at the reception. All beds are singles and must be put together to make a double. The restaurant, integrated into the 2-story lobby under high-beamed ceilings, looks inviting. The pool has a sunny disposition. Standard doubles run about $41, deluxe doubles $47. 42 apartments. *Moderate. Cards: AE, MC.*

Praia Center Hotel
Rua Fabricio Pedrosa, 45 (Praia dos Artistas); ☎ *222-6764*

Two years old, this hotel is centrally located, near Praia dos Artistas. Breakfast is taken downstairs in a covelike salon overlooking the pool. Air conditioning is cold, but rooms are on the smallish side. Suites are the best deal with two rooms and extra space. 35 apartments. *Moderate. Cards: AE, MC.*

Outside the City
★ Pousada Vila do Sol
Loteamento Tabu, QD 9 (Genipabú); ☎ *225-2132*

Owned by a young American named Ron whose hippie parents moved to Brazil in the 1950s, this moon-shaped pousada is located on Rio Ceara Mim where the river meets the sea. Entranced by the unusual ecological conditions, beachcombers love to walk here because there is no pollution and you can even catch crabs by hand in the nearby *mangue* (mangrove swamp). The basic 15 apartments are fan-cooled, with tile floors and private baths; the daily rate includes breakfast. Restaurants are about half a mile walk to Genipabú beach, or the pousada will transport you to Genipabú Hotel for a fine dinner. A lot of employees from the American Embassy in Brasília come here in July, but most guests are Brazilians. Doubles are $30 in high season, with a 20 percent discount in low season, Fielding's readers 30 percent discount. 12 apartments. *Inexpensive.* Cards: AE.

Genipabú

Highway to Genipabú; ☎ *221-5672. Reservations:* ☎ *221-6378*

Located 2 kilometers from the center of the village of Genipabú, this hotel is a fabulous option for families or anyone in search of tropical tranquility. Situated on a hill surrounded by dunes and groves of trees, the hotel is more like an upper-class pousada, dominated by a racing-size pool shaded by grass umbrellas. Apartments, complete with verandas, are either spacious doubles or duplexes with 3 beds in the lower level. The chic native style is carried through the lounge and restaurant with its wicker furniture, woven rugs, and folkloric paintings. Nearby, beaches may be reached with the help of the hotel's jeep, or you may roam the countryside on horseback. The Brazilian-Japanese owner, who speaks English, and her French husband lend their charming personalities to the homey ambiance and will fill any reasonable requests. Buses leave for downtown every hour, and free airport transfers are provided. Standard doubles run about $47. Fielding's readers receive a 50 percent discount. 24 apartments. *Moderate–inexpensive. All cards.*

WHERE TO EAT

Except for the restaurant Raízes, Natal is not particularly noted for outstanding cuisine. Due to electrical problems, food is often served lukewarm, and meat, if ordered rare, nearly always arrives "medium." Fish in this seaside town is your best bet, but excellent *carne de sol* can be found at the restaurant aptly named Carne de Sol.

Expensive -------------- **Over $10**

Moderate --------------- **$5–$10**

Inexpensive ------------ **Under $5**

★ Raízes

Avenida Campos Sales, 609 (Petrópolis); ☎ *222-7338. Daily 11:30 a.m.–3:00 p.m., 6:00 p.m.–11:00 p.m., closed Sunday.*

Perhaps the best native kitchen in the Northeast, Raízes is a must for those daring enough to try the almost forgotten art of Northeastern cuisine. The native-born owner, who spent 20 years in the south, finally came home to revive the kind of food he'd eaten at his grandfather's home. The chic native decor, folkloric paintings, and traditional shutters provide a warm counterpart to delicacies such as *carne de sol*, *canjica* (a dessert with corn and coconut milk that takes all day to prepare), and *carimã* (sun-dried cakes of pressed manioc). Start with a *mangaba* fruit cocktail (it will need sugar), then follow up with lamb or *carne de sol* (dried salted meat). A treat here is the *manteiga do sertão*, a cholesterol-laden liquid butter that looks like congealed fat but is frighteningly delicious. À la carte dishes run $4–$12. Many come just for Café Sertanejo ($6), which includes an impressive buffet of sweets and breads. During high season, poets known as *cantadores* or *repentistas* go tableside, improvising bawdy songs and stories about the guests. After-dinner liqueurs, especially the *cajú* (cashew), are delicious. An excellent deal is the buffet for $8. Children under 5 are free; children 5–12 are half price. *Moderate. All cards.*

Camarões Restaurant
Avenida Eng. Roberto Freire, 2610 (Ponta Negra); ☎ *219-2424. Daily 11:30 a.m.–4:00 p.m., 6:00 p.m.–midnight, closed Monday, only Sunday lunch.*
Sit on the veranda overlooking Ponta Negra Beach or inside this fan-cooled restaurant with white brick walls and a few greens to offset the red tablecloths. The specialty is shrimp—15 kinds—from *gratinado* (broiled under fire) to *empanado* (fried with flour). Try *camarões ao champagne* flambéed with champagne or the *camarão sertanejo*, sauteed with herbs and *nata do sertão*, a typical regional butter. As with most restaurants in Natal, dessert concludes with Italian ice cream concoctions. *Moderate. All cards.*

Xique Xique
Avenida Afonso Pena, 444 (Petrópolis); ☎ *222-4426. Daily 11:00 a.m.–4:00 p.m. and 6:00 p.m.–midnight, closed Sunday.*
Would-be plantation owners will love this white colonial house with its calm, sophisticated ambiance and top-class service. The folk paintings of Nilton Navarro make a fine setting for such seaside delicacies as *delícias do mar*, a delicate broth of lobster, fish, and shrimp. *Risoto de polvo* (with octopus) is excellent as is the Lobster Thermidor (even if the menu's pigeon English translates it as "with ketchup"). Entrées, which also include chicken and pasta, range from $7–$12. Before or after dining, sip a tropical cocktail on the veranda. *Moderate. All cards.*

★ Marenosso
Rua Aderbal de Figueiredo (Centro de Turismo) (Petrópolis); ☎ *221-4022. Daily Monday–Saturday 11:00 a.m.–7:00 p.m., Friday 11:00 a.m.–11:00 p.m.*
Located in the Centro de Turismo (the arts and crafts market), this restaurant opens its traditional green-shuttered windows to the sea, with golden corn fields waving in the foreground. Regional food like *carne de sol*, *paçoca* (a dish made of meat with manioc meal), and *galinha ao molho pardo* (chicken cooked in its own blood) are specialties. Every Thursday night, a *forró* dance with big band kicks in from 10:00 p.m.–2:30 a.m. In high season, folkloric dances are held every afternoon at 3:30 p.m. and at night in the inner courtyard. Taxis are usually waiting outside the market. *Moderate. All cards.*

Chaplin
Avenida Pres. Café Filho, 27 (Praia dos Artistas); ☎ *222-0217. Daily 11:00 a.m.–2:00 a.m.*
Dedicated to Chaplin memorabilia, this restaurant overlooking Artist's Beach is as elegant as Natal gets; in fact, anyone who's anyone comes for happy hour. The dining room upstairs is air-conditioned and serves an international menu starting at $6. Specialty is shrimp à Greta Garbo flambéed in a salmon bisque. Beef and chicken dishes are prepared with similar élan. You can also sit outside on the windy veranda for beer and hors d'oeuvres. *Moderate. All cards.*

Calamari
Praia dos Artistas. Daily 11:00 a.m.–midnight, Saturday till 2:00 a.m.
Room to dance at this informal open-air eatery with live music Sunday afternoon and Tuesday and Saturday nights. Lobster runs about $15; the house shrimp is cooked empanada style, with Greek-style rice, cheese puré, and rice for about $8. The location on Artist's Beach is central, in the area of Rua Governador Silva Pedrosa. *Moderate. No cards.*

Nemésio
Rua Rodrigues Alves, 546 (Petrópolis); ☎ *222-4658. Daily noon–3:00 p.m., 6:00 p.m.–midnight, closed Sunday.*
The only place that serves codfish in Natal, this wood-beamed restaurant with rustic chandeliers offers Spanish-flavored cuisine at moderate prices. Sangria arrives in large jars, a mixture of chilled red wine and tropical fruits. Spanish paella for two at $24 is extremely good, as is the *Pupurry Marinho*, a potpourri of fish, lobster, oysters, and fish for about $10. A grand piano provides music nightly. *Moderate. All cards.*

Italia '90
Praia dos Artistas
The waiters are young and flirty at this beachside, all-you-can eat pizza-and-pastaria, with posters of Sophia Loren sobbing on the strand. Simple chairs, wood ta-

bles—the only thing missing is a real view, but for $4, the all-inclusive price can't be beat. Afterwards, walk catty-corner to **Gelare** *Avenida Gov. Silvio Pedroza, 134* an Italian ice cream parlor with 31 types of sundaes, including one with champagne. Eat it in or take it out. "Para viajar" means "to go." *Inexpensive. No cards.*

Carne de Sol
Rua Dionisio Filgueira, 799;
☎ *222-9627. Daily 6:00 p.m.–last client, weekends 10:00 a.m.– 4:00 a.m.*
Walking distance from Praia dos Artistas, this stone-floor, open-air restaurant has a *piaçava*—a typical straw roof made from palm trees. The menu is nearly unilateral: *carne de sol* and *frango de sol* but famous citywide. The meats are salted and left to dry for a week, then grilled with *manteiga da terra*, a cholesterol-laden butter that easily becomes addictive. One portion, big enough for two, comes with french fries. The house style here is to stuff the *carne de sol* with cheese, which makes it exceedingly tasty. *Inexpensive. All cards.*

A Macrobiótica
Rua Princesa Isabel, 524 (Centro);
☎ *222-0217. Daily 11:00 a.m.–2:00 p.m.*
Macrobiotic regime for lunch only. *Inexpensive. No cards.*

NIGHTLIFE

The best nightclub is located at the **Natal Othon Hotel** *Avenida Presidente Café Filho, 822;* ☎ *222-2140. Thursday, Friday, Saturday 11:00 p.m.–4:00 a.m.*
The most popular dance hall for lambada can be found at **Mandacaru** *Avenida do Jiqui, 201 (Neópolis);* ☎ *217-3008* across from the Shopping Center Cidade Jardim. A 1-hour folkloric show features young sexy dancers who actually look like they're having a good time. Order wine, drinks, and hors d'oeuvres before you're pulled up to dance. Weekends are crowded, maybe because of the neon Love Motel sign that blinks in the background.
To dance *forró*, the native dance of the Northeast, head for **Casa da Música Popular Brasileira** *Rua 25 de Dezembro (Praia do Meio);* ☎ *222-6277. Friday and Saturday 9:00 p.m.–4:00 a.m.*

SPIRITUALISM

For several generations, the family of **Dona Jânia** has dedicated itself to a form of spiritualism in which troubled departed spirits are healed through group intervention. Only Portuguese is spoken, but if you contact the family directly, they may let you attend one of their sessions. The work, done with impressive commitment, is performed free of charge. For more information contact **Jânia Góis de Muora** *Rua Dr. Luiz Antônio, 500 (Natal);* ☎ *222-7425.*

SHOPPING

Housed in the antiquated house of detention, the **Centro de Turismo do Natal** *Rua Aderbal de Figueiredo, 1976* now encloses the city's major arts and crafts enclave. Most of the small stores (housed in the original cellblocks) accept credit cards, though you're better off paying in cash. Traditional buys include wicker baskets and hats made out of *palha* (straw), as well as *feijoada* earthenware. *Nas coxinhas*—small phallic symbols made out of clay—are hot items here, as are tiny bottles of *cachaça* with pornographic labels. In the art gallery upstairs, antique sculptures of Catholic saints (which can be custom-made) make memorable purchases, as do *cordels*, the Northeast's version of dime-store novels.
Few tourists head downtown for shopping, but there are some artisan *barracas* across the street from Praça JFK.

HANDS-ON NATAL

Airlines

Varig
Avenida João Pessoa, 308; ☎ *221-1535.*
VASP
Avenida João Pessoa, 220; ☎ *222-7500.*
Transbrasil
Avenida Deodoro, 363; ☎ *221-1895.*

Arrival

The local airport **Aeroporto Augusto Severo** *Rua Eduardo Gomes;* ☎ *272-2811* is located about 9 miles from the center of town.

Taxis are plentiful.
The main bus station **Rodoviária** is located some distance from town at *Rua Capitão-Mór Gouveia, 1237;* ☎ *231-1170.* Catch local buses into town on the far side of the street; those marked "*Via Costeira*" (the principal beach drag) run along the southern coast to Ponta Negro Beach.

Car Rental
Dudu
Avenida Rio Branco, 420 (downtown); ☎ *222-4144.* Also at the airport.

Climate
The highest temperature in summer is about 84°F, with constant winds cooling the air. Winter is so-named not because of a drop in temperature but because it is more likely to rain. Because of its proximity to the Equator (three degrees), the city enjoys up to 15 hours of sunlight daily.

Tourist Agency
Natal Tur
Avenida Deodoro, 424; ☎ *(84)222-5401, FAX 221-5956* offers city tours, as well as trips to the more exotic beaches, such as Jenipabú, Litoral Sul, Praia de Pipa, and Praia Maria.

Tourist Information
The **Center of Tourism** (Centro de Turismo) *Rua Aderbal de Figueiredo, 980 (Petrópólis);* ☎ *231-6729* is situated in the old prison on the top of the hill overlooking the city. Brochures, maps, and assistance (sometimes in English) can be found Monday–Saturday 2:00 p.m.–8:00 p.m. There is also an enclave of artisan stores and a lively restaurant. Information booths are also located at the airport.
EMPROTURN (the state tourist board) is located at *Avenida Deofore, 249;* ☎ *221-1452.*

512 FIELDING'S BRAZIL 1994

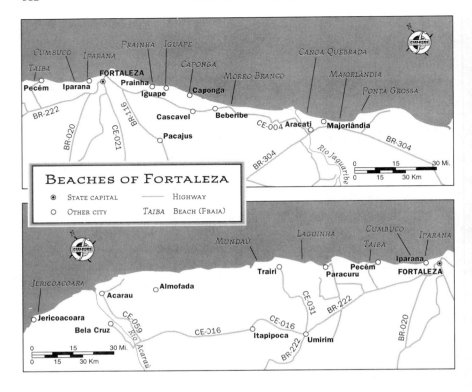

FORTALEZA

Like many of the states in the Northeast, the state of **Ceará** has long been subject to the hard facts of water—the deadly absence of it in the interior and the glorious abundance along the Atlantic Coast. Ever since its colonization in the late 18th century, the state has been the victim of severe droughts that parched the *sertão* and left millions of people starving and desperate for livelihood. And yet in one of those ironies of nature, Ceará also boasts some of the most beautiful beaches in all of the Northeast—almost 400 coastal miles of swaying palm trees, multi-colored sand dunes, dramatic cliffs, and rocky coves formed by the eternal rush of sea and air. No matter how stunning the natural resources are, however, it's in the gentle coastal fishing villages where the true spirit of Ceará can be felt. Village women, famous for their delicate artistry, still fashion lacework from century-old patterns while their fishermen husbands sail out to sea on homemade *jangadas*, their fishing nets resembling enormous silvery spider webs against the azure-blue sea.

The capital of Ceará is **Fortaleza**, by far its largest metropolis in the Northeast, with over 2 million inhabitants. With perpetual sunshine and an exciting nightlife, the city rates as one of the best resort cities in the country. But wealth and poverty co-exist closely here, and homeless beggars can be frequently seen asking for money. Since most of the beaches are polluted on the eastern shore, many tourists head out to the beaches beyond the city limits for swimming and such exotic adventures as dune surfing. Within the city, however, even the polluted beachfronts are the site of continuous activity, with tourists crowding the arts and crafts fair along **Avenida Presidente Kennedy** or settling into one of the numerous *barracas* and bars for a plate of fried crab legs and *chopp*. *Not to be missed is the return of the local fishermen from the open sea (around 4:00 p.m.), when they dock their jangadas, roll up their nets, and clean their daily catch right on the beach.*

HISTORY

The first inhabitants of the Cearense region—the **Tabajara Indians**—did not easily give up their territory to the first Portuguese settlers, who arrived in 1603. In fact they killed and ate the first bishop (a fate the laity in Belém shared as well). The **Dutch** forced the remaining

Portuguese out in 1637 and erected a fortress against the natives in 1639. Seventeen years later, the **Portuguese** returned in victory, founding their own fort (Fortaleza means "fortress"), around which a settlement grew.

Independent political fortitude has continued to mark Cearense history. In 1824, Fortaleza was one of the few places where the continental Portuguese tried to quell the growing Brazilian independence movement, massacring the local patriots before being decimated themselves several months later. The state of Ceará was also the first to **abolish slavery** (although the absence of sugar plantations and the low number of blacks tended to make the noble act seem somewhat less than sacrificial). As Fortaleza became prosperous at the end of the 19th century, the backlands of Ceará also gained national prominence when a humble parish priest, **Padre Cícero Romão Batista**, effected a seeming miracle when the communion wafer he was administering to one of his flock turned to blood in her mouth. Overnight, the dusty village of **Juazeiro** became the site of religious pilgrimages while Padre Cícero himself came to be worshipped as a near saint, despite the Church's attempt to quell his religious influence. Until his death in 1934, Padre Cícero maintained intense political power, and at one point his followers even marched on Fortaleza and brought about the downfall of the state. Today, the city of Fortaleza remains a destination for thousands of migrants who arrive from the dusty, parched interior looking for a better life.

SIGHTS

The best **view** of the city is situated on a cliff overlooking the twinkling lights of

Conjunto Santa Teresinha. Below the rocky embankment lies a lower–class neighborhood from where the sounds of *candomblé* drums can be heard deep into the night. Atop the cliff is a complex of open–air restaurants frequented by the cognoscenti, who enjoy the terrific view, the fabulous sunsets, and the cool, windy nights. Here, at the

Mirante Restaurant *Daily 6:00 p.m.-midnight, closed Monday.* you can sit under a tiled roof or on the romantic terrace overlooking the hill; just don't miss the huge phallic–like totem in the back room. Specialties here come *na telha* (baked in a clay boat) but if you're brave, order the *arraia*, a special fish said to be decended from an underwater bat. Also in the area is the **Mirante Bar**, with a stunning view of the ocean and the city's port. The trip by car from **Avenida Presi-**

dente Kennedy takes about 10 minutes (I don't suggest walking because you'll have to pass through lower–class *bairros*, though the cityscape from this perspective can be quite enlightening). Taxis are usually waiting outside the restaurant for the return trip.

BEACHES IN FORTALEZA

The good news in Fortaleza is that at least 19 beaches can be found along its eastern and southern shores, as well as points beyond the city limits. The bad news is that most of the inner–city beaches (with the exception of **Praia do Futuro**) are now too polluted to accommodate swimmers. This doesn't stop the continuous promenade of tourists down the still–picturesque strands; they come to watch the sun set, contemplate the dramatic rocky vistas, embark on *jangada* trips, and cruise the art and crafts fair that is held nightly along Avenida Presidente Kennedy.

The city's most traditional beach is **Praia de Iracema**, located 10 minutes from downtown at the beginning of Avenida Presidente Kennedy. The rocky landscape acts as a natural breakwater, though swimming is not suggested. A few kilometers south is **Praia do Meirles**, where the majority of hotels are located. The artisan fair is held here along Avenida Presidente Kennedy.

Further east, *jangada* sails, lobster boats, and the movement of local fishermen make colorful activity at **Praia do Mucuripe**. Photo ops abound around 4:00 p.m., when the fishermen, mostly residents from the poor *bairro* on top of the hill, return from the open sea and sort through their day's catch. Not surprisingly, most of the best fish restaurants are located here, as is a statue of Iracema, considered the folkloric mother of Ceará, in front of the Yacht Club.

On the eastern coast of the city, **Praia do Futuro** runs 5 kilometers long from Avenida Zezé Diogo to Clube Caça e Pesca. Crowded on the weekends, "Future Beach" is the only city beach where you can swim. Every few yards you'll find open–air bars, restaurants, and hotels that serve excellent crabs, fried fish, and the best *batidas*.

Located where the Ceará River empties into the Atlantic Ocean, **Praia da Barra do Ceará** is a lovely stretch of sand and an excellent place to take a boat ride.

Excursions: The travel agency **MARTUR** *Avenida Presidente Kennedy, 4301;* ☎ *244-6203* offers schooner trips disembarking from Beira–Mar 100 meters from the Statue of Iracema. Two–hour boat trips also leave from Mucuripe and go to Praia Mansa, where you jump off the boat and spend about 20 minutes on the small, deserted beach. The best time to go is between 10:00 a.m. and noon, or for the sunset cruise at 4:00 p.m. The cost is about $10. Diving courses and fishing expeditions can also be arranged.

BEACHES BEYOND FORTALEZA

An alternative to the city beaches is the more commercially developed **Beach Park**, located 12-1/2 miles from Avenida Beira Mar. A brainchild of 2 Brazilian entrepreneurs who fell in love with Florida's Wet 'n Wild, this complex features its own exquisite beach *and* a massive water park with wave pools and slides. Equipment for all water sports (including ultraleves, jetski buggies, kayaks, and surfboards) can also be rented. *Barracas* line the strand, employing enthusiastic young boys as waiters, and a good restaurant offers a cool refuge from the sun. An interesting boutique hawks overpriced bathing suits, T-shirts, and practically the only M&Ms I ever saw in Brazil. No regular buses come here; you'll have to hire a private car or take an excursion through a travel agency.

Fifty-four miles north of Fortaleza lies **Morro Branco**, one of the most publicized beaches in the country due to a TV soap opera in the early 1980s. The original settlement sprang up among petrified dunes, and today has become famous for its natural springs, monazitic sand, and spectacular *jangada* rides over red, yellow, white, black, and gray-tinted dunes. (The bottled sand paintings you see in crafts stores come from this region.) During high season, four daily buses leave from the Fortaleza terminal (note that the 2-1/2 hour trip will be hot, crowded, and uncomfortable). Dune buggies can be hired for sightseeing at the restaurants fronting the beach.

Excellent for camping is **Praia da Lagoinha** *(Litoral Norte)*, about 62 miles from Fortaleza. Full of coconut trees, the beach gets its name from the small, but very deep lake surrounded by dunes. The minimal infrastructure includes only two pousadas and very simple restaurants.

Down the Litoral Sul, 100 miles from Fortaleza, is **Praia da Canoa Quebrada**, in the municipal of **Aracatí**—a favorite resort among Europeans. During the 1960s, people from the interior moved to this paradisiacal retreat in search of tranquility, remaining to this day in harmony with the native Potangi Indians. Buses that go to the village are always met by local dune buggies.

A mere 177 miles from Fortaleza lies one of the most beautiful beaches in all Brazil. Now the in-spot of the Northeast, **Jericoacoara** mixes the starkness of the *sertão* with the voluptuousness of wind-swept dunes that reflect a rainbow of colors at sunset. Here, the dramatic sea carves masterful designs into the rocky formations already sculptured by thousands of years of wind and surf. The fisherman's village still retains its local charm, though there are many bars to waste away hours and a very famous hall to see real *forró* dancers in action.

As it usually goes with most elite beaches in Brazil, Jericoacoara is not easy to get to. It's possible to take a local bus to **Gijoca**, but the trip will take at least 8 hours since the driver stops at every village on the way. Best to sign up for a private excursion that includes direct transportation and 2-night accommodations in simple pousadas. The **Hippopotamus Pousada** provides transportation from Fortaleza Friday-Sunday and Tuesday-Thursday for a $53 inclusive rate. (In Fortaleza contact **Hippopotamus Turismo** *Avenida Santos Dumont, 2459;* ☎ *244-9191.*) Also, the **Pousada Matusa** offers a similar transfer with accommodation package, including horsebackriding, diving, and dune buggying. Contact in Fortaleza **Matusa Turismo** *Avenida Dom Luís, 383, sala 2;* ☎ *240-6500.*

It's also possible to stay at the simple dwellings of fishermen. Offer them some money and they'll probably show you to a hammock strung up on their porches. If you go this route, you'll have to rent your own dune buggy to get around; lots of Toyotas are usually waiting at the bus station.

EXCURSION

DUNE SURFING

Anyone with a yen for scaling the dunes should head for **Cumbuco Beach**, 45 minutes from Fortaleza. Despite its rapid development in the past years, the beach has retained its natural beauty, with coconut palms peppering the dunes and wild pigs strolling along the shoreline. Settle in under the shaded roof of the restaurante **Sol e Sol** for a *bolinho de camarão* (a shrimp roll) and a quick *caipirinha*, then hire a dune buggy (and driver) for a screaming-meemies adventure over the rolling sand dunes. The buggies stop along the **Lagoa de Banana**, where a mule team will be waiting; if you want to ride, tip the muleteer, but be careful getting on (I would have fallen right over the mule's ears if the muleteer hadn't pulled me back by my belt). The *pièce de resistance* of this trip is the dune surfing over a substantial hill that requires the participant to stop himself just seconds before falling into a glorious azure lake—takers are thrown a rope to drag themselves back up the hill. Most people go tumbling into the lake, but I once saw a talented native boy stop on a dime at the foot of the hill. Even if you don't want to dune–surf yourself, the scenery alone is spectacular, and just watching the bikini–clad surfers is always a riot. After the excursion, head back to the **Sol e Sol Restaurant** for a large plate of *mariscos*, fried crab claws, or a fine grilled lobster for a mere $10. *Pargo frito* is a huge fried fish suitable for two because it has few bones. If you decide to stay in Cumbuco, the **Hotel Tendas do Cumbuco**, ☏ *231-5249 or 224-1670,* comes highly recommended. Nearby, the village women offer a variety of handmade crafts.

Getting There

The easiest way to experience Cumbuco is to book a day–excursion through a local travel agency. Otherwise, you'll have to catch a bus to **Caucaia** at the *Praça Estação* in Fortaleza, then catch another bus to Cumbuco (which runs every 3 hours). Thirty minutes beyond Cumbuco is one of Fortaleza's most exotic beaches— **Taíba** —a fishermen's village where at ebb tide visitors can enter the numerous grottoes hollowed out in the rocks by the sea. The mile-high dunes here are separated from the sandy coastal plains by blue lagoons surrounded by greenery. At twilight, the landscape turns lunar as the mountainous dunes and craters form mysterious shadows under the illumination of the moon.

Safety Tips for Dune Buggy Drivers:

Unless you're an expert, driving your own buggy over these dunes can be treacherous. Even Brazilians on weekend joy-rides have tipped over. Note that only 4–wheel drive and special tires can safely navigate these beaches. And remember to cross rivers only at ebb tide because the mouths become too broad and deep to traverse at high tide. If your dune buggy does get bogged down, lower the pressure of the rear tires. Never speed on a beach, and when driving over dunes, don't go over 12 miles per hour; the sun creates optical illusions, flattening out the slopes.

THE ESSENTIAL FORTALEZA

WHERE TO STAY

Most of the best hotels in Fortaleza are located along Avenida Presidente Kennedy; unfortunately most of the beaches here have been polluted from overuse. You'll save a few dollars with smaller hotels and pousadas a few blocks away. If you prefer more rustic accommodations in fishing villages outside the city, head for beaches like Cumbuco or Jericoacoara.

Esplanada Praia Hotel
Avenida Presidente J. Kennedy, 2000 Meireles); ☎ *244-8555, FAX 244-8555*
You'll find the Varig crew staying at this top 5-star, located on Meireles Beach, the city's main drag, close to the hub of Fortaleza's nightlife. The sprawling lobby, full of abstract art and modern tapestries, is split-level, with various areas bordered by leather chrome chairs and massive couches. The spacious apartments all have tubs and sport magnificent verandas that look onto the ocean; standards and superiors differ only in the size of the balcony. The reception and corridors are not air-conditioned, though the rooms are well cooled. The coffee shop offers a fine breakfast (including hard-to-find cornflakes) and overlooks the sea. Pool, beauty salon, and boutiques are also on premises. Ask in advance for an airport transfer. Superior doubles run $90, exec suites $207. 244 apartments. *Expensive. All cards.*

Imperial Othon Hotel
Avenida Presidente J. Kennedy, 2500 (Meireles); ☎ *244-9197*
This 5-star Othon located on Meireles Beach isn't as luxurious as similar Othons further south, but it does provide a full array of services and entertainment. During high season, a special *lazer* girl whips ups aerobic classes and parties, and a winding staircase from the tree-lined pool area leads to an underground mall of boutiques and crafts stores. There's also a beauty salon, sauna, and nightclub, and a doctor on 24-hour call. Standards are decorated simply with white walls, white spreads, and red rugs; more preferred are the larger deluxes with wonderful sea views. Bathrooms are luxurious. Every floor has a small living room, though not air-conditioned; neither is the lobby. The pleasant coffee shop, with a veranda overlooking the sea, also functions for dinner and a well-received folkloric show nightly. Thirty percent discount offered Friday-Sunday, 10 percent in low season. 264 apartments. *Expensive. All cards.*

Hotel Praia Centro
Avenida Mons Tabosa, 740 (Iracema); ☎ *211-9644, FAX 252-3501*
A few blocks from Iracema beach, the Praia Centro is a spiffy, well-serviced hotel with a remarkable mid-range rate. Sunsets from the rooftop pool area are so spectacular that even nonguests should drop by for a drink. Standards are not only attractive but surprisingly ample; deluxes are not substantially bigger. The piano bar with live bands is a reasonable place to hang out at night; live music accompanies lunch and dinner. *Feijoada* is served on Monday from 10:00 p.m.-3:00 a.m. Doubles range from $70-$90. 190 apartments. *Moderate-Expensive. All cards.*

★ Colonial Praia Hotel
Rua Br. de Aracati, 145 (Meireles); ☎ *211-9644, FAX 252-3501*
This 4-star, with its white stucco walls, graceful arches, and tiled roof has the charm and repose of a country pousada. A tropical garden shades the attractive, but irregular-shaped pool and children's pool, set far back from the bustle of city traffic. Standards and deluxes differ only in location; none have views. Colorful woven bedspreads coordinate tastefully with the brown carpet and exposed brick walls; bathrooms are small but clean, with hot and cold water. Tennis courts are available to clients. The restaurant serves all three meals. Standard doubles run about $50, deluxe doubles $52. 99 apartments. *Moderate. All cards.*

★ Hotel Praia Verde
Avenida Dioguinho, 3860 (Praia do Fu-

turo), 16 kilometer; ☎ 234-5233
Situated on Future Beach, this is one of Fortaleza's best bets, with medium–range rates, 5–star service, and a 2–level architecture that resembles a resort. The lobby is a breezy sprawl of white couches and marble, dominated by a wild carving of a nature spirit emerging from a piece of bark. The beautiful pool area is shaded by palm trees and graced by a voluptuous, but tortured statue of Iemanjá. A small intimate bar offers live music in high season. The pleasant, air–conditioned apartments differ only in view. *Luxe vento* ($41) has a view of the dune and lots of wind; *luxe dunas* ($57) has only dunes, and the *luxe* ($81) has a sea view obscured by palm trees. A small mall holds several boutiques, hair salon, tapestry store, and travel agency. There is no elevator. During low season, all clients receive a 30 percent discount. During high season, Fielding's readers receive a 20 percent discount. Across the street is the great musical bar Chico e Caranguejo. 150 apartments. *Moderate. All cards.*

Samburá Praia
Avenida Presidente Kennedy, 4530 (Meireles); ☎ 224-8929
The small homey lobby has a tiled floor, framed by leather and woodframe couches and a protecting saint. Standards ($47) are small, with no view; deluxes ($52) look to the sea, superiors ($47) have a side view. The best bets are rooms with two windows, from where you can look down on the fishing villages. Little decoration adorns the air-conditioned rooms except a color TV and minibar, but they are spunky clean. The pool is tiny, but located next to a covered area with a fantastic view of the fishing huts and sea. There's a very attractive, if slightly kitschy restaurant. Low season discounts can range up to 40 percent. 35 apartments. *Moderate. All cards.*

St. Tropez des Tropiques
Avenida dos Coqueiros, 4000; ☎ 211-9644. *(Write to Hotel Colonial Praia, see address above.)*
Now reopening with its own freshwater lake, this rustic complex of grass–hut chalets on its own exquisite, deserted beach offers attractive accommodations that can sleep 4. Unless you have wheels, you'll be dependent on the hotel's kitchen for meals, but spending the day slunk in a hammock or sipping a drink in the open–air bar couldn't prove all bad. The hotel is a favorite among the French, for whom Air France arranges direct flights. *Moderate. All cards.*

Hotel Nossa Pousada
Avenida da Abolição, 2600; ☎ 261-4699
This budget–styled property doesn't exactly retain the charm of a pousada, but its prices are low. Rooms are carpeted and include a minibar, but you must pay extra for TV. Showers have no curtain and practically rain down on the toilet. Breakfast is included, though the room is not spectacularly clean. Its prime advantage is that it's located one block from the beach. Twenty-five percent discounts are available in low season. Apartments with air–conditioning run $28, with fan $19. 20 apartments. *Inexpensive. All cards.*

Turismo Praia Hotel
Avenida Presidente Kennedy, 894; ☎ 231-6133
The Turismo Praia is only recommended for those on a minute budget or blessed with a backpacker's mentality. Rooms are small and the minibar rusty, but the bathrooms are tolerable. All have air–conditioning and phones. One person runs $24, 2 persons $34; with 20 percent discount during low season. *Inexpensive. No cards.*

WHERE TO EAT

Expensive ------------- **Over $15**

Moderate -------------- **$6–$15**

Inexpensive ----------- **Under $5**

O Alfredo
Avenida Presidente Kennedy, 4616 (Mucuripe); ☎ 261-3818. *Daily 11:00 a.m.– 1:00 a.m.*
A popular open–air fisheria on the main beach drag, from where you can watch fishermen arrive with their day's catch, as well as sailboats struggling to stay afloat. A nice

grilled fish runs about $6. Try the *peixada*, fish, potato, and vegetable in a thin souplike sauce, or the *ensopado*, more like a stew. *Moderate. No cards.*

Peixada do Meio
Avenida Presidente Kennedy (Mucuripe), 4632; ☎ *224-2719. Daily 11:00 a.m.–2:00 a.m.*
Practically the same restaurant and menu as O Alfredo next door, but with the added oomph: hanging fish nets and a tiny waterfall with lobster cages. Lobsters run about $15. Steaks and chicken are also available, but take a leap and try the *Peixe Big Surpresa*: fish stuffed in a fried crust full of shrimp and cheese. *Moderate. No cards.*

La Trattoria
Rua dos Pacajus, 125; (Iracema); ☎ *252-3666. Daily 6:00 p.m.-midnight, Sunday 11:00 a.m.-2:00 p.m., 4:00 p.m.-midnight*
A charming Italian adega where the waiter's shirts match the red–and–white tablecloths. Italian–born owner Alfio claims he started the city's first Italian restaurant 13 years ago because the "Cearenses didn't have any food." At least you won't go hungry now: the garlic bread is delicious, 12 kinds of pizza are cooked in a brick oven over natural fire, and the *antipasti diversi*—a fantastic buffet of about 30 dishes—can be a complete meal for about $3. Best bet for two is to order an antipasto plate, split a lasagna, and go for the marvelous desserts, like the *cassata*, ice cream with crystallized fruit and liqueur, drizzled with chocolate. Reserve on weekends. Some American friends love the bar next door, named Casbar. *Moderate. All cards.*

Rancho Gaúcho
Avenida Presidente Kennedy next to the beach. Daily 11:30 a.m.-last client
This open–air steak houses serves a la carte beef from Argentina and Rio Grande do Sul, the best on the continent. Order side dishes separately, such as french fries, *farofa*, and *macaxeira frita*. Live music during high season on weekends. *Moderate. Cards: DC.*

★ Sandra's
Avenida Eng. Luis Vieira, 555 (Future Beach); ☎ *234-6555. Daily 11:30 a.m.-midnight, weekends 11:30 a.m.-3:00 a.m.*
Surrounded by high–class beach homes 15 minutes from downtown, Sandra's is about as classy as an open–air restaurant gets. Under typical wood-beamed roofs and white stucco arches, diners enjoy a panoramic view of the city with the roaring ocean behind; waiters in white coats offer impeccable service. For starters, octopus salad is a true delicacy; main courses run from $3 for grilled chicken to $8 for fish and $13 for lobster. Small and cavelike is an inner salon with faux Indian calligraphy; there's also an air–conditioned dining area with cushy banquettes. After dining, just sit outside under the gorgeous palm tree and meditate. *Moderate. All cards.*

Sabor da Terra
Avenida Presidente Kennedy, 1695 (Meireles). Daily 24 hours
An open–air restaurant that ranks on the far side of casual. Not everything is available on the menu, but you should always be able to count on *picanha* with *macaxeira* (about $6) or the *panelada* (cooked intestines) for about $3. *Galinha do Sertão e Capote* is made from chickens raised in the countryside. An exceedingly fine side dish is the rice and beans spiked with cilantro. Out-of–tune local singers (who will seem charming after you've had a few beers) dominate the small stage, but I'm told anyone can get up to sing. *Inexpensive. All cards.*

★ London London
Avenida Dom Luiz, 131, (Aldeota). Daily 6:00 p.m.-3:00 a.m., weekends until 5:00 a.m.
Playboy magazine called this bar, open–air restaurant, and pizzeria the place to flirt in Brazil. Besides serving 24 kinds of pizza, 4 lasagnas, 6 pastas, and filet mignon, waiters deliver personal messages written on printed cards from other diners; if you don't get at least one per night, you're considered a drip. Fueled by a great *forró* and lambada band, Sunday nights get so full that people dance in the street and cars can't pass. The bar serves 17 kinds of special cocktails; take a swig of the Lady Di with gin, cointreau, *creme de leite*, and sugar. During the week, a

different type of music booms nightly from the DJ's control board suspended over the bar. Video TVs hanging from catwalks and MTV on a satellite dish add to the "cool." *Moderate. No cards.*

Ice Cream
Tropical Sorveteria
Avenida Presidente Kennedy, 4690
A necessary pit stop on Mucuripe Beach, featuring 50 different flavors, including such tropical fruits as *goiaba*, *melão*, *manga*, *tangerina*, *coco*, and *abacaxi*. Also ice-cold water!

NIGHTLIFE

Teatro José de Alencar
Praça do Alencar; Monday-Friday 8:00 a.m.-11:00 a.m., 2:00 p.m.-6:00 p.m.
This metallic Art Nouveau theater was built in 1910 but looks like something out of the boardwalk in Atlantic City, with its military green grillwork, cut-glass dome, and antique street lamps. All types of shows, from folklore to popular singers, are presented here. The view from the stage is awesome.

Oba Oba
Avenida Washington Soares, 3199; ☎ *234-4030. Daily Thursday-Saturday.*
A venue for major musical shows, featuring singers from all over Brazil. Styles include lots of *forró* and lambada. Make sure to catch the singer Beto Barbosa, a part owner, who was born in Belém but became famous in Fortaleza for singing lambada.

★ Chico e Caranguejo
Avenida Zezé Diogo, 6801 (Future Beach). Daily 9:00 p.m.-2:00 a.m.
A riotous outdoor bar on Future Beach, where the best live music is performed nightly. The scene is like a big party, with everyone dancing between the tight tables and throwing their crab claw shells into green plastic tubs. All stages of flirting seem to be allowed. Next door is a similar scene at **Lua e Luar**. Check the daily papers to see who is playing. *Inexpensive. No cards.*

Itaparik255 Bar
Avenida Zezé Diogo, 6801 (Future Beach); ☎ *234-6061*
This huge straw-roofed bar on Future Beach is packed on weekends (day and night) with families and bikini-clad teens. You must like people to come here, however, because the wood chairs and tiny tables are packed knee-to-knee. Little boys take your order and bring back the goods; the ones wearing white-and-green T-shirts will sell you coconut juice. Best thing to order are *caranguejos* (crabs), which you crack open with a wood pestle. Live music happens on Thursday nights, but dancing, strangely, is not permitted.

Forró and Lambada
Pirata
Rua dos Tabajaras, 3235 (Praia de Iracema); ☎ *231-4030*
Waiters are dressed like pirates in this restaurant/theater, where singers perform on a stage set that looks like the backyard of a house. Shows start at 9:30 p.m.; Mondays feature *forró* and lambada (when the entrance fee is $5). Menu is basically brick-oven baked pizza and appetizers. Apparently, this is the only place anything happens on Monday nights in Fortaleza. *Inexpensive. No cards.*

Folklore
Don't miss the **Guarani Grupo de Danças Folclóricas,** who perform native dances in traditional costumes accompanied by instruments like the *ganza* (a big bass drum), triangle, accordion, and *pandeiro* (a large, flat tambourine). They perform every Saturday night at 9:15 p.m. at the Othon Hotel. If you go for dinner, the show is free.

Live Music
Chopin Bach
Avenida Des Moreira, 1025; ☎ *244-3823. Thursday-Saturday.*
Live singers.

GAY FORTALEZA

Boite Africa and **Los Angeles** near the Avenida Presidente Kennedy cater to gays. **Praça do Ferreira** also tends to be a hangout at night (during the day the plaza is filled with old men kibitizing over politics).

SHOPPING

Centro de Turismo
Avenida Senador Pompeu, 350, ☎ 231-3566

The old public jail, constructed in 1850, was used for over 120 years before it was transformed into the Center of Tourism. It took three years to clean up the jail, whose former cells now house a complex of artisan and handicraft shops. Stop first in the Tourist Office for maps and brochures, then browse through the corridors. Wood carvings of Padre Cícero go for about $1-$3, and interesting sculptures and lacework can be found here, but in general the quality is kitschy. Bargaining is expected. Best prices for lace can be found downtown at the **Mercado Central**. Do stop by the **Sorveteria Doce Sabor**, a stand across the street from the theater, and pick up a bottle of *cajuina Nordeste* (a tangy fruit juice made from the cashew tree; when it's chilled, it tastes like alcohol but isn't). Also, roasted and raw cashew nuts from this tiny stand are delicious.

Located upstairs from this complex is the **Museu de Arte e Culturas Populares** *Avenida Sen. Pompeu, 360. Daily 7:00 a.m.-6:00 p.m.* This historical museum of popular culture doesn't exactly overwhelm with interest, but it does show a good model of a *jangada*, a 40-year-old weaving machine for hammocks, and an authentic raft made out of logs. Some visitors slip money under Padre Cicero's statue for good luck.

CEARTE
Monday-Thursday 9:00 a.m.-6:30 p.m., Friday and Saturday 9:00 a.m.-8:00 p.m.

Opened in May 1991, this complex of 14 stores was established by the government to promote native handicrafts in Fortaleza. The remarkable wood-beam and cut-glass structure also houses a restaurant for typical foods and a gallery. Good buys include leather moccasins, sand paintings made inside bottles, crochet rugs, woven baskets, and large painted pottery from the city of Cascavel (the leaf design is its signature). A natural food store sells *cachaça* with fermenting fruits, roasted cashews, and *doce de cajú com castanha*, a sweet loaf of jelly-like substance made from the cashew fruit. Brightly colored hammocks go for about $55 (you can find them cheaper in Belém). Folkloric shows are presented at night only in high season.

Mercado Central
Rua Gen. Benzeril (downtown). Monday-Saturday 8:00 a.m.-5:00 p.m.

Hot, crowded, and exotic, these 600 stalls, featuring everything from clothes to live animals for dinner, is straight out of a Turkish bazaar. If you want to see how the general population shops, this is it. Bargaining is expected, and the best prices for lace are here. But watch your purse and backpacks.

Feira de Artesanato
Beginning in front of the Praiano Palace Hotel along Avenida Presidente Kennedy, starts putting up its tents at 5:30 p.m. All the crafts from Ceará are represented here. Bargaining is essential, and time is needed to scout out the blocks-long fair to find good buys. Make a stop at the stand called "Mágica" and you'll be treated to a series of Brazilian magic tricks. The area also has a snack bar and tables, and there is an information post in the center.

Iguatemi Shopping Center is the best shopping mall in Fortaleza.

The **Antique Fair** is held at *Shopping Aldeota*. Friday 5:00 p.m.-10:00 p.m.

HANDS-ON FORTALEZA

Airlines
Varig
Rua Miguel Calmon, 19; ☎ 243-1344.
VASP
Rua Chile, 216; ☎ 243-7044.
Transbrasil
Rua Portugal, 3; ☎ 241-1044.

Arrival
Taxis from the **Aeroporto Pinto Martins** *Praça Eduardo Gomes,* ☎ 227-8066 to downtown charge a fixed rate of about $8; buses, about 30 cents, run every 20 minutes. As you leave the lobby young boys will aggressively try to help you with luggage, but don't be intimidated. They are usually extremely poor and just trying to make a

buck, but they are not official. If you accept their help, however, you should tip them. The main bus terminal *Rodoviária* is located at *Avenida Borges de Melo;* ☎ *186.*

Car Rentals
Locatur Hertz
Avenida Br. Studart, 3330; ☎ 272-4333.
Buggy Tur
(only buggies) *Avenida Antônio Justo, 2236;* ☎ *224-5000.*

City Transportation
Taxi
Rádio Taxi
☎ *241-2266.*
COOMETAS
(special taxi) ☎ *244-4500.*
Air Taxi
☎ *227-5511.*

Bus
Buses running along the beach strand are labeled according to the beach: Meireles, Mucuripe, Praia do Futuro, Caça e Pesca. After dark, take a cab; they're cheap and safer.

Climate
Located 3 degrees below the equator, Fortaleza averages between 90°F and 97°F the year round, with high humidity. Nights are windier and cooler. July is considered summer since it tends to rain (a daily 15-minute spritz). High season is considered to be July, January, and February, when the most tourists come. The *maresia* (sea wind) is strong and tends to rust equipment.

Money Exchange
Accountur Câmbio e Turismo
Avenida Monsenhor Tabosa, 1600 (Meireles); ☎ *261-3444*
Dollars are exchanged here (cash to cruzeiros only). For traveler's checks, call the Tourist Board for information.

Points Beyond
Air service and bus service is available to Recife, Rio, Bélem, and other major cities. Express bus service includes Recife (12 hours) and Rio (48 hours).

Security
Tourists need to be careful downtown, especially at night. However, Avenida Presidente Kennedy, where most visitors stroll, is safe due to the heavy presence of police. Watch your backpacks and purses at Future Beach and the Mercado Central.

Tourist Information
CODITUR
Avenida Senador Pompeu, 350, ☎ *231-3566*
Located in the ex-municipal prison, Coditur offers information assistance, as well as a gallery of artisan shops. Ask to see the office's notebook with photos of Jericoacoara, Praia Lagoinha, Canoa Quebrada, and other beach destinations. Maps with some English are available.
Posto Fortaleza Turística
Avenida Presidente Kennedy; ☎ *261-4221. Daily 7:00 a.m.-midnight*
This tourist information center, which looks like a caved-in grass hut, is located in front of the Nautical Club. Here, you can pick up brochures on beach excursions, as well as stock up on cigarettes, cachaça, maps, newspapers, and postcards. There's also a phone company where you can make long-distance and international calls.

Travel Agency
Ego Turismo
Rua Barão de Aracati, 644 (Aldeota); ☎ *221-6461; FAX 231-3672*
offers city tours and excursions to Beach Park and other beaches.

When to Visit
Festas Juninas takes place the first 2 weeks of June, with natives dressed in old-fashioned costumes performing *quadrilhas* (Northeastern square dances). Dedicated to Santo Antônio, the patron saint of marriages, the festival celebrates the tradition of sticking a knife into a banana tree overnight to find out the name of one's future mate. The **Regata de Jangada Dragão do Mar,** a well-known regatta race, is held on July 29 in front of the Nautical Club. On August 15, *umbanda* groups celebrate the **Festival of Iemenjá** on Praia do Futuro, filling the strand from dusk to dawn with rituals, drumming, and offerings that they throw into the sea.

FERNANDO DE NORONHA

Three hundred and twenty–six miles north of Recife and 217 miles north of Natal is one of the last great, untouched paradises of the Southern Hemisphere. A miniature archipelago of 16 islands, **Fernando de Noronha** is also the name of the principal island first discovered by Amerigo Vespucci in 1503. Almost 500 hundred years later, the island has retained its pristine eco–system, despite having weathered a spooky history as a penal colony. Today, it harbors some of the rarest species of fish and fowl in the world; one bird species, called *vireo gracilirostris*, a small brown brush bird, can only be found on this island. With a year–round visibility of over 300 feet, the island is considered by divers as one of the greatest sites in the world for both scuba and snorkeling.

The fragility and preciousness of Fernando has fortunately been recognized by the Brazilian authorities. In 1988, the military returned control of the island to the civilian government, which was persuaded by conservatives to declare 70 percent of the archipelago a national marine park. Today the island is under the jurisdiction of IBAMA, the national environmental protection agency, who tightly controls the waters and regulates the number of visitors. Since 1984, underwater fishing has been outlawed, which has inspired a profusion of tropical fish to proliferate, from queen angels, butterflies, and honeycombs to yellow goats and parrot fish. Although the Bay of Dolphins has been closed to divers, they may swim outside the immediate boundaries of the bay, where many dolphins can be encountered.

Anyone wanting to meet human beings unpolluted by modern culture should come to Fernando de Noronha. Of the 1,600 residents (most of whom are descendants of the prisoners who inhabited the penal colony during the 18th and 19th centuries), about 800 are children; very few are educated and those who do not work for the hotel subsist off the land or from welfare. Almost none have ever left the island, and there is no TV anywhere in sight. The natives, however, are very friendly to visitors, and crime is virtually unheard of.

PAST GLORIES

In 1503, the great astronomer and mathematician **Amerigo Vespucci** miscalculated his bearings on his fourth voyage to the New World and rammed into a rock at Fernando de Noronha. Immediately he sailed on to Cabo Frio, Brazil, where he paraded his hard-earned maps entitled "Land of the Americas" before the German government, thus altering the course of American history. In the early 1600s and 1700s, the Dutch and French repeatedly seized the island, using it as a springboard for invasions of the mainland. After expelling the last foreign occupiers in 1736, the Portuguese colonial authorities completed the island's fort, whose cannon barrels still stand watch over the trans–Atlantic yachts anchored below in Santo Antônio harbor.

In the early 1700s, Fernando de Noronha became a highly feared Devil's Island. Situated along a cliff overlooking a beautiful bay, a prison was built with stone beds, barred windows, and ghastly holes for solitary confinement. The worst punishment was considered to be abandonment on Rat Island, far out to sea. In 1832, **Charles Darwin** sailed around the island and noted in his diaries that it was covered with vegetation. Twenty years later, another visitor remarked that the only trees to be found were in the prison governor's garden; all the others had been cut down to prevent the prisoners from building escape rafts. Until 1817, women were banned from the community until inspectors complained repeatedly to the Portuguese crown of widespread homosexuality.

Incredibly, the **American influence** on this totally primitive island is omnipresent, though hardly mainstream. During World War II, the U.S. Army established a base to transport planes to Africa, and today their quonset huts have been appropriated by locals as igloo–type homes. The 2-mile airstrip now used by tourist flights was built by American engineers. Most of the inhabitants receive power from a diesel station installed by Americans, and they drink water from an American–made cement rainwater catch basin. The summit of the island's landmark, the **Pico**, is reached by a series of cast–iron ladders riveted to the rock by American soldiers.

SIGHTS

Rising up like a fertility god, **Pico Rock** stands as the major icon of the island—a 1,060-foot tall finger-shaped rock formed by millions of years of erosion. Visitors first glimpse the extraordinary protrusion from the plane, as it rises high above the green foliage surrounded by a shoreline of white coral sand and large crescent-shaped bays. As is common in Brazil, many locals have claimed to have seen strange lights emanating from the center of the natural structure. For those who want to enjoy the spectacular 360-degree view from the top, the peak can be climbed with the help of cast-iron ladders that were attached to the rock by American soldiers stationed on the island. It would be a good idea, however, to wear a climber's belt with clamps that hook to the ladder.

Dolphin Bay is the only place outside Kealakekua Bay, Hawaii, where **whitebelly spinner dolphins** are known to live year round. Spotted here since 1700, the community of about 600 dolphins are *famous for their gravity-defying acrobats in mid-air*; one biologist has actually recorded dolphins performing up to 5 somersaults, 14 leaps with body twists, and 10 consecutive leaps. Visible in the bay about a third of the year, they are best sighted between dawn and 3:00 p.m. The hotel can arrange a driver and car, which leaves at dawn and makes the 1-1/2-hour trek (including climbing) up the bay's 350-foot cliff. Since the dolphins use the bay for mating, breeding, and nourishment, park authorities have banned swimming and boating here within demarcated buoys.

Leão Beach, built up by sand dunes, faces 2 small rocky islands known as the **nesting place** for the rare blue-faced booby. At the southern end of the beach, *waves rushing the naturally formed reefs explode in 30-foot high fountains.* From January–March this beach is also the scene of a thousand-year-old ritual. Paddling feverishly from Ascension Island 900 miles to the west, **green turtles** return every year, dragging themselves exhaustedly onto the beach to lay their eggs. The TAMAR project, a national turtle preservation foundation, has been instituted here to protect the hatchlings. *(From February-May, authorities have banned visiting the beach from 6:00 a.m.-6:00 p.m.)*

Bird-watchers will appreciate the gentle walk at low tide from Porcos Beach past **American's Beach** to **Boldró Beach**; sightings of boobies and frigate birds patrolling the crashing surf are common.

Sunsets on the windblown western side of the island facing Africa are fantastic. Also, check out Suest Beach, a calm bay about a 2-mile walk from the hotel, where the Dutch landed in the early 17th century.

THE ESSENTIAL FERNANDO DE NORONHA

WHERE TO STAY

Virtually all visitors stay at **Hotel Esmeralda** *Al. do Boldró;* ☎ *(81) 549-1138* which offers little more charm than it did when it was the American Army base. Visitors are lodged in squarebox rooms, furnished with at least 2 single beds, with no cross–ventilation, no window screens, and total dependence on air–conditioning (it only runs between 10:00 p.m. and 7:00 a.m.). Single guests should expect to share rooms with the same sex. Only cold-water showers are available, and cleanliness is such that you will want to wear sandals when you bathe. The only place to eat on the island is the hotel, which flies in fish from Recife or Fortaleza, served with tropical fruits from the island. The bar is well stocked with sodas, beer, and basic hard liquor.

Insider Tip:
Bring your own soap, towel, and hard liquor. You will also be glad to have packed your own stock of chocolate, nuts, raisins, instant oatmeal, etc. Drink only bottled water.

Some accommodations may be made with local residents, but reservations and confirmation must be made in advance. Don't expect anyone to speak English. **Dona Zeta's house** ☎ *549-1242* has 4 rooms. The rate is $15 a night, including 3 meals.

Located next to the church, **Dona Pituca's house** ☎ *549-1201* has 4 rooms, at $15 a night, including meals.

HANDS–ON FERNANDO DE NORONHA

Arrival

Nordeste Airlines flies from Recife to Fernando de Noronha, leaving daily at 12:30 p.m. and returning around 3:30 p.m. Two flights are made on Sunday. Flights are also available from Natal. Since regulations keep visitors to a maximum of 100, park police will not allow you out of the air terminal without a confirmed reservation. No camping is allowed.

Accommodations

Brazilian Scuba and Land Tours *5254 Merrick Road, Suite 5, Massapequa, NY 11758;* ☎ *(800)722-0205, (516) 797-2133; FAX (516) 797-2132* offers an excellent 10–day package including 3 nights in Recife, 6 nights in Fernando, 5 days of diving, accommodations at the Hotel Esmeralda, all meals, tour of the bay and islands, and roundtrip airfare for $1,999.

Insider Tip:
Because of the visitors' quota, it will be considerably easier to book a package deal rather than arrange accommodations on your own.

Climate

The island is blessed with 200 days of sunshine. The rainy season peaks between March and May, when the rain leaves most roads unpassable, but turns the island into a bright green paradise. Between September and February (called the dry season), the island takes on a dusty brown shade. Daytime temperatures hover around 78°F, never dipping below 64°F. Since the island is only 3.5 degrees from the equator, the UV rays are among the most intense on the planet, so sun hats, coverups, extra–strength tanning lotion, and extreme caution are mandatory.

Getting around

Aguas Claras is the dive operation owned by Randall Fonseca, who owns three dive boats. At the end of the dive, clients are awarded with popsicles and ice cream made of avocados, peanuts, and native graviola fruit.

Bill Guarda rents a battered military jeep and driver for $35 a day. You can also pick up fins, snorkel, and mask for about $3.

Time
One hour ahead of Recife.

When to Visit
The open Atlantic side of the islands can be dived only from January-March due to sea conditions. (Note: From December through March, Brazilian tourists descend on the island, and prices may be higher.)

SÃO LUIS

São Luis is the capital of **Maranhão**, a state laden with Nordestino culture despite a climate and geography that nearly belongs in Amazônia. From the moment you step off the plane, the hot (very hot) humid air smacks you in the face, and if you visit from January–June, you will understand the meaning of rain. West of São Luis, you'll find the beginnings of the rain forest, yet the southern coastline has often been called the "Pantanal of the Northeast," because between July and December the land becomes so dry you can ride a truck over what was formerly water. Despite being one of the poorest states in Brazil, Maranhão has some of the most fertile plains in the Northeast, particularly along the banks of the **Tocantins**, a powerful tributary of the Amazon River.

As a tourist destination, São Luis is slowly crawling out of obscurity. The city has always boasted fine beaches, even if the weather can turn oppressively hot. Today, the interest is leaning towards the historical. The **Reviver Project**, funded by the state, has poured more than 25 million dollars over the last 15 years into restoring the grand old mansions that once marked São Luis as a center of the aristocracy. Even cobblestone streets that were being decimated by heavy traffic have been closed to vehicles and transformed into pedestrian malls. Today a very viable colonial area makes for picturesque strolling, and at night, the cobblestone streets, illuminated by authentic 19th–century gas lamps, resembles Bourbon Street, with local musicians and artists hanging out in the neighborhood bars and open–air eateries.

Bumba-meu-boi Festivities

During the month of June, it's worth catching the **bumba–meu–boi** festivities, one of the most authentic folkloric events in the Northeast. The festivities occur all month, but peak around June 24, when the interior towns send their troops of dancers and musicians into São Luis to perform outside the churches of **São João Batista** and **Santo Antônio**. The festival's folklore revolves around the story of a bull that dies while under the care of a slave and then is magically resurrected. Center stage in the dancing is the *boi*, or bull—an enormous black velvet–and–sequined puppet, which whirls around to the beat of the hypnotic *bumba* drums and the Mediterranean twangs of the *mandolin*. During the rest of the month, folkloric dances, typical foods, and native crafts are exhibited at the **Parque Folclórico**.

PAST GLORIES

São Luis possesses the historical oddity of being the only Brazilian capital founded by the French. The expedition, which arrived in 1612, was headed by **Daniel de la Touche, Senhor de la Ravadiére**, whose three ships maneuvered through the Bay of São Marcos to establish an island fort they dubbed Saint Louis in honor of the King of France. The land, however, already belonged to the Portuguese, who eventually expelled them, only to be taken over again by the Dutch in 1641. Three years later, the Portuguese regained control and initiated the expansion of a new city, whose streets were designed to take advantage of whatever refreshing wind blew in from the sea. During the 18th and 19th centuries, the majority of the great colonial mansions were built and decorated with imported blue tiles from Portugal called *azulejos*, thus giving the city its nickname: *cidade de azulejos* (City of Tiles).

SIGHTS

The old city of São Luis is a marvelous area to tour on foot. In fact, it's the only way to see the colonial area since the Reviver Project has prohibited traffic over a 4-street complex that includes **Rua Portugal, Rua Estrela, Rua Giz, and Rua Humberto de Campos.** The following walking tour will give you a glimpse of some of the main attractions, including museums and marketplaces, but pace yourself because the heat may become oppressive. Along the way you'll pass numerous bars and restaurants where you can find a cool drink. And remember to wear good walking shoes for the cobblestone streets and slightly steep slopes.

ON FOOT

Begin the tour at

Praça João Lisboa, where the **SEMATUR/MARATUR** Information Office is located, in the **Casa da Cidade de São Luis.** This is the main square of the city, which during colonial days featured the *pelourinho*, a whipping post for renegade slaves. In the middle of the square is a statue of **Jõao Francisco Lisboa,** a great journalist and historian who started the first newspaper of Maranhão called *Timon*. In this square is also the **Igreja do Carmo** and **Convento do Carmo,** as well as the offices of Transbrasil and VASP. Down the block from MARATUR is the post office called **Correios e Telegraphos.**

Cross the *Praça* to

Rua Osvaldo Cruz. To the right, the houses in extreme disrepair look barely inhabitable, but they are actually lawyers' and engineers' offices, as well as well–known **boutiques with 200–year–old tiles**. Turn left on Rua Osvaldo Cruz, the main commercial street, its cobblestones now closed off to all but pedestrians. On both sides of the street are wonderful, though ill–kept examples of **Art Nouveau;** notice the wooden shutters, the molded emblems, and the grilled balconies on the second stories. At the **Aky Disco** record store, you'll find the latest regional cuts.

To go directly to the restored part of the city, take a right on Rua Humberto de Campos, which arrives at Rua do Giz, Rua Estrela, and Rua Portugal. Or turn left from Rua da Cruz at **Unibanco** (on the corner), then right to Rua 13 de Maio to reach the

Museu de Arte Sacra at #500. In front of it is the **Igreja de São João**, built by the governor Ruy Vaz de Siqueira in 1665 in penitence for a dalliance with a married noblelady that resulted in a child. Continue until **Praça de Santo Antônio**, where there is a **19th–century monastery and church** by the same name, notable for its pink–winged angels on the main altar. Next, turn left on **Rua Santo Antônio** to **Rua Ribeirão**, where you will arrive at the

Fonte do Ribeirão (1796). Sunk into a cobblestone square, this **intricately carved fountain** features a statue of Neptune flanked by two young imperial palms. (Many Maranhão natives believe that a legendary serpent sleeps with his head under the fountain and his tail under the cathedral; when he wakes up, he supposedly shakes the entire city.) Across the street is **Solar do Ribeirão**, an excellent stop for lunch in an authentic 19th–century mansion.

From the fountain take a right on Rua do Sol. You'll pass the salmon–colored

Teatro Artur Azevedo, which may be in the throes of restoration but boasts a beautiful facade. Cross the **Rua do Egito** and you will be face to face with *one of the most beautiful glazed–tile facades in the colonial city*—the **Caixa Econômica Federal Bank**. Take a rest on the benches next to the old men and the young boys chanting out their wares. On this traffic–less cobblestone street called **Rua de Nazareth e Odylo**, notice the antique lamps. Cross to the

Praça Benedito Leite, a plaza teeming with fruit stands, jewelry counters, and shoeshinemen. This is a great place to pick up a bag of cashew nuts or Brazil nuts to munch on. There are also handicraft stores and an ice cream stand that features such tropical fruit flavors as *cupuaçu*, *bacurí*, and *graviola*.

Praça Dom Pedro Segundo is the site of both touristic and political activity. The square is circled by the **Hotel Central** (the city's *oldest*), the **Hotel Vila Rica** (*5-star*), and the **Lord Hotel** (*2-star*). As it has for centuries, the café next to the Hotel Central remains a favorite place to meet. The **Varig** office is also located here, a pink–and–white restored building with splendid grilled-work windows. The **cathedral** here is distressingly unattractive, but the government buildings that stretch out before it on *Avenida Dom Pedro Segundo* are impressive leftovers from the pre–Baroque colonial era. Dating from 1688, the oldest building, next to the Panorama Café, still houses the mayor's office and is called **Palácio La Ravadière,** after the French buccaneer who founded São Luis (his pirate–like bust can be found on the sidewalk). Next door is the state governor's residence, the

Palácio dos Leões *Monday, Wednesday, and Friday 3:00 p.m.-6:00 p.m.* built between 1761 and 1776. Originally a French fort, it now boasts sumptuous rooms fit for a king, with 200–year–old hardwood floors, portraits of Dom Pedro I, and a fabulous courtyard overlooking the bay. The gardens, juxtaposing limpid pools and islands of trees, were landscaped by the famous Roberto Burle Marx. Tours are usually given on *Monday and Wednesday 3:00 p.m.-6:00 p.m., but ask in advance at MARATUR.*

From the **Praça Dom Pedro II,** you can reach the Reviver either through **Rua Estrela** or through the **Beco Catarina Mina.**

The **Rua da Estrela** will take you to the

Fundação da Memoria Republicana, a museum featuring the worldly goods and tomb-to-be of the still-living ex-President José Sarney (who left office with few fans, but is still in politics as a senator from Amapá). Along this street there are also lots of artisan shops featuring straw and leather crafts, as well as an *umbanda* store called **Ogun Yara,** which features the tricks of the voodoo trade.

If you take the **Beco Catarina Mina** from **Dom Pedro Praça,** you'll go through the heart of

the Zona, block after block of historic buildings, some crumbling, others being revitalized. In general, however, what were once colonial mansions are now tenements, inhabited by very poor people whom you may see sitting on their porches or hammering on their houses.

The Old City's Marketplace

From here you can reach the large grilled archway of the

Feira da Praça Grande, next to the building with the sign called "*Casa de Sucos e Produtos Regionais.*" Here, in the old city's marketplace, ripe with fish smells and damp from constant washings, you'll find all sorts of regional products, from dried fish to exotic spices to Brazil nuts. The game the young boys are playing around the counters is a type of checkers called *jogo de damas*.

Walk down to

Centro de Criatividade de Odylo *Costa Filho Rampa do Comércio, 200;☎ 222-4844*, a very old, restored building that used to be a warehouse and is now an art center, with a cinema, restaurant, artists' ateliers, and a theater that hosts Segundo Arte, a Monday night musical show. Walk around to the painting and ceramic classes and watch the students at work; you'll be welcomed. There's also a bookstore, where you can buy books on folklore and *bumba-meu-boi* records.

Nearby, at the

Museu de Arte Visuais *Rua Portugal, 289. Monday-Saturday 1:00 p.m.-6:00 p.m.*, you'll find a full exhibit of **Maranhão tiles** from the 18th to 20th centuries. The building is a 19th-century house beautifully restored by the engineers from the Reviver project. Upstairs are contemporary paintings from Maranhão artists, including lithographs and oil pastels. On the third floor is a fabulous view of the city's rooftops.

Next door to the museum is one of the city's most historically ambient restaurants, **Alcântara**, a restored house with a towering roof and ox-cart tables that hang from the ceiling by chains. On Friday nights, troubadors sing *serestas* and there's even a bingo game played called *sorteios*.

On this same street the

Secretaria da Cultura is one of the most charming buildings in town, with blue Portuguese tiles and antique-grilled balconies. At the end of *Rua Portugal*, the **Cooperative Reggae** is open for reggae on Thursday and Friday night.

If you turn left onto *Rua Estrela*, then another left on *Rua João Gualberto*, you'll discover a wonderful used bookstore at #52 with used Brazilian records and paperbacks on all topics. Pick up a small newspaper called *O Tambor*, written in *São Luis*, covering the city's reggae scene, as well as *Folha de Gaia*, a paper about tourism and ecology in Brazil.

BEACHES

São Luis has a fine chain of beaches, easily reachable by local bus. At high tide, the water reaches all the way to the rock embankments, forming natural pools. Sometimes even small fish and shrimp appear. At low tide, bathers are treated to enormous expanses of sand.

Now extremely crowded, **Ponta d'Areia** has become the beach of the masses, who have recently been provided transportation from the suburbs. The stone sculptured mermaid adorning the beach was made in 1983 by Cherubino, an eccentric ex–priest whose "castle" you may visit (see below). A direct walk from Ponta d'Areia is the highly inviting **Calhau** beach, where the Sofitel Quatro Rodas Hotel is located—a scenic 2-kilometer walk from Olho d'Agua when the tide is low. Full on the weekends, the beach is lined with *barracas* offering all kinds of snacks.

Olho d'Agua is the best known beach in the entire state. The strand itself is extremely wide, and the activity colorful; donkey carts vie for space with speeding Volkswagens. An excellent *barraca* for seafood is **Roseangelas**. The elite of Maranhão head for **Aracagí** (about 9 miles out of town), which has the cleanest water and no crowds.

To rent a catamaran at the **Yacht Club**, either contact the English-speaking guide **Simão Ramos** ☎ *236-4069* or come to the club at *Praia da Ponta d'Areia* and talk directly to the salesman. The cost for a full day (to Alcântara and nearby islands) runs about $60 and is a wonderful way to spend a hot day in Maranhão. Rumor is that guests rarely get sick because catamarans are propelled by motor.

EXCURSIONS

ALCÂNTARA

If you've made it as far as São Luis, a side excursion to the glorious ruins of **Alcântara**, 11 miles across the Bay of São Marcos, is a must. Formerly the center of the aristocracy in northern Brazil, the village today could be the setting of a ghost story about 17th–century spirits. Crawling ivy nearly obscures the once magnificent facades of colonial mansions; cobblestone streets are now fully overgrown with grass. A mysterious hush seems to prevail over the entire 10–block historical area, and even the town's 2,000 inhabitants seem a bit other-worldly. If the delapidated shutters and crumbling fountains could talk, they would surely tell quite a story.

Officially founded in 1612, and named Alcântara in 1648, the area was originally wrested from the **Tupinambá Indians** by the Portuguese, who slaughtered them to make way for their own sugar, rice, cotton, and salt plantations. To facilitate production, thousands of African slaves were imported, many of whose descendants are still living in the village today. When slavery was abolished, the thriving metropolis (and the first capital of Maranhão) seemed to vanish against time. Although the state government these days is making stabs at restoration, the majority of the colonial houses, cathedrals, Portuguese-tile facades, and iron balconies remain in awesome, but strangely beautiful delapidation. Ironically, this village, lost in the 17th century, has also been designated as a special site for spaceship launching, due to its special equatorial location.

Though Alcântara has no real touristic infrastructure, you may be approached by young boys who will offer to guide you about (note that practically no one speaks English here). A visit can start at **Ladeira do Jacaré**, the main road, including a stop at the **Igreja de Nossa Senhora do Carmo** (the main cathedral), the **Igreja do Desterro**, the unfinished **São Francisco de Assis**, and the **Fonte das Pedras** (Fountain of Stones). Built in 1648, the main square, **Praça da Matriz**, was finally restored in 1948 after being buried underground for 50 years. Try to find **Rua da Amargura**, once a large promenade now completely covered with grass and weeds, though some of the most impressive ruins are located there, like the **Passo** (Step of the Cross) at one end. On the principal street, **Rua Grande**, you'll find the **Pousada do Mordomo**, as well as **Casa do Divino**, a center of artisanry, where you might find a native woman sewing lacework on a wooden loom. Most of all, just wander around and snatch glimpses of a village life that has remained as primitive as you'll ever find in Brazil.

Museu Histórico de Alcântara *Praça Gomes de Castro. Daily 9:00 a.m.-2:00 p.m.* features native pottery, primitive sculptures, and excellent black–and–white photos of religious festivals attended by native Indians in full regalia.

Local cuisine is simple but delicious: *arroz cuxá* (rice mixed with a special spicy sauce and *torta de camarão* (shrimp pie). Try the mangoes, which are always superb. For a fabulous pit stop, settle in with an ice–cold coconut juice at the **Pousada Pelourinho** and order a sweet called *espécie*, a kind of coconut macaroon so utterly delicious that folks from Maranhão come just to take home a sack.

Local handicrafts (pottery, wood, straw) can be bought on the streets and squares.

> **Insider Tip:**
> Drink only water that has been bottled, if you can find it.

THE ESSENTIAL ALCÂNTARA

Getting There

The easiest way to get to Alcântara is by private plane (there are no regularly scheduled flights). For information regarding the 8-minute trip, contact the fine pilot **Ilmo Antônio Klamt** at **CERTA**, located at the airport in São Luis; ☎ *225-4519*, or *225-0819* at night.

The really exotic way to reach Alcântara is by boat, which departs from the **Governador Luiz Rocha Terminal Hidroviário** *sometimes* at 7:00 a.m., 9:00 a.m., and 10:00 a.m. and *sometimes* returns at 2:00 p.m. or 3:00 p.m. The "sometimes" depends on the tides, and incredibly enough, nobody seems to know exactly when that will be. You'll have to return to the terminal several times to ask in advance, but be careful: It's a colorful, though rather seedy port, and brawls among drunken sailors tend to break out easily. The 90-minute "cruise" in the 2-level wood schooners tend to get rough, so arm yourself with whatever seasickness remedies you believe in. (A Brazilian once taught me to suck on a lemon and it worked.)

Telephones

None on the island.

Where to stay

Simple pousadas are the only official offerings here, but local families also provide room and board for tourists. Contact **MARATUR** in São Luis.

Pousada Pelourinho
Praça Gomes de Castro, 15
This beautiful, sprawling fazenda-like house looks out on the principal square. Rooms are huge, but primitive, with traditional beam roofs. The top floor is the best bet, with a full suite for $8. Other rooms are about $4. None have air-conditioning. 13 apartments. *Inexpensive. No cards.*

Pousada do Mordomo Régio
Rua Grande, 134. Reservations in São Luis: ☎ *(98) 222-3093*
Doubles for $12, with air-conditioning $15.

Where to eat

The best eateries—all simple and unpretentious—are the **Josefa Rua Direita**. *Daily 11:30 a.m.-2:00 p.m., 6:00 p.m.-11:00 p.m., closed Friday* and the restaurant at the **Pousada Pelourinho** *Praça Gomes de Castro, 15. Daily 2:00 p.m.-9:00 p.m.*

When to visit

A marvelous festival to catch is the **Festa do Divino Espírito Santo** from *May 8-19*.

PARQUE NACIONAL DOS LENÇOIS

Surely one of the most exotic landscapes in Brazil are the voluptuous white dunes and dark green oases of the **Parque Nacional dos Lençóis**. Called the "Brazilian Sahara," Lençóis is actually a desert without a desert: a veritable dance between dune and *mangue*, the latter a kind of swamp vegetation teeming with marine life and small verdant shrubbery. Although about 70,000 inhabitants (mostly fishermen) live in this 155,000-hectare national park, the only way to experience the landscape is from the air in a 4-seater plane. The trip, however, will be forever etched in your memory. About 2 hours from **Barreirinhas**, thousands of freshwater lakes nestling between the dunes begin to make a hypnotic design of sensuous proportion, and if you look hard you might even glimpse a stray cow or the tiny figure of a fisherman on his boat. Between January and June, fishermen improvise boats made of straw; when dry season comes, they bundle up their belongings and head for the closest municipal for small–plot farming.

Getting There

The very first inroads are now being made into this park by anyone other than the farmer-residents, who have existed precariously on its dunes for hundreds (if not thousands) of years in severe isolation. The nearest city to the park is Barreirinhas (about 30 minutes by air from São Luis), a municipality of 40,000 people which boasts a mere landing strip for air arrivals. (The city itself has a few small hotels and restaurants.)

Bus trips from São Luis (about 4 hours), arranged through a travel agency, run about $50 per person (minimum of 9 people) and take about 4 hours. From Barreirinhas, you may enter the park on a 3–hour boat tour that includes stopping at the sensuous sand dunes and swimming in freshwater (*aguá doce*) lagoons. This should prove to be a simply marvelous excursion, and since this dune park was just recently "discovered" by Fernando César Mesquita, Secretary of Tourism of Maranhão, you will be among the very first tourists on the entire planet to visit. So go with respect and ecological care. For more information, contact **Atlântica Turismo** *Rua 14 de Julho, 20 (in São Luis);* ☎ *(98) 232-1965/222-8585.*

TUTÓIA

If you decide to fly over Parque Nacional dos Lençois, carry on a few miles further (toward the border of the state of Piaiú) to **Tutóia**, a coastal city more than 400 years old, which has not yet even made it to the *Guia Quatro Rodas*, Brazil's travel Bible. That means the native fishermen won't even know what to charge you for a day excursion around the untouched islands, and the only hotel may not even have clean sheets. Women still wash their clothes in the river, children play nude in the streams, and a secret grotto bears excellent mineral water (when I was there, Maranhão's Secretary of Tourism actually declared it drinkable with one hefty gulp, but frankly, you couldn't have paid me to taste it). Most charming are the little pigs that run around town with lamp–shade type collars to keep them from slipping under the log fences.

If you decide to visit Tutóia, you must first contact the **Secretary of Culture** Maria José, who will pick you up at the airport and fully arrange your stay. (American and Japanese scientists have visited the area to research the fishing industry, but few tourists are ever sighted, and nobody around here speaks English.) Negotiate with a resident to rent his mule for a tour around the town, although you'll be surprised to be passed by a few roaring motocycles. The church, built in 1724, features a wonderful ceiling painting of a frolicking Jesus who looks like he's dancing through heaven. The beaches surrounding the city are nearly pristine, though you may have to share strand space with some wandering boars. The prettiest island to visit by boat is **Cajú**, nearly deserted, so you must bring your own food and water. The only restaurant on the beach of Tutóia is **Embarcação**, which serves hearty platters of fried fish and rice. Ask if you can see some folkloric dances, which will probably be the most authentic you'll ever see. The city is very proud that it has had phones for the last 8 years, but there are only 2 lines: *(98) 471-1271 and 471-1027.*

Getting There

Flights over Parque Nacional dos Lençois and to Tutóia from São Luis are offered 2 times a week, on Monday and Friday. Private planes may also be hired. For reservations call **CERTA** at the airport in São Luis; ☎ *(98) 225-4519* or *225-0819* at night. The contact is **Ilmo Antônio Klamt**. Private flights can also be arranged.

Where to Stay

O Manelão *Rua Senador Leite, 178* is the simplest of accommodations; you should probably bring your own sheets. All apartments have a bed and a hammock. Doubles go for $13, a shared room with two beds and no bath runs $4. For reservations, call the Tutóia operator and leave a message, or better yet, contact the Secretary of Culture.

THE ESSENTIAL SÃO LUIS

MUSEUMS

Museu de Arte Sacra
Rua 13 de Maio, 500. Monday–Friday 1:00 p.m.–6:00 p.m.

A project of Reviver, this colonial mansion boasts a fine collection of sculptured saints from the 17th-19th centuries. The extraordinary vista of the city from the top floor shouldn't be missed.

Centro de Cultura Popular Domingos Vieira Filho
Rua do Giz, 221; ☎ *222-4599. Monday–Friday 8:00 a.m.-5:00 p.m.*

Free Near the Praia Grande market, this museum in a preserved colonial mansion features stunning folkloric costumes and other *artisanato* of the region. Front and center are the elaborately sequined *bois* (or bulls), as well as a full cast of characters that parade through the streets of São Luis during the June *bumba-meu-boi* festivals.

Museu do Negro
Rua Jacinto Maia, 43. Monday-Friday 1:30 p.m.–5:00 p.m.

This former slave market called *Cafuá das Mercês*, or Hovel of Mercies, has now been transformed into a homage to black culture in Maranhão. Signs of the house's former function can be seen in the disturbing displays of manacles and chains that kept the newly arrived African slaves immobile until they were sold at auction. Upstairs, the indomitable spirit of the race can be seen in the black–and–white photos of the spiritual leaders of *Tambor de Mina*, Maranhão's version of *candomblé*. Notice the strength in the faces of these *mães* and *pais de santo* (mothers and fathers of the saints, as they are called), who by the sheer force of their personality and connection to the spirits were able to influence the moral outlook of their enslaved people. If you would like to attend a session of *tambor de mina*, inquire of the staff here.

WHERE TO STAY

Expensive -------------- Over $70
Moderate --------------- $40–$70
Inexpensive ------------ Under $40.

★ **Sofitel Quatro Rodas São Luis**
Avenida Aviscência; ☎ *(98) 227-0244, FAX 227-4737*

Iguanas and peacocks roam this 5–star resort on Calhau Beach, where the philosophy is Club Med without the frenzy. Folkloric programs throughout the week keep guests entertained with dance performances, typical foods, and hot bands. The extensive pool complex invites all–day tanning, but the palm–tree grounds lead directly to the lovely beach, where all manners of watersports can be enjoyed. Rooms are large and well furnished, though the *maresia* wind tends to leave a musty smell in some carpets. The restaurants, though not inexpensive, offer excellent cuisine, attended by folklorically dressed waitresses. 195 rooms. *Expensive. All cards.*

Hotel Vila Rica
Praça Dom Pedro II, 299 (Centro); ☎ *(98) 232-3535*

This 5–star is situated right next to the Archbishop of Maranhão, but that doesn't stop it from being a fine leisure hotel. The ice–cold lobby (a relief in São Luis) is constructed around a variety of intimate areas that resemble a private living room. The coffee shop, where breakfast is served, opens onto an exceedingly pleasant pool complex lined with coconut and palm trees and bouquets of tropical flowers. A fine international–style meal can be had at Restaurante dos Arcos, which strangely resembles the inside of a castle. Lushly decorated 2–room executive suites sleep 4; standards are more simply appointed with 2 sofa beds, color TV, and bamboo closet. Clients may patronize the beauty salon, sauna, massage, and small boutique. An attractive playroom looks out onto the bay, where guests may play pool and bridge. Singles run $80, doubles $93, 30 percent discount for cash. 213 apartments. *Expensive. All cards.*

★ **Pousada do Francês**
Rua da Cruz, 121; ☎ *(98)222-0334*
I saw this pousada in its last stages of construction but it promises to become one of the most charming accommodations in the city. Located in the old city on a street replete with colonial grillwork and wonderful old arches, the original house dates back to 1712. Owner Airton Abreu has worked hard to follow the strict laws regulating historical renovation, including preservation of the original facade and typical tiled roof. Walls have been painted with oxidized whale oil to retain a warm burnish glow, and antique lamps have been preserved. Because no walls can be knocked down, rooms follow the eccentricities of the original architecture; hence, some of the 30 apartments are quite small while others are spacious. All apartments are air–conditioned with color TV and minibar; the bathrooms are small but modern. Best bet is to check out the available rooms on arrival and take your pick, but reservations in advance are recommended. Room prices were not designated at press time, but should be in the moderate range. *Moderate. All cards.*

★ **Araçagy Praia Hotel**
Praia da Araçagy, 12 kilometer; ☎ *(98) 226-3299*
Built in 1989, this 3–story property boasts some of the most pleasant apartments in the city, if not the cleanest. The hotel is equipped with verandas that provide a distant glimpse of the sea, all rooms are air–conditioned and come with wood–frame beds, color TV, minibar, and tiled bathroom. A good-sized pool and tanning patio provides an attractive alternative to the beach, which is only a 5–minute bus ride away. Next door is a water park with numerous swimming pools, slides, and tennis courts, which hotel guests may utilize free of charge. The restaurant serves lunch and dinner, as well as *feijoada* on Saturday. Singles run $22, doubles $27. 66 apartments. *Inexpensive. Cards: AE.*

★ **Pousada Olho d'Agua**
Avenida Atlântica, 200 and Rua dos Magistrados, 28; ☎ *(98) 226-0435*
This extended private home, transformed into a pousada, offers a homey seaside option. From the backyard, you can walk right onto Olho d'Agua beach, one of São Luis' most popular, where donkey–drawn carts vie with Volkswagens for space on the huge strand. Semi–erotic nude paintings adorn the open–air breakfast room; neighboring rooftops are so close one could nearly make a historical study of the city's architecture. The attractive apartments, built around the cubbyholes of the house, are air–conditioned with private baths, several have color TVs, 3 have verandas. A few have minibars. Room 201, the best, boasts an exquisitely carved bureau and bed, traditional shutters, and wood-carved doors. The Olho D'Agua restaurant is a point. Most rooms run $14-17, #201 runs $20. *Inexpensive. No cards.*

Ilha Bella Hotéis
Praça da Matriz, (São Francisco); ☎ *(98) 227-0921*
A 10–minute walk to Ponta d'Areia Beach, this budget hotel opened in 1991 with 5 apartments; it should have 15 by 1992. The lobby is brief but clean; the rooms are all huge, with fine wood floors and nicely tiled (though small) bathrooms. No closets, but all rooms have air–conditioning and phones; you pay a extra couple of bucks for TV and minibar. Singles start at $17, doubles $22. *Inexpensive. All cards.*

Chale de Lagoa
Praia do Araçagi; ☎ *(98) 226-4916*
A funky down–scale pousada, the Chale de Lagoa on the outside looks like a tiny charming village with traditional tile roofs and tropical vegetation. Inside, the apartments range from simple to questionable, but they are perfect for backpackers or those who don't mind bringing their own sheets. The owners, who are involved in *Tambor de Mina* (a form of *candomblé*, or voodoo worship) have named their apartments after the saints of the religion. Rooms have tiled floors, private baths, fan, and a sheet of burlap that passes for a closet. Prices range from

$13-$28, breakfast included. The pousada is next door to Castello, a castle–like private home built by an eccentric, but very friendly ex–priest turned architect. *Cheap. No cards.*

WHERE TO EAT

Churrascaria Pavan
Avenida dos Holandeses (Calhau), 9 kilometer; ☎ *226-3085. Daily 11:00 a.m.- 3:00 p.m., and 6:00 p.m.–11:00 p.m., closed Monday.*
A no–fanfare *rodízio* with 12 kinds of meat, 12 salads, and 12 desserts (including watermelon) for a reasonable $8. Painted scenes of the old city adorn the walls; a large wood–beam roof and traditional tile roof keeps the joint cool without air–conditioning. Pavan is also one of the few places in the Northeast where you can find a Diet Coke. *Moderate. All cards.*

★ Tia Maria
Avenida Nina Rodrigues, 1 (Ponta d'Areia), 4 kilometer ; ☎ *227-4338. Daily 11:00 a.m.–2:00 a.m., Sunday 11:00 a.m.–8:00 p.m.*
With one of the most beautiful vistas in the city, Tia Maria is a step away from the beach at Ponta d'Areia. At night, the twinkling lights of the city reflected on the water make a stunning panorama. Hanging lamps of woven rope and raw wood tables add to the rustic allure, but there's also room to dance to languorous Brazilian ballads played by live bands nightly. The menu includes 14 kinds of fish, 12 kinds of shrimp, 10 kinds of crabs, 4 types of oysters, as well as *Hapossay*, a kind of paella with squid, shrimp, chicken, *sururu* (a mollusk), vegetables, and mushrooms in a Japanese sauce. Most famous is the *ensopado de caranguejo no leite de coco* (a kind of crab stew with coconut milk) The specialty of the house is homemade *batidas* made with *pitanga* and vodka; the chocolate was so good I walked out with a bottle for about $12. After dinner, take a turn in the double-seated love swing or just kick up some sand on the beach. *Moderate. Cards: AE.*

★ Solar do Ribeirão
Rua do Ribeirão, 141; ☎ *222-3068. Daily 11:30 a.m.–3:00 p.m., 7:00 p.m.–11:00 p.m., closed Sunday.*
Overlooking the Fonte do Ribeirão, this restored colonial mansion dates back to 1884 and is a lovely place to dine a la 19th century. Specialties are regional delicacies like *cuxá com peixe frito* (fried fish) and *caldeirada* (fish stew). A lunch buffet with chicken and beef runs about $6.50. *Moderate. All cards.*

Hibiscus
Avenida dos Franceses (Vila Palmeira); ☎ *223-2830. Daily noon–3:00 p.m., 7:00 p.m.–midnight*
Next to the Folkloric Park where the *bumba meu boi* festivities are held, this tropical chic eatery serves politicos like Sarney who indulge in the *peixe frito com cuxá*. Friday and Saturday you can dine to live *música romantica* from 9:00 p.m.-2:00 a.m. Try the *taioba*, a kind of mussel that comes in a tiny shell with a touch of cilantro. *Moderate-Expensive. No cards.*

Olho d'Agua
Avenida Atlântica, 200 and Rua dos Magistrados, 28; ☎ *226-0435*
Located on Olho d'Agua beach at the pousada of the same name, this funky, open–air eatery is one of the most popular in the area. Locals adore the drink called "Jesus"—an exceedingly sweet soft drink that nearly made me sick. Try the *torta de camarão*, a delicious shrimp pie for under $4. *Feijoada* is served on Sundays for a reasonable $4. *Inexpensive. Cards: AE.*

Base do Germano
Avenida Venceslau Brás (Canto da Fabril); ☎ *222-3276. Daily 11:00 a.m.–4:00 p.m., 6:00 p.m.–1:00 a.m., Sunday 6:00 p.m.–1:00 a.m.*
Legendary for its *caldeirada de camarão*, a steamy shrimp soup. *Moderate. No cards.*

Naturista
Rua do Sol. Monday-Sunday 11:00 a.m.–11:00 p.m. Macrobiotic menu. Inexpensive. No cards.

SHOPPING

CEPRAMA
Monday-Saturday 9:00 a.m.–8:00 p.m., Sunday 4:00 p.m.–8:00 p.m.
The handicraft center run by the state in a re-

stored textile plant in the Madre de Deus district. Good buys are canned regional fruits made by Tia Noca, leather-worked jewelry boxes, lacework, leather sandals, straw baskets, pottery, and Indian crafts from tribes in the interior. If you can stick it in your luggage, splurge on a "Rain stick," a long bamboo-type stalk filled with seeds that gives the impression of rain; it's become a staple among Latin percussionists. I found a good one at "Box da Tribo Guarajaras."

HANDS-ON SÃO LUIS

Arrival

Flights daily into São Luis are provided by **Varig**, **VASP**, and **Transbrasil**. The airport, **Tirirical** ☎ *225-0049* is located 18 kilometers from the center of the city. Taxis are plentiful.

City Transportation

Bus:

Adequate bus service is available to the various beach fronts.

Taxi:

Rodotaxi
☎ *223-5904.*
Cobras
(airport) ☎ *225-1317.*

Climate

Equatorial—which means hot and very humid. Rainy season peaks between January–April, though it rains for short periods during the rest of the year. The coolest month is September. From January–July it rains some every day.

Money Exchange

Baespa
Rua do Sol, 404 (downtown);
☎ *222-1281.*
BASA
Avenida Dom Pedro II, 140 (downtown).

Travel Agency

Praia Tur
Avenida São Marcos (Ponta d'Areia);
☎ *227-0331.*

When to Visit

June is the traditional month of festivities, with the most *bumba–meu–boi* celebrations in the Northeast. *Tambor de Mina* (homage to São Sebastião) is held January 19–20.

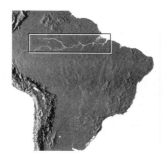

AMAZÔNIA

The Amazon

"How do I convey the scent of the wet forest, as ineffable as a mixture of crushed herbs?"
Loren McIntyre, photojournalist

"The Amazon is the last unwritten page of Genesis."
Euclides da Cunha, geographer and novelist

"Imagine if all the people in Amazônia decided in the next decade that they didn't want to treat the places they lived in as a commodity but as a sacred place."
Ailton Krenak, Krenak Indian

To travel through the great Amazon River region is a nature experience you will never forget. The innate wisdom of the forest—its voluptuous beauty, the life-and-death dramas of millions of species—are realities that will literally enter your bones as you tramp through the rainforest, cruise down the tributaries, or raft over rapids. The Amazon is about challenge, and ever since the first explorers stepped forth on the banks of the newly discovered continent, the dark, mysterious rainforest has inspired countless numbers to sacrifice life and limb for a little excitement and the promise of treasure.

These days, of course, travel through the Amazon need not be life-threatening, though it's still exciting, unpredictable, and full of challenge. Despite all the recent political controversy, there's still a lot of poetry left in the rainforest: the liquid rustle of treetops, the elusive shadows of animals, the cries of unseen birds. But for most travelers, the most memorable part of a jungle adventure are the people—the locals who toil day by day in the jungle; *caboclo* fishermen who live like Indians along the river shores; old ladies who have fled to the jungle to escape city violence; little girls who paddle to school every morning and brush their teeth in the river. There are also Indians, those living on protected reservations, as well as those trying to survive halfway between "civilization" and tribal security. Add to that botanists and biologists and scientific photographers who are trying to capture the miracle of the ecosystem. And finally, there are the goldminers, rubber tappers, ranchers, and industrialists—all, in their own way, attempting to bend the will of nature to their own commercial desires. A circus of cross-purposes, yes, but no matter what one's political allegiance is, each "jungle" person you meet will only add to your understanpding of what the Amazon rainforest is and why it has become such a fragile paradise.

Traveling through the Amazon is not for couch potatoes, and you may have to do some solid soul-searching to see if you'll make a good candidate. (The "Should I Go to the Amazon?" quiz will separate the gnats from the gnus.) The best way to indoctrinate yourself is rent a few videos *(The Emerald Forest, Arachnophobia, At Play in the Fields, Medicine Man)* or dive into travel-adventure narratives and novels that will let you feel the thrills without the thorns. Some of the best books are *Running the Amazon* by Joe Kane, *The Cloud Forest* by Peter Matthiesson, *Amazon Beaming* by Petru Popescu, Amazônia by Loren McIntyre, and (for laughs) *Holidays in Hell* by P. J. O'Rourke.

A BIRD'S EYE VIEW

Maybe it was all those Tarzan movies, but to most people the phrase **The Amazon** has come to suggest a vast, humid jungle. Technically, the phrase "The Amazon" refers only to the river itself, including more than 1000 tributaries that stretch some 4000 nautical miles from the Atlantic Ocean to its source, Lago Lauricocha, high in the Peruvian Andes. Resembling a large funnel, the Amazon flows in a Y-shaped system into which its headwaters, the Negro-Branco, from the northwest, and the Madeira, from the southwest, converge. When the main trunk reaches the Brazilian border, it turns into the **Solimões**, a so-called "white river," dense with silt and microorganisms, until it meets the darker and clearer **Rio Negro**. Long a point of fascination among visitors, the "dark" and "light" rivers run parallel for several miles without mixing until they finally blend, forming the pale-brownish Amazon, as it is called until it empties into the Atlantic. The term Amazonas refers to Brazil's largest state (of which Manaus is the capital), which is part of Amazônia, a vast basin of forests and wetlands occupying about half of the South American continent (75 percent of Brazil, as well as parts of Venezuela, Ecuador, Peru, Suriname, Guyanas, and Colombia). Within Brazil itself, Amazônia embodies the states of Amazonas, Acre, Rondônia, parts of Pará, Mato Grosso, and Maranhão, and the territories of Roraima and Amapá.

Amazonian Facts

- Amazônia is the world's largest rainforest, covering 2.5 million square miles in countries.
- The Amazon River system is the planet's largest body of fresh water.
- The Amazon Basin, with 6 million square kilometers of river and jungle, is the world's largest in terms of volume and drainage. The basin holds two-thirds of all the flowing water in the world.
- Besides the Amazon River, there are 1,100 tributaries (17 of which are more than 1,000 miles long). All totaled, there are 48,000 miles of navigable rivers.
- The Amazon River is at times so wide (up to 7 miles) that you can't see the other side of the shore.
- The flow of the Amazon River is 12 times that of the Mississippi.
- There are 15,000 known animal species, 1,800 species of butterflies, 1,200–2,000 species of fish, 4

types of big cats and 200 mosquitoes. One-quarter of the world's 8,600 bird species live in the Amazon.

PAST GLORIES

It was myth that seduced the first European explorers to the Amazon. Four centuries ago, the most prevailing one was that of El Dorado, a tribal chieftain whose wealth was so vast that he supposedly tattooed his body daily with gold-dust. In 1540, **Gonzalo Pizarro**, the brother of the conqueror of Peru, launched an expedition with Ecuadoran general Francesco Orellana to conquer the lands of El Dorado and the cinnamon forests. Confronted by disease and imminent starvation, Orellana broke off from the main troops and led a hunting party into the jungle, eventually discovering the mouth of the Amazon River. Although he never found gold, Orellana did tangle with fierce tribes, who told him about a community of women warriors who once a year invited male adults to participate in their mating rituals. Orellana may never have actually met these women, but the story soon became bloated with retelling and enflamed numerous *bandeirantes* and booty-seekers to follow in his footsteps. Later, Spanish scholars dubbed the region and its massive river the Amazon, in honor of the women warriors of Greek mythology who removed their right breast so that they could more easily use a bow and arrow.

BOTANISTS, BIOLOGISTS, AND SHUTTERBUGS

Imagine the courage of those first Amazon explorers who didn't have the advantage of a travel guide, let alone good maps. Among the most intrepid were the 19th-century botanists and biologists, whose journals recorded their profitable, but harrowing journeys. The Prussian naturalist **Alexander von Humboldt** was the first to prove that the Orinocco and Rio Negro-Amazon rivers sprang from the same source in the Parima Range, but he soon lost his enthusiasm when the crocodile grease he daily smeared on his body failed to ward off mosquitoes. A half-century later, English scientist **Alfred Russel Wallace** forged his way up the Rio Negro, experienced firsthand the "survival of the fittest," and eventually co-authored the theory of evolution with Charles Darwin. Henry Walter Bates, the founder of protective mimicry, walked around the forest like a human pincushion, collecting over 14,712 species (8,000 which were new to science), but even he was unnerved by the screeching of howler monkeys and other mysterious sounds, like the clanking of iron. Perhaps the best description of the frustration scientists felt came from Englishman Richard Spruce, who wrote: *"Save willing Indians to run like cats or monkeys up the trees for me . . . the only way to obtain the wildflowers and fruits was to cut down the tree, but it was long before I could overcome a feeling of compunction at having to destroy a magnificent tree, perhaps centuries old, just for the sake of gathering flowers."*

The tallest tales of the jungle came from **Percy H. Fawcett**, a retired British army colonel sent to the upper Amazon in 1906 to resolve the overlapping claims of Bolivia and Peru arising from the rubber boom. Fawcett reported rumors of anacondas swallowing cattle whole and picking men right out of canoes at night, and he even claimed he once smelled a penetrating fetid odor emanating from one, *"probably its breath,"* he wrote, *"which is known to have a stupefying effect."* Fawcett also complained about the anacondas' melancholy wails at night—a phenomenon never proven by scientists. Certainly a colorful figure, Fawcett carried no radio during his expeditions, which didn't seem to matter since several spiritualists, including his wife, claimed to be in psychic contact with him. Ever in search of the lost city supposedly discovered by the Portuguese explorer Francisco Raposo in 1754, Fawcett was eventually found dead near the mouth of the Xingú River, most probably murdered by Kalapalo tribesmen.

In this century, one of the last great Amazon explorers is **Loren McIntyre**, a world-class photographer for *National Geographic* who has done more to capture the ever-changing Amazon than any other chronicler. A must-read is Petru Popescu's **Amazon Beaming,** a riveting account of McIntyre's capture by an isolated Amazonian tribe and his subsequent involuntary descent into their shamanistic reality. McIntyre's own coffee-table book, **Amazônia,** is a thrilling visual testimony to the region and its people.

RUBBER BOOM AND BUST

It was rubber, not gold, that transformed the face of Amazônia. Contrary to popular belief, the rubber trade in Amazônia started long before Charles Goodyear accidentally discovered rubber in 1839. As early as 1750, Dom José, King of Portugal, was sending his boots to be waterproofed in Pará, and by 1800 Belém was exporting rubber shoes to New England. The famous Amazonian rubber boom, however, was fueled by the debt peonage of isolated *seringueiros* (rubber tappers) and *caboclos* (backwoodsmen) who sold their balls of latex to the trading post for mere pittance. It's been estimated that in 1850 there were 5200 rubber men, by 1912 when the boom peaked, no less than 190,000 Brazilians were tapping 88 percent of the world's rubber. During these giddy years, Manaus became a boom city, its wealth concentrated in the hands of about 100 men—so-called "rubber barons," who drank Hennesey brandy, dined on Irish linen, and built palatial homes. Soon, electricity was installed and the first tramway in South America initiated. The crowning glory in Manaus was a massive customs building modeled on that of New Delhi, prefabricated in England and shipped to Brazil piece by piece.

In 1870, a young Englishman named **Henry Wickham,** in cahoots with the Royal Botanic Gardens at Kew, conspired a scam that would totally puncture the rubber future of Brazil. Working with the Tapiu Indians, a detribalized tribe, Wickham raced to gather *hevea* seeds at their prime, smuggled them past customs with a large dose of charm, then nursed them across the Atlantic to Le Havre, where a special chartered train delivered them to Kew. From there, the seedlings were rushed to Ceylon, where in the swampy fields of Sri Lanka, the few that survived came to form the basis of the great rubber plantations of Malaysia. In a mere 24 years, the trees matured, outstripping the Amazonian market, which burst totally in 1923. With frightening speed, tycoons, speculators, traders, and prostitutes departed from the tropics, leaving behind them decayed palaces, a boarded-up opera house, and cobblestones full of weeds. The only beneficiaries were the native people, who would be left in peace for another half-century.

THE LAST GREAT GOLD RUSH

In 1979, the owner of a two-bit cattle ranch, **Gensio Ferreira da Silva**, discovered that his scrubby grasses and skinny cows were astride the most important gold strike in Amazonian history. By 1985, over 500,000 prospectors were toiling up and down the vast pits dug into the mountainside—a frightening tableau of human mudmen right out of a Brueghel painting. The federal government, worrying about the potential danger of so many unruly men near Carajás, the largest iron development in the world, finally sent in troops. In May 1984, the military occupied the Serra Pelada, led by Major Curió, who, descending from his helicopter, flashed his Magnum and cried, "The gun that shouts loudest is mine." Though the military occupation brought a much needed health center, bank, post office, telephone line, and wholesale government store, the *garimpeiros* staged a rebellion down the Belém-Brasília highway, eventually forcing the government to retreat.

THE INDIAN ISSUE

The real history of the Amazon region belongs to its native peoples—a subject that deserves not a few paragraphs but tomes (among the best of which are *Red Gold* and *Amazon Frontier: The Defeat of the Brazilian Indians* by John Hemming.) When the first explorers arrived in 1500, there were 6–9 million Indians in the Amazon basin; by 1900 they had been reduced to 1 million; today, there are less than 200,000. The Jesuit missionaries were only one form of unnatural control. What truly undermined the Indian was *cachaça*, happily provided by the *bandeirantes*, who soon discovered that liquor was the only way to press-gang the natives into submission. The tribes that escaped such ignominy, including the rape of their women, the theft of their children, and a legacy of incurable alcoholism, retreated deeper and deeper inside the forest.

In the 20th century, the onslaught of "progress" has continued to devastate the native population. The construction of two highways—the **Transamazônica** and the **Cuiabá-Santarém**—has dislocated over 10,000 families (50,000 originally intended), and nearly wiped out through disease the tribes of the Araba, Parkana, Kreen Akarore, and Txukarramae. During the 1980s, Indians began to display political self-determination when a group of **Txukarramae** from the Xingú River basin held the director of the Xingú Park hostage to demand demarcation of their lands, severed from the rest of the park by Highway BR-080. For a short term, a Xavante Indian chief even enjoyed his own seat in Congress. In 1989, President Sarney brought national attention to the plight of the **Yanomami Indians** when their 9,000-sq. kilometer reserve on the border between Brazil and Venezuela was overrun by goldminers. Military troops were sent in, but in the end the army simply refused to confront 45,000 burly *garimpeiros*, even though they were poisoning the Yanomami rivers with mercury and attracting new strains of malaria. Today, some 70 percent of the Yanomami reservation has already been confiscated by mining concerns, but even more tragic has been the physical devastation brought on by constant contact with the outside world; among their tribesmen the first case of AIDS has already been reported. In the future, the Yanomamis will be facing the federal government's own *Calha Norte* plan to populate the Brazil's remote borders with frontiersmen.

In February 1989, in the town of **Altamira,** over 500 Indians from Amazon tribes gathered together with international environmentalists to protest the Brazilian **Eletronorte's Xingú HEP Dam scheme.** Few who were present (or saw the documentary film) will ever forget the sight of a Kayapó woman brandishing a machete at Eletronorte's CEO and fervently crying, "Do you think we are so stupid that we don't know your plans for us, for this forest?"

In the last few years, a **Kayapó** Indian chief—**Paulinho Paiakan**—has emerged as a worldwide icon of native power. Touted as Brazil's wealthiest Indians, the 5,000 Kayapó Indians earn millions of dollars a year in royalties from gold and mahogany reserves in central Brazil. Most recently, the chief has solicited the support of the rock star Sting, who founded the Brazilian Rainforest Foundation, and he even managed to sell brazil–nut oil to The Body Shop, an international cosmetic chain. But on the eve of a $40-million movie to be made of his life (not to mention numerous international awards), Chief Paiakan was abruptly arrested when the 19-year-old white Portuguese-language tutor of his children accused him of rape. In Brazil, a national furor erupted, turning environmentalists against feminists (the latter enraged that rapists rarely are punished in Brazil), and raising the ire of industrialists who were lying in wait to discredit the Indian rights movement. By press time, the crisis remained unresolved.

AMAZON HEROES

The Amazon has given birth not only to exploiters, but also to heroes. One of the greatest champions of Indians was the **Cândido Mariano da Silva Rondôn,** the highest ranking officer in the Brazilian army and a great explorer who led Teddy Roosevelt on an historic expedition down the Amazon. (A river discovered on that mission, first called River of Doubt, was later renamed Rio Roosevelt.) In 1961, three brothers named **Orlando, Claudio,** and **Leonardo Villas-Boas** persuaded the government to create a national park for the Xingú tribe, whose lands during WWII had been invaded by the construction of military airstrips connecting Rio to Manaus. Entranced by native life, the Villas-Boas brothers not only fought for native rights but also managed to live with various tribes for many years. Until they succumbed to old age and malaria, the brothers fought valiantly to secure FUNAI's protection of the area from rubber tappers, hunters, industrialists, journalists, missionaries, and even anthropologists, but in 1971, builders overrode public sentiment and drove Highway BR-080 right through the park.

The most prominent name in recent Amazonian activism is that of **Chico Mendes,** a poor rubber tapper born in Seringal, Cachoeira. Illiterate until the age of 18, he gained most of his worldly education from listening to Radio Moscow, Voice of America, and the BBC Portuguese Service; when he finally learned to read, he discovered the price of rubber was being outrageously exploited by the *seringalistas*. As ranchers and settlers came to clear the rainforest, the rubber tappers were forced to leave, but Chico refused, urging his fellow workers to unionize. With no knowledge of Gandhi or Martin Luther King, Mendes naturally hit upon the idea of nonviolent resistance, and in 1976 organized a series of human stand-offs that prevented work crews from using their chainsaws. In 1989, Indians joined the lobby in favor of extractive reserves set aside for use by rubber tappers and gatherers of nuts, fruits, and fibers; today over 5 million acres of forest have been preserved. In December 1988, after returning home from a labor-organizing trip, Mendes stepped into his backyard and was fatally blasted by a shotgun at close range. The 21-year-old son of a rancher who hated Mendes finally confessed to the murder, but general opinion conceded that his father, Darli Alves, was to blame. In 1993, father and son escaped from a loosely secured prison in Rio Branco, Acre, and have not been found. Following the murder of Mendes, Hollywood descended on his family and his wife, Ilzamar, who is reported to have received a million dollars for the rights to his life story. A film by Warner Bros. is expected soon.

LEGENDS OF THE AMAZON

Legends and superstitions seem to lurk behind every plant or animal in the Amazon jungle; don't hesitate to ask locals about their folk beliefs. Among the most "enchanted" of jungle beings are *botos,* or dolphins, who are thought to transform themselves at night into white-suited cads and seduce young virgins. It's even said that *botos* are particularly attracted to the scent of menstrual blood—a folk belief so powerful that girls often refuse to bathe in the river during their periods.

The *japiim*, an Amazonian bird, also enjoys a notorious reputation. Legend has it that in the early days of the jungle, the *japiim* had a very beautiful voice, which secured him a place in Heaven right next to God. One day he came to earth and tried imitating the songs of the other male birds. When he started attracting all the females, their enraged spouses told him to get lost or reap the punishment. Desperate, the *japiim* turned to the bees for help, who allowed him to make his nest right next to theirs. As such, you can always find a bee hive near the nest of a *japiim*, whose song is often mistaken for that of other birds.

The mystical origin of the **lily pad** is particularly evocative. Once a beautiful but ambitious girl named Arari wanted to be just like the moon. She tried climbing a great mountain to reach it, but finally jumped to her death from despair, falling into a glimmering lake. The moon, who had a bigger heart than most imagined, took pity on the girl and decided to transform her into a part of the forest. Hence was born the lily pad, which is formed from a blossom that sinks to the bottom of the river, then resurfaces.

A QUICK RAINFOREST TOUR

To the uninitiated, the jungle looks like so much green mess, but actually the terrain that runs through the Amazon river system is extremely diverse. Some soils are deeply fertile, others approach bleached sand; along the Negro River, the vegetation is stunted, whereas in southeastern Pará, the forest, with its purplish-red soil, abounds with wildlife. There are also huge areas of wetlands and large expanses of savannah.

The rainforest itself grows in distinct layers, a natural hierarchy formed by the access (or lack of access) to the sun. Most of the activity take place in the luxuriant canopy, 100–130 ft. above the forest floor, where plants complete for sunshine and where the majority of animals and birds live. Above the canopy poke the trees that form the skyline of the forest. A poorly defined middle layer of understory merges with the canopy, hosting a variety of epiphytes—plants that derive moisture and nutrients from the air and rain but live on the surface of other plants. About 50 to 80 feet above ground spreads a tangle of seedlings, saplings, bushes, and shrubs. On the forest floor, plant life is limited because the thick vegetation of the canopy blocks out all but 1–2 percent of available sunlight. Ants and termites live here among the scattering of leaves and decaying plant matter.

TYPES OF FOREST There are three types of Amazon forest: *várzea*, or floodplain, regularly flooded by the rivers; the *igapós*, which are occasionally flooded; and the terra firme, generally unflooded land that forms the majority of the surface area. Much of the *terra firme* is high forest where animal life exists as much in the canopy as on the ground. When the forest is destroyed, the land turns to scrub since its fertility is bleached out.

WHY PRESERVE THE FOREST? Rainforests are intimately tied to global weather conditions, and their preservation helps prevent the global warming trend known as the Greenhouse Effect. Deforestation causes up to 30 percent of all human-produced carbon dioxide to the atmosphere, as well as unknown amounts of methane and nitrous oxide—gases that exacerbate global warming and threaten the quality of life worldwide. Rainforests also provide a natural defense against hurricanes, cyclones, and typhoons, absorbing the punch of howling winds and preventing storm tides from eroding beaches.

The products that come from the rainforest are part and parcel of our daily lives. As a fantastic natural pharmacy, the forest is home to thousands of medicinal plants that can be turned into antibiotics, painkillers, heart drugs, and hormones. The National Cancer Center in the U.S. has identified 3,090 plants as having anti-cancer properties—70 percent of which come from the rainforest. Other products that can be taken from the forest without destroying it range from cosmetics to automobile tires.

Tropical forests also provide the planet with much of its biological diversity. Every species that lives there is a living repository of genetic information, i.e., the building blocks of life. If the food chain that binds them together in a complex web of relationships is disturbed, it is not clear that humankind itself could survive. At the very least, we'd be facing the future with a shrunken world, a hostile climate, and a genetic base vulnerable to mutations.

Last but not least, the forest is home to millions of indigenous people, who have known no other way of life for thousands of years.

Within their memory banks is a trove of natural wisdom, including how to use plants medicinally, that can never be reduplicated once they pass from the earth. With very few exceptions, the forced relocation of indigenous forest people in the face of the bulldozer has invariably spelled disease, despair, and death.

IS ECO-TOURISM KOSHER? Many eco-conscious travelers ponder whether joining the rank and file of tourists tramping through the rainforest will ultimately endanger it. Truly in Brazil, the phrase eco-tourism has become the buzz word for the 1990s, though in many cases it's merely a marketing device referring to any outdoor adventure, be it beach, mountain, or forest. There are a select number of travel agencies and operators, however, who are deeply dedicated to preserving not only the forest but also its native peoples. Among these are **Expeditours** in Rio, **Lago Verde Turismo** in Santarém, and **Ariaú Jungle Tower** outside Manaus. A prevailing philosophy in Brazil these days is that eco-tourism actually serves to preserve the forest by giving its residents another way of making a living besides cutting down trees. Of course, one need only imagine the trash and debris that could clog the mighty Amazon and its tributaries when gum-chewing, smoking, beer-drinking tourists hit its banks. The nightmare needn't happen, however, if each traveler takes responsibility for his or her actions.

Eco Alert

The best way to preserve a rainforest is to travel with a conscience. Here are some Do's and Don'ts for visiting national reserves:

1. Don't give food to the local animals.
2. Don't hunt.
3. Don't destroy trees or break branches.
4. Don't throw litter.
5. Don't kill turtles, fish, birds, or other animals except in self-defense.*
6. Don't mistreat animals.
7. Don't make a fire.
8. Always have a reliable guide.
9. Do not cross into Indian reserves without special permission from FUNAI (nearly impossible to get). This law protects native people from unwanted diseases and cultural disturbance.

*Federal law prohibits the killing of dolphins, turtles, alligators, peixe boi (cowfish), tortoises, birds, and capybaras. Any animal that lives in the forest belongs to the state. Anyone caught red-handed by IBAMA agents is sent to prison from 3 months to 1 year.

OPTIONS FOR TRAVEL

In all honesty, it takes a certain kind of traveler to enjoy a jungle adventure. Sometimes, however, human beings can vastly surprise themselves. I, who was nearly sent home in tears from Girl Scout camp, immensely enjoyed my Amazonian treks, but they were not always easy, nor was I left with an overriding desire to return for the *unbeaten* tracks. (The beaten tracks were plenty exciting.) On your first trip to the jungle, I would not suggest braving it alone or with unreliable guides; believe me, you will want to feel there is someone looking after your welfare. Good guides (usually those officially trained) know the trails where you are least likely to meet poisonous snakes, voracious ants, man-eating piranha, and malaria-infested pools, not to mention mudslides and other debacles of nature. As for travel options, there is such a variety of possibilities that anyone from senior citizens to responsible children (nine and older) can make the grade. My suggestion is to plan a number of different treks that will give you a multi-dimensional perspective of Amazonian life. Among the possibilities:

- **Packaged boat tours** (or special charters) through the *igarapés* (streams) shooting off from the Amazon, near Belém, Manaus, or Santarém.
  Advantage: Good for those with limited schedules; trips usually last between 4 and 48 hours. Can include fishing, jungle walks, and overnight stays in the forest. Best trip is out of Belém, with Amazon Star Turismo. Travelers seeking air-conditioned cabins should investigate the 22-passenger "Tuna" or the 8-passenger "Hawk," which conduct 3-day and 6-day cruises out of Manaus. For more information contact **Brazil Nuts** ☎ *(203) 259-7900* in the U.S.

- **2–3 day stays at lodges built inside the jungle**, mostly accessible by boat from Manaus.
  Advantage: Secure accommodations with adequate to good food, bath, and organized excursions day and night.

- **2–3 day trips down the Amazon on public river boats** (the region's buses), like the *Cisne Branco,* which goes between Santarém and Manaus.

Advantage: Slow, relaxing, requires no effort, and gives you a chance to hobnob with locals. Best for those who speak Portuguese.

- **Sidetrip excursions to river beach sites** such as Alter de Chão near Santarém, and Marajó Island near Belém.

  Advantage: Change of greenery, cooling beaches, and exotic culture.

- **Luxury resorts**, like the Floresta Amazônica in Alta Floresta, Mato Grosso where you can sleep in comfort and take expeditions into the forest, down the river, to neighboring farms, and even to gold mines.

  Advantage: Offers the greatest options of adventures and the largest perspective of Amazonian lifestyles.

Will I Get Bitten by Snakes?

Snakes are an Amazon reality, but poisonous serpents are rare in the forest where official tours go. The most feared, however, is the *surucucu* (bushmaster), the largest venomous snake in Brazil, which measures up to 10 ft. Also common is the the *sucuri* (anaconda), the largest snake in the world, though not poisonous. Silverish-green in color, it's a member of the boa family, meaning it kills its prey by constriction and suffocation, feeding on fish, birds, mammals, and alligators. Don't worry.

Do beware, however, that some rainforest plants and animals mimic each other in order to hide from predators or sneak up on prey. Snakes, in particular, love to look like vines. For protection, wear ankle-high boots and tuck in your pants.

Will I Get Eaten by Piranha?

Pira means fish and *rana* means tooth—nasty, toothy little fish found throughout the rivers and lakes of the Amazon basin. Their viciousness, though exaggerated, is not exactly unfounded. Piranha only become dangerous when trapped in lagoons during dry season or when they smell blood. Waters in the Rio Negro around Manaus are harmless, but in general avoid swimming with open sores.

Squeamish tourists should enter the the water only after their guide dives in first. More feared than piranha is the *candirú açu*, a minute catfish that forces its way into the urethra of the bather, making itself difficult to extract. Don't worry.

"Should I Go to the Amazon?" Test

Take the following quiz to determine if you are a good candidate for an Amazon adventure. Don't cheat or it will come back to haunt you. If you rate more than 6 "Trues," sign up immediately; you'll probably actually enjoy yourself.

1. You are in good physical shape (heart and lungs), though you needn't be able to jog 5 miles.
2. You are able to withstand intense heat and humidity while trekking through a rugged forest on relatively flat land.
3. You do not flinch in the face of flying bugs, ticks, gnats, ants, or spiders, and will not faint at the sight of a dead snake (screaming in the face of a live snake is permitted, but not encouraged).
4. You can endure less than haute cuisine for a few days, and, if you're traveling on a boat, severely cramped quarters.
5. Seasickness is not a problem for you, nor are you scared of small canoes with bad motors.
6. You are not overly allergic to bees or bug bites.
7. You are prepared to come home with arms and legs eaten up by mosquitoes.
8. You like mud.
9. You can handle intense, frequent rain.
10. You know how to psyche yourself to withstand "green overload," fear of the unknown, and that kind of squishy, moldy feeling that comes from being rained on and not able to change your clothes immediately.

THE AMAZON SURVIVAL KIT

MOSQUITOES AND BUGS

Almost all lodges near Manaus were chosen for their mosquito-free locations. Even so, independent-party mosquitoes always managed to find me, especially on my boat cruise from Santarém to Manaus. Off-the-beaten trekkers must be careful; some areas of the Amazon are so ridden with mosquitoes that few human beings venture there. In his book *The Amazon* (Time-Life), Tom Sterling recalls how he had to wear a bathing cap to protect his bald head in the notorious Jari River region.

Yellow fever, transmitted by mosquitoes, is considered endemic in Brazil, except around the coastal shores.

Health authorities advise that the most infected areas are Acre, Amazonas, Goiás, Maranhão, Mato Grosso, Mato Grosso do Sul, Pará, Rondônia, and the territories of Amapá and Roraima. Vaccinations

THE AMAZON SURVIVAL KIT

are good for 10 years, and are essential if you are traveling either to the Amazon or the Pantanal. You may be required to show proof of vaccination when entering the country from Venezuela, Colombia, Ecuador, or Bolivia; it's best to always travel with it. (For more information, see the *Health Kit* in the back of the book.

PHOTOGRAPHIC EQUIPMENT

I went down the Amazon River with a professional German photographer who didn't give a whit about humidity-rot, bugs, or human carelessness—until I nearly knocked his equipment overboard. Truth is, bugs and infintesimal-sized tics are rampant on these boats and fungus abounds; the spray from the river alone is enough to render delicate mechanisms inactive. To avoid ruined film, keep rolls tightly secured in waterproof baggies and store all equipment with a small packet of silica gel. At least once a week expose lenses and camera to direct sunlight (minus the film!). Also, remember to develop film promptly (Manaus has some good 24-hr. processing shops), and if your camera allows for exposure adjustments, underexpose a 1/4 F-stop.

IN PREPARATION

Be in good physical shape; even though the terrain is more or less flat, hiking through a humidity-intense jungle can be exhausting. (In contrast, river trips border on the soporific.) Time your vaccinations over the month before you leave because you can't take them all at the same time. To ward off mosquitoes, many people swear by taking daily doses of Vitamin B 2 weeks to a month before the trip (and during) to ward off critters. Some professionals even believe that forgoing sugar helps. If you are particularly allergic to bees, make sure you travel with your own remedies (emergency medical assistance will probably be miles away). And above all, break in your new boots before leaving.

WHAT TO PACK

Swiss Army knife, canteen or plastic water bottle, thermos (with cup big enough to eat from), compass, binoculars, journal, pens, small backpack, and collapsible fishing gear. Pack water purification pills (but use in emergencies only; it's better to drink bottled water). If you plan to take river trips on the public boats, a hammock is advisable, even if you secure a private cabin. Mosquito nets are not generally needed, unless you venture out into the jungle on your own. Take plenty of bug repellant (see *Health Kit* in the back of the book) and reapply especially at dusk and before going to sleep. A fellow traveler in the Pantanal swore by Avon Skin-So-Soft bath oil as a natural repellant (available through Avon Products). Suntan lotion with a high SPH is an absolute must; the sun at the equator is the hottest in the world, and the river water will reflect it even more intensely. You should wear sun-block even in the tree-shaded jungle. Pack extras of all personal medicines, contact lenses, and glasses, etc. If you're taking a 2-3 day cruise down the Amazon, a juicy paperback will be deeply appreciated after 2 hrs.

WHAT TO WEAR

Light cotton clothing. Although native people walk through the rainforest barefoot and in shorts, I

THE AMAZON SURVIVAL KIT

don't suggest it for foreigners, whose immune systems are unaccustomed to jungle life. Wearing jeans (tucked into boots) and light cotton long-sleeved shirts (with roll-up sleeves) will cut down on scratches and snake and bug bites. In both wet and dry seasons you'll need sturdy tennis shoes and/or waterproof hiking boots (I loved my lightweight, waterproof Merrell boots made of Goretex). Heavy-treaded soles are needed to help you balance on tree logs. On any river trips you'll need a sunhat and good sunglasses with a strap to keep them from falling off. Kerchiefs are excellent for wiping sweaty brows. In rainy season, take a lightweight hooded rain poncho and an extra pair of clothes for when you get soaking wet. A swimsuit will come in handy, but pack a coverup. Some agencies supply rain gear (rubber boots and ponchos) when necessary.

MALARIA

To take malaria pills or not to take—that is the question that doctors, north and south of the equator, are still debating. On the con side: Prophylactics tend to mask symptoms; once the illness is diagnosed, they make it more difficult to treat. Also, new species of mosquitoes (from which malaria is contracted) are always developing and the latest medicines are not usually up to date. On the pro side: Pills give you some peace of mind. What's best is to wear strong repellant and avoid areas commonly known as breeding grounds, particularly stagnant water. Personally, I took every form of vaccination possible before leaving for Brazil including yellow fever (required), tetanus, and gammaglobulin (for Hepatitis B) as well as a complete round of malaria pills before, during, and after my trip to the jungle. For the latest official advisories, contact the Centers for Disease Control, Atlanta, GA 30333 (Parasitic Division, Center for Infectious Diseases). (Also see *Health Kit* in the back of the book.)

FOOD AND WATER

Meals cooked by private agencies are usually edible, but public river boats are notorious for food you wouldn't feed your dog. (One look at the boat's chef slicing raw beef from a carcass swarming with mosquitoes was enough to make me dive for my stash of oranges and cashew nuts (bought at port). Consider bringing from home some instant rice-and-bean mixes (found in health food stores) that need only hot water, as well as instant soups like miso, instant oatmeal, and dried seaweed (always good for energy). Always peel fruits. Bottled water, as well as hot boiling water, can be usually obtained on public river boats. Most even have snack bars with soda pop, candy, and beer. When trekking in the jungle, guides tend to forget to take along water, so remember to fill your own canteen with bottled water or stash a bottle of mineral water in your backpack. You will need it within 15 min. of hiking through the rainforest.

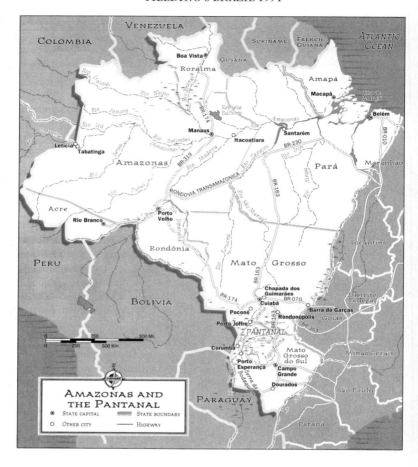

SANTARÉM

Located near the western border of the state of Pará, **Santarém** is the major city in the **Tapajós River Basin**—an enchanting, near magical region distinct from other Amazon terrains. Also called the **Lower Amazon,** this area is a verdant, almost continuous plain, rarely exceeding 300 meters high, and overlaid with lakes, tributaries, island rivers, and narrow streams called *igarapés*. During low tide (July–December), vast stretches of fine white sand and green water graced by pink porpoises turn the Tapajós into an Amazonian resort. Though there are roads in the region, they are torturous to traverse during rainy season, so most people travel by way of the *estradas líquidas* (liquid highways). Travelers can pick from every kind of water transport imaginable—from flat-bottom barges to diesel-powered canoes to *gaiolas* ("water buses") where everyone, from teens to salesmen to old ladies with grandchildren hang up their hammocks and settle in for the two to three day journeys.

Santarém is situated at the exact point where the Tapajós River pours its greenish waters into the brownish waters of the Amazon. For more than 300 years the region lived on a natural abundance of fish and wild game, which at one time seemed inexhaustible. Today the economy is based more on the processing of fruits and wood and cattle-raising. Despite its population of more than 300,000, Santarém would have been forgotten in the wake of the region's most recent gold rush if not for its location midway on the river route between Belém and Manaus. Unfortunately, little of the money made in the gold rush has returned to Santarém, which today is suffering from a severe depression.

Still, Santarém is a lovely Amazonian port to visit. Along the **Avenida Tapajós** you'll see hundreds of boats loaded with goods that are sold to villagers within moments of arrival. Even large luxury cruise ships have started to dock at port, taking advantage of the nearby primitive community **Alter de Chão,** known for its "illusory" lakeside beach. Santarém itself boasts a colorful wharfside market, a few imposing colonial houses, and several sleepy baroque squares. The best way to see this Rip Van Winkle city is to hire a languorous cow-drawn cart and go rambling down the dusty, cobblestone streets.

From an ecological viewpoint, Santarém can be seen as a microcosm of the Amazon, where all three types of jungle systems can be fully experienced: *várzea, terra firme,* and *igapó.* Extra excursions can be made to **Alenquer,** a former Indian village, where an impressive assembly of hieroglyphics leaves no doubt of an ancient civilization. Also a few hours away by boat is the community of **Monte Alegre,** a region ripe with rock paintings as well as amethyst mines and an unusual ecosystem: Its meadows, part of the Great Lake, boast semi-submerged forests and an enormous variety of fish.

Insider Tip:

Typical of the region are enormous water lilies that look like saucers right out of *Alice in Wonderland.* Called *Vitória Régia,* this lily has bright green leaves that measure almost 2 meters in diameter and a flower of 30 centimeters, making it the largest in the Americas.

PAST GLORIES

Prior to the European discovery, the Lower Amazon was inhabited by several indigenous groups, including the **Tupayos,** from which the Tapajós River got its name. In 1661, an Indian mission was founded, and in 1758 the name of the burgeoning settlement was changed to Santarém, after the town in Portugal. If you come across a few locals with last names like Vaughn or Steele, that's because two years after the American Civil War, one 100 **Confederates** immigrated to the region straight from the southern United States. (Sadly, practically none of their descendants speak English today.) Between 1821 and 1912, nearly half a million people from the Northeast migrated to the region in a desperate bid to flee a ravaging drought, helping the region become the world's prime producer of natural rubber. In 1927, the most curious jungle saga began when American mogul Henry Ford, after researching sites around the world, decided that the Tapajós Valley was the best region in which to cultivate rubber trees on an international scale. (Curiously, no Brazilian had ever given it much thought.) Capitalizing on a contract that awarded him 110,000 kilometers of forest for 50 years, Ford actually transported an entire prefabricated city into the jungle, complete with all the modern facilities. The community, appropriately named **Fordilândia,** was light years ahead of other cities in the Amazon basin: Workers reaped the benefit of free housing, electric light, running water, telephones, schools, theater, nurseries, orchards, and the best equipped hospital in the state of Pará. What Ford didn't anticipate was an explosion between the social classes, including an outbreak (known as the "saucepan-breaking incident") when the native workers demanded back their old food—beans, manioc flour, and *cachaça*—instead of the protein-enriched American rations. The real downfall of the enterprise, however, was attributed to a fungus known as leaf blight that devastated the plantation. In 1934, the same venture was attempted in another tract of land 60 kilometers south of Santarém (called **Belterra**), but it, too, was attacked by the same fungus as well as caterpillar blight. Today ecologists understand that the root of the disasters was monoculture—the lack of any other species that could balance the delicate ecosystem of the jungle. After 17 years the Ford company finally gave up the enterprise and "presented" the government of Brazil with the remains of the two communities for $250,000 (a loss of more than $20 million). Today, Fordilândia, though still inhabited, resembles a ghost town, with its deserted sheds and picket-fence houses—a mere shadow of the imposing structures erected during the '20s and '30s.

In 1958, the Lower Amazon was shaken by another explosion: an enormous vein of gold discovered in the upper Tapajós river valley, from Itaituba northwards. In 1969 the Santarém-Cuiabá highway was opened, enabling makeshift towns and villages to multiply as thousands hurried to the river and its tributaries to "*bamburrar*," or get-rich-quick. Today, more than 200,000 gold prospectors are still scattered over the region, contaminating the rivers with mercury, a deadly by-product of their primitive mining methods.

A BIRD'S EYE VIEW

To get a pleasant picturesque view of Santarém, walk down **Av. Tapajós**—past the river boats, chicken coops, and floating gas station to where you can view the meeting of the Amazon and Tapajós River. From July to January, the beach in front of the avenue is full of sand and lined with mango trees. A night tour to scope out alligators can be taken to Ilha de Ponta Negra, an area known for its cattle and huge water lily lake. Early morning trips are best for bird-watchers. Beaches near Santarém are exquisite. Located about three hrs. by boat, the **Arapiuns River** is reputed to be the most beautiful beach in the area, with 40 meters of white sand and dark rocks and excellent resources for fishing in unpolluted waters. Three or four kilometers into the forest, you'll discover a stunning waterfall. Four kilometers from Santarém is **Maracanã Beach,** which local people frequent. Among the chic beaches is **Pajussara,** about 30 minutes by boat from the city, full of lovely summer homes and palm-lined white sands. You must take your own food.

SIGHTS

ON FOOT

Santarém is a cinch to see on foot; just be careful about the heat, or the rain (during the rainy season). Start at the marketplace along the wharf near

Praça de Relógio, where from 6-10 a.m. you'll find the perfect picture-postcard version of an outdoor third-world marketplace. Nearby is the indoor **Mercado Modelo;** between the two you'll find everything from live chickens to tropical fruits to hammocks, which run about $16-$17. Then walk up **Rua Siqueira Campos** to the cathedral,

Nossa Senhora da Conceição, whose original structure was built in 1711 by French architects, but had to be rebuilt 20 years later when it collapsed. The fully clothed model of Jesus holding the Cross in the front right vestibule is paraded during the Círio festival (for more explanation, see under "Belém"). In front of the church is the **Praça da Matriz,** where about 60 years ago, a band used to perform. Walking down **Rua Siqueira Campos** (the main shopping avenue), you'll pass two record stores with good discount bins as well as recordings by regional musicians like Ray Brito and Tinha. Even if you're not heading out on a river trip, an interesting stop is the supermarket on this street called **Formigão** (Big Ant). You can stock up on beer, cookies, crackers, and especially Tang™ (the American orange drink mix, good for dehydration). On the next block you'll find the **Varig** office *(Rua Siqueira Campos, 277. Daily 7:00–11:30 a.m., 2:00–5:30 p.m., closed Sun.).* Across the street is **Pastelândia,** a clean and airy snack bar specializing in *pastéis* (baked dough pastries filled with meat or cheese), cooked right under your eyes. Camera and film stores are next door. Along Siqueira Campos are also several drugstores that may exchange dollars; talk to the owner.

Turn left on **Rua 15 de Novembro** past more shops, then right on **Rua do Comércio,** a pedestrian mall full of sportwear stores. On the right is the

Mascote Bar, a good stop for lunch. Nearby, at Rua Sen. Lam Bittencourt, 31 (the street running into Rua Comércio) is one of the best artisan stores (for more information, see under "Shopping").

Turning left from Rua do Comércio onto **Rua Francisco Correia,** walk up the steep hill for a wonderful view of the *meeting of the waters;* you'll see the blue of the Tapajós River and the brown of the Amazon. Fortunately, there's also a cool breeze here, perhaps the only one in the city. The odd illusion is that you'll feel as if you are looking out onto the ocean; the water is so clear because the river is full of plankton (plants) and, therefore, does not allow for the penetration of light. Walk back to Siqueira Campos and turn left, passing the only banana stand in the city. Walk straight to the

Museu dos Tapajós, also called **Casa da Cultura** *Av. Borges Leal, 6390;* ☎ *522-6390. Hours: 7 a.m.–5 p.m.* passing a stand that sells soda and *tacacá,* a Northeastern delicacy that is loaded with pepper and served piping hot. The museum is a small two-room affair that features pre-Columbian ceramics, Indian crafts from the Tapayo tribes, 400-year-old pottery, and the 300-year-old remains of an Indian girl. There's also a good view of the meeting of the waters here. Formerly the city hall, the building has a lobby lined with portraits of former mayors. To end this tour, walk back along the wharf. The best place to see the sun set is at

Mascotinho, an open-air café where you can indulge in pizza and beer. Next door there's a small park with swings for children. You'll also find an ice cream parlor where you can stock up on sweets and pastries, especially great if you're planning a boat trip. Along the wharf you'll see cows tied to carts, still used for transporting goods and people. If you would like a tour through the city on a cow, contact **Lago Verde Tourism** ☎ *522-1645* and they'll round one up.

BY CAR

Aparecida Hammock Factory Thousands of redes (or hammocks) are handmade daily at this factory *Av. Borges Leal, 2561;* ☎ *522-1187. Daily 7:30-11:30 a.m., 1:30–6 p.m.* where you can watch artisans work (until 3 p.m.) on looms imported from Southern England. Excellent quality is assured here, and you're sure to find all varieties and colors (if you're looking for cheap, better go to the Mercado Modelo). At Aparecida, you can pick up a single hammock for $11, a double for $20 (good for one large person), and a child's for about $7; all profits go to support social-welfare programs. If you're making any jungle trips—by land or water—a hammock helps beat the heat. Do practice slowly getting in and out; many a gringo has fallen flat on his or her face, to the enormous amusement of locals, who do it so gracefully. (One hint: The safest way is to lie down diagonally.) Before you invest, note that a hammock takes up considerable bulk in a suitcase but will fit nicely in a backpack.

Herb Farm For the past 15 years, **Farmácia Viva,** a dirt-road community of 3,000, has supported this herb cooperative famous for its medicinal remedies. The village, about 10 minutes from the Tropical Hotel, is full of ethereal-looking children with curly, bright-golden hair that no one can explain, but the old ladies who tend the garden seem like the salt of the earth. They'll love to show you their patches of patchouli, *capim santo*, and other herbs whose tart aromas fill the air. And they'll be even more delighted if you buy some of their homemade tonics (usually under $1). The *banho capilar* is reported to grow hair on a bald head, and there's even a plant called "Vick" that's good for headaches. Stomach ailments, colds, cysts—just name the ailment and you'll get an herbal cure. Since the way to the plantation often confuses even locals, you'll probably have to go with a guide, but be careful about getting stuck in the mud (though, if you do, the whole community will turn out to help). To get there, take the road to Cuiabá, turn left on Av. (MORP) Moaçara, right on Trav. Rouxinol and Rua Maravilha. And keep asking.

National Forest Sixty-two kilometers by good road from Santarém is the **Floresta Nacional de Tapajós,** a virgin forest where you can see a variety of animals, including gangs of wild pigs, monkeys, and tropical birds. Ornithologists often come to research South American landbirds, which appear in volumes in the early mornings. To visit the park, call **IBAMA** ☎ *522-3032* and speak to Ronaldo Almeida, director of the the National Forest. You must provide your own transportation (boat, plane, or jeep) and translator, but you are also required to be officially accompanied by one of their guides.

EXCURSION

ALTER DE CHÃO

Thirty-five kilometers from Santarém is **Alter de Chão,** Santarém's weekend resort. It's an outgrowth of a village of the Borari Indians, a place of magical leisure because of the still-native community and unusual beaches that spread over the bay of the Tapajós River. Alongside the village is

Muiraquitãs Lake, whose folklore is the most important in the region, especially the celebration of the **Festa da Sairé** in June. Slowly the village has been surrendering to modernism. Today, most of the locals, who used to fish and hunt, live mainly off tourism, and their clay homes are now being squeezed in between more modern summer homes. During high season the city is so crowded you can barely walk through the dusty streets; at other times it looks deserted. Despite the city government's attempt to pave over the streets, even the beachside avenue has remained dirt. The city's "gar-

bage collectors" can be seen flying over the city—huge black vultures called *urubus*. (They're also called turkey vultures because their heads look like turkeys.) The main square,
Praça de Nossa Senhora da Saude, is fronted by a native church and shaded by big-leafy jambeiro trees, whose fruits are quite tasty. Here, you'll also find native women selling *tacacá*, a native dish usually served in coconut shells. On the far side of the plaza, down **Travessa dos Martines** (a side street from the beach), is an area of rubber trees, where at 4 p.m. every day, the seeds blow up and explode, sounding just like a revolution breaking out.

Between January and June, an island in the bay appears out of nowhere with 40 meters of sand, becoming the makeshift summer residence for about 1,000 *caboclos*. For about a dollar each way, little boys will ferry you in rickety canoes across to the island; there you'll find *barracas* for drinks, snacks, and barbecue fish and chicken. It's best to avoid swimming on the river side (south); instead head for the north side of the island, where trees are growing out of the lake and the water is cooler and cleaner. Windsurfing is excellent (though you must have your own equipment). A very healthy hike can be taken up the no-name mountain with a cross on top (about 45 min. one way). At the peak, you'll get an impressive view of **Piranha Lake**.

Buffalo fanatics can head for the fazenda of **Wil Ernesto Leal,** whose 1,000-hectare farm also houses the **Instituto de Pesquisa Amazônica,** the most famous research institute in the area. The land is primarily savanna, a vegetation uncommon to the Amazon, comprised of thin tall trees around which scamper monkeys, capybaras, and exotic birds. Presently, Senhor Leal is looking for American investors to make a pousada there. For more information contact **Lago Verde Tourism** ☎ *(91) 522-1645* or **Wil Ernesto Leal** *Rua Tapajós, 47;* ☎ *(91) 522-5094, FAX 522-6588.*

Getting There

Many cruises anchor in Santarém, where passengers then take a bus to Alter de Chão, and then are picked up by the ship. Other tourists may take the split-level cruising boat provided by the Tropical Hotel. The breezy 2-hour trip passes through the Tapajós River, cruising by islands that look exactly like the shape of alligators. You can also take a rough-and-rugged trip by car, where you'll catch glimpses of the edge of the forest. The road is gravel, but has been improved of late.

Hotels/Restaurants/Crafts

If you stay over night during high season, you'll have to reserve a hotel in advance. Only primitive pousadas are available. Try the

Pousada Alter de Chão ☎ *101, ramal 2* where you can find a room for $7 per person, including breakfast, bathroom, but no air-conditioning. 12 apts. *Inexpensive. No cards.*

Best restaurant lakeside is **Lago Verde** *Daily 7 a.m.–6 p.m., weekends, open at 6 a.m.* Try the regional *tucunaré* (a family of black bass) or the *bolinho de pirarucú*, (an extremely tender fish wrapped in a crispy fried crust).

Arte Grupo Lago Verde, a handicraft store, features an interesting snack called *beijos de moço* (kisses of a young boy), a kind of tapioca flour baked into crispy crackers. Also stock up on jars of *doce de cupuaçu* or *licor de cajú*, sweets and liquers made out of regional fruits. Native crafts include hand-painted logs and twigs found in the forest—a little kitschy for my taste since the local style is to paint over the natural bark with artificial colors.

EXCURSION PACKAGES

A few good tour operators can be found in Santarém; the most reliable is **Lago Verde Turismo**, whose various options can be tailored to your time, budget, and interest. (Also see "Travel Agencies" under *Hands-On Santarém*.)

An excellent 3-day/2-night package that could serve as an exotic honeymoon starts from the airport, where you transfer to a 10-person boat and head up the

River Curuana. Here, a canoe with outboard motor will be awaiting you for navigation through the numerous *igarapés* full of water lilies, pink dolphins, alligators, and birds. The region is known for having more native trees than any other, and as the river meets the Amazon, *varzea* appears, which is good for piranha fishing. After lunch you return to the regional boat and go up river to visit

Vila Pacoval, a village founded by runaway black slaves originally from Guyana. At dusk (5:30–6:30 p.m.), small canoes are taken out for alligator hunting. Afterwards, a special candlelit dinner is served in the middle of the forest. The next morning you visit the outdoor and indoor labs of **SUDAM**, a research center for reforesting projects. Then you cruise down river to

Alter de Chão, arrive at dawn, and breakfast on the island. After breakfast, you are invited to climb the mountain; successful trekkers are feted with ice cream and champagne. The rest of the day is spent at Alter de Chão (at the beach or in canoes); then you may either head for the airport in the evening or spend the night in a hotel. Groups of 8 to 10 people run $300 per person. A private package for 2 people runs about $1,900.

MONTE ALEGRE

Heading down the Amazonas River between Santarém and Belém is the town of **Monte Alegre**. Etched into the Ererê and Paituna mountain ranges are caves, rock formations, and primitive designs and paintings belonging to pre-historic Amazônia. Two hundred meters from the port is one of the largest egret rookeries in the region. At dawn and dusk, millions of birds can be seen flapping their wings in a magnificent display. Another attraction is the thermal springs, where pools of sulfurous water are used to treat skin diseases. For more information contact the **Secretaria da Cultura e Turismo/ Prefeitura Municipal de Monte Alegre** *Av. Presidente Vargas;* ☎ *(92) 533-1147, Santarém, PA.*

ALENQUER

Nicknamed the "City of the Gods," **Alenquer** can be found upstream on the Amazon River between Santarém and the border of Pará. About an hour from the town are lakes and streams with giant waterlilies. A family of rock pedestals with smaller stones in identifiable shapes can be found in Morada dos Deuses. There is also a tall cliff in a valley that forms a canyon with a waterfall. The folklore event **Festa do Marambiré** is held every June.

Lago Verde Turismo also offers excursions to both Monte Alegre and Alenquer on a 3-day package. (For address and telephone, see under "Travel Agencies" in *Hands-On.*)

THE ESSENTIAL SANTARÉM

WHERE TO STAY

In Santarém, there is the Tropical Hotel, and then there are the others—a gap of about 3 stars. If you're rugged enough to spend a few days in the jungle, you may be perfectly happy with lower-class accommodations in the city, but there's nothing like coming back to clean sheets, civilized service, and reliable air-conditioning.

Expensive -------------- Over $50

Inexpensive ------------- Under $20

★ Santarém Tropical

Av. Mendonça Furtado, 4120; ☎ *522-1533, FAX 522-2631*

Not as elegant as the Tropical in Manaus, but it is the best hotel here. It's also owned by Varig, so you'll find an airline office in the lobby and a travel agency that can book jungle tours. Rooms are tiled to accommodate jungle trekkers, and every effort is made to maintain high standards of cleanliness. 122 apts. *Expensive. All cards.*

Santarém Palace Hotel

Av. Rui Barbosa, 726; ☎ *522-5285*

The best of the budgets offers rooms that are spacious to a fault, with painted corridors and carpeted floors. All rooms are air-conditioned and come with color TV, telephone, and minibar; even the lobby is air-conditioned. Local tours are offered in the lobby. Singles run $14, doubles $16. 47 apts. *Inexpensive. No Cards.*

Brasil Grande Hotel

Trav. 15 de Agosto, 213; ☎ *522-5660*

Nearly a "dive," but at least it's clean and efficiently run. A favorite among locals, the fan-cooled restaurant with MTV serves regional fish for $5. Across the street is the Mascote Ice Cream Parlor, with exotic Popsicles. Standards with fan, color TV, and minibar run $12 for one person, $15 for two; suites with air-conditioning, color TV, and minibar run $14-$16. Rooms with only fan and collective bathroom run $7. 20 apts. *Inexpensive. No Cards.*

City Hotel
Trav. Francisco Corrés, 200/212; ☎ *522-4719*
Funky on the verge of sleazy. What's called a suite has a double and single bed in one air-conditioned room, with a color TV and minibar. Since rooms vary in size, check out what's available when you arrive. The lobby is dominated by a color TV, dirty plastic plants, and a grungy aquarium. Laundry service available. Suites run $15, double deluxes $14, standards $11. The simplest rooms, with fan and minibar, run $8-$10. *Inexpensive. No cards.*

WHERE TO EAT

Moderate---------------- $5–$10

Inexpensive------------- Under $5

Mascote Restaurante
Praça do Pescador, 10; ☎ *522-1997. Daily 11 a.m.–midnight*
Santarém is not the culinary king of the Amazon, but a good meal can be had here for under $5. Pizzas are good, as is the *Peixe de Tucunaré*, a fish similar to black bass that arrives in a light soup. The service is not fast, but you can spend the wait gazing out the window at the *gaiolas* loading up. *Inexpensive. All Cards.*

Mutuny
Est. Santarém/Curuá-Una, 6 kilometers; Daily 10 a.m.–2 p.m., 5 p.m.–1 a.m.
Set outdoors in the middle of a forest about 10 kilometers from the city, this is a great place to see the Amazon moon and stars. During the day, you can swim in a natural pool made from an *igarapé* or cool off at the big canopied tables. Local families crowd in on the weekend to feast on great barbecued chicken and beef. Plates run about $3, no desserts. *Inexpensive. No Cards.*

Mascotinho
Riverside
The "little" version of Mascote, perched on the bank, perfect for pizza, sandwiches, and dock-watching. Sunsets are spectacular here. *Inexpensive. No Cards.*

Lumi
Av. Cuiabá, 1683, ☎ *522-2174. Daily: 11 a.m.–2 p.m., 6 p.m.-11 p.m*
Authentic Japanese cuisine made by the descendants of immigrants who arrived during the rubber boom. *Moderate. No cards.*

Storil
Rua Turiano Meira, 115; ☎ *522-3159. Daily: 11 a.m.–3 p.m., 6 p.m.–midnight, closed Monday.*
Regional food. *Moderate. No Cards.*

Insider Tip

Bolo de Macacheira (Macacheira cake) is a delicious sweet heavy cake made of shredded macacheira root (the non-poisonous variety of cassava root), sugar, eggs, coconut, and butter. You're not likely to find this on any menu, so stop by Dona Antônia's **Lanchonete Quero Mais** *Av. Rui Barbosa, 23.*

NIGHTLIFE

With chagrin, locals have confessed to me that Santarém at night is no stranger to boredom. Decent clubs are few and far between, but nationally known musicians do appear periodically at the auditorium; check the newspaper.

Carinhoso
Wharfside. Daily 6 p.m.–6 a.m.
Owned by a businessman, journalist, and lawyer, this musical bar is *the* after-hours spot. On the menu are pizza, beer, and big sandwiches on white bread. Musicians who present shows in the area jam here with locals. Tues.-Sun. features a great local MPB singer. Across the street is a magnificent

"horizontal" mango tree that's over 100 years old.

> **Insider Tip**
>
> Ask about Sebastião Tapajós, a fantastic local guitarist who's become well known in France and Switzerland for regional Amazon folk music.

SHOPPING

Santarém is just finding its sea legs touristically speaking, so the likelihood of finding serviceable souvenirs at the marketplace is negligible. Normal goods, such as sandals, can run outlandishly high here (what costs $20 in Manaus goes for $60 here). The following stores offer some unique crafts made by isolated artisans. Also, check record stores on **Rua Siqueira Campos** for regional music.

Cerâmica Art Sousa
Av. Gonçalves Dias, 747
Pottery specialists José Aniceto and his son Joel sell mainly to arts and crafts shops throughout the Amazon Region, but they welcome visitors. Joel was an exchange student/professor at the University of Missouri-Rolla in 1981.

Artisanato Dica Frazão
Rua Floriano Peixoto, 281
Since 1949 Dona Dica has been creating her own cottage industry, crafting natural bark, root, and vine fibers gathered by Indians on the upper Tapajós River into dresses, tunics, purses, and fans.

Livraria e Papelaria Ática
Trav. 15 de Novembro, 193; ☎ *522-2745*
Stationary, fine gifts, and books by regional authors such as Benedito Monteiro, João Santos, and Wilde da Fonseca.

Prönatus
Rua Galdino Veloso, 278. Mon.-Sat. 8 a.m.–noon, 2–6 p.m.
Across the street from the Brasil Grande Hotel, this store sells natural products from the Amazon, such as herb soap, shampoo, and various herb capsules for impotency, urinary problems, etc.

Cabana
Travessa 15 de Agosto, 211. Mon.-Fri. 8 a.m.-noon, 2–6 p.m., Sat. 8 a.m.–noon
An endlessly fascinating store that sells *umbanda* and *candomblé* paraphernalia, including statues of Christian and African saints, incense, candles, and all types of potions. (I once spied a very serious middle-aged man buying a potion to attract love.)

Manipulação
Trav. Francisco Correa, 168, ☎ *522-1303*
A homeopathic store selling brown rice, homeopathic medicines, and anti-diabetic teas.

HANDS-ON SANTARÉM

Arrivals

Air:
Flights are available from Belém, Campo Grande, Cuiabá, Alta Floresta, Manaus, Rio Branco, Salvador, São Paulo, and a few other cities. The airport is located 13 kilometers from town. Taxis to downtown are readily available at the airport: the Tropical Hotel provides complimentary shuttle bus service for its guests. Airlines that fly into Santarém are: **Varig/Cruzeiro** *Rua Siqueira Campos, 227;* ☎ *522-2084 and 522-1084* (at the airport) and **VASP** *Av. Rio Barbosa, 786;* ☎ *522-1680*.

Boat: See "River Cruises" below.

Bus: The *Rodoviária* ☎ *522-3392* is located on the Santarém-Cuiabá highway. Conditions permitting, bus service is available to Belém (through connections) and other points.

Car Rentals

Localiza/National *Av. Borges Leal, 1826;* ☎ *522-1130.*

City Transportation

Aquila *(air and land taxis)* ☎ *522-1848;* ☎ *522-2596 (at the airport).*

Climate

Tropical temperatures vary between 72 degrees and 94 degrees F. The dry season runs July–Dec.; the rainy season from July to Jan., when it precipitates copiously. March receives the most rain and, therefore, is the coolest month. The annual alternation of low and high tide that occurs every 6 months makes for exuberant ecological contrasts. From July-Dec., the meadows become excellent pastures for cattle and buffalo; between Jan.–July, wildlife must swim through swamps or be transported to *terra firm*.

Medical Emergencies

José Garcia, M.D. ☎ *522-1044* specializes in tropical diseases and speaks English and Spanish.

Paulo Sérgio Pimentel, M.D. ☎ *522-4293/522-4782* specializes in internal medicine.

Money Exchange

No one officially changes money in Santarém (better to come with a sufficient pile of *cruzeiros*), but in emergencies, drugstores along Rua Siqueira Campos may comply; inquire of the owners.

Post Office

Correio *Praça da Bandeira, 81.*

Private Guide

A good English-speaking guide is **Fernando Guarany Filho** *TV. NS-4, no. 82 COHAP* a young Brazilian chap who loves Lou Reed and whose veddy British accent was honed in parochial school. He can also be contacted through **Lago Verde Turismo** ☎ *522-1645.*

River Cruises

The oldest and still most common mode of travel in the region is boat, as witnessed by the 7,000 vessels operating in the municipality, from small wooden diesel-powered crafts to large catamaran passenger ships owned by the ENASA Company. Luxury liners from the States and Europe are becoming a more frequent sight.

Larger boats and ships dock at the deep-water pier **(Docas do Pará),** located at the far northern end of the Santarém-Cuiabá Highway. Most other boats leave from the area between the Market Place and the Praça do Pescador (Fisherman's Square). Though they are not always safe, 2-decker *gaiolas* are the most popular way to journey downriver. Some have been known to sink from being overloaded with chickens, pigs, and produce, but better precautions are taken these days to avoid the kind of tragedy that befell the *Cisne Branco* about 8 years ago. (On a special New Year's cruise the ship sank, drowning everyone aboard when all the passengers moved to the right side at the same time to see the approaching port of Manaus. I must add, however, in 1991 I daringly took a cruise on the resurrected *Cisne Branco* and happily survived.) For any bookings for river cruises, contact **Lago Verde Turismo** or contact ENASA directly (see page 491).

Most boats headed for Manaus or Belém offer a limited number of private cabins, and should be reserved as early as possible. The cabins in **gaiolas** are extremely small, but their virtue is privacy; if you rent one, you may also want to hang a hammock in the main galley to lounge during the hot days. Usually, there is an upper deck with a snack bar where you can sit and watch the banks pass by. More often than not, the price of the ticket includes meals, but do take a pile of bananas, oranges, and cashews because the food may not be up to your personal standards of cleanliness.

Travel time by boat from Santarém: Belém 75 hrs., Manaus 75 hrs., Alenquer 6 hrs., and Monte Alegre 10 hrs.

Enasa Boats may or may not be running in 1994, but they have been one of the most popular tourist excursions between Belém and Manaus (with stops in Santarém). Made for touring, the boats boast air-conditioned cabins with private bathroom, restaurant, telephone, video lounge, bar, sun-deck, and swimming pool. The trip from Belém to Santarém runs 3 days; Santarém to Manaus 2 days. Schedules in the past have run once a month.

In Santarém contact **Agência de Navegação Marítima Tapajós** *Av. Tapajós, 905, second floor, room 2;* ☎ *(91) 522-1138;* in **Belém** *Av. Presidente Vargas, 41;* ☎ *(91) 223-3011;* in **Manaus** *Rua Mal. Deodoro, 61;* ☎ *(92) 232-4280.*

Telephone Company

Local and international phone calls may be made at **TELEPARA** *Av. São Sebastião, 913.*

Time

Santarém is 1 hour earlier than Belém—a fact that sometimes confuses even airline officials.

Tourist Information

PARATUR *Praça Kennedy, 66030;* ☎ *224-9633* may have tourist brochures or information. Some souvenir shops may sell *Alexander's Guide to Santarém*, a small booklet with a map and other information (mostly included here).

Travel Agencies

Lago Verde *Rua Galdino Veloso, 664;* ☎ *522-1645* One of the premier agencies in Santarém, Lago Verde offers personalized packages to large and small groups. Good English-speaking management and guides are available for fishing, trekking, scientific expeditions, photographic projects, and nature studies.

Agências Tropicais de Turismo/Hotel Tropical *Av. Mendonça Furtado, 4120,* ☎ *522-1533* provides transfers from the airport to the hotel for its guests, as well as a variety of group tours, including half-day city tour, Alter de Chão, Meeting of the Waters, Belterra, piranha fishing, and nighttime alligator hunts.

Amazon Turismo Ltda. *Trav. Turiano Meira, 1084;* ☎ *522-2620, FAX 522-1098* offers overnight trips to Monte Alegre in a jeep, and Alenquer in a wooden riverboat, as well as daytrips to Fordilândia and the National Park.

When to Go

From August–January, the flowers become increasingly more profuse and there's more sand on the beach. January is peak time, with **New Year's Day** celebrated with big bashes. **Festa do Sairé** occurs the first week in July. On June 29, a procession of *bumba-meu-boi* takes place during the **São Pedro** festival. In September there is the **International Tucunaré Fishing Championship.**

BELÉM

Belém effectively entered the 20th century in 1961, when Juscelino Kubitschek's highway from Brasília reached its final destination. For centuries prior, however, the city, strategically placed on the Amazon estuary close to the mouth of the Rio Tocantins, had served nobly as a natural port for the steady stream of products extracted from the Amazon. Dating back to 1621, the city of Belém, which is also the capital of the state of Pará, was christened on the feast day of St. Mary of Bethlehem, and at times is still referred to by its long nomenclature: **Nossa Senhora do Belém do Grão-Pará** or, at least, **Belém do Pará**. The state, which is larger than most European countries, is the wealthiest in Brazil in regards to ore; even Indian tribes, such as the Kayapó, are sitting on some of the richest mahogany and gold reserves in the country.

It was the 19th-century rubber boom that transformed this natty little port into a graceful, Victorian city of *fin de siècle* arches and Italianate palazzos. What makes Belém truly beautiful are its avenues and plazas, shaded with magnificent *mangueiras* (mango trees) that cool the cobblestones when temperatures soar above 80 degrees. Even today, the historic quarter, which retains much of its Art Nouveau and Neo-classical structures, is a pleasure to stroll through, butted on all sides by a thriving market. One need only step inside the famed **Teatro da Paz**, the city's all-purpose theater, to appreciate the ingenuity of the rubber barons who longed to recreate European culture in the middle of the jungle. Yet it is the **Ver-o-Peso** market, facing the waterfront, which outclasses any other outdoor marketplace in Brazil, and perhaps in South America. Crammed, chaotic, and totally confusing to the uninitiated, the Ver-o-Peso is a veritable lion's den of exotic sights and smells that could take days to exhaust.

Although most jungle-destined tourists have traditionally headed for Manaus, Belém shouldn't be missed. Not only is the city more navigable by foot, but the jungle expeditions I experienced here should be considered some of the best in the region. Like Manaus, Belém is hot and humid, but the locals here have developed a sense of humor: They refer to themselves as fish because they feel they breathe more water than air.

SIGHTS

ON FOOT

Belém is a perfect city to stroll through. Start your walking tour in front of the **Hilton Hotel**. (If you're not staying there, you might take a peek at the lush breakfast buffet, open to the public but free for guests.) Directly across the street is the **Praça da República**. Once dense with tropical forest, the site was cleared in the 17th century to make way for Belém's first cemetery; later it became the city's principal park. There's even a *coreto*, an iron-grilled pagoda where brass bands used to entertain. Dominating the square is the city's pride and joy, the **Teatro da Paz** *Mon.–Fri. 8 a.m.–noon, 2–6 p.m.*), an unabashedly neoclassical opera house surrounded by Greek columns and adorned at its entrance with the four busts of the Muses. Inaugurated in 1878, the plush theater, with its bronze staircases and fabulous tiled floors was fueled by the ostentatious passions of the rubber barons who continually looked to Europe for style. Consequently, the foyer's crystal mirrors are Italian, the massive chandelier in the lobby German, the pastel, fluted light fixtures Art Deco. The theater's ceiling is an amazing marriage of Italianate painting and grillwork from which is suspended an 8-tiered, 1-1/2 ton crystal chandelier. The adjacent Salão Nobre is absolutely charming, once a salon for the elite balls and now the stage for chamber concerts and voice recitals. Note that the salon's ceiling painting is not from the original construction but was designed in 1960 by São Paulo artist Armando Balloni to reflect the wealth of Amazonian animals. Walk out to the balcony and look up to see the four Muses: from right to left, Comedy, Poetry, Music, and Drama. In 1986 the building, after laboring under a blue facade for many years, was restored to its original pink color. Backstage, you'll see plaques honoring performances by the great ballerina Anna Pavlova in 1918 and the great Brazilian soprano Bidu Sayão. If you have the opportunity to catch a performance of theater or music, grab it; merely ask your concierge or check the daily newspapers for listings. Free tours are given continuously throughout the day, though only in Portuguese.

On the side of the theater near the Hilton is the **Bar do Parque**, an outdoor café where the city's artists, singers, and streetwalkers gather until the wee hours of morning. Nearby is a kiosk that sells bread and coffee in the morning and beer and *caipirinhas* in the afternoon.

Walking down **Rua Presidente Vargas**, you'll come upon the **Teatro Experimental Walder Henrique** *Rua Pres. Vargas, 645;* ☎ *222-4762*. Started in 1979, this experimental theater is a showcase for avant-garde music, plays, and dance, with preference given to artists who are not yet professionals. Due to their struggling budget, shows are not given daily; they start around 9 p.m. when they do happen. Seats go for about $1.50.

Walk down **Av. Presidente Vargas** to the right of the theater, passing a travel agency, the **Varig** office at #363, and the **Monopólio Turismo Câmbio** (for exchanging money) at #325. Turn left on **Rua Santo Antônio**, a cobblestone street with no cars, down the middle of which are the remains of 19th-century trolley tracks. As the principal shopping avenue of the city (also called Comércio) the street overflows with shops and vendors hawking all kinds of third-world quality goods. As you wander, look up at the second-story houses, once 19th-century fashionable homes and still adorned with exquisite tile work and pastel-colored balconies and shutters. At #264, you'll find the **Restaurante Vegetariano e Mercadinho Natural**, a vegetarian market where you can stock up on natural shampoos, whole foods, and Amazon teas. Upstairs, the restaurant serves only lunch Mon.-Fri. from 11:30 a.m.-3 p.m. Down the street, do peek inside the **Paris N'América**, today a dry goods store but once a beautiful home constructed in 1906 for Francisco Castro by the Portuguese master Ricardo Salvador Fernandes Mesquita. From the sculptured ceilings to the dramatic grilled stairway, many of the details of the original architecture are still intact. The steel was imported from Scotland, the ceramic-tiled floor and mechanical clock from Germany, the bronze light fixtures from France, the crystal mirrors from Belgium, and the outside wall tiles from Portugal.

A few steps further on, you'll reach **Praça Mercês**, home to many finely restored buildings. Dominating the plaza is the church known as **Mercês**, founded in 1640. Despite the graffiti, you can see that the facade is still intact. This may be just the time that you need a ice-cold *água de coco*, which can be bought in front of the church.

Next, walk in front of the church on Rua Gaspar Viana and turn right on **Travessa Frutuoso Guimarães**. At #63, you can pick up decent mosquito nets and hammocks for about $6–14; white canvas hammocks with lace go for about $40.

VER-O-PESO MARKET

Nearby, along **Av. Castilhos** facing the pier, you'll enter into one of the great third-world marketplaces of all time. To a first-world eye, the open-air market may look like a den of iniquity, but it's actually the epitome of Amazonian life: hundreds of tiny stalls selling anything and everything that floats up the river—from fruits and vegetables and Brazil nuts to snake skins, turtle soap, and dolphin eyes (the last three all contraband materials). Begun as a checkpoint in 1688, the market received its name ("watch the weight") from the Portuguese habit of weighing all merchandise that passed through the port so that a tax could be charged. Today, the market is also a food bazaar, with scores of native women cooking aromatic dishes for the workers who cram into the tiny pathways. The air in the market is hot and dense and barely conducive to dining, but if you're brave enough, browse around until you find something that looks edible. The dark-maroon, soup-like juice sitting in the large tin pans is *açaí*, a true Amazon delicacy made with sugar and manioc juice (it tastes a bit like avocado and goes well with fried fish). Take a moment to watch the workers squeeze the water out of the ground manioc with a long straw tool called *tipiti* that works something like an accordion. As you walk through the market, each section will resound with its own sounds and smells. Daily life, not just business, is carried on here, with lots of flirting and cursing going on between stalls. A perusal of the tropical fruit stands will give you an idea of the enormous variety available here; note the Brazil nuts that come lodged in big brown shells, just as they're found in the forest. The large green spiny-looking fruit is a *graviola*. The herb section is particularly ripe with superstition and folklore. Good buys are small bottles of concentrated oils like *baunilha* (vanilla) and jasmin, or more potent love potions like the "*Corre Atrás*" designed to make a man "Run After" you. *Tamaquaré* powder is a cooked lizard powder sprinkled on husbands to get to them calm down sexually—a hot-selling item in the Amazon. (Some women actually buy the live lizards you see in the market and cook them into potions themselves. Another trick is to place the live lizard in the same water where the man regularly washes his clothes.) On the opposite extreme, stall

#54 sells perfume that comes complete with a boa constrictor inside, well known as a "fatal attraction" potion.

> **Insider Tip**
>
> *Due to the tight space and general mayhem, this market can be dangerous. Go with little money on you, do not wear gold chains or jewelry, keep your bags close to you at all times, and be cautious about taking photos. Since a number of vendors trade in contraband items (particularly endangered species), they do not care to have their business recorded.*

Don't miss the **meat market** nearby, a chrome-grilled structure brought from England in 1909; its cast-iron frame and Victorian turrets are souvenirs from the time when the British built most of the port a century ago. Inside, individual stands are manned by brawny workers who constantly yell at each other while slicing carcasses hanging from wires. The wet, smelly fish market in the same complex opens in the early morning and closes by 1 p.m.; here you can view full-sized samples of the region's most typical fish. Buyers receive their merchandise wrapped in large leaves from the *guarumã* bush, then supply their own plastic bag—a traditional Amazonian way of economizing on paper.

In general, the entire area near the pier is endlessly fascinating and ripe with photo ops. Outside the market you may see baby monkeys for sale (illegal) or even baby sloths (also illegal). Make sure you walk down **Boulevard Castilhos França** next to the bay, where fishermen and merchants dock their schooners and canoes laden with goods. Unfortunately, a lot of trash litters the portside here, even though (or because) many people use their boats as floating lodges. You may even see rats scurrying about these barges to no one's apparent dismay. Do note the Texaco floating gas station in the bay, an omnipresent reminder of Western influence.

Across from the pier near the market, the **Praça do Relógio**, with its large, monumental clock tower, is often used by guides as a meeting place.

> **Insider Tip**
>
> *ENASA boats to Marajó Island leave from the port on the other side of the market.*

Walk from the market past the mango and bamboo tree-filled Dom Pedro II Park to the **Praça Frei Caetano Brandão**, dominated by the 19th-century **Catedral de Nossa Senhora da Graça**. Sadly run-down on the outside, the cathedral boasts some of Brazil's finest paintings inside, though the lights are rarely turned on. *Hours for mass are Tues.–Thur. 5:30 p.m., Sat. 6:30 a.m. and 7 p.m., and Sun. 7 a.m., 9 a.m., 5 p.m., and 8 p.m.* It's from here that nearly one million strong begin their journey to the Basílica each year during the Círio festival.

A good place to end the walking tour is at the **Forte do Castelo**: open *daily 8 a.m.–noon, 2-6 p.m.: restaurant 11:30 a.m.–3 p.m., 6:30–11:30 p.m.* This fort marks the city's founding, as it was the first building constructed in Belém, strategically located at the confluence of the Guajará Bay and Guamá River on a hill commanding a view of the bay. Once headquarters for the military operations that expelled the English, French, and Dutch, it also provided a refuge for the Caabanagem revolutionaries. Now the fort houses the **Circulo Militar Club and Restaurant**, open to the public. Actually, there's nothing to do here but sit and drink (better at night when the weather is cooler, though during the day the view of the port below is fantastic). From the perimeter of the fort you can also see the **Feira d'Açai** down below, where boats loaded with raw *açaí* start arriving as early as 4:30 a.m. You can also see large cargo boats transporting ceramics from the nearby islands and returning home laden with mineral water and sodas.

The **Cidade Velha** (Old City) around the market and cathedral are full of quaint squares and colonial homes with grilled balconies and colorful shutters. Browse at will, but do try to avoid **Rua da Ladeira**—not a safe street to walk through due to the prostitutes and homeless who frequent its alleyways. (During the day, it's more or less okay, but avoid completely at night.)

MORE SIGHTS

Basílica de Nossa Senhora de Nazaré • *Praça Justo Chermont. Daily 6:30–11:30 a.m., 3–9 p.m.* • One of the most stunning churches in Brazil, this basilica is the end point for the annual procession of Círio de Nazaré on the second Sun. in Oct. The church, which was initiated in 1909, took 40 years to build—a majestic blending of Italian granite and mosaics, French stained glass, and a ceiling of red cedar taken from the forest. The idolized statue of the Madonna, which is carried through the streets, rests above the altar in a circle of cherubs (a photo showing details can be found to the right of the altar). Devotion to the statue is so intense that you might see petitioners dragging themselves on their knees to the altar in payment of a promise. In front of the basilica is a modern, open-air complex consisting of high altar, ampitheater, pantheon, and war monument, where mass during the Círio festival is held.

MUSEUM

Museu Paraense Emílio Goeldi • *Parque Zoobotânico, Av. Magalhães Barata, 376;* ☎ *224-9233. Tues., Wed., Thurs., and Sat. 9 a.m.–noon, 2–5 p.m. (Tues. and holidays free in the a.m.), Fri. 9 a.m.–noon, Sun., 8 a.m.–5:45 p.m. Closed Mon.* • Belém's premier museum was initiated in 1866 to record the richness of Amazônia's flora, fauna, rocks, indigenous culture, and folklore. The multi-media complex embraces a park, zoo, and indoor museum. The park, planned after an Amazonian jungle, has fewer trees per square foot than the forest, but offers more species, including rubber trees, *guaraná* (from which the herbal stimulant is taken), *pau-brasil, cedro vermelho, castanha-do-pará* (Brazil nut), and the huge *sumaumeira* (the biggest tree in the South American jungle). At the desk of the permanent exhibition, ask for a guide book in English, then tour the fine displays of stuffed birds, basketry, Indian artifacts, and jewelry. Running freely outside in the zoo are *cutias* (a type of anteater with the frisky personality of a racoon).

TROPICAL PARK

Parque dos Igarapés • *Conjunto Satélite WE 12, # 1000, Ananindeua, Pará. Office: Rua Manoel Barata, 704, Edifício Paes de Carvalho, # 403, Belém, CEP 66020;* ☎ *235-1910, 223-8324, 227-2588. Reserve only on Sun. or groups* • This tropical park owned by a private family is a welcome respite from the heat of the city and the ruggedness of the jungle. The ten-dollar entrance fee can go toward food and beverages taken in the excellent open-air restaurant or beside the natural swimming pool (whose water was pronounced cleaner than the drinking water in Belém). Ecological walks can be taken through the forested grounds or you can hop in a canoe and navigate the narrow *igarapés* (streams) that seem to go everywhere and nowhere. Children will love the wood-log playground and there are so many animals here (including an *atú* (armadillo), *creatipurí* (squirrel), and *preguiçosa* (sloth) that a staff vet is required by law. Belemites flock to this complex on weekends, when live bands turn the main arena into a outdoor nightclub.

EXCURSIONS

A JUNGLE ADVENTURE

Jungle adventures start early in Belém—4 a.m. at the Hilton, when my young guide Tony Rocha picks me up, threading his way through late-night revelers on their way to bed. We drive to the docks at the Novotel Hotel, then board a skiff in the moonlight, the humidity dense around us. Illuminating our way with flashlights, we set off down the Guamá River, passing *caboclos* already on their way to market. Just 15 minutes later, Tony points out a brand-new island, recently sculpted by the 6-hour tides that continually change the face of the Amazon. As the sky turns luminescent pink we settle in front of another island called Ilha dos Papagaios and watch as thousands of green parrots wake up, then fly off squawking in pairs. As the sun rises we catch glimpses of river life—women carrying baskets, children paddling to school. Soon we bank and I take my first plunge into the jungle. The feeling of being surrounded by literally millions of life forms—trees, shrubs, vines, birds, ants, bugs, and whatever is flying in my face—is thrilling, if not a bit scary. Cutting the path with a machete, Tony points out the *sumaumeira* tree, an elephantine-like monster, whose trunks are used by natives to beat out messages. We inspect the leaves of the guaramá tree, which is used to wrap fish at market, and another tree whose bark exudes a drinkable milky substance. My boots sink deep into fungus. Despite the incessant cawing of birds, it's difficult not to appreciate the eery silence of the forest—what Peter Mathiesson once described as the "stillness of a cathedral."

Cruising down the river again, we make a pitstop at a riverside grocery—a mere counter crammed with *pinga*, the jungle's cure-all. The owners are an elderly couple, whose eyes are incredibly similar—wet and shining. "Maybe we're brother and sister," Senhor Tomé laughs. "When we were young, my father was very active." Their grandchildren, visiting from the city, scamper about in their marvelous backyard—the jungle. Don Palmira talks about the time she saw a white-suited stranger dive into the river late at night (obviously an enchanted *boto*, or dolphin). As a full eclipse of the sun is about to occur, we rush to the pier of an abandoned pepper plantation to catch the fantastic darkening over the river. At dusk, our boatman, named Branco, invites us to sleep at his river-side house.

The moment the sun sets, mosquitoes attack us in droves, but we bat them off long enough to devour an excellent dinner of fried catfish cooked by his wife. Before retiring, we pump Branco for tales of the *curupira*, the legendary master of the forest whose feet are turned backwards and who loves to befuddle humans. Branco tells of his troubles with a *matinta pereira*, a forest witch, who would never leave him alone until he finally married his present wife. At midnight I wake up terrified, since my hammock, which is strung over a boat anchored far up on the bank, is swinging wildly for no reason. Soon Tony's hammock goes out of control, too, driving us both to hysterics, when suddenly, both hammocks stop as fast as they started. At breakfast, Branco looks at us darkly and mumbles that the *matinta pereira* had paid us a visit. We don't laugh.

After breakfast, we head out for the tiny streams called *igarapés*, overhung with luscious green vines, just like in a Tarzan movie. Branco's 9-year-old nephew Fernando shows us how to climb a palm tree with a rope made from leaves. After a hot, sweaty trek over *terra firma*, we reach a *casa de farinha*, a manioc plantation, run by Dona Paula, a heavy-set woman with two grown daughters. Incredibly, the talk turns to the Gulf War, which she has just watched on her battery-powered TV. Before we head back, after a plate of hot manioc and beans, she warns us to watch for cobras—not a happy thought. By the time we return to the dock only 24 hours after we began, it feels like we've been gone a few lifetimes.

Something similar to the above tour can be arranged through (**Amazon Star Turismo** *Rua Carlos Gomes, 14;* ☎ *and FAX 224-6244*) who offers 4 kinds of tours: a half-day tour around Belém, in front of the Guamá River, including a forest walk, about $28 per person, including hotel transfer and two guides; an 8-hr. (full-day) tour down the Guamá and Acará rivers, including a walk in the forest and lunch, about $48 per person; an overnight stay on the Guamá River and Parrot Island, about $70; and an early morning jaunt to Parrot Island, leaving at 4:15 a.m. and returning 8:30 a.m., about $38. Arrangements with Amazon Star Turismo can also be made in Rio through **Expeditours** *Rua Visconde de Pirajá 414;* ☎ *(21) 208-5559*.

MOSQUEIROS ISLAND

Eighty-two kilometers from Belém is **Mosqueiros Island**, the main bathing beach of the capital. Back in the 19th century, the first tourists to the island were Portuguese, French, and English rubber barons enjoying the boom; today most of the village has still retained its mud-hut look. The hour's drive from the city takes you over a decent highway (BR 360) lined with verdant forests full of *açaí* and *dendê* palm trees (the red flag in front of houses signify they sell *açaí*); after you pass over the 1,485-meter bridge, you'll be beseiged by young boys hawking beer and bags of sun-dried shrimps. The bus from Belém stops at **Areão Beach**, where the city's main square and market is located, but most of the popular beach action takes place at Farol Beach, where the strand is the widest and rock concerts happen at night. The water here is a bay, where all rivers meet and flow to the ocean, causing an intense wave reaction big enough for surfing. **Murubira Beach** is considered the chic beach, where most of the jetskiers, ultraleve daredevils, and windsurfers hang out.

Since there are 16 *igarapés* in the middle of the island, the landscape is perfect for short jungle tours, which can be arranged through Carlos Alberto Ribeiro, owner of the **Maresia Restaurant**. For a mere $15 for 4-1/2 hours, you can tour the *igarapés* by canoe, visit a *caboclo*'s house and wheat plantation, and fish for fresh shrimp (you must provide your own transportation to the island). If you would like to spend the night, Senhor Carlos Alberto's colonial-style pousada offers an exotic hideaway on the beach for remarkably low prices (about $30). The restaurant itself, located on Farol Beach, serves a fine *caldeirada* (soup stew with fish, octopus, egg, potatoes, onions, shrimps, and manioc flour) and a delicious *peixe tropical*, fish with Brazil nuts and the cream of Brazil nuts. Buffalo steak, another rare delicacy, must be ordered 4-5 hours in advance. For reservations for the tour and pousada contact the **Restaurante Maresia** *Av. Beira Mar, 29;* ☎ *771- 1463*.

When To Go

Mosqueiros Island seemed even hotter to me than Belém. After it rains at 1 or 2 p.m. (every day), the temperature cools a bit, making strolling more palatable. (In Belém the same shower is called the "three o'clock rain.") Oct. is the hottest month, when crabs appear in the saltier water. High season lasts from July to Nov., with the best months of sunshine being Aug. and Sept. The months notorious for rain are Jan. and Feb.

How To Go

Buses leave hourly from the bus station in Belém (during vacations, every 15 min.). The trip takes about 1-1/2 hour by bus, or one hour by car.

MARAJÓ ISLAND

Just across the bay from Belém is Marajó, an island the size of Switzerland, and fast becoming the major tourist destination of the North. The major attraction are the water buffalo ranches, where enormous herds graze the open plains—a species that first came to the island by way of shipwreck. Also in profusion are hundreds of rare bird specimens, as well as numerous alligators and monkeys, more easily seen here than in the jungle. Those who choose to stay along the coast are awarded with a roiling sea, whose crashing waves result from the confluence of the inland rivers and the ocean seas.

Those who want to truly feel the life of Marajó should go to **Bonjardim**, the most famous of the buffalo ranches. The owners, Eduardo and Eunice Ribeiro, are a charming couple who speak English, French, and Spanish and love to sit down to lunch and dinner with their guests (invariably a groaning table of fine delicacies). During the day you can ride the range with the staff, birdwatch, and fish for piranha; at night there are organized alligator hunts. Bookings can be made most easily through **Amazon Star Turismo** ☎ *(91) 224-6244.*

Beyond the ranch, the best pousada in the main town of Soure is the **Marajoara Pousada**, *Quarta Av. ;* ☎ *(91) 741-1472*, walking distance from the waterfront and center of town. If you would prefer to stay on the beach, **Pousada Guarás** is your only choice, located in Salvaterra on the other side of the island. (Rooms are air-conditioned and have private baths.) Unfortunately, transportation throughout the island is painstakingly slow. Since there are very few roads, you must take boats that run about 10 miles per hour; it takes 2 or 3 days just to reach the next city.

How To Go

The fastest way to get to Marajó Island is by plane. Air taxis, which can be reserved for any time, run about $200. Much cheaper are the regularly scheduled flights on TABA (about $30), which leave Mon. and Wed. from Belém at 7 a.m. and return at 7:40 p.m. from Soure. On Fri. the flight leaves Belém at 4 p.m. and returns on Sun. at 4 p.m.

You can also go by bus. Service leaves from Belém's bus terminal at 5 a.m., and includes a bus to Iguraci, a ferry boat to Câmara (across the Marajó Bay, about 3 hrs.), then a bus to Salvaterra and a small ferry to Soure. The return trip leaves from Soure at 2 p.m. Mon.–Sat.

ENASA boats leave Belém Wed. and Fri. at 8 p.m. and return on Thurs. and Sun. at 4 p.m., as well as Saturday at 2 p.m., returning at 5 p.m. or 6 p.m. (from Soure). The trip is colorful, usually accompanied by screaming babies, squawking chickens, and quacking ducks. Regional class is about $8, but tourist class (much preferred) runs about $18.

The easiest way to visit Marajó is to arrange a package deal through **Amazon Star Turismo** 25 *FAX 224-6624* • who will provide transfer to the pier in Belém, trip by ferry boat to the island (3 hrs., two buses) or boat (5 hrs.), city tour, lodge with breakfast, 1/2-day tour to a fazenda to see buffalos and horses, stops at one or two beaches, and a folklore show on Sat. night.

THE ESSENTIAL BELÉM

WHERE TO STAY

Accommodations in Belém run from the ever-efficient, luxurious Hilton to the modest pousada. Air-conditioning is *de rigeur*.

Expensive -------------- **Over $75**

Moderate --------------- **$50–$75**

Inexpensive ------------ **Under $30**

★ Hilton International Belém

Av. Presidente Vargas, 882 (Praça da República) (Centro); ☎ *(91) 223-6500*
The Hilton is Belém's first and only 5-star—a luxurious relief from the heat and humidity of the cityscape. Service is geared towards those who wake up at dawn for river tours or stay up till dawn to dance; breakfast opens at 4 a.m. An impressive underground mall of stores includes a deli, famous for salamis, cheeses, and exquisite pastries. The pool is small, but unusually shaped and is a magnet on the weekends for chic cruisers. The gym is the best in the city, with free weights, aerobic classes, sauna, and massage. An elegant club serves exotic tropical drinks and offers live music on the weekends. Apartments are plush, with marble-topped bathrooms and comfortable beds. Normal rates for June 1994 are projected at $110 for singles, $140–$150 for doubles. Fielding's readers receive the following discount: $85 for singles or doubles. 361 apts. *Expensive. All cards.*

Equatorial Palace

Av. Braz de Aguiar, 612 (Nazaré); ☎ *(91) 241-2000, FAX (091) 223-5222*
This traditional 4-star is located in a prime area of shady streets and chic stores, four blocks from downtown. Smaller and more intimate than the Hilton, the hotel boasts a fine, old-world restaurant, called 1900, famous for its Portuguese codfish. The circular, blue-tiled swimming pool is surrounded by a *churrascaria* and pool bar. The romantic piano bar is a favorite in the city. The older rooms, mostly used for long-term residences, have an old-world charm the newer apartments lack. Ignore the tacky lobby. Singles run $75, doubles $87. Fielding's readers receive 20 percent discount. 296 apts. *Expensive. All cards.*

Novotel Hotel

Av. Bernardo Sayão, 4804 (Guamá), 4 kilometer; ☎ *229-8011, FAX 229-8707*
Near the University of Belém, the Novotel is a good, medium-priced hotel, particularly suitable for families who make a one-day stop in Belém; most 3-hr. river tours leave from the harbor located in the hotel's backyard. The pool area, lined with *açaí* trees, is extensive, with a children's pool, playground, and volleyball court. All rooms are air-conditioned, and come with 2 double beds and an extra couch bed, color TV, and a large desk. Make sure you ask for a room with a view to the river. Laundry service available. Standard doubles run $57, suites $73. Fielding's reader's receive 20 percent discount if they pay in cash. 121 apts. *Moderate. All Cards.*

Zoghbi Park Hotel

Rua Pe. Prudêncio, 220 (Centro); ☎ *241-1800*
This small but adequate three-star offers a good low-priced option for discerning travelers. Rooms, all air-conditioned, are nearly monklike, but clean, with finely finished wood doors, closets, and headboards. A good buy is the *especial*, with a fascinating view of the city's back streets. The bar doubles as a TV lounge. All room keys are electronic and safes are available at reception. Standard doubles run about $27, special doubles $32. 33 apts. *Moderate. Cards: V.*

Regente Hotel

Av. Gov. José Malcher, 485 (Centro); ☎ *224-0755, tlx. 1796, FAX 224-0343*
Centrally located within walking distance of the Praça da República, the Regente is a reliable low-priced hotel; nearby is the fine restaurant Lá Em Casa. Apartments, with color TV and minibar, are cheerful and overlook the city's rooftops. A good budget idea is the standard central for $23. Noise from the city

traffic may filter up to the rooms. The restaurant offers standard fare without much style. Safes at reception. 149 apts. *Inexpensive. All cards.*

Vidonha's
Rua O de Almeida, 476 (Centro); ☎ *225-1444*
A simple, small hotel that isn't at all seedy, Vidonha's has rock-bottom rates that can't be beat. Apartments come with minibar and color TV, and furniture in good condition. The only drawback are the small windows. Safes at the reception. Standard singles run $12, doubles $16, specials, which hold 3 beds and a partial front view, run $18. 48 apts. *Inexpensive. Cards: DC, MC, V.*

WHERE TO EAT

Expensive	Over $15
Moderate	$5–15
Inexpensive	Under $5

★ Lá Em Casa
Av. Gov. José Malcheer, 24 (Centro); ☎ *223-1212. Daily noon-3 p.m., 7 p.m–midnight*
Some folks say the only "native" food in Brazil can be found in Belém, where it was taught to the first colonists by the Indians. Owner Ana Maria Martin, who learned to cook from her grandmother (and even went upstream to the family farm to learn from Indian women) has received international raves for her *maniçoba*, a concoction of meat or fish mushed with manioc leaves that must be cooked for 4-5 days to extract the poison. Warm and voluble, Dona Ana Maria has installed 2 restaurants in this colonial-style house: the air-conditioned salon, called O Outro (The Other), which serves hot and cold buffets, and the back patio, called *Lá em Casa* (There at Home), with its gargantuan *flamboyante* tree in the middle. The *Menu Paraense*, for about $10, gives you a chance to try all the different regional tastes. A special lunch plate is a steal at $4. *Pato no Tucupi* (duck made with a manioc sauce available only in Belém) and *patinhas de carangueijo à Milanesa* (fried crab legs) are excellent. The fish *tucunaré* is best eaten in Santarém. *Moderate. All cards.*

Restaurante Círculo Militar
Praça Frei Caetano Brandão (Forte de Castelo); ☎ *223-4374. Daily noon-3:00 p.m. and 7 p.m.-midnight*
With its balcony-like salon overlooking the bay, this is the perfect place to lunch away from the hubbub of the marketplace. Located in the Castelo Fort, it's especially romantic at night. A light lunch might be a crabmeat omelette, for under $6. *Polvo* (octopus), cooked in tomato sauce with potatoes and cooked eggs, is hearty. *Lagostim*, for about $7, is a small freshwater shrimp breaded with egg and stuffed with cheese. Try the native fruit juices like *cupuaçu* or *taperebá*, from the cashew family. *Moderate. All Cards.*

Augustus
Av. Almirante Barroso, 493 (S. Brás); ☎ *226-8317. Daily noon-2:30 p.m., 7 p.m.-midnight, Sat. 7 p.m.–midnight*
Dark wood-beamed ceilings vye with tropical gardens in this chic restaurant. Beef, fish, and shrimps run about $10 a plate. A specialty is *Brochette misto à Piamonteza*, a mixed grill of steak, pork, and sausage. Don't miss the *coco branco*, an intensely sweet concoction of shredded coconut glazed in sugar and spiked with cloves. *Moderate. All Cards.*

Miralha Bar e Restaurante
Av. Doca de Souza Franco, 194; ☎ *241-4832. Daily 8 a.m.-4 a.m.*
Hip Belemites come to this tropical beer garden after work for a drink (and a pickup). Families, however, will also feel at home. Music (usually MPB) is the best in the city with live bands starting at 9:30 p.m.; a $3 cover must be paid after 9:45 p.m. The special is Japanese food: *camarão na chapa miralha* comes with super-sized shrimp, vegetables, and fries on a simmering grill. The bar is located near the docks in the Umarizal district. *Moderate. No Cards.*

Hilton Delicatessen
Av. Presidente Vargas, 882 (Praça da República). Daily 11 a.m.–9 p.m., Sun. 10 a.m.–2 p.m
Takeout deli in the Hilton Hotel. Excellent

pastries, salamis, and cheese. Stock up if you're planning a river trip. *Moderate. All Cards.*

Vegetarian
Alternativa Natural
Rua O. de Almeida, 306. Mon.–Fri. 11:30 a.m.-3 p.m., lunch.
A nice, quick alternative for vegetarians—a natural foods buffet, including tropical fruit juices, noodles, soy meat, fried macaxeira, soup, salad, and dessert for about $2. Unfortunately, the rice is white. The post office on Rua Santo Antônio is nearby. *Inexpensive. No Cards.*
Nutribem Ltda.
Rua Santo Antônio, 264; ☎ *224-3429*
Vegetarian restaurant and market for natural products.

Ice Cream
One can't come to the Amazon without trying its most famous delicacy—ice cream made from tropical fruit flavors. Needless to say, it's the best way to beat the heat (and the parlors are usually air-cooled), but the flavors alone are unforgettable—ranging from delicate to sensuously ripe.
Tip Top
Travessa Pariquis at the corner of Padre Eutiquip (Batista Campos)
A tip-top ice cream parlor 4-1/2 blocks from the Hilton, with more than 150 exotic flavors. *Bacuri*, made from the hard-shelled fruit, is particularly delicious.

Street Food
You're sure to see folks on the street slurping something from a shell. It's *tacacá*, made with dried shrimps and *tucupí* (a sauce made from manioc), served in a *cuia*, the dried shell of the fruit of the *calabaça* tree. *Tacacá* runs hot (both in temperature and in spices), and if you add pepper, you'll have even more sweat running down your brow—an effect strangely adored by locals.

NIGHTLIFE

Sabor da Terra *Av. Visconde de Souza Franco, 685;* ☎ *223-8620. Mon.–Sat. 9:00 p.m. Fee: $17 table, $5 tickets.* Come to dine on traditional Amazonian dishes or just enjoy the city's best folklore show, featuring backland dances like xote, forró, lundi, carimbó, and lambada. The 8 dancers are young and attractive and not at all bored. The show lasts about two hours; one fine number is a cowboy dance with lassos straight from Marajó Island.

Boite Lapinha *Trav. Ferreira Pena, 352;* ☎ *241-4104. Shows: Mon.-Sat. 8:30 p.m. Fees: $16 table for 4, tickets $5.50, bermudas not allowed for men.* The city's most famous nightclub hangs somewhere between funky and old-fashioned. A statue of Iemanjá surrounded by live ducks greets arrivals while inside, a 50s silver ball dominates the stage. The shows change every half hour, from comedy to live bands to striptease after 11:30 p.m., all introduced by a transvestite MC. The specialty is língua de boi (bull tongue), served with mashed potatoes. Dancing is fun, but beware of mosquitoes and be extra careful when you go to the bathroom: There are three of them (men, women, and "others"), considered a major accomplishment by gays in Belém

Insider Tip

Check the newspaper for listings of local musicians like Nilson Choves, a singer/guitarist; **Jane du Boc**, *an ex-volleyball player who sings like Zizi Possi;* **Rosanna**, *a wonderful singer of all types of music,* **Alibi de Orfeu**, *who sings Portuguese blues;* **Debson Tayonara**, *who sings MPB; and* **Oficina de Samba**, *an 8-man group that performs popular sambas.*

SHOPPING

Markets
The main city market is the **Ver-o-Peso** (see under "Walking Tour"). There's also an **artisan Fair** *Praça da República. Fri.-Sat*, not so big but worth a look. Good buys are drums, flutes, handmade jewelry, and semi-precious stones. In the middle of the square is a monument to Brazil's independence. The **Palha**

Market takes place every day near the Novotel Hotel—small but exceedingly third-world, with the intense smell of fish and dried spices.

Crafts

Cacique *Av. Presidente Vargas, 892;* ☎ *222-1144* The best artisan shop in Belém.

> **Insider Tip:**
>
> Among local crafts are aromatic essences of oil, like Cheiro de Pará, made from Amazonian plants. Many of these oils are related to candomblé practices and often come packaged with promises of love, money, or good health. Roots and barks are also ground into pleasant-smelling powders and fashioned into dolls or simple sachets. Other good buys are leather-tooled jewelry, wood carvings, and fiber crafts.

If you're in the market for an Amazonian icon, look for a *muiraquitã*—a piece of green jade (or ceramic) in the shape of a frog. Legend has it that once upon a time in the middle of the Amazon forest, a tribe of female warriors were desperately in search of men for reproduction. One full moon they waited for Yara, goddess of the water, who unearthed some green stones from the depths of the river. The women dived into the river to retrieve the stones, then shaped the jade (or malachite) into a frog, which they then wore as an amulet. (Since the jungle later became populated, we can assume the fetish worked.) Anyone who wears it today is said to enjoy protection and good luck. (Specimens in the museum were found on Marajó Island by the Aruã tribe who used them).

Herbs

Casa das Ervas Medicinais *Rua Gaspar Viana, 230* This "House of Medicinal Herbs" is veritably crammed with wooden bins of dried leaves, herbs, barks, and seeds for every illness imaginable—even cancer. The owner has been in business for years, and even makes mixtures that come refrigerated in tall glass bottles (the tonic I bought did wonders for me). You can also buy a two-volume book (Portuguese only) called *A Flora Nacional na Medicina Doméstica*, which tells the story of each herb and what disease it cures.

Perfumaria Chamma *Rua Boaventura da Silva, 606;* ☎ *224-7298* and **Artesanato Juruá**, across the street from the Equatorial Palace Hotel on Avenida Brás de Aguiar, are both well known for natural soaps, shampoos, cosmetics, and perfumes made from Amazonian plants. Celebrities and actresses, in particular, swear by the products at Juruá.

Pottery

Stúdio Rosemiro Pinheiro *# 100, Soledade (past Espírito Santo)* On a back dirt road about 18 kilometers from downtown Belém (half-hour by car) is the village of **Icoracy**, an unusual community of craftsmen who maintain the age-old tradition of handmade pottery. One of twenty-odd master artisans in the area, 50-year-old Rosemiro Pinheiro works in a rundown shack that belies the extraordinary output of his "factory." (He personally makes 200 vases a day, while his 25-man team produces over 2,300 pieces a month.) Young boys take their canoes down the igarapé in the backyard to find suitable clay, which is then brought back to be cleaned, fashioned on wheels, and baked in brick ovens fueled by wood scraps. Children play around Senhor Pinheiro's feet while he fashions vases in the Marajó style, a technique he learned from his father, though he is constantly experimenting with new designs. In the front room is a showcase, from which you may purchase 45-piece feijoada sets, vases of all sizes, commemorative plates, and even erotic beer mugs. Prices are extraordinarily low; shipping to the U.S. doubles the price.

HANDS-ON BÉLEM

Airlines

Varig/Cruzeiro
Av. Presidente Vargas, 768/3363 (across

from the Praça da República); ☎ 225-4222.
TABA
Av. Gov. José Malcher, 883; ☎ 223-6300.
Transbrasil
Av. Presidente Vargas, 780; ☎ 224-6977.
VASP
Av. Presidente Vargas, 620, loja B; ☎ 224-5588.
Air France
Rua Boaventura da Silva, 11457; ☎ 223-7547.
TAP
Rua Senador Manoel Barata, 704, room 1401; ☎ 222-5304.

Arrivals
Cooperativos Taxis ☎ 233-4941 at the airport runs about $11–$12 and can be hired at the last counter near the Paratur office. Buses run every 5 min. from the airport for about 25 cents. The name of the bus to downtown is "Perpétuo Socorro" (Perpetual Help).

Car Rental
Avis Av. Brazil de Aguiar, 621; ☎ 225-2237; also **Hilton Hotel** ☎ 223-1276, ext. 7573.

City Transportation
Taxis ☎ 224-5444, 226-1000, 229-4799.

Climate
Temperatures range from 82 degrees F. in the Amazonian winter (June-Aug.) to 90-93 degrees F. in summer (Dec.-Jan.). Rain occurs nearly every day around 3 p.m.; the months with heaviest rainfall are Jan. and Feb.

Consulates
U.S.A.
Av. Oswaldo Cruz, 165; ☎ 223-0800.
Great Britain
Rua Gaspar Viana, 490; ☎ 223-4353.
South Africa
Av. Presidente Vargas, 351; ☎ 224-8282.

Money Exchange
Casa Francesa
Padre Prudêncio, 40; ☎ 241-2716.
Carajás
Av. Presidente Vargas, 762; ☎ 225-1550.

Monopólio Turismo e Câmbio
Av. Pres. Vargas, 325; ☎ 223-3177.

Points Beyond
The **Rodoviária** ☎ 228-0502 is located at the end of Av. Gov. José Malcher 5 kilometers from downtown. Buses are available to Brasília, Santarém, Salvador, Recife, Fortaleza, and Belo Horizonte, among others.

Police
POLITUR ☎ 224-9469 is a special division of the local police force that provides security for tourists.

Private Guide
Tony (Antônio) Rocha, Filho Av. Antônio Everdosa, 1660 (Pedreira); ☎ 233-1627 gets my vote for best English-speaking guide in Brazil. A tall order to live up to, but his charm, knowledge, and consideration made my first foray into the jungle a joy to remember. He can also be reached through **Amazon Star Turismo** ☎ 224-6244.

River Transportation
The most utilized form of transportation in this region is boat. Wooden multi-deck cruisers called *gaiolas* regularly make trips down the Amazon River from Belém to Santarém and Manaus—a colorful way to make friends and enter into the heart of Amazonian life. Along with grandmothers, babies, and traveling salesmen, you might share quarters with dogs, chickens, and the family pig. Some boats rent only hammock space (you must provide your own hammock); others offer a few private cabins just big enough for a sink and two bunk beds, with a key to the private toilet. (Note well that the communal toilet is usually *beyond* description.) You might consider renting a cabin (for the privacy and the bathroom) and also hang your hammock in the main galley. During sunlight hours, the boats usually cruise near the banks so you can spot wildlife and peek inside the native homes; most people hang out on the top deck where you can buy beer and snacks. Most exciting are the brief stops at port, where you can watch lovers parting, children hawking fruits and homemade foods, and dockworkers loading the

ship's goods.
For information about ENASA boats, see "River Cruises" in the section *Hands-On Santarém*.

Time

Belém is one hour later than Santarém.

Tourist Information

A visit to **PARATUR** *Praça Kennedy;* ☎ *224-9633* won't be your typical boring trip to the tourist office. An ancillary park is full of native animals, particularly little monkeys called *saguis*, who will come eat from your hand. (They love peanut candy.) The primary handicrafts of the area are sold in an adjacent gallery. Of particular value are the ceramics, whose designs are native to the area. The style called *tapajónica* is characterized by fine line carvings and sculptured decorations, originally from Santarém but now made in Belém; they often resemble ceramics made by ancient civilizations. Of wider, heavier design, more colorful, and slightly more modern is the *marajoara* style. It can be recognized by its low relief sculptures, often brightly patterned in red, black, and white. You can also stock up on machetes and bows and arrows authentically crafted by natives tribes in Amazonas. Brochures in English can be picked up at the information desk in the artisan store.

Travel Agency

Most hotels do not have sufficient information regarding river and jungle tours. For the best service in Belém, contact **Amazon Star Turismo Ltda**. *Rua Carlos Gomes, 14;* ☎ *and FAX 224-6244*. Owned by French immigrant Patrick Barbier, the agency offers 4 kinds of river/jungle tours as well as package deals to Marajó and Mosqueiros islands. Special chartered tours can be arranged for specific needs. (For more information, see under "Excursions," below.)

When to Go

Best season to come to Belém is June–Aug., when there is sun in the morning and a little rain in the afternoon. Dec.–Mar. you'll experience the very wet side of the rainforest and will need rubber boots and ponchos.

MANAUS

Cruising into Manaus along the Rio Negro is an awesome sight after spending even a few days in the jungle. I've often wondered what Indian or *caboclo* children feel when they first glimpse that skyline of twenty skyscrapers, the yellow construction cranes stretching to heaven, the improbable gold dome of the opera house, all towering over the pastel-colored shacks that cling precariously to the hillside. How could they possibly grasp the meaning of all that black smoke pouring from the refineries, the multi-colored boats bobbing in the floating docks, the *desfile* of cars and trucks on the steel-girded bridge? One look, I think, and some of them must go reeling straight back to the forest.

For others, however, Manaus is the technological oasis of the Amazon. Located on the left bank of the Rio Negro, just above its junction with the Amazon River, Manaus is not only the political capital of Amazonas, it's practically the only city with any gusto of civilization. During the rubber boom, it enjoyed a few decades of nouveau-riche expansion; after a long decline, it's been gaining a grittier, if just as economically voracious, reputation ever since being declared a free trade zone in 1966. Just a few hundred meters from the docks, the center of the city is a beehive of activity—noisy stalls and shops selling everything from knock-off electronic equipment to Persian rugs and Taiwanese toys. As such, you'll always see Brazilians from all over the country dashing madly about trying to find the best price; the international airport (built in 1976) usually resembles the remains of a wholesale festival as passengers try to board planes loaded with enormous packages.

The eccentricities of the Rio Negro's ebb and flow sculpt the ever-changing face of Manaus' port. Subject to biannual tides, the river rises and falls as much as 40 feet within a 6-month period; hence, the necessity of **floating docks**, a marvelous feat of British engineering (installed during the rubber boom) that responds to the tiniest variation of volume change. Many huts along the shore are actually built on rafts, some merely strung together by chains.

For many, the so-called **"meeting of the waters"** is an awe-inspiring sight—the junction of the Rio Negro and the Amazon, where two rivers of different colors flow together without mixing for miles. Blessed with a mosquito-free environ, the jungles around Manaus attract most of the Amazon's tourists, who usually head for the jungle lodges located three to six hours away by boat. Many visitors spend their first night in Manaus at the famed Tropical Hotel—a veritable palace replete with its own zoo. My suggestion is to stay there *after* your jungle expedition—to slowly acclimate yourself back to the luxuries of civilization.

Nineteenth-century biologists Wallace, Bates, and Spruce all set out from Manaus; today the city is home to several hundred international scientists who actively study the forest in the hope of preserving both its fauna and flora. Though severely underfunded, INPA, the National Institute of Amazonian Research, staunchly perseveres in its multi-dimensional projects, including raising manatees, dolphins, and rare sea otters that have been confiscated from illegal fishing expeditions. Many are on display to the public, and a swim-with-the-dolphins project is presently being planned, though its future may be bleak: Brazilians are uncommonly suspicious of the breed.

Unfortunately, the prospects for seeing substantial number of animals in their natural habitat near Manaus are somewhat discouraging. Frightened by loud motors and the sound of crunching boots, the smaller, more timid animals have for the most part retreated from the banks of the river while most of the birds are so high up in the canopy they are difficult to see. (If you are desperate for fauna, better go to the Pantanal.) Sadly, many animals in the Amazon have already become extinct; the endangered manatee, common in the time of Henry Bates, is now being illegally slaughtered by *caboclo* fishermen, who often torture the babies to attract the mother. More often seen on excursions (and definitely heard) are screeching howler monkeys and also capybaras, who can sometimes be glimpsed poking their snouts into vegetation. Jaguars are rarely encountered by tourists, but I was once lucky enough to be handed a live sloth to cuddle—an experience no one should ever pass up.

SIGHTS

TEATRO AMAZONAS *Praça Sebastião;* ☎ *234-2776. Daily 9 a.m.-6 p.m.*
Imagine the chutzpah, the ingenuity, and the sheer persistence it took to build a grand opera house in the middle of the jungle. Inaugurated after 12 years of construction on Dec. 31, 1896, the Teatro Amazonas (700 seats, 800 boxes) is still a wonder of artful design,

constructed completely with materials imported from Europe, except for the wood, which came from the Amazon forest. The original curtains, still intact, were painted by the Brazilian artist Crispim do Amaral in 1896 and represent the meeting of the waters of the Rio Negro and the Rio Solimões (the goddess in the middle is Yara, the water princess). The bronze chandeliers, which descend for cleaning, are from France; the pillars are made of English cast iron; and the ceiling was painted in Paris by 2 Italians, showing the arts of opera, tragedy, dance, and music. Except for the theater chairs, everything in the house is original (the old wood and cane chairs were replaced when air-conditioning was installed under the seats). The ballroom, now only used as a showpiece, consists of 12,000 pieces of Amazon mahogany. The wrought-iron staircases are covered with *guaraná* plants. The wall painting showing a group of Indians saving some desperate-looking Europeans is a scene from the Brazilian opera *I Guarani*, by Carlos Gomes. In olden times, musicians used to serenade guests from the balcony. In 1947 the Governor declared all public buildings should be colored gray; it wasn't until 40 years later that the front facade was restored to its original light mauve. The first opera given in the house was *La Gioconda*, performed by an Italian troupe imported for the occasion. Tours are given throughout the day at regular intervals (though rarely in English). The air-conditioning is only turned on for performances, so bring a fan and prepare to swelter. The view from the balcony is wonderful, but be careful of flying pigeons, who may decide to use your shirt as a toilet.

THE PORT

The docks in Manaus often look like somebody threw all the people and goods up in the air and then let them fall back down willy-nilly, but actually there's a consumer's intelligence organizing the activity lining the waterfront. A stroll down the waterfront to the Municipal Market may well be one of your best moments in Manaus, as you elbow past brawny dockmen, tired fishermen, and even steely-eyed sailors eyeing the crowd for a little companionship. If you're daring, ask around to see which boats may be going out for the day; you could probably hitch a ride or, at the very least, charter one. During the day, walking around here is reasonably safe, but at night do avoid looking like you're loitering. Despite the enormous fluctuation in river volume, these floating docks, a miracle of British invention, can accommodate anything from canoes to ocean liners all year round. Nearby is the Customs House, prefabricated in Britain, then shipped to Manaus piece by piece.

FISH TERMINAL

Around 10 p.m. nightly a fantastic commotion takes place behind the Municipal Market as the port fills up with fishermen unloading their day's catch from canoes. Often the fishermen throw some of their fish away, and dolphins lurking nearby leap out of the water to catch them. You can even rent canoes here and row around to inspect the activity. Make sure, however, that your boat doesn't have a hole in it, and take precautions with your valuables. To get there: Take Travessa Tabelião Lessa behind the Mercado, then walk along the wood plank on the left side of the canal, following under the bridge to the floating platform.

MERCADO MUNICIPAL

Located at the corner of Rua Rochas dos Santos and Rua dos Barés, the Mercado Municipal is a concrete-and-steel structure built in 1906 and painted the pastel gray of all government buildings. Small cubbyholes manned by swarthy-looking merchants sell fruits, beans, wheat, sweets, and popcorn in big burlap sacks; it's a good place to stock up on supplies if you're headed for the jungle. You can also buy camping gear here, including paddles and hammocks. Good prices for Indian and *caboclo* crafts also can be found here (bargaining is de riguer). Check out Store #67, teeming with fresh and dried herbs for medicinal purposes; #30 is an *Umbanda* store selling candles, incense, and other paraphernalia for calling up the spirits. Be careful with your own wordly goods here, however. A merchant cautioned me to carry my backpack in *front* of me because several persons were eyeing it longingly.

FISH MARKET

The fish market next door to the Mercado Municipal is wet and slimy, full of merchants, women, and children all juggling for a good price. Here you'll see *pirarucu* just off the boat, as well as many fresh counterparts to the stuffed fish on view at the Science Museum.

MUSEUMS

Flora and Fauna

Museu de Ciências Naturais (Museum of National Science) *Colônia Cachoeira Grande (Aleixo);* ☎ *244-2799. Tues.–Sun. 9 a.m.–5 p.m., closed Mon. Fee: adults $2, children $1.30* Founded in 1988, this exceedingly creative and well-maintained museum was the brainchild of a Japanese businessman who came to Brazil 15 years ago and immediately fell in love with Amazônia's flora and fauna. Located 15 min. from downtown, the museum is situated in a Japanese community where children still speak Japanese and traditional customs are maintained. The museum's air-conditioning makes it a most attractive location to plant an overheated nervous system, and if you're heading off for some serious fishing, this is great place to get oriented. All notations are in English, Japanese, and Portuguese. Among the 20 stuffed and 15 live species of fish housed in a gorgeous outdoor aquarium you'll see the *pirarucu*, the largest scaled fish in the world (up to 440 lbs.); the vicious *canjirú*, a small leathery fish that is extremely carnivorous (the species of the *gnus Vanellia* are feared by people living along the river because they can enter the genitals of unsuspecting swimmers); the *tucunaré*, a very delicious fish whose coloring confuses other fish as to which end is its head. The insect room is straight out of a horror movie, featuring locusts, scarabs, and elephantine-like beetles. The butterfly mounts are extraordinary, including some species whose coloring resembles leaves and owls. The souvenir shop is one of the finest artisan stores in Manaus; though the goods are pricey, the quality is superlative. No cards are accepted, but traveler's checks, dollars, and yen are welcome. Groups may make arrangements to come at night.

INPA *Al. Cosme Ferreira, 1756;* ☎ *236-9400. Mon.–Fri. 8 a.m.– noon, 2 p.m.–6 p.m. Tours 9 a.m.–11 a.m. only. Free lectures (some in English) are given every Tues. at 3 p.m.* The Instituto Nacional Pesquisada Amazônia (the National Institute of Amazonian Research) is a forested park utilized by research scientists who are studying the survival and maintenance of the Amazon region. Many foreign scientists are working here, and guests are welcome during the morning hours (9 a.m.-11 p.m.), when free tours are given. You may see manatee pups in captivity that have been saved from fishermen who tried to use them as bait to capture their mothers, and there are usually several tanks of dolphins. A good show is always given by the *arainha*, a diva-like otter who seems to have a special ability to amuse itself in front of adoring onlookers. In the past, tours of the sawmill belonging to Center for the Study of Forest Products have been given upon request, and guests have sometimes been presented with free boxes containing many different types of Amazonian wood. Fine T-shirts with slogans like "Preserve the Manatee" can be purchased on the grounds. Permission to enter the INPA grounds must be obtained from the security police at the front gate.

Noé's Park *Fundação Vitória Amazônica, Av. Darcy Vargas, 520;* ☎ *642-1336, FAX 642-2255* Located some 23 miles from Manaus on BR-174, this 35,000-hectare reserve is a unique refuge created to harbor Amazonian animals, particularly those confiscated from poachers. It also serves as a research station to breed endangered species and reacclimate animals into the wild. Visitors are encouraged to spend a few hours roaming the paths, where you may come into close contact with a wide variety of animals, including monkeys, parrots, toucans, and parakeets, as well as sloths, anteaters, deer, and giant anteaters. The park (Noé is Portuguese for Noah) was the brainchild of Dutch primatologist Marc von Roosemalen, who has long been studying Amazon monkeys. The income generated by tourists supports environmental education programs for poor children.

Native Crafts

Museu do Homem do Norte *Av. 7 de Setembro, 1385 (Centro);* ☎ *232-5373. Mon. 8 a.m.–noon, 3–6 p.m., Wed.–Fri. 9 a.m.–noon, 2–6 p.m. Fee: about 30 cents* This hot and sweaty, two-room museum was founded in 1985 to show the culture and way of life in the north. If you can brave the heat, you'll find the Indian artifacts fascinating, especially those from the Xingú tribe, which Noel Nutel collected over a 30-year period. Most impressive are the ritual clothes and masks, among them an exquisitely beaded mask used to celebrate a girl's passage to puberty, and an ant-filled glove called *Luva de Tocandira*, into which young boys put their hands in order to prove their manhood. There is also a room full of *bumba-meu-boi* costumes and a typical manioc house. A guaraná display shows the development of the plant as well as its many uses. There is no guide, but we did locate a worker who spoke a little English.

Museu do Índio *Rua Dq. de Caxias/Av. 7 de Setembro;* ☎ *234-1422. Mon.–Fri. 8 a.m.–noon, 2–5 p.m., Sat. 8 a.m.–noon. Fee: about 75 cents. To film or take pictures, you must pay an extra 30 cents* Another non-air-conditioned museum in Manaus—this one owned by the Salesian nuns who run an Indian mission along the Rio Negro. Each of the 6 rooms is dedicated to various facets of Indian life; there are fantastic ceramics, baskets, and weapons, and even a model of a Yanomami house, a circular, straw-roofed dwelling where between 30–250 people live. The museum's store sells crafts from tribes up the Rio Negro and from *cablocos*. Rumor has it you can buy here the best *guaraná* (an herbal stimulant) in Amazonas (called Marou de Maués). One interesting novelty is a *Pega Moça* ("catch the girl"), an Indian wedding ring that looks like a Chinese knot and is placed on the woman's finger to pull her along. Also fascinating is the display of a *paje's* instruments—the magical tools of the tribal shaman, including various powders, rattles, and medicine pouches. Among the musical instruments are panpipes, maracas, turtle-shell rattles, rain sticks, and instruments made out of the brain of a buck. The last room is full of neon-colored butterflies and humongous-sized creepy crawlers.

> **Insider Tip**
>
> Ponta Negra, the river beach next door to the Hotel Tropical, is the city's hot spot on weekends. Between Oct.–Mar., when the river is low, you'll even find sand for fresh-water swimming.

JUNGLE EXCURSIONS

What's the best way to "do" the jungle near Manaus? You have basically two choices: lodges or package cruises. Jungle lodges are pousada-type accommodations located deep in the jungle (usually near the shore of a tributary), where trekkers stay for two to three days. Quality ranges from the semi-luxurious to the primitive; meals are generally served in an open-air communal dining room. If you like to cruise, you may be happier (and cooler) if you take a package boat tour where you sleep in tight (usually "cramped") quarters and take meals on board prepared by a crew member. (The schedule may include a night of sleeping in the forest.) Excursions from both the lodge and the boat tours are usually similar: canoe treks through tiny streams, piranha fishing in the afternoon, alligator hunts at night, and the proverbial walk through the forest. During rainy season, consider that the lounging space on a boat becomes even *more* cramped. Private boat cruises usually sleep up to eight, not including crew.

There is a third category of tourists who fantasize about renting their own canoes, meeting up with crazy explorers and riding the rapids to the mouth of the Amazon. Before you do, make sure you read Joe Kane's compelling account of his own hazardous trip in *Running the Amazon*. The Polish daredevils he traveled with now have their own agency called **CanoAndes** *310 Madison Avenue, NY, NY 10017;* ☎ *212-286-9415* They arrange trekking, rafting, and wildlife and cultural expeditions for all levels of fitness and expertise. Just be forewarned that their guides run on the wild side.

THE ESSENTIAL MANAUS

Jungle Lodges

Ariaú Jungle Tower *2 kilometers from the archipelago of Amanilhanas, 60 kilometer from Manaus (3 hrs. by boat)* The Amazon jungle's premier accommodation, Ariaú is the brainchild of a Brazilian businessman who longed to be not only in the jungle but above it. The entire complex of 45 wood apartments are interlinked by wooden catwalks between the trees, affording a unique communication with the flora and fauna. Towering 35 meters (130 ft.) above ground is an observation deck (the only one in Amazonas), which allows you to see the magnificent canopy of the forest from above—a thrilling experience. A special Tarzan House on top of a 120-ft. chestnut tree was especially erected for guests who want to live out tree house fantasies. All rooms, with air-ventilators only, have private bathrooms and verandas. The duplex Presidential Suite, where the owner stays when he visits, boasts a downstairs dining room, TV, VCR, and lush leather furniture. Upon arrival from the river, you'll no doubt be greeted by the resident monkeys, macaws, and *coatis* (charming anteaters with racoon tails); just watch out for the monkeys, who love to rip off eyeglasses and throw them in the water. Two day/one night packages for about $280 include all meals (except drinks), a visit to a *caboclo* village, an alligator hunt at night, forest walks, and fishing. One warning: the manager was dumbfounded as to why Americans never seemed to eat their food. For reservations contact the main office in Manaus ☎ *(92) 234-7308; FAX (92) 233-5615.*

Amazon Lodge *Lago do Juma, about 100 kilometers from Manaus (4-1/2 hrs. by boat)* This is a 2-story rustic pousada that actually floats on the water. The 17 apartments share 2 bathrooms (cold water only) and use candles for illumination. Various treks into the jungle are part of a package. In U.S. contact **Brazil Nuts** ☎ *(800) 533-9959* or **Expeditours** in Rio ☎ *(21) 287-9697, FAX 521-4388.*

Amazon Village *Lago do Puraquequara, 60 kilometers from Manaus (2 hrs. by boat)* These 64 wood apartments in neat cabanas are favorites of Germans and Swiss who appreciate the excellent service and reputedly good food. Perched on a small hill at the bend of an *igarapé*, it's located 2–4 hrs. from Manaus, depending on the river's condition. There are no electric lights, no air-conditioning, no doors, and no windows. The "main building" is a large, open-thatched shed with a dining area, living room, bar and mini-museum, all open to the wind. Guests sleep in cottages scattered around the main building, easy to find with flashlights. The house jaguar even eats in the dining area and loves to be stroked like a kitten. A 5-star banquet can be held in the middle of the jungle if you ask. In the States contact **Brazil Nuts** ☎ *(800) 533-9959* or **Expeditours** in Rio ☎ *(21) 287-9697, FAX 521-4388.*

Acajatuba Jungle Lodge *Lago Acajatuba, Rio Negro, 70 kilometers from Manaus (4 hrs. by boat)* More primitive than the Ariaú, these recently built 16 apartments are contained in 3 grass-roofed huts with private bathrooms, all illuminated by gas lanterns. Two day/one night packages for $140 include all food and mineral water, as well as piranha fishing, alligator hunt, river tour, and jungle walk. *No cards* accepted, but traveler checks, dollars, and *cruzeiros* are welcome. Contact **Expeditours** in Rio ☎ *(21) 287-9697, FAX 521-4388* or **Amazon Explorers** in Manaus ☎ *(92) 232-3052.*

Pousada dos Guanavenas *Ilha de Silves, 320 kilometers from Manaus (4-1/2 hrs. by car)* The Hilton Hotel of jungle lodges, these 20 apartments overlooking the Urubu River sometimes embarrass tourists who come to the forest to escape air-conditioning, minbars, and excellent food. On the other hand, the 2-story roundhouse with screened porches and hewn-log verandas has received architectural raves for its structure made entirely from regional materials. From Manaus, it's a 3-1/2-hour trip by jitney to

Itaquatiara, where you must board a flat-bottomed boat for another 1-1/2-hr. ride. You may also arrive by sea plane or take a bus to Itacoatiara and continue by boat. Packages include all meals and guided jungle excursions, such as alligator hunts and piranha fishing. In Manaus contact the main office: Rua Ferreira Pena, 755; ☎ *233-5558* or **Expeditours** in Rio ☎ *(21) 287-9697, FAX 521-4388.*

WHERE TO STAY

Manaus is one of the hottest places in the world (and I grew up in Houston!). So, there are several points to remember in selecting a hotel. 1. The air-conditioning must work; 2. A good pool will be appreciated; 3. Cleanliness is sacred (this close to the jungle, you should think twice about what bugs end up in your bed); 4. Laundry (no one has ever returned from the jungle without the devastating need to wash clothes). Considering all that, good deals can be found in Manaus, but at least one night at the Tropical is *de rigeur*. If you can't afford that, at least drop by for a drink beside the fantastic wave-pool.

Very Expensive--------- Over $100

Expensive --------------- $75–$100

Moderate---------------- $40–$75

Inexpensive------------- Under $15

Tropical Manaus
Estrada da Ponta Negra (Ponta Negra), 18 kilometer, ☎ *(92) 238-5757*
The palatial oasis of the Amazon jungle—if you have the money, spend it here. The hacienda-like hotel is a sprawling maze of 608 rooms; a newer building built 6 years ago doubled the capacity. Dominating the lobby is an 3-story atrium housing a great white heron and tropical ducks who do tricks between 6-7 a.m. A magnificent pool complex famous throughout Brazil sports waterfalls gushing over rock cliffs. A mini-zoo features jaguars and pumas. Minimal differences exist between standard and deluxe rooms, both lavishly appointed, with a chic-rustic allure. (Rooms in the older section are slightly more expensive, but sometimes retain a musty smell that cannot be removed.) The 3 restaurants are spectacular: a barbecue buffet poolside for about $16, a candelit gourmet restaurant, and a charming coffee shop. Tennis courts are open from 9 a.m.–9 p.m. daily. A travel agency arranges river and jungle tours, and a Varig office is open during business hours. Standard doubles run $118, superiors $142, deluxes $165, suites $236–$284. 605 apts. *Very expensive. All cards.*

Taj Mahal Continental
Av. Getúlio Vargas, 741 (Centro); ☎ *(92) 233-8900*
Opened in 1991, the Taj Mahal is the premier property of a famous Indian family who also owns the Plaza and the Imperial. All apartments have a view of the city; standards and deluxes barely differ. Furniture is stream-lined and functional. Special rooms are equipped for the handicapped. The roof pool is about 3 strokes long. A nightclub is being built. The restaurant delivers a fantastic view of the Opera House, and an upper level slowly rotates for a panoramic view. Standard doubles run $92, deluxe doubles $106. 190 apts. *Expensive. All cards.*

Imperial Hotel
Av. Getúlio Vargas, 227 (Centro), ☎ *(92) 233-8711*
Brass sculptures of the Buddah adorn the lobby of this Indian-owned hotel in downtown Manaus. Standard rooms sport brightly flowered spreads, but the rugs are not uniformly clean. The medium-sized pool looks up to the hanging laundry of the neighboring apartment. The best *tacacá* in Manaus—a native dish of tapióca, manioc juice, garlic shrimps, and pepper—is located right outside the front door, between the Plaza and the Imperial. Doubles run $90-$102. 100 apts. *Expensive. All cards.*

Plaza Hotel
Av. Getúlio Vargas, 215 (Centro), ☎ *(92) 233-8900*
Owned by the same family as the Taj Mahal, the Plaza carries over the Indian decor in its colorful tapestries and bedspreads. Service is friendly. Superior rooms are substantially larger than deluxes, with an extended area

for an extra couch bed. Although the rooms are well cooled, the corridors are as hot as a sauna. A rectangular pool is covered by a glass ceiling, which keeps the pollution out. Laundry service, a travel agency, and an imported-foods store are also on premises. Deluxe doubles run about $71, superiors about $86. Fielding's readers receive a 20 percent discount. 80 apts. *Moderate. All cards.*

Hotel Amazonas
Praça Adalberto Vale (Centro), ☎ *(92) 234-7679*
This 4-star seems to be particularly accommodating to children, who were running their electric cars all over the lobby when I visited. Best bets are deluxes, with verandas offering a fantastic view of the port; standards are a bit depressing. Special discounts are available for those who eat lunch and dinner. A hair salon, barbershop, pool, luncheonette, and drugstore accommodate guests. Children up to 5 are free. Children 5–12 years old are half price. Standard doubles run about $76, deluxe $92. 182 apts. *Moderate–Expensive. All cards.*

Slaass Flat Hotel
Av. Boulevard Alvaro Maia, 1442; ☎ *(92) 233-3525/3519, FAX 234-8971*
This gorgeous 3-star is such a steal for its price that one is left wondering, what's wrong with this picture? Built initially as an apart hotel (with kitchenettes), the Slaass, about 6 minutes by car from downtown, suggests an elegance almost unknown in Manaus. Doubles are incredibly spacious, with attractive wood floors and a breezy veranda overlooking the city's rooftops. Apartments for 4 include 3 bedrooms, 2 bathrooms, kitchen, and living room. Special long-term rates are available. The rooftop bar makes a great perch. A pool and shopping center are being planned. Restaurants within walking distance include Florentina (Italian), Canto do Peixada (fish), and Miako (Japanese). Singles run $40, doubles $47. *Inexpensive. All cards.*

Hotel Monaco
Rua Silva Ramos, 20 (Centro); ☎ *(92) 232-5211*
The classic Hotel Monaco is something out of a Jim Jarmusch movie, where the receptionist resembles a hooker and the quirkiest people emerge from the rooms. Still, the rooftop restaurant is one of the great spots to witness the city's fabulous sunsets, and you're sure to meet characters. Standard doubles run $52, deluxe doubles $56. 112 apts. *Moderate. No cards.*

Pousada Monetmurro
Rua Emilio Moreira, 1442 (Praça 14 de Janeiro); ☎ *(92) 233-4564*
This pousada, in a middle-to-low-class residential neighborhood, is a viable budget option. A white stucco building holds 6 kitchenettes and 3 suites, all air-conditioned, with sculptured stained-glass windows. Suites are the best bet, with an outer room that includes a couch, dining table, and crazy photos of the Swiss Alps. All apartments have color TV and tiled bathrooms; only the suite has a phone. Breakfast (included in the rate) is the only meal served, but a tiny luncheonette is located across the street. A sunning patio with potted plants relieves any sense of claustrophobia. Singles run $10.50, doubles $13, suite $20. *Inexpensive. No cards.*

Hotel Dona Joana
Rua dos Andrades, 553; ☎ *(92) 233-7553*
If you're looking for a cheap night, this simple 3-story pension might do, but check your room before you sign on; grunginess is in the mind of the beholder. There's no elevator, and the stairs are steep, but the deluxe on the third floor has a good breeze and great view of the river. You pay extra for hot water but the spacious rooms should all have air-conditioning. Across the street is a famous fish restaurant. The lobby is more funky than tasteless, but do note: This is no place to leave valuables. Deluxe doubles run $13, (extra bed $4); suites with hot water, minibar, and color TV $18. 60 apts. *Inexpensive. No cards.*

Hotel Rio Branco
Rua dos Andradas, 484; ☎ *(92) 233-4019*
Located across the street from the Dona Joana Hotel, this pension is the hangout for hard-core adventurers, with 90 percent of the clientele European. All rooms have private bathrooms, and if you're seriously back-

packing, who cares if the rooms are a little musty, the showers cold, and the breakfast room small? PR man Christopher Charles Gomes organizes jungles tours with expert guides; among his best is Jerry Hardy (part Brit, Indian, and Brazilian) who owns his own boat. Three day/two night tours run about $150. Reports from the bush have been raves. Doubles with air-conditioning run $10, with fan $8, singles $5-$6. Bedrooms with 3 or 4 beds, a *coletiva*, run $5 per person; all rates include breakfast (coffee, bread, and milk only). A pay telephone, which you can use for 3 minutes a shot, is in the lobby, as are safes. *Inexpensive. No cards.*

Hospedaria de Turismo Dez de Julho
Rua 10 de Julho, 679; ☎ *(92) 232-6280*
Located walking distance from downtown, this youth hostel for all ages is perfect for trekkers. All rooms are air-conditioned, and come with tile floor, 2 beds, and clean baths. Breakfast is included, and laundry service is available. Pay phone in the lobby. Janete Tôrres the director, is a lovely, gray-haired lady who speaks some English. Singles go for $16, doubles $18. 13 apts. *Inexpensive. No cards.*

WHERE TO EAT

No one really goes to Manaus for a memorable meal. However, if you're just coming out of the jungle, any food that's more sophisticated than a ham sandwich will probably taste great. The finest cuisine can be found at the Tropical Hotel, which features an impressive (but pricey) outdoor barbecue, indoor Italian restaurant, coffee shop, and several bars, all open to the public. Throughout the Amazon region be careful to avoid raw vegetables, salads, sushi, and unpeeled fruits.

Expensive --------------- **Over $15**

Moderate ---------------- **$5–$15**

Inexpensive ------------- **Under $5**

La Barca
Rua Recife, 684 (Parque 10); ☎ *236-6964. Daily 11:30 a.m.-3:30 p.m., 7 p.m.–midnight, Sun. 11:30 a.m.-4 p.m.*
This popular fishery is set in an open-air, white stucco building, with a glimpse of the encroaching forest seen through open arches. *Costela de tambaqui grelhado* (grilled fish) is native to the Amazon—big enough for 3, and one of the best fish I had in Brazil. People with colds (everyone seems to get one in Manaus because of the heat and the air-conditioning) will love the steaming bowl of *canja da galinha* (chicken soup). Beef, chicken, strogonoff, and omelettes are also available. Those who can't take take the heat or the traffic noise can escape into an airconditioned salon. *Inexpensive-Moderate. All cards.*

Churrasco/Tropical Hotel
Estrada da Ponta Negra (Ponta Negra); ☎ *238-5757. Daily 7 p.m.-midnight*
This barbecue buffet held under a tent-like roof is a little steep at $16, but the quality of the meats, fish, chicken, and salad bar is superb. One meal could last you 2 days. *Expensive. All cards.*

Caçarola
Av. Maués, 188-A (Cachoeirinha); ☎ *234-6964 Daily 11 a.m.-3 p.m., 6 p.m.-midnight, Sun. 11 a.m.-4 p.m.*
Ten minutes from the docks, this humble abode with a stone floor, porch, and odd local art excels in regional food. The owner/chef started a restaurant in her home 9 years ago that got so popular she finally had to buy another house. Try the *caldeirada*, a fabulous fish stew, or the *tambaqui ao molho escabeche*, a native fish fried with a tomato and onion sauce. But don't pass up the freshly squeezed fruit juices, especially the *jenipapo*. *Moderate. No cards.*

Búfalo
Rua Joaquim Nabuco, 628 (Centro); ☎ *232-3373. Daily 11 a.m.-3 a.m., 6 p.m.-midnight, Sun. 11 a.m.-3 p.m.*
An Air-conditioned *rodízio*—all-you-can-eat meat for about $14 per person. *Moderate. All cards.*

Tarumã
Tropical Hotel, Estrada da Ponta Negra; ☎ *238-5757. Daily 7 p.m.-midnight*

Old-world romance with Spanish-style lanterns and high-beamed ceilings makes a welcome, i.e., air-conditioned, oasis. The cuisine rates as one of the best in the city: roasted duck with a cashew-spiked sauce was memorable. Desserts are first-class. Music from a grand piano and strings wafts down from the upper staircase. *Moderate. All cards.*

Fiorentina

Rua José Paranaguá, 44 (centro); ☎ *232-1295. Daily 11:30 a.m.–11 p.m.*
In the heart of the duty-free zone, this is the closest you'll get to an Italian cantina in the Amazon—cheerful tablecloths, bustling waiters, wood-slat chairs, and the inevitable fan. Air-conditioned room upstairs. Menu in English and Portuguese, with pizzas ranging from $6-$12. *Moderate. All cards.*

Hakata

Rua Jonathas Pedrosa, 1800; ☎ *233-3608. Tues.–Fri. 11:30 a.m.–2 p.m., 6:30 p.m.–10:30 p.m., Sun. 11:30 a.m.–3 p.m.*
"*Na chapa*" (or table-grilled) is the specialty at this air-conditioned Japanese restaurant. *Camarão na chapa* comes with 6 shrimps, fried cabbage, and fried rice—a bit greasy. but filling. *Moderate. No cards.*

Vegetarian

Rua Costa Azevedo, 105 (Centro); ☎ *234-6788. Mon.–Fri. lunch only 11 a.m.–2:30 p.m.*
A clean, airy, if warm luncheonette, serving brown rice, beans, vegetables, and pizza slices in a counter-style buffet. The banana cake was tasty, but the salads looked iffy. Excellent tropical juices. *Inexpensive. No cards.*

Bar "Galo Carijó"

Rua dos Andradas, 536. Daily 10:30 a.m.–3 p.m., 5:30 p.m.–9 p.m., closed Sun.
Also known as O Rei Jaraqui Frito, this open-air dive across from the Hotel Dona Joana is just a roof and tables, but it's famous citywide for fish. The ones I saw were bigger than the plates, with the head and tail hanging over. Tastiest is the *pirarucú*, one of the largest fresh-water species, for about $5; the small *jaraqui* runs about $2.50. Fish is normally served lightly fried, with tomatoes, onions, and a mixture of rice and beans. *Inexpensive. No cards.*

Ice Cream

Beijo Frio Ice Cream Parlor

Av. Getúlio Vargas, 1289 (Centro). Daily 8 a.m.-midnight
People go to Manaus just to indulge in the numerous tropical fruit-flavored ice creams. This air-cooled parlor features 36 exotic tastes like *cupuaçu, goiaba, tucumã, tapioca, graviola, castanha de cajú, açaí,* and *maracujá* as well as 5 diet flavors. Scoops run about $1; sundaes and banana splits are delicious. Take your time tasting flavors.

Alema

Rua José Paranaguá at the corner of Doutor Moreira
Located near the Free Zone, this is a good pit stop for cold tropical juices, desserts, and ice cream.

Insider Tip

Do try tacacá–*a street dish famous in the region, made with tapioca, cupí (manioc juice and pepper), garlic, and shrimps. The most famous vendor is located on the corner between the Plaza and Imperial Hotels.*

NIGHTLIFE

A slave to fast-moving trends, Manaus boasts a nightlife that starts on Thur. and runs through Sat. Dancing lasts until the wee hours of dawn. Among the more popular places:

Kalamazon

Highway to Itacoatiara. Thur., Fri. and Sat., action starts after midnight. Fee: about $4
This is the best club to dance *lambada* and *forró*, situated on the road to Itacoatiara—a substantial taxi drive from downtown. All ages are welcome and sometimes folklore bands from Paratins perform *toadas*, songs from the *boi* festivities.

Consciente Bar

Av. Joaquim Nabuco, 1425; ☎ *232-1425*
Good MPB bands at this lively hangout near

the red-light district. The tiny dance floor gets crowded fast.

Jet Set

Rua 10 de Julho, 439; ☎ *234-9309*

Manaus' version of tropical strip-tease; women welcome. Locals consider the show "cold," but tourists seem to get a kick out of it.

Starship

Rua Constantino Nery, at the corner of Rua Leonardo Malcher; ☎ *232-9343*

Teens to 28-year-olds head to this popular disco, particularly on Fri. after 11 p.m.

Insider Tip

Live bands can be often found at Praia da Saudade on the weekends.

SHOPPING

Downtown

The main street downtown is **Rua Eduardo Ribeiro**, full of large department stores like **Mesbla** (the Macy's of Brazil) and the even cheaper **Lojas Americanas**. The majority of banks are located along **Rua Djalma Batista**. Duty-free shopping (not of particular value to the foreign tourist) in concentrated in the Calçadão area around the streets of Doutor Moreira, Marcilio Dias, and Guilherme Moreira, crossed by Quintino Bocaiuva.

Native Crafts

Casa do Beija-Flor

Rua Quintino Bocaiuva, 224; ☎ *234-2700. Mon.–Sat. 8 a.m.–6:30 p.m., Sat. till noon*

Named House of the Hummingbird, this artisan shop is the best in the city, featuring Amazonian arts and handicrafts made by local tribes and other regional artists. Stock up on Indian musical instruments like the *pau de chuva* (rainstick) and a large variety of flutes as well as weapons like the *zarabatana* (blow gun). Huge (dead) beetles are an option, and the store even gives away free *pirarucú* scales as nail files. Prices are fixed (don't insult anyone by bargaining) and the minimum rate to send to the U.S. is $50. No cards, but dollars, cruzeiros, and traveler checks accepted.

Centro de Artesanato Banco e Silva

Rua Recife (no number); ☎ *236-1241. Mon.–Fri. 8 a.m.–7 p.m. and Saturday 8 a.m.–1 p.m.*

Located in Parque 10 de Novembro, these 20 stores carry various indigenous Indian and *caboclo* artisanry.

Museu do Índio

Av. 7 de Setembro at the corner of Duque de Caxias

Fine Indian artisanry, such as headdresses, bows and arrows, and jewelry, have been collected by the Salesians nuns who run the museum. Reasonable prices and considerably cheaper than the Science Museum store.

Herbs, Cosmetics, and Whole Foods

Chapaty

Rua Saldanha Marinho, 702-A (Centro), ☎ *233-7610*

This natural health food store specializes in herbal medicines, teas, whole breads, whole wheat pastas, and natural sweets. Also, extraordinary shampoos made from Amazon products.

Prönatus do Amazonas

Rua Costa Azevedo, 11 (Centro), factory at Rua Visconde de Porto Alegre, 440 (Centro); ☎ *234-8754*

Inspired by the richness of Amazônia, this company has developed an exclusive line of herbal pills and cosmetics culled from the plants and fruits of the jungle. All products are hypo-allergenic, and their processing is all done with respect to the cycles of the forest. Soaps and shampoos made from tropical herbs make great gifts, as do herbal formulas for anything from impotence and diabetes to weight control.

Fairs

An outdoor **Art Fair** takes place on Sun. (5 p.m.-on) at Praça da Saudade near the Monaco Hotel, in cooperation with ASSOCI-ART. Crafts, beer, native foods, children's rides, and general mayhem prevail.

> **Insider Tip**
>
> Best place to buy hammocks is along Rua dos Bares. For international magazines and newspapers, try the Livraria Nacional on Rua 24 de Maio and the kiosk near the Teatro Amazonas.

HANDS-ON MANAUS

Arrivals
Aeroporto Internacional Eduardo Gomes
Av. Santos Dumont; ☎ 212-1431 receives flights from Rio, Belém, Brasília, Campo Grande, Cuiabá, Fortaleza, Natal, Recife, Porto Velho, Recife, Rio Branco, Salvador, Santarém, São Luis, São Paulo, and a few others. From the United States, Varig flies direct from Miami, and a new flight was recently installed from San Francisco and Los Angeles.

The Hotel Tropical provides shuttle service (bus) to and from the airport for guests.

Varig Rua Guilherme Moreira, 278/86; ☎ 234-1425.
VASP Rua Guilherme Moreira, 179; ☎ 234-1266.
Transbrasil Rua Guilherme Moreira, 150; ☎ 232-1000, 232-5206.
TABA Av. Eduardo Ribeiro, 664 (Ed. Zulmira Bittencourt); ☎ 232-0676, ☎ 232-0806.
Air France Rua dos Andradas, 371, first floor, ☎ 234-2798.

Business Hours
Mon.–Fri. 8 a.m.–noon, 2 p.m.–6 p.m. Banks are open Mon.–Friday 9 a.m.–3 p.m. Stores are also open Sat. from 8 a.m.–1 p.m.

City Transportation
Car Rentals
Hertz ☎ 232-8155.
Nobre ☎ 233-6056.

Taxis
Amazonas ☎ 232-3005.
Taxi Aéreo (for the airport) ☎ 212-1370.

Buses
City buses run from 5 a.m.–midnight.

Climate
Manaus is a sauna-hot and humid all year long with temperatures that start at 80 degrees and rise without mercy. Nov.–Mar. is the rainy season, with precipitation a daily occurrence. Temperatures are a bit cooler in May and June, with the water level reaching its peak in June, Dry season occurs July–Nov. During dry season, you may have to change routes. Canoe trips may be cancelled in downpours. In an open river with a real storm, don't go out in a canoe because of high winds.

Consulates
U.S.A.
Rua Dr. Machado, 106; ☎ 234-4546 (during office hours); ☎ 232-1611 (after-hours).
England
Rua Eduardo Ribeiro, 520, room 1202; ☎ 234-1018.
Germany
Rua Barroso, 355; ☎ 232-0890.

Exchange House
Casa Cortez Rua Dr. Moreira, 105; ☎ 232-2695.
Banco do Brasil Rua Marechal Deodoro and at the *airport* (24 hrs.) exchanges dollars at the tourist rate.

Guides
Emamtur, the official tourist board, requires officially sanctioned guides to take 3 months of training, including courses in history, jungle survival, ecology, and Red Cross. If you hire a nonofficial guide, make sure he is reliable and knowledgeable or you will regret it dearly. Some recommended private guides are: **John Harwood** ☎ 236-5133 a British scientist, formerly at INPA, who now works with cruise lines as well as individuals; Brazilian-born **Claudia Roedel** ☎ 244-2455 formerly an ecology student who now guides treks into the jungle with her husband. **Christopher Charles Gomes** conducts tours and individual expeditions that may be reserved through the **Hotel Rio Branco** Rua

dos Andradas, 484; ☎ 233-4019. (See more information under "Hotels").

Special interest groups may contact **Sherre P. Nelson** at **Solução** *Rua Monsenhor Coutinho, 1141;* ☎ *234-5955, 5400.*

Luxury Cruise Liners

A number of luxury cruise liners dock in Manaus or travel up the Amazon River, among them: Odessa America Service Co., Sun Line Cruises, Regency, Royal Viking, Ocean Princess, Society Explorers, Saga Fjiord, Stella Solaris, Berlim, and Fairwind. (For more information, see "Cruises" under *Specialty Tours* in the back of the book.)

Mosquitoes

The Amazon River has an acidity content that prevents the breeding of mosquitoes, but the white waters of the Solimões are seriously infested. There, mosquitoes attack mostly at dusk and after dark, when repellant is absolutely necessary. Most legitimate tours avoid this area at those times. (Also see the "Amazon Survival Kit," in *Amazônia*.)

Yellow fever, transmitted by mosquitoes, is considered endemic in Brazil, except around the coastal shores. Health authorities advise that the most infected areas are Acre, Amazonas, Goiás, Maranhão, Mato Grosso, Mato Grosso do Sul, Pará, Rondônia, and the territories of Amapá and Roraima. Vaccinations are good for 10 years and are essential if you are traveling either to the Amazon or the Pantanal. You may be required to show proof of vaccination when entering the country from Venezuela, Colombia, Ecuador, and Bolivia; it's best to always travel with the document. (For more information on malaria, see the "Amazon Survival Kit".)

For a list of other gruesome diseases carried by bugs, see Alex Bradbury's book *Backcountry Brazil* (Hunter Publishing, 1990). As far I could tell, I never encountered any of these bugs on the normal tourist excursions, except perhaps for a few tics.

Photo Development

Foto Nascimento *Av. 7 de Setembro, 1194;* ☎ *234-4660, 234-4995* Film development in 1 hr. Major makes of cameras are for sale.

Telephones

To make international calls, head for the telephone company **Tele Amazonas** *Rua Guilherme Moreira, 326 (downtown). Daily: 6 a.m.–11:30 p.m.* Another branch is located on the corner of Av. Getúlio Vargas and Leonardo Malche. Both are downtown.

Time

Manaus is 1 hr. behind Brazilian standard time (2 hrs. behind between Oct.–Mar., when the rest of Brazil is on summer time).

Tourist Information

Emamtur (state tourist board) *Av. Tarumã, 379 (Praça 24 de Outubro);* ☎ *234-2252, FAX 233-9973* An information post is also located at the airport Eduardo Gomes. For information regarding native tribes and permission to visit reservations, contact **FUNAI** *Rua dos Andradas, 473;* ☎ *234-7632.*

Travel Agencies

Amazon Explorers *Rua Quintino Bocaiúva, 189;* ☎ *232-3052/8543* arranges boat excursions, overnight jungle treks, fishing trips, city tours, and excursions specially tailored to the needs of clients. English-speaking staff available.

The **Hotel Tropical** ☎ *238-5757* maintains a fine agency for guests and non-guests alike. Another full-service agency is **Selvatur** *Praça Adalberto Vale (Hotel Amazonas);* ☎ *234-8984.*

When to Go

June 12-30 *Folklore Festival of Paratins* Often as spectacular as Carnaval in Rio, these festivities divide the cities into rivaling groups with parades, typical foods, and music. Best time to go is the last 3 days.

July 15-30 *Folklore Festival of Amazonas.*

September 21-28 *Agricultural Fair.*

September 27-29 *Itacoatiara Festival of Song.*

ALTA FLORESTA

In the southernmost part of the state of Mato Grosso, the grit-and-grizzle town of **Alta Floresta** is something right out of the Old West. The business at hand is gold. For the last twenty years, thousands have converged on the area to try their luck; some make it after two years; others are still following pipe dreams. Luck, not persistence, seems to be the deciding factor in these parts, and as one local explained, a kind of inbred culture prevails where rules are not made to be broken. "There are no thieves here," he told me matter-of-factly, "because if someone takes something, he dies." A pale orange dust storm seems to have perpetually enveloped the city; even the children playing outside are covered with it. The major activity during the day takes place at the **Aurim Gold Exchange**, where *garimpeiros*, from the slick to the mud-slung, come to exchange their gold nuggets for cash. Around 10:30 in the morning, you'll see *garimpeiro* wives, dressed in cut-offs, high heels, and lots of gold jewelry, forking over the husbands' hard-earned nuggets to be weighed and processed.

Alta Floresta is also fascinating because you can actually see rainforest burning. Perhaps that's not everyone's dream vacation, but there's nothing like ramming home the reality of the earth's plight than by seeing it close at hand. Just traveling the roads out of town will bring you past scorched earth and burnt trunks, and you'll no doubt see not only smoldering grass but groves of trees and shrubs in actual flames. I actually saw one farmer setting fire to a plot of land so he could plant cotton, but the most shocking scene I witnessed was that of a three-year-old playfully setting a tiny pile of twigs on fire with a match—just like his dad.

There is, however, access to a wonderful jungle near Alta Floresta and the best way to see it is to book a stay at the **Floresta Amazônica Hotel**. This resort, unusually stylish for the area, is located on the junction of the **TeleSpires** and **Cristalina Rivers** and is owned by a large landholder who is passionate about preserving the forest (she even hires as guides young professional botanists who do extensive research over their six-month internships). The complex is most unique for the multidimensional perspectives of Amazonian life it offers its guests, who can look forward to widely different adventures, depending on the season (routes navigated during the dry season by jeep are cruised by canoe during the rainy season.) A day trip may be taken to a nearby *fazenda* that features an unusual zoo as well as an exciting display of *garças* roosting in the leafy trees at dusk. Other excursions include a coffee plantation and the muddy dregs of a gold mine, where you'll probably get a chance to speak with miners. Overnight excursions into the jungle are the most exciting: Guests are escorted down the Cristalina in a canoe to a location in the jungle, where they bed down dormitory-style (beds or hammocks). Just waking up to the symphony of cawing birds will be thrilling, not to mention the nightly orchestra of bullfrogs. Fishing expeditions and fresh-water swimming are also available. This resort is particularly fine for families.

CULTURE

THE FOREST PEOPLE

The following interview was made with Luiz Pereira Andrade, a 57-year-old guide who lives with his wife, daughter, son-in-law, and grandchild in the forest connected to the Floresta Amazônica Hotel. He is a big, burly man with gray, bushy eyebrows and a paunch that pushes out of his shirt. He has lived in the forest for twenty years.

"Here, in Alta Floresta, we call the *matinta pereira* the *pai do mato* (father of the forest). The first clue to being in contact with him is when you are in the forest and suddenly feel lost. You go home and get something to give him—food or anything—and put it where you felt strange. If you don't do this, you'll be lost forever and won't find your way back home. He's invisible but you can feel him. When I fish at night, sometimes I hear strange sounds, like tools falling, or somebody coughing, but there's nothing there. I never feel afraid—I just don't know what it means. Many times I've seen strange lights. When I'm fishing at night, a spot of light, yellowish with a blue tail, comes up behind me, goes to the river, then disappears in the water. This light is very strong and illuminates the whole river. Some people say it's the Gold Mother. Me, I don't know.

"Do trees and animals have spirits? *Com certeza*. If they are alive, they have spirits. Trees have a natural capacity to take energy, others to receive. When I embrace a tree, I feel it. I learned this by myself because one time I went to the shade of a tree when I was very nervous and suddenly calmed down. You saw that when you went to hug the *embauba* tree, it released your negative energy and when you hugged the *castanha* it gave you positive energy. How could trees do this if they don't have souls?

"When you go to the forest and watch birds, they are happy so you start to be happy. You start to join with their happiness. When you are unhappy and you go to the forest and look around, you feel human is not that big. You are just a small piece in this world. I will live in this forest till I am 90 because here the old people become young. We don't miss anything from the city. I just feel unhappy I didn't come sooner."

A GOLD MIND

The following interview was made with the owner of a gold mine in Alta Floresta, a well-dressed man in his late 50s who was waiting to exchange gold. His slicked-back gray hair, good linen clothes, diamond ring, and gold watch made a sharp contrast to the rough, desperate-looking young men with muddy feet who were also waiting in line.

"I came here nine years ago from Paraná just for gold—eight in the mine, one year making money. In the beginning you don't know much. You usually lose money. You get friends to work for you, but usually they steal from you. But I was lucky. I have a good life now—a good house, car. I was rich also in Paraná—I had a shop of tools for cars. But I think life was better there. The city here doesn't have much society, but my wife likes it better here because it's hotter. I had malaria five times. Only last year did I have it badly—at Christmas, I was very ill. Is it worth the pain? For me it's been good. *Garimpo* is like a vice. When you start you can't stop. And sometimes you lose all your money just because you have to reinvest it to try again."

THE ESSENTIAL ALTA FLORESTA

WHERE TO STAY

Floresta Amazônica Hotel

Av. Perimetral Oeste, 2001; ☎ *(65)521-3601*

A clean, cheerful resort that is about as comfortable as you'll find for thousands of miles. An outdoor dining area looks out onto a pleasant pool complex; meals can also be eaten inside a stylishly rustic restaurant. Excursions include jungle hikes, coffee farm, and gold mine. The landscape is an ebullient profusion of pink and blue flowers, and the lobby sports a few caged spiders and snakes. Trained biologists serve as guides. Fishing and fresh-water swimming included. Reservations can be made through Expeditours in Rio ☎ *(21) 287-9697, FAX 521-4388.* The following rates contain a 50 percent discount: single deluxes run $24, doubles $30, VIP apartment $43. *Moderate. Cards: V.*

Getting There
Air:

Alta Floresta is serviced by the airline **TABA** *Av. Ariosto de Riva;* ☎ *(65)521-3222, 5521-3360 (airport)* with flights from Altamira, Belém, Cuiabá, Itaituba, Jacareacanga, Juará, and Santarém.

Bus:

Connections can be made from Campo Grande, Cuiabá, Paranaiba, and others. If you take the bus from Cuiabá, some parts of the road are not paved and you may feel like you will never see civilization again. "Luxury" buses called *leitos* are available from São Paulo to Cuiabá, where you must change buses. At Colida, you change to an even more primitive bus for another 3 hours (total trip from São Paulo runs 12–14 hrs., about $76).

Air Taxis:

Aeorobleto ☎ 521-2693.

When to Go

The rainy season runs Oct.–Mar.; mosquitoes are rampant after heavy rains. Best time to visit is May–Oct. The coolest months are Aug.–Oct.

Insider Tip

Mato Grosso is one of the most malaria-infected states in Brazil, and Alta Floresta has its fair share (mostly around the gold mines). Do come protected with prophylactics and wear plenty of mosquito repellant, reapplying it before dusk. Keep windows shut at night. (Personally, I never had a problem, but I did take prophylactics.) (See Health Kit in the back of the book.)

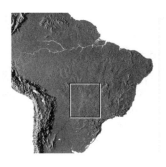

THE PANTANAL

Caiman Crocodile

Although nearly obscured by the eco-media's blitz on the Amazon rainforest, the Pantanal—an immense kidney-shaped swampland in Western Brazil—is perhaps the country's greatest natural resource. Officially known as *O Grande Pantanal*, the region, which cuts across the states of Mato Grosso and Mato Grosso do Sul (as well as western Bolivia and northeastern Paraguay) is a multifaceted ecosystem that changes its alluvial face every six months—not unlike the Everglades in Florida. During the rainy season (October to March), torrential rains inundate up to 85 percent of the region, causing rivers, lakes, and ponds to merge into an inland sea. Five months later, the effect of the burning tropical sun and the north-south flow gives way to verdant grassy plains dotted by water holes teeming with fish, tall wading birds, and alligators. As such, the Pantanal during the dry season becomes an acutely visible arena for the playing out of Mother Nature's food chain. Simply, what the Amazon is to flora, the Pantanal is to fauna. If you want to see Brazilian wildlife at its most exotic, come to the Pantanal. Although the word "pantanal" is usually translated as swampland, in actuality the Pantanal is a sedimentary basin into which drain numerous rivers, including the Rio Paraguay and its tributaries, as they make their way south to the Rio de la Plata and the Atlantic Ocean. More than 65 million years ago, the region was completely ocean; 7,500-year-old animal bones have been found here, as well as the remains of a 10,000-year-old human fetus. As recent as 500 years ago, Kayapó, Iguato, and other tribes were known to migrate along the border with Amazonas. In the early 18th century, rumors of fist-sized emeralds and diamonds magnetized the first *bandeirantes* from São Paulo, though it was gold that was finally discovered along the banks of the Cuiabá River. After a 30-year rush, most miners moved on, but the few who stayed started sugarcane plantations and huge cattle ranches, piquing the interest of the King of Portugal, who established a captaincy in 1719 to collect taxes.

A Wild West Fantasy

It would take another century until anyone intentionally returned to the Pantanal. As 17th- and 18th-century expeditions found the way nearly impassable, the region gained a certain wildcat reputation. In 1925, Lt. Colonel Percy Fawcett, one of the most indefatigable explorers, mysteriously disappeared while searching for the legendary city of El Dorado, but that didn't deter big-city slickers during the 1930s and 1940s from zooming down in their German-made seaplanes to fish and bag game. With the construction of the highways between Cuiabá–Santarem and Cuiabá–Porto Velho, the Pantanal's fortunes, and especially those of Cuiabá (Mato Grosso's capital) improved dramatically. The booming frontier town, situated on the banks of the Cuiabá River, became a symbol of Manifest Destiny, a Wild West fantasy for those trapped in the drought–ravaged Northeast. Roads were planned for 150,000 new residents, but many more thousands were spellbound by the lure of gold, lumber, cattle, and diamonds. Nearly all had to pass through Cuiabá on their way to the yellow-brick plains.

Today, as the Pantanal loses its reputation as an intractable swamp, it is fast becoming the focus of enormous political and economic intrigue. Although two Brazilian areas are officially protected—a remote national park near Bolivia and a small ecological reserve in Mato Grosso—the rest remains the property of private cattle ranches where frontier law prevails. Illegal hunters, miners, and commercial fishermen continue to blatantly exploit the region in the face of lax federal enforcement. The health of residents is threatened by mercury poisoning from goldmining, agrochemical pollution from crops, and malaria epidemics. Violent outbreaks take place daily between goldminers and native tribes, the latter which are being forced further and further into the interior. Sadly, with the exception of Pantanal Alert, an activist group made up of artists and musicians in São Paulo, there are very few private organizations dedicated to conserving the Pantanal with the same fervor as that of the Amazon rainforest.

Whether the land in the Pantanal is even economically viable is being hotly debated today behind closed doors. Although most of the land had been traditionally owned by a few families, it is now being divvied up into smaller plots, at great loss to the new owners. Rumor has it that, since such a large percentage of the land is flooded for most of the year, substantial agriculture is nearly impossible, and the exorbitant cost of constantly relocating grazing cattle makes for unprofitable business. Some factory owners are now using their newly claimed property merely as tax dodges. Beyond the great ranches, the only other residents of the region are poor fishermen, who eke out a subsistence level of existence. Eco-tourism is the Pantanal's brightest hope for the future.

HOW TO VISIT

THE TRANSPANTANEIRA HIGHWAY

There are many ways to visit the Pantanal—all of them rugged, muddy affairs, but well worth the effort for a die-hard eco-tourist. At least once in your stay, you must traverse the grand **Transpantaneira Highway**, a feat of civil engineering completed during the dictatorship (1964–85) that unwittingly created a stunning ex post facto reserve. The 150-kilometer road, elevated two to three meters above the flooded plains, starts right after the quaint village of Poconé, where the asphalt road suddenly turns into what Pantanal vets sardonically call an "all-weather" highway. In the rainy season, the road becomes a linear refuge for wildlife; when the waters recede, millions of fish are trapped in the roadside trenches, offering a smorgasbord for predator and scavenger alike. During the dry season, riding over the bumpy highway with its bomb-sized craters is like journeying through a zoo on the moon—every few meters, another "oh-oh-oh" experience. Large mounds become islands of refuge for snakes, capybaras, antbears, and jaguars, while caimans and great wading birds retreat to the artificial pools below to wait out the dry season. Seeds borne on the wind and in the guts of birds create the landscape of squat trees and scrub—a dried-out *cerrado* that nearly resembles parts of East Africa. The highway ends abruptly 150 kilometers south of Poconé at Porto Jofre on the banks of the Cuiabá River.

There are few people and no other towns in the Pantanal, so a look around Poconé is well warranted. Dating back to the 18th century, Poconé is a picturesque, well-kept colonial town, where most of the houses have traditional roofs and horse-drawn carts still meander down the cobblestone streets. A blue church dominates the main square, around which are situated general stores and the mayor's office. Just as it was 150 years ago, gold was "rediscovered" in Poconé about five years ago, turning the town upside down. Convinced there was gold hidden in the walls of the church, miners actually tore it down, finding only enough to rebuild a new church. Today, signs of *garimpeiros* are everywhere, from the picks and axes in the country stores to the smell of mercury in the air.

RIVER EXCURSIONS AND LODGES

Besides trekking the Transpantaneira Highway, there are several other travel options in the Pantanal. Cuiabá is only one of three gateways to the Pantanal; the other jumping-off points are Campo Grande and Corumbá. From any one of these cities you can journey into the interior and choose among several types of accommodations. Favorite among fishermen and birdwatchers are the 2-4 day river cruises in **botels** (floating lodges, really just boats), like the one I took with Expeditours. Or you can choose to stay in a **rustic lodge** from where you can initiate treks by foot, horseback, or canoe—usually preferred by those who sleep more comfortably on dry land. A variety of lodges in all price ranges are available, from the most primitive ranches, where meals are cooked over an open fire, to the luxurious Pousada Caiman, the most famous lodge in the Pantanal.

Package deals are usually the cheapest and the most sensible way to go; just make sure the lodge provides transfer from the airport.

The **independent's way** to see the Pantanal is to combine different options. First, hire a good guide who is ready to go anywhere, then improvise. You can go by car from Poconé to Barão de Melgaço, then rent kayaks and paddle to Porto Cercado, or if you're crazy enough, all the way down to Porto Jofre (about 4-5 days). This way you can stop and take time to talk to the locals, who are usually friendly. Have a car waiting at Porto Jofre and go over the Transpantaneira Highway to Pixaim, camping or staying at a lodge. To do it right, you'll need about 8-10 days. The price for such a trip with guide and transportation will probably cost as much as an Expeditours boat tour for four days, but you must come prepared with your own food. To find a guide, call a travel agency and just ask for the names of reliable guides without explaining exactly what you want, then make private arrangements with the guide.

Insider Tip:

Hitchhiking the Transpantaneira Highway (as opposed to traversing it in a prearranged tour) seems to be the beloved pastime of male travel writers and photojournalists who are mad for adventure and great photo-ops. Maybe I'm a sissy, but frankly, I wouldn't suggest hitchhiking, at least not on your first trip to the region. Sure, you'll find a friendly ride eventually, and you'll meet lots of colorful cowboys, native fishermen, and even a few federal agents, but in the meantime you could be overcome by sunstroke, exhaustion, bee attacks, hungry capybaras, dazed jacarés, and swarms of malaria-ridden mosquitoes, not to mention sudden floodings. You might even stumble on illegal poachers who would like to scramble you for breakfast. Better on your first attempt to go with a reputable guide, in well-maintained vehicles (trucks, boats, planes) with responsible drivers who know the terrain. The driving is rough; even Brazilian tourists have been known to topple over their jeeps. Since there are no towns, no restaurants, and no phones on the highway, getting stuck will mean a very long wait.

PANTANAL SURVIVAL KIT

BEES Anyone going to the Pantanal should read Vic Banks's riveting description of the "bees from hell" in his book *The Pantanal* (Sierra Club, 1991). According to Banks, 300-400 people a year die from bee stings in Brazil, more than from any other animal attack. In the Pantanal, Europa honeybees have interbred with African killer bees, making them capable of attacking aggressively en masse, even if just one drone is disturbed. Truly, Banks' encounter was most unfortunate, but I frankly never met one bee in the Pantanal.

CLIMATE *Between April–October,* which is the dry season, temperatures average between 68°F and 75°F, but temperatures can rise over 50 degrees in just a matter of hours. The hottest months in the Pantanal are *December–February,* when temperatures average between 110°F and 112°F. During dry season it's important to drink lots of liquids to avoid dehydration. Starting in *November,* weather alternates between torrential rains and scalding sun. The most animals can be seen in *December and January.*

MEDICAL EMERGENCIES It's best not to have them while you're in the Pantanal. Decent hospitals will probably be boats, planes, and torturous jeep rides away. Take your own medicine kit (including gauze, antiseptic, allergy pills and antihistamines, calamine lotion, aloe vera lotion for cuts and bruises, a snake bite kit, TANG™ for dehydration, and Pepto–Bismol™ for diarrhea, etc. Make sure you've had all the necessary innoculations (tetanus, yellow fever, typhoid, polio). And pray. (Hospitals are listed under *Hands–On Cuiabá.*)

WHAT TO PACK Follow guidelines for Amazon treks (see *Amazônia* chapter), but also dress in layers (for cool nights, a jean jacket and sweater is sufficient). Binoculars, telephoto lenses, and high-speed film are essential in the Pantanal. (Those magnificent closeup shots of birds seen in books and brochures are surely taken by professionals who spend days waiting silently under a bush for just the right moment.)

CUIABÁ

The capital of Mato Grosso, **Cuiabá** (pronounced Kwee–ah–bah) is the major gateway to the Pantanal, located about 102 kilometers from the northern entrance of the Transpantaneira Highway. Even so, it's not exactly a destination in itself, though a day or two stuck here won't feel like the end of the world. Most visitors use Cuiabá as a trampoline to visit other parts of the region, like the magnificent rock sculptures in the **National Park** and the caves and waterfalls of **Chapada dos Guimarães**, one of the most beautiful sites in all Brazil. Once a frontier town, Cuiabá has boomed to over 330,000 people (some reports claim up to one million in the surrounding area); you will discover fine regional restaurants here, as well as some of the best crafts stores for Indian artifacts in the region.

The first *bandeirantes* in the early 18th century came in search of Indian slaves but soon forgot their objective when they discovered gold. A Paulista, Pascoal Moreira Cabral, established the first settlement in 1719, having braved disease, mosquitoes, floods, and intense heat through his arduous 5-month journey from São Paulo. Soon, thousands more were traveling the 3,000-kilometer route, boosting the population of Cuiabá far beyond that of São Paulo between 1719–1730. Because of the navigation systems, however, ties with Bolivians, Paraguayans, and Argentinians soon became tighter than with fellow Brazilians, resulting in a kind of trans-Latino culture. The flotillas of canoes and medium-sized ships that arrived laden with supplies and slaves invariably departed from Cuiabá groaning with gold.

In 1979, **Mato Grosso** was divided into two states, Mato Grosso in the north and Mato Grosso do Sul in the south. Since then, Cuiabá has enjoyed enormous development in education, tourism, and construction. In 1989–1990, three shows on TV claiming that gold had been found on the streets (!) of Cuiabá magnetized a stream of Northeasterners and Mineiros, who arrived with little more than dreams in their pockets. As a result, a rash of frontier towns rose up, most of them approximating slums. One such town is **Cangas**, ten minutes from Cuiabá on the Cuiabá-Santarém highway, the site of six or seven **gold mines**. Founded about seven years ago, *Cangas today is a scene straight out of a Wild West movie, with two big bars, three small snack bars, one school, three churches, three gas stations, and*

a single public phone (for all 5,000 people). As one local told me, *"There's only one phone because most people here have no one to call."*

> **Insider Tip:**
>
> During the dry season, airplane descents into Cuiabá can be turbulent due to the smoky warm air from fires set by cattle ranchers every dry season to burn off undesirable vegetation and promote fresh grass for fodder. August is the peak month for these fires, and sometimes flights are canceled for several weeks, forcing travelers to take 5-hour bus trips from the nearest open airport. During the rainy season, flights may be delayed due to inclement weather.

A BIRD'S EYE VIEW

Cuiabá is nicknamed the Garden City because of its many trees, including 200-year-old palms. The main plaza, Praça da República, is dominated by an old church, the city, the Hotel Excelsior, and a 12-story television tower on a nearby hill. Next to the tower is the alabaster minaret of a Muslim temple. From the Igreja de Bom Jesus dos Passos, an 18th-century church with an exquisite Gothic facade, you can see a vista of the city. The tourist office, TURIMAT, is located off the main plaza near the Igreja Matriz.

SIGHTS

GEODESIC CENTER Although the *mirante* in Chapada is considered a more scenic representation of the geodesic center of South America, the exact point is located at the Praça Moreira Cabral in Cuiabá. The site is marked by a monument and pyramid in a small concrete park facing the Legislative Assembly and is considered to include a 50-kilometer radius (of which Chapada forms one end). The Praça can be entered from Rua Barão de Melgaço.

FISH MARKET Buying and selling the day's fresh catch takes place along the Rio Cuiabá daily from 4:00 a.m.–6:00 p.m.

CITY PARK Horto Florestal Bairro Coxipó, *at the confluence of the Rio Coxipó with Rio Cuiabá; access through Avenida Fernando Correa da Costa. Daily 7:00 a.m.–5:30 p.m. Guides available 2:00 p.m.–5:00 p.m.* The future park of the city is being planned on this tropical landscape where children can scamper around playgrounds made from logs. On the docket for the future is an orchid greenhouse, an exposition of seeds and plants natural to the forest, and a special display of medicinal plants.

CRAFTS COMMUNE *Comunidade São Gonçalo,* located near the Fazenda de Mato Grosso, is a primitive community on the banks of the Rio Cuiabá that supports itself totally through artisanry (especially pottery) and folkloric presentations. Visitors are always welcome; just seeing the rural lifestyle should prove fascinating. The community's major festival is held on January 10, the Feast of São Gonçalo, when colorful boats proceed upriver to herald the arrival of the saint.

> **Insider Tip:**
>
> *If you want to eat regional food, see a folkloric museum, and buy regional crafts all in one stop, try the complex that houses the Casa do Artesão, the Museu de Artesanato, and the Regionalissimo restaurant, located on Praça Maj. João Bueno.*

MUSEUMS AND ZOO

Museu de Artesanato *Rua 13 de Junho, Praça Maj. João Bueno. Tuesday–Sunday 10:00 a.m.–3:00 p.m., 6:00 p.m.–11:00 p.m.* Next door to the Casa do Artesão (a fine crafts store) is a museum of folkoric art situated in a frontier-styled, brick-and-wood house, complete with an antique kitchen. Featured are ornaments and weapons from the Xavantes and other Mato Grosso tribes, as well as leather goods from the home-on-the-range culture. Especially intriguing is the leather *bornal,* a contraption that was strapped around a horse's mouth so it could walk and eat millet at the same time.

Museu do Indio Marechal Candîdo Rondôn at the University Federal of Mato Grosso displays artisanry, weapons, and ornaments crafted by the state's indigenous peoples.

Mini Zoo Universidade Federal do Mato Grosso (UFMT), *Avenida Fernando Correa da Costa,* displays the fauna and flora of the region in an outdoor natural environment. On the far side of well-secured fences, animals such as capybaras, egrets, garças, alligators, and land turtles all seem to live in harmony, although some tend to look collapsed from the heat. Best times to visit is *6:00 a.m.–8:00 a.m. and 3:30 p.m.–7:00 p.m. to avoid your own sunstroke (1:00 p.m. is deadly).* An indoor environ is open daily *7:00 a.m.–11:00 a.m. and 1:30 p.m.–7:00 p.m., closed Monday* and features snakes, jaguars, monkeys, birds, and ostriches. A university restaurant near the parking lot goes on strike a lot but is a nice place to meet young people. To reach the zoo, take the city bus labeled *"Copamel Universidade"* or *"Santa Cruz."*

THE ESSENTIAL CUIABÁ

WHERE TO STAY

If you don't want to find a veritable zoo in your hotel room (i.e., frogs in your toilet and cockroaches the size of capybaras in the closet), you'll have to pay for a bug-free environment in Cuiabá. In the hot clime, air-conditioning is essential, and if you are returning from an excursion, you'll appreciate a good laundry service.

Expensive -------------- $30–$50

Moderate ---------------- $10–$30

Inexpensive ------------- Under $10

★ **Veneza Palace Hotel**
Avenida Coronel Escolástico, 738 (Bandeirantes); ☎ *(65) 321-4847*
This perfectly respectable, impeccably clean 3-star has an oriental lobby and a genial staff. The carpeted apartments are small, but the air-conditioning is ice-cold, and the wood furniture attractive. All rooms come with color TV, minibar, and carpet. Safes are at the reception. Laundry is available. The restaurant, which favors international cuisine, serves an excellent *canja de galinha* (chicken soup). There's also a pool, TV/playroom, and an American bar. Superior singles run $46, doubles $61. 78 Apts. *Moderate. All Cards.*

Hotel Fazenda de Mato Grosso
Rua Antônio Dorileo, 1200 (Coxipó)
Located only 6 kilometers from the city, this farm-like complex is surrounded by 19 hectares of forested land—a kind of "civilized wilderness." The rustic apartments are housed in 1- and 2-story buildings with traditional tiled roofs; all have air-conditioning, color TV, minibar, and phone. Clean and attractive, the bathrooms are appointed in tile and marble. On the grounds is a mini-zoo with snakes, garças, and capybaras; there's also a large pool and playground surrounded by tropical vegetation. Horses, paddle boats, and other sports are included in the daily rate, as is breakfast. Transportation to the city is provided for groups who hold conventions here. 46 apartments. *Moderate. All cards.*

JJ Palace Hotel
Rua Alziro Zarur, 312; (Boa Esperança); ☎ *(65) 361-1858*
For budget travelers only. A single in this 3-story hotel is absolutely basic—little closet space, a slight mustiness, somewhat dirty walls, but a well-equipped minibar. Location is near a pharmacy and several restaurants. Singles with fan run about $10, doubles with air-conditioning $20. *Inexpensive. No Cards.*

WHERE TO EAT

Moderate ---------------- $5–$15

Inexpensive ------------- Under $5

Recanto do Bosque
Rua Cândido Mariano, 1040;
☎ *323-1468. Noon–3:00 p.m., 5:00 p.m.–midnight*
Trees grow right through the middle of this open-air restaurant, the best rodízio in town, situated under a grass roof. Eighteen cold salads and all-you-can-eat meat; Saturday features *feijoada*. After 5:00 p.m., beer is half price and barbecued fish is included. Buffet runs about $4–$5 per person, discounts for groups of 15 or more. *Moderate. All cards.*

★ **Taberna Portuguesa**
Avenida XV de Novembro, 40;
☎ *321-3661. Daily 10:30 a.m.–2:00 p.m., 6:00 p.m.–midnight*
Located about 1 kilometer from the center of town, this cozy, air-conditioned Portuguese tavern is piquant with the smells of home cooking. Codfish runs about $9, *caldeirada* (a thick fish soup made with white wine, potatoes, onions, pimentos, and tomato sauce) runs about $13, an award-winning paella about $20. Dishes usually serve two. *Moderate. No cards.*

O Regionalíssimo
Rua 13 de Junho (Praça João Bueno);
☎ *322-3908. Daily: 11:30 a.m.–2:30 p.m., 7:30 p.m.–11:00 p.m., live music Thursday–Sunday, closed Monday.*
Situated next to the Casa do Artesão, this

charming adega features some of the best regional cuisine in Cuiabá. Local folkloric musicians serenade the buffet, which changes daily; you might find fried fish, *peixe ensopado, farofa de banana, carne de sol,* and other delicacies. Alas, no air-conditioning, but a steady breeze whips through the open brick arches. *Moderate. No cards.*

Mamma Aurora
Rua Miranda Reis, 386; ☎ *322-4339. Daily: 6:00 p.m.–midnight*
Best pizzeria in town. *Inexpensive. No cards.*

NIGHTLIFE

Nightlife in Cuiabá is as hot as you will find in the Pantanal, or even in Mato Grosso—north or south. Best disco for the 18–40 set is **Discoteca Logan.** Another dance spot is **Get Up Dance**
Avenida Fernando Corrêa da Costa, 1953; ☎ *323-3335*
For local bands and solo singers performing MPB, try the
Mirante Bar
Avenida Miguel Smith, in front of the Plaza Motel.

SHOPPING

Casa do Guaraná
Avenida Mário Corrêa, 310; ☎ *321-7729*
Situated in the *bairro* of Porto, the oldest district in Cuiabá, this "House of Guaraná" makes a facinating showcase for Brazilian ingenuity, featuring products made from the plant most known for its stimulating kick to the nervous system. Here you can buy "sticks" of guaraná that you can grate into a powder in the traditional way, or you may buy the powder already formed. *Xarope de guaraná* is a syrup that is drunk as juice (just add water). The store also features *licor de Pequi* (a liqueur made from a typical fruit of the *cerrado*), as well as *serrinhas de unha* (nail files made from fish scales). You can also stock up on natural herb shampoos and cosmetics, as well as stunning Pantanal T-shirts.

Casa do Artesão
Rua 13 de Junho, 315; ☎ *322-3908, 321-0603*

Founded in May 15, 1975, this store, situated in an 18th-century blue-and-white colonial house, features some of the best crafts for sale in the region. Good buys include ganzas (scraper-like percussion instruments made of wood) and handmade pottery. Absolutely exquisite are the embroidered hammocks that go for about $200—steep, but so lovely you could hang them on the wall as decoration. Also for sale are indigenous Indian crafts such as bows, arrows, and basketry. A special room features homemade sweets and liqueurs; don't miss the antique sugarcane machine in the garden. Next door is the Regionalíssimo restaurant.

Artíndia
Rua Comandante Costa, 942;
☎ *321-1348, near the Praça Rachid Jaudy*
The artisan store of FUNAI features crafts from the indigenous tribes of the Pantanal.

Mercearia Banzai
Avenida Generoso Ponce (no number), Mercado Municipal Box 1/2/3 (downtown); ☎ *321-7518*
Macrobiotic and natural products including brown rice, miso, and tofu are sold here.

HEALERS

Cuiabá and Chapada dos Guimarães have attracted a steady stream of holistic health practitioners during the last 10 years. Among the best are:

Centro de Vivências Para Integração do Ser
Rua Balneário São João, 323 (Coxipó da Ponte); ☎ *361-2215*
The city's most active alternative health center, offering a fine acupuncturist, Décio Cesar da Silva, as well as other practitioners in the fields of rebirthing, oki-yoga, massage, etc.

Ma Prem Dwari
Rua Doze, 297 (Boa Esperança);
☎ *361-5274*
Excellent masseuse and practitioner of Bach Flower Remedies.

HANDS–ON CUIABÁ

Airlines

Flights to Cuiabá can be arranged from Alta

Floresta (TABA), Belém, Belo Horizonte, Brasília, Campo Grande (Varig), Natal, Porto Alegre, Rio Branco, Rio de Janeiro, Salvador, Santarém, and São Paulo, among others.

Varig/Cruzeiro
Rua Antônio João, 258; ☎ 321-7238.

VASP
Rua Pedro Celestino, 32 (Downtown); ☎ 624-1313, ramal 112.

Transbrasil
Rua Barão de Melgaço 3508; ☎ 624-2000.

TABA
Airport; ☎ 381-2233.

Arrivals

Aeroporto Marechal Rondôn
is situated at Avenida Governador Ponce de Arruda (Várzea Grande); ☎ 381-2211. The Rodoviária (bus station) is located at Avenida Mal. Rondôn (on the road to Chapada dos Guimarães); ☎ 321-4703/4603. For more information see Points Beyond below.

Car Rentals and Air Taxis

Nobre can be found at the airport; ☎ 381-1651. There is also an office at Avenida Governador Ponce de Arruda, 980; ☎ 3811-2821.

Localiza Nacional
Avenida Dom Bosco, 965; ☎ 381-3773; at the airport, open 24 hours.

AIR TAXIS:

Abelha
☎ 381-122.

Jáo
☎ 381-1067.

Scala
☎ 381-2491.

Climate

Weather can change very quickly within hours in Cuiabá. Basically, summers (December–February) are hot and humid (temperatures over 100°F) while winters (June–August) are cool and dry (temperatures dropping to 60°F).

Money Exchange

If you're flying into the state of Mato Grosso from a major Brazilian city, it's best to exchange money before you arrive; rates will undoubtedly be better. Traveler's checks can be exchanged at

Banco do Brasil
Rua Barão de Melgaço, 915
Good exchange rates for dollars are offered at the **Abudi Palace Hotel.**

Medical Emergencies

Hospitals are generally to be avoided in this region. For emergencies:

Hospital Geral e Maternidade
Rua 13 de Junho, 2101; ☎ 323-3322.

Pronto–Socorro Municipal
Rua Gen. Valle; ☎ 321-7404.

Pharmacies

Drogaria Avenida
Avenida Getúlio Vargas, 280;
☎ 624-1305.

Farmácia Bezerra de Menezes
Avenida Ten. Cel. Duarte, 326; ☎ 322-7779.

Points Beyond

Buses
run regularly between Cuiabá and Chapada dos Guimarães. (For times, see under Hands-On Chapada). Buses are also available to São Felix do Araguaia, São José dos Quatro Marcos, Guiratinga, Rio do Casca, Paranatingam, Paxaréo, and D. Aquino, among others. You can also reach the Véu de Noiva (a waterfall and mountain) by local bus, which will leave you off after Buriti, if you tell the driver in advance.

Airplane flights
are available to Alta Floresta, Belém, Brasília, Belo Horizonte, Corumbá, Fortaleza, Manaus, Porto Alegre, Recife, Porto Velho, Rio Branco, Rio de Janeiro, Salvador, Santarém, São Paulo, and others.

Private Guides

For the names of city guides who speak English, call the president of the Guide Association,

Amilton Martins da Silva
☎ 322-3702

who is a very good guide himself. Another English-speaking guide is

Carlos Wolff

☎ 661-1469.

Telephone
Local and international phone calls can be made from the telephone company **Telemat** *Rua Barão de Melgaço, 3195* during commercial hours. There is also an office located at the bus station and the airport.

Travel Agency
Cidade Turismo
Rua Duque de Caxias, 59 (Alvorada); ☎ *(65) 322-3702.*
Director Amilton Martins da Silva specializes in cinematography, film crews, ecological tours, and VIP service. Arrangements for treks by boat, jeep, or plane can also be made. 4-hour city tours run about $37, including lunch at a regional restaurant.

Expeditours
Avenida Ponce de Arruda, 670 (near the airport); ☎ *(65) 381-4959, 381-5674*
Perhaps the leading eco-tour agency in Brazil, Expeditours mans an office in Cuiabá near the airport, where clients headed for Pantanal river cruises and Chapada dos Guimarães are received. (Their base office is in Rio.) One of the most serious eco-tour operators in Brazil, owner André von Thuranyi is not only deeply commited to preservation, but is also well tuned to the mystical aspects of the countryside. His efficient English-speaking staff can arrange accommodations at any of the pousadas listed below, as well as transportation and accommodations throughout the country, including the Amazon.

Tourist Information
The state tourist board **Turimat** is located at *Praça da República, 131 (downtown);* ☎ *(65) 322-5363.* Information booths can also be found at the airport and the bus station. You'll find maps and some general assistance on car rentals and hotels. For major excursions, it's best to contact the travel agencies above.

628　　　　　　　　　FIELDING'S BRAZIL 1994

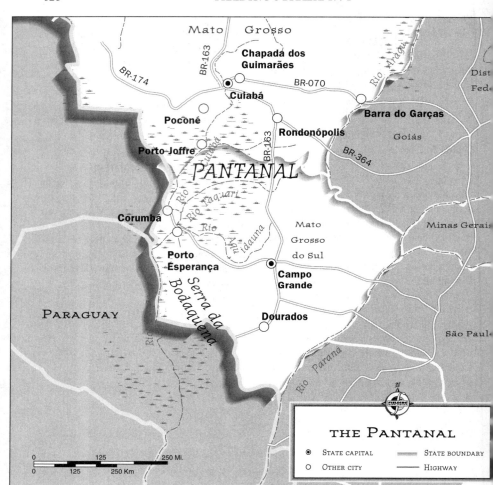

CHAPADA DOS GUIMARÃES

Chapada dos Guimarães is simply an extraordinary place. More than 800 meters above sea level, it boasts a variety of microclimates that allows for the coexistence of an enormous variety of plants and animals. Geological studies have shown that life existed here over 45,000 years ago, and mystics predict that future civilizations will be born here. Exactly what that means for the average visitor remains obscure, but it can't be denied that most tourists immediately feel a strong sense of clarity and well-being here, and many are inclined to stay longer than they had initially planned. Frankly, it's my favorite place in Brazil, if not the world.

Chapada's recorded history began when the Jesuits built a little chapel in 1751. By 1779, Chapada had become a primitive baroque city, its newly built cathedral marked by two imposing towers that were later felled by heavy rains. *Bandeirantes* from São Paulo swarmed over the area, looking for gold to mine and Indians to subjugate; the first sugarcane plantation was established, later becoming famous for its *cachaça*. Supplies were so limited in this isolated region that locals were often forced to trade large hunks of gold for the simplest foods imported from São Paulo.

In the 1930s, a group of Americans left Bahia to found an evangelical mission at Buriti, Chapada's first farm. Today, the pastoral estate is an agricultural school, but the American-made church and colonial houses still look like something out of New England. In more recent times, *Chapada has become famous for its waterfalls, rock formations, and UFO sightings*. Every year a Winter Festival brings artists and craftspersons to the region during the month of July.

ON THE WAY TO CHAPADA

The drive from Cuiabá to the National Park of Chapada dos Guimarães offers some of the most thrilling vistas in Brazil. Taking MT–2551 (Cuiabá–Chapada Road), you'll first pass verdant rolling hills and glimmering lakes, behind which looms a massive mountain range washed in purples and blues. Suddenly, the rocky skyline is accentuated by vertical cliffs standing like sentinels—a dramatic contrast to the shrunken brown-and-green shrubbery lining the highway. This is the beginning of the **Planalto Central** (Central Plains) of

Brazil, 10,000 years ago a magnificent inland sea that gradually dried to its present state.

The first stop you must make is at **Salgadeira**, originally built by the government as a weekend spot for tourists, but now a private enterprise. Nicknamed the "Beach of Mato Grosso," the area boasts a stupendous man-made waterfall where bathers can take a dip, as well as a restaurant complex with four bars, ice cream stands, bathrooms, and playground. Walking along a path into the forest, you'll come upon a turbulent double waterfall, and at every angle another mystical nature scene, including steamy falls, natural grottoes, and macumba offerings tucked inside coves. Campgrounds are available, but please don't litter; policemen keep close watch. A few years back, the "Green" community made a fuss here when trees were cut down to build the complex, but the environs are still so beautiful that it's hard to complain.

Nearby is **Portão do Inferno** (Hells' Gate), a truly awesome canyon sculpted into dramatic shape more than a thousand years ago by natural erosion. The lookout point, a few meters beyond, is replete with gossip. Legend has it that the federal police threw "undesirables" off this cliff during the dictatorship, and at the beginning of Sarney's administration, a lot of Brazilians were rumored to have thrown *themselves* off when they lost all their money. Even today, a yellow car can be seen at the foot of the pit, reputed to have accidentally veered off the cliff, killing four or five people. These days, police maintain strong surveillance against further incidents, but locals claim they can still hear the spirits of the departed crying at night. Three to four centuries ago, Indians roamed these areas, and the rock formations, which rise like phallic symbols along the highway, have given rise to various legends. Local mystics like to think they are street signs for landing extraterrestrials. The big holes in the ground, however, are definitely made by local rodents. If you're intent on climbing these hills, be careful because the rock is soft.

Six kilometers after Salgadeira, take a right turn onto a red dirt road to **Cachoeira Véu de Noiva**, a few hundred meters from the rock formations. The road takes you down to an open canyon graced with a slender 60-meter waterfall that looks like the veil of a bride (hence its name). During rainy season, the fall is more voluminous, but can become yellow and dirty-looking; in August, when I saw it, it was simply stunning, rivaling Iguaçu Falls, perhaps not in volume, but at least in grace. Sturdy trekkers will love the half-hour climb down to the foot of the waterfall (one hour back), but be forewarned: the inclines are abrupt. (Also, the route back may be deceiving because it doesn't look the same going—just stick to the wall on the right.) The fall is actually a big lake, which you can only see from the base, and the water and surrounding air are always cold, no matter the season. The canyon itself is a natural wonder, embraced by a forest and accentuated by vertical backdrops of red rocks. A snack bar serves beer, snacks, and *galinha com arroz* (chicken with rice) for $2.

Eight kilometers before you reach the city of Chapada (and an easy 1-hour trek from Véu de Noiva) is a smaller waterfall called **Cachoerinha** (Little Waterfall). The *mata* here is being reforested by locals, since destruction of this environment could endanger the entire microsystem of the Pantanal. Walking down an idyllic woody path, you'll come upon a small waterfall jutting out of a rocky embankment; facing it is a most idyllic beachlet. A thatched-roof restaurant surrounded by a mixture of rain forest and cerrado is a perfect place to let the sound of crashing rivulets wash over you. It's also a great place to sun, but weekends are packed. The path to the left above the waterfall goes to Véu de Noiva.

Insider Tip:

*Buses that run between Cuiabá and Chapada dos Guimarães do not stop at the above sites; in fact, you'll see little of the marvelous countryside from a bus. The **Expeditours** travel agency in Cuiabá offers tours of the area, or you can take the bus to Chapada and sign up for treks at **Eco Turismo**, off the main square. Anyone who plans to travel the swampy Pantanal by boat, truck, or foot should absolutely make time to enjoy these contrasting environs between Cuiabá and Chapada. (For more options see under* Chapada dos Guimarães.*)*

A BIRD'S EYE VIEW

The town of Chapada is located 73 kilometers north of Cuiabá, (with access on MT 251). No one quite knows how many people live there; some say about 6,000, but it's rumored another 15,000 live in the surrounding area. The main square is full of flowers and trees and makes a peaceful core to the town; the main restaurants are located here, as well as the oldest church in Mato Grosso, the Igreja de Senhora Sant'Ana, built in 1779 with the help of the local Indians. Today chickens scratch around in its courtyard, but inside is a magnificent dusty old chapel. Of particular note is the statue of Joseph wearing boots, a symbol of the goldminers who lived in the area. During my visit, an old couple was valiantly trying to clean the church from the soot that continually blows in from the burning fields—a sad reminder of the forest's destruction.

MYSTICAL THEORIES OF CHAPADA

Chapada is located at the 15th degree parallel, on line with such cities as Porto Seguro, Bahia (the birthplace of Brazil), Brasília (the futuristic capital), and Ilhéus, Bahia (near the site of the Transamérica Hotel, the most luxurious resort in Brazil). Such a location is rendered symbolic among Brazilians; many prophecies have suggested that Chapada dos Guimarães will be the birthplace of the Third Millenium. If you're a fan of Sedona, Arizona, you might recognize some of the same kinds of "vibrations"—a mixture of gorgeous landscape and mystical energy generated by numerous psychics, healers, and "Green People" who have moved to Chapada over the last 15 years. Not surprisingly, spiritual beliefs run rampant here. Some locals even believe there's a magnetic "hole" over Chapada that allows for communications with extraterrestrials. Indeed, something magnetically fishy is going down here since car batteries and cameras are notorious for malfunctioning on cloudy days (mine did). Without much effort, you're sure to find residents who claim to have personally tape-recorded conversations with ETs; the topics generally seem to concern saving the environment.

SIGHTS

MIRANTE Considered the "picturesque" geodesic center of South America, this magnificent rocky cliff and mountain range is felt by many to be a point of high magnetic energy and one of the best places to sight **UFOs**, particularly at night. At the very least, on a clear day you can see Cuiabá—50 kilometers to the southwest. Do take the exhilarating walk down the rocky path to the right, until you reach the 700-meter drop-off plateau; the trip back up is tiring but worth it. Hopefully, the litter marring the landscape has been picked up; be careful with cigarettes since fires start fast. Near the rock formations there is a large amount of burned land that can't be attributed to any reason other than human carelessness.

NATIONAL PARK

Founded about three years ago, the **Parque Nacional** covers about 33,000 hectares but is a national park in name only (the government does little to nothing to maintain it). Eco Turismo is the only agency that conducts tours to the park's wonderful **Cidades das Pedras**, seven "cities" of rock formations situated among the gnarled trees of the *cerrado*. During the rainy season, this route, which must be navigated by truck or 4-wheel drive, is considerably less dusty than in dry season, and more animals, such as pigs, foxes, jaguars, tapirs, wolves, and coatis can be seen scurrying over the landscape. But even dry season is exciting. In August, the stunted cerrado lends an other-worldly air to the forbidding rock formations, which can look variously like sacrificial altars, alligators, or Indian faces. Animals do approach at times; we clocked an *emu* (ostrich) running chase in front of our truck at 80 kilometers an hour. Many of the rocks are over 3 million years old; on their side you can often see stratification lines where the ocean left its indelible marks. It's even possible to find chips of hematite and crystals embedded in the ground, as well as fossils engraven with fish shapes. At the **Nascente do Rio Claro,** you can walk to the edge of a 350–meter cliff and witness an awesome vista of rivers and plateaus that could keep you mesmerized for days. The most unforgettable site I saw here is the **Casa de Pedra**, a natural house of stone situated over a running stream that was surely the home of native peoples thousands of years ago. I dream of making an overnight camp-out here; the nearby waterfalls boast such clean water you could probably safely drink it. Our final trek in Chapada took us down a slightly torturous descent to what must be the most perfect cove in Brazil—a gorgeous waterfall embraced by a thumb-sized strand of beach, behind which is a craggy outcropping of rock.

> **Insider Tip:**
>
> *If you have rugged desires, do arrange a 2-3 day trekking expedition through this region, which could include camping out at one of the above sights. Backpacks are required, but all other equipment, tents, and food are supplied. Wear good hiking boots, take your swimsuit, and dress in layers (nights get nippy).*

EXCURSIONS

THE CAVES

Eco Turismo's trek to the Caverns is not to be missed. In late August we start out by jeep over a rollicking dusty road hugged on one side by flat dry plains and on the other by tall willowy soyfields. Just at the moment I think we're in Oklahoma, we begin to pass miles of burnt land and scorched trees, and as the road turns into white sand, it winds around countryside that looks like the aftermath of World War III. As Jorge parks his truck, seemingly in the middle of nowhere, we hop out, following his energetic lead for 20 minutes up a torturous hill. At the first cavern, armed with flashlights, we wade through a dark gallery, feeling our toes squish into ankle-high mud. Apparently, native peoples lived here thousands of years ago, their spirits nearly still palpable. The hot afternoon sun calls us out and we start trekking again, this time through a sudden crop of rainforest obscuring the second cave. Another dry forest leads us into a humid one in a matter of a few feet, our arrival greeted by a raucous outburst of birds. The climax of the hike is Blue Lake (not exactly the luminescent color of its name), provocatively set inside an outcropping of rock connected to a swimmable tunnel. After taking a dip, we beat a fast path back to the car since the terrain is too rough to negotiate after dark. As the moon rises, the ride back to Chapada on the dark highway turns even eerier, evoking the kind of atmosphere where any moment you expect to see strange colored lights pulsing in front of you. What we actually do witness is the spontaneous combustions of fires exploding all along the highway, making us even more aware of the fragility of the landscape.

THE FAZENDA EXPERIENCE

I step off a 10-seater plane in Corumbá and find a rugged, silent-type cowboy waiting for me in the lobby. He piles my gear in the back of his truck, and soon we're off on wildly bumpy ride to reach the **Fazenda Xaraes**. *During rainy season, more than half this trek would be made by canoe, when the annual rains flood the plains leading to the farm.*

After a dead-to-the-world sleep in my air-conditioned cabana, I fortify myself with a mule-teamer's breakfast, then hop in a truck to see the countryside. Julio, our driver, seems to have a preternatural sense where the wild animals are, even before he sees them; along the highway we discover cobra skins, contemplate the jaws of alligators from bridges overhead, nearly get crushed by herds of cattle running Pamplona style. Capybaras sometimes plant themselves in our way; birds fly right in front of the windshield, barely surviving. If we were traveling at night, our guide informs us, we'd run smack into gators looking for food. Twice we see toucans streaking past. In mid-sentence Julio jumps out of the running jeep to race after an armadillo, catching him by the tail so we can inspect the armored body. If you go to Bolivia by train, he says, they'll serve you armadillo na casca *(in the shell). Soon we discover it's not just humans who scavenge the Pantanal. We drive past about 20 black* urubus *(vultures) feasting on the remains of a* jacaré *(crocodile).*

In the afternoon, a canoe trip takes us through the leafy waterway of an igarapé—*a miraculous vista at dusk when a crop of trees lining the banks becomes home to roosting* garças *who fly in for the night. The next day we comb the enormous grounds of the Xaraes Fazenda on both horseback and foot, exploring forests that seem nearly prime-*

val—home to hundreds of monkeys, capybaras, and rodents who scurry under the brush as we approach. From our guide, we learn that the only way to hear the voice of the Pantanal is to descend into silence—a kind of Zen in the wild. Crouching down behind bushes, we suddenly hear the terrifying screech of howler monkeys, a sound that even unraveled the botanist Henry Bates.

Fazenda Xaraes

Rio Abobral, 130 kilometers from Corumbá. Reserve in Campo Grande ☎(67) 242-1102 or São Paulo ☎(11) 246-9934, or through Expeditours in Rio ☎(21) 287-9697, FAX 521-4388. This well-maintained, 3-star lodge is rustic enough to be authentic and clean enough to be comfortable. Owned by the same group as the Nacional Hotel in Corumbá, it features wood-and-tiled rooms with shutters open to the river. The air-conditioning is solid, and whatever dirt you trail in seems to mysteriously disappear in a matter of hours. The dining room is surrounded by screens so you can see and hear the chirping birds. Most impressive is the salt-of-the-earth staff, some of the nicest people I met in Brazil. Packages include all meals and a variety of daily excursions. Rates per person per night range from $57.85 (doubles $51.05); transfers from Corumbá $61 per person or $40 for doubles; 3-hour horse treks for 2-1/2 hours run $8, boat trip, $40. 2–day/1–night package, including one boat tour, runs $89; 3–days/2–nights per person is $200 (doubles $162).

Getting There

If you arrive in Corumbá, the staff will pick you up and transfer you by truck (or canoe during rainy season) to Fazenda Xaraes. You can also take the bus to Morro do Azeite, which leaves you out in the middle of the road, 31 kilometers (45 minutes) from Xaraes, where the staff will pick you up.

Flights to Corumbá are offered by VASP from Belo Horizonte, Brasília, Campo Grande, Cuiabá, Goiânia, and São Paulo.

Insider Tip:
Avoid January when there are the most mosquitoes. August-September are the coolest months.

OTHER FAZENDAS

Pousada Caiman *236 kilometers from Campo Grande, Mato Grosso do Sul* The 5-star accommodation of the southern Pantanal, situated on a serious working ranch, is the eco-dream of Roberto Klabin, the energetic scion of a rich Brazilian family who wanted to create for his friends and tourists the height of luxury-in-the-wild. Of the ranch's 53,000 hectares, 7,000 (15,400 acres) has been set aside as an ecological reserve, but much of the land remains range for the 65 staff cowboys who live in a village adjacent to the lodge. The U-shaped hacienda (formerly the Klabin's family residence) houses 22 guests and offers every deluxe amenity, from swimming pool and Italian-tiled floors, to comfy leather furniture, satellite-dish TV, and stylish apartments with excellent air-conditioning; the cuisine is superb. The grounds have been called "an oasis for birds," since a large variety of species can easily be seen. Guests are led on morning and afternoon excursions on horseback, in canoe, and on foot. The lodge is located about four hours by car from Campo Grande; transfers by air-conditioned micro–buses are offered every Saturday and Wednesday from Campo Grande between 1:30 p.m.–2:00 p.m., and after breakfast from the lodge. (Campo Grande may be reached by commercial flights from Belém, Brasília, Corumbá, Cuiabá, Rio Branco, Santarém, São Paulo, and others.) 3-day packages run from Wednesday-Saturday; 4 nights from Saturday to Wednesday. In New York, contact **Brazil Nuts** (see the chapter, *Specialty Tours*, for address). In São Paulo, contact **Roberto Klabin Hotéis e Turismo** *Rua Pedrosa Alvarenga, 1208, first floor, CEP 045531;* ☎ *(11) 883-6566.* In Rio contact **Expeditours** ☎ *(21) 287-9697, FAX 521-4388.*

Fazenda Boa Sorte Região de Abobral (in Corumbá) ☎ *231-1120* A rustic (read "primitive") farm without frills near the Fazenda Xaraes gives you a home-on-the-range ambiance. Sleep outdoor in hammocks, inside tents, or under grass-roofed huts with wood-slat floors. If you don't want to bathe in the river, there's a communal bath. Three daily meals are cooked over a wood fire; don't pass up a glass of freshly milked cow juice. The farm's parrots will sit happily on your shoulder and even the wild ducks and toucans are friendly. During the day you can make excursions on horseback, sleep in other fazendas, and take canoe trips. A 3-day package for $70 includes all meals and treks. Arrangements can be made through **Expeditours** ☎ *(21) 287-9697 (Rio) or (65) 381-4959 (Cuiabá).*

Fazenda Beira Rio *Rod. Transpantaneira, 150 kilometers from Poconé, 205 kilometers from Cuiabá* Located on 3,700 hectares of land right off the Transpantaneira Highway, this is considered the best pousada in the region for cleanliness and trek options. The hotel is two years old, owned by the grizzly but *simpático* Senhor Valdo de Luis. Running next to his property is the Pixaim River, which you can traverse by motor boat ($25 an hour), or canoe (monkeys upstream, herons downstream). You can also rent horses ($7 per hour) or explore the grounds by foot. Guides accompany guests without charge. Housed in a 1-story white stucco building with traditional tile roofs, the simple rooms are all air-conditioned and come with minibar, TV, and attractive tile floors. Suites sleep five. If you come through a travel agent, the package deal includes horse treks and boat excursions; otherwise, you pay extra. There are no phones, but there is radio communication with Cuiabá. Rates are about $50 per day, including all three meals; packages available. Reserve ☎ *(65) 322-0948, or* ☎ *(11) 35-4157 (in São Paulo), or* ☎ *(67) 725-5267 (in Campo Grande),* or through **Expeditours** ☎ *(21) 287-9697, FAX 521-4388. 13 apartments. Moderate.*

Hotel Santa Rosa do Pantanal

Transpantaneira Highway, 150 kilometers from Poconé. Reserve in Cuiabá ☎ *(65) 322-0513/0077; in São Paulo (11) 231-4511*
Once a luxurious (for the region) hotel, this is still the best in Porto Jofre, located at the end of the Transpantaneira Highway on the banks of the Cuiabá River. One travel option is to trek or hitch your way here, then rent boats, horses, or guides at the hotel. The owner of the nearby campgrounds also rents boats. 54 apartments. *Moderate. No cards.*

NEW FOR 1994

After nearly 20 years of working in the Pantanal, André Von Thuranyi of **Expeditours travel agency**, has now started his own lodge program in collaboration with native farmers in the Pantanal wetlands. While I plan to check this accommodation out for the '95 edition, I can heartily recommend any travels with **Expeditours**, who are totally committed to preserving the ecology through conscientious tourism. A 3-day/2-night package at the Araras Farm lodge, a private reserve off the Transpantaneira Highway, offers treks by foot, canoe, horseback, and jeep. An extra night in Cuiabá and/or a tour of Chapada dos Guimarães (highly recommended) may be added. Transports to the lodge leave the Expeditours office in Cuiabá every day at 3:30 p.m. For more information, contact **Expeditours** *Rua Visconde de Pirajá, 414 (Ipanema), Rio de Janeiro;* ☎ *(21) 287-9697, FAX 521-4388, or in Cuiabá: Avenida Governador Ponce de Arruda, 670;* ☎ *(65) 381-4959/381-5674 in Cuiabá.*

BOTELS AND BOAT CRUISES

An alternative to bunking down at lodges is to take a package cruise. Expeditours offers the Pantanal Ecological triangle tour, a fine 5-night/4-day package on the Pantanal Explorer, a modest, low draft boat that sleeps 12 including crew (four air-conditioned bunks for passengers, with two shared bathrooms, sun deck, and kitchen/bar). During the day, you can sight birds and other wildlife from the top deck of the boat; at night special alligator expeditions are conducted in canoes. Tight quarters make sociable personalities a must, but humor is provided by outgoing guides who are able to identify most of the animals and birds sighted. Food is surprisingly good: a mixture of beef, fish, chicken, and pasta. The most exciting part of the trip is the roller-coaster ride over the Transpantaneira Highway—a must for Pantanal-goers. Among animals to be sighted are savanna hawks, Amazon kingfishers, snowy egrets, toco toucans, black-headed vultures, wood storks, herons, parrots, woodpeckers, cormorants, marsh deer, capybaras, caimans, iguanas, and lizards. The highway's 114 bridges are sometimes portraits of imminent disaster—weatherbeaten washboard planks crossed by moldy timbers, but the anything-can-happen ambiance is part of the fun. An hour and a half beyond Poconé you'll pass the São João ranch owned by Sebastião Camargo Correia, one of the five richest men in the world. Ask if you can visit. A stop at the gold mines near Cangas, 10 minutes from Cuiabá, is also an eye-opener. For more information, see *Hands-On Cuiabá*.

Insider Tip:

If you are traversing the Transpantaneira in a group tour, make sure the driver and your guide know you want to savor every scene. This will slow down the trip considerably, so if you have flights to catch later in the day, leave a few hours earlier. You may never see anything like it again.

THE ESSENTIAL CHAPADA DOS GUIMARÃES

WHERE TO STAY

Chapada is a rustic town; so are the hotels. Fortunately, with such cool temperatures, air-conditioning is not necessary. No pousada or hotel in Chapada has telephones inside the room.

Expensive --------------- $27–$32

Moderate ---------------- $10–$20

Inexpensive ------------- Under $10

★ Pousada da Chapada

Rodovia MT–251, kilometer 63, Estrada Chapada dos Guimarães/Cuiabá, 2 kilometer, ☎ 791-1171. Reservations: SP ☎(11) 231-4511

The nicest hotel in Chapada is unfortunately 800 meters from the city (not walking distance), but the hotel provides free transportation. The red-tile, white stucco complex of 4 buildings retains a frontier colonial charm. Apartments, with raw wood furniture, are spacious, and tiled floors cut down on dirt. The deluxe suite, which sleeps 4, is unusually elegant. On premises is a playground and outdoor pool, and a restaurant that serves all 3 meals. The owner also runs the Fazenda Porto Joffre in the Pantanal, as well as the Selva Turismo travel agency. Singles with fan run $27, doubles $32, double the price for air-conditioning. Fielding's readers receive a 10 percent discount. 38 apartments. *Moderate. No Cards.*

Rios Hotel

Rua Tiradentes, 333; ☎ 791-1126

Among the lesser-priced hotels, Rios rates as the best. A block from the bus station and near the telephone company, it looks like a private residence. Families stay here, as do the kind of hippie clientele that sport feather earrings. Bathrooms are reasonably clean. Prices are rated according to the presence of air-conditioning and TV. Singles with air-conditioning run $17, doubles $22. 18 apartments. *Inexpensive. Cards: V.*

Hotel Turismo

Rua Fernando C da Costa 1065; ☎ 791-1176

From the street, this small hotel looks like a residential house, complete with crowing roosters; the rooms are simple and clean, if overpriced. The dining room serves lunch and dinner (a small breakfast of fruit, bread, and coffee). Sunday features all-you-can-eat *comida caseira* (home-cooked). Air-conditioned rooms with minibar and TV run about $25, with fans $20. 14 apartments. *Moderate. No cards.*

Pensão do Povo

Rua Fernando Corrêa, 825

Located behind the church, Chapada's cheapest rooms are for those who don't care what bites them after they drop dead asleep. One communal bathroom for most rooms; 2 apartments have private bath. Some rooms have 4 beds, but no phones. About $3 a night. *Cheap. No cards.*

WHERE TO EAT

Taberna Suiça

Rua Fernando Corrêa. Friday, Saturday, and Sunday

Open only on the weekends, but insiders consider this to be the best restaurant in town for international cuisine. Friday serves only dinner. *Inexpensive. No cards.*

★ Nivio's Tour Restaurante

Praça Bispo Dom Wunibaldo, 631; ☎ 791-1206

Don't let the word "tour" discourage you. This Portuguese-styled house with blue-tiled walls and white stucco arches offers a veritable feast. No one ever knows what will be served, but it's invariably a full table with two main courses and several side dishes of vegetables and rice. Saturday features *feijoada*. There's also a short list of French and German wines. Rates per person run $4–$5. *Inexpensive. No Cards.*

Véu de Noiva Restaurante

Rua Penna Gomes, 535. Daily 11:00 a.m.–10:00 p.m.

Grungy walls and a cracked stone floor, but the ambiance is very *caseira* in this one-room house. If temperatures rise too high inside, you can sit outside on the veranda on a residential side street overlooking the public swimming pool. (The natural water is piped in from the Prainha River 200 meters away.) Chicken and rice dishes are excellent, as is the *prato feito* (meal of the day) for about $2.50 per person. *No cards.*

Costelão
Road to Cuiabá, 2 kilometer (Aldeia Velha); ☎ *791-1102. Daily 11:00 a.m.–3:00 p.m., 7:00 p.m.–9:00 p.m.*
Good barbecue styled in a typical *gaúcho* house. *No cards.*

Amarelinho
Rua Dom Wunibaldo. Daily lunch and dinner
Regional food.

Gaia Bar
Off the main plaza
This green-and-orange house is the denizen for the local "Green People," who are still reading Herman Hesse. Outsiders are sometimes scowled at, but yell out "Preserva natureza!" and you'll be fine.

★ Borboleta Casa de Chá
Rua Fernando Corrêa, 446-B; ☎ *321-5307*
A civilized tea house in this dirty-boots wilderness is definitely refreshing. Indulge in *bolos* (cakes), *docinhos* (sweets), and *salgadinhos* (salty pastries), washed down with tea or cold beer.

SHOPPING

Achei Novidades
Praça D. Wunibaldo. Daily 8:00 a.m.–8:00 p.m.
Next to the Gaia bar off the main *praça*, this is the city's premier crafts store featuring jewelry made by the Xavantes Indians (situated about 1,250 kilometers from Chapada) and pottery from the Carajas tribe in the state of Pará. Other great buys are homemade liqueurs with *pequi cristalizado* (a tree typical of the *cerrado*). You can also buy modern art from regional artists. *No Cards.*

HEALERS

Chapada, like Cuiabá, has a strong Green movement, as well as a New Age/alternative health community. If you ask around, you can easily meet students of various gurus (like Rajneesh, called Osho here), Zen meditators, yoga enthusiasts, massage therapists, acupuncturists, and even psychic healers. There may also be a few lingering souls who speak Esperanto. The small brochure-like magazine *Tempo de Crescer!* lists various professional holistic practitioners and organizations in the Cuiabá-Chapada region.

HANDS-ON CHAPADA DOS GUIMARÃES

Arrival
The **Rodoviária** (bus station) is located at *Rua Cipriano Curvo*. Buses run regularly between Cuiabá and Chapada dos Guimaráes, starting at 7:30 a.m., 8:00 a.m., 10:00 a.m., noon, 2:00 p.m., 3:00 p.m., 4:00 p.m., and 7:00 p.m., and returning at 6:00 a.m., 9:00 a.m., noon, 1:00 p.m., 1:30 p.m., 2:00 p.m., 4:00 p.m., and 6:00 p.m. Buses also run to Brasilândia, Paranatinga, and others.

Climate
Between April–October, which is the dry season, temperatures average between 68 and 75 degrees fahrenheit, but temperatures can rise over 50 degrees in just a matter of hours. The hottest months in the Pantanal are December–February, when temperatures average between 110°F–112°F. During dry season, it's important to drink lots of liquids to avoid dehydration. Starting in November, weather alternates between torrential rains and scalding sun. The most animals can be seen in December and January.

Credit Cards
Chapada seems to have trouble processing **American Express** cards. A few businesses take **VISA**. (See *Money Exchange* below.)

Money Exchange
Do come with a full stash of cruzeiros. You'll be hard put to find anyone who will accept dollars or credit cards. Even the Banco Brasil will not exchange dollars, though it is ru-

mored the **Hotel Turismo** will, located on *Rua Fernando C. da Costa, 1065,* ☎ *791-1176.*

Taxis
There's only one taxi in Chapada. Call **Eco Turismo**
☎ 791-1393
to find out who owns it that week.

Telephone
Posto Telefônico
Rua Tiradentes, 390.

Travel Agency
Eco Turismo Cultural
Praça Dom Wunibaldo, 464; ☎ *(85) 791-1393, 791-1305*
One of Chapada's premier trek agencies is owned by Jorge Belfort Mattos Jr., a university professor who, despite his Santa Claus girth, scampers up and down steep hills like a master. All his trips last between 4–6 hours, including transportation, light lunch, and water. Three main tours include the Parque Nacional (with the Véu de Noiva), the Caverna Aroe Jari with the Lagoa Azul, and the Cidades das Pedras (City of Rocks). Exciting 2–5-day packages, from $100–$282, including breakfast and one meal a day, can also be arranged (accommodations at Hotel Pousada or Turismo). 5-day tours include city tour and geodesic site, caverns, National Park, Cidades das Pedras, and horseback riding. *Cards: V only.*

When To Go
July 1994
A superb festival celebrating 500 years of South American history will encompass exhibitions, typical foods, folklore, dances, and special courses for the entire month.

SPECIALTY TOURS

Chapada de Guimaraes, Mato Grosso

Specialty tours, especially through the Amazon, are often the easiest and safest way to travel. The following agencies, most of them based in the U.S., are all reputable, but do take precautions. Cancellations and price changes are a way of life in Brazil; you might even consider taking out insurance *against* cancellation. And do read the fine print of any contract; usually you are required to take responsibility for your own health and property.

TRAVEL EXPERTS

Brazil Nuts
79 Stanford St., Fairfield, CT 06430;
☎ *(203) 259-7900, or toll free (800)* *553-9959* Owner Adam Carter is a passionate Braziliophile who offers packaged tours of Rio, the Pantanal, the Amazon, Carnaval in

Salvador, and others. Independent travelers can also take advantage of the "Rio Like a Native" program on a day-by-day basis, that includes various excursions to tourist sights and evening performances. To contact the office in Rio upon arrival, call ☎ 255-6692.

International Expeditions
One Environs Park, Helena, Alabama 35080; ☎ *(205) 428-1700*
This company usually offers trekking journeys through the Amazon basin in Peru, but may have now extended trips into Brazil.

ICS Scuba and Travel
5254 Merrick Road, Suite 5, Massapequa, NY 11758; ☎ *(516) 797-2133; (800) 722-0205*
This company specializes in scuba expeditions throughout the world, including an extensive program in Fernando de Noronha. (For more information, see the section on Fernando de Noronha.)

Special Expeditions
720 Fifth Avenue, New York, NY 10019; ☎ *(212) 765-7740; (800) 762-0003*
This company, aimed at the more adventurous tourist, offers remarkable 16-day voyages aboard the 80-passenger M.S. Polaris from Manaus to Ciudad, Venezuela, traversing a thousand miles on the Amazon. Cost begins at $5,030 per person, double occupancy, including everything but airfare.

Ecotour Expeditions
P.O. Box 1066, Cambridge MA 02238; ☎ *(617) 876-5817*
A 3-year-old company, Ecotour offers a 9-day Amazon journey with 3 meals a day, including a tour of Manaus. The cost is about $1,895 (plus airfare to Brazil).

Rainforest Alliance
270 Lafayette Street, Suite 512, New York, NY 10012; ☎ *(212) 941-1900*
One of the leading organizations dedicated to the preservation of the rainforest will be leading small trips on the Amazon in February and June of 1994. In October 1994, an 80-passenger ship will cruise up the Amazon to Iquitos, Peru, departing from Manaus. All trips are conducted by Alliance staff members and local naturalists. For more information contact Paul Ewing.

International Study Tours
225 W. 34th Street, Suite 913, New York, NY 10122; ☎ *(212) 563-1202*
Now offered to tourists of all ages are educational and cultural tours of Brazil. Trips for 1994 will include a rainforest expedition out of Manaus; a combination package including Manaus, the Pantanal, Iguaçu Falls, and Rio; and an "Art in Brazil" tour, including stops in Rio, Brasília, and Ouro Preto. Trips run from 7–13 nights. Lecturers are professors from universities in Brazil.

The American Museum of Natural History Discovery Tours and Cruises
Central Park West at 79th Street, New York, NY 10024; ☎ *(212) 769-5700*
The museum offers a cruise down the Amazon on the M.S. Polaris November 7–21, 1994. Lectures will be given by a team from the museum. The price for 1993 was $5,700–$9,600 (air included).

New York Botanical Garden
Travel program/New York Botanical Garden, Bronx, NY 10458-5126; ☎ *(212) 220-8700, FAX (212) 220-6504*
Special Amazonian tours for groups of 8–20 are planned for the early dry season of each year. Cruises are taken on a small river boat built especially for the program, accompanied by guides who lecture on the botanical aspects of jungle life. Fee, including roundtrip airfare from Miami to Manaus, all meals, transfers, expeditions, and reading material, is $2,495.

Brazilian Views, Inc.
201 East 66th Street, Suite 21G, New York, New York 10021; ☎ *(212) 472-9539*
This New York–based specialty consulting firm has previously offered serveral types of expeditions including a 10-day birdwatching tour in the Pantanal, a (4-day minimum) fishing expedition to the Pantanal, a garden tour of Brazil and Argentina, sponsored by four South American garden clubs, and a decorative fiber arts and folk crafts tour of the cities of Belém, Recife, Salvador, Belo Horizonte, Rio de Janeiro, and São Paulo. Write for more current information.

F & H Consulting
*2441 Janin Way, Solvang, CA 93463;
☎ (800) 544-5503, FAX (805) 688-1021*
This extremely reputable firm, co-owned by Claudio Heckmann, a native-born Brazilian, works exclusively with 5-star hotels in Brazil and Brazilian-owned properties. He also acts as the coordinator for the Brazilian Tourism Information Center in the U.S. Contact F & H for the most up-to-date information on resort facilities, spas, and private islands and the Ariau Jungle Tower outside Manaus.

Ocean Line Cruises
The following companies offer cruises that make port in various Brazilian cities, including Rio de Janeiro, Manaus, Recife, Salvador, and Santarém.

Holland America Line
300 Elliott Avenue West, Seattle, WA 98119; ☎ (206) 681-3535.

Odessa America Cruise Company
250 Old Country Road, Mineola, NY 11501; ☎ (516) 747-8880.

Ocean Cruise Lines
1510 S.E. 17th Street, Fort Lauderdale, FL 33316; ☎ (305) 764-3500 or (800) 556-8850.

Regency Cruises
*260 Madison Avenue New York, NY 10016;
☎ (212) 972-4499.*

Royal Viking Line
*95 Merrick Way, Coral Gables, FL 33134;
☎ (305) 447-9660; for reservations
☎ (800) 422-8000; for brochures
☎ (800) 448-4785.*

Sun Line Cruises
1 Rockefeller Plaza, Suite 315, New York, NY 10020; ☎ (212) 397-6400 or (800) 872-6400, outside New York City.

Also see "Travel Agencies" under *Rio Hands-On* and in the various *Hands-On* sections of each city in the Amazon and the Pantanal.

LANGUAGE

Outdoor Food Market in Bahia

It's been often said that Portuguese is one of the sexiest languages in the world. If you are planning to spend any time in Brazil, it's well worth studying it seriously, even for a few months. Those who do are usually deeply moved by the sensuosity of the cadences and the vibrant vowel sounds—surely the secret behind the beauty of Brazilian music. Accents notwithstanding, continental Portuguese (that which is spoken in Portugal), varies only slightly in word usage, although natives from Portugal are constantly lamenting the damage Brazilians have wrought on the mother tongue over their 500-year history. (Brazilians, for their part, consider their contributions enlivening.) Among other things, Brazilians have usurped a lot of Tupi, Arabian, and French words, not to mention English phrases, particularly in the field of advertising. Don't be surprised if, in the middle of a whirl of Portuguese, you suddenly hear more familiar words like "know–how," "marketing," "design," "outdoor," and "brainstorm" —all somewhat mangled by the Portuguese accent. (For more information, see under "Language" in the Directory.)

The easiest way to reap a smile from a Brazilian is to learn one choice phrase of slang and use it at just the right time.

Slang

Cool, neat (literally, legal)	Legal! (leh–gow)
How great!	Que legal!
Really, really great!	Tri–legal!
How neat!	Bacana!
What a joy! Neat! Cool! Fantastic!	Jóia!
Wow! No kidding.	Puxa! (or Puxa vida!)
Oh, my gosh (literally, Our Lady)	Nossa Senhora (or Nossa)
Keep cool.	Fica frio.
Keep it going. Chill out.	Fica numa nice.
expert (adjective)	craque
You said it!	Falô!

Super (and even hiper, which is bigger and better) can be added to any word in Portuguese, i.e., supermercado (supermarket), hipermercado (even bigger supermarket), super legal (better than great), and super bonita (really beautiful).

Proverbs

These three proverbs should cover almost any situation you will encounter in Brazil.

Don't create a tempest in a teacup.	Não fazer tempestade em copo d'água.
One who doesn't have a dog hunts with a cat (in other words, make do with what you have).	Quem não tem cão caça com gato!
A man is a devil that no woman can deny, but every woman wishes for a devil to take her away.	O homem é um diabo não há mulher que o negue, mas toda mulher deseja que um diabo a carregue.

Airplane/Customs

Have you anything to declare?	Tem alguma coisa a declarar?
One suitcase of mine is missing.	Faltame uma mala.
Smoking is not allowed.	É proibido fumar.
I feel air-sick.	Sinto-me enjoado(a).

Common Questions and Phrases

Where is the bathroom?	Onde fica o toilete (banheiro)?
Flirting Hello	Alô
Hi, hey	Oi
Oops	Opa
Bye	'Tchau (as in ciao)
Good-bye	Até logo
Good morning	Bom dia
Good afternoon	Boa tarde
Good night (good evening)	Boa noite
What's your name?	Qual é seu nome?
My name is . . .	Meu nome é . . .
How are you?	Como vai?
I'm fine, thank you.	Bem, obrigado(a).
Thank you (very much).	Obrigado (muito).
You're welcome.	De nada.
Excuse me (apology).	Desculpe.
Excuse me (to pass by someone in your way).	Com licença.
Where are you from?	De onde você é?
I'm from . . .	Sou de . . .
Do you speak Portuguese/English/Spanish?	Você fala português/inglês/espanhol?
I don't speak Portuguese.	Não falo português.
Do you understand?	Você entende?
I don't understand.	Não entendo.
Please speak more slowly.	Por favor, fale mais devagar.
How do you say . . . ?	Como se diz . . . ?
What do you call this in Portuguese?	Como se chama isto em português?
What does "—" mean in Portuguese?	Que quer dizer "—"?
Want to go out with me?	Quer sair comigo?

Common Questions and Phrases

Want to have a drink?	Quer tomar alguma coisa?
You're very beautiful.	Você é muito bonito (a).

Insider Tip:

Gosto de você *is perhaps the most misunderstood phrase in Brazilian Portuguese. Depending on the tone, the body gesture, and the look in the eye, it can variously mean* I like you *(you're a nice person)*, I like you a lot *(I hope we see other again)*, I really like you a lot *(let's be friends for life)*, *or* I really, really like you a lot *(do you want to go to bed with me?)*.

Direction

left	esquerda
right	direita
here	aquí
there (where you are)	aí
over there or yonder	lá
pull	puxe
push	empurre

Brush-offs for Street Punks

Leave me alone.	Deixe-me em paz.
Go away.	Vá embora.
Don't touch me.	Não me toque.
Don't bother me.	Não me chateie.
Don't bother me (stronger).	Não enche.
Help!	Socorro!

Date

Monday	segunda-feira (written as 2a)
Tuesday	terça-feira (3a)
Wednesday	quarta-feira (4a)
Thursday	quinta-feira (5a)
Friday	sexta-feira (6a)
Saturday	sabado

Date

Sunday	domingo
weekend	fim de semana
yesterday	ontem
today	hoje
tomorrow	amanhã
the day	o dia
the month	o mês
the year	o ano

Numbers*

1	um/uma		17	dezessete
2	dois/duas		18	dezoito
3	três		19	dezenove
4	quatro		20	vinte
5	cinco		21	vinte e um
6	seis		30	trinta
7	sete		40	quarenta
8	oito		50	cinquenta
9	nove		60	sessenta
10	dez		70	setenta
11	onze		80	oitenta
12	doze		90	noventa
13	treze		100	cem
14	quatorze		101	cento e um
15	quinze		500	quinhentos
16	dezesseis		1,000	mil

*Numbers in Portuguese use periods instead of commas, and commas instead of periods. For example, cr $3.500,75.

Time

What time is it?	Que horas são?
At what time?	A que horas?
How long does it take?	Leva quanto tempo?
When?	Quando?
Which day?	Que dia?

Time

Official time in Brazil (buses, airplanes, etc.) is reported on a 24–hour system. Midnight is meia noite; one, two, three o'clock in the morning is uma hora, duas horas, três horas, etc., until noon, which is meio dia. One o'clock in the afternoon is reported as treze horas, two o'clock as quatorze horas, etc. In general conversation, use the 12–hour system (i.e., you'll meet for dinner at oito horas (eight o'clock).

at 1:00 AM	a uma hora
at 3 PM (official)	às quinze horas (15:00 hours)
an hour from now	daqui a uma hora
yesterday	ontem
today	hoje
tomorrow	amanhã
this week	esta semana
last week	semana passada

Dining

Waiter	Garçon
Maitre d'	Maitre
The menu, please.	O cardápio, por favor.
What's the specialty?	Qual é a especialidade da casa?
I don't eat meat/fish.	Não como carne/peixe.
A little more.	Um pouco mais.
The bill, please.	A conta, por favor.
Is service included?	O serviço está incluido?
I want a receipt.	Quero recibo, por favor.
I want my change.	Quero meu troco, por favor.
The meal was superb.	A refeição estava ótima!
I'm full.	Estou satisfeito (a).
breakfast	café da manhã
lunch	almoço
dinner	jantar
a napkin	um guardanápio
a plate	um prato
a glass	um copo
a cup	uma xícara

Beverages

mineral water	água mineral
carbonated	com gás
noncarbonated	sem gás
coffee	café
tea	chá
milk	leite
black coffee in demitasse	cafezinho
soda pop	refrigerante
beer	cerveja
draft beer	chopp
wine	vinho
red wine	vinho tinto
white wine	vinho branco
with ice	com gelo
without ice	sem gelo

Cover/Condiments/Hors d'Ouevres

cover	couvert
bread	pão
butter	manteiga
salt	sal
pepper	pimenta
sugar	açúcar
oil	azeite
vinegar	vinagre
sauce	molho
without sugar	sem açúcar

Fruits

fruits	frutas
apple	maçã
banana	banana
grapes	uvas
lemon	limão
melon	melão
orange	laranja

Fruits

pear	pêra
strawberries	morangos
juice	suco
orange juice	suco de laranja
smoothie with fruit, juice, often milk and sugar	vitaminas

Seafood

seafood	frutos do mar
codfish	bacalhau
crab	siri
marsh crab	caranguejo
lobster	lagosta
octopus	polvo
oysters	ostras
shrimp	camarão
sole	linguado
squid	lula

Beef

beef	bife
chicken	frango/galinha
chops	costeletas
goat	bode
ham	presunto
lamb	carneiro
pork	porco
rabbit	coelho
sausage	linguiça
turkey	peru
veal	vitela
barbecue	churrasco
all–you–can–eat	rodízio

Vegetables

salad	salada
carrot	cenoura
cucumber	pepino
green beans	vagens
lettuce	alfaçe
tomato	tomate
cooked vegetables	legumes cozidos

Beans and Pasta

bean	feijão
pasta	massa

Money

cash	dinheiro
credit card	cartão de crédito
traveler's check	traveler's check (cheque de viagem)
exchange house	câmbio
I want to exchange money.	Quero trocar dinheiro.
Do you exchange money?	Você troca dinheiro? (dólares)
What is the exchange rate?	Qual é o câmbio?
Can you cash a traveler's check?	Pode trocar um traveler's check (cheque de viagem)?

Getting Around/Directions

Where is the . . . ?	Onde é o (a) . . . ?
I want to go to . . .	Quero ir para . . .
How can I get to . . . ?	Como posso ir para . . . ?
Does this bus go to . . . ?	Este ônibus vai para . . . ?
Please, take me to . . .	Por favor leve–me para . . . ?
airport	aeroporto
bathroom	toilete
beach	praia
bus station	rodoviária
bus stop	ponto de ônibus
embassy/consulate	embaixada/consulado

Getting Around/Directions

gas station	posto de gasolina
supermarket	supermercado
market/ street market	mercado/ feira
street arts fair	feira hippie
movies	cinema
police station	delegacia de polícia
post office	correio
subway station	estação de metrô
theatre	teatro
train station	estação de trem
Please stop here.	Por favor pare aqui.
Please wait.	Por favor espere.
I want to rent a car.	Quero alugar um carro.

Driving

Danger	Perigo
Dangerous bend	Curva perigosa
Service station	Posto

At the Doctor's

Call for the doctor.	Chame o médico.
I have a . . .	Estou com dor . . .
headache	de cabeça
sore throat	de garganta
stomach ache	de estômago
toothache	de dente
backache	nas costas
I have a bad sunburn.	Estou queimado(a) do sol.
sunstroke	insolação
food poisoning	intoxicação alimentar
I have a fever.	Estou com febre.
I sprained my arm/ankle.	Torci o braço/o tornozelo.
injections	injeções
cough medicine	xarope
aspirin	aspirina
tablets	comprimidos
ointment	pomada

At the Doctor's

tonic	tônico
vitamins	vitaminas
I need to go to the hospital.	Preciso ir ao hospital.

At the Hotel

I have a reservation.	Tenho uma reserva.
I want to make a reservation.	Quero fazer uma reserva.
I want to see the room.	Quero ver o quarto.
I want to talk to the manager.	Quero falar com o gerente.
a single room	um quarto de solteiro
a double	um quarto de casal
double room with bath	quarto de casal com banheiro
triple	triplo
with air–conditioning	com ar condicionado
minibar	frigobar
safe	cofre
key	chave
What time is breakfast served?	A que horas é o café da manhã?
Can you wake me up at seven?	Pode me acordar às sete horas?
I need another pillow/blanket.	Preciso de outro travesseiro/cobertor.
Where can one hire a car?	Onde se pode alugar um automóvel?
The air–conditioning/ central heating is not working.	O ar condicionado/ aquecimento central não está funcionando.
Does that include all service and taxes?	Estão incluídos o serviço e o imposto?
Where is the manager?	Onde está o gerente?
I enjoyed my stay.	Gostei da estadia.
Thank you for your help.	Obrigado/a pela sua ajuda.

Shopping

Brazilians salespersons, especially those barely out of their teens, are sometimes overly eager to help. To have some breathing space, it's absolutely necessary to learn the password "Só olhando," or "just looking." Other helpful phrases are:

How much?	Quanto?
How much does it cost?	Quanto custa?

Shopping

That's too expensive.	É muito caro.
I want something cheaper.	Quero alguma coisa mais barata.
Can I try this on?	Posso provar?
I want to buy (this).	Quero comprar (isto).
Do you sell film?	Vende filme?
batteries	pilhas
cassette	fita cassete (k–7)
Where can I buy . . . ?	Onde posso comprar . . . ?
postcards	cartões postais
soap/shampoo	sabonete/xampu or champoo
toothpaste/sunscreen	pasta de dente/filtro solar
stamps	selos
condom	camisinha
newspaper	jornal
shoe store	sapataria
These shoes do not fit me.	Estes sapatos não me servem.
What size do you take in shoes/clothes?	Qual é o tamanho/número que calça/que veste?
This color does not suit me.	Esta cor não me fica bem.
This coat is tight on me.	Este paletó está apertado.
silk	seda
cotton	algodão

Clothes

suit	terno
skirt	saia
jacket	casaco
dress	vestido
trousers	calça
swimsuit/bikini	maiô/ fio dental/tanga
blouse	blusa
raincoat/umbrella	capa de chuva/guarda–chuva
girdle/stockings/panties/bras	cinta/meias/calcinha/soutien
socks/nightgown	meias/camisola
tie/shirt	gravata/camisa

HEALTH KIT FOR THE TROPICS

Jet Lag

Overnight overseas flights to Brazil (9 hours from New York to Rio) can easily cramp your style by the time you arrive. The time change from the East Coast is minimal (2 hours); it's the long hours spent cramped in a seat, the night of lost sleep, and the rich food and drinks that may get you down. Here are some tips to minimize discomfort:

- Minimize alcohol before and during flights.
- Avoid large meals for several hours after landing to shrink your stomach to its normal size.
- Chew gum slowly only to relieve ear discomfort.
- Avoid gas–producing and greasy foods.
- Eat small portions starting 2 hours before takeoff. Eat high-fiber foods to avoid constipation.
- Drink 1 pint of liquid for every 3 flying hours to counteract the dryness of the cabin. Best are water and fruit juices.
- Use eyedrops for dry eyes and take off your contact lenses.
- Eat simply and sparingly the first few days in Brazil.

Traveler's Diarrhea

Traveler's diarrhea is not preordained, though few escape it. It's usually caused by ingesting contaminated food and water or by placing your contaminated fingers in your mouth. The rule for all travelers: Boil it, cook it, peel it, or forget it. Also:

- Avoid street foods, shellfish, and any uncooked or undercooked foods. Be careful which restaurants you choose. Deluxe international hotels are usually your best bet, since most use modern refrigeration, purify local water, protect foods from insects, wash vegetables in chemical solutions, and cook food properly.
- Eat only fruit with thick skins that you peel yourself. Don't drink milk in Brazil after noon (since it is rarely refrigerated and is delivered only in the morning).
- Avoid salads and uncooked vegetables. Do not eat raw fish or meat, and avoid shellfish.
- Wash your hands always before eating. Germs are picked up through handling money, souvenir shopping, door knobs, sand, and ocean, etc. In remote areas, carry your own soap, toilet tissue, and handiwipes.
- Drink only bottled water. The carbonation in water (água com gas) acidifies it and kills microorganisms that may have gotten into the water prior to boiling. Be suspect of juices or fruit drinks not prepared in your presence.
- Minimize the water you swallow when swimming.
- Use bottled water when you brush your teeth (found in the minibar).

If you do get Montezuma's Revenge, minimize food intake for several meals and drinks lots of liquids. Medications that you should pack are Pepto Bismol (over the counter), Imodium (over the counter), Bactrim (prescription), and Lomotil (prescription). If you have bloody stools or fever, feel unusually weak, or if your symptoms continue for 3 days, see a doctor immediately. Dehydration is a severe risk. Drink fruit juices, carbonated soft drinks, or mix 8 ounces of carbonated or boiled water with 1/4 tablespoon of baking soda alternated with a mixture of orange juice, 1/2 teaspoon of honey or corn syrup, and a pinch of salt. Drink alternately from each glass until thirst is quenched, and supplement with carbonated beverages, water, or boiled tea. (Information courtesy of the Centers for Disease Control, Atlanta, GA.)

Tips for Drinking Water

- Always order mineral water (*sem gás*, without gas, or *com gás*, with gas). Insist it be opened in front of you.

- Avoid ice cubes in any drink; they are usually made from tap water. If you must have ice, put them in a small, clean, leak-proof bag inside your glass.
- Tie a colored ribbon around the bathroom faucet to remind yourself not to drink tap water.
- Carry an electric immersion coil for boiling water—to brush teeth or make tea or coffee. You will most likely need a current converter and a plug adapter available in department stores and travel boutiques.
- Carry a small (unbreakable) bottle of chlorine bleach or tincture of iodine to disinfect water when boiling is not feasible. Add 2 drops of 5 percent chlorine bleach or 5 drops of 2 percent tincture of iodine to a quart of clear water. Let stand for 30 minutes. Commercial tablets available in the U.S. to disinfect water are Halazone, Globaline and Potable–Agua.
- Travelers using filters to purify river water may find them hopelessly clogged with sediment and thus be forced to drink river water straight—a perfect way to contract amebiasis. Best to take a safe water supply with you.

Immunizations

Yellow fever is endemic in the northern half of Brazil, Vaccines are recommended for those going to jungle or rural areas. Suggested, but not required are hepatitis and typhoid immunizations when traveling to areas of sub–standard sanitation outside the usual tourist routes. Persons working extensively in the countryside and on working assignments in remote areas should be vaccinated. Tetanus shots should always be updated.

Malaria

Malaria is transmitted by the bite of the female Anopheles mosquito, which feeds from dawn to dusk. You can also get malaria from blood transfusions, or from using contaminated needles and syringes. Not every mosquito carries malaria, but one bite can give you the disease. The Centers for Disease Control in 1994 believes that all travelers to the Amazon Basin will be exposed to what is called chloroquine-resistant malaria. The recommended prophylactic is mefloquine, taken weekly and continued for 4 weeks after leaving the malarious area. You can also carry a treatment of Fansidar or doxycycline alone, taken daily. If you are pregnant or are planning to fly a plane or undertake any task requiring fine coordination, you should not take mefloquine since small doses have been known to cause dizziness and/or gastrointestinal upset.

Other Bug-Transmitted Diseases

Other mosquito–transmitted diseases found in jungle areas are: **dengue fever** (flulike symptoms, with rash, over in about a week; antibiotics do not help and no vaccine available; beware of hemorraghing); **leishmaniasis** (avoid sandfly bites which attack most frequently at dusk and dawn); **filariasis** (caused by larvae of worms injected into the body through the bite of a mosquito; usually only heavier exposure causes symptoms; treat with Hetrazan); **onchocerclasis** (a form of filariasis, or river blindness, borne by flies that breed in rivers; if parasites invade the eyes, total blindness can occur; treat with Ivermextin early); and **Chagas' disease** (spread by the reduid bug usually found on roofs and walls of native huts). For more information, see the *International Travel Health Guide* by Stuart R. Rose, M.D.

Prevention

Cut down on your chances of catching mosquito–transmitted diseases by protecting yourself. Search your sleeping quarters and bed for hidden insects. Use insecticides, preferably pyrethrum-based, in your living and sleeping quarters (RAID Formula II Crack and Crevice Spray is good). And protect your bed (if outdoors) with mosquito netting (spray the inside of the netting with RAID Flying Insect Spray).

Mosquito and tick bites can be reduced greatly by using the appropriate repellants. Insect repellants with a DEET percentage between 35–50 is recommended. Clothing may be sprayed with DEET-containing repellants and the insecticide permethrin, available in many states as Permanone, or PermaKill 4 Week Tick Killer. If you are using a mosquito net, spray it with the same product. A good, lightweight, compact mosquito net well suited for the vagabond traveler is "The Spider." Contact **Thai Occidental** *5334 Yonge Street, Suite 907, Toronto M2N 6M2, Ontario, Canada (416) 498-4277, price $69.95.*

Cholera

Cholera is an acute diarrheal disease caused by bacteria found in water contaminated by sewage. Although there have been serious outbreaks of cholera during the last few years in many Latin American countries, including Brazil, few Western travelers ever get seriously ill. Most illness occurs in native people who are undernourished and who regularly ingest large amounts of contaminated water. The main symptom is explosive, though painless diarrhea, which if left untreated, may lead to fatal dehydration. Treating loss of fluids immediately is primary to recovery. A good idea is to carry Oral Rehydration Salts mixture distributed by the World Health Organization, which you should mix with safe drinking water and consume after every loose stool. If you can't drink enough to replace lost fluid because of vomiting or weakness, get to a hospital immediately. The best prevention is to pay attention to what you eat and drink.

Other Diseases

Wading or swimming in fresh water can put you at risk for **schistosomiasis**, caused by parasitic blood flukes called schistosomes. The tiny larvae of these creatures bore into the skin and mature within the body. Some people disregard the initial symptom—a rash at the site of penetration—but 4–12 weeks later, fever, malaise, and coughing, along with diarrhea, usually sets in abruptly. It's often curable, but if left untreated can progress to more severe stages.

Hepatitis A can be transmitted by person-to-person contact or by contaminated food, water, or ice. The flulike symptoms don't appear typically for 2–6 weeks and are soon followed by jaundice. The CDC recommends a gamma globulin vaccination for each 3-month period. There's no specific treatment and normally healthy people recover on their own, but do see a doctor.

Hepatitis B is high risk for travelers to the Amazon basin. Vaccinations are not required, but the CDC recommends one for health-care workers, long-term travelers, or anyone expecting to have intimate relations with locals in rural areas. The virus is transmitted through the exchange of blood products, daily physical contact, and sexual intercourse. The vaccine involves a series of 3 intramuscular doses, which should be begun 6 months before travel; the series should be begun even if it cannot be completed before travel begins.

Typhoid Fever is at risk in Brazil for travelers to small cities, villages, and rural areas. Although not required, the CDC recommends a vaccination for those straying from the regular tourist itinerary or staying more than 6 weeks. The disease is transmitted through contaminated food and water. Currently, the vaccine only protects 70–90 percent of cases, so continue to drink only boiled or bottled water and eat well-cooked food, even if you've taken the vaccination.

AIDS Information for Travelers
(Also see "Diseases" under Directory)

As of press time, Brazil does not require foreign travelers to take AIDS tests. For a free 4-page leaflet on how to travel abroad and not bring home acquired immuno-deficiency syndrome, write **Global Programs on AIDS, World Health Organization** *Avenue Appia, 1121; Geneva 27, Switzerland.*

Other Information

For the most current information on traveling to tropical countries, contact the **Centers for Disease Control** ☎ *(404) 332-4559* using a touch-tone phone 24 hours a day. A recorded voice will direct you through a menu of information.

For an excellent bimonthly newsletter on travel precautions, write **Traveling Healthy** *108-48 70th Road; Forest Hills, NY 11375.*

An excellent 51-page booklet published by the **American Society of Tropical Medicine and Hygiene** discusses such topics as pre-trip preparations, immunizations, malaria prevention, traveler's diarrhea, etc. Write: Karl A. Western, MD c/o **ASTMH** *6436-31st Street, N.W., Washington, D.C. 20015-2342. Price $4.00.* Everything you need to know about the latest travel-health requirements worldwide (updated annually) can be found in *International Travel Health Guide*, by Stuart R. Rose, M.D. Published by **Travel Medicine, Inc.** *351 Pleasant Street, Suite 312, Northhampton, MA 01060.*

Post-Trip Checkups

Many specialists feel there is no reason to have a post-tropics checkup if you are feeling well. In some cases, however, symptoms don't appear for weeks, months, or a year after the trip; you may even suffer intermittent attacks followed by periods of subsidence. The incubation period for malaria varies from five days to a month, and longer in some cases. In its initial stages, it causes flulike symptoms, and if treatment is delayed, it can become potentially fatal. If you have any of the following symptoms, don't delay seeking immediate medical attention:

- gastrointestinal distress (if diarrhea, loose stools, abdominal pain, or excessive flatulence continues for a week or more, you could be harboring parasites);

- fever (never ignore fever coming out of the tropics—it could be malaria, schistosomiasis, roundworms, hepatitis A, or a sign of tuberculosis);
- rashes, change in skin pigmentation, or swelling;
- persistent coughs, possibly due to parasitic worms in the lungs or tuberculosis;
- unexplained weight loss. In all cases, it is best to go to a tropical disease specialist straightaway.

To find one in your area call the local health department or the tropical disease unit of a nearby hospital. The new **International Society of Travel Medicine** *Box 150060, Atlanta, GA 30333;* ☎ *(404) 486-4046* should have a list of specialists. (To request a nationwide directory of tropical disease specialists, send a stamped, self-addressed business-size envelope to **Dr. Leonard C. Marcus** *148 Highland Avenue, Newton, MA 02165.*

BOOKS AND FILMS

THE ESSENTIAL COLLECTION

BOOKS

Luso-Brazilian Books *Box 170286, Brooklyn, NY 11217;* ☎ *(718) 624-4000, toll free* ☎*(800) 727-LUSO, FAX (718) 858-0690* is one of the leading distributors of Brazilian and Portuguese–oriented material. Write for a free catalogue.

Photography

Manor, Graciela, text, and Mann, Hans, photos. *The Twelve Prophets of Aleijadinho.* Austin & London: University of Texas Press, 1976. Black and white photos, a short text, and a poetic essay by Carlos Drummond de Andrade on the character of Minas Gerais as seen through the eyes of the Baroque sculptor Aleijadinho.

Verger, Pierre. *Historical Center of Salvador (Centro Histórico de Salvador 1945–1950).* Rio de Janeiro: Câmara Brasileiro do Livro, 1989. Black and white photos by a French documentary photographer in the 1940s whose reminiscences are still fresh.

Bruce Weber. *O Rio de Janeiro.* New York: Knopf, 1986. A sensual photographic journal by one of the world's leading photographers.

History

Alden, Dauril., ed. *Colonial Roots of Modern Brazil.* Berkeley: University of California Press, 1973.

Burns, E. Bradford. A *History of Brazil.* New York: Columbia University Press, 1980. Perhaps the most readable history of Brazil readily available in bookstores.

Conrad, Robert Edgar. *World of Sorrow: The African Slave Trade in Brazil.* Baton Rouge & London: Louisiana State University Press, 1986. A rich resource of details and culture, particularly helpful for anyone writing an historical novel.

Diffie, Bailey W. A *History of Colonial Brazil 1500–1792.* Malabar, Florida: Robert E. Krieger Publishing Co., 1987.

Freyre, Gilberto. *Order and Progress: Brazil from Monarch to Republic.* Berkeley and Los Angeles: University of California Press, 1986. A 3-volume masterpiece by the premier Brazilian sociologist.

Freyre, Gilberto. *The Mansions and the Shanty: The Making of Modern Brazil.* Berkeley and Los Angeles: University of California Press, 1986.

Freyre, Gilberto. *The Masters and the Slaves:*

A *Study in the Development of Brazilian Civilization.* Berkeley and Los Angeles: University of California Press, 1986.

Maxwell, Kenneth. *Conflicts and Conspiracies: Brazil and Portugal 1750–1808.* Boston: Cambridge University Press, 1973. Interesting analysis explaining why Brazil adopted a monarchical system of government instead of fragmenting into numerous separate states like other areas in Latin America.

Street Life

De Jesus, Maria. *Child of the Dark: The Diary of Carolina Maria de Jesus.* New York: Penguin, 1963. An extraordinary diary of a poor woman living in a São Paulo ghetto, written originally on scraps of paper. After her writings were discovered by a journalist, they were first serialized in the newspaper, then made into an instant bestseller. Nothing more honest and direct exists to describe the day-to-day struggle of living in a *favela*.

Dimenstein, Gilberto, introduction by Rocha, Jan. *Brazil: War on Children.* London: Latin America Bureau, 1991. One of Brazil's most outstanding journalists investigates the tragic world of underaged pimps, muggers, prostitutes, and petty criminals—all homeless children who live in fear of sudden death at the hands of vigilantes.

Trevisan, João, translated by Martin Forman. *Perverts in Paradise.* London: GMP Publishers, 1986. Written by one of the founders of the Brazilian gay movement, this is a fascinating, if severely biased, history of the development of homosexuality in Brazil, from the Papal Inquisition to today's pop music idols. A provocative analysis of how homosexuality dovetails with the Brazilian traits of extravagance and social repression is followed by a startling interview with a gay *candomblé* priest. Write: GMP Publishers, LTD., P.O. Box. 247, London N15 6 RW, England.

Native Peoples

Davis, Shelton H. *Victims of the Miracle: Development and the Indians of Brazil.* Boston: Cambridge University Press, 1977, reprinted in 1988. An anthropologist examines contemporary Indian policy in Brazil and discusses the devastation wrought on tribal life by highway construction and mining.

Hemming, John. *Amazon Frontier: The Defeat of the Brazilian Indians.* London: Macmillan London Ltd., 1987. Covering the period from the mid-18th century to the early 20th century, this compelling analysis explains how and why native cultures fell into demise. The author is Director and Secretary of Royal Geographic Society.

The Amazon

Head, Suzanne and Heinzman, Robert, editors. *Lessons of the Rainforest.* San Francisco: Sierra Club Books, 1990. Essays from 24 leading authorities (biologists, ecologists, economists, and political activists), all committed to finding alternatives to rainforest decimation.

Hecht, Susanna and Cockburn, Alexander. *The Fate of the Forest: Developers, Destroyers and Defenders of the Amazon.* New York: Harper Perennials, 1990. A deeply informed and searing work exploring the history of the rainforest from the conquistadors to the goldminers to the military dictatorship. It also sheds new light on the role of Chico Mendes and other activists.

Miller, Cristina G. and Berry, Louise A. *Jungle Rescue: Saving the New World Tropical Rain Forests.* New York: Atheneum, 1991. A thought-provoking and entertaining book for children, explaining the complexities of the rain forest and its relationship to the Western Hemisphere.

Lamb, F. Bruce. *Wizard of the Upper Amazon, The Story of Manuel Córdova-Rio.* Boston: Houghton-Mifflin, 1975. Written by a Peruvian healer held captive by Amazonian Indians, this is a mesmerizing document of life in a South American tribe, including descriptions of *ayahuasca* rituals—a hallucinogenic tonic made from two Amazonian plants.

Lewis, Scott, preface by Robert Redford.

The Rainforest Book: How You Can Save the World's Rainforests. Los Angeles: Living Planet Press, 1990. An extremely easy-to-read book that explains how rainforests are being destroyed, why we should preserve them, and what we can do.

Kane, Joe. *Running the Amazon*. New York: Knopf, 1989. A must-read for anyone looking for arm-chair adventure, this eye-witness account of traversing the Amazon River was written by a formerly office-bound journalist whose pre-trip naiveté was matched only by his unexpected fearlessness.

Matthiessen, Peter. *The Cloud Forest*. New York: Penguin, 1961, 1989. Zen master Matthiessen crisscrossed 20,000 miles of South American wilderness, from the Amazonian rainforests to Machu Picchu and Mato Grosso. Stylish, ironic, and insightful.

Popescu, Petru. *Amazon Beaming*. New York: Viking, 1991. When world–class photographer Loren McIntyre was kidnapped by an Amazonian tribe, he found himself descending, unwillingly, into another level of perceptual reality that ultimately changed his life. This amazing "Twilight Zone" story is told with style by Romanian filmmaker Petru Popescu.

Shoumatoff, Alex. *The Rivers Amazon*. San Francisco: Sierra Club Books, 1978 and 1986. A staff writer for the New Yorker and a premier commentator on Brazilian affairs resolved to spend his thirtieth birthday in the Amazon. His reminiscences of negotiating headwaters, mosquitoes, exotic vegetation, and wildlife, as well as all manners of *bureaucratic* red tape lie somewhere between poetry and science.

Pantanal

Banks, Vic. *The Pantanal: Brazil's Forgotten Wilderness*. San Francisco: Sierra Club Books, 1991. Photojournalist and cinematographer Vic Banks chronicles his lively adventures in the Pantanal, accompanied by photos of the region. Also included is a good overview of the political dilemmas of the region.

Art and Architecture

Epstein, David. *Brasília: Plan and Reality. A Study of Planned and Spontaneous Urban Development*. Berkeley: University of Press, 1973.

Holston, James. *Brasília: The Modernist City. An Anthropological Critique*. Chicago & London: University of Chicago Press, 1989.

Music

McGowan, Chris and Ricardo Pessanha. *The Brazilian Sound*. New York: Billboard Books, 1991.

Perrone, Charles. *Masters of Contemporary Brazilian Song: MPB 1965–1985*. Austin: University of Texas Press, 1989.

Roots and Culture

Amado, Jorge. *Bahia de Todos Os Santos (Guia de ruas e mistérios)*. A mystical guide to Salvador's streets and icons by Brazil's most foremost novelist. (Portuguese)

Religion

Brumana, Fernando Giobellina and Elda Gonzales Martinez. *Spirits from the Margin: Umbanda in São Paulo*. Stockholm: Wicksell International, 1989.

Bastide, Roger, translated by Helen Sebba. *The African Religions of Brazil: Toward a Sociology of the Interpretation of Civilizations*. Baltimore and London: Johns Hopkins University, 1960. The leading analysis of Brazilian religious cults by a noted French social scientist.

Galembo, Phyllis. *Divine Inspiration: Benin to Bahia*. New Mexico: University of Albuquerque Press, 1993. An exquisite photo album with a foreword by David Byrne and various essays celebrating the ritualistic "theater" of African and Afro-Brazilian trance cult religions. The folklore-rich photos help explain how African traditions, as living elements transmitted orally, were adapted in Brazil without losing their sacred fire.

McGregor, Pedro. *Jesus of the Spirits*. New

York: Stein & Day, 1966. An interesting analysis of African myths and ritual and their influence on the religious beliefs of Brazilians.

O'Gorman, Frances. *Aluanda: A Look at Afro-Brazilian Cults.* Rio de Janeiro: Livraria Francisco Alves Editora S.A., 1979.

St. Clair, David. *Drum & Candle.* New York: Doubleday, 1971. An American journalist made a personal investigation into the psychic/spiritual side of Brazil and came out a believer.

Wofer, Jim. *The Taste of Blood: Spirit Possession in Brazilian Candomblé.* Philadelphia: University of Pennsylvania Press, 1991.

Samba/Carnaval

Guillermoprieto, Alma. *Samba.* New York: Random House, 1990. A marvelous account of one year in the life of Rio's Mangueira samba school, written by a former journalist with the soul of a poet.

Gardel, Luis. *Escolas de Samba.* Rio de Janeiro: 1967. Subtitled "A Descriptive Account of the Carnival Guilds of Rio," this book is a bit out of date, but the historical details of Carnaval are interesting. (The English edition is available in Rio's best book stores; try the one next door to the Copacabana Palace Hotel).

Dance

Bira, Almeida. *Capoeira: A Brazilian Art Form: History, Philosophy, and Practice.* Berkeley: North Atlantic Books, 1986. The student of one of the great capoeira masters of the 20th century and now a master teacher himself in California, the Brazilian-born author writes poignantly about the history, philosophy, and form of the country's premier martial art. The book is filled with legends, songs, and tricks of the trade—valuable for anyone interested in ethnocultural studies.

Cuisine

Rojas-Lombardi, Felipe. *The Art of South American Cooking.* Harper Collins, 1991. Innovative Latin cooking by the late Peruvian owner of The Ballroom restaurant in New York City. Recipes for Brazilian delicacies are superb.

Health

Rose, Stuart R., MD. *International Travel Health Guide.* Northampton: Travel Medicine, Inc., 1991. Written by a physician who is a member of the AMA and the American Society of Tropical Medicine and Hygiene, this book gives excellent advice about traveling in third-world countries and tropical jungles. Specific guidelines for individual countries, including Brazil, are denoted in detail.

Guides

The Best of São Paulo. Hard-cover pocket-size guide written by a native Paulistano. Price, including shipping and handling, is $10. Write to: Editora Marca D'Agua, Avenida Cidade Jardim 427 #124, São Paulo, Brazil 01453; ☎ (11) 881-0753, FAX (11) 883-5965.

Humor

O'Rourke, P. J. *Holidays in Hell.* New York: Vintage, 1989. An irreverent and world-weary foreign correspondent for *Rolling Stone* reports from hellholes and other fun spots around the world. His chapter about driving on third-world roads is required reading for anyone heading for the Amazon or Pantanal.

Films

Available on video:

Black Orpheus

Directed by Marcel Camus, with music by Antônio Carlos Jobim and Luis Bonfá, this stunning movie retells the Orpheus tale through the eyes of a carioca streetcar conductor who figuratively descends into hell to save the woman he loves. A lush, if fantastical, view of Carnaval during the 1960s. Portuguese with English subtitles. (Available from Luso-Brazilian Books, see address above.)

At Play in the Fields of the Lord
Directed by Hector Babenco, this 1991 film preserves the moral intelligence of Peter Mathiessen's 1965 novel but loses some of the adventure. Aidan Quinn plays a nerdy evangelist sent to convert an Amazonian tribe, which is also being invaded by a half-Cheyenne mercenary with his own savior complex. The footage of the jungle near Belém is colossal.

Medicine Man
New York magazine called this film "the most enjoyable bad movie in some time"—a big, messy emotional drama starring Sean Connery as a research scientist obsessed with finding a cure for cancer in the Amazon jungle. The shots of Connery and his sidekick, Lorraine Bracco, swinging over the forest on cables is exciting, but her jungle attire is all wrong.

Blame It on Rio
Michael Caine plays a businessman in São Paulo seduced by the nubile virgin daughter of his best friend. The film gives a beautiful view of Grumari Beach, but the token toplessness is not authentic to the region. Anyone going to Rio for the first time might tolerate the horrible script for the cultural glimpses of *candomblé*, *capoeira*, and samba.

Flying Down to Rio
This 1933 music and dance extravaganza featuring Fred Astaire and Ginger Rogers is unabashedly fun, especially the chorus line dancing samba on the wings of the airplane. Unfortunately, the music is more mariachi than Brazilian.

The Emerald Forest
A marvelous, near-mythical tale of a Amazonian Indian who tries—literally—to scale civilization. The score alone is superb, and the clash between the white and native cultures is thought-provoking.

Rainforest Information

Organizations involved in saving tropical rainforests include:

Conservation International
1015 18th Street NW, Suite 1002, Washington, D.C. 20036.

Friends of the Earth/U.S.
218 DD, SE Washington, DC. 20003.

Greenpeace
1436 U Street NW, Washington, DC 20009.

National Resources Defense Council
40 W. 20th Street, New York, NY 10011.

Rainforest Action Network
3301 Broadway, Suite A, San Francisco, CA 94133.

Rainforest Alliance
270 Lafayette St, Suite 512, New York, NY 10012.

Sierra Club
730 Polk Street, San Francisco, CA 94109.

World Wildlife Fund/U.S
Panda House, Godalming, Surrey GGU 7 1 XRR United Kingdom.

COICA
(Coordinating Body for the Indigenous Peoples' Organizations of the Amazon Basin) *Jiron Almagro 614, Lima 11, Peru.*

Amanaka's Amazon Network
494 Broadway, 3rd floor, New York, NY 10012; ☎ (212) 219-2204, FAX 274-1773 is a nonprofit organization that sponsors an annual Amazon Week to promote public dialogues between Amazon leaders and their U.S. supporters. Amanaka also publishes a quarterly newsletter on Amazon-related issues.

SELECTED DISCOGRAPHY

The following records were selected with regard to quality and availability. Recent releases have been emphasized. Stars represent Fielding's choice.

Singer/Songwriters

★ Ben, Jorge. *Benjor*. Tropical Storm/WEA, 1989.
   Ben Jorge and Gilberto Gil. *Gil Jorge*. Polygram/Verve, 1975.
   Ben, Jorge. *Live in Rio*. Warner Bros., 1992.
★ Bethânia, Maria. *Álibi*. BR/Philips, 1988 (rpt.)
   Bethânia, Maria. *Memória da Pele*. BR/Philips, 1989.
   Bethânia, Maria. *Personalidade*. Polygram/Brazilian Wave.
   Biglione, Victor. *Baleia Azul*. Tropical Storm/WEA, 1989.
★ Bonfá, Luiz. *Non Stop to Brazil*. Chesky Records, 1989.
★ Bosco, João. *Odilê Odila*. Polygram/Verve, 1991.
   Buarque, Chico. *Construção*. BR Philips, 1980.
   Buarque, Chico. *Malandro*. Barclay, 1985.
   Buarque, Chico. *Personalidade*. Polygram/Brazilian Wave, 1987.
   Buarque, Chico. *Vida*. BR/Philips, 1980.
   Carlos, Roberto. *Roberto Carlos*. BR/CBS, 1986.
   Djavan. *Lilás*. CBS, 1984.
★ Djavan. *Luz*. BR/CBS, 1982.
   Djavan. *Não é Azul, Mas é Mar*. CBS, 1987
   Djavan. *Seduzir*. World Pacific, 1990 (rpt).
★ Gil, Gilberto. *Dia Dorim Noite Neon*. Tropical Storm/WEA, 1985
   Gil, Gilberto. *Parabolic*. Tropical Storm, 1992.
   Gil, Gilberto. *Raça Humana*. Tropical Storm/WEA, 1984.
★ Gil, Gilberto. *Realce*. Tropical Storm, 1979.
   Gil, Gilberto. *Um Banda Um*. Tropical Storm, 1982.
   Gilberto, João. *Chega de Saudade*. BR/EMI, 1959.
   Gilberto, João. *Interpreta Tom Jobim*. BR/EMI, 1985.
★ Gilberto, João. *The Legendary João Gilberto*. World Pacific, 1990.

Gilberto, João. *Live in Montreaux*. Elektra/Asylum, 1987.
★ Gonzaga, Luiz. *O Melhor de Luiz Gonzaga*. BR/RCA, 1989.
Gonzaguinha, *É*. World Pacific, 1990 (rpt.)
★ Horta, Toninho. *Diamond Land*. Polygram/Verve, 1988.
Horta, Toninho. *Moonstone*. Polygram/Verve, 1989.
Joyce. *Language and Love*. Verve, 1991.
Joyce. *Music Inside*. Verve, 1991.
Lins, Ivan. *Awa Yiô*. Reprise, 1991.
Lins, Ivan. *Harlequin*. GRP, 1986.
Lins, Ivan. *Love Dance*. Reprise, 1989.
★ Lins, Ivan. *O Talento de Ivan Lins*. EMI. Maria, Tânia. Bela Vista. Capitol, 1990.
Maria, Tânia. Love Explosion. Concord, 1984.
★ Moraes, Vinícius de & Toquinho. *Vinícius e Toquinho*. BR/Philips, 1985.
★ Nascimento, Milton. *Anima*, 1982.
★ Nascimento, Milton. *Ao Vivo*. Polygram, 1983.
★ Nascimento, Milton. *Clube da Esquina 2*. BR/EMI, 1978.
★ Nascimento, Milton. *Geraes*. BR/EMI, 1976.
★ Nascimento, Milton. *Milagre dos Peixes*. Intuition Records, 1992 (reissued).
Nascimento, Milton. *Missa dos Quilombos*. Polygram/Verve, 1982.
Nascimento, Milton. *Txai*. CBS, 1992.
Nascimento, Milton. *Yuareté*. CBS Discos, 1987.
Toquinho. *Canta Brasil*. CGD, 1989.
Toquinho. *Made in Coração*. Elektra, 1990.
Toquinho e Vinícius. *Personalidade*. Polygram/Brazilian Wave.
Valença, Alceu. *7 Desejos*. EMI, 1992.
★ Veloso, Caetano. *Cinema Transcendental*. BR/Philips, 1979.
★ Veloso, Caetano. *Circuladô*. Elektra, 1992.
Veloso, Caetano. *Estrangeiro*. Elektra/Musician, 1989.
★ Veloso, Caetano. *Personalidade*. Polygram.
★ Veloso, Caetano. *Totalmente Demais*. Verve, 1987.
Vila, Martinho da. *Martinha da Vida*. CBS, 1990.
Viola, Paulinho da. *O Talento de Paulinho da Viola*. EMI Odeon.

Singers

Alcione. *Emoções Reais*. RCA, 1990.
Alcione. *Fogo da Vida*. RCA, 1985.
Andrade, Leny. *Embraceable You*. Timeless Records, 1991.
Barbosa, Beto. *Beto Barbosa*. BR/Continental, 1988.
Belém, Fafá de. *Atrevida*. BR/Som Livre, 1986.
★ Calcanhoto, Adriana. CBS Discos, 1992.
Caram, Ana. Rio After Dark. Chesky Records.
Carvalho, Beth. "Das Bênçãos que virão com os novos amanhã." RCA, 1985
Carvalho, Beth. *O Carnaval de Beth Carvalho and Martinho da Vila*. BMG, 1990.
Caymmi, Nana. *Atrás da Porta*. BR/CID, 1977.
★ Costa, Gal. *Bem Bom*. RCA, 1985.
★ Costa, Gal. *Gal Canta Caymmi*. Verve, 1976.
Costa, Gal. *Personalidade*. Polygram/Brazilian Wave.
Gilberto, Astrud. *Astrud Gilberto Plus the James Last Orchestra*. Polydor,

1987.
Kenia. *Initial Thrill*. MCA, 1987.
Leão, Nara. *Personalidade*. Polygram/The Best of Brazil.
Lee, Rita. *Rita Lee*. BR/Som Livre, 1986 (rpt.).
Matogrosso, Ney. *Matogrosso & Mathias, vol. 14*. Chantecler.
Menezes, Margareth. *Kindala*. Mango, 1991.
Menezes, Margareth. *Elegibo*. Mango, 1989.
Miranda, Carmen. *Carmen Miranda*. BR/RCA, 1989.
★ Monte, Marisa. *Marisa Monte*. BR/EMI, 1988.
Purim, Flora. *Midnight Sun*. Virgin Records, 1988.
Purim, Flora. *Queen of the Night*. Sound Wave Records, 1992.
Ramalho, Elba. *Personalidade*. Polygram/The Best of Brazil series.
Regina, Elis. *Elis*. BR/Philips, 1988 (rpt.).
★ Regina, Elis. *Elis & Tom*. Verve, 1974.
★ Regina, Elis. *Essa Mulher*. WEA Latina, 1988
★ Regina, Elis. *Fascinação*. BR Philips, 1988.
Regina, Elis. *Falso Brillhante*. BR/Philips, 1988 (rpt.).
Regina, Elis. *Nada Será Como Antes*. Fontana, 1984.
Regina, Elis. *Personalidade*. Polygram/Brazilian Wave, 1987.
★ Regina, Elis. *Samba Eu Canto Assim*. 1983.
★ Sá, Sandra. *Sandra!* BMG Ariola Discos, 1990.
Simone. *The Best of Simone*. Capitol Records, 1991.

Rock

Baby Consuelo. *Sem Pecado E Sem Juízo*. BR/CBS, 1985.
★ Cazuza. *Burguesia*. BR/Philips, 1989.
Kledir. *Kledir Ao Vivo*. Som Livre, 1991.
Lobão. *Sob O Sol de Parador*. BMG/RCA, 1989.
Paralamas do Successo. *Bora Bora*. Capitol/Intuition, 1989.
Paralamos do Successo. *Selvagem?* EMI, 1989.
RPM. *Rádio Pirata Ao Vivo*. BR/CBS, 1986.

Gaúcho

Borghetti, Renato. *Renato Borghetti*. BR/RCA, 1987.
Gaucho da Fronteira. *Gaitero, China e Cordena*. Chantecler.
Gildo de Freitas. *Successos Imortais de Gildo Freitas*.

Minas School

Azul, Paulinho Pedra. *Sonho de Menino*, 1988.
Azul, Paulinho Pedra. *Uma Janela Dentro dos Meus Olhos*, 1984.
Franco, Tadeu. *Captivante*. Barclay, 1983.
★ Franco, Tadeu. *Animal*. Barclay, 1989.
Guedes, Beto. *Viagem das Mãos*. EMI, 1987.
Guedes, Beto. *Alma de Borracha*. EMI, 1986.

Instrumentalists

Airto, Moreira. *Samba de Flora*. Montuno Records, 1988.
★ Moreira, Airto. *Identity*. Arista, 1975.
★ Moreira, Airto and Flora Purim. *The Colours of Life*. W. Germany/In + Out, 1988.
★ Assad, Sérgio and Odair. *Alma Brasileira*. Elektra/Nonesuch, 1988.

Alameida, Laurindo & Carlos Barbosa-Lima, Charlie Byrd. *Music of the Brazilian Masters.* Concord Picante, 1989.
Alemão (Olmir Stocker). *Longe dos Olhos, Perto do Coração.* Happy Hours Music.
Banda Savana. *Brazilian Movements.* Libra Music (Denmark)
Barbosa-Lima, Carlos & Sharon Isbin. *Brazil, with Love.* Concord, 1987.
Biglione, Victor. *Victor Biglione.* Tropical Storm, 1987.
★ Castro-Neves, Oscar. *Maracujá.* JVC, 1989.
★ Castro-Neves, Oscar. *Oscar!* Living Music. 1987.
Cayymi, Dori. *Brasilian Serenata.* Qwest/Warner, 1991.
★ Elias, Eliane. *Eliane Plays Jobim.* Blue Note, 1990.
Elias, Eliane. *So Far So Close.* Blue Note, 1989.
★ Favero, Alberto. *Classical Tropico.* Tropical Storm/WEA Latina, 1989.
★ Gandelman, Leo. *Leo Gandelman.* Secret Records, 1989.
★ Geraissati, André. *Dadgad.* Tropical Storm/WEA, 1989.
Gismonti, Egberto. *Amazônia.* EMI, 1991.
★ Gismonti, Egberto. *Dança das Cabeças.* ECM, 1977.
Gismonti, Egberto. *Dança das Escravos.* ECM, 1989.
★ Gismonti, Egberto. *Sol do Meio Dia.* ECM, 1978.
Gismonti, Egberto and Nana Vasconcelos. *Duo Gismonti-Vasconcelos.* Jazz Bühne Berlin/Repertoire Records, 1990.
★ Jobim, Antônio Carlos. *Passarim.* Polygram/Verve, 1987.
Jobim, Antônio Carlos. *Personalidade.* Polygram/Brazilian Wave.
Jobim, Antônio Carlos. *Urubu.* BR/WEA, 1985 (rpt.).
★ Jobim, Antônio Carlos & Gal Costa. *Rio Revisited.* Verve, 1989.
Lyra, Carlos. *Carlos Lyra: 25 Anos de Bossa Nova.* 3M, 1987.
Tiso, Wagner. *Baobab.* Antilles/Island, 1990.
Silveira, Ricardo. *Sky Light.* Polygram/Verve, 1989.
Vasconcelos, Naná & the Bushdancers. *Rain Dance.* Antilles/Island, 1988.

Compilations

Alô Brasil. Tropical Storm/WEA Latina, 1989.
Afro Brasil. Verve, 1990.
Bahia Black Ritual Beating System. Island Records, 1992.
Black Orpheus (soundtrack). Verve, 1990 (rpt.).
Brazil Classics 1: Beleza Tropical, compiled by David Byrne. Luaka Bop/Sire, 1989.
Brazil Classics 2: O Samba, compiled by David Byrne. Luaka Bop/Warner, 1989.
Brazil Classics 3: Forró, etc., compiled by David Byrne. Luaka Bop/Warner, 1989.
Brazil Classics 4: The Best of Tom Zé, compiled by David Byrne. Luaka Bop/Sire, 1990.
Brazil is Back. Braziloid Records, 1987.
Djavan, João Gilberto, Toninho Horta. Capitol Records, 1990.
Lambada Brazil, featuring Caetano Veloso and Margareth Menezes. Polygram, 1990.
Nordeste Brazil. Verve, 1991.
Samba Brazil, Verve, 1991.
Sampler '89. Tropical Storm/WEA, 1989.

Sounds of Bahia Volume 2. Sound Wave records, 1991.
★ *Violões.* Banera. (São Paulo), 1991.

For Brazilian-influenced recordings by non-Brazilians, check out the releases of Stan Getz, Pat Metheny, Basia, Chick Corea, Ella Fitzgerald, Manhattan Transfer, Dave Grusin, Lee Ritenour, Sara Vaughan, Weather Report, and Paul Winter, among others.

Best cities to buy and hear music in Brazil are Rio and São Paulo (all genres), Belo Horizonte (especially the Mineiro School), Fortaleza (*forró and lambada*), Salvador (*afoxé*), Recife/Olinda (*forró*).

INDEX

A

Abraão, 219
Accommodations, 7
    See also Hotels and Lodges
Aerolinas Argentinas, 10
AIDS, 94, 664
Air taxes, *See* taxes
Air travel, 8–10
Airlines, 9
    Alta Floresta, 614
    Belém, 592
    Brasília, 408
    Cuiabá, 625
    Fernando de Noronha, 528
    Fortaleza, 523
    Natal, 510
    Porto Seguro, 462
    Recife, 498
    Rio, 191–193
Airports
    Alcântara, 538
    Belém, 593
    Belo Horizonte, 248
    Brasília, 407
    Búzios, 210
    Fortaleza, 523
    Maceió, 483
    Manaus, 608
    Natal, 510
    Praia do Forte, 457
    Recife, 498
    Rio, 191
    Salvador, 443
    Santarém, 573
    São Luis, 544
Aleijadinho (Antonio Francisco Lisboa), 232, 239, 250, 254, 284–286
Alenquer, 571
Alta Floresta, 611–614
Alvares, Diogo, 37
Amazon, 4, 545–614
Amazônia, 6, 545–614
American Airlines, 10
Angra dos Reis, 215, 217
Apartments (apart-hotels), 8
    Belo Horizonte, 242
    Rio, 151
Aracajú, 6

Architecture
    Joinville, 348
    Ouro Preto, 252
    Salvador, 422
Arco de Telles, 102
Arpoador, 128
Arraial d'Ajuda, 465–468
Arrivals, 9
Art
    Congonhas, 286
    Olinda, 491
    Parati, 224
    Rio, 141
    See also under specific buildings
Astronomy, 136
Asturias Beach, 325
Augusto de Lima, 236
Avenida Atlântica, 143
Avenida Nossa Senhora de Copacabana, 142
Avenida Rio Branco, 105

B

Baby-sitters, 119
Bahia, 6, 409–470
Bandeirantes, 39, 621
Bar do Arnaudo, 111
Barra, 427–428
Barra da Lagoa, 343
Barra da Tijuca, 95, 118, 132
Basílica, 287
Bay of Ilha Grande, 215
Beaches, 6, 34
    Arraial d'Ajuda, 465
    Barra, 427
    Barra da Tijuca, 118, 132
    Búzios, 210
    Camboriú, 355
    Flamengo, 114
    Florianópolis, 343
    Fortaleza, 515–518
    Guarajá, 325
    Ilha Grande, 219
    Maceió, 476
    Natal, 502–506
    Paquetá Island, 115
    Rio, 95, 120–133
    Salvador, 418–420
    São Conrado, 131

São Luis, 535–536
São Paulo, 304
Torres, 375
Vidigal, 130
Before you go, 7–8
Belém, 4, 577–592
Belo Horizonte, 5, 235–248
Bento Gonçalves, 385–386
Best of Brazil, 33–34
Best time to visit, 11
   Alcântara, 538
   Alta Floresta, 614
   Arraial d'Ajuda, 468
   Belém, 594
   Blumenau, 354
   Brasília, 403
   Camboriú, 356
   Caxambú, 299
   Chapada dos Guimarães, 641
   Congonhas, 289
   Fernando de Noronha, 529
   Florianópolis, 345
   Fortaleza, 524
   Iguaçu Falls, 338
   Ilha Grande, 220
   Joinville, 350
   Maceió, 483
   Manaus, 609
   Mariana, 269
   Nova Petrópolis, 373
   Porto Alegre, 363
   Praia do Forte, 457
   Recife, 499
   Rio, 96
   Santarém, 575
   São João del Rei, 271, 278
   São Luis, 544
   Torres, 378
Bethânia, Maria, 81
Beto Guedes, 235
Bicho Solto, 112
Bird's-eye view
   Amazon, 546
   Brasília, 393
   Brazil, 5
   Chapada dos Guimarães, 631
   Congonhas, 284
   Cuiabá, 622
   Maceió, 476
   Natal, 502
   Ouro Preto, 252
   Recife, 486
   Rio, 94–95
   Salvador, 417
   Santarém, 565

São João del Rei, 272
São Paulo, 308–309
Blumenau, 342, 351–354
Boat rentals, 216
Boat tours
   Búzios, 210
   Cuiabá, 637
   Iguaçu Falls, 332
   Ilha Grande, 220
   Parati, 224
   Porto Seguro, 463
   Salvador, 430–431
Bolsa de Valores, 102
Books, 667–672
Botafogo, 95, 129–130
Botanical gardens, 113
Braganças, 41
Brasília, 6, 389–408
Brazilian American Cultural Center, 15
Brazilian Miracle, 45
Buddha's Birthday, 309
Bus tours, 112
Buses, 19, 30
   Alta Floresta, 614
   Brasília, 408
   Búzios, 210
   Cachoeira, 451
   Caxambú, 299
   Congonhas, 288
   Fortaleza, 524
   Green Rio, 112
   Guarujá, 325
   Iguaçu Falls, 333, 337
   Itaipu Dam, 334
   Leitos, 31
   Manaus, 608
   Mariana, 269
   Ouro Preto, 262
   Parati, 223
   Petrópolis, 203
   Rio, 97, 194
   Salvador, 443
   Santarém, 573
   São João del Rei, 277
   São Lourenço, 293
   São Luis, 544
   São Paulo, 322
   Trancoso, 470
Business hours, 20
Butantã Institute, 309
Búzios, 209–213

C

Cabanagem Rebellion, 41
Cachoeira, 447–451

INDEX

Cachoeira Véu de Noiva, 630
Cachoerinha, 631
Café do Teatro, 106
Caigangue tribe, 330
Cals, 591
Camboriú, 355–356
Caminho dos Pescadores, 125
Camping
    Brasília, 405
    Pantanal, 619, 633
    Praia do Forte, 456
Campos do Jordão, 305
Cândido Mendes Escola Técnica de Comércio, 101
Candomblé
    Cachoeira, 447, 450
    Rio, 184
    Salvador, 414–415, 422
Canela, 365–369
Cangas, 621
Canto, 219
Capoeira, 415
Car rentals, 24
    Belém, 593
    Belo Horizonte, 248
    Búzios, 210
    Camboriú, 356
    Cuiabá, 626
    Florianópolis, 345
    Fortaleza, 524
    Joinville, 350
    Manaus, 608
    Mariana, 269
    Natal, 511
    Porto Alegre, 362
    Rio, 194
    Salvador, 443
    Santarém, 573
Caramuru, 37
Carlos Barbosa, 387
Carnaval, 2, 67–76
    Bahia, 74
    History, 68
    Hotel reservations, 75
    Parade, 71–72
    Pernambuco, 74–75
    Rehearsals, 76
    Sambódromo, 70
Casa de Pedra, 633
Casa de Santos Dumont, 205
Casa do Baile, 236
Casa Franca–Brasil, 103
Cascatinha de Taunay, 112
Castro, Domitila de, 40
Catedral São Francisco Xavier, 348

Cathedral de São Pedro de Alcântara, 205
Caxambú, 295–299
Caxias do Sul, 379–380
Cemitério do Imigrante, 348
Chácara do Céu Museum, 110
Chapada dos Guimarães, 621, 629–641
Children
    Parati, 225
    Rio, 118
    São Lourenço, 294
Chimarrão, 358
Cholera, 11, 662–663
Christ the Redeemer, 88, 95
Churches
    Brasília, 399–401
    Camboriú, 355
    Olinda, 491
    Ouro Preto, 254–256
    Pampulha, 236, 237
    Parati, 224
    Petrópolis, 205
    Rio, 107–110, 141
    Salvador, 421, 423–425, 426
    São João del Rei, 273–275
    Tiradentes, 280
Churrascaria, 55
Cidade das Flores, 347
Cidades das Pedras, 633
Circuito Inferior, 333
City transportation
    Belo Horizonte, 248
    Brasília, 407
    Fortaleza, 524
    Maceió, 483
    Mariana, 269
    Porto Seguro, 463
    Recife, 498
    Salvador, 443
    Santarém, 573
    São Lourenço, 293
Ciudad Presidente Stroessner, 330
Climate, 21
    Arraial d'Ajuda, 467
    Belém, 593
    Brasília, 408
    Caxias do Sul, 380
    Chapada dos Guimarães, 640
    Congonhas, 288
    Cuiabá, 626
    Fernando de Noronha, 528
    Fortaleza, 524
    Manaus, 608
    Mariana, 269
    Natal, 511
    Nova Petrópolis, 373

Pantanal, 620
Porto Alegre, 363
Recife, 498
Rio, 195
Salvador, 444
Santarém, 573
São Luis, 544
São Paulo, 322
Torres, 377
Clothing, 17–18, 121, 560, 620
Club Med, 215
Collor Plan, 46
Colonists, 38
Commendatuba Island, 435
Comondatuba Island, 34
Computers, 21
Condoms, 23
Confeitaria Colombo, 105
Congonhas, 233, 239, 283–289
Consulates, 11
    Belém, 593
    Brasília, 408
    Iguaçu Falls, 337
    Manaus, 608
    Recife, 498
    Rio, 195
    Salvador, 444
    São Paulo, 322
Copacabana, 95, 123–125
Copacabana Beach, 88, 160, 161, 172
Corcovado, 95
Cost, 4–5
Costa do Sol, 201, 209–213
Costa Verde, 201, 215–217
Crafts commune, 623
Credit cards, 14
    Chapada dos Guimarães, 640
    Rio, 195
    Salvador, 444
Crena, 219
Crime, 16
Cruises, 645
    Costa Verde, 216
    Manaus, 609
    ocean liners, 645
Cruz, Ilha da, 36
Cuiabá, 4, 621–627
Cuisine, 55–58
    Rio, 164–179
    São Paulo, 304
Culture, 49–53
    Alta Floresta, 612
    Ouro Preto, 240
Curral del Rey, 235
Currency, 14, 21

Customs, 11, 19

D

Dancing, 185
Dangerous animals, 558
Democracy, 45–46
Diana Turismo, 216
Diarrhea, 659–661
Discography, selected, 673–677
Diseases, 11, 23, 662, 663–664
Djavan, 82
Doctors, 23, 620
Dona Marta Mirante, 111
Driving, 24
Dumont (coffee farm), 307
Dutch West Indies Company, 38
Dutra, Marechal Eurico Gaspar, 44

E

Eco tourism, 33
    Amazon, 556
    Caxambú, 297
    Chapada dos Guimarães, 633
    Florianópolis, 343
    Iguaçu Falls, 332
    Itaipu Dam, 333
    Pantanal, 615–617
    Pão de Açúcar, 97–99
    Praia do Forte, 454
    Serra da Bocaina, 227
    Tijuca Forest, 111
    Tiradentes, 279
Electricity, 25
Embassy, 11
Eroticism, 188–189
Espaço Cultural dos Correios, 103
Exchanging money, 21
Excursions
    Chapada dos Guimarães, 633–635
    Green Rio, 111–115
    Maceió, 477
    Pantanal, 618
    Santarém, 568, 570
    São Luis, 536
Exotiquarium, 310
Expeditours, 199
    Green Rio, 112
    Pantanal, 618

F

F & H Travel Consulting, 645
Fairs
    Rio, 149
    São Paulo, 321
Farroupilha, 381

Fast food, 170
Favela, 112, 115–117
Fazenda Alegria, 118
Fazenda Beira Rio, 636
Fazenda Boa Sorte Região de Abobral, 636
Fazenda Xaraes, 635
Feijoada, 56
Feijoadas, 170
Fernando de Noronha, 525–529
Ferries
    Arraial d'Ajuda, 467
    Costa do Sol, 219
Festa do Colono Alemão, 204
Festival of the Stars, 309
Festivals
    Blumenau, 351
    Guarujá, 325
    Joinville, 347
    São Paulo, 309
Figueiredo, João Baptista, 45
Film, 16
Films, 119, 667–672
Fishing
    Caxambú, 297
    Serra da Bocaina, 227, 229
Flamengo Beach, 95, 114, 129
Flamengo Park, 114, 118, 129
Flights, 25
Florália, 204
Florianópolis, 339, 343–346
Fonseca, Marechal Deodoro da, 42
Forests, 111, 554–556
Fortaleza, 4, 6, 513–524
Fountains, 296
Foz do Iguaçu, 329–338
Franco, Itamar, 47
Freguesia Island, 219

G

Galeria Paulo Fernandes, 103
Galetos, 172
Garganta del Diablo, 333
Garibaldi, 383–384
Garota de Ipanema, 127
Gaúcho, 358
Gay
    Belo Horizonte, 246
    Brasília, 403
    Fortaleza, 522
    Maceió, 482
    Rio, 190–191
    Salvador, 441
    São Paulo, 321
Geodesic Center, 622
Geyser at Caxambúr, 297

Gil, Gilberto, 79–80
Gold
    Alta Floresta, 611
    Amazon, 550
Golf courses, 131
Goulart, João, 45
Gramado, 365–369
Greener Rio, 90, 201–229
Grumari, 95
Grumari Beach, 133
Grupo Corpor, 235
Guanabara Bay, 88
Guarajá, 325–327
Guaratiba, 95
Guarujá, 304
Guides
    Iguaçu Falls, 332
    Manaus, 608

H

Hair salons, 25, 323
Hang gliders
    Rio, 137
    São Conrado, 131
Healers
    Chapada dos Guimarães, 640
    Cuiabá, 625
    Vale do Amanhecer, 402
Health, 659–665
Health clubs
    Rio, 138, 215
Helicopter flights, 138
Helisul Taxi Aeréo, 331
Hepatitis, 663
Heroes, 552
Hiking
    Iguaçu Falls, 333
    Pantanal, 617
    Rio, 138
Hippie fair, 127
Historical sites, 34
History, 35–47
    Amazon, 548–554
    Belo Horizonte, 235
    Brasília, 390–393
    Cachoeira, 448
    Chapada dos Guimarães, 629
    Congonhas, 283
    Cuiabá, 621
    Fernando de Noronha, 526
    Fortaleza, 513–514
    Iguaçu Falls, 330
    Joinville, 347
    Mariana, 263
    Olinda, 485–486

Ouro Preto, 250
Pampulha, 238
Pantanal, 616–618
Recife, 485–486
Rio, 91–94, 134–135
Salvador, 413–414
Santarém, 564
São João del Rei, 272
São Luis, 532
São Paulo, 307–308
Hitching, 345
Holidays, 20
   Ouro Preto, 250
   Salvador, 445–446
Horse racing, 138
Horse-and-carriage, 325
Horseback
   Belo Horizonte, 240–241
   Caxambú, 298
   Pantanal, 618
   São Lourenço, 294
   Tiradentes, 281
Hotels, 33
   Alcântara, 538
   Alta Floresta, 614
   Arraial d'Ajuda, 466
   Barra da Tijuca, 132
   Belém, 589–590
   Belo Horizonte, 242–243
   Bento Gonçalves, 385
   Blumenau, 352
   Brasília, 404–405
   Búzios, 211–212
   Cachoeira, 451
   Camboriú, 355
   Canela, 367–368
   Caxambú, 298
   Caxias do Sul, 380
   Chapada dos Guimarães, 639
   Congonhas, 288
   Copacabana, 125
   Costa Verde, 217
   Cuiabá, 624
   Fernando de Noronha, 528
   Flamengo, 129
   Florianópolis, 344
   Fortaleza, 519–520
   Garibaldi, 383–384
   Gramado, 367–368
   Guarujá, 326
   Iguaçu Falls, 335–336
   Ilha Grande, 221
   Ipanema Beach, 127
   Joinville, 349
   Leblon, 128
   Leme Beach, 126
   Maceió, 479–481
   Manaus, 603–605
   Mariana, 268
   Natal, 506–508
   Nova Petrópolis, 372
   Olinda, 495–496
   Ouro Preto, 258–260
   Parati, 226
   Porto Alegre, 361–362
   Porto Seguro, 461
   Praia do Forte, 456
   Recife, 494–495
   Rio, 150–163
   Salvador, 432–435
   Santarém, 571
   São Conrado, 131
   São João del Rei, 277
   São Lourenço, 293
   São Luis, 541–543
   São Paulo, 312–315
   Serra da Bocaina, 228
   Teresópolis, 207
   Tiradentes, 281
   Torres, 376–377
   Trancoso, 469
   Vidigal, 130
How to use this guide, 6

I

Ibirapuera Park, 310
Ice cream, 173, 606
Igreja de São Francisco, 236
Iguaçu Falls, 6, 329–338
Ilha Grande, 219–221
Immunizations, 560, 661
Incas, 37
Inconfidência Mineira, 39
Indians, 348, 551
International Folklore Festival, 325
Ipanema, 95, 126–128
Ipanema Beach, 98, 120, 127
Ipanema Tours, 16
IRFFI, 235
Itaipu Dam, 333
Itajaí River, 351
Italian food
   Rio, 173
   São Paulo, 316

J

Jaganda party, 478
Japanese food, 317
Jaraguá Peak, 310
Jardim Botânico, 113

Jardim Zoológico, 113, 118
Jazz clubs, 182
Jequiti-mar Beach, 325
Jesuit missionaries, 37
Jet lag, 13, 659
Jet ski, 138
Jewish food, 318
João Leite da Silva Ortiz, 235
João Pessoa, 6
Joaquina, Carlota, 40
Jobim, Antônio Carlos, 79, 93, 127
Jogo do Bicho, 104
Joinville, 342, 347–350
Jungle adventures
　Serra da Bocaina, 229
　Amazon, 557
　Belém, 584–585
　Manaus, 601–603
Jurerê, 343

K
King João III, 38
Kubitschek, Juscelino, 44

L
Ladatco, 15
Lagoa da Conceição, 343
Language, 13, 647–658
Leblon, 95, 128
Legends, 553
Leme Beach, 125–126
Leopoldina, Dona, 347
Levy, Ricardo Carvão, 236
Liberdade, 309
Libraries
　Green Rio, 113
　Rio, 106
Livraria São José, 105
Lodges, 34
　Amazon, 557, 601
　Pantanal, 618
Lokau, 118
Lopes, Túlio Marques, 240–241
Luggage, 26

M
Maceió, 4, 6, 475–483
Macumba Beach, 133
Mail, 26
Malaria, 561, 661
Manaus, 4, 595–609
Manoel da Costa Athaíde, 239
Marajó Island, 587
Marechal Deodoro, 477
Maria Fumaça train, 275–276

Mariana, 232, 233, 239, 263–269
Markets, 34
Marx, Roberto Burle, 236
Mato Grosso, 621
Mayrink Chapel, 112
Medical, 23
　Cuiabá, 626
　Pantanal, 620
　Rio, 196
　Salvador, 444
　Santarém, 574
　São Paulo, 323
Médici years, 45
Meditation, 141
Mello, Fernando Collor de, 46
Mello, Zélia Cardoso de, 47
Mesa do Imperador, 111
Metropolitan Cathedral, 108
Mexican food, 175
Minas Gerais, 4, 5, 223, 231–302
Mini–Rio Barra Shopping, 118
Mint at Ouro Preto, 256
Mirante da Mata, 238
Mirante das Mangabeiras, 238
Missionaries, 37
Money, 14, 21
Money exchange
　Belém, 593
　Belo Horizonte, 248
　Blumenau, 354
　Brasília, 408
　Chapada dos Guimarães, 640
　Cuiabá, 626
　Florianópolis, 345
　Fortaleza, 524
　Iguaçu Falls, 338
　Maceió, 483
　Ouro Preto, 262
　Porto Alegre, 363
　Porto Seguro, 463
　Recife, 498
　Rio, 196
　Salvador, 444
　Santarém, 574
　São João del Rei, 277
　São Luis, 544
　São Paulo, 323
　Torres, 378
Monroe, President James, 40
Monte Alegre, 571
Monumento à Paz, 236
Morais, Prudente de, 43
Mosqueiros Island, 585

Mountains
  Rio, 201
  São Conrado, 131
  Serra da Bocaina, 227
MPB, 78–86
Museu Arqueológico de Sambaqui, 348
Museu de Arte Sacre, 224
Museu Nacional de Imigração e
  Colonização, 347
Museums
  Belém, 583
  Cuiabá, 623
  Green Rio, 113–114
  Itaipu Dam, 334
  Joinville, 348
  Manaus, 598–601
  Museu von Matius, 206
  Pampulha, 238
  Parati, 225
  Petrópolis, 204
  Recife, 488
  Rio, 106, 119, 133–136
  Salvador, 422, 428–430
  Santa Teresa, 110
  São Luis, 541
  São Paulo, 311–312
Music, 77–86, 673–677
  Rio, 135
  São Paulo, 319
Musical theaters, 184

N

Nabuco, Joaquim, 42
Nacional Museu, 113
Naipí, 330
Nas Rocas, 202
Nascente do Rio Claro, 633
Nascimento, Milton, 81
Natal, 4, 6, 501–511
National Park, 621
National unity, 41
National War Memorial for the Dead
  of the Second World War, 129
Neves, Tancredo, 45, 232
New Year's Festival, 309
Newspapers, 26
  Rio, 196
  São Paulo, 323
Niemeyer, Oscar, 236, 389, 391, 392, 393,
  397, 398, 399
Nightlife
  Arraial d'Ajuda, 467
  Belém, 591
  Belo Horizonte, 246
  Blumenau, 353

Brasília, 402
Búzios, 210
Cachoeira, 451
Camboriú, 356
Caxambú, 299
Cuiabá, 625
Florianópolis, 345
Fortaleza, 522
Guarujá, 327
Iguaçu Falls, 337
Joinville, 350
Maceió, 482
Manaus, 606
Mariana, 268
Natal, 510
Olinda, 497
Ouro Preto, 261
Parati, 226
Porto Alegre, 362
Porto Seguro, 462
Recife, 497
Rio, 180–189
Salvador, 440–441
Santarém, 572
São Paulo, 319–321
Nordestinos, 43
Northeast, 6, 471–544
Nossa Senhora da Boa Viagem, 237
Nossa Senhora do Carmo da Antiga Sé, 103
Nova Petrópolis, 371–373

O

Oktoberfest, 351
Olinda, 485–499
Oriental Fair, 309
Oriental Festival, 309
Oriental food
  Rio, 175
  São Paulo, 317
Ouro Preto, 232, 233, 239, 249–262

P

Package deals, 8, 15
Painters, *see* Museums
Palácio de Cristal, 205
Palácio Imperial, 101
Pampulha, 236–237
Pantanal, 4, 6, 615–641
Pão de Açúcar, 97–99
Paquetá Island, 115
Paraná, 5
Parati, 215, 223–226
Parks
  Chapada dos Guimarães, 629, 633
  Cuiabá, 622

Iguaçu Falls, 330
Pampulha, 237
Rio, 118
São Paulo, 310
Serra da Bocaina, 227
Teresópolis, 206
Parque do Flamengo, 114, 187
Parque dos Fontes, 291
Parque Florestal das Mangabeiras, 237
Parque Nacional, 633
Parque Nacional dos Lençóis, 538
Party Bahia
    Arraial d'Ajuda, 465–468
    Porto Seguro, 459–463
    Trancoso, 469–470
Party towns, 34
Passport, 12
Patrones, 204
Paulista Plateau, 307
Paulistanos, 325
Pedra da Guaratiba, 133
Pedra do Leme, 126
Pedro, 40, 41
Pedro Alvares Cabral, 36
Peixoto, Marechal Floriano, 43
Petrópolis, 203–206
Pharmacies, 23
Photography, 16
    Belo Horizonte, 247
    Manaus, 609
Piano bars, 182
Pitangueiras, 325
Pizza
    Rio, 175
    São Paulo, 318
Planalto Central, 6, 629
Planetariums (Planetário), 118
Playcenter, 310
Police, 26
    Belém, 593
    Salvador, 444
Pomerode, 342
Pope's Square, 236
Portão do Inferno, 630
Portinari, Cândido, 237
Porto Alegre, 361–363
Porto Seguro, 36, 459–463
Portobello, 215
Portuguese food
    Rio, 175
    São Paulo, 315
Post Offices, 574
Pousada Caiman, 635
Pousada do Vale dos Veados, 202
Praça da República, 109

Praça Floriano, 105
Praça N.S. de Guia, 223
Praça Tiradentes, 256
Praça XV, 101
Praia Canasvieiras, 343
Praia da Joaquina, 343
Praia do Campeche, 343
Praia do Forte, 453–457
Praia Juerê, 343
Praia Vermelha, 130
Prainha, 133
Precautions, 561
Prescription drugs, 24
Prince of Joinville, 347
Private guides
    Belém, 593
    Brasília, 408
    Mariana, 269
    Ouro Preto, 262
    Petrópolis, 203
    Rio, 197
    Salvador, 444
    Santarém, 574
Puerto Canoas, 333
Puerto Iguazú, 333

Q

Quadros, Jânio, 45
Quinta da Boa Vista, 113

R

Rainforest
    Amazon, 554–561
    Atlantic, 111–112
Rasa Island, 209
Recife, 4, 6, 485–499
Recreio dos Bandeirantes, 95, 133
Regina, Elis, 79
Religion, 59–65
Resorts, 34
    Costa do Sol, 217
    Costa Verde, 217
    Salvador, 435–436
    São Paulo, 304
Restaurants, 33
    Alcântara, 538
    Arraial d'Ajuda, 467
    Barra da Tijuca, 132
    Belém, 590–591
    Belo Horizonte, 243–246
    Bento Gonçalves, 385–386
    Blumenau, 352–353
    Botafogo, 130
    Brasília, 406–407
    Búzios, 212–213

Cachoeira, 451
Camboriú, 356
Canela, 368
Caxambú, 298
Caxias do Sul, 380
Chapada dos Guimarães, 639–640
Congonhas, 288
Copacabana, 125
Cuiabá, 624
Flamengo, 129
Florianópolis, 345
Fortaleza, 520–522
Gramado, 368
Guarujá, 326–327
Iguaçu Falls, 336–337
Ilha Grande, 221
Ipanema Beach, 128
Joinville, 349
Leblon, 128
Leme Beach, 126
Maceió, 481–482
Manaus, 605–606
Mariana, 268
Natal, 508–510
Nova Petrópolis, 372
Olinda, 497
Ouro Preto, 260–261
Pampulha, 236
Parati, 226
Porto Alegre, 362
Porto Seguro, 462
Praia do Forte, 456–457
Recife, 496–497
Rio, 167–179
Salvador, 436–439
Santarém, 572
São Conrado, 131
São João del Rei, 277
São Luis, 543
São Paulo, 315–319
Teresópolis, 207
Tiradentes, 281
Torres, 377
Trancoso, 470
Vidigal, 130
Restrooms, 27
Rio de Janeiro, 4, 5, 87–200
Rio Grande do Sul, 6
River cruises
Belém, 584
Pantanal, 637
Santarém, 574
River transportation
Amazon, 557
Belém, 593

Rock and video, 184
Romantic things
Iguaçu Falls, 330
Pão de Açúcar, 98
Rio, 181, 187
Rua Amendoim, 237
Rua do Ouvidor, 102, 105
Rua Galvão Bueno, 309
Rua Princesa Isabel, 347
Rua Visconde de Pirajá, 127

S

Safety, 16
　Fortaleza, 524
　Salvador, 418
Salvador, 4, 6, 410, 411–446
Samba
　Rio, 183, 186
　Roots, 69
　São Paulo, 320
Santa Catarina, 5, 339–342
Santa Teresa, 110–111
Santarém, 4, 563–575
São Conrado, 95, 131
São João del Rei, 233, 239, 271–278
São Lourenço, 291–294
São Luis, 6, 531–544
São Paulo, 4, 5, 303–323
São Tomé das Letras, 233, 301–302
São Vicente, 38
Sarney, José, 46
Savassi, 235
Scandinavian food, 318
Scuba diving
　Fernando de Noronha, 525
　Rio, 139
Security, 16–17
Serra da Bocaina, 227–229
Serra de Tiradentes, 279
Serras, 201
Shoes, 18
Shopping, 27, 34
　Belém, 591–592
　Belo Horizonte, 235, 247
　Blumenau, 353–354
　Brasília, 403
　Búzios, 211
　Canela, 368–369
　Caxambú, 299
　Caxias do Sul, 380
　Chapada dos Guimarães, 640
　Congonhas, 288
　Cuiabá, 625
　Fortaleza, 523
　Gramado, 368–369

INDEX

Guarujá, 327
Iguaçu Falls, 337
Joinville, 350
Maceió, 482
Manaus, 607
Mariana, 268
Natal, 510
Nova Petrópolis, 372
Ouro Preto, 261
Petrópolis, 205
Porto Alegre, 363
Porto Seguro, 462
Recife, 497
Rio, 118, 119, 127, 142–149
Salvador, 425, 441–443
Santarém, 573
São Lourenço, 293
São Luis, 543
São Paulo, 321–322
Tiradentes, 281
Torres, 377
Sights
  Belém, 578–583
  Belo Horizonte, 236
  Blumenau, 352
  Brasília, 396
  Cachoeira, 448
  Camboriú, 355
  Canela, 365
  Chapada dos Guimarães, 632
  Costa Verde, 215–216
  Cuiabá, 622–623
  Fernando de Noronha, 527
  Fortaleza, 514–515
  Gramado, 366
  Iguaçu Falls, 333
  Joinville, 347–348
  Manaus, 596–598
  Mariana, 264–267
  Nova Petrópolis, 371
  Olinda, 488
  Ouro Preto, 252
  Parati, 224–225
  Petrópolis, 204
  Porto Seguro, 460
  Praia do Forte, 454–455
  Rio, 95–97
  Salvador, 420–423
  Santarém, 566–568
  São Luis, 532–535, 538
  São Paulo, 309–311
Simba Safari, 310
Skiing, 305
Slavery, 42
Sousa, Martim Afonso de, 38
Sousa, Tomé de, 38
Spa Towns, 290–302
Spas
  Canela, 367
  Gramado, 367
  São João del Rei, 276
Spiritual sites, 34
Spirituality, 59–65
  Brasília, 402, 404
  São Lourenço, 292
Sports
  Belo Horizonte, 247
  Brasília, 408
  Búzios, 211
  Petrópolis, 205
  Rio, 137–139
  Salvador, 443
Steps of the Cross stations, 285–286
Sugar Loaf Mountain, 88, 98–99
Surfing, 343
Survival kit
  Beach blanket, 122–123
  Pantanal, 619

T

Tai Chi Chuan, 127, 139
Tarobá, 330
Taxes, 19
Taxis, 19, 27
  Búzios, 210
  Chapada dos Guimarães, 641
  Fortaleza, 524
  Joinville, 350
  Manaus, 608
  Mariana, 269
  Porto Alegre, 363
  Rio, 193
  Salvador, 443
  São Luis, 544
  São Paulo, 322
Teatro Municipal, 106
Telephones, 28–29
  Alcântara, 538
  Chapada dos Guimarães, 641
  Cuiabá, 627
  Manaus, 609
  Rio, 198
  Salvador, 444
  Santarém, 574
  Trancoso, 470
Tennis, 139
Teresópolis, 206–207
Theft, 16
Tijuca National Park, 111

Time
  Belém, 594
  Santarém, 574
Time zones, 29
Tipping, 30
Tiradentes, 232, 233, 239, 279–282
Tivoli Parque, 118
Tombo Beach, 325
Toninho Horta, 235
Topelem, Rubéms, 112
Torres, 375–378
Tourist info
  Belém, 594
  Belo Horizonte, 248
  Brasília, 408
  Cachoeira, 451
  Caxambú, 299
  Caxias do Sul, 380
  Congonhas, 288
  Cuiabá, 627
  Fortaleza, 524
  Iguaçu Falls, 338
  Itaipu Dam, 334
  Joinville, 350
  Maceió, 483
  Manaus, 609
  Mariana, 269
  Natal, 511
  Nova Petrópolis, 373
  Ouro Preto, 262
  Porto Alegre, 363
  Porto Seguro, 463
  Recife, 498
  Rio, 99, 198–199
  Salvador, 445
  Santarém, 575
  São Lourenço, 294
  São Paulo, 304, 323
  Serra da Bocaina, 229
  Tiradentes, 282
  Torres, 378
Tours, 643–645
  Búzios, 210
  Costa Verde, 216
  Favela, 115–117
  Ilha Grande, 220
  Pão de Açúcar, 97
  Serra da Bocaina, 228
  Teresópolis, 207
Trains, 31, 408
Trancoso, 469–470
Transamérica Hotel, 34, 435

Transpantaneira Highway, 617
Travessa do Comércio, 102
Tupí-Guaraní, 37
Typhoid, 663

U

UFOs, 3, 34, 301–302, 629
United Airlines, 10
Urca, 95

V

Vaca, Alvaro Nunes Cabeza de, 330
Vaccinations, 17
Vargas, Getúlio, 43
Varig Airlines, 8, 19
Vegetarian food
  Rio, 176
  São Paulo, 318, 319
Vegetarians, 166
Veloso, Caetano, 79–81
Vidigal, 130
Vila Brumado, 267
Visas, 12, 333
Vista Chinesa, 111

W

War of Triple Alliance, 42
Water, 31, 660–661
Waves, 310
What to pack
  Amazon, 560
  Pantanal, 620
What to wear
  Amazon, 560
  Brasília, 403
  Rio, 200
  São Paulo, 323
Where to stay
  São Paulo, 312–315
Wine-Tasting
  Bento Gonçalves, 385
  Garibaldi, 383
  Torres, 376
Women, 32, 144
World War II, 43–44

X

Xavier, Francisco Cândido (Chico), 63

Y

Yoga, 141
Youth hostels, 32
  Rio, 163
  Salvador, 435

Z

Zona Norte, 94
Zona Sul, 94
Zoological Gardens, 310
Zoos
    Cuiabá, 623
    Green Rio, 113
    Parati, 225
    Rio, 118
    São Paulo, 310

Introducing the 1994 Fielding Travel Guides—fresh, fascinating and fun!

The travel guide series that started truth in travel is back.

An incisive new attitude and an exciting new look! All-new design and format. In-depth reviews. Fielding delivers travel information the way frequent travelers demand it—written with sparkle, style and humor. Candid insights, sage advice, insider tips. No fluff, no filler, only fresh information that makes the journey more fun, more fascinating, more Fielding.

Australia 1994	**$16.95**
Belgium 1994	**$16.95**
Bermuda/Bahamas 1994	**$16.95**
Brazil 1994	**$16.95**
Britain 1994	**$16.95**
Budget Europe 1994	**$16.95**
Caribbean 1994	**$16.95**
Europe 1994	**$16.95**
Far East 1994	**$16.95**
France 1994	**$16.95**
The Great Sights of Europe 1994	**$16.95**
Hawaii 1994	**$16.95**
Holland 1994	**$16.95**
Italy 1994	**$16.95**
Mexico 1994	**$16.95**
New Zealand 1994	**$16.95**
Scandinavia 1994	**$16.95**
Spain & Portugal 1994	**$16.95**
Switzerland & the Alpine Region 1994	**$16.95**
Worldwide Cruises 1994	**$16.95**
Shopping Europe	**$12.95**

To place an order: call toll-free
1-800-FW-2-GUIDE
add $2.00 shipping & handling, allow 2-6 weeks.

FIELDING'S TRAVEL SECRETS

For Travel Insiders Only!

FIELDING'S TRAVEL SECRETS is the insider's travel guide, available only to travel professionals and a very limited number of Fielding Travel Guide readers. Created by Fielding's experienced staff of writers and released in six bi-monthly installments per year, the insider's report is packed with timely travel information, trends, news, tips and reviews. Enroll now and you will also receive a variety of significant discounts and special preview information.

Due to the sensitive nature of the information contained in these reports, subscriptions available to non-travel industry individuals are limited to the first 10,000 subscribers. The annual price for all six installments is $60. This offer also comes with an unconditional money-back guarantee if you are not fully satisfied.

To Reserve Your Subscription
1-800-FW-2-GUIDE

Favorite People, Places & Experiences

ADDRESS:	NOTES:

Name

Address

Telephone

Name

Address

Telephone

Name

Address

Telephone

Name

Address

Telephone

Name

Address

Telephone

Name

Address

Telephone

Name

Address

Telephone

Favorite People, Places & Experiences

ADDRESS:	NOTES:

Name

Address

Telephone

Name

Address

Telephone

Name

Address

Telephone

Name

Address

Telephone

Name

Address

Telephone

Name

Address

Telephone

Name

Address

Telephone

Favorite People, Places & Experiences

ADDRESS:	NOTES:

Name

Address

Telephone

Name

Address

Telephone

Name

Address

Telephone

Name

Address

Telephone

Name

Address

Telephone

Name

Address

Telephone

Name

Address

Telephone

Favorite People, Places & Experiences

ADDRESS:	NOTES:

Name

Address

Telephone

Name

Address

Telephone

Name

Address

Telephone

Name

Address

Telephone

Name

Address

Telephone

Name

Address

Telephone

Name

Address

Telephone

Favorite People, Places & Experiences

ADDRESS:	NOTES:

Name

Address

Telephone

Name

Address

Telephone

Name

Address

Telephone

Name

Address

Telephone

Name

Address

Telephone

Name

Address

Telephone

Name

Address

Telephone

Favorite People, Places & Experiences

ADDRESS:	NOTES:

Name

Address

Telephone

Name

Address

Telephone

Name

Address

Telephone

Name

Address

Telephone

Name

Address

Telephone

Name

Address

Telephone

Name

Address

Telephone

Favorite People, Places & Experiences

ADDRESS:	NOTES:

Name

Address

Telephone

Name

Address

Telephone

Name

Address

Telephone

Name

Address

Telephone

Name

Address

Telephone

Name

Address

Telephone

Name

Address

Telephone

Favorite People, Places & Experiences

ADDRESS:	NOTES:

Name

Address

Telephone

Name

Address

Telephone

Name

Address

Telephone

Name

Address

Telephone

Name

Address

Telephone

Name

Address

Telephone

Name

Address

Telephone

Favorite People, Places & Experiences

ADDRESS:	NOTES:

Name

Address

Telephone

Name

Address

Telephone

Name

Address

Telephone

Name

Address

Telephone

Name

Address

Telephone

Name

Address

Telephone

Name

Address

Telephone

Favorite People, Places & Experiences

ADDRESS: NOTES:

Name
Address

Telephone

Name
Address

Telephone

Name
Address

Telephone

Name
Address

Telephone

Name
Address

Telephone

Name
Address

Telephone

Name
Address

Telephone